THIRD EDITION

W9-CDU-137

Cambridge Preparation for the TOEFL® Test

JOLENE GEAR and ROBERT GEAR

CAMBRIDGE
UNIVERSITY PRESS

CAMBRIDGE UNIVERSITY PRESS
Cambridge, New York, Melbourne, Madrid, Cape Town, Singapore, São Paulo

Cambridge University Press
40 West 20th Street, New York, NY 10011–4211, USA

www.cambridge.org
Information on this title: www.cambridge.org/9780521784016

First edition published 1993

Second edition published 1996

Third edition published 2002
7th printing 2005

Printed in the United States of America

Library of Congress Cataloging in Publication data

Gear, Jolene.
   Cambridge preparation for the TOEFL test / Jolene Gear and Robert Gear. – 3rd ed.
      p. cm.
ISBN-13   978-0-521-78401-6 book and CD-ROM
ISBN-10   0-521-78401-8 book and CD-ROM
   1. Test of English as a Foreign Language – Study guides. 2. English
language – Textbooks for foreign speakers. 3. English language – Examinations – Study
guides. I Gear, Robert. II. Title

PE1128.G35   2002
428'.0076 – dc21   00-031217

ISBN-13   978-0-521-78401-6 Book/CD-ROM
ISBN-10   0-521-78401-8   Book/CD-ROM
ISBN-13   978-0-521-78399-6 Audio CDs
ISBN-10   0-521-78399-2   Audio CDs
ISBN-13   978-0-521-78400-9 Audio Cassettes
ISBN-10   0-521-78400-X   Audio Cassettes
ISBN-13   978-0-521-78396-5 Book/CD-ROM/Audio CD Pack
ISBN-10   0-521-78396-8   Book/CD-ROM/Audio CD Pack
ISBN-13   978-0-521-78397-2 Book/CD-ROM/Audio Cassette Pack
ISBN-10   0-521-78397-6   Book/CD-ROM/Audio Cassette Pack
ISBN-13   978-0-521-78398-9 CD-ROM
ISBN-10   0-521-78398-4   CD-ROM

Book design: McNally Graphic Design
Layouts and text composition: Dewey Publishing Services

ACKNOWLEDGMENTS

We would like to thank those people who made the publication of the Third Edition of this book possible. Our deepest appreciation goes to Sylvia Bloch, Patti Brecht, Liane Carita, Jeff Chen, Tünde Dewey, Susan Dodson, Laura Dorfman, Deborah Goldblatt, Arley Gray, Nadia Kalman, Andrew Libby, Kathy Niemczyk, Bill Paulk, Howard Siegelman, and Jennifer Wilkin of Cambridge University Press for their combined efforts and painstaking care in helping to bring the Third Edition into print. A special word of thanks also goes to our colleagues and students at the University of Oulu, Finland, and Arron Grow and his students and colleagues at Pierce College, Lakewood, Washington, for their help with field-testing the Third Edition.

We would also like to express our gratitude to those people who helped with the First and Second Editions: These include Sandra Graham of Cambridge University Press who assisted us throughout the preparation of the First Edition; John Haskell, our ETS consultant, who read and commented on the early drafts of the First Edition; William Gear for his continuous support and encouragement throughout the preparation of both editions; Ahmed Gomaa and our colleagues and students at the University of Kuwait for initial piloting and suggestions; Ted Quock for his helpful comments in the pilot study; Karen Davy who assisted us in the preparation of the Second Edition; our colleagues and students at the University of Bahrain for piloting material for the Second Edition; and those teachers and students from the following institutions who took part in the initial field-testing of the book and cassettes:

American Language and Culture Institute – CSU, California, USA
Cambridge Centre for Languages, Cambridge, England
CES Inc., New York, USA
Ecole Centrale de Lyon, France
Ecole des Cadres, Paris, France
ESARC–ESSIGE, St. Clément, France
D. B. Hood Community School, Toronto, Canada
Instituto Americano, Florence, Italy
ISMRA, Caen, France
Kyoto YMCA English School, Japan
Mohawk College, Hamilton, Canada
Nichibei Kaiwa Gakuin, Tokyo, Japan
San Jose State University, California, USA
Sankei International College, Toyko, Japan
Sheridan College, Mississauga, Canada
Simul Academy, Tokyo, Japan
Temple University, Tokyo, Japan
Trident College, Hiroshima, Japan
Université Paris – Dauphine, France
University of Arkansas at Little Rock, USA
University of California Extension – Davis, USA
University of Florida, USA
University of Washington, USA
Vincennes University, Indiana, USA

We gratefully acknowledge permission to use the following materials:

Pages 50–53; CD-ROM Test 1, reading passage for questions 1–11. The reading on interviewing is adapted from Stuart Sutherland, *Irrationality: Why We Don't Think Straight,* copyright © 1992 by Stuart Sutherland. Printed by permission of Rutgers University Press and Constable Publishers.

Pages 159, 582; CD-ROM Test 2, lecture for questions 35–40. The talk about the "War of the Worlds" radio broadcast is used by permission of the *Skeptical Inquirer* magazine.

Page 304, Exercise R3, reading passage for example on screen. Article about mounties was originally published on the Royal Canadian Mounted Police Internet site. RCMP/GRC © 1996–1999.

Pages 305–306, Exercise R4, reading passage for questions 1–4. This article was adapted from the Web site of the Rubber Pavements Association and used with its permission.

Pages 379–382; CD-ROM Test 2, reading passage for questions 28–39. The reading on resolutions is adapted from Stuart Sutherland, *Irrationality: Why We Don't Think Straight,* copyright © 1992 by Stuart Sutherland. Printed by permission of Rutgers University Press and Constable Publishers.

Pages 462, 588–589; CD-ROM Test 4, lecture for questions 34–38. The talk about the fossil record is used by permission of the *Skeptical Inquirer* magazine.

CD-ROM Test 5, lecture for questions 39–45. The talk in an economics class is a summary of Chapter 2 in Richard J. Maybury, *Whatever Happened to Penny Candy?* published by Bluestocking Press, PO Box 2030, Dept. TL, Placerville, CA 95667-1014, USA, and is used with permission of the author and publisher.

CONTENTS

TO THE USER

About the book and CD-ROM

Cambridge Preparation for the TOEFL® Test helps you build the skills necessary to answer the questions on the TOEFL® Test successfully. Also, it thoroughly familiarizes you with the TOEFL® Test format and suggests test-taking strategies to help you improve your scores.

The book and its accompanying CD-ROM, which features seven practice tests, may be used as a classroom text or for self-study. An extensive audio program is also available on audio cassette or audio CD. You may also wish to use the text to review or refresh your English-language skills.

Important features of this program

- An **Introduction** that explains what the TOEFL® Test is and other information that you need to know about the test.

- A **Tutorial** that explains how to answer questions on the Computer-Based TOEFL® Test.

- A comprehensive **Table of Contents** that identifies the content of each exercise in the text.

- An accompanying **CD-ROM** for additional practice that features seven practice tests in the Computer-Based TOEFL® Test format.

- A **Diagnostic Test**, which helps you to pinpoint your weaknesses in English and then directs you to the exercises that will strengthen those areas. This test corresponds to Test 1 on the CD-ROM. You may take it on a computer, or as a paper-based test in this book.

- Test-taking **strategies** for each of the four sections of the TOEFL® Test – Listening, Structure, Reading, and Writing.

- **Exercises** that isolate and gradually build upon specific skills needed for success on the TOEFL® Test.

- Several **mini-tests** in each section that use the TOEFL® Test format and allow you to check your mastery of a particular set of skills.

- A complete **section practice test** in the TOEFL® Test format at the end of the Listening, Structure, Reading, and Writing Sections. Each of these tests indicates whether you have mastered the skills in that section. These section practice tests are combined to form one complete practice test that is included on the CD-ROM as Test 2.

- Two full-length **Practice Tests** at the end of the book, which give you further practice with the TOEFL® Test format and test-taking strategies. The answer keys to the Practice Tests direct you to the exercises that will help you strengthen those areas that are causing you difficulties. These tests correspond to Tests 3 and 4 on the CD-ROM.

- An Answer Key, which explains the correct answers for many exercises and tests.

- A complete listening program (available as audio cassettes or audio CDs)* that includes all the Listening exercises and Listening test material in the text. Like the actual TOEFL® Test, many different native American English speakers have been used in the recording to give you the opportunity to hear a wide selection of voices.

- Complete Scripts of all the Listening exercises and Listening test materials on the cassettes or audio CDs. The scripts aid you in checking your answers by allowing you to compare your responses with what you actually heard.

- An Index that allows you to easily locate exercises that build specific skills (for example, making inferences), or grammar points (for example, subject-verb agreement).

- Extended practice exercises, which provide additional work in some skill areas.

- Cross-references, which indicate the pages where explanations, scripts, or other related exercises can be found.

  *The listening program is available separately for classroom use, or as part of a pack for self study. A list of ISBNs is included on the copyright page of this book.

Important features of the CD-ROM

- Seven computer-based practice tests, which consist of the four tests that are found in the book (the Diagnostic Test, End-of-Section Tests, and two Practice Tests) and three additional tests that are not included in the book. All of the tests on the CD-ROM are designed to simulate the experience of taking the actual Computer-Based TOEFL® Test.

- A Full Tutorial and a Quick Tutorial that explain how to answer questions on the Computer-Based TOEFL® Test.

- The same icons as on the Computer-Based TOEFL® Test to familiarize you with the appearance of the computer screens on the test.

- Two options that give you the choice of taking the test either as a simulated TOEFL® Test (Full Practice Tests) or with access to answers and explanations during or following the test (Practice and Study).

- A bookmark option that allows you to stop the program during a test and come back to the same place to continue later.

- A section choice option in Practice and Study that allows you to choose a particular section where you may want to focus more attention.

- A show text option in Practice and Study that allows you to read the script as you listen.

- An Answer Key that explains the correct answers.

How to use *Cambridge Preparation for the TOEFL® Test*

1. Go through the Tutorial that starts on page 13 or on the CD-ROM to learn how to answer the types of questions you will see on the TOEFL® Test.

2. Complete the computer-based Diagnostic Test (Test 1) on the CD-ROM or the paper-based Diagnostic Test beginning on page 35. This will highlight areas that you need to concentrate on the most so that you will not spend time studying material you already know.

3. The computer-based Diagnostic Test (Test 1) will give you a good idea of the areas where you need more practice. Answer feedback will direct you to relevant skill-building exercises in the book.

   If you take the paper-based Diagnostic Test, check your answers using the Answer Key starting on page 495. For every wrong answer you choose, the Answer Key will direct you to exercises that will build the skills you need in order to answer that type of question correctly.

4. Read the strategies at the beginning of the Listening, Structure, Reading, and Writing Sections.

5. Work through the exercises that concentrate on the skills you need to develop. Take the mini-tests as you proceed through a section to check your progress.

6. When you have finished all the necessary exercises in a particular section, take the test at the end of that section or take the appropriate section test on CD-ROM Test 2. For example, once you have worked through the Listening exercises, take the Listening Section Practice Test at the end of the Listening Section or do the Listening Section of Test 2 on the CD-ROM.

7. Take the Practice Tests. You may want to take one halfway through your course of study to confirm your progress. You may want to leave one to take as a final check before taking the actual TOEFL® Test.

8. If you take the CD-ROM Practice Tests, the program will give you answer feedback that will direct you to skill-building exercises in the book.

   If you take the paper-based Practice Tests in the book, check your answers using the Answer Key. In many cases, the Answer Key will direct you to exercises that will help you build the skills you need in order to answer that type of question correctly.

Notes: It is probably not necessary for you to do every exercise in this book in preparation for the TOEFL® Test, so concentrate on the exercises covering your weaknesses as indicated by the Diagnostic Test and the Practice Tests. Moreover, it is not necessary for you to complete all of the items within an exercise. If you discover that an exercise is too easy for you, go on to exercises that will be more challenging.

On the CD-ROM, you can move through the questions at your own pace. In order to complete all of the questions in a timed test, you should try to pace yourself by paying attention to the number of questions and time remaining.

On the cassettes or audio CDs, all Listening tests and mini-tests give you the same amount of time (12 seconds) to answer the questions as on the Paper-Based TOEFL® Test. In the skill-building exercises, pause the cassette or audio CD after each question if you need more time to answer or if the question requires a written answer.

TO THE TEACHER

- The Diagnostic Test will show you the areas that your students need to concentrate on the most. Don't feel that every exercise, or all items within an exercise, must be completed.

- If you are preparing students for the Computer-Based TOEFL® Test, you may want to encourage them to take some of the tests in simulation mode (Full Practice Tests), which mimics the same test conditions that they will experience during the actual test, and some of the tests in practice mode (Practice and Study), which gives students the option of checking each answer while going through the test.

  If you are preparing students for the Paper-Based TOEFL® Test, provide the same test conditions while they are doing the exercises and tests in the TOEFL® Test format that they will experience during the actual test (i.e., use answer sheets, play the cassettes or audio CDs without pauses, and allow only one section to be worked on during the time allotted).

- In listening skill-building exercises, pause the cassette or audio CD after each question if students need more time to answer or if the question requires a written answer. In order to manage time efficiently on the Computer-Based TOEFL® Test, students should become accustomed to checking the time and number of questions remaining. There are about 30 seconds allotted for Listening questions. Encourage students to answer items in the Paper-Based TOEFL® Test format within 12 seconds. This is the time allowed on the Paper-Based TOEFL® Test.

- Use the exercises in all sections to build skills in other areas.

  There may be many unfamiliar words throughout the sections, which would be useful to learn in order to improve not only reading and listening skills, but also to build word-form recognition skills for grammar items. Help students to identify which of the words are useful and which may never be encountered again.

  Making inferences, drawing conclusions, and identifying topics are important skills to acquire for success in both listening and reading comprehension.

  Understanding the grammatical structure of a sentence is important for determining the meaning of a Listening Section item.

  The formats of the Listening lectures, the Reading passages, and the Writing essays are similar; that is, they all begin with an introduction that includes the topic, continue with ideas that support the topic, and end with a conclusion.

- In class, focus on areas that the Diagnostic Test has indicated most students are having trouble understanding. Homework assignments can be individualized so that each student can focus on his or her specific areas of difficulties.

- Stress to students that all English-language experience is useful in studying for the TOEFL® Test. In addition to the exercises in the book, you may wish to assign related homework or in-class activities. Watching an English-language movie or television program, reading articles in an English-language newspaper or magazine, and listening to English-language radio programs are all helpful in improving students' knowledge of English.

INTRODUCTION TO THE TOEFL® TEST

Reasons for taking the TOEFL® Test

The Test of English as a Foreign Language (TOEFL®) is an examination that is administered by the Educational Testing Service (ETS) and used to evaluate a nonnative English speaker's proficiency in the English language. Many North American colleges and universities, as well as a large number of institutions, agencies, and programs, ask for official TOEFL® Test score reports. An acceptable score on the TOEFL® Test depends on the specific requirements of the particular institution or agency involved.

To be admitted to a North American college or university, you will probably need a computer-test score of 150 to 215 (or a paper-test score of at least 475 to 550). Although some colleges accept students with a score under 130 (computer test) or 450 (paper test), usually those students are required to enroll in remedial classes or in ESL classes as part of their course of study. Other colleges and universities require a higher score (250+ on the computer test or 600+ on the paper test). This score is frequently required for students who wish to work at the graduate level. A few colleges and universities do not require nonnative English-speaking students to take the TOEFL® Test. They may, however, have their own English proficiency exam that students are required to take upon arrival. Because these exams test the same skills as the TOEFL® Test, preparing yourself for the TOEFL® Test is a good way to prepare for any English proficiency exam.

The TOEFL® Information Bulletins

Two TOEFL® information bulletins include the necessary registration forms and instructions for completing the forms, as well as information concerning methods of payment, special services, identification requirements, testing sites, and refund policy. If you are preparing for the computer-based test, you will need the *TOEFL® CBT Bulletin*. If you plan to take the paper-based test, you will need the *Supplemental Paper TOEFL® Bulletin*. To receive a copy of either information bulletin, write to ETS at the following address and specify which bulletin you need.

TOEFL/TSE Services
P.O. Box 6151
Princeton, NJ 08541-6151
USA

If you have access to the Internet, you can order or download either of these bulletins. The TOEFL® Web site address follows.
http://www.toefl.org

You can also contact TOEFL/TSE Services using the following e-mail address.
toefl@ets.org

Depending on where you live or the circumstances in which you are taking the test, you will have to take either the computerized test or the paper test. You should find out which test you will be taking so that you can become familiar with its requirements and test format.

Information about the Computer-Based TOEFL® Test

Unlike the Paper-Based TOEFL® Test, you can schedule an appointment for the computer-based test at the testing center on the day you want to take the test. However, since there is no guarantee that there will be an available workstation, you may want to set up an appointment in advance by phone, fax, or mail. For information about availability, contact the appropriate Regional Registration Center (RRC) for the country you are testing in. A list of these centers can be found on the TOEFL® Web site (http://www.toefl.org).

On the Paper-Based TOEFL® Test, the Writing test is a separate test and is scored separately. However, on the Computer-Based TOEFL® Test, the score for Writing is a component of the score for the Structure Section. Even though the college or university where you are applying may not require a score for Writing, you will have to write the essay to complete the Computer-Based TOEFL® Test.

Plan on being at the test center for up to five hours. On the day of the test, you will be required to go through several tutorial lessons that teach you basic computer skills and how to answer the test questions. You can spend as much time on the tutorials as you want. The total time for taking the Computer-Based TOEFL® Test is under four hours; the Writing test takes approximately thirty minutes. Remember that in addition to the actual test-taking time, time is needed for checking identification, following the score reporting procedures, taking the ten-minute break, and so forth.

You cannot take the TOEFL® Test more than once a month. Colleges and universities usually consider only the most recent score. ETS keeps records of scores for two years. You will probably have to take the TOEFL® Test again if your score report is more than two years old.

Computer-Based TOEFL® Test format

Table 1 shows the format and the number and types of questions you can expect to see on the Computer-Based TOEFL® Test.

TABLE 1

Listening*	Number of passages	Number of questions per passage	Total number of questions	Time
Short dialogues	11–17	1		
Short conversations	2–3	2–3	30–59	40–60 minutes
Lectures and discussions	4–6	3–6		

Structure		Number of items	Total number of questions	Time
Completing sentences correctly		10–15	20–25	15–20 minutes
Identifying errors		10–15		

Reading	Number of passages	Number of questions per passage	Total number of questions	Time
Reading comprehension	4–5	10–12	44–55	70–90 minutes

Writing		Number of essays		Time
		1		30 minutes

*The Listening Section will have between thirty and fifty-nine questions. You will have fifteen to twenty-five minutes to answer the questions. The clock does not run while you are listening to the spoken passages and questions, only when you are answering the questions.

Information about computer-adaptive tests

The Computer-Based TOEFL® Test has two sections that are computer adaptive – the Listening Section and the Structure Section. The Reading Section is not computer adaptive.

Computer adaptive means that the questions you receive are based on how you answer. Your first question will be of moderate difficulty. If you answer correctly, the next question you receive will be of greater or equal difficulty. In contrast, if you answer incorrectly, the next question you receive will be of lesser or equal difficulty. The computer is programmed to continuously present questions of appropriate difficulty for test-takers of all performance levels.

Since the computer must score each question in order to select the next one, you must answer each question as it is presented. You cannot skip questions or return to a previous question to change an answer in the Listening or Structure Sections.

Since the Reading Section is not computer adaptive, you can skip questions and return to previously answered questions. How you answer one question in the Reading Section does not affect the difficulty level of the following question.

Scoring information

In the sections that are computer adaptive, your section scores are based on how well you answered the questions. You are given more credit for the right answer on a hard question than for one on an easy question. For test-takers who have the same number of correct responses, the one who answered the greatest number of difficult questions correctly will receive the highest score. For test-takers who have correctly answered questions of equivalent difficulty, the one who answered the most questions within the time limits will receive the highest score.

Your score for the Structure Section is combined with the rating on your essay. Because your essay will be read later, you will receive a score that indicates the range in which your final score will fall. Your score for the Reading Section is based on the number of questions answered correctly and converted by statistical means to a scaled section score.

Most colleges accept only the official score report received directly from ETS. After the test, you will have the option of viewing your score range on the computer screen. After viewing your scores on screen, you may choose up to four institutions or agencies as score recipients. You may also cancel your scores if the score range does not satisfy the minimum requirement of your chosen institutions.

If you use the CD-ROM, your approximate score will be calculated for you. However, if you take the tests in *Cambridge Preparation for the TOEFL® Test* in paper form, first use Table 4 on page 9 to convert your Practice Test scores into a paper-based test score. Then use Table 2 to convert your paper-test score to a computer-based test score. This will give you the approximate score range that you could expect to achieve on the TOEFL® Test.

TABLE 2

Total Score from Table 4	Approximate corresponding Computer-Based Score
677	300
673	297
670	293
667	290
663	287
660	287
657	283
653	280
650	280

(continued)

TABLE 2 (*continued*)

Total Score from Table 4	Approximate corresponding Computer-Based Score
647	277
643	273
640	273
637	270
633	267
630	267
627	263
623	263
620	260
617	260
613	257
610	253
607	253
603	250
600	250
597	247
593	243
590	243
587	240
583	237
580	237
577	233
573	230
570	230
567	227
563	223
560	220
553	217
550	213
547	210
543	207
540	207
537	203
533	200
530	197
527	197
523	193
520	190
517	187
513	183
510	180
507	180
503	177
500	173
497	170
493	167

(*continued*)

TABLE 2 (*continued*)

Total Score from Table 4	Approximate corresponding Computer-Based Score
490	163
487	163
483	160
480	157
477	153
473	150
470	150
467	147
463	143
460	140
457	137
453	133
450	133
447	130
443	127
440	123
437	123
433	120
430	117
427	113
423	113
420	110
417	107
413	103
410	103
407	100
403	97
400	97
397	93
393	90
390	90
387	87
383	83
380	83
377	80
373	77
370	77
367	73
363	73
360	70
357	70
353	67
350	63
347	63
343	60

(*continued*)

TABLE 2 (*continued*)

Total Score from Table 4	Approximate corresponding Computer-Based Score
340	60
337	57
333	57
330	53
327	50
323	50
320	47
317	47
313	43
310	40

Note: The scores you receive in this program are approximate only and are provided to give you a better idea of your potential TOEFL® Test score.

Writing scoring information

The Writing test is scored on a scale from 1 to 6. A score of 6 shows strong writing abilities, 5 average writing abilities, and 4 minimal writing abilities. A score of 3, 2, or 1 shows a lack of writing technique.

Your essay will be read by two testing evaluators. Each one gives your essay a score. The two scores are averaged to produce your final Writing score. If the evaluators are more than 1 point different in their assessment, a third evaluator will score the essay. In the Computer-Based TOEFL® Test, the Writing score is part of your Structure score and, therefore, affects your total TOEFL® Test score. However, in the Paper-Based TOEFL® Test, the Writing score does not affect your total TOEFL® Test score.

For the practice TOEFL® Test essays in this book, we suggest that you have a native speaker of English – preferably a writing instructor – evaluate your essay using the Writing scoring guide that follows.

Writing scoring guide*

6 An essay at this level
   – effectively addresses the writing task
   – is well organized and well developed
   – uses clearly appropriate details to support a thesis or illustrate ideas
   – displays consistent facility in the use of language
   – demonstrates syntactic variety and appropriate word choice
5 An essay at this level
   – may address some parts of the task more effectively than others
   – is generally well organized and developed
   – uses details to support a thesis or illustrate an idea
   – displays facility in the use of the language
   – demonstrates some syntactic variety and range of vocabulary
4 An essay at this level
   – addresses the writing topic adequately but may slight parts of the task
   – is adequately organized and developed

*TOEFL® materials are reprinted by permission of Educational Testing Service, the copyright owner. However, the test questions and any other testing information are provided in their entirety by Cambridge University Press. No endorsement of this publication by Educational Testing Service should be inferred.

  – uses some details to support a thesis or illustrate an idea
  – demonstrates adequate but possibly inconsistent facility with syntax and usage
  – may contain some errors that occasionally obscure meaning

3 An essay at this level may reveal one or more of the following weaknesses:
  – inadequate organization or development
  – inappropriate or insufficient details to support or illustrate generalizations
  – a noticeably inappropriate choice of words or word forms
  – an accumulation of errors in sentence structure and/or usage

2 An essay at this level is seriously flawed by one or more of the following weaknesses:
  – serious disorganization or underdevelopment
  – little or no detail, or irrelevant specifics
  – serious and frequent errors in sentence structure or usage
  – serious problems with focus

1 An essay at this level
  – may be incoherent
  – may be undeveloped
  – may contain severe and persistent writing errors

0 An essay will be rated 0 if it
  – contains no response
  – merely copies the topic
  – is off-topic, is written in a foreign language, or consists only of keystroke characters

Information about the Paper-Based TOEFL® Test

Because you cannot register at the testing center on the test date, you must register in advance using the registration form provided in the *Supplemental Paper TOEFL® Bulletin*. You should register in advance of the given deadlines to ensure a place because the test centers have limited seating and may fill up early. Tests are administered only several times each year. Check the *Bulletin* to confirm that the center(s) in your area will be open on the date(s) you select. Some colleges and universities require their prospective students to take the Writing test. This test is administered with the Paper-Based TOEFL® Test.

Test scores are sent to you and to any colleges and universities you have indicated on the registration form. Most colleges accept only the official score report received directly from ETS.

Plan on being at the test center for up to 4 hours. The total time for taking the TOEFL® Test is under 3 hours; the Writing test takes approximately 30 minutes. Remember that in addition to the actual test-taking time, time is needed for checking identification, going over the instructions, and filling out the personal information sheet.

You can take the TOEFL® Test as many times as you wish. However, colleges and universities usually consider only the most recent score. ETS keeps records of scores for two years. You will probably have to take the TOEFL® Test again if your score report is more than two years old.

Paper-Based TOEFL® Test format

Table 3 gives the general outline for the Institutional Testing Program (ITP). This TOEFL® Test is used by institutions and businesses. It is administered only to students in English programs that have made special arrangements with ETS. The scores from ITP are usually not considered valid for university admission requirements.

The Paper-Based TOEFL® Test administered for the Institutional Testing Program usually has the same format and length as the Paper-Based TOEFL® Test administered for university admissions.

TABLE 3   Paper-Based TOEFL® Test Format

Section		Number of items	Time
Listening			
Part A	Questions about short conversations	30	
Part B	Questions about longer conversations	8	
Part C	Questions about lectures or talks	12	
	Total	50	30–40 minutes
Structure and Written Expression			
	Completing sentences correctly	15	
	Identifying errors	25	
	Total	40	25 minutes
Reading Comprehension			
	Questions about Reading passages	50	
	Total	50	55 minutes
Test of Written English			
	One essay, 250–300 words		30 minutes

Information about the answer sheet

When you take the TOEFL® Test, you should not mark your answers in the test book. You will receive an answer sheet. This answer sheet will have one of two different formats – horizontal and vertical.

Horizontal

1. Ⓐ Ⓑ Ⓒ Ⓓ
2. Ⓐ Ⓑ Ⓒ Ⓓ
3. Ⓐ Ⓑ Ⓒ Ⓓ
4. Ⓐ Ⓑ Ⓒ Ⓓ

Vertical

1	2	3
Ⓐ	Ⓐ	Ⓐ
Ⓑ	Ⓑ	Ⓑ
Ⓒ	Ⓒ	Ⓒ
Ⓓ	Ⓓ	Ⓓ

Answer the questions in the following way:

1. Use a #2 or HB black-lead pencil.

2. Find the row with the same number as the number of the question you are answering.

3. Answer the item by filling in the oval corresponding to the letter on the answer sheet. The scoring machine cannot read light marks or partially filled ovals. Be sure to make dark marks and completely fill the oval.

4. Mark only **one** answer to each question.

5. If you change your mind, be sure to erase the old answer completely.

6. Erase all extra marks completely before the end of the test.

Scoring information

Sections 1, 2, and 3 (Listening, Structure, and Reading)

The score you receive on the TOEFL® Test is not the percentage of correct answers. Your score is converted to take into account the fact that some tests are more difficult than others. The converted scores correct these differences. Therefore, the converted score is a more accurate reflection of your ability than the correct answer score is.

As explained on page 3, if you take the practice tests on the CD-ROM that accompanies this book, your approximate score will be calculated for you. However, if you take the tests in *Cambridge Preparation for the TOEFL® Test* in paper form, use Table 4 to convert your Practice Test scores into a corresponding TOEFL® Test score. This will give you the approximate score range that you could expect to achieve on the actual Paper-Based TOEFL® Test.

Remember that the scores you receive in this program are approximate only and are provided to give you a better idea of your potential TOEFL® Test score.

TABLE 4   Paper-Based Practice Test Score Conversion Chart

Correct answer scores	Converted scores		
	Section 1	Section 2	Section 3
48–50	66–68		65–67
45–47	62–65		60–64
42–44	59–61		57–59
39–41	57–58		55–56
36–38	55–56		53–54
33–35	53–54		50–52
30–32	51–52		48–49
27–29	49–50		46–47
24–26	47–48		44–45
21–23	45–46		41–43
18–20	43–44	61–68	38–40
15–17	41–42	54–60	35–37
12–14	36–40	48–53	31–34
9–11	32–35	42–47	29–30
6–8	30–31	36–41	26–28
3–5	27–29	26–35	24–25
0–2	24–26	20–25	21–23

Example for calculating your score

If you had 40 correct in Section 1, 16 correct in Section 2, and 35 correct in Section 3, enter those numbers in the "Correct answer score" column in Table 6. Now find "40" (the number of correct answers for Section 1) in the "Correct answer scores" column in Table 4, and look across to the converted scores in the "Section 1" column: "57–58." Write "57" and "58" in the "Converted score" column in Table 6. Do the same for the correct answer scores for Sections 2 and 3. Add the converted scores, multiply them by 10, and then divide that number by 3. Round off to the nearest number. Your Practice Test score will be between these two numbers. Table 5 shows the example described above.

TABLE 5   Example of a Score Conversion

	Test 1	
	Correct answer score	Converted score
Section 1	40	57 – 58
Section 2	16	54 – 60
Section 3	35	50 – 52
Total of converted score		161 – 170
Multiply by 10		1610 1700
Divide by 3		536.7 566.6
Practice Test score		537 – 567

Your total score will probably be between 537 and 567.

Worksheets for calculating your scores

Use Table 6 to determine your paper-test scores for the Diagnostic Test, the Section Tests, and Practice Tests 1 and 2 in this book. Use Table 2 to convert your paper scores to computer scores.

TABLE 6

	Diagnostic Test		Section Tests	
	Correct answer score	Converted score	Correct answer score	Converted score
Section 1 (Listening)	_____	_____ - _____	_____	_____ - _____
Section 2 (Structure)	_____	_____ - _____	_____	_____ - _____
Section 3 (Reading)	_____	_____ - _____	_____	_____ - _____
Total of converted score		_____ - _____		_____ - _____
Multiply by 10		_____ _____		_____ _____
Divide by 3		_____ _____		_____ _____
Practice Test score		_____ - _____		_____ - _____

	Practice Test 1		Practice Test 2	
	Correct answer score	Converted score	Correct answer score	Converted score
Section 1 (Listening)	_____	_____ - _____	_____	_____ - _____
Section 2 (Structure)	_____	_____ - _____	_____	_____ - _____
Section 3 (Reading)	_____	_____ - _____	_____	_____ - _____
Total of converted score		_____ - _____		_____ - _____
Multiply by 10		_____ _____		_____ _____
Divide by 3		_____ _____		_____ _____
Practice Test score		_____ - _____		_____ - _____

How to take the TOEFL® Test successfully

Preparing for the TOEFL® Test

1. If you do not have a sound basic knowledge of English, it is best to take English language courses before taking a TOEFL® Test preparation course. Preparation materials are designed to help you improve your scores through reviewing English and becoming familiar with the testing procedures and format.
2. Begin your TOEFL® Test studies as soon as you decide to take the exam. It will not be useful to try to learn everything the week before the exam date.
3. Study on a regular basis. Thoroughly studying a small amount of material daily is more effective than insufficiently or inaccurately studying a large amount at one sitting.
4. All English practice is helpful. Listening to a movie or radio program in English is good for building your listening comprehension skills. Reading English-language newspaper or magazine articles will improve your reading comprehension skills. Systematically add new words to your vocabulary. Even though these activities are not directly related to the TOEFL® Test, they will help you.
5. Work carefully through the exercises in *Cambridge Preparation for the TOEFL® Test* that were indicated by the Diagnostic Test as your weak areas. Once you have

mastered the skills in your weak areas, you may want to skim other exercises to improve your stronger skills even further. However, it is best to concentrate the most effort on your weak areas.

Studying for the TOEFL® Test

1. Practice budgeting your time. Both the Computer-Based TOEFL® Test and the Paper-Based TOEFL® Test are taken under time-limit pressures. Time management is a key to doing well on the TOEFL® Test. Learn to use your time wisely so that you can complete each section.
2. If you are taking the Computer-Based TOEFL® Test, use the Tutorial that starts on page 13 or that is included on the CD-ROM to become familiar with the test format and how to answer the different kinds of questions in each section.
3. Identify your problem areas. Concentrate on those areas, but review other areas as well.
4. Know your goals. Write to the admissions office of the college or university of your choice, and ask for their entrance requirements. The college or university will confirm the minimum TOEFL® Test score required for admission.

Taking the Computer-Based TOEFL® Test

1. The test-center staff will tell you where to sit. You will have your own workstation and can control the volume of the Listening Section before the test starts.
2. Listen to and read the instructions carefully. If you don't follow the instructions correctly, you will get a computer message directing you to go back and follow the instructions.
3. After you have chosen an answer in the Listening or Structure Sections, you should click on the Next icon. If you click on the Next icon before you answer the question, you will get a computer message telling you that you must answer the question first.
4. In the Listening and Structure Sections, you will then need to confirm your answer before the computer will take you to the next question. Be sure of your choice before you click on the Answer Confirm icon because you cannot go back to change your answers.
5. You can skip questions or change answers in the Reading Section. However, to return to a question, you have to page back through all of the questions between the one you have skipped and the one you are on. Since this is time-consuming, it is best to complete the questions covering one reading passage before moving on to the next passage.
6. Pace yourself so that you will have enough time to think about and answer the questions. There is a clock icon that you can show and hide. The time display will flash when there are only five minutes left. You cannot hide the timer during the last five minutes.

Taking the Paper-Based TOEFL® Test

1. The test-center staff will tell you where to sit. You can ask for the volume of the cassette to be adjusted at the beginning of the test administration, but remember that it may not be possible to adjust the volume to suit all test-takers.
2. Listen to the instructions carefully. The cassette or audio CD will explain how to complete the personal data sheet and how to mark your answer sheet. It is important that you follow these instructions.
3. If you need to erase, do so thoroughly using a clean eraser.
4. Work quickly through the easy items. Be sure to skip a space on the answer sheet when you skip a difficult item. After you answer the easy items, return to the ones you skipped.
5. Do not underline any words in the test book or make any notes either in the test book or on the answer sheet. A light check mark on your answer sheet by any item you wish to recheck should be carefully erased before the end of the test.

6. If you finish one of the sections early, you may go back through that section to double-check your answers. Do not work on any other section of the test. This is not permitted. If you are caught working on the wrong section, your test will be invalidated.

7. Be prepared for changes. Occasionally a TOEFL® Test has a change in format or more items to answer in a longer period of time.

8. Answer all questions. However, do not waste time on difficult items. Eliminate as many answer choices as you can and then select one that you think may be correct and go on. If you simply don't know, you should guess. You are not penalized for guessing, and your guess may be correct.

TUTORIAL FOR THE COMPUTER-BASED TOEFL® TEST

This book tutorial will show you how to answer questions on the Computer-Based TOEFL® Test. The CD-ROM that accompanies this book also has tutorials that give you similar information. You may take the Quick Tutorial, which will take approximately 7 minutes, or the longer Full Tutorial, which will take approximately 30 minutes. It is recommended that you take the Tutorial on the computer if you have access to one.

If you do not have access to a computer as you prepare to take the Computer-Based TOEFL® Test, read these pages carefully. When you go to the testing center, you will be able to work through similar tutorials on the computer there before taking the actual test.

Using the Mouse

In the Listening, Structure, and Reading Sections of the Computer-Based TOEFL® Test, you will use a mouse to select the answers to the questions. (In the Writing Section, you will write an essay, which you may compose using the computer or a typewriter, or by writing it out by hand.)

A mouse is a device that allows you to make choices on the computer screen. As you hold the mouse in your hand and move it around on a smooth surface, an arrow on the computer screen moves correspondingly. This arrow is called the *mouse pointer.*

The mouse has two "buttons" on it (see illustration). To make a choice, you will position the mouse pointer over the answer you want on the computer screen and then gently press and release the left mouse button. This is called "clicking" the mouse. Always use the left button. The right button does not do anything when pressed on the Computer-Based TOEFL® Test.

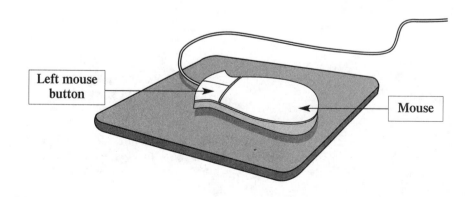

Left mouse button

Mouse

Here is an example of a typical question on the Computer-Based TOEFL® Test.

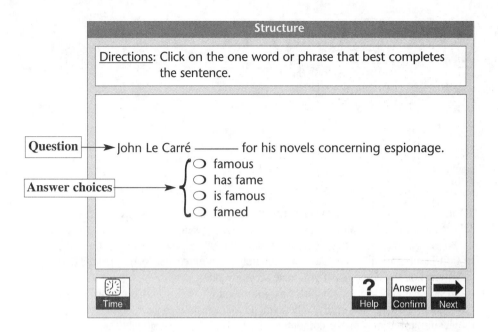

To answer the question, move the mouse until the mouse pointer is over the oval next to the choice that you want, or over the answer text itself. Then click the mouse. As shown below, the oval will darken to show your selection. If you change your mind, click on another answer choice. The oval next to your new choice will then darken.

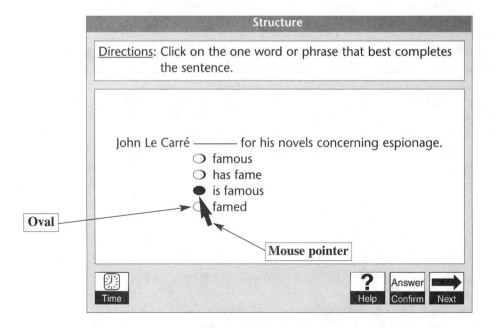

There are several different types of questions in the Listening, Structure, and Reading Sections of the Computer-Based TOEFL® Test, and you will answer all of them by pointing to your choices and clicking the mouse. This tutorial will show you all of the question types.

Listening

Part A

Part A of the Computer-Based TOEFL® Test consists of short conversations, each followed by one multiple-choice question with four answer choices. First, you will listen to a conversation. While you are listening, you will see a photograph of two people talking. This photograph is not important to answering the question. Concentrate on what the people are saying.

You will hear:

(man)	*I dropped my physics course because I discovered it didn't meet my degree requirements. You wouldn't know anyone in the class who would like to buy the course book, would you?*
(woman)	*Not offhand. But if you bought it new and kept the receipt, I'm sure you could get your money back or exchange it for one you do need.*
(man)	*I did buy it new, but I thought that the bookstore wouldn't refund money on textbooks.*
(woman)	*They will if you take it back within a reasonable time period. If I were you, I'd go there as soon as possible.*
(man)	*Right. Thanks for the tip.*

At the end of the conversation, you will see and hear the question. Then the answer choices will appear. Each answer choice has an oval next to it.

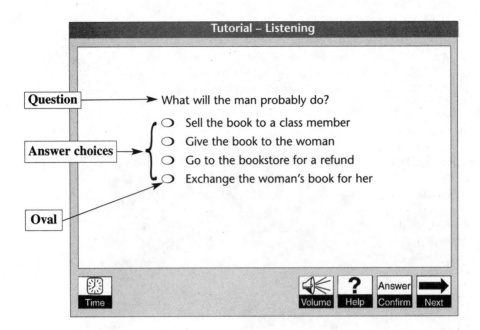

This question requires you to select the one best answer. To answer this question, position the mouse pointer over the answer of your choice and click the mouse.

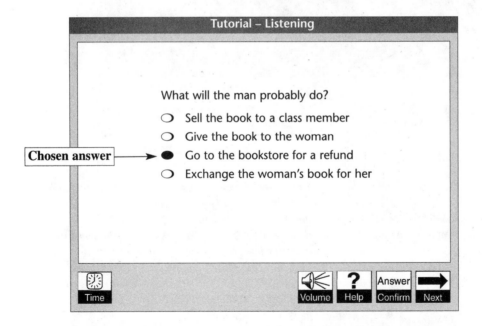

If you change your mind, click on another answer. When you are sure that you have selected the answer you want, click on the Next icon. Then click on the Answer Confirm icon. After you click on Next and Answer Confirm, the computer will go on to the next conversation and question. You will not be able to return to the question that you have just answered.

Part B

In Part B of the Computer-Based TOEFL® Test, you will hear longer conversations as well as academic discussions and classroom lectures.

Academic discussions and lectures are preceded by one or two sentences that tell you the subject matter of the listening passage you are about to hear. Pay attention to these introductions because they can help you understand what the speakers are talking about.

As you listen to academic discussions and lectures, you will see photographs of professors and students, and sometimes you will see illustrations that help the speakers make their point. The photographs of the people are not important in answering the questions, but you should pay attention to the illustrations because they can help you understand what the speakers are saying. Note that the illustrations are not visible throughout the lecture. They appear on the screen only when the speakers are referring to them.

At the end of the listening passage, you will be presented with a number of questions, one at a time. Some of the questions are like the ones in Part A, but there are additional types which are demonstrated on the pages that follow.

Here is an example of an academic discussion.

You will see:

Only one photograph is shown above. When taking the Computer-Based TOEFL® Test, you may see several photographs and sometimes illustrations as the talk progresses.

You will hear:

Listen to part of a discussion in an Earth Sciences class. The participants are talking about atmospheric phenomena.

(woman 1)	*Of course, you are all familiar with rainbows, perhaps the most beautiful of atmospheric phenomena. However, there are other interesting but less common phenomena that are produced when light from the sun or the moon passes through ice crystals associated with high-level clouds. The crystals bend the light at different angles, depending on their orientation to the surface of the earth.*
(woman 2)	*That sounds as though the crystals act like prisms, bending each wavelength of light at a different angle.*
(woman 1)	*That's right. Now, if the light enters these tiny ice prisms at just the right angle, it is scattered around the sun or moon in a ring of light called a halo. These halos occur when the ice crystals, through which the light shines, are randomly dispersed. Now, sometimes the ice crystals are aligned horizontally instead of randomly. This causes a different phenomenon to occur. If the sun is low in the sky and its light shines through these horizontal ice crystals, we see two bright spots, one on either side of the actual sun.*
(man)	*Are those what are known as sun dogs?*
(woman 1)	*Yes. And, like halos, sun dogs are caused by the bending of light.*
(man)	*Isn't there a phenomenon called a sun pillar?*
(woman 1)	*I was coming to that. A sun pillar is a vertical shaft of light extending upwards or downwards from the sun – just like a pillar, in fact. It occurs when sunlight reflects off the horizontally aligned ice crystals. Sun pillars tend to occur around sunrise or sunset. I must point out that all of these sights can be very spectacular, and I hope you are all fortunate enough to witness them at some time.*

At the conclusion of the lecture, you will see and hear the questions, presented one at a time. Here are examples of the question types.

Multiple Choice/One Correct Answer

This question asks you to select one answer. To answer this question, position the mouse pointer over the oval next to the answer that you want. Then click the mouse. To change your answer, click on another oval.

When you are satisfied with your answer, click on ▮Next▮ and then on ▮Answer Confirm▮ to move on to the next question. The example that follows shows the correct answer selected.

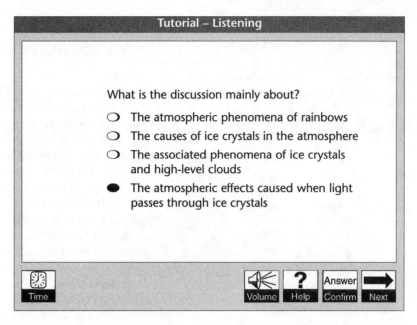

Multiple Choice/Two Correct Answers

This question asks you to select more than one correct answer. You must select two answers in order to continue. Click on the answers you think are correct, or click on the boxes next to the answers. To erase a selection, click on it again.

When you are ready to go on to the next question, click on Next and then on Answer Confirm.

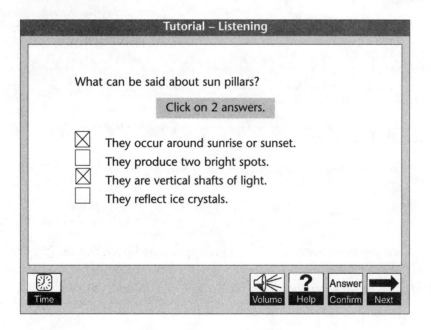

Multiple Choice/Picture or Graph

This question asks you to select an answer by clicking on a picture or graph. Click on the picture or graph that answers the question. After you click on a picture, a dark frame will appear around it, as shown below. To change your answer, click on another picture.
When you are satisfied with your answer, click on Next and then on Answer Confirm.

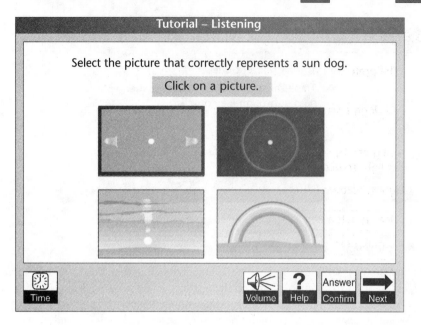

Ordering

In Ordering questions, you must put four phrases or sentences in order of their occurrence, from the first to the last. To answer this kind of question, click on each phrase or sentence and then click on the space where it belongs. The answer choice will appear in that box. For example, if you think that the upper-right-hand statement comes first, click on the sentence and then click on the box labeled "1." Proceed with the other sentences until you have placed all of the sentences in the correct order.

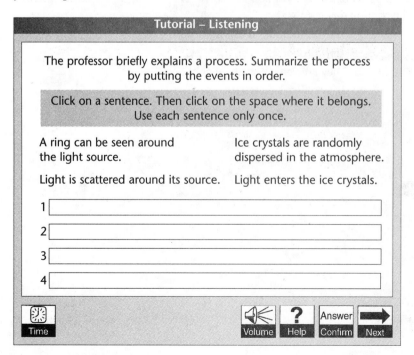

When all answers are completed, the screen will look like the one below. To change an answer, click on the box where the sentence appears. The sentence will disappear. Then click on the sentence that you want and click on the box again. The new sentence will appear in the box. When you are ready to go on to the next question, click on Next and then on Answer Confirm.

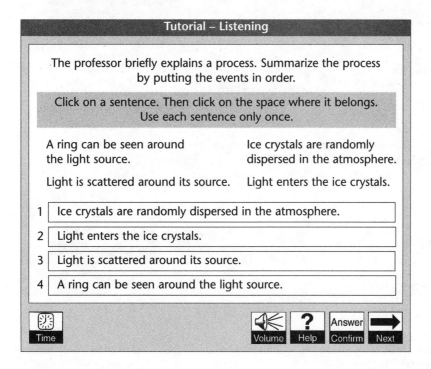

Match the Terms

Match-the-Terms questions present a group of words or phrases and ask you to match them with definitions, descriptions, or illustrations in a chart. Select your answers by clicking on one of the words or phrases at the top. Then click on the space below the description that goes with it. The word or phrase will appear in the space.

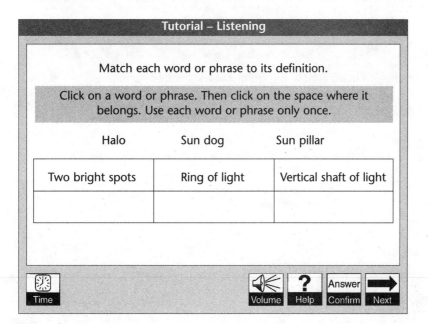

When all answers are completed, the screen will look like the one below. To change your answer, click on the box that contains the word or phrase you want to change. It will disappear. Then click on another word or phrase at the top and click in the box again. To go on to the next question, click on Next and then on Answer Confirm.

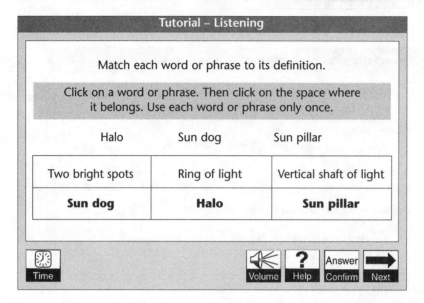

Structure

There are two question types in the Structure Section: Complete the Sentence and Identify the Error.

Complete the Sentence

To answer a Complete-the-Sentence question, you must read the sentence and decide which of the four answer choices completes the sentence correctly. Click on the answer choice or the oval next to your choice. The oval will darken, as shown below. To change your answer, click on another choice. When you are ready to go on to the next question, click on Next and then on Answer Confirm.

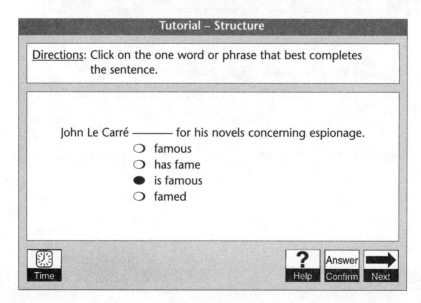

Identify the Error

In Identify-the-Error questions, one of the underlined parts of the sentence must be changed for the sentence to be correct. You will click on the underlined word or phrase that must be changed. When you click on an underlined part of the sentence, it will darken, as shown below. To change your answer, click on another underlined word or phrase. To go on to the next question, click on **Next** and then on **Answer Confirm**.

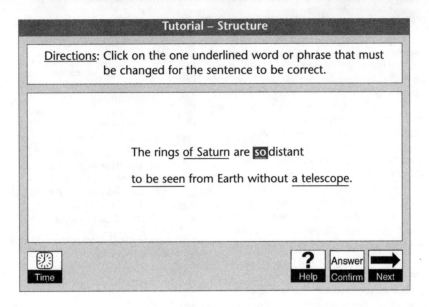

Reading

The Reading Section of the Computer-Based TOEFL® Test is different in some ways from the Listening or Structure Sections. Look at the following screen.

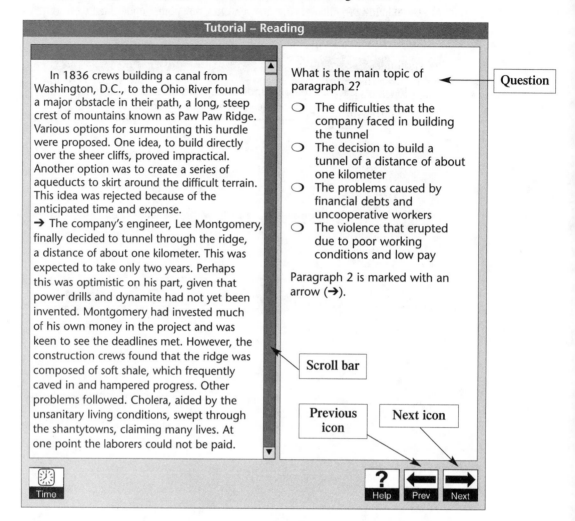

The reading passages appear in the left part of the screen. The questions following each passage appear in the right part of the screen. The passages are usually too long to fit on the screen. To read the entire passage, you must scroll down the screen. You can scroll down in two ways. First, you can place the mouse pointer over the down arrow at the bottom of the scroll bar and click the mouse repeatedly (or hold the mouse button down to scroll fast). As you do this, the lines "below" the screen will become visible. The other way to scroll down is to place the mouse pointer over the square button within the scroll bar, hold down the mouse button, and move the square button down.

As you scroll down, the text at the top of the screen disappears. To see this text, you have to scroll up. This is the reverse of scrolling down: Click on the up arrow (or place the mouse pointer over the button on the scroll bar, hold down the mouse button, and move the square button up).

The first time that you see a selection, the computer will not allow you to proceed until you scroll down to the bottom of the text. If you try to proceed without scrolling down, the computer will give you a message telling you to scroll down to the bottom of the passage.

Unlike in the Listening and Structure Sections, you can skip questions and return to them later in the Reading Section. You can also change your answers to questions that you have already answered. To do this, click on Prev (Previous) to go back. Click on Next to go forward.

In the Reading Section, there are four types of questions.

Multiple Choice

A Multiple-Choice question asks you to select the one correct answer from among four choices. To answer the question, click on the answer choice or on the oval next to your choice. If you change your mind, click on another choice. Click on Next to go on to the next question.

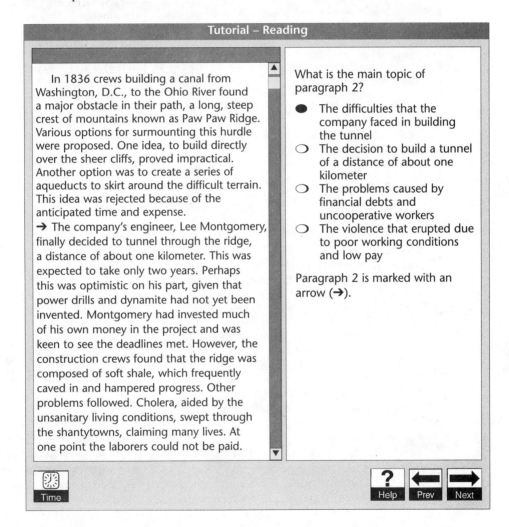

Sometimes, multiple-choice answers are pictures or graphs rather than words. To answer these questions, click on one of the four choices. To change your answer, click on another choice. Click on Next to go on to the next question.

Click on a Sentence or Paragraph

Click-on-a-Sentence or Click-on-a-Paragraph questions ask you to find the sentence in a paragraph, or the paragraph in the passage, that answers the question. To answer a click-on-a-sentence question, first find the correct paragraph in the selection in the left part of the screen. It will be preceded by an arrow (➔). The sentence that answers the question will be in that paragraph. When you find the sentence you want, click anywhere in the sentence. The sentence will become highlighted, as shown below.

To change your answer, click on another sentence. When you are satisfied with your answer, click on Next to go on to the next question.

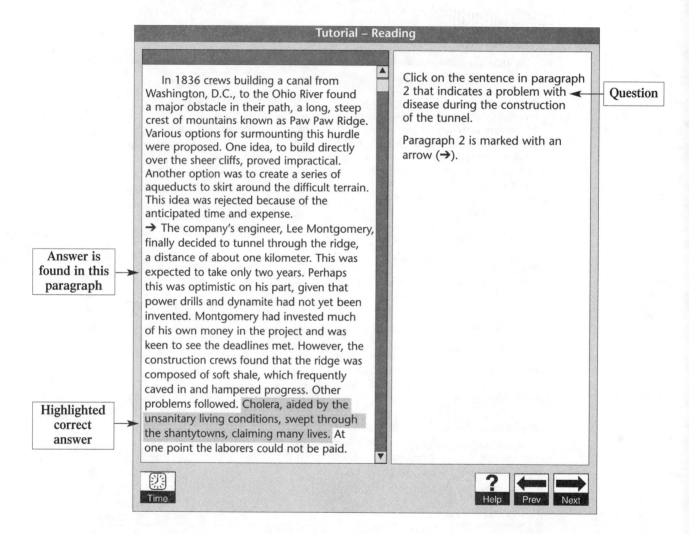

Sometimes, you will be asked to find and click on a paragraph instead of a sentence. The paragraph can be located anywhere in the passage, so remember to scroll so that you can see all of the paragraphs. When you find the one that answers the question, click on it. If you change your mind, click on another paragraph. When you want to go to the next question, click on Next.

Click on the Word or Phrase

Click-on-the-Word or Click-on-the-Phrase questions ask you to identify a word or a phrase in the **bold** text. Sometimes, as in the example below, the question asks you to find a synonym. In other questions, you must find a word that is OPPOSITE in meaning to the word highlighted in the question. Other questions give you a word (usually a pronoun such as *they*) and ask you to find the word or phrase in the **bold** text that the word refers to. In all cases, you answer the question by reading the part of the selection that appears in **bold** text.

Bold text →

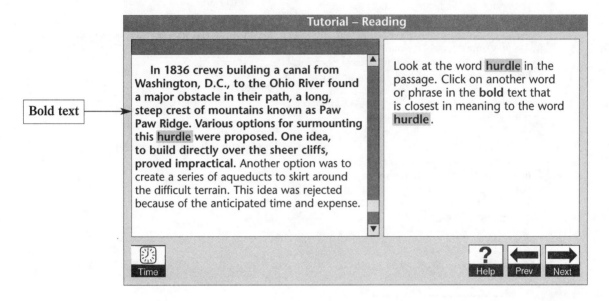

When you find the word or phrase that answers the question, click on it. The word or phrase will become highlighted, as shown below. If you want to change your answer, click on another word. When you are finished answering the question, click on Next to go on to the next question.

Highlighted answer choice →

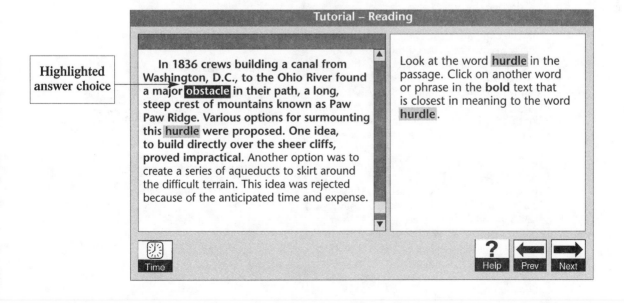

Add a Sentence

Add-a-Sentence questions ask you to find the best place in a paragraph to put a new sentence. Answer the question by clicking on the black square in the paragraph that shows where the sentence could best be added.

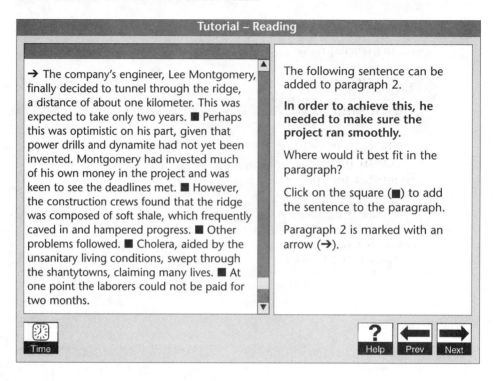

When you click on a square, the sentence will appear in the paragraph. It will be highlighted so that you can see it, as shown below. To change your answer, click on another black square. When you are ready to move on to the next question, click on Next.

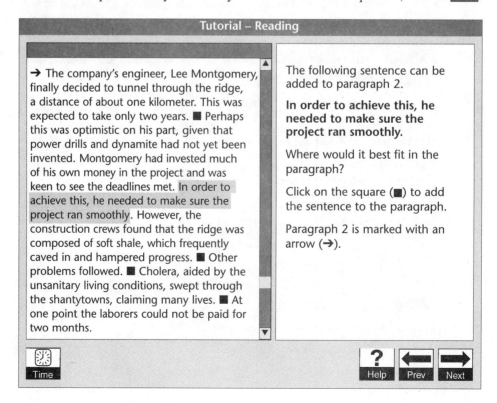

Writing

This part of the Tutorial shows you how to write your essay on the computer. Note that you may also write the essay out by hand or use a typewriter.

Understanding the Writing Screen

Here is an example of a Writing screen.

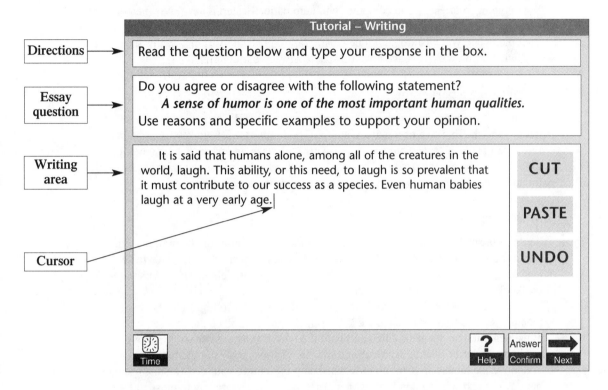

The directions and essay question with the topic that you are to write about appear at the top of the screen. The area that you will write in is below the topic. In the example above, the test-taker has begun the essay. Note the vertical line after the last word. This is called the *cursor*. On the computer, the cursor blinks constantly so that you can locate it easily. The cursor shows you where you are in the text. If you type a letter, it will always appear to the left of the cursor.

Using Special Keys on the Computer Keyboard

Here is an example of a typical keyboard. Moving around on the screen and typing and deleting text using these special keys is explained in detail on the following page.

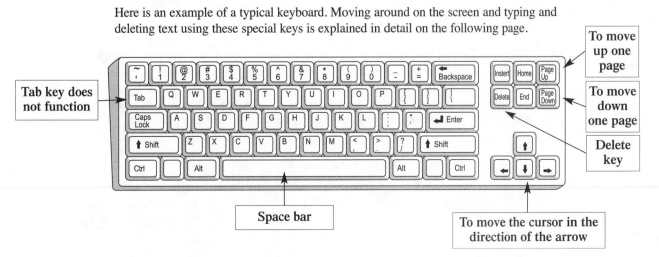

1. Moving around on the screen

Once you have started typing your essay, the writing area will fill up quickly. To see the part of your essay that is above and below the writing area, you can use the **Page Up** and **Page Down** keys on the computer keyboard. You can also use the arrow keys on the keyboard, or use the mouse to reposition the cursor.

2. Starting a new line

When typing your essay, the computer will automatically start a new line when you get to the end of a line. If you want to start a new line before you get to the right margin (for example, when you wish to start a new paragraph), press the **Enter** key. Press the **Enter** key twice if you want to leave an extra space between paragraphs.

3. Indenting a paragraph

If you want to indent your paragraphs (that is, leave a blank space between the left margin and the first line of a new paragraph), first press the **Enter** key to start a new line. Then press the space bar five times. This will make an appropriate indentation for your new paragraph. (*Note:* The **Tab** key on the keyboard, which is normally used to indent paragraphs, does not work in this word-processing program.)

4. Deleting text

To delete a small amount of text, position the mouse pointer at the beginning of the text you want to delete. Click to make the blinking cursor appear. Press the **Delete** key on the keyboard one time for each letter or space that you want to delete. The letters to the right of the blinking cursor will be deleted.

To delete a larger amount of text, it is sometimes faster to highlight the text and then press the **Delete** or **Backspace** key. To highlight text, place the mouse pointer at the beginning of the text. Click and hold the mouse button down as you move the mouse to the end of the text you want to delete. The text will become highlighted as you move the mouse. When you have finished highlighting your text, release the mouse button. The text will remain highlighted. Then press the **Delete** key to erase the text that you highlighted.

Using the Word-Processing Menu

Some of the features that are available on other word-processing programs can also be used in the Writing test. You can use the **Cut**, **Paste**, and **Undo** options to make writing on the computer easier.

1. Cut and Paste

When you *cut* words or sentences from your essay, they disappear from the screen and are placed in the computer's temporary memory. When you *paste* words or sentences, they are retrieved from memory and put back into your essay. This feature is helpful when, for example, you wish to move a sentence from one place in your essay to another. The examples on the following pages show how to cut and paste.

First, highlight the text that you want to cut, as shown below.

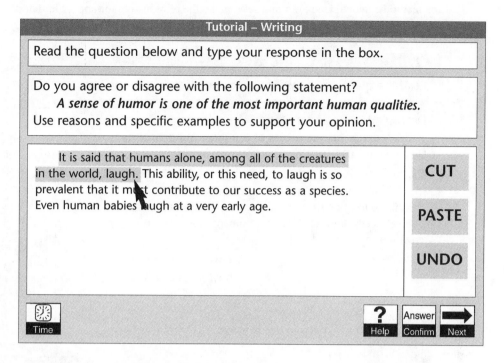

Next, click on the **Cut** button on the word-processing menu. The text will disappear.

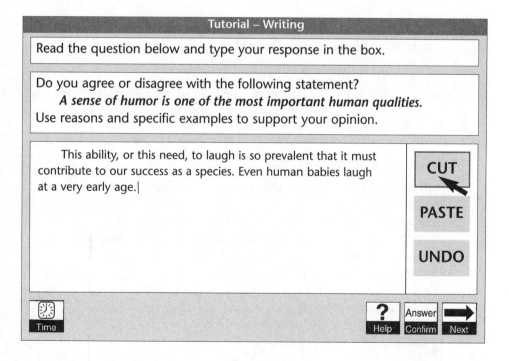

You can use the **Cut** function simply to delete text. If that is all you want to do, continue writing. But if you want to place the text somewhere else in your essay, you can use the **Paste** function.

To place text that you have cut elsewhere, position the mouse pointer where you want the text to be added. Click the mouse to make the blinking cursor appear in that place. Then click on the **Paste** button. The text will reappear in its new location.

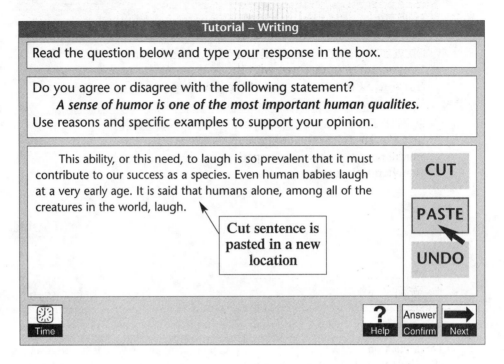

2. Undo

If you click on **Undo**, the computer will reverse your last action. If you have just typed some words, they will disappear when you click on **Undo**. If you have just cut or pasted text, that action will be reversed. Clicking on **Undo** again will return your text to its previous state. If you click on **Cut** to erase text and then click on **Undo**, the text will reappear. If you click on **Undo** again, the text will disappear again. In the example below, the highlighted text will disappear.

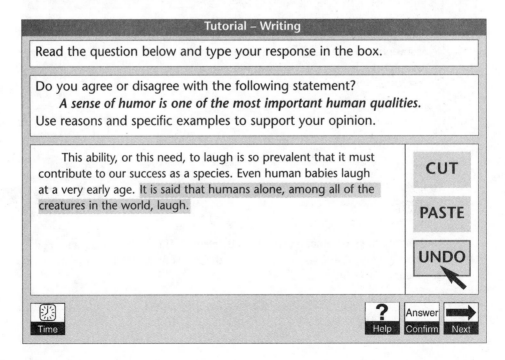

In this example, the sentence has disappeared because the previous paste function has been undone.

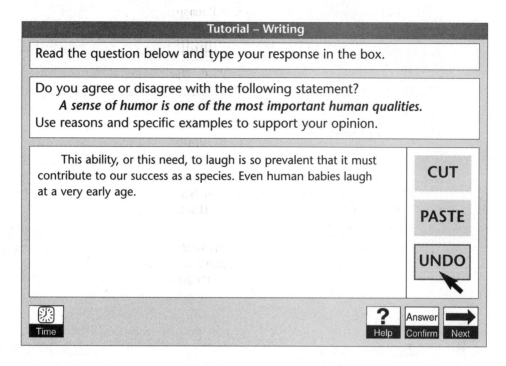

By clicking on **Undo** again, the sentence will reappear, as shown below.

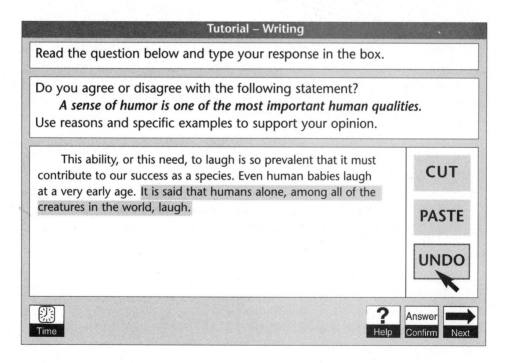

3. Save

When using the CD-ROM that accompanies this book, you can save your essay on your computer by clicking on the **Save** button. Your computer will ask you where you want to save the essay.

4. Print

If you have a printer, you can print your essay by clicking on the **Print** button.

Completing Your Essay

When you have finished your essay, you must click on Next , and then on Answer Confirm. Reread your essay carefully. You may not make further changes after you have clicked on Answer Confirm.

DIAGNOSTIC
· TEST ·

Before you use this book, take the Diagnostic Test, which is Test 1 on the CD-ROM that accompanies this book. Alternatively, you can take the Diagnostic Test on the pages that follow.

Take this test as if you were taking an actual TOEFL® Test. If you are unsure of TOEFL® Test procedures, read the instructions on pages 11–12 of the Introduction to this book.

Taking the Diagnostic Test on the Computer

If you have access to computer equipment on which to use the CD-ROM, it is suggested that you take the Diagnostic Test (Test 1) on the computer. This will allow you to experience a close approximation of the actual Computer-Based TOEFL® Test.

Before taking a test on the computer, arrange to have a quiet place where you will not be disturbed for the duration of the test. The Diagnostic Test will take approximately three hours.

The CD-ROM will pace you through the test, and it will provide you with an approximate score. After you have finished the test, you can see a list of the questions that you answered incorrectly. If you review the questions, you will be referred to a section of the book that will help you answer questions of this type. For example, you may see: See Exercises L1–L8.

During the Listening and Structure Sections of the actual Computer-Based TOEFL® Test, you may not go back to check your work or change your answers. However, you may go back to review your work in the Reading Section before time is called.

Taking the Diagnostic Test on Paper

If you do not have access to a computer, take the Diagnostic Test that follows in this book. The presentation of the questions in the book is similar to the way they will look on the computer screen. Before taking one of the tests, make the following preparations:

1. Arrange to have a quiet room where you will not be disturbed for the duration of the test. The Diagnostic Test will take approximately three hours.
2. Bring the following items: a cassette or CD player; the cassette or CD that contains the Diagnostic Test; two sharpened black-lead pencils with erasers; and a watch, a clock, or a timer.
3. Bring extra paper if you do not want to write in the book. You will also need paper on which to write your essay.

When you have completed the test, check your answers against the Answer Key that starts on page 495. If you marked a wrong answer, the Answer Key will tell you which exercises in the book will help you improve in that area. For example, you may see: See Exercises L1–L8.

LISTENING
Time – approximately 60 minutes

This section measures your ability to understand spoken English. There are fifty questions in this section. The listening material and questions about it will be presented only one time. You may not take notes.

Part A

In this part, you will hear short conversations between two people. Each conversation is followed by a question about it. Each question in this part has four answer choices. Choose the best answer to each question. Answer the questions on the basis of what is <u>stated</u> or <u>implied</u> by the speakers.

 Now we will begin Part A with the first conversation.

1. What does the man mean?
   (A) Tom's part in the play included mime.
   (B) Tom lifted an iced drink.
   (C) It was kind of Tom to make the offer.
   (D) Tom waved his hand as he parted.

2. What does the woman mean?
   (A) They shipped her the gift.
   (B) They broke what was in the package.
   (C) They arranged to go away.
   (D) They shared the cost of the gift.

3. What does the woman mean?
   (A) Hardback books cost twice as much as before.
   (B) The cost of hardback books goes up two or three times a year.
   (C) The cost of hardback books has gone up twice in the last three years.
   (D) Two years ago hardback books cost a third as much as now.

4. What does the woman mean?
   (A) She thinks they didn't go to the Supreme Court.
   (B) She can't believe they went to the Supreme Court.
   (C) It doesn't seem possible to her that they missed the Supreme Court.
   (D) Their going to the Supreme Court seems unbelievable.

5. What does the woman imply?
   (A) He passed by a narrow margin.
   (B) He was close to a passing mark.
   (C) He will be called into the physics office.
   (D) He shouldn't shout in the hallway.

6. What does the man imply?
   (A) He doesn't want the woman to visit him.
   (B) It's easy to find his house.
   (C) The woman wouldn't be able to find the parking lot.
   (D) It's difficult to explain how to get to his house.

7. What does the woman say about Scott?
   (A) He finished working on his dissertation more than five years ago.
   (B) He has taken less than five years to write his dissertation.
   (C) He began writing his dissertation more than five years ago.
   (D) He will be writing his dissertation for at least five more years.

8. What does the woman mean?
   (A) They need to buy some gasoline.
   (B) They should ask for directions.
   (C) They need to check their headlights and taillights.
   (D) They should pull off the road.

9. What does the woman imply?
   (A) She needs to get a haircut.
   (B) She's going to visit Barbara.
   (C) She wants to see Jim.
   (D) She's on her way to exercise.

10. What does the woman mean?
    (A) She is surprised he didn't finish.
    (B) She is surprised he took so long to finish.
    (C) She is surprised the exam was so easy.
    (D) She is surprised the exam took hardly any time at all.

11. What does the woman imply the man should do?
    (A) Ask about bus routes at the information desk
    (B) Refer to the map at the bus station
    (C) Pick up a map from the information desk
    (D) Map out the routes in the Student Union

12. What does the woman imply?
    (A) Her sister cut her hair.
    (B) Her sister works at home.
    (C) Her sister will cut his hair.
    (D) Her sister needs more practice.

13. What does the woman mean?
    (A) She's upset with Jill about not giving her notes back.
    (B) She wants to give Jill another piece of information.
    (C) She's thinking about binding her notes.
    (D) She wouldn't mind going to see Jill about the notes.

14. What does the man mean?
    (A) He's heard about Sue's great ideas.
    (B) He agrees with Sue's ideas for the project.
    (C) He thinks Sue's ideas are impractical.
    (D) He finds some of Sue's ideas agreeable.

15. What does the woman mean?
    - (A) She can't believe that Bob has already completed his work.
    - (B) She knows that Bob won't be able to go back to the library.
    - (C) She doesn't know that Bob didn't finish the assignment.
    - (D) She's certain that Bob shouldn't have gone back to the library.

16. What can be inferred about the woman?
    - (A) She would probably rather walk to the university than take the bus.
    - (B) She is probably very studious and wants to be far away from campus life.
    - (C) She would probably like to commute to Los Altos from a quiet suburb.
    - (D) She probably has to commute to the university campus frequently.

17. What does the man mean?
    - (A) Dan's leave-taking surprised him.
    - (B) It wasn't true that Dan asked him to make a speech.
    - (C) He was amazed at the way Dan defended him.
    - (D) He didn't know what to say when Dan accused him.

18. What does the woman mean?
    - (A) Ted could set up a good deal for the man.
    - (B) The man should consider driving a bus.
    - (C) Ted would be interested in buying the man's car.
    - (D) The man could get good information about bicycles from Ted.

This is the end of Part A.
Go on to Part B.

Part B

In this part, there are several talks and conversations. Each talk or conversation is followed by several questions. The conversations and talks are about a variety of topics. You do not need special knowledge of the topics to answer the questions correctly. Rather, you should answer each question on the basis of what is <u>stated</u> or <u>implied</u> in the conversation or talk. You may not take notes.

🎧 Now we will begin Part B with the first conversation.

19. What is the main topic of the conversation?
    (A) The birthday gift for Phil
    (B) The man's fencing class
    (C) The time and place to meet
    (D) The best place to park

20. Why does the woman want to go downtown?
    (A) She wants to buy a present for Phil.
    (B) She needs to pick up her new contact lenses.
    (C) She has to pay a fine for a traffic ticket.
    (D) She wants to help the man buy a present.

21. Where are the people going to meet?
    (A) In front of the gym building
    (B) In the fencing class
    (C) On the one-way street
    (D) In the student parking lot

22. What happened to the woman?
    (A) She didn't complete her assignment.
    (B) She reported to Dr. Reed.
    (C) She waited in line to meet Dr. Reed.
    (D) She got an extension.

23. What did Dr. Reed give the woman?
    (A) A new deadline
    (B) A different assignment
    (C) Some organizational tips
    (D) Some ideas for the report

24. What does the man want?
    (A) A copy of the assignment
    (B) The due dates for future reports
    (C) The main points of the assignment
    (D) Advice on organizing his material

25. What is the man going to do during the summer?
    (A) Attend classes
    (B) Hold down a part-time job
    (C) Go camping in Colorado
    (D) Dig on an archaeological site

26. What is NOT done at Copper Mountain?
    (A) Fossil collecting
    (B) Mapping strata
    (C) Laboratory analysis
    (D) Fieldwork

27. According to the man, why can't some of the summer classes be held during the academic year?

    Choose 2 answers.

    A   Because too many students are interested in taking them
    B   Because field trips would keep students away from regular classes
    C   Because professors are too busy to help students
    D   Because weather conditions can make it difficult to work

28. What objects might be found at a buffalo-kill site?
    (A) Buffalo bones and flint knives
    (B) Buffalo skins and rifles
    (C) Buffalo herds grazing near cliffs
    (D) Buffalo meat being dried

29. What does the man imply about summer classes?
    (A) They're more interesting than regular classes.
    (B) They're more work than regular classes.
    (C) They're more expensive than regular classes.
    (D) They're more challenging than regular classes.

Now get ready to listen.

Now get ready to answer the questions.

30. What are the people discussing?
    (A) A well-known painting
    (B) A painting that thieves favor
    (C) A popular painting among the public
    (D) The most valuable painting
        in the museum

31. How long had the painting been missing?
    (A) For 3 years
    (B) For 4 years
    (C) For 5 years
    (D) For 20 years

32. What reason is given for the painting's popularity among thieves?
    (A) It's a Rembrandt.
    (B) It's worth $5 million.
    (C) It's easily recognized.
    (D) It's 9 by 11 inches.

33. What is the professor uncertain about?
    (A) How thieves can steal the painting
    (B) Why someone would buy a painting
    (C) How many times the painting has
        been taken
    (D) How much a stolen painting sells for

34. Select the work of art below that thieves would be attracted to.

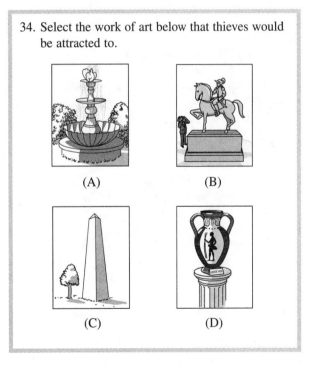

(A)   (B)

(C)   (D)

Now get ready to listen.

Now get ready to answer the questions.

35. What is the purpose of the talk?
    (A) To examine the causes of population movement
    (B) To explain why humans started leaving Africa
    (C) To show how North America was settled
    (D) To outline the history of human migration

36. How did people survive the Ice Age in northern Europe and Asia?
    (A) They moved south to avoid the cold.
    (B) They made shelter, clothes, and fire.
    (C) They hunted migrating animals.
    (D) They took over unused land.

37. What does the speaker say about the invasion of occupied land by human groups?
    (A) It is not related to human migration.
    (B) It is one form of human migration.
    (C) It occurred mainly in Europe.
    (D) It was practiced only when there was no free land.

38. What does the speaker say about human migration?
    (A) It was done mainly by early tribal societies.
    (B) It appears to no longer be common.
    (C) It seems to be a basic human instinct.
    (D) It has been done only at certain times in history.

39. The professor briefly explains a series of human migrations. Put the migrations in chronological order.

    Write the letter of each sentence in the space where it belongs. Use each sentence only once.

    | A | Humans crossed the Bering land bridge and spread throughout the Americas. |
    | B | Humans migrated from the savannahs of Africa into Europe and Asia. |
    | C | Humans spread through eastern Asia and south to Australia. |
    | D | Humans have continued to migrate throughout the world. |

1	
2	
3	
4	

Now get ready to listen.

Listening	Listening	Listening
American Literature **Jack London**		

Now get ready to answer the questions.

40. What is the main topic of the professor's discussion?
    (A) Jack London's works
    (B) Jack London's life
    (C) Jack London's politics
    (D) Jack London's family

41. Why did London become a writer?
    (A) Because of his failure in becoming a political leader
    (B) To avoid working in a factory
    (C) Because he was an avid reader
    (D) To cover the costs of his kidney illness

42. According to the professor, where did London get his ideas for his publications?

    Choose 2 answers.

    A He retold stories written by other authors.
    B He told the stories of people he met when he was a factory worker.
    C He used material from his own experiences.
    D He created stories from his imagination.

43. Why does the professor mention London's novel *The Call of the Wild*?
    (A) To give an example of London's diverse experiences
    (B) To name a work that showed London's anticapitalist ideas
    (C) To name the work that brought London fame
    (D) To give an example of London's disciplined approach to writing

44. According to the professor, in what ways was London inconsistent and self-contradictory?

    Choose 2 answers.

    A In his support for socialism
    B In his support for women's rights
    C In his support for the prohibition of alcohol
    D In his innovative ideas

45. The professor describes London's life chronologically. Summarize his life by putting the events in order.

    Write the letter of each sentence in the space where it belongs. Use each sentence only once.

    A London worked at becoming a successful writer.
    B London introduced practical innovations on his ranch.
    C London's family settled in Oakland after having moved around.
    D London's working life as a young man was very diverse.

1	
2	
3	
4	

Now get ready to listen.

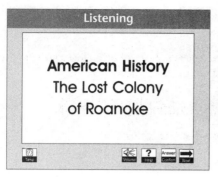 

Now get ready to answer the questions.

46. What is the lecture mainly about?
   (A) Theories of the Roanoke episode
   (B) Scholars' claims about the Lost Colony
   (C) The return of the original Roanoke colonists
   (D) The events surrounding the Roanoke mystery

47. According to the professor, what did the people on the relief vessels find in Roanoke?

   Choose 2 answers.

   A The 100 new pioneers
   B An abandoned fort
   C Cut-down entrance posts to the fort
   D A mysterious clue

48. Which of the following may explain what happened to the Roanoke settlers?
   (A) They returned to England for supplies.
   (B) They moved to a nearby fort.
   (C) They married into the native population.
   (D) They got involved in the war with Spain.

49. What happened to each of the three groups of people left at Roanoke?

   Write the letter of each phrase in the space where it belongs. Use each phrase only once.

   A were found dead
   B disappeared
   C returned to England

The original settlers	The holding force of fifteen men	The 100 new settlers
1.	2.	3.

50. Why does the professor refer to Roanoke as an enigmatic episode in early American history?
   (A) Because Roanoke had been abandoned
   (B) Because there was not a trace of the settlers on the island of Croatoan
   (C) Because what happened to the settlers is a mystery
   (D) Because the story is fascinating for history students

This is the end of the Listening Section.
Turn off your cassette or audio CD player now.

Go on to the Structure Section.

STRUCTURE

Time – 15 minutes

This section measures your ability to understand the structures of standard written English. There are twenty questions in this section. There are two types of questions.

The first type of question consists of incomplete sentences. Beneath each sentence there are four words or phrases. You will select the one word or phrase that best completes the sentence.

Example:

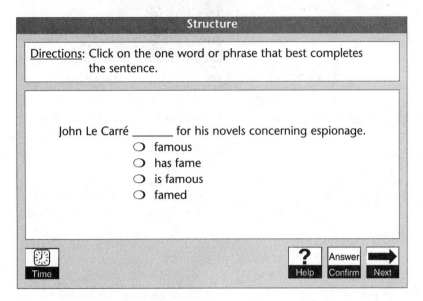

The second type of question consists of a sentence with four underlined words or phrases. You will select the one underlined word or phrase that must be changed for the sentence to be correct.

Example:

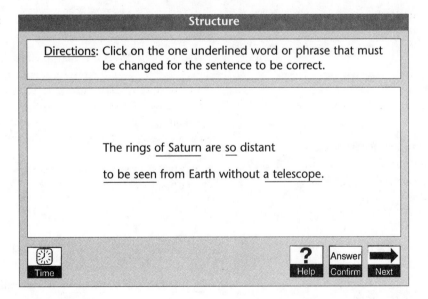

Now begin working on the Structure questions.

1. Not all birds _____ .
   (A) flying
   (B) fly
   (C) to fly
   (D) flown

2. Natural predators, <u>disturbing</u> from tourists,
                            A

   and pollution <u>have</u> all <u>contributed</u>
                   B   C

   to the <u>decline</u> of the California condor.
              D

3. A construction kit consists of parts that can
   be _____.
   (A) together they are fitted
   (B) that when fitted together
   (C) fitted together
   (D) together are fitted

4. The Soay sheep, the <u>old</u> breed of sheep in
                          A

   existence, <u>has changed</u> little <u>since</u> 3500 B.C.E.
        B   C   D

5. The Swedish scientist _____ to people
   who have done something important
   to help humankind.
   (A) left money to be awarded
       to Alfred B. Nobel
   (B) Alfred B. Nobel left to be awarded money
   (C) Alfred B. Nobel left money to be awarded
   (D) awarding money to Alfred B. Nobel
       to be left

6. A traveler can <u>reach</u> some of <u>the village</u> along
                    A   B

   the Amazon <u>only</u> by <u>riverboat</u>.
                 C   D

7. The western part of Oregon generally receives
   more rain than _____ the eastern part.
   (A) in it does
   (B) does
   (C) it does in
   (D) in

8. Fiber <u>is important</u> element <u>in</u> nutrition, and it
              A   B

   aids in <u>protecting</u> the digestive tract <u>as</u> well.
                 C   D

9. _____ porpoises and dolphins, whales
   are mammals.
   (A) As
   (B) Also
   (C) Like
   (D) When

10. <u>The first</u> European <u>settlement</u> of Australia
         A   B

    <u>left</u> the city of Portsmouth <u>in</u> May 1787.
       C   D

11. _____, Luxor did not reach preeminence until about 2000 B.C.E.
    (A) Many centuries earlier it was founded
    (B) The city founded centuries earlier
    (C) Although founded many centuries earlier
    (D) Founding the city centuries earlier

12. Starches <u>provide</u> people <u>with</u> important
              A   B

    nutrients <u>which</u> they need <u>them</u>.
           C   D

13. _____ living in Birmingham, England, that the American writer Washington Irving wrote *Rip Van Winkle.*
    (A) It was
    (B) There he was
    (C) It was while
    (D) While he was

14. The Bactrian, <u>or</u> Asian, camel <u>can be</u> <u>identified</u>
                  A   B   C

    by <u>their</u> two humps.
       D

15. _____ known as "Stonehenge" has never been determined.
    (A) Who built the stone circle
    (B) The stone circle
    (C) That the stone circle
    (D) There is the stone circle

16. <u>A</u> trade center since <u>antiquity</u>, Catalonia <u>itself</u>
     A   B   C

    has often been ruled by <u>outsider</u>.
                        D

17. Certain Paleolithic artifacts are given special terms _____.
    (A) which indicating their location of discovery
    (B) whose locations are indicating their discovery
    (C) what the location of their discovery is
    (D) indicating the location of their discovery

18. <u>Early</u> balloonists remained aloft <u>in the air</u>
      A   B

    for <u>relatively</u> short <u>periods</u>.
           C   D

19. No matter _____, Mozart was an accomplished composer while still a child.
    (A) how remarkable it seems
    (B) how seems it remarkable
    (C) it seems remarkable how
    (D) how it seems remarkable

20. <u>At</u> space camp, <u>youngsters</u> go through
     A   B

    <u>concentrated</u> astronaut training <u>but</u> shuttle
          C   D

    simulations.

This is the end of the Structure Section.
Go on to the Reading Section.

READING

Time – 80 minutes
(including the reading of the passages)

In this section, you will read several passages. Each passage is followed by ten to fifteen questions. There are fifty questions in this section. You should answer all questions following a passage on the basis of what is <u>stated</u> or <u>implied</u> in that passage. For each question, select or write the correct answer.

Now begin reading the first passage.

Questions 1–11

Experiments have shown that in selecting personnel for a job, interviewing is, at best, a hindrance and may even cause harm. These studies have disclosed that the judgments of interviewers differ markedly and bear little or no relationship to the adequacy of job applicants. Of the many reasons why this should be the case, four in particular stand out. The first reason is related to an error of judgment known as the "halo effect." If a person has one noticeably good trait, his or her other characteristics will be judged as better than they really are. Thus, an individual who dresses smartly and shows self-confidence is likely to be judged capable of doing a job well regardless of his or her real ability. The "horns effect" describes essentially the same error, but focuses on one particularly bad trait. Here the individual will be judged as incapable of doing a good job because of one flaw.

Interviewers are also prejudiced by the "primacy effect." This error occurs when interpretation of later information is distorted by earlier related information. Hence, in an interview situation, the interviewer spends most of the interview trying to confirm the impression given by the candidate in the first few moments. Studies have repeatedly demonstrated that such an impression is unrelated to the aptitude of the applicant.

The phenomenon known as the "contrast effect" also skews the judgment of interviewers. A suitable candidate may be underestimated because he or she is different from a previous one who appears exceptionally intelligent. Likewise, an average candidate who is preceded by one who gives a weak showing may be judged as more suitable than he or she really is.

Since interviews as a form of personnel selection have been shown to be inadequate, other selection procedures have been devised that more accurately predict candidate suitability. Of the various tests devised, the predictor that appears to do this most successfully is the applicant's cognitive ability as measured by a variety of verbal and spatial tests.

1. This passage mainly discusses the
   (A) effects of interviewing on job applicants
   (B) weaknesses of the job interview process
   (C) judgments of interviewers concerning job applicants
   (D) techniques interviewers use for judging job applicants

→ Experiments have shown that in selecting personnel for a job, interviewing is, at best, a hindrance and may even cause harm. These studies have disclosed that the judgments of interviewers differ markedly and bear little or no relationship to the adequacy of job applicants. Of the many reasons why this should be the case, four in particular stand out. The first reason is related to an error of judgment known as the "halo effect." If a person has one noticeably good trait, his or her other characteristics will be judged as better than they really are. Thus, an individual who dresses smartly and shows self-confidence is likely to be judged capable of doing a job well regardless of his or her real ability. The "horns effect" describes essentially the same error, but focuses on one particularly bad trait. Here the individual will be judged as incapable of doing a good job because of one flaw.

2. The word hindrance in paragraph 1 is closest in meaning to
   (A) encouragement
   (B) assistance
   (C) procedure
   (D) interference

Paragraph 1 is marked with an arrow (→).

Experiments have shown that in selecting personnel for a job, interviewing is, at best, a hindrance and may even cause harm. **These studies have disclosed that the judgments of interviewers differ markedly and bear little or no relationship to the adequacy of job applicants. Of the many reasons why this should be the case, four in particular stand out. The first reason is related to an error of judgment known as the "halo effect." If a person has one noticeably good trait, his or her other characteristics will be judged as better than they really are.** Thus, an individual who dresses smartly and shows self-confidence is likely to be judged capable of doing a job well regardless of his or her real ability. The "horns effect" describes essentially the same error, but focuses on one particularly bad trait. Here the individual will be judged as incapable of doing a good job because of one flaw.

3. Look at the word they in the passage. Select another word or phrase in the **bold** text that they refers to.

4. According to the passage, the halo effect
   (A) stands out as the worst judgment error
   (B) only takes effect when a candidate is well dressed
   (C) exemplifies how one good characteristic colors perceptions
   (D) increases the interviewer's ability to judge real potential

➔ Interviewers are also prejudiced by the "primacy effect." This error occurs when interpretation of later information is distorted by earlier related information. Hence, in an interview situation, the interviewer spends most of the interview trying to confirm the impression given by the candidate in the first few moments. Studies have repeatedly demonstrated that such an impression is unrelated to the aptitude of the applicant.

5. The word confirm in paragraph 2 is closest in meaning to
   (A) verify
   (B) conclude
   (C) recollect
   (D) misrepresent

Paragraph 2 is marked with an arrow (➔).

6. According to the passage, the first impression
   (A) can easily be altered
   (B) is the one that stays with the interviewer
   (C) is unrelated to the interviewer's prejudices
   (D) has been repeatedly demonstrated to the applicant

➔ The phenomenon known as the "contrast effect" also skews the judgment of interviewers. A suitable candidate may be underestimated because he or she is different from a previous one who appears exceptionally intelligent. Likewise, an average candidate who is preceded by one who gives a weak showing may be judged as more suitable than he or she really is.

7. The word skews in paragraph 3 is closest in meaning to
   (A) biases
   (B) opposes
   (C) improves
   (D) distinguishes

Paragraph 3 is marked with an arrow (➔).

Since interviews as a form of personnel selection have been shown to be inadequate, **other selection procedures have been devised that more accurately predict candidate suitability. Of the various tests devised, the predictor that appears to do this most successfully is the applicant's cognitive ability as measured by a variety of verbal and spatial tests.**

8. Look at the word **this** in the passage. Select another word or phrase in the **bold** text that this refers to.

[1] Experiments have shown that in selecting personnel for a job, interviewing is, at best, a hindrance and may even cause harm. These studies have disclosed that the judgments of interviewers differ markedly and bear little or no relationship to the adequacy of job applicants. Of the many reasons why this should be the case, four in particular stand out. The first reason is related to an error of judgment known as the "halo effect." If a person has one noticeably good trait, his or her other characteristics will be judged as better than they really are. Thus, an individual who dresses smartly and shows self-confidence is likely to be judged capable of doing a job well regardless of his or her real ability. The "horns effect" describes essentially the same error, but focuses on one particularly bad trait. Here the individual will be judged as incapable of doing a good job because of one flaw.

[2] Interviewers are also prejudiced by the "primacy effect." This error occurs when interpretation of later information is distorted by earlier related information. Hence, in an interview situation, the interviewer spends most of the interview trying to confirm the impression given by the candidate in the first few moments. Studies have repeatedly demonstrated that such an impression is unrelated to the aptitude of the applicant.

[3] The phenomenon known as the "contrast effect" also skews the judgment of interviewers. A suitable candidate may be underestimated because he or she is different from a previous one who appears exceptionally intelligent. Likewise, an average candidate who is preceded by one who gives a weak showing may be judged as more suitable than he or she really is.

[4] Since interviews as a form of personnel selection have been shown to be inadequate, other selection procedures have been devised that more accurately predict candidate suitability. Of the various tests devised, the predictor that appears to do this most successfully is the applicant's cognitive ability as measured by a variety of verbal and spatial tests.

9. The author mentions all of the following reasons why interviewing is not an accurate way to predict candidate suitability EXCEPT the
(A) halo effect
(B) primacy effect
(C) contrast effect
(D) cognitive effect

10. Select the number of the paragraph in which the author discusses the effect of comparing two candidates.

11. The paragraphs following the passage would most likely discuss which of the following?
(A) Other reasons for misjudgments of applicants
(B) More information on the kinds of judgments interviewers make
(C) More information on cognitive-ability tests
(D) Other selection procedures included in interviewing

Questions 12–25

A variety of experiments can be performed to illustrate the nature of light, but perhaps the most well known is the classic "double-slit experiment" first performed by Thomas Young in 1803. In the first part of this experiment, a light is shone through a tiny vertical slit in a screen and allowed to pass on to a second detecting screen. The light spreads out after passing through the hole, and a large illuminated area that fades into darkness at the edges shows up on the detecting screen. To form this pattern, the light actually bends or diffracts when passing through the slit.

In the second part of the experiment, light is shone through two parallel slits. This time the light passes through the slits, but instead of creating a large lighted area, the detecting screen now shows alternating bands of light and darkness. The band in the center is the brightest. Around that are alternating bands of light and darkness with the light bands becoming less intense the farther away they are from the central one.

What is happening is called the "phenomenon of interference." The waves of light from the two slits interfere with each other. Like all waves, light waves have crests, their highest points, and troughs, their lowest points. In places where the crests coming from one slit extend over the crests coming from the other slit, the result is an intensification of light, and light bands appear on the detecting screen. In places where the crests from one slit overlap the troughs from the other slit, they cancel each other out, and the result is an area of darkness on the detecting screen.

But what happens if particles of light, or photons, are shot one after the other through the slits? If only one slit is open, these photons build up the same pattern as that of the beam of light. The fascinating thing is that if two slits are open and photons are fired one at a time through either of them, the pattern that builds up on the detecting screen is the same pattern obtained when a beam of light is shone through two slits. In other words, a single photon appears to "know" whether one slit or two are open.

12. With what topic are the first two paragraphs mainly concerned?
(A) Thomas Young's various illustrations
(B) The significance of photon interference
(C) The classic double-slit light experiment
(D) The double slit of light on a detecting screen

A variety of experiments can be performed to illustrate the nature of light, but perhaps the most well known is the classic "double-slit experiment" first performed by Thomas Young in 1803. **In the first part of this experiment, a light is shone through a tiny vertical slit in a screen and allowed to pass on to a second detecting screen. The light spreads out after passing through the hole, and a large illuminated area that fades into darkness at the edges shows up on the detecting screen.** To form this pattern, the light actually bends or diffracts when passing through the slit.

13. Look at the word slit in the passage. Select another word or phrase in the **bold** text that is closest in meaning to the word slit.

In the second part of the experiment, light is shone through two parallel slits. **This time the light passes through the slits, but instead of creating a large lighted area, the detecting screen now shows alternating bands of light and darkness. The band in the center is the brightest. Around that are alternating bands of light and darkness with the light bands becoming less intense the farther away they are from the central one.**

14. Look at the word one in the passage. Select another word or phrase in the **bold** text that one refers to.

15. Select the drawing that shows which pattern of light emerges on a detecting screen when a single photon is fired through two open slits.

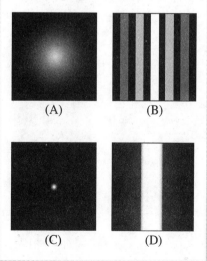

(A) (B)

(C) (D)

What is happening is called the "phenomenon of interference." The waves of light from the two slits interfere with each other. Like all waves, light waves have crests, their highest points, and troughs, their lowest points. In places where the crests coming from one slit extend over the crests coming from the other slit, the result is an intensification of light, and light bands appear on the detecting screen. In places where the crests from one slit overlap the troughs from the other slit, they cancel each other out, and the result is an area of darkness on the detecting screen.

16. Look at the phrase **each other** in the passage. Select the word or phrase in the **bold** text that **each other** refers to.

→ What is happening is called the "phenomenon of interference." The waves of light from the two slits interfere with each other. Like all waves, light waves have crests, their highest points, and troughs, their lowest points. In places where the crests coming from one slit extend over the crests coming from the other slit, the result is an intensification of light, and light bands appear on the detecting screen. In places where the crests from one slit overlap the troughs from the other slit, they cancel each other out, and the result is an area of darkness on the detecting screen.

17. Why does the author mention crests and troughs in paragraph 3?
    (A) To explain what all waves are like so that the reader will understand waves
    (B) To inform the reader what the highest points and the lowest points in a wave are called
    (C) To explain why the physical aspects of a wave are important for the movement of light
    (D) To give background information that the reader needs to understand the phenomenon of photon interference

Paragraph 3 is marked with an arrow (→).

What is happening is called the "phenomenon of interference." The waves of light from the two slits interfere with each other. Like all waves, light waves have crests, their highest points, and troughs, their lowest points. **In places where the crests coming from one slit extend over the crests coming from the other slit, the result is an intensification of light, and light bands appear on the detecting screen. In places where the crests from one slit** overlap **the troughs from the other slit, they cancel each other out, and the result is an area of darkness on the detecting screen.**

18. Look at the word **overlap** in the passage. Select another word or phrase in the **bold** text that is closest in meaning to the word **overlap**.

→   1 What is happening is called the "phenomenon of interference." 2 The waves of light from the two slits interfere with each other. 3 Like all waves, light waves have crests, their highest points, and troughs, their lowest points. 4 In places where the crests coming from one slit extend over the crests coming from the other slit, the result is an intensification of light, and light bands appear on the detecting screen. 5 In places where the crests from one slit overlap the troughs from the other slit, they cancel each other out, and the result is an area of darkness on the detecting screen.

19. Select the number of the sentence in paragraph 3 that describes what happens when the crest of a wave extends over the trough of another wave.

Paragraph 3 is marked with an arrow (→).

But what happens if particles of light, or photons, are shot one after the other through the slits? If only one slit is open, these photons build up the same pattern as that of the beam of light. The fascinating thing is that if two slits are open and photons are fired one at a time through either of them the pattern that builds up on the detecting screen is the same pattern obtained when a beam of light is shone through two slits. In other words, a single photon appears to "know" whether one slit or two are open.

20. Look at the word **photons** in the passage. Select another word or phrase in the **bold** text that is closest in meaning to the word **photons**.

➜   But what happens if particles of light, or photons, are shot one after the other through the slits? If only one slit is open, these photons build up the same pattern as that of the beam of light. The fascinating thing is that if two slits are open and photons are fired one at a time through either of them the pattern that builds up on the detecting screen is the same pattern obtained when a beam of light is shone through two slits. In other words, a single photon appears to "know" whether one slit or two are open.

21. What does the author mean by the statement a single photon appears to "know" whether one slit or two are open in paragraph 4?
    (A) A single photon behaves as if other photons were causing interference.
    (B) A single photon can predict photon and light-beam behavior.
    (C) A single photon has the ability to think about whether one slit or two are open.
    (D) A single photon knows how the other photons will behave and alters its behavior accordingly.

Paragraph 4 is marked with an arrow (➜).

A variety of experiments can be performed to illustrate the nature of light, but perhaps the most well known is the classic "double-slit experiment" first performed by Thomas Young in 1803. [1] In the first part of this experiment, a light is shone through a tiny vertical slit in a screen and allowed to pass on to a second detecting screen. The light spreads out after passing through the hole, and a large illuminated area that fades into darkness at the edges shows up on the detecting screen. [2] To form this pattern, the light actually bends or diffracts when passing through the slit.

In the second part of the experiment, light is shone through two parallel slits. This time the light passes through the slits, but instead of creating a large lighted area, the detecting screen now shows alternating bands of light and darkness. [3] The band in the center is the brightest. Around that are alternating bands of light and darkness with the light bands becoming less intense the farther away they are from the central one.

What is happening is called the "phenomenon of interference." [4] The waves of light from the two slits interfere with each other. Like all waves, light waves have crests, their highest points, and troughs, their lowest points. In places where the crests coming from one slit extend over the crests coming from the other slit, the result is an intensification of light, and light bands appear on the detecting screen. In places where the crests from one slit overlap the troughs from the other slit, they cancel each other out, and the result is an area of darkness on the detecting screen.

But what happens if particles of light, or photons, are shot one after the other through the slits? [5] If only one slit is open, these photons build up the same pattern as that of the beam of light. The fascinating thing is that if two slits are open and photons are fired one at a time through either of them the pattern that builds up on the detecting screen is the same pattern obtained when a beam of light is shone through two slits. In other words, a single photon appears to "know" whether one slit or two are open.

22. The passage discusses all of the following experiments EXCEPT
   (A) shining light beams through a single slit
   (B) shining light beams one at a time through two slits
   (C) shining photons one at a time through a single slit
   (D) shining photons one at a time through two slits

23. With which of the following statements would the author most probably agree?
   (A) The physics of light has been understood since the first experiment in 1803.
   (B) There still exist unexplained phenomena in the study of light behavior.
   (C) Photons cannot make patterns unless they can overlap each other.
   (D) The intensification of light bands is dependent on the strength of the light beam.

24. The following sentence can be added to the passage.

This is fairly easy to replicate in a classroom setting.

Where would it best fit in the passage?

Select the square (□) that shows where the sentence should be added.

[1] A variety of experiments can be performed to illustrate the nature of light, but perhaps the most well known is the classic "double-slit experiment" first performed by Thomas Young in 1803. In the first part of this experiment, a light is shone through a tiny vertical slit in a screen and allowed to pass on to a second detecting screen. The light spreads out after passing through the hole, and a large illuminated area that fades into darkness at the edges shows up on the detecting screen. To form this pattern, the light actually bends or diffracts when passing through the slit.

[2] In the second part of the experiment, light is shone through two parallel slits. This time the light passes through the slits, but instead of creating a large lighted area, the detecting screen now shows alternating bands of light and darkness. The band in the center is the brightest. Around that are alternating bands of light and darkness with the light bands becoming less intense the farther away they are from the central one.

[3] What is happening is called the "phenomenon of interference." The waves of light from the two slits interfere with each other. Like all waves, light waves have crests, their highest points, and troughs, their lowest points. In places where the crests coming from one slit extend over the crests coming from the other slit, the result is an intensification of light, and light bands appear on the detecting screen. In places where the crests from one slit overlap the troughs from the other slit, they cancel each other out, and the result is an area of darkness on the detecting screen.

[4] But what happens if particles of light, or photons, are shot one after the other through the slits? If only one slit is open, these photons build up the same pattern as that of the beam of light. The fascinating thing is that if two slits are open and photons are fired one at a time through either of them the pattern that builds up on the detecting screen is the same pattern obtained when a beam of light is shone through two slits. In other words, a single photon appears to "know" whether one slit or two are open.

25. Select the number of the paragraph that describes what happens when a light beam is projected through a single slit.

Questions 26–38

It was once believed that being overweight was healthy, but nowadays few people subscribe to this viewpoint. While many people are fighting the battle to lose weight, studies are being conducted concerning the appetite and how it is controlled by both emotional and biochemical factors. Some of the conclusions of these studies may give insights into how to deal with weight problems. For example, when several hundred people were asked about their eating habits in times of stress, 44 percent said they reacted to stressful situations by eating. Further investigations with both humans and animals indicated that it is not food that relieves tension but rather the act of chewing.

A test in which subjects were blindfolded showed that obese people have a keener sense of taste and crave more flavorful food than people who are not extremely overweight. When deprived of variety and intensity of tastes, obese people are rarely satisfied and consequently eat more to fulfill this need. Also, blood samples taken from people after they were shown a picture of food revealed that overweight people reacted with an increase in blood insulin, a chemical associated with appetite. This did not happen to average-weight people.

In another experiment, results showed that certain people have a specific, biologically induced hunger for carbohydrates. When people eat carbohydrates, the level of serotonin, a neurotransmitter in the brain, rises. Enough serotonin produces a sense of satiation, and, as a result, their hunger for carbohydrates subsides.

Exercise has been recommended as an important part of a weight-loss program. However, it has been found that mild exercise, such as using the stairs instead of the elevator, is better in the long run than taking on a strenuous program, such as jogging, which many people find difficult to continue over long periods of time and which also increases appetite.

26. What is the main purpose of the passage?
    (A) To discuss the health problems caused by being overweight
    (B) To recommend a weight-loss program for the obese
    (C) To help overweight people overcome their eating problem
    (D) To present research into the factors causing obesity

27. The author mentions people's eating habits during times of stress to show that
    (A) overweight people are tense
    (B) thin people don't eat when under stress
    (C) a large percentage of people deal with stress by eating
    (D) 56 percent of the population isn't overweight

→ A test in which subjects were blindfolded showed that obese people have a keener sense of taste and crave more flavorful food than people who are not extremely overweight. When deprived of variety and intensity of tastes, obese people are rarely satisfied and consequently eat more to fulfill this need. Also, blood samples taken from people after they were shown a picture of food revealed that overweight people reacted with an increase in blood insulin, a chemical associated with appetite. This did not happen to average-weight people.

28. The word crave in paragraph 2 is closest in meaning to
(A) devour
(B) absorb
(C) season
(D) desire

Paragraph 2 is marked with an arrow (→).

→ A test in which subjects were blindfolded showed that obese people have a keener sense of taste and crave more flavorful food than people who are not extremely overweight. When deprived of variety and intensity of tastes, obese people are rarely satisfied and consequently eat more to fulfill this need. Also, blood samples taken from people after they were shown a picture of food revealed that overweight people reacted with an increase in blood insulin, a chemical associated with appetite. This did not happen to average-weight people.

29. Paragraph 2 supports which of the following conclusions?
(A) Thin people don't enjoy food as much as overweight people do.
(B) A variety of foods and strong flavors satisfy heavy people.
(C) Overweight people have an abnormal sense of taste.
(D) Deprivation of food makes people fat.

Paragraph 2 is marked with an arrow (→).

30. According to the passage,
(A) insulin increases in the bloodstream when people eat large amounts of food.
(B) insulin can be used to lessen the appetite.
(C) insulin causes a chemical reaction when food is seen.
(D) insulin levels don't change in average-weight people who see food.

Diagnostic Test – Reading **63**

→ In another experiment, results showed that certain people have a specific, biologically induced hunger for carbohydrates. When people eat carbohydrates, the level of serotonin, a neurotransmitter in the brain, rises. Enough serotonin produces a sense of satiation, and, as a result, their hunger for carbohydrates subsides.

31. It can be inferred from paragraph 3 that for certain people
    (A) eating carbohydrates eliminates hunger
    (B) carbohydrates biologically induce hunger
    (C) carbohydrates don't satisfy a hungry person
    (D) carbohydrates subside when serotonin is produced

Paragraph 3 is marked with an arrow (→).

In another experiment, **results showed that certain people have a specific, biologically induced hunger for carbohydrates. When people eat carbohydrates, the level of serotonin, a neurotransmitter in the brain, rises. Enough serotonin produces a sense of satiation, and, as a result, their hunger for carbohydrates subsides.**

32. Look at the word **their** in the passage. Select another word or phrase in the **bold** text that **their** refers to.

→ In another experiment, **results showed that certain people have a specific, biologically induced hunger for carbohydrates. When people eat carbohydrates, the level of serotonin, a neurotransmitter in the brain, rises. Enough serotonin produces a sense of satiation, and, as a result, their hunger for carbohydrates subsides.**

33. Look at the word subsides in paragraph 3. Select another word or phrase in the **bold** text that is OPPOSITE in meaning to the word subsides.

Paragraph 3 is marked with an arrow (→).

34. What can be said about serotonin?
    (A) It is a chemical that increases appetites.
    (B) Only certain people produce it in their brains.
    (C) It tells the brain when a person is full.
    (D) It neurotransmits carbohydrates to the brain.

→ Exercise has been recommended as an important part of a weight-loss program. **However, it has been found that mild exercise, such as using the stairs instead of the elevator, is better in the long run than taking on a strenuous program, such as jogging, which many people find difficult to continue over long periods of time and which also increases appetite.**

35. Look at the word strenuous in paragraph 4. Select another word or phrase in the **bold** text that is OPPOSITE in meaning to the word strenuous.

Paragraph 4 is marked with an arrow (→).

1. It was once believed that being overweight was healthy, but nowadays few people subscribe to this viewpoint. While many people are fighting the battle to lose weight, studies are being conducted concerning the appetite and how it is controlled by both emotional and biochemical factors. Some of the conclusions of these studies may give insights into how to deal with weight problems. For example, when several hundred people were asked about their eating habits in times of stress, 44 percent said they reacted to stressful situations by eating. Further investigations with both humans and animals indicated that it is not food that relieves tension but rather the act of chewing.

2. A test in which subjects were blindfolded showed that obese people have a keener sense of taste and crave more flavorful food than people who are not extremely overweight. When deprived of variety and intensity of tastes, obese people are rarely satisfied and consequently eat more to fulfill this need. Also, blood samples taken from people after they were shown a picture of food revealed that overweight people reacted with an increase in blood insulin, a chemical associated with appetite. This did not happen to average-weight people.

3. In another experiment, results showed that certain people have a specific, biologically induced hunger for carbohydrates. When people eat carbohydrates, the level of serotonin, a neurotransmitter in the brain, rises. Enough serotonin produces a sense of satiation, and, as a result, their hunger for carbohydrates subsides.

4. Exercise has been recommended as an important part of a weight-loss program. However, it has been found that mild exercise, such as using the stairs instead of the elevator, is better in the long run than taking on a strenuous program, such as jogging, which many people find difficult to continue over long periods of time and which also increases appetite.

36. The author suggests that it might be good for extremely overweight people wanting to lose weight to do all of the following EXCEPT
   (A) jog fifteen miles daily and look at pictures of food
   (B) walk up stairs instead of using the elevator
   (C) eat plenty of chewy carbohydrates
   (D) avoid stressful situations and eat spicy foods

37. Which one of the following exercises might be best for an overweight person to engage in daily?
   (A) A stroll
   (B) A long swim
   (C) Cross-country skiing
   (D) A 10-mile bicycle ride

38. Select the number of the paragraph in which the author discusses a nutritional substance that reduces hunger.

Questions 39–50

In June 1863 a Confederate army under the command of General Lee encountered a Union army commanded by General Meade near the town of Gettysburg in Pennsylvania. The ensuing battle, which lasted three days, is considered the single most important engagement of the American Civil War.

On the morning of July 1, the battle opened with Confederate troops attacking a Union cavalry division to the west of the town at McPherson Ridge. Reinforcements came to both sides, but eventually the Union forces were overpowered and were driven back to the south of Gettysburg. They formed defensive positions along Cemetery Ridge, a long rise of land running southwards from outside the town, and on two hills just to the north and east of the ridge. The whole army formed a defensive arc resembling a fishhook. The Confederate forces, about a mile away, faced the Union positions in a larger arc from the west and north.

Throughout the day of July 2, Lee's forces attacked, leaving thousands of dead on both sides. The Confederates overran the Union's advance lines in the southern part of their "hook," but they failed to dislodge the Union forces from their main positions. A strategically important hill known as Little Round Top on the Union's left flank was stormed unsuccessfully by the Confederates with a devastating number of casualties on both sides.

On the third day of battle, Lee decided to concentrate his attack on the center of the Union forces that ranged along Cemetery Ridge. As a prelude to the attack, the Confederate artillery bombarded the ridge for two hours but inflicted less damage than they had expected, due to poor visibility. When the bombardment ceased, a Confederate infantry force of twelve thousand men charged courageously across the open land toward the Union lines. They were subjected to heavy artillery and rifle fire and sustained a huge number of casualties. This attack, now known as Pickett's Charge after the general whose division led it, failed in its objective to break the Union line. After this failure General Lee decided to withdraw his army toward safer territory in the South. Both sides had suffered huge losses of men, but the Union had succeeded in preventing the Confederates from successfully invading the North, and so Gettysburg proved to be a decisive turning point in the Civil War.

39. The passage is mainly about
(A) the defeat of the Confederate army in the American Civil War
(B) the battle between the Confederate and Union forces at Gettysburg, Pennsylvania
(C) the attack known as Pickett's Charge, when General Lee invaded the North
(D) the skillful deployment of Union forces at the battle of Gettysburg

→ On the morning of July 1, the battle opened with Confederate troops attacking a Union cavalry division to the west of the town at McPherson Ridge. Reinforcements came to both sides, but eventually the Union forces were overpowered and were driven back to the south of Gettysburg. They formed defensive positions along Cemetery Ridge, a long rise of land running southwards from outside the town, and on two hills just to the north and east of the ridge. The whole army formed a defensive arc resembling a fishhook. The Confederate forces, about a mile away, faced the Union positions in a larger arc from the west and north.

40. The word Reinforcements in paragraph 2 is closest in meaning to
(A) additional troops
(B) subsidiary branches
(C) armored divisions
(D) inexperienced conscripts

Paragraph 2 is marked with an arrow (→).

On the morning of July 1, the battle opened with Confederate troops attacking a Union cavalry division to the west of the town at McPherson Ridge. Reinforcements came to both sides, but eventually the Union forces were overpowered and were driven back to the south of Gettysburg. They formed defensive positions along Cemetery Ridge, a long rise of land running southwards from outside the town, and on two hills just to the north and east of the ridge. The whole army formed a defensive arc resembling a fishhook. The Confederate forces, about a mile away, faced the Union positions in a larger arc from the west and north.

41. Look at the word They in the passage. Select another word or phrase in the **bold** text that They refers to.

→ 1 On the morning of July 1, the battle opened with Confederate troops attacking a Union cavalry division to the west of the town at McPherson Ridge. 2 Reinforcements came to both sides, but eventually the Union forces were overpowered and were driven back to the south of Gettysburg. 3 They formed defensive positions along Cemetery Ridge, a long rise of land running southwards from outside the town, and on two hills just to the north and east of the ridge. 4 The whole army formed a defensive arc resembling a fishhook. 5 The Confederate forces, about a mile away, faced the Union positions in a larger arc from the west and north.

42. The following sentence can be added to paragraph 2.

Throughout the night the remainder of Meade's forces arrived in large numbers, strengthening these positions.

Where would it best fit in the paragraph?

Select the square (□) that shows where the sentence should be added.

Paragraph 2 is marked with an arrow (→).

→ ☐1 On the morning of July 1, the battle opened with Confederate troops attacking a Union cavalry division to the west of the town at McPherson Ridge. ☐2 Reinforcements came to both sides, but eventually the Union forces were overpowered and were driven back to the south of Gettysburg. ☐3 They formed defensive positions along Cemetery Ridge, a long rise of land running southwards from outside the town, and on two hills just to the north and east of the ridge. ☐4 The whole army formed a defensive arc resembling a fishhook. ☐5 The Confederate forces, about a mile away, faced the Union positions in a larger arc from the west and north.

43. Select the number of the sentence in paragraph 2 in which the author mentions a Confederate success.

Paragraph 2 is marked with an arrow (→).

→ Throughout the day of July 2, Lee's forces attacked, leaving thousands of dead on both sides. The Confederates overran the Union's advance lines in the southern part of their "hook," but they failed to dislodge the Union forces from their main positions. A strategically important hill known as Little Round Top on the Union's left flank was stormed unsuccessfully by the Confederates with a devastating number of casualties on both sides.

44. The word stormed in paragraph 3 is closest in meaning to
(A) diverted
(B) attacked
(C) dislodged
(D) avoided

Paragraph 3 is marked with an arrow (→).

→ On the third day of battle, Lee decided to concentrate his attack on the center of the Union forces that ranged along Cemetery Ridge. As a prelude to the attack, the Confederate artillery bombarded the ridge for two hours but inflicted less damage than they had expected, due to poor visibility. When the bombardment ceased, a Confederate infantry force of twelve thousand men charged courageously across the open land toward the Union lines. They were subjected to heavy artillery and rifle fire and sustained a huge number of casualties. This attack, now known as Pickett's Charge after the general whose division led it, failed in its objective to break the Union line. After this failure General Lee decided to withdraw his army toward safer territory in the South. Both sides had suffered huge losses of men, but the Union had succeeded in preventing the Confederates from successfully invading the North, and so Gettysburg proved to be a decisive turning point in the Civil War.

45. The word sustained in paragraph 4 is closest in meaning to
(A) nourished
(B) defended
(C) established
(D) suffered

Paragraph 4 is marked with an arrow (→).

→ On the third day of battle, Lee decided to concentrate his attack on the center of the Union forces that ranged along Cemetery Ridge. As a prelude to the attack, the Confederate artillery bombarded the ridge for two hours but inflicted less damage than they had expected, due to poor visibility. When the bombardment ceased, a Confederate infantry force of twelve thousand men charged courageously across the open land toward the Union lines. They were subjected to heavy artillery and rifle fire and sustained a huge number of casualties. This attack, now known as Pickett's Charge after the general whose division led it, failed in its objective to break the Union line. After this failure General Lee decided to withdraw his army toward safer territory in the South. Both sides had suffered huge losses of men, but the Union had succeeded in preventing the Confederates from successfully invading the North, and so Gettysburg proved to be a decisive turning point in the Civil War.

46. The author mentions the poor visibility in paragraph 4 to help explain why
    (A) the attack failed to attain its objectives
    (B) the men charged across the open land
    (C) the Union lines sustained a large number of casualties
    (D) General Lee withdrew his troops to safer territory

Paragraph 4 is marked with an arrow (→).

47. What does the author mean by saying Gettysburg was a decisive turning point in the Civil War?
    (A) It was at Gettysburg that the Union troops forced the Confederates to flee to the South.
    (B) It was the battle in the American Civil War that turned the public opinion against supporting the war.
    (C) It was the place where the most devastating number of casualties on both sides occurred.
    (D) It was because of events at Gettysburg that the Union was eventually victorious.

In June 1863 a Confederate army under the command of General Lee encountered a Union army commanded by General Meade near the town of Gettysburg in Pennsylvania. The ensuing battle, which lasted three days, is considered the single most important engagement of the American Civil War.

On the morning of July 1, the battle opened with Confederate troops attacking a Union cavalry division to the west of the town at McPherson Ridge. Reinforcements came to both sides, but eventually the Union forces were overpowered and were driven back to the south of Gettysburg. They formed defensive positions along Cemetery Ridge, a long rise of land running southwards from outside the town, and on two hills just to the north and east of the ridge. The whole army formed a defensive arc resembling a fishhook. The Confederate forces, about a mile away, faced the Union positions in a larger arc from the west and north.

Throughout the day of July 2, Lee's forces attacked, leaving thousands of dead on both sides. The Confederates overran the Union's advance lines in the southern part of their "hook," but they failed to dislodge the Union forces from their main positions. A strategically important hill known as Little Round Top on the Union's left flank was stormed unsuccessfully by the Confederates with a devastating number of casualties on both sides.

On the third day of battle, Lee decided to concentrate his attack on the center of the Union forces that ranged along Cemetery Ridge. As a prelude to the attack, the Confederate artillery bombarded the ridge for two hours but inflicted less damage than they had expected, due to poor visibility. When the bombardment ceased, a Confederate infantry force of twelve thousand men charged courageously across the open land toward the Union lines. They were subjected to heavy artillery and rifle fire and sustained a huge number of casualties. This attack, now known as Pickett's Charge after the general whose division led it, failed in its objective to break the Union line. After this failure General Lee decided to withdraw his army toward safer territory in the South. Both sides had suffered huge losses of men, but the Union had succeeded in preventing the Confederates from successfully invading the North, and so Gettysburg proved to be a decisive turning point in the Civil War.

48. The author discusses all of the following tactics EXCEPT
   (A) the defensive positions taken by the troops
   (B) a courageous charge across open ground
   (C) the importance of espionage in determining position
   (D) a bombardment concentrated on the Union's forces

49. From which direction did Pickett's Charge originate?
   (A) Northeast
   (B) Northwest
   (C) Southeast
   (D) Southwest

50. According to the passage, the battle at Gettysburg was
   (A) a huge success for the Union army
   (B) the most important battle in the Civil War
   (C) a devastating defeat for Pickett
   (D) General Lee's greatest engagement

This is the end of the Reading Section.
Go on to the Writing Section.

WRITING

Time – 30 minutes

Read the essay question carefully.

Think before you write. Making notes may help you to organize your essay. It is important to write only on the topic you are given.

Check your work. Allow a few minutes before time is up to read over your essay and make changes.

You have thirty minutes to complete the essay. On the real test, if you continue to write, it will be considered cheating.

Set your clock or watch for thirty minutes.
Now get ready to begin.

Directions: Read the question below and write an essay on a separate sheet of paper.

Do you agree or disagree with the following statement?

Childhood is the happiest time of a person's life.

Use reasons and specific examples to support your opinion.

NOTES

Use this space for essay notes only. On the day of the Computer-Based TOEFL® Test, work done on the worksheet will not be scored.

This is the end of the Writing Section.

SECTION
·1·
LISTENING*

The Listening Section of the Computer-Base TOEFL ® Test measures your ability to understand spoken English. It contains listening passages and questions about each passage.

PART A

In Part A of the Listening Section of the Computer-Based TOEFL® Test, you will see two people on your computer screen and hear a short conversation between them. As Part A progresses, the conversations will become slightly longer. You must listen carefully because you will hear each conversation only once. After the conversation, you will hear and see a question on the screen. The question will be about what was stated or implied in the conversation. Then you must choose the correct answer from among four choices on the computer screen by clicking on the oval in front of the answer of your choice (or on the answer text itself). After you choose your answer, you must then click on the Next icon. You are given the opportunity to check your answer and then click on the Answer Confirm icon. You must confirm your answer in order to go on to the next conversation.

STRATEGIES TO USE FOR LISTENING, PART A

Concentrate on the Conversation

1. Focus all your attention on the conversation.

Each speaker speaks only once in a short conversation, but may speak more than once in a longer conversation. Do not be distracted by the speakers you see on the screen. The questions will be about what is stated or implied in the conversation. The questions will not be about what is happening on the screen.

2. Concentrate on the context and the details.

The language in the conversations is usually rather informal and frequently concerns topics common to the everyday life of young adults enrolled in a university. It is not necessary to have previous knowledge of the subject matter discussed in the conversations. All the information needed to answer the questions is included within the conversations. Try to remember the details in context so as not to get confused.

In the short conversations in Part A, the first speaker sets the context, and the question usually relates to how the second speaker responds. Look at this example:

    (man)   I've just locked my car keys in the trunk.
    (woman)   Don't worry. I've got my set.
    (narrator) What does the woman mean?

In this conversation, the man sets the context – he's locked his keys in the trunk of his car. The woman's response indicates that she is not concerned about the incident because she has her own set of keys to the car.

---

* Students using this book for self-study will require a copy of the listening program (available as audio cassettes or audio CDs). Please refer to the copyright page of this book for a list of ISBNs.

In the longer conversations of Part A, the first speaker often gives the context. In the course of each conversation, several details may be mentioned. Look at this example:

(woman)	*Have you decided to change your major?*
(man)	*Well, the Engineering Department will accept most of the work that I did toward my physics degree, so I switched to engineering just last week.*
(woman)	*But won't the change set you back as far as graduating is concerned?*
(man)	*It looks like I will be able to catch up with most of the engineering courses by next year, so it really won't set me back too much. Besides, I think that I will be happier in the engineering field.*
(narrator)	*What is the woman concerned about?*

In this conversation, the woman sets the context – the man's change of major. The man answers her question and gives information about his decision. She wonders how this will affect him. His response indicates that he is confident about his decision.

3. Concentrate on the purpose.

Many of the questions concern the speakers' purpose. The first person might be extending an invitation, and the second person might be accepting or declining it. Concentrate on details that indicate apologies, requests, offers, or opinions. Look at this example:

(man)	*I can't get this printer to feed the paper through.*
(woman)	*Don't look at me. I'm hopeless at these things.*

In this conversation, we can infer that the man is seeking help to solve his problem. The woman's response indicates that she cannot help him.

4. Listen for meaning.

A wrong answer choice may confuse you by having words that sound similar to (or the same as) those in a spoken statement in the conversation. Look at these examples:

(A)   The **moss** is on the wall.
(B)   The **moth** is on the wall.

"Moss" and "moth" may be confused because they are similar in sound.

(C)   We **rode** in the boat.
(D)   We **rowed** the boat.

"Rode" and "rowed" are pronounced the same but have different meanings.

(E)   Can Bob ever play tennis!
(F)   Can Bob ever play tennis?

The two sentences are the same in wording, but the first is an exclamation that means "Bob plays tennis very well." The second sentence is a simple question that means "Does Bob ever get a chance to play tennis?"

5. Listen for vocabulary.

A wrong answer choice may confuse you by using the same words as the correct answer but in a different way.

(A)   Jill **overcooked** *Tony's* dinner.
(B)   Jill **cooked** the dinner **over** at *Tony's*.

The words in bold do not mean the same thing in each sentence. "Overcooked" means "cooked too long," but "cooked over at Tony's" means "made at Tony's house." The meanings of the italicized words might also be confused. "Tony's" in the first sentence refers to "Tony's dinner" while "Tony's" in the second sentence means "Tony's house."

    (C)   Betty **slipped out** during Conrad's speech.
    (D)   Betty **slipped up** during Conrad's speech.

Be aware of expressions or word combinations that are similar but have differences. For example, in (C) and (D) the expressions in bold do not mean the same thing. "Slipped out" means "left quietly and quickly" while "slipped up" means "made a mistake."

6. Listen for structure.

A wrong answer choice may confuse you by having a slightly different word order from the correct answer. Also a wrong answer may contain slight changes in the words used.

    (A)   Never have I been so worried.
    (B)   I have never been worried.

Although both of these statements include a negative adverb and the same subject and verb, they do not mean the same thing. The first sentence means "I have never been this worried before." The second sentence means "Nothing has ever worried me."

    (C)   Sue does better in math than science.
    (D)   Sue does better in math and science.

Although both sentences make a comparison, they do not have the same meaning. The first sentence compares how well Sue does in math with how well she does in science (she does not do as well in science as she does in math). The second sentence compares how well Sue does in math and science with how well she does in other, unnamed courses.

Concentrate on the Question and the Answer Choices

1. Listen to and read the question carefully.

It is important to be certain what is being asked before you read the answer choices.

2. Read the answer choices carefully.

Remember that the answer choices may have similar-sounding words, vocabulary items, or structures that can make an incorrect answer seem correct.

3. Pay attention to time.

Look frequently at the question number and the amount of time you have remaining. Be sure you are pacing yourself well in order to complete all the questions.

4. Answer every question.

You cannot go on to the following question until you have answered a question and confirmed it. If you try to do so, you will lose valuable time when you have to click through the computer "error" message to get back to the question you tried to skip. If you don't know an answer, eliminate those answers you know are incorrect and then take a guess from the remaining choices.

5. Check your answer.

Since you cannot go back and change an answer, be sure you have clicked on the answer you want before you click on the **Answer Confirm** icon.

Read the directions to each exercise. When you understand what to do, start the recording. You will hear the exercise title and then the question number. The directions and the example are <u>not</u> on the recording.

Start the recording when you see the symbol and the word **START**.

Stop or pause the recording when you see the symbol and the word **STOP** or **PAUSE**.

PRACTICE WITH SOUNDS

Many items are difficult because of sound or word confusion. Use Listening Exercises L1–L8 to develop the following skills:

1. Understanding words that sound similar
2. Understanding intonation
3. Understanding words that sound the same as other words but have different meanings
4. Understanding the correct meaning of words that have several different meanings

Exercise L1   *Identifying the correct sound*

Read the following pairs of sentences. Then listen to the spoken sentence. Circle the letter of the sentence with the same meaning as the sentence you heard.

Example   You will hear: *I saw the pear.*

           You will read: (A)   I saw the fruit.
                            (B)   I saw the animal.

You should circle (A) because a "pear" is a fruit.

 START

1. (A) Did you see the boat?
   (B) Did you see the animal?

2. (A) He gave me something to ring.
   (B) He gave me something to pay.

3. (A) I didn't have any idea.
   (B) I didn't have any paste.

4. (A) The army officer was sitting at his desk.
   (B) The city official was sitting at his desk.

5. (A) Where did she put the object to cook in?
   (B) Where did she put the object to write with?

 STOP

Answers to Exercise L1 are on page 499.

Exercise L2   ***Recognizing questions and statements***

Sometimes intonation determines the meaning of a sentence. Listen to the spoken sentence. Write "Q" if you heard a question and "S" if you heard a statement.

Example   You will hear: *What a good book!*

You will write: _S_

You should write "S" because the sentence is a statement and not a question.

 START

1. _____   5. _____
2. _____   6. _____
3. _____   7. _____
4. _____   8. _____   **STOP**

 Answers to Exercise L2 are on page 499.

Exercise L3   ***Identifying words that are pronounced the same but have different meanings***

Practice with statements

The following pairs of words are pronounced the same but have different meanings.
Listen to the spoken sentence and circle the word you heard in the sentence.

Example   You will hear: *Put the book here.*

You will read: (here)   hear

You should circle "here" because the word you heard refers to location.

 START

1. right   write   4. hour   our
2. feet   feat   5. heir   air
3. weight   wait

 PAUSE

Practice with conversations

The following pairs of words are pronounced the same but have different meanings.
Listen to the spoken conversation and circle the word you heard in the conversation.

Example   You will hear: (man)   *Where shall I put this vase?*
                                   (woman)   *Right here on the table.*

You will read: (here)   hear

You should circle "here" because the conversation refers to location.

 START

6. dye   die   9. lone   loan
7. breaks   brakes   10. hole   whole
8. won   one   **STOP**

 Answers to Exercise L3 are on page 499.

Exercise L4   ***Identifying the meaning of the word in the conversation***

In your book are the definitions of two words that are pronounced the same but spelled differently. Listen to the word, followed by a short conversation. Circle the letter of the definition of the word as it is used in the conversation you heard.

Example   You will hear: *tow*
            (man)   *My car broke down on Grand Avenue during rush hour.*
            (woman)   *I bet it was expensive to tow it.*

    You will read: (A) pull
            (B)   appendage of the foot

You should circle (A) because "pull" is the definition of "tow" used in the conversation. (A "toe" is an appendage of the foot.)

 START

1. (A) encounter
   (B) animal flesh

2. (A) exchange of goods for money
   (B) sheet of canvas used to catch the wind

3. (A) people who work on a ship or on a plane
   (B) trip on a ship

4. (A) seven days
   (B) fatigued

5. (A) letters
   (B) man

 STOP

Answers to Exercise L4 are on page 499.

Exercise L5   ***Identifying which meaning is correct***

Practice with statements

Read the following list of words and the four possible meanings for each. Listen to the spoken sentence and circle the letter of the meaning that is used in the sentence you heard.

Example   You will hear: *He runs a small business.*

    You will read: runs
            (A) meets
            (B) moves quickly
            (C) operates
            (D) elapses

You should circle (C) because "runs" means "operates" in the spoken sentence.

 START

1. simple
   (A) easy
   (B) plain
   (C) innocent
   (D) feebleminded

2. board
   (A) piece of wood
   (B) get on a transportation vehicle
   (C) meals supplied on a regular basis
   (D) group of people controlling a business

3. kid
   (A) baby goat
   (B) young child
   (C) tease
   (D) leather

4. beat
   (A) route
   (B) rhythm
   (C) hit
   (D) defeat

5. common
   (A) ordinary
   (B) ill-bred
   (C) general
   (D) shared

 PAUSE

Practice with conversations

Read the following list of words and the four possible definitions for each. Listen to the spoken conversation and circle the letter of the meaning that is used in the conversation.

Example   You will hear: (man)   *How often do you go skiing?*
                                 (woman)   *About three times a month.*

              You will read: times
                                (A) occasions
                                (B) multiply
                                (C) durations
                                (D) tempos

You should circle (A) because "times" in the conversation means "occasions."

 START

6. degree
   (A) step
   (B) academic qualification
   (C) angle
   (D) level of heat

7. major
   (A) army officer
   (B) musical scale
   (C) more important
   (D) a student's field of study

8. spring
   (A) time of year
   (B) stream
   (C) leap
   (D) coil

9. volume
   (A) loudness
   (B) large mass
   (C) amount of space
   (D) one of a set of books

10. sound
    (A) noise
    (B) healthy
    (C) dependable
    (D) body of water

 STOP

Extended practice: Make your own sentences using each of the meanings for these ten words.

Answers to Exercise L5 are on page 499.

Exercise L6   *Identifying multiple meanings*

In your book is a list of words and one of their meanings. For each word, you will hear two sentences. Write the letter of the sentence that uses the meaning given in your book.

Example   You will hear: (A) *The house needs a new coat of paint.*
                                (B) *Ted's family has a coat of arms.*

             You will read: *A*   coat = thin layer

You should write "A" in the space because "coat" means "thin layer" in that sentence.

 START

1. _____   light = be known

2. _____   strike = attack

3. _____   note = take notice of

4. _____   spring = jump suddenly

5. _____   exercise = make use of

 STOP

Answers to Exercise L6 are on page 499.

Exercise L7   *Matching words*

In your book is a list of sentences with an underlined word in each. You will hear two spoken sentences. Write the letter of the sentence that uses the underlined word in the same way as the sentence in your book.

Example   You will hear: (A) *Peter's dog heels very well on command.*
                                (B) *The horse kicked up its heels as it crossed the pasture.*

             You will read: *B*   I've got painful blisters on my heels.

You should write "B" in the space because "heels" in the sentence "The horse kicked up its heels as it crossed the pasture" has the same meaning as "heels" in the sentence "I've got painful blisters on my heels."

START

1. _____ The llamas were surefooted along the steep <u>pass</u>.

2. _____ Mr. Turner is a <u>just</u> man and can give you good advice.

3. _____ Ron caused the boat to <u>tip</u> over.

4. _____ The children <u>filed</u> out calmly during the fire drill.

5. _____ The incorrect answers have a <u>check</u> by them.

 STOP

Answers to Exercise L7 are on page 499.

Exercise L8   *Practice with conversations*

To answer the questions in Part A of the Computer-Based TOEFL® Test, you must listen to a short conversation between two people. The computer screen will show the people who are talking. The computer screen will look like this.

On the recording, you will hear:	(man)	*Would you like cream in your coffee?*
	(woman)	*No, thank you. I'll take it black.*
	(narrator)	*What does the woman mean?*

After the conversation, you will hear the narrator read the question as it appears on the computer screen. You will also be shown the answer choices. The computer screen will look like the one on the next page.

Listening

What does the woman mean?

○   She plans to have coffee.

○   She's going to take a bag.

○   She doesn't want anything in her drink.

○   She thinks the coffee is too black.

| Time | | Volume | Help | Answer Confirm | Next |

To answer this question, you would click on the oval next to the sentence "She doesn't want anything in her drink" because to take coffee "black" means that nothing extra is put in the drink. She declines the man's offer of cream because she doesn't want anything in her coffee. The oval you click on will become dark. When you are sure of your answer, click on the Next icon. Check your answer and then click on the Answer Confirm icon.

In the following exercise, listen to the spoken conversation. Circle the letter of the statement that answers the question.

 START

1. What is the man's problem?
    (A) He'll be gone for a week.
    (B) He doesn't have much strength.
    (C) His timing is bad.
    (D) He's been sick four times.

2. What does the woman mean?
    (A) She can't lend him money.
    (B) She doesn't want to join the group.
    (C) She doesn't know how to clean the engine.
    (D) She doesn't want to change the parts.

3. What are the people doing?
    (A) They're ordering two steaks.
    (B) They're collecting the essays.
    (C) They're trying to prove what was stated.
    (D) They're looking for errors in a paper.

4. What does the woman mean?
   (A) Carmen is bored with serving the boat club directors.
   (B) Carmen arranges meetings for the directors of the boat club.
   (C) Carmen is a waitress on board the ship called *Directors*.
   (D) Carmen is one of the directors of the boat club.

5. What does the woman say about Ted?
   (A) He lets the yolks sink to the bottom.
   (B) He understands after he thinks about things.
   (C) He doesn't realize the eggs stink.
   (D) He takes time to wash in the basin.

 STOP

Answers to Exercise L8 are on page 499.

PRACTICE WITH IDIOMS AND PHRASAL VERBS

Idioms and phrasal verbs are seen frequently on the Computer-Based TOEFL® Test. Misinterpreting their meaning may lead to the wrong choice of answer. Use Listening Exercises L9–L11 to develop your skills in identifying the correct meaning of these phrases.

1. Idioms

An idiom is a group of words that together have a different meaning from the individual words.

Examples   **shoot one's mouth off** (talk in an opinionated and loud manner)
Ted shot his mouth off at the meeting, and no one else had
a chance to speak.
(Ted talked in such a way that no one else was able to put forward
his or her own views.)

be hard up (lack money)
I'm sorry, I can't lend you $10 because I'm really hard up this month.
(I have very little money this month.)

Remember: The meaning of an idiom cannot be figured out by putting together the meanings of the individual words. Instead, the group of words as a whole has a special meaning, which you need to learn.

2. Phrasal verbs

A phrasal verb (also called a two-word verb or a three-word verb) is a verb + preposition (e.g., "take after") or a verb + adverb (e.g., "take apart") that together have a special meaning. Phrasal verbs can also be three words (e.g., "take out on").

Examples   Sue **takes after** her father. (Sue resembles her father.)

I'll have to **take apart** the engine to fix it. (I'll have to separate
the engine into its different parts in order to fix it.)

He was angry about failing the exam and **took** it **out on** his friend.
(He showed his disappointment at failing the exam by being angry
with his friend.)

Exercise L9   **Understanding idiomatic expressions**

Practice with statements

Listen to the spoken statement. Circle the letter of the sentence that is true based on the sentence you heard.

Example   You will hear: *He caught the drift of the conversation.*

You will read: (A) He was ill.
(B) He understood.

You should circle (B) because the idiom "caught the drift" means "understood."

 START

1. (A) Marsha has to swim regularly.
   (B) Marsha swims as much as she wants.

2. (A) Jim was very worried.
   (B) No one besides Jim was worried.

3. (A) Gordon becomes ill easily.
   (B) Gordon thinks ball games are easy.

4. (A) I'll take care of that problem later.
   (B) I'll propose crossing the bridge.

5. (A) Sue got into everything.
   (B) Sue didn't help at all.

6. (A) The movie is frightening.
   (B) The movie is boring.

 PAUSE

Practice with conversations

Listen to the spoken conversation. After each conversation, you will hear a question. Circle the letter of the sentence that answers the question correctly.

Example   You will hear: (woman)   *This class will be a breeze.*
(man)   *I agree.*
(narrator) *What does the woman mean?*

You will read: (A) The class work will be easy.
(B) The classroom will be windy.

You should circle (A) because the idiom "be a breeze" means "be easy."

 START

7. (A) The woman wants to break the bottle open.
   (B) The woman wants to try opening the bottle herself.

8. (A) The man will register for the music course.
   (B) The man won't register for the music course.

9. (A) The woman might know Cindy.
   (B) The woman doesn't know Cindy.

10. (A) He had to run to the registration office.
    (B) He had difficulty with the registration personnel.

 PAUSE

Practice with short test-like conversations

Listen to the spoken conversation. Circle the letter of the sentence that answers
the question.

Example   You will hear: (man)   *It's a long drive from your hometown
to the university.*

(woman)   *Yeah. I headed out before dawn.*

(narrator)   *What does the woman mean?*

You will read: (A)   She drove to Dawn's house four times.
(B)   It wasn't yet sunrise when she left.
(C)   She was yawning when she started out.
(D)   She headed the membership drive in her hometown.

You should circle (B) because the expression "to head out" means "to begin a journey."

 START

11.   (A)   There was an explosion in the chemistry classroom.
(B)   The teacher was angry because they hadn't done the work.
(C)   The students didn't understand what caused the explosion.
(D)   The instructor misunderstood the students' answers.

12.   (A)   Play catch on campus
(B)   Go to campus with Gus
(C)   Give Gus a ride to campus
(D)   Ride the bus to campus

13.   (A)   She thinks he must be rich.
(B)   She thinks he wants her to pay.
(C)   She's afraid he'll get burned.
(D)   She wonders how he can afford it.

14.   (A)   He prefers the color of the dress.
(B)   He thinks she would look better in a suit.
(C)   He doesn't care for her dress.
(D)   He prefers the blue suit.

 PAUSE

Practice with longer test-like conversation

Listen to the spoken conversation. Circle the letter of the sentence that answers
the question.

Example   You will hear: (woman)   *Hey, you're late. You just missed our football
team's kickoff. Where's Robin?*

(man)   *I came alone.*

(woman)   *I thought you were going to come with Robin.*

(man)   *I did, too, but she stood me up.*

(narrator)   *What does the man mean?*

You will read: (A)   Robin didn't come to meet him.
(B)   Robin stood beside him.
(C)   Robin went to the football game.
(D)   Robin was at the kickoff.

You should circle (A) because "to stand someone up" means "to not meet that person
at the prearranged time." He came alone because Robin didn't meet him as planned.

START

15. (A) Mike could make her feel better.
    (B) Mike always has good ideas.
    (C) Mike wouldn't laugh at her.
    (D) Mike could use some cheering up.

16. (A) Ann will visit her during spring break.
    (B) Ann will take her to the airport.
    (C) Ann will go home with her.
    (D) Ann will say good-bye to the man for her.

17. (A) Janet has gone ahead to the campsite.
    (B) Janet has the idea to go camping.
    (C) Janet is joining a summer camp.
    (D) Janet is doing research at the university campsite.

18. (A) She thinks he is a dedicated professor.
    (B) She thinks he is young for his age.
    (C) She thinks he is too old to continue teaching.
    (D) She thinks he should be approved for promotion.

 STOP

Answers to Exercise L9 are on page 500.

Exercise L10   ***Identifying the correct idiom or phrasal verb***

Practice with statements

Listen to the spoken statement. Circle the letter of the expression that could be substituted in the spoken statement.

Example   You will hear: *I don't let anyone treat me unfairly.*

You will read: (A) take after me
    (B) push me around
    (C) push my luck
    (D) run into me

You should circle (B) because "push me around" means the same as "treat me unfairly."

 START

1. (A) put up with the idea
   (B) put the idea together
   (C) put the idea across
   (D) put away the idea

2. (A) see the light
   (B) see the light at the end of the tunnel
   (C) light up
   (D) go out like a light

3. (A) was in over his head
   (B) was head over heels in love
   (C) lost his head
   (D) had a big head

4. (A) footing the bills
   (B) on his toes
   (C) pulling my leg
   (D) underfoot

5. (A) put that bicycle together
   (B) put that bicycle aside
   (C) put that bicycle down
   (D) put that bicycle out

6. (A) test the waters
   (B) be a test case
   (C) be put to the test
   (D) stand the test of time

7. (A) held it against her son
   (B) held on to her son
   (C) got hold of her son
   (D) held her son up

8. (A) give me a run for my money
   (B) make my blood run cold
   (C) run me ragged
   (D) put me in the running

 PAUSE

Practice with conversations

Listen to the spoken conversation. Circle the letter of the sentence containing the idiom or phrasal verb that could be substituted in the conversation.

Example   You will hear: (man)   *Did the professor collect the assignment?*
                                  (woman) *No, but I gave him mine anyway.*

                You will read: (A) But I handed in mine anyway.
                                  (B) But I gave him a hand anyway.
                                  (C) But I went hand in hand with him anyway.
                                  (D) But I put my hands on it anyway.

You should circle (A) because the idiom "handed in" could have been used instead of "gave him."

 START

9. (A) Because I have fallen behind.
   (B) Because I have fallen asleep.
   (C) Because I have fallen in love.
   (D) Because I have fallen apart.

10. (A) He always weighs his words.
    (B) He always gains weight.
    (C) He always throws his weight around.
    (D) He always pulls his weight.

11. (A) She may, on the off chance.
    (B) She stands a good chance.
    (C) She may chance upon it.
    (D) She may chance it.

12. (A) The professor called it a day.
    (B) The professor called a halt to it.
    (C) The professor called my bluff.
    (D) The professor called attention to it.

13. (A) Janet and Mike were turning the other cheek.
    (B) Janet and Mike were speaking tongue in cheek.
    (C) Janet and Mike were dancing cheek to cheek.
    (D) Janet and Mike were being cheeky.

14. (A) You just saw the last of it.
    (B) You were seeing things.
    (C) You saw your way clear to do it.
    (D) You saw the daylight.

15. (A) Don't let her throw cold water on it.
    (B) Don't let her throw a party.
    (C) Don't let her throw in the towel.
    (D) Don't let her throw it away.

16. (A) You might as well.
    (B) You will come off well.
    (C) You should leave well enough alone.
    (D) It's just as well.

 STOP

Answers to Exercise L10 are on page 500.

Exercise L11   *Identifying the correct meaning of expressions*

Practice with statements

Listen to the spoken statement. Circle the letter of the sentence that is true based on the information you heard.

Example   You will hear: *The professor would have let the student stay late*
to complete the exam, but he finished ahead of time.

You will read: (A) The student stayed late in order to finish the exam.
                 (B) The professor made the student stay after class
                     because he didn't arrive on time.
                 (C) The student was ahead of the professor in meeting
                     the deadline to finish the test.
                 (D) The student completed the test early.

You should circle (D) because if the student finished "ahead of time," he completed the test early.

 START

1. (A) Sue and Mary had an accident in the parking lot.
   (B) Sue and Mary jogged together at the mall.
   (C) Sue happened to meet Mary at the mall.
   (D) Sue ran into the mall to see Mary.

2. (A) Since John is doing the best, he'll win.
   (B) John has the best chance of winning.
   (C) Although John is trying very hard, he won't win.
   (D) John can't stand metal.

3. (A) Bess works out by going jogging.
   (B) Bess will run all the way to work.
   (C) Eventually, everything will turn out well.
   (D) Long runs are the best way to get a good workout.

4. (A) Rebecca did all right on her entrance exams.
   (B) Rebecca passed the entrance on the right.
   (C) Rebecca did everything correctly.
   (D) Rebecca immediately let her parents know about the tests.

5. (A) Bill didn't take the test because of the time.
   (B) Bill didn't take the test although he wasn't late.
   (C) Bill checked the test out for a short time.
   (D) Bill used his identification card to take the test.

 PAUSE

Practice with short test-like conversations

You will hear a spoken conversation. After each conversation, you will hear a question.
Circle the letter of the answer that is true based on the conversation you heard.

Example   You will hear: (woman)   *Why did your flight take so long?*
                               (man)   *There was a four-hour layover in Chicago for refueling.*
                               (narrator) *What reason does the man give the woman?*

               You will read: (A) The flight personnel were discharged.
                               (B) They spent the night in Chicago.
                               (C) The plane needed fuel.
                               (D) There was fog over Chicago.

You should circle (C) because if there was a "layover" (a stop) for refueling, it was
because the plane needed fuel.

 START

6. (A) He's going to get things organized.
   (B) He's going to get a good seat in the stands.
   (C) He's going to avoid standing in long lines.
   (D) He's going to help put the TV sets in the recording studio.

7. (A) The woman made an ethical mistake.
   (B) The woman got a point wrong on the exam.
   (C) The woman missed a very good speech.
   (D) The woman didn't understand the lecture.

8. (A) The doctor told her to run in order to lose weight.
   (B) She ran so quickly to the doctor's office that she arrived panting.
   (C) She discovered how to lose weight in a brochure at the doctor's.
   (D) The doctor was cross with her for not exercising and watching her diet.

9. (A) She votes well.
   (B) She can do a good job.
   (C) She takes what she can.
   (D) She takes elections seriously.

10. (A) He doesn't have the approval to begin.
    (B) He's ahead of the committee on the project.
    (C) The head of the committee is going away.
    (D) He has to turn in the project ahead of time.

PAUSE

Practice with longer test-like conversations

You will hear a spoken conversation. After each conversation, you will hear a question. Circle the letter of the answer that is true based on the conversation you heard.

Example   You will hear: (woman)   *I didn't recognize Ned when I saw him in the cafeteria. Have you seen him?*

(man)   *No, I haven't. Has he cut his hair or something?*

(woman)   *No. He spent the summer taking tourists hiking, and all that exercise has made a new person of him.*

(narrator)   *What does the woman mean?*

You will read: (A)   Dealing with tourists has improved Ned's personality.
(B)   Ned has a new haircut that makes him unrecognizable.
(C)   Ned has changed so much that he seems like a different person.
(D)   Ned has a new person in his life.

You should circle (C) because being "made a new person" means that a person has changed and now seems different.

 START

11.   (A)   He's taken up smoking.
(B)   He's worn out from smoking.
(C)   He's given up smoking.
(D)   He's sworn at smokers.

12.   (A)   He is turning in the form in plenty of time.
(B)   He is holding on to a difficult job.
(C)   He is taking on work on a farm.
(D)   He is wasting his time applying for a loan.

13.   (A)   She might find it difficult to work and study.
(B)   She could get good teaching practice.
(C)   She would make a good assistant.
(D)   She may have to make a difficult decision.

14.   (A)   She fell on the road across from the second-hand store.
(B)   She saw a building on Main Street tumble.
(C)   She found the used-clothing store by accident.
(D)   She had the second hand on her watch fixed.

STOP

Answers to Exercise L11 are on page 501.

CHECK YOUR PROGRESS

Check your progress in understanding similar words and sounds (Exercises L1–L11) by completing the following mini-test. This exercise uses a format similar to that used in Part A of the Listening Section of the Computer-Based TOEFL® Test. If you are unfamiliar with how to answer questions on the Computer-Based TOEFL® Test, see the Tutorial on pages 15–16.

Exercise L12   Mini-test

Listen to the conversation and question. Then select the letter of the best answer choice.

Now get ready to listen.

 START

1. What does the man mean?
   (A) He doesn't enjoy going climbing.
   (B) He plans to take the airplane.
   (C) He doesn't want to use the steps.
   (D) He thinks they fly too often.

2. What are the people discussing?
   (A) Replacing a picture
   (B) Taking a class photo
   (C) Framing a painting
   (D) Buying some glass

3. What are the people discussing?
   (A) An extra tire
   (B) A bathroom plug
   (C) A clogged drain
   (D) An odor

4. What does the man mean?
   (A) The woman should close her eyes.
   (B) The woman should get some sleep.
   (C) The woman should turn off the light.
   (D) The woman should close up her house.

5. What does the man want to do?
    (A) Pack up a dinner for the party
    (B) Return to the party after dinner
    (C) Avoid going to the dinner party
    (D) Have dinner in the backyard

6. What can be inferred about the man?
    (A) He isn't letting his bad grade upset him.
    (B) He hasn't studied hard enough.
    (C) He has broken the lamp in the sociology class.
    (D) He didn't write darkly enough on the score sheet.

7. What does the woman mean?
    (A) She thinks he should brush up on his social skills.
    (B) She understands why it can't be hurried.
    (C) She agrees that there are reasons not to talk about it.
    (D) She thinks people should know about the experiment.

8. What does the man mean?
    (A) Some people are put on TV.
    (B) Some people are screamed at.
    (C) Some people eat ice cream.
    (D) Some people are disqualified.

9. What does the man say about Neil?
    (A) He usually feels sticky after class.
    (B) He usually meets Rick after class.
    (C) He's usually stuck up after class.
    (D) He usually stays after class.

10. What can be inferred about Professor Jenson?
    (A) He returned the class papers.
    (B) He wasn't well.
    (C) He passed everyone in the course.
    (D) He taught the course in the past.

11. What does the man want to do?
    (A) Go to space
    (B) Return to class
    (C) Pack his glass
    (D) Carry the pack

12. What needs to be done to the jacket?
    (A) It needs to be cleaned.
    (B) It needs to be made smaller.
    (C) It needs to be returned.
    (D) It needs to be mended.

13. What does the woman mean?
    (A) She thought the man didn't want the tags.
    (B) She thought the man didn't get along
        with Cindy.
    (C) She thought the man didn't price
        the books.
    (D) She thought the man didn't want them
        to come.

14. What has the instructor done?
    (A) Simplified his course
    (B) Watered his horse the required amount
    (C) Required a change of courses
    (D) Dropped his course requirements

15. What are the people going to do?
   (A)   Play pool
   (B)   Take a cab
   (C)   Cool the car
   (D)   Go swimming

Answers to Exercise L12 are on page 503.

🎧 **STOP**

PRACTICE WITH VARIOUS STRUCTURES

The following structures occur with some frequency on the Computer-Based TOEFL®
Test. Use Listening Exercises L13–L18 to develop your skills in understanding the
meaning of these structures. Study the following examples.

1.   *Statements that contain time, quantity, or comparison information*

TIME – Time can be expressed through verb tense or time expressions.

   (man):   Do you know when Mary will finish the project?
(woman):   She said she **would be finished** within the week. (Mary will be
             finished sometime during the week.)

Although the tense "would be finished" may appear to be an action occurring in the past,
it was Mary's statement concerning an action in the future that was said in the past.

   (woman):   I am **not** going to the library **until** after lunch. (The woman will go
              to the library after lunch.)

no(t) sooner than	not before	no(t) more than	no(t) later than	not until
the day after tomorrow	by tomorrow	in two days		
the week after next	by Tuesday	in three weeks		
the following month	by March 1	after next month		
for many years	many years ago	since		

**QUANTITY – Quantity can be expressed through amounts, numbers,
              or frequency.**

   (man):   How much of this medicine can I take?
(woman):   **Up to six** doses **daily**. (The man can take no more than six doses
             in one day.)

   (man):   You look discouraged.
(woman):   That's because I have**n't** sold **a single** raffle ticket for the Economics
             Department fund-raiser. (The woman has not sold any tickets.)

double	twice as much	two times as much	half as much
triple	three times as much	a third of	
quadruple	four times as much	a fourth	a quarter

a couple more	up to (no more than the number given)
a few more	at least (no less than the number given)
several more	and then some (the number given + more)

few = not many (almost none)
a few = some (more than none)
quite a few = lots
not a single / not one = none

little = not much (almost none)
a little = some (more than none)
quite a lot / quite a bit = a large amount

Words that indicate two	Words that indicate more than two
either	every
neither	some
both	any
between	among
each	each

daily = once a day
every other day = on alternating days
weekly = once a week
monthly = once a month
yearly (annually) = once a year

COMPARISONS – Comparisons are expressed through comparative and superlative structures.

(man):   Sue's **better** in math **than** science.
(woman):   Maybe, but she's **better** in math and science **than** the rest of the class.

The man compares Sue's abilities in math to her abilities in science. The woman compares Sue's abilities in both math and science to the other class members' abilities in math and science.

(man):   Was the ecology exam difficult?
(woman):   Yes, it was **the most** difficult one yet.

The woman is comparing one ecology exam to all the other ecology exams given so far in one particular course.

(woman):   How many people should we have fill in the questionnaire?
(man):   Well, **the more** people we ask to fill it in, **the more** reliable our statistics will be.

The man is making a double comparison. The number of people who take part in the study will directly affect the reliability of their statistics.

2.   *Verbs that show the idea that someone or something caused ("get," "make," "have"), requested ("ask"), or permitted ("let") something to happen*

CAUSE

Andy **got** Bill to do the work. (Bill did the work because Andy either persuaded or paid him to do it.)

The teacher **made** Susan rewrite the essay. (Susan rewrote the essay because her teacher required her to do so.)

Mary **had** Tim get a haircut. (Mary asked Tim to get a haircut, and he did.)

I **got** my flat tire fixed. / I **had** my flat tire fixed. (I caused my flat tire to be fixed by asking/paying someone to do it.)

REQUEST

Jack **asked** Marvin to bring a hammer. (If Marvin brought the hammer, it was because Jack asked him to bring it. It was Marvin's choice whether or not to do this.)

PERMISSION

I **let** Becky have the cake. (Becky had the cake because I told her she could have it.)

3. *Words that express a negative meaning*

Sue **seldom** does her homework. (Sue doesn't do her homework very often.)

Rick **neither** jogs **nor** swims. (Rick doesn't jog and he doesn't swim.)

Robin **didn't** work quickly. (Robin worked slowly.)

It is **unlikely** that Tom brought the game. (Tom probably didn't bring the game.)

4. *Modals: "can," "could," "had better," "may," "might," "must," "ought to," "shall," "should," "will," "would" (special auxiliary verbs that indicate a speaker's attitude or mood about what is being said)*

Ms. Jones **can** do the typing. (Ms. Jones is able to do the typing.)

Can I give the report now? (I want permission to give the report now.)

Jane **could** buy the television. (I think Jane is able to buy the television.)

Could you close the door? (A polite request meaning "I want you to close the door.")

Mr. Smith **may** come to the opening. (It is possible that Mr. Smith will come to the opening.)

Lee **might** have written down the assignment. (It is possible that Lee wrote down the assignment.)

Ann **must** have gone to the fair. (I think that Ann has gone to the fair.)

Frank **should** have been at the concert. (Frank wasn't at the concert, but it was advisable for him to be there.)

Should you have any trouble, call me. (If you have trouble, call me.)

Will you please speak quietly? (A polite request meaning "I want you to speak quietly.")

5. *Conditional sentences (which indicate a possible situation and its consequences)*

If it rains, we will go to the shopping mall. (There might be rain. In that case, we are going to go to the mall.)

If he had bought the book, I would have read it. (He hasn't bought the book. Therefore, I haven't read it.)

If they had followed my advice, they wouldn't have had that problem. (They didn't follow my advice. Therefore, they had that problem.)

Had we left at 4:00, we would have missed seeing Rob. (We stayed, and therefore, we did see Rob.)

6. *Ways of expressing causes and results*

We left because the noise was bothersome. (The bothersome noise caused us to leave. Our leaving was a result of the noise's being bothersome.)

Joan was **so** happy, she hugged everyone. (Joan's happiness caused her to hug everyone. Her hugging everyone was the result of her happiness.)

It was **such** an extraordinary movie that we watched it twice. (Our watching the movie twice was a result of the movie's being extraordinary.)

Now that Fred has a part-time job, he will have the money to buy that car. (Fred's having the money to buy the car is a result of his getting a job.)

It was difficult to drive **due to** the fog. (The fog made it difficult to drive.)

After the bypass was built, the traffic passing through the city center was more manageable. (The traffic's being more manageable in the city center is a result of the bypass's being built.)

7. **Reflexive pronouns (used to indicate that the person doing the action is the same as the person receiving the action; also used for emphasis)**

I bought **myself** a new watch. (I was the person who bought the watch, and I was the person who received the watch.)

Jack cut **himself** while shaving. (Jack was the person who did the cutting, and Jack was the person who got cut.)

Linda painted the picture **herself**. (Linda's painting the picture without help from anyone else is being emphasized.)

8. **Verb + infinitive (e.g., "stopped to rest") or verb + gerund ("stopped resting")**

Chris **stopped to buy** some matches. (Chris stopped somewhere and bought some matches there.)

Chris **stopped buying** matches. (Chris doesn't buy matches anymore.)

Liz **remembered to bring** the chairs. (Liz didn't forget to bring the chairs. She brought them.)

Liz **remembered bringing** the chairs. (Liz knows that she brought the chairs because she remembers having done so.)

9. **"Used to" (a habitual action in the past) versus "be used to" (be accustomed to)**

Dick **used to** jog in the mornings. (Dick regularly went jogging in the mornings. This is no longer his habit.)

Susan **is used to** singing on stage. (Susan is accustomed to singing on stage.)

10. **"Was to have" (was supposed to)**

I **was to have done** the assignment. (I was given the assignment to do, but I didn't do it.)

I **was supposed to have done** the assignment. (I was given the assignment to do, but I didn't do it.)

Exercise L13   *Practice with time, quantity, and comparisons*

Practice with statements

Listen to the spoken statement. Circle the letter of the sentence that is true based on the information you heard.

Example   You will hear: *When the new regulation goes into effect, no more extensions will be given.*

You will read: (A) After the new regulation goes into effect, extensions will be given.
(B) After the new regulation goes into effect, extensions will not be given.

You should circle (B) because first the new regulation will go into effect. Then, no more extensions will be given.

 START

1. (A) It's too late to tell me tomorrow.
    (B) It's too late to tell me after tomorrow.

2. (A) Tom stopped studying at midnight.
    (B) Tom started studying at midnight.

3. (A) Alice needs about two credits to graduate.
    (B) Alice doesn't need more credits to graduate.

4. (A) Professor Merrill has written thirty or more articles on art history.
    (B) Professor Merrill has not written more than thirty articles on art history.

5. (A) The fog is usually heavier than it is tonight.
    (B) There is more fog tonight than there usually is.

 PAUSE

Practice with conversations

Listen to the spoken conversation. Circle the letter of the sentence that is true based on the information you heard.

Example   You will hear: (man)   *Are you still going to Aspen?*
(woman)   *I don't know. The more we discuss the trip, the less we agree on it.*

You will read: (A) They agree on the trip.
(B) They don't agree on the trip.

You should circle (B) because the more they discuss the trip, the more they do not agree on it ("the less we agree on it").

 START

6. (A) He didn't buy as many books last semester as this semester.
    (B) He bought more books last semester than this semester.

7. (A) He spent less than two hours on his speech preparation.
    (B) He spent more than two hours on his speech preparation.

8. (A) The people don't understand an example.
    (B) The people don't understand two examples.

9. (A) The woman would prefer a big box.
    (B) The woman would prefer a better box.

10. (A) A few students couldn't get loans.
     (B) A lot of students couldn't get loans.

 PAUSE

Practice with short test-like conversations

Listen to the spoken conversation. Circle the letter of the sentence that answers the question.

Example   You will hear: (woman)   *Jane only needs about a third of the food*
                                             that she bought for the picnic.
                              (man)   *Don't you believe it! Those guys could empty*
                                             a grocery store.
                              (narrator) *What does the man mean?*

           You will read: (A) Jane bought three times as much food as necessary.
                            (B) Jane almost bought all the food in the grocery store.
                            (C) Jane didn't buy too much for the picnic.
                            (D) Jane only bought a third of the groceries,
                                 and the guys bought the rest.

You should circle (C) because "those guys could empty a grocery store" indicates that they can eat a lot. Therefore, the woman is wrong to think that Jane bought too much.

 START

11. (A) She needs a minimum of twelve folders to get organized.
    (B) The organization will take care of the project's expenses.
    (C) They've tried a dozen times to get the project started.
    (D) The number of files needed for the organization has increased.

12. (A) She has a computer exam to finish.
    (B) She has finished two programs.
    (C) She's trying to finish her work.
    (D) She's too busy to study for her finals.

13. (A) The woman should stop working for a while.
    (B) The woman should work on the fifth problem.
    (C) The woman should not let the problem get her down.
    (D) The woman should let the man sort it out for her.

 PAUSE

Practice with longer test-like conversations

Listen to the spoken conversation. Circle the letter of the sentence that answers the question.

Example   You will hear: (woman)   *The cafeteria sure is crowded today.*
                              (man)   *I'll say. We could go over to that new campus*
                                             snack bar.
                              (woman)   *I've heard that a meal there is almost twice*
                                             as expensive as one in the cafeteria.
                              (man)   *I bet it is twice as good, too. I'd rather pay*
                                             double and be able to find a place to sit
                                             and enjoy my meal.
                              (narrator) *What does the man mean?*

           You will read: (A) He'll make two bets with the woman about the
                                 quality of food.
                            (B) He paid almost double for the food in the new
                                 campus snack bar.
                            (C) He'd prefer to pay more and in return get quality
                                 and comfort.
                            (D) He is willing to pay for his own meal as well as
                                 the woman's meal.

You should circle (C) because the man is comparing the quality of the food and is saying that he would pay for a comfortable place to eat.

 START

14. (A) Tony ate a couple of pizzas.
    (B) Tony worked extra hours.
    (C) Tony put two pizzas in the oven.
    (D) Tony's been late over three times.

15. (A) The man couldn't have been mistaken.
    (B) Sue got back last Monday.
    (C) Sue's roommate was at the bookstore.
    (D) The man probably didn't see Sue.

 STOP

Answers to Exercise L13 are on page 504.

Exercise L14   **Understanding causatives**

Practice with statements

Listen to the spoken statement, followed by the question. Circle the letter of the correct answer.

Example   You will hear: (woman)   *Tom will advise Nick to buy that car.*
                                (narrator)   *Who might buy a car?*

             You will read: (A) Tom
                              (B) Nick

You should circle (B) because Nick might buy the car that Tom recommends.

 START

1. (A) Kathy   3. (A) Mary
   (B) John   (B) Dan

2. (A) Vicky   4. (A) Nancy's
   (B) Ann   (B) Jeff's

 PAUSE

Practice with conversations

Listen to the spoken conversation. Circle the letter of the correct answer.

Example   You will hear: (man)   *Is Ron or Vicky giving the introductory speech?*
                                (woman)   *Since Ron isn't available that evening,*
                                          I asked Vicky.
                                (narrator)   *Who will give the speech?*

             You will read: (A) Ron
                              (B) Vicky

You should circle (B) because according to the conversation, Vicky was asked to give the introductory speech.

START

5. (A) Joe
    (B) Fred

6. (A) Mike
    (B) Tom

7. (A) Ms. Jones
    (B) Dr. Welsh

8. (A) Rebecca
    (B) Barbara

 PAUSE

Practice with short test-like conversations

Listen to the spoken conversation. Circle the letter of the sentence that answers the question.

Example   You will hear: (woman)   *Wow! What a bizarre paint job you've had done to your car. Did your cousin who works for Galaxy Auto Repair do it?*

(man)   *No, but they have a man there who specializes in designer paint jobs.*

(narrator)   *What does the man mean?*

You will read: (A) His cousin specializes in painting designs on cars.
(B) The people at Galaxy Auto Repair wouldn't paint his car.
(C) He had a specialist paint his car.
(D) He asked his cousin to recommend a car painter.

You should circle (C) because a man who specializes in designer paint jobs painted the man's car.

 START

9. (A) Jane got the form for him.
    (B) Jane will help him apply.
    (C) He picked Jane up this morning.
    (D) He thinks Jane will get a loan.

10. (A) Tom has never been a reliable plumber.
    (B) The plumber couldn't take care of the problem.
    (C) The job didn't need to be done by a professional.
    (D) Tom couldn't have fixed the pipe himself.

11. (A) Marie gave Rick's speech.
    (B) Rick gave Marie his speech.
    (C) Rick got a speech for Marie.
    (D) Marie wrote the speech for Rick.

 PAUSE

Practice with longer test-like conversations

Listen to the spoken conversation. Circle the letter of the sentence that answers the question.

Example   You will hear: (woman)   *Did you ask Bill to photocopy the notes Jane took at that business studies seminar?*

(man)   *Yes, I did. I also asked him to see if his uncle would lend us the management book he told you about.*

(woman)   *Good. I'm glad Bill is in our group. With his contacts we'll have our Management Studies project done in no time.*

(narrator)   *What does the woman imply?*

You will read: (A) Bill is going to do the project for them.

(B) Bill knows a lot of people who can help them.

(C) Bill works hard when he is in a group project.

(D) Bill's uncle will manage the project for them.

You should circle (B) because a person who has contacts knows people who can help.

 START

12. (A) Ellen's father is taking care of her injured finger.

(B) Ellen's father has agreed with her mother.

(C) Ellen's father will help her get a driver's permit.

(D) Ellen's father will let her use the car.

13. (A) Someone from the small-claims court could take care of the dispute.

(B) It would be advisable for Mrs. Jones to hand in the claim.

(C) The student legal-aid adviser could deal with the problem.

(D) The tenant has a problem with the small-claims court.

14. (A) The secretary will bring the paper to him on Friday.

(B) The secretary will make the final revisions for her.

(C) The secretary will correct her paper while he's in Chicago.

(D) The secretary will give him the paper when he gets back.

 STOP

Answers to Exercise L14 are on page 504.

Exercise L15   ***Understanding negative meaning***

Practice with statements

Listen to the spoken statement. Circle the letter of the sentence that is implied in the statement you heard.

Example   You will hear: *Never have so many people been unemployed.*

You will read: (A) There is a lot of unemployment.

(B) There is little unemployment.

You should circle (A) because the statement "Never have so many people been unemployed" suggests that "many people are unemployed."

 START

1. (A) I never catch the number 9 bus.

(B) I often catch the number 9 bus.

2. (A) Motivation is often the reason for success.

(B) Experience is often the reason for success.

3. (A) My suggestions usually aren't taken seriously.

(B) My suggestions usually are taken seriously.

4. (A) There isn't enough bread.

(B) There is just enough bread.

 PAUSE

Practice with conversations

Listen to the spoken conversation. Circle the letter of the sentence that is true based on the conversation you heard.

Example   You will hear: (man)   *I've never had such a bad headache.*
                                 (woman)   *Maybe you should see a doctor about it.*

                You will read: (A)   The man has never had a headache.
                                 (B)   The man has never had a headache as bad as this one.

You should circle (B) because, according to the conversation, the man has a bad headache.

 START

5. (A)   The man had a lot of trouble with the exercises.
   (B)   The man had some trouble with the exercises.

6. (A)   The woman saw more than one course she wanted to attend.
   (B)   The woman saw no courses she wanted to attend.

7. (A)   Mark is tense about the test.
   (B)   Mark isn't tense about the test.

8. (A)   There was enough equipment.
   (B)   There wasn't enough equipment.

 PAUSE

Practice with short test-like conversations

Listen to the spoken conversation. Circle the letter of the sentence that answers the question.

Example   You will hear: (man)   *Professor Adams has just announced there*
                                            will be a quiz next Monday.
                                 (woman)   *Oh, not another one.*
                                 (narrator) *What does the woman imply?*

                You will read: (A)   There's not really going to be a quiz.
                                 (B)   Professor Adams gives too many quizzes.
                                 (C)   She knew about the quiz.
                                 (D)   She's never taken one of Professor Adams's quizzes.

You should circle (B) because the woman's complaint about yet another quiz indicates
she thinks there are too many quizzes.

 START

9. (A)   She thinks the man would be a good model.
   (B)   She doesn't appreciate art.
   (C)   She doesn't think the man can paint.
   (D)   She's surprised by the man's decision.

10. (A)   Everyone has paid their membership dues.
    (B)   They can't sponsor the tournament unless everyone pays their dues.
    (C)   They're going to charge an admission fee for the tournament.
    (D)   The Fencing Club needs to hold a membership drive.

11. (A)   Robert needs to study hard to stay in the university.
    (B)   Robert has gotten into a lot of trouble.
    (C)   Robert seldom has a problem he can't solve.
    (D)   Robert dropped out of the last course.

 PAUSE

Practice with longer test-like conversations

Listen to the spoken conversation. Circle the letter of the sentence that answers the question.

Example   You will hear: (man)   *Did you hear that Nancy sold her car?*
                                (woman)   *That lemon? I sure wouldn't have bought it.*
                                (man)   *Well, she had no problems selling it.*
                                (narrator) *What does the man mean?*

You will read: (A)   Nancy couldn't sell her car.
                 (B)   Nancy wouldn't sell her car.
                 (C)   There was nothing wrong with Nancy's car.
                 (D)   Nancy sold her car easily.

You should circle (D). Since Nancy had no problems selling her car, she sold it easily.

 START

12. (A) Jim's not a good athlete.
    (B) Jim doesn't go out for sports.
    (C) Jim couldn't qualify to be on the team.
    (D) Jim has a good position on the football team.

13. (A) Dan discussed the problem with Maria.
    (B) The department head explained the situation to Dan and Maria.
    (C) The problem isn't as bad as Dan and Maria think.
    (D) Dan and Maria complain far too much.

14. (A) Go to the mall
    (B) Go to the farmer's market
    (C) Go downtown
    (D) Go to the town hall

 STOP

Answers to Exercise L15 are on page 504.

Exercise L16   ***Understanding modals***

Practice with statements

Listen to the spoken statement. Circle the letter of the sentence that is closer in meaning to or implied in the statement you heard.

Example   You will hear: *Jane should have stayed in bed after her operation.*

You will read: (A)   Jane stayed in bed.
                 (B)   Jane didn't stay in bed.

You should circle (B) because "should have stayed" means "Jane didn't stay in bed."

 START

1. (A) We'll meet once a week.
   (B) We won't meet once a week.

2. (A) Ben heard the talk.
   (B) Ben didn't hear the talk.

3. (A) Please call tomorrow.
   (B) Please don't call tomorrow.

4. (A) Jill most likely went back to the dorm.
   (B) It was necessary for Jill to go back to the dorm.

 PAUSE

Practice with conversations

Listen to the spoken conversation. Circle the letter of the sentence that is true based on the conversation you heard.

Example   You will hear: (man)   *Joyce must have dropped the class.*
                               (woman)   *I don't think so. She's been very ill recently.*

               You will read: (A) Joyce has dropped the class.
                               (B) Joyce is sick.

You should circle (B) because, according to the conversation, Joyce has been ill.

 START

5. (A) The woman will be attending the ceremonies.
   (B) The woman may not be attending the ceremonies.

6. (A) Jim probably called a plumber.
   (B) Jim probably didn't call a plumber.

7. (A) The woman doesn't think she'll have Professor Roth for biology.
   (B) The woman thinks she'll have Professor Roth for biology.

8. (A) The woman has been married for ten years.
   (B) The woman hasn't been married for ten years yet.

 PAUSE

Practice with short test-like conversations

Listen to the spoken conversation. Circle the letter of the sentence that answers the question.

Example   You will hear: (woman)   *Do you know anyone who can work overtime this weekend?*
                               (man)   *What about John? I heard he's short on cash.*
                               (narrator) *What does the man mean?*

               You will read: (A) John might want to do the work.
                               (B) John has to work this weekend.
                               (C) The woman should pay John better.
                               (D) The woman could work overtime for John.

You should circle (A) because the man means John needs some money and, therefore, may want to work overtime.

 START

9. (A) The man should rewrite his essay.
   (B) The man should go over the problems again.
   (C) The man should have been given more time.
   (D) The man should look over his paper again.

10. (A) Their car has been hauled away.
    (B) They can't get a good trade-in.
    (C) Their car is unreliable.
    (D) They can't afford a new car.

11. (A) The woman shouldn't read frightening books.
    (B) He doesn't like romance novels.
    (C) There must be a romantic element in the story.
    (D) The woman reads too many horror stories.

 PAUSE

Practice with longer test-like conversations

Listen to the spoken conversation. Circle the letter of the sentence that answers the question.

Example   You will hear: (man)   *This weather is unbelievable.*
                               (woman)   *That's for sure. The fog is so heavy that you can't see the other side of the street.*
                               (man)   *I wouldn't want to drive in it.*
                               (narrator) *What does the man mean?*

               You will read: (A) He doesn't want the woman to drive.
                               (B) He thinks that the fog could cause driving difficulties.
                               (C) He wants her to pull over to the other side of the street.
                               (D) He doesn't want to continue driving in the fog.

You should circle (B) because by saying that he wouldn't want to drive in the fog, he is implying that the fog would make driving difficult.

 START

12. (A) She would be able to go abroad if she wanted.
    (B) She couldn't take off two weeks because of her job.
    (C) She should stay home and work during the summer.
    (D) She should quit her job with the travel agency.

13. (A) There's no way the man can finish the project in time.
    (B) Jerry will never help the man finish the project.
    (C) With Jerry's help, the man could finish the project.
    (D) The man could help Jerry finish the project on time.

14. (A) Stop and take a rest
    (B) Go a little farther
    (C) Continue past the bus stop
    (D) Go until she's tired

 STOP

Answers to Exercise L16 are on page 505.

Exercise L17   *Identifying conditions*

Practice with statements

Listen to the spoken statement. Circle the letter of the sentence that is closer in meaning to or implied in the statement you heard.

Example   You will hear: *If you have a boarding pass, please get in line.*

               You will read: (A) You must stand in line if you have a pass.
                               (B) You must stand in line if you don't have a pass.

You should circle (A) because those people who have a boarding pass should get in line.

START

1. (A) Sarah got a raise.
   (B) Sarah didn't get a raise.

2. (A) Mary's mother was in Spain.
   (B) Mary's mother wasn't in Spain.

3. (A) I drank a lot of coffee.
   (B) I didn't drink a lot of coffee.

4. (A) Ted will bring sandwiches.
   (B) Ted might bring sandwiches.

 PAUSE

Practice with conversations

Listen to the spoken conversation. Circle the letter of the sentence that is true based
on the conversation you heard.

Example   You will hear: (woman)   *Would you mind if I didn't come?*
                              (man)   *No, of course not.*

              You will read: (A) The woman won't go with the man.
                               (B) The woman didn't go with the man.

You should circle (A) because the woman is asking the man to excuse her from going.

 START

5. (A) The man didn't meet Helen Martin.
   (B) The man met Helen Martin.

6. (A) Sue is on probation.
   (B) Sue isn't on probation.

7. (A) Marion didn't attend the march.
   (B) Marion attended the march.

8. (A) The man has taken a walk.
   (B) The man hasn't taken a walk.

 PAUSE

Practice with short test-like conversations

Listen to the spoken conversation. Circle the letter of the sentence that answers
the question.

Example   You will hear: (man)   *Would you like a piece of my mom's wonderful*
                                          homemade spice cake?
                              (woman)   *It sounds tempting, but if I even smell cake,*
                                          I gain five pounds.
                              (narrator) *What does the woman mean?*

              You will read: (A) She doesn't like to make cakes.
                               (B) She thinks the cake smells good.
                               (C) She can't go to his mother's house.
                               (D) She doesn't want any cake.

You should circle (D) because the woman has stated her concern about gaining weight
as a way to say that she doesn't want any cake.

START

9. (A) The experiment will fail.
   (B) He's certain everything will be all right.
   (C) The woman shouldn't worry about the experiment yet.
   (D) They can always do the experiment later.

10. (A) The final will cover only Unit 10.
    (B) The woman is better prepared for the final.
    (C) The final will be very difficult.
    (D) The woman doesn't have to study Unit 10.

11. (A) Give the keys to the owner
    (B) Leave the keys where she found them
    (C) Take the keys to the security office
    (D) Leave the keys in the car

 PAUSE

Practice with longer test-like conversations

Listen to the spoken conversation. Circle the letter of the sentence that answers the question.

Example   You will hear: (woman)   *I missed my afternoon French literature class because my flight didn't get in until 2:00 P.M.*

(man)   *I thought you were arriving on Flight 219 out of Denver. Doesn't that arrive in the morning?*

(woman)   *Yes, and I would have been on that flight had I not missed my connecting flight.*

(narrator)   *What does the woman mean?*

You will read: (A) She didn't board Flight 219.
                 (B) She didn't miss the connection.
                 (C) She boarded the wrong flight.
                 (D) She must have boarded connecting Flight 219.

You should circle (A) because the woman missed the connecting flight, and therefore, she couldn't get Flight 219.

 START

12. (A) He had enough money to help Marvin.
    (B) He would have gone with Marvin.
    (C) He offered to pay Marvin.
    (D) He shouldn't have gone with Marvin.

13. (A) The man can't write reports very well.
    (B) The woman may have difficulty reading the man's handwriting.
    (C) It is impossible to write a report so quickly.
    (D) It is impossible to type a report so quickly.

14. (A) She would have liked some jam from the cupboard if she weren't so full.
    (B) The cupboard was so full she found the door jammed.
    (C) The cupboard wasn't full, so she was able to find the jam.
    (D) The cupboard is so full she can't find the jam.

 STOP

Answers to Exercise L17 are on page 505.

Exercise L18   *Identifying causes and results*

Practice with statements

Listen to the spoken statement. Write "C" in the space if the phrase in your book contains the cause, and write "R" if it contains the result.

Example   You will hear: *I had to work late last night because I had to finish that report.*

You will read: __C__ I had to finish that report

You should write "C" in the space because "I had to finish that report" is the cause of "I had to work late."

 START

1. _____ Paul didn't finish it

2. _____ you're a math major

3. _____ we stayed at home and watched TV

4. _____ The instructor didn't come

 PAUSE

Practice with conversations

Listen to the spoken conversation. Write "C" in the space if the phrase in your book contains the cause, and write "R" if it contains the result.

Example I   You will hear: (woman)   *I had such a bad day that I came home and yelled at my roommate.*
                                 (man)   *So that's why she's so upset.*

You will read: __R__ she's so upset

You should write "R" in the space because the roommate is upset as a result of the woman's yelling at her.

Example II   You will hear: (man)   *Now that Pat is married, we hardly see her.*
                                  (woman)   *You can't expect her to continue the life of a single woman.*

You will read: __C__ Pat is married

You should write "C" in the space because Pat's marriage is the cause of the speakers' not seeing her very often.

 START

5. _____ the movie at the Student Union is free

6. _____ Monday is a national holiday

7. _____ I went to the library

8. _____ My parents are going to call tonight

 PAUSE

Practice with short test-like conversations

Listen to the spoken conversation. Circle the letter of the sentence that answers the question.

Example   You will hear: (woman)   *Have you made our reservations yet for the ski trip?*
                                  (man)   *Not enough students have paid their deposit for the flight, so it looks like our trip will fall through.*
                                  (woman)   *There's time yet. Don't forget that many students have part-time jobs and are waiting for payday.*
                                  (narrator) *What does the woman mean?*

                You will read: (A) The trip might not be canceled.
                                  (B) The students will have to work.
                                  (C) The flight will be delayed.
                                  (D) The deposit should be returned.

You should circle (A) because enough students might pay the deposit after payday for the trip not to be canceled.

 START

9. (A) He prefers not to wait for tea.
    (B) He likes his coffee very hot.
    (C) The coffee is too strong.
    (D) He'll get the tea ready for the woman.

10. (A) The art museum is temporarily out of operation.
    (B) More students will see the exhibit in the Student Union.
    (C) The prints need to be repaired this summer.
    (D) The art museum has been permanently relocated to the Student Union.

11. (A) He's been preoccupied with a problem.
    (B) He's been developing some film techniques.
    (C) He's been practicing his part in a drama.
    (D) He's very nervous about being on stage.

 PAUSE

Practice with longer test-like conversations

Listen to the spoken conversation. Circle the letter of the sentence that answers the question.

Example   You will hear: (woman)   *Well, I'm off to the library. See you later.*
                                  (man)   *I thought you and Kim were going on a picnic in the park today.*
                                  (woman)   *We were. But it is such a cloudy day that Kim decided to call it off.*
                                  (narrator) *What does the woman mean?*

                You will read: (A) Kim called them to go on a picnic.
                                  (B) The picnic was canceled due to the weather.
                                  (C) Kim decided it was a good day for an outing.
                                  (D) Kim wanted the outing on a cloudy day.

You should circle (B) because the picnic was called off due to the weather.

 START

12. (A) He has always been a good cook.
    (B) He thinks the woman should learn how to cook.
    (C) He understands the problems of apartment living.
    (D) He learned to cook out of necessity.

13. (A) She lost her job at the bookstore.
    (B) She finished working at the library.
    (C) She had applied for a job in the library.
    (D) She had been unemployed for a while.

14. (A) His indecisiveness is affecting the date of his graduation.
    (B) He has already completed his courses for graduation.
    (C) He has to repeat the classes he has failed before graduating.
    (D) His graduation is taking place in a year.

 STOP

Answers to Exercise L18 are on page 505.

CHECK YOUR PROGRESS

Check your progress in understanding the various structures covered in Exercises L13–L18 by completing the following mini-test. This exercise uses a format similar to that used in Part A of the Listening Section of the Computer-Based TOEFL® Test. If you are unfamiliar with how to answer questions on the Computer-Based TOEFL® Test, see the Tutorial on pages 15–16.

Exercise L19   Mini-test

Listen to the conversation and question. Then select the letter of the best answer choice.

Now get ready to listen.

 START

1. What does the man mean?
   (A) When he gets a car, he'll offer the woman a ride.
   (B) If he's going to campus, he'll get a car.
   (C) Whether he has a car or not, he'll take her.
   (D) If they're going at the same time, he'll take her.

2. What does the woman say about Peter?
   (A) He barely passed the exam.
   (B) He must not have passed the exam.
   (C) He didn't pass the exam.
   (D) He did very well on the exam.

3. What is the woman's problem?
    (A) She's in the University Health Center.
    (B) She wants Tom to give her the card.
    (C) She won't be able to visit Tom.
    (D) She needs to make a get-well card.

4. What does the woman mean?
    (A) She's going to quit taking her class next month.
    (B) Mary's quit her class for a month.
    (C) She quit Mary's class in order to take aerobics.
    (D) She will resume her class in a month.

5. What does the man mean?
    (A) He's surprised by the results.
    (B) He wouldn't go over the statistics.
    (C) He doesn't believe the computations.
    (D) He hasn't looked at the results.

6. What does the woman mean?
    (A) She had to finish by Monday.
    (B) She finished last Monday.
    (C) She finishes on Monday.
    (D) She finished by Monday.

7. What does the man say about Julia?
    (A) She can't remember if she signed the paper.
    (B) She forgot to signal to the man in uniform.
    (C) She didn't remember the sign about applications.
    (D) She didn't write her name on the form.

8. What does the man mean?
   - (A) Dr. Roberts gave Andy's newsletter to Sue.
   - (B) Sue got the newsletter from Andy.
   - (C) Andy gave Dr. Roberts Sue's newsletter.
   - (D) Sue gave Dr. Roberts the newsletter.

9. What does the man mean?
   - (A) Jim wants at least twenty-five guests.
   - (B) Bob wants as many guests as possible.
   - (C) Bob doesn't want more than twenty-five people to be invited.
   - (D) Jim wants to invite as many guests as Bob.

10. What does the man say about David?
    - (A) He has never had a serious problem.
    - (B) He hardly ever makes it to his classes.
    - (C) He has never been more serious about attending classes.
    - (D) His physical condition doesn't stop him from going to classes.

11. What does the man mean?
    - (A) The professor left the testing center.
    - (B) The student wasn't permitted into the center.
    - (C) The student left the center to get his card.
    - (D) The professor forgot the student's card at the center.

12. What does the woman say about Rick?
    - (A) He put two volumes into the library book drop.
    - (B) He returned two library books.
    - (C) It took him several hours to walk to the library.
    - (D) He spent a couple of hours at the library.

13. What does the woman want to do?
    (A) Have a talk
    (B) Go to the library
    (C) Study something
    (D) Get a book

14. What does the woman say about Nancy?
    (A) She used to dance a lot.
    (B) She is not accustomed to dancing.
    (C) She doesn't find it difficult to dance.
    (D) She isn't dancing as much as she used to.

15. What does the man mean?
    (A) The test should have been taken months ago.
    (B) The test he took was probably harder than any other he's taken before.
    (C) He must take the most difficult exam.
    (D) He should have taken the most difficult exam.

Answers to Exercise L19 are on page 505.

 STOP

PRACTICE WITH UNDERSTANDING MEANING FROM CONTEXT

In conversations, people have many different reasons for speaking to each other. For example, a first speaker may ask for some information. The second speaker may either provide the information, apologize for not knowing the information, or give a suggestion concerning where the information can be found. Look at the following example.

You will hear: (woman)   *Would you like to go to the Barnacle for dinner tonight?*
                (man)   *I'm never eating there again.*
             (narrator) *What does the man mean?*

1. Concentrate on the purpose of the conversation.

The woman's question sets the context: She is suggesting a place where they can have dinner.

2. Concentrate on the context.

We can guess that the Barnacle is a restaurant because the woman wants to go there for dinner and the man mentions "eating there."

3. Concentrate on the response.

We can understand that the man doesn't like eating there. Perhaps he doesn't like the food there, or maybe the service isn't good.

4. Concentrate on the question.

We can assume that since the man doesn't like the restaurant, he is opposed to the woman's suggestion.

Use Exercises L20–L24 to develop your skills in deriving meaning through context.

Exercise L20   *Identifying the purpose*

Listen to the spoken sentence. Identify the person's purpose for speaking.

Example   You will hear: *Are you up to helping me with this chemistry assignment?*

You will read: The speaker is
    (A) requesting help.
    (B) offering help.

You should circle (A) because the speaker needs help on an assignment and is asking if the other person is "up to helping" (able to help).

 START

1. The speaker is
    (A) asking for information.
    (B) making a request.

2. The speaker is
    (A) asking for information.
    (B) giving an opinion.

3. The speaker is
    (A) making an offer.
    (B) making a request.

4. The speaker is
    (A) confirming a belief.
    (B) stating a fact.

5. The speaker is
    (A) giving advice.
    (B) stating a complaint.

6. The speaker is
    (A) complaining.
    (B) apologizing.

7. The speaker is
    (A) postponing an assignment.
    (B) mentioning an obligation.

8. The speaker is
    (A) stating a regret.
    (B) making an apology.   **STOP**

Answers to Exercise L20 are on page 506.

Exercise L21   *Understanding responses*

Listen to the spoken conversation. Circle the letter of the sentence that is true based on the conversation you heard.

Example   You will hear: (man) *I think I'm catching a cold.*
                (woman) *Maybe you should take some vitamin C.*

You will read: (A) The woman is making a suggestion.
                (B) The woman is making an offer.

You should circle (A) because the woman is suggesting that the man take some vitamin C for his cold.

START

1. (A) The woman is correcting a misunderstanding.
   (B) The woman is disagreeing with the man.

2. (A) The woman is ill.
   (B) The woman is complaining.

3. (A) The man is accepting an invitation.
   (B) The man is rejecting an invitation.

4. (A) The man agrees.
   (B) The man doesn't agree.

5. (A) The man is accepting dessert.
   (B) The man is declining dessert.

6. (A) The woman agrees to the request.
   (B) The woman does not agree to the request.

7. (A) The woman is criticizing the man.
   (B) The woman is disagreeing with the man.

8. (A) The woman is offering the man some cookies.
   (B) The woman is refusing to help.

 STOP

Answers to Exercise L21 are on page 506.

Exercise L22   Identifying what people are doing

Listen to the spoken conversation. Identify what the two people in the conversation are doing.

Example   You will hear: (man)   *Shall we go to the amusement park or the beach?*
                                 (woman) *It's up to you.*

You will read: The man is   The woman is
                 (A) suggesting some options.   (C) letting the man decide.
                 (B) giving an opinion.   (D) declining his offer.

You should circle (A) because the man has suggested either going to the amusement park or going to the beach. You should circle (C) because the woman's remark means that it is for him to decide.

START

1. The man is   The woman is
   (A) expressing uncertainty.   (C) asking for permission.
   (B) extending an invitation.   (D) accepting an offer.

2. The woman is   The man is
   (A) gossiping.   (C) expressing doubt.
   (B) complaining.   (D) giving encouragement.

3. The man is   The woman is
   (A) giving an excuse.   (C) apologizing for an action.
   (B) breaking a date.   (D) expressing sympathy.

4. The man is   The woman is
   (A) expressing disappointment.   (C) suggesting a time.
   (B) arranging an appointment.   (D) organizing a trip.

5. The woman is
    (A) explaining a situation.
    (B) asking for help.
    The man is
    (C) making a joke.
    (D) asking for a choice.

6. The man is
    (A) making a criticism.
    (B) giving advice.
    The woman is
    (C) agreeing.
    (D) refusing politely.

7. The man is
    (A) causing an argument.
    (B) expressing confusion.
    The woman is
    (C) advising the man.
    (D) forgiving the man.

8. The man is
    (A) stating a problem.
    (B) expressing thanks.
    The woman is
    (C) paying a compliment.
    (D) giving a suggestion.

 STOP

Answers to Exercise L22 are on page 506.

Exercise L23   *Drawing conclusions*

Listen to the spoken conversation. Circle the letter of the answer that is probably true.

Example   You will hear: (man)   *Are you coming for a walk with me?*
                                 (woman)   *I really have my hands full with this typing.*

               You will read: (A) She probably will go with the man.
                                 (B) She probably won't go with the man.

You should circle (B) because you can conclude that she won't go with the man because she has so much typing to do.

 START

1. (A) The people probably will go get something to drink.
    (B) The people probably won't go get something to drink.

2. (A) The woman probably drank the milk.
    (B) The woman probably broke the glass.

3. (A) The man is probably good at math.
    (B) The man probably has trouble with math.

4. (A) Chris probably does well on exams.
    (B) Chris probably doesn't do well on exams.

5. (A) The man probably will invite Tim.
    (B) The man probably won't invite Tim.

6. (A) The class will probably have started.
    (B) The class probably won't have started.

7. (A) The man probably has sales experience.
    (B) The man probably doesn't have sales experience.

8. (A) The woman probably wouldn't like what he wrote.
    (B) The man probably hasn't written anything.

 STOP

Answers to Exercise L23 are on page 507.

Exercise L24   *Making inferences based on context*

Listen to the spoken conversation. Circle the letter of the statement that is implied in the conversation.

Example   You will hear: (man)   *Could you answer my telephone while I go downstairs to pick up the mail?*

                                     (woman)   *You'll have to keep your door open so I can hear it.*

                                     (narrator)   *What does the woman imply?*

You will read: (A)   She can't hear over the telephone.
                          (B)   She doesn't want to pick up the mail.
                          (C)   She'll answer the phone for the man.
                          (D)   She'll keep his mail downstairs.

You should circle (C) because the woman is asking the man to leave the door open so she can hear the telephone, indicating that she will answer if it rings.

 START

1. What does the woman imply?
   (A)   She always dumps her ashtray.
   (B)   She thinks he should quit smoking.
   (C)   She doesn't smoke.
   (D)   She's thrown out the ashtray.

2. What does the woman imply?
   (A)   The hedge gets broken down.
   (B)   The hedge causes traffic problems.
   (C)   The hedge needs to be cut down.
   (D)   The hedge serves many purposes.

3. What does the man imply?
   (A)   The woman should know what he wants to see.
   (B)   The woman shouldn't ask for his opinion.
   (C)   The woman can choose for herself.
   (D)   The woman should see what else is on.

4. What does the man imply?
   (A)   He doesn't agree with the woman's description.
   (B)   He won't move the sculpture.
   (C)   He shouldn't have gotten a good grade.
   (D)   He thinks the woman should move it.

5. What does the man imply?
   (A)   He doesn't have enough money to go.
   (B)   He doesn't like cake and ice cream.
   (C)   He doesn't want to go for a treat.
   (D)   He'd prefer an ice-cream soda.

6. What does the man imply?
   (A)   He organized the debate in no time.
   (B)   He's no longer on the committee.
   (C)   The organization only recently held the debate.
   (D)   The committee organized the debate before he joined.

7. What does the man imply the woman should do?
   (A)   Follow the computer instructions for purchasing books
   (B)   Use the computer to locate the materials she needs
   (C)   Look at the biography on the computer screen
   (D)   Inspect the fully computerized library

8. What does the woman imply?
    (A) She probably hasn't visited Anita.
    (B) Anita has probably never lived in the dorm.
    (C) Anita has probably moved out of the dorm.
    (D) Anita has probably dropped out of the university.

 STOP

Answers to Exercise L24 are on page 507.

CHECK YOUR PROGRESS

Check your progress in understanding meanings from context (Exercises L20–L24) by completing the following mini-test. This exercise uses a format similar to that used in Part A of the Listening Section of the Computer-Based TOEFL® Test. If you are unfamiliar with how to answer questions on the Computer-Based TOEFL® Test, see the Tutorial on pages 15–16.

Exercise L25   *Mini-test*

Listen to the conversation and question. Then select the letter of the best answer choice.

Now get ready to listen.

 START

1. What does the woman mean?
    (A) She's frightened of eating out.
    (B) She's afraid of writing a bad report.
    (C) She's busy this evening.
    (D) She'll go out after she's written the report.

2. What does the man imply?
    (A) It takes more than an hour to get home.
    (B) They should leave the concert early.
    (C) The concert will end very late.
    (D) Midnight is too late to get home.

3. What does the man mean?
   (A) There is little to worry about.
   (B) The exam is important to him.
   (C) The exam will be short.
   (D) He's never had a scholarship before.

4. What does the man imply?
   (A) Dr. Mason's accent is unidentifiable.
   (B) Dr. Mason speaks like a native.
   (C) He can't understand Dr. Mason's accent.
   (D) He thought Dr. Mason was a foreigner.

5. What does the woman imply?
   (A) Her watch is missing.
   (B) She's misplaced her watch.
   (C) She doesn't own a watch.
   (D) She needs her watch in the afternoon.

6. What does the woman imply?
   (A) She needed to wait for the light to change.
   (B) She didn't know how much the drink cost.
   (C) She didn't have the right coins to buy the drink.
   (D) The drink machine was out of order.

7. What does the man mean?
   (A) He stayed at Bill's party all night.
   (B) He couldn't sleep because he felt sick.
   (C) He had a disagreement with Bill.
   (D) Someone at Bill's party upset him.

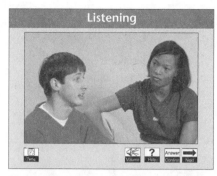

8. What does the man mean?
   (A) He doesn't like either movie.
   (B) He doesn't know how to make movies.
   (C) He doesn't like the movie either.
   (D) He doesn't like sequels to movies.

9. What does the woman mean?
   (A) She doesn't know anything about the project.
   (B) A good project hasn't been decided on.
   (C) They've decided to postpone doing the project.
   (D) They've decided to keep their project a secret.

10. What will the man probably do?
    (A) Go to the museum
    (B) Join the group
    (C) Meet them at the airport
    (D) Pick up his mother

11. What does the woman imply?
    (A) She finds economics boring.
    (B) She didn't get enough sleep.
    (C) She's sure the man enjoyed it.
    (D) She's certain it was very interesting.

12. What does the woman mean?
    (A) Sue might have already left.
    (B) The man could possibly go with Sue.
    (C) Sue is giving her a ride to the theater.
    (D) The man could probably help her with makeup.

13. What will the woman probably do?
    (A) Write out a check for the book
    (B) Help the man get the book out
    (C) Browse through the magazines
    (D) Buy a magazine for the man

14. What does the woman imply about Sally?
    (A) She must have met Jack already.
    (B) She's probably still around.
    (C) She probably walked to Jack's.
    (D) She didn't remember the meeting.

15. What does the woman mean?
    (A) There is no chance of her getting a job at the factory.
    (B) Many factory workers are taking the summer off.
    (C) The factory is closing down for the summer.
    (D) The factory isn't a good place to work.

Answers to Exercise L25 are on page 507.

🎧 **STOP**

PART B

In Part B of the Listening Section of the Computer-Based TOEFL® Test, you will see two or more people on your computer screen and hear longer conversations, academic discussions, and mini-lectures or talks. Each academic discussion or talk begins with a spoken statement that sets the context. For example, you will hear: "Listen to part of a discussion in a microbiology class. The professor is talking about cell structure." When listening, you must focus your attention and concentrate carefully on the passage because you will hear it only once, and taking notes is not permitted. After each passage, several questions are asked about what was stated or implied. You must then choose the correct answer to the question from the choices on the computer screen by either clicking on the best choice of four possible answers or by following the special directions that appear in a box on the computer screen. After you choose your answer, you must click on the Next icon. You are given the opportunity to check your answer and then click on the Answer Confirm icon. You must confirm your answer in order to go on to the next question or to listen to the next conversation or talk.

STRATEGIES TO USE FOR LISTENING, PART B

Concentrate on the Conversation or Talk

1. Focus all your attention on the conversation or talk.

Most of the questions concern what the people are talking about (the topic and details of the conversation or talk). Other questions are based on what is implied, but not stated. Some questions require you to draw a conclusion. Concentrate on the details and clues that reveal the information that is necessary to answer the questions.

2. Understand the purpose of the visuals.

You will see two different types of visuals: (a) pictures of people representing the speakers are shown to help you determine the context and the role of the speakers – no questions are asked about these people; (b) other illustrations or graphs that support the content of the discussion or lecture may be shown on the computer screen during the talk. These visuals contain key information. Focus your attention on what is being said about them.

3. Concentrate on the context and the details.

The main idea is usually found in the first sentence of the conversation or talk. The language in the conversations may be informal and may concern topics common to the everyday life of young adults enrolled in a university. The language in the academic discussions and talks is more formal and usually concerns an academic topic. It is not necessary to have previous knowledge of life in a North American university or of the subject matter discussed in the talks. All the information needed to answer the question is included within the conversations or talks. Try to remember the details in context so as not to get confused.

Concentrate on the Question and the Answer Choices

1. Listen to and read the question carefully.

It is important to be certain what is being asked before you read the answer choices.

2. Read the special instructions.

Some of the items have special instructions, such as "choose two answers." If you do not follow these instructions, you will get a computer "error" message telling you what you need to do. You will lose valuable time when you have to click through the computer message to get back to the question you did not answer in the correct way.

3. Read the answer choices carefully.

All correct and incorrect answers include details mentioned in the conversation or talk. An incorrect answer may contain information that is true according to what was said yet does not answer the question. Sometimes an incorrect answer contains information that has been stated in a way that changes its meaning and, therefore, does not answer the question.

4. Pay attention to time.

Look frequently at the question number and the amount of time you have remaining. Be sure you are pacing yourself well in order to complete all the questions.

5. Answer every question.

You cannot go on to the following question until you have answered a question and confirmed it. If you try to do so, you will lose valuable time when you have to click through the computer "error" message to get back to the question you tried to skip. If you do not know an answer, eliminate those answers you know are incorrect and then take a guess from the remaining choices.

6. Check your answer.

Since you cannot go back and change your answer, be sure you have clicked on the answer you want before you click on the `Answer Confirm` icon.

PRACTICE WITH TOPICS

Immediate identification of the topic will help you to anticipate the information you will hear and that you will need to retain in order to answer the question.

1. The topic is what the conversation or talk is about. It is usually found at the beginning of the conversation or talk.

Example

(man) *Arthritis is one of the oldest complaints that has tormented not only humans but animals as well. Even dinosaurs suffered from it millions of years ago. The earliest known example of one with arthritis is the platycarpus. So it is natural that you will also see arthritis in the animals that are brought into pet clinics. Today we will be comparing slides of the bone structure of healthy animals and arthritic animals to help you in future diagnosis of arthritis.*

The topic of arthritis is stated in the beginning of the lecture. Although the speaker discusses different aspects of the topic, arthritis remains the main topic of the lecture.

2. **Sometimes it appears that the speaker or speakers are going to discuss one topic, but then that topic is changed. Sometimes a broad topic is narrowed down to a specific topic.**

Example

(woman)	*Before we start today, I would like to remind you that the video conference of the debates between the candidates for the upcoming election will be shown in the Franklin Auditorium starting at 2:00 this afternoon.*
(man)	*Will we be able to ask the speakers questions or take part in any of the discussions?*
(woman)	*No, we won't. Some of the larger state universities will be able to take part, but we only have the facilities to listen to the debates and questions.*
(man)	*Is the university doing anything toward improving our facilities?*
(woman)	*Yes, in fact they are budgeting a large sum of money in order to build a conference center here on campus. This center would include all the facilities needed.*
(man)	*Is there a proposed date for these facilities to be ready for use?*
(woman)	*Well, yes, but I'm afraid they will probably be open after you have graduated because the building will take a couple of years to complete.*

Although the first speaker introduces the first topic of the discussion – a video conference of debates between candidates for an election – the topic changes to the facilities for video conferencing at the speakers' university. The remainder of the conversation concerns the university's plans for improving its facilities.

Use Listening Exercises L26–L29 to develop your skills in identifying topics.

Exercise L26   Predicting the topic from the first statement

Listen to the spoken statement. Predict the topic to be discussed and write your prediction in the space provided.

Example   You will hear: *The molecular structure of synthetic vitamins is the same as that of natural vitamins.*

You will write: *vitamins*

The lecture will probably continue with more information about vitamins.

🎧 **START**

1. _____   4. _____

2. _____   5. _____

3. _____   6. _____   🎧 **STOP**

Answers to Exercise L26 are on page 508.

Exercise L27   Identifying the topic from the first statement

Listen to the first statement of the conversation or talk. Circle the letter of the answer that states the topic.

Example   You will hear: *Of all nonprofessional architects, Michelangelo was the most adventurous.*

You will read: (A) professional architects
(B) adventurous architects
(C) Michelangelo's architecture
(D) Michelangelo's adventures

You should circle (C) because the speaker will probably continue the talk by explaining in what way Michelangelo's architecture was adventurous.

 START

1. (A) uses of acupuncture in the West
   (B) China in recent years
   (C) the practice of acupuncture
   (D) ancient cures for arthritis

2. (A) fabric
   (B) muscles
   (C) millimeters
   (D) lengths

3. (A) communications technology
   (B) challenges in communications
   (C) educational satellites
   (D) educational possibilities

4. (A) the Spanish literature seminars
   (B) the Spanish courses offered
   (C) the history of Spain
   (D) the Golden Age of Spanish literature

5. (A) the signs and symptoms of influenza
   (B) the signs and symptoms of the common cold
   (C) similarities between the common cold and influenza
   (D) highly contagious diseases

6. (A) the lack of human protein in diets
   (B) causes of malnutrition in the world
   (C) serious world problems
   (D) deficiency of animal protein in the human diet   STOP

Answers to Exercise L27 are on page 509.

Exercise L28   ***Determining if the topic is stated in the first sentence of the passage***

Sometimes the topic is not stated at the beginning of the passage. Listen to the conversation or talk. Write "yes" in the blank if the topic can be identified in the first sentence. Write "no" if it cannot.

Example   You will hear: *When a disaster such as an earthquake or a flood strikes,*
time is often a critical factor in providing needed shelter
for people who are suddenly homeless and exposed to the
elements. Ideally, the erection of a shelter should take a short
time. The emergency use of tents has been the conventional
answer to these situations. However, in many cases, those
left homeless are in need of shelter for an extensive period
of time. The temporary and insufficient nature of tent housing
does not meet these longer-term requirements.

You will write: *yes*

The talk is mainly about "shelters," which are mentioned in the first sentence of the talk.

🎧 **START**

1. _____   4. _____

2. _____   5. _____

3. _____   🎧 **STOP**

Answers to Exercise L28 are on page 509.

Exercise L29   **Identifying a change in topic**

Listen to the conversation or talk. Write its topic in the space.

Example   You will hear: *Hygiene was almost unheard of in Europe during the Middle Ages. Consequently, millions of people died during various epidemics that raged throughout Europe. The worst outbreak of plague, called the Black Death, struck between the years 1347 and 1351. The populations of thousands of villages were wiped out. In fact, it is thought that about one-third of all the people in Europe perished during the Black Death.*

You will write: *the Black Death*

Although the speaker begins by discussing hygiene, the talk is mainly about the epidemic of plague called the Black Death.

🎧 **START**

1. _____   3. _____

2. _____   4. _____   🎧 **STOP**

Answers to Exercise L29 are on page 509.

CHECK YOUR PROGRESS

Check your progress in identifying the topic of the conversation or talk (Exercises L26–L29) by completing the following mini-test. This exercise uses a format similar to that used in Part B of the Listening Section of the Computer-Based TOEFL® Test. If you are unfamiliar with how to answer questions on the Computer-Based TOEFL ® Test, see the Tutorial on pages 17–22.

Exercise L30   **Mini-test**

Listen to the conversation or talk. Then select the letter of the best answer choice for each question following the passage.

Now get ready to listen.

 START

1. What are the people discussing?
   (A) Getting presents
   (B) Purchasing books
   (C) Pasting checkout sheets
   (D) Working in a library

2. What is the talk mainly about?
   (A) American sharpshooters
   (B) The czar of Russia
   (C) Buffalo Bill's "Wild West Show"
   (D) European heads of state

3. What does the speaker mainly discuss?
   (A) The turn of the century
   (B) Ragtime in America
   (C) Band concerts in America and Europe
   (D) Early American musical forms

4. What is the main purpose of this talk?
   (A) To describe the proposed
       fine-arts building
   (B) To demonstrate the usefulness
       of an exhibition hall
   (C) To discuss the several stages
       for theater classes
   (D) To propose the construction
       of a building for fine-arts majors

 STOP

Answers to Exercise L30 are on page 509.

PRACTICE WITH DETAILS

In a conversation or talk, several details may be mentioned. There are different types of questions that deal with these details.

1. Referents – *Sometimes instead of repeating a detail, the speakers use pronouns and short phrases to refer to the details. These are called "referents" and may refer back to a previously mentioned word or phrase, or they may anticipate a detail to be mentioned.*

Example   You will hear: (man)   *Twenty people are coming to our graduation party, so we'd better get some plastic cups.*

(woman)   *There are a dozen in this package. We could buy two of them.*

(man)   *Hmm. That would be only four extra cups. Do you think we might need more than that?*

When the woman suggests buying a dozen, she is referring to cups. When she suggests buying two of them, she is referring to the packages, not to the cups. When the man is concerned that they might need more than that, he is referring to more than four extra cups. There are twenty people who will need a cup and the two packages each contain twelve cups – a total of twenty-four. This amount may not be enough.

When answering the questions, it can be important that you understand the meanings of these referents. (For more information, see Practice with Understanding Details and Restatements, item 1, pp. 316–317.)

2. Restatements – *Sometimes the possible answers give the correct detail using different words. Sometimes the same words are used, but a change in their order has made a change in their meaning.*

Example   You will hear: (man)   *What did you do over the summer, Donna?*
(woman)   *Mostly I helped my father in his dress shop.*
(man)   *I can't imagine you selling dresses.*
(woman)   *I didn't. Remember, I'm studying accounting. I helped him with the bookkeeping. Also, I put price tags on the new clothes and designed the window displays.*
(narrator)   *What did Donna do over the summer?*

You will read: (A)   She helped her father do the accounting.
(B)   She sold dresses in her father's store.
(C)   She displayed prices in the windows.
(D)   She designed new clothes.

You should circle (A) because Donna helped her father with the bookkeeping. This means the same as helping him do the accounting. Donna told the man that she didn't sell dresses. She designed window displays, not clothes, and she put prices on new clothes, not prices in the window.

3. Two correct answers – *Sometimes numerous details are mentioned, which are frequently confused in the answer choices. These questions have boxes instead of ovals in front of the answer choices on the screen.*

Example   You will hear: (man)   *Why hasn't Frank come yet? He told me he'd be here first thing in the morning.*

(woman)   *I'm sorry. Didn't I tell you he called and said he couldn't make it until this afternoon?*

(man)   *No, you didn't. What time did he say he'd be here?*
(woman)   *About four o'clock.*

(man)   *Four o'clock! That means we'll be working on this report until midnight.*

(narrator)   *What did Frank tell the woman about coming to meet the people?*

You will read: ☐ He'd be there first thing in the morning.

☒ He couldn't make it first thing in the morning.

☒ He would come in the afternoon.

☐ He could stay from four o'clock until midnight.

You will see and hear the question. The answer choices are in the above format and special instructions to choose two answers appear on the screen.

4. Ordering – Sometimes you hear information about a series of events that can be put into order. All answer choices are correct, but they are not in the correct order.

Example   You will hear: (man)   *Tomatoes are usually picked green. They are washed and sorted according to size and quality, and then they are packaged and sent to supermarkets. During transportation the tomatoes ripen to the bright red color we are accustomed to seeing.*

(narrator)   *The professor briefly describes a process. Summarize the process by putting the events in order.*

You will see and hear the question. The answer choices are in a different format and special instructions to put the answers in order appear on the screen.

5. Matching – Sometimes descriptions are given in the talk. You must use this information in order to match given words or phrases with illustrations or phrases.

Example   You will hear: (woman)   *The fork, knife, and spoon are the most common eating utensils. These instruments all consist of a handle, which is basically the same. They differ from each other in their use and the shape that use has dictated. The knife has a sharp blade for cutting and is not normally used for transferring food from the plate to one's mouth. The fork has three to four prongs, which are used to secure food that needs to be cut. It is used to take more solid kinds of foods to the mouth. The spoon has a bowl shape in order for its user to consume liquid or semi-liquid food.*

(narrator)   *Based on the professor's description, identify the following utensils.*

You will see and hear the question. The answer choices are in a different format and special instructions for matching the choices appear on the screen.

6. Labeling – Sometimes a description of an illustration is presented during the talk. You must use this information in order to label the illustration or to choose a selected part of the illustration to answer the question.

Example   You will hear: (woman)   *The fork has three to four prongs, which are used to secure food that needs to be cut, and a handle, which is gripped in the left hand.*

(narrator)   *What part of the fork is a prong?*

You will see and hear the question. The illustration and special instructions for answering the question appear on the screen.

Use Listening Exercises L31–L36 to develop your skills in understanding details.

Exercise L31   ***Understanding referents in a conversation or talk***

Listen to the complete conversation or talk for each item. Pause the recording while you write in the space the word or phrase that the referents refer to. After you have completed all the items, listen to the recording a second time to check your answers. (For additional practice, see Exercises R9–R11, pp. 318–321.)

Example   You will hear: (man)   *I've never been to Scandinavia, so I've decided to spend the summer there.*

(woman)   *That will be expensive, won't it?*

(man)   *Not really. My grandfather is from a small Swedish town near the Norwegian border. He still has a sister there.*

(woman)   *Will you stay with her?*

(man)   *For some of the time. The expensive part will be my stay in Denmark. I don't know anyone there.*

You will read: (A) he   *the man's grandfather*

(B) her   *the grandfather's sister*

(C) some of the time   *the summer in Scandinavia*

🎧 **START**

1. (A) them _____

(B) these problems _____

(C) their _____

🎧 **PAUSE**

2. (A) this climb _____

(B) it _____

(C) these _____

🎧 **PAUSE**

3. (A) this calculator _____

(B) mechanical one _____

(C) this machine _____

🎧 **PAUSE**

4. (A) it _____

(B) one _____

(C) that _____   🎧 **STOP**

Answers to Exercise L31 are on page 509.

Exercise L32   *Understanding restatements*

You will hear a statement. Circle the letter of the answer that gives the same information as the spoken statement.

Example   You will hear: *Minute as atoms are, they consist of still tinier particles.*

You will read: (A) Atoms are made up of even smaller particles.
(B) Small particles consist of minute atoms.

You should circle (A) because it gives the same information in different words.

🎧 **START**

1. (A) In Homer's time, the people used many old words from the Kárpathos dialect.
   (B) The people in Kárpathos use many words that were used in Homer's time.

2. (A) In 1783, a Frenchman made the first manned flight in a hot-air balloon.
   (B) In 1783, a Frenchman made a twenty-five-minute flight in the first hot-air balloon.

3. (A) The Aztec word for "beautiful bird" is "quetzal," which means "tail feather."
   (B) The Aztec word for "tail feather" is the name given to one of the world's most beautiful birds – the quetzal.

4. (A) After an all-night march, twenty-two men stormed onto the Luding Bridge, thus cutting off the escape route of Mao Tse-tung's forces.
   (B) After an all-night march, twenty-two men captured the Luding Bridge to secure an escape route for Mao Tse-tung's forces.

5. (A) Centers were established to relieve those people stricken by the drought.
   (B) The drought-stricken areas set up many relief centers.

6. (A) The human past has been revolutionized by our concept of recently discovered fossils.
   (B) Our concept of the human past has been revolutionized by recently discovered fossils.

7. (A) In March 1783 explorers had not been able to locate the island that was vividly described in the captain's log.
   (B) In the captain's log, dated March 1783, is the vivid description of an island that explorers have been unable to locate.

8. (A) That numerous dead fish, dolphins, and whales have been spotted off the East Coast was reported by the authorities.
   (B) The authorities have spotted and reported numerous dolphins, whales, and dead fish off the East Coast.

🎧 **STOP**

Answers to Exercise L32 are on page 510.

Exercise L33   *Getting all the facts*

To answer some of the questions on the Computer-Based TOEFL® Test, you must listen to a discussion or lecture and then choose two correct answers. The computer screen will show the people who are talking.

On the recording, you will hear:

> *The black bear may seem friendly, but it is a dangerous animal that can maim or kill easily. If a bear is disturbed during the hibernation period, it is easily angered, and it is very hazardous to come between a mother and her cubs at any time. Because of the risk, it is never advisable to go closer than one hundred meters to a bear in the wild.*

After the discussion or lecture, you will hear the narrator read each question as it appears on the computer screen. You will also be shown the answer choices. The computer screen will look like this.

Listening

When is the black bear most dangerous?

Click on 2 answers.

- ☐ When it maims someone
- ☐ When it is separated from its cubs
- ☐ When it is closer than one hundred meters
- ☐ When it is awakened from its sleep

Time   Volume Help Answer Confirm Next

To answer this question, you would click on the boxes in front of the following two sentences: "When it is separated from its cubs" and "When it is awakened from its sleep." An ☒ will appear in the boxes you click on. Be sure that you have clicked on two boxes. When you are sure of your answer, click on the Next icon, check your answer, and then click on the Answer Confirm icon to go on to the next question.

In the following exercise, listen to the conversation or talk. Answer the question that follows by selecting the two best answers.

 START

1. What can be said about fish rubbings?

   A The art was practiced in various cultures.
   B The prints were slimy.
   C It is an ancient art.
   D It is a dying art.

2. What is true about Mughal Emperor Jehangir?

   A He was from Baghdad.
   B He did not follow minting traditions.
   C He issued coins in the caliph's name.
   D He encouraged many art forms to flourish.

3. How is a metallurgical microscope different from an optical microscope?

   A It can measure three-dimensional objects.
   B It allows fine-tuning for unwieldy samples.
   C It is more delicate.
   D It has inadequate illuminating systems.

4. What is true about communication disorders?

   A A problem with speech or hearing mechanisms is often caused
      by communication disorders.
   B Communication disorders can result from emotional or psychological
      problems.
   C Speech pathologists can help people with communication disorders
      improve their ability to communicate.
   D Communication disorders frequently result from the normal functioning
      of the brain.

 STOP

Answers to Exercise L33 are on page 510.

Exercise L34   **Organizing details**

To answer some of the questions on the Computer-Based TOEFL® Test, you must listen to a discussion or lecture and then put the events or information in order. The computer screen will show the people who are talking.

On the recording, you will hear:

> *Pioneers wanting to reach the West Coast of North America arrived by riverboat at Missouri River towns in the early spring. They hoped to cross the plains during the summer, when the prairie grass would provide food for their animals. They needed to cross the plains quickly because it was essential to get through the Rocky Mountains and arrive in California before the winter snows closed the mountain passes. Those who didn't make it through were stranded in the mountains without sufficient provisions for the entire winter.*

After the discussion or lecture, you will hear the narrator read each question as it appears on the computer screen. You will also be shown the answer choices. The computer screen will look like this.

Listening
The professor briefly describes a process. Summarize the process by putting the events in order.
Click on a sentence. Then click on the space where it belongs. Use each sentence only once.

The pioneers arrived by riverboat at the Missouri River.　　　　The pioneers crossed the plains.

The pioneers arrived in California.　　　　The pioneers went through the Rocky Mountains.

1	
2	
3	
4	

Time　　　　　　　　　　Volume　Help　Answer Confirm　Next

To answer this question, you would click on the sentence "The pioneers arrived by riverboat at the Missouri River" and then click on the first box. The sentence you selected will be inserted into the box you clicked on. Click on "The pioneers crossed the plains" to place it in box 2, "The pioneers went through the Rocky Mountains" to place it in box 3, and "The pioneers arrived in California" to place it in box 4. When you are sure of your answer, click on the Next icon, check your answer, and then click on the Answer Confirm icon to go on to the next question.

In the following exercise, listen to the conversation or talk. Put the letter of the sentences in the spaces according to the order asked for in the question.

 START

1. The speaker gives a brief account of Victoria C. Woodhull's life. Summarize the events by putting them in order.
   (A) Woodhull ran as a presidential candidate.
   (B) Woodhull started a political journal.
   (C) Woodhull cofounded a brokerage firm.
   (D) Woodhull adopted a modest public life.

1	
2	
3	
4	

2. Put these statements about fox hunting in the correct order.
   (A) Recently people have been offended by the sport of fox hunting.
   (B) Fox hunting may soon be a sport event of the past.
   (C) Sabotage activities have ended in court cases.
   (D) Fox hunting has been practiced for centuries.

1	
2	
3	
4	

3. In which order should the diving teacher's instructions be carried out?
   (A) Swim along the reef
   (B) Watch for instructor's signal to return
   (C) Find a diving partner
   (D) Check all diving equipment

1	
2	
3	
4	

4. What is the order of events in the hundredth-monkey phenomenon study?
   (A) Some monkeys on an island were taught a different way to eat sweet potatoes.
   (B) Other monkeys on the island mimicked the behavior.
   (C) Monkeys on another island began to eat sweet potatoes in the new way.
   (D) Soon 100 monkeys were copying the behavior.

1	
2	
3	
4	

 STOP

Answers to Exercise L34 are on page 510.

Exercise L35   ***Focusing on details***

To answer some of the questions on the Computer-Based TOEFL®Test, you must listen to a discussion or lecture and then match words to phrases or illustrations. The computer screen will show the people who are talking.

On the recording, you will hear:

> *It is often said that no two snowflakes are exactly alike. In fact, they can be classified into several basic types, all of which have six sides. The most familiar are, perhaps, the star, which looks like the common picture-book depiction of a real star with six points; the plate, which looks like a tiny, hexagonal dinner plate; and the column, which is a solid prism shape, rather like a section cut through a lead pencil.*

After the discussion or lecture, you will hear the narrator read each question as it appears on the computer screen. You will also be shown the answer choices. The computer screen will look like this.

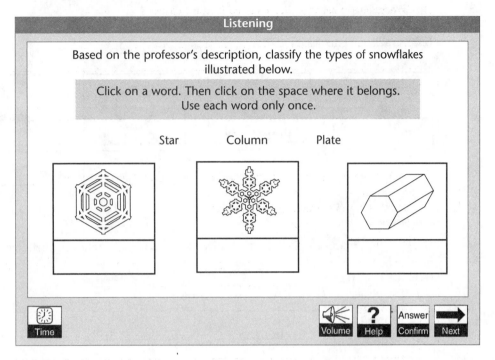

To answer this question, you would click on the word "Star" and then on the box under the second illustration; click on the word "Column" and then click on the box under the third illustration; and click on the word "Plate" and then click on the box under the first illustration. The word you click on will be inserted in the box you click on. When you are sure of your answer, click on the Next icon, check your answer, and then click on the Answer Confirm icon to go on to the next question.

In the following exercise, cover the answer choices. After the lecture is over, stop the tape and look at the answer choices for the lecture you heard. Answer the question by writing the letter of the word or phrase in the box where it belongs.

Questions 1–3

 START

Based on the professor's description of birds, answer the question about which flying bird is the largest.

(A) South African bustard
(B) Albatross
(C) South American vulture

The bird with the longest wingspan	The bird with the largest wings	The heaviest bird in the world
1.	2.	3.

Questions 4–7

Based on the professor's description of several gears, identify the following gears.
(A) Spur gear
(B) Worm gear
(C) Bevel gear
(D) A rack and pinion

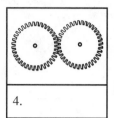

4.

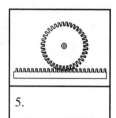

5.

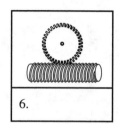

6.

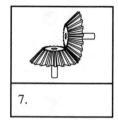

7.

Questions 8–10

Based on the professor's discussion, identify the city where the following bells can be found.
(A) The Emperor Bell
(B) Great Paul
(C) The Liberty Bell

London	Philadelphia	Moscow
8.	9.	10.

Questions 11–13

Based on the professor's description, identify the following puppets.
(A) Hand puppet
(B) Marionette
(C) Shadow puppet

11.

12.

13.

 STOP

Answers to Exercise L35 are on page 510.

Exercise L36   *Using details*

To answer some of the questions on the Computer-Based TOEFL® Test, you must listen to a discussion or lecture and then label an illustration. The computer screen will show the people who are talking.

On the recording, you will hear:

> *Over the ages, people have invented machines to make their work easier. One of the simplest machines is the lever. Each kind of lever has a pushing force or effort, a pivot point called the fulcrum, and the load where the resistance takes place.*

During the talk, you may see pictures that the speaker uses to illustrate points in the discussion or lecture.

After the discussion or lecture, you will hear the narrator read each question as it appears on the computer screen. You will also be shown the answer choices and a picture. The computer screen will look like this.

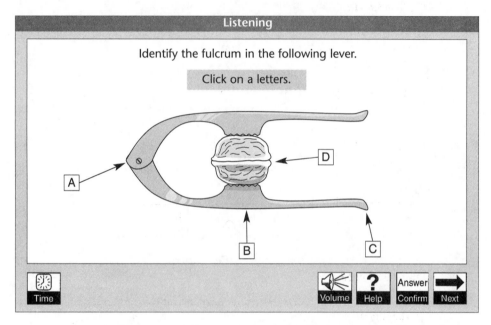

To answer this question, you would click on box "A" because this is the location of the fulcrum. When you are sure of your answer, click on the Next icon, check your answer, and then click on the Answer Confirm icon to go on to the next question.

In the following exercise, cover the answer choices. After the lecture is over, stop the tape and look at the answer choices for the lecture you heard. Select the letter of the correct answer choice.

 START

1. Identify the stringer in the stairway.

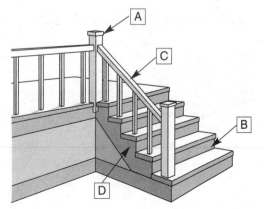

 STOP

START

2. Identify the pipe organ's stops.

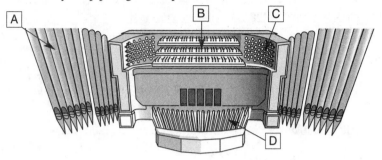

 STOP

 START

3. Identify the serving on the bow.

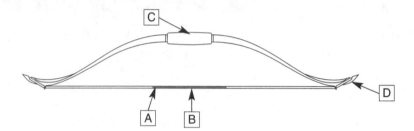

 STOP

 START

4. Identify the pit in the Elizabethan theater.

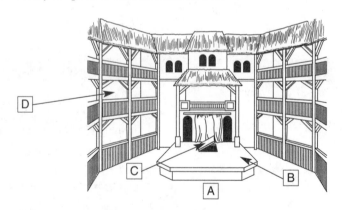

 STOP

Answers to Exercise L36 are on page 510.

CHECK YOUR PROGRESS

Check your progress in understanding details in the conversation or talk (Exercises L31–L36) by completing the following mini-test. This exercise uses a format similar to that used in Part B of the Listening Section of the Computer-Based TOEFL® Test. If you are unfamiliar with how to answer questions on the Computer-Based TOEFL ® Test, see the Tutorial on pages 17–22.

Exercise L37   Mini-test

Listen to the conversation or talk, and the questions about it. Then select the letter of the best answer choice.

Now get ready to listen.

 START

Now get ready to answer the questions.

1. What was the Boston Tea Party?
   (A) An act of defiance
   (B) A social event
   (C) A group of Native Americans
   (D) A cargo of tea

2. According to the passage, when did the Boston Tea Party take place?
   (A) During the American War of Independence
   (B) In 1773
   (C) When Americans began drinking coffee
   (D) At night

3. Why did the Boston Tea Party take place?
   (A) Because Americans were drinking coffee
   (B) Because the tea was too highly taxed
   (C) Because the colonists were taxed without being represented
   (D) Because Native Americans were revolting against the invasion of Europeans

4. Who threw the cargo overboard?
   (A) The British rulers
   (B) King George III
   (C) Native Americans
   (D) Prominent citizens

5. Which person or group of people is identified in the boxes?

   Write the letter of each phrase in the space where it belongs. Use each phrase only once.

   (A) American colonists
   (B) George III
   (C) Disguised prominent citizens

The king the British parliament was under	The people defying the British rulers
1.	2.

The people attending the Boston Tea Party
3.

Now get ready to listen.

Now get ready to answer the questions.

6. What has happened to the man's car?
   (A) It was stolen.
   (B) It was towed away.
   (C) It was vandalized.
   (D) It was wrecked.

7. Where did the man leave his car?
   (A) At home
   (B) Under an oak tree
   (C) At Jim's place
   (D) Near the Geology Building

8. What does the woman suggest the man do?
   (A) Call Jim's Wrecker Service
   (B) Call the City Roads Department
   (C) Check the records
   (D) Report the theft at the station

9. In what order did the following events occur?

   Write the letter of each sentence in the space where it belongs. Use each sentence only once.

   (A) The car was reported missing.
   (B) The man left the car near the Geology Building.
   (C) Oak Street was resurfaced.
   (D) The car was towed away.

1	
2	
3	
4	

Now get ready to listen.

Now get ready to answer the questions.

10. Which societies are faced with the problem of aging?
    (A) Those with a large population of elderly people and a low birthrate
    (B) Those with an excessive social-security expenditure
    (C) Those with an excessive national income
    (D) Those with skyrocketing medical costs

11. According to the talk, what do older people need?
    (A) More social security taxes
    (B) More medical attention
    (C) Higher national incomes
    (D) Larger families

12. According to the talk, what burden frequently falls on the state?
    (A) Paying the elderly to look after themselves
    (B) Solving long-term medical problems
    (C) Finding the families of the elderly
    (D) Financing care for the elderly

13. Which graph represents the age structure discussed in the talk?

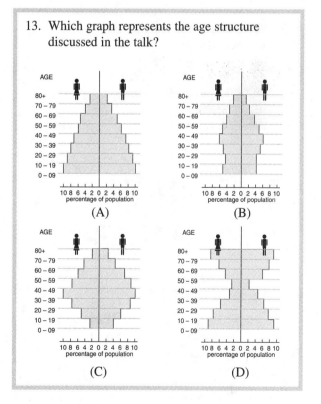

Now get ready to listen.

Now get ready to answer the questions.

14. What did photographs used to provide?

   Choose 2 answers.

   A   An unreliable source of historical information
   B   Images of people from past generations
   C   A way to document past events
   D   Extraordinary details of preservation techniques

15. According to the talk, nineteenth-century photographs may differ from contemporary photographs in which way?
   (A)   They have not been altered.
   (B)   They have extraordinary detail.
   (C)   They show deeds of the famous.
   (D)   They show the faces of the unknown masses.

16. What has electronic imaging done to contemporary photographs?
   (A)   Made them unequaled in excellence
   (B)   Made them unreliable as historical documents
   (C)   Made the images more effective to the modern eye
   (D)   Made them more popular for contemporary photographers

STOP

Answers to Exercise L37 are on page 510.

PRACTICE WITH INFERENCES

When you hear a conversation, some things are not stated but they can be understood through details that are expressed or through general knowledge.

Example I   You will hear: (woman)   *My favorite experiment at the fair was the one where the man produced electricity with a potato.*

(man)   *I liked the computer that ran on solar power.*

What kind of fair are the people discussing?
(A)   An arts and crafts fair
(B)   A science fair
(C)   An agricultural fair
(D)   A computer fair

Although the answer is not stated, we can understand that the particular fair the people are discussing is a science fair because experiments of the nature described would most likely be presented in a science fair.

Example II   You will hear: (woman)   *I heard the fire was devastating.*
(man)   *It was. It swept through the house and destroyed almost everything.*

What may have survived the fire?
(A)   The wooden staircase
(B)   The marble fireplace
(C)   The children's toys
(D)   The people's clothes

We can understand that some things survived the fire because the man's saying "almost everything" implies that a few things were not destroyed. Because of our general knowledge about fires, we can assume that a fireplace made of marble (a kind of stone) is the only object mentioned that would not burn or melt in a fire.

Use Exercises L38–L40 to develop your inference skills.

Exercise L38   *Understanding inferences*

Listen to the following conversations or talks. Answer "yes" or "no" to the statement that follows each conversation or talk.

Example   You will hear: *In a recent survey on smell, men and women were asked to smell samples of scents and to identify them. It was established that women in general have a more acute sense of smell than men unless they are pregnant when, contrary to popular belief, a temporary loss of smell occurs.*
(narrator)   *Both pregnant and nonpregnant women probably took part in the survey.*

You will write: *yes*

You should write "yes" in the space because women in both conditions must have taken part in the survey in order for the researchers to discover that nonpregnant women have a more acute sense of smell than men and that pregnant women have a less acute sense of smell than men.

🎧 START

1. _____   4. _____

2. _____   5. _____

3. _____

🎧 STOP

Answers to Exercise L38 are on page 510.

Exercise L39   *Drawing conclusions*

To answer the questions in Part B of the Computer-Based TOEFL® Test, you must listen to longer conversations, academic discussions, and mini-lectures. The computer screen will show the people who are talking. The computer screen will look like this.

On the recording, you will hear:	*"Moonshiner" was the name given to a person who made illegal alcohol. Many people preferred the taste of whiskey made in the old-fashioned way from recipes and techniques dating back to America's earliest Scotch-Irish pioneers.*
(narrator)	*What might have been the reason the makers of illegal alcohol were called "moonshiners"?*

After the passage, you will hear the narrator read each question as it appears on the computer screen. You will also be shown the answer choices. The computer screen will look like this.

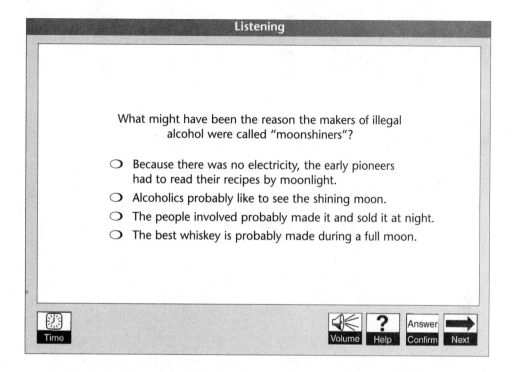

To answer this question, you would click on the oval next to the sentence "The people involved probably made it and sold it at night." Since the makers of illegal alcohol were breaking the law, they probably did so during the night, when there was less chance of being caught. They would have had to work by moonlight because candlelight or lamplight could have been seen by the authorities. The oval you click on will become dark. When you are sure of your answer, click on the **Next** icon. Check your answer and then click on the **Answer Confirm** icon.

In the following exercise, listen to the talks and questions. Circle the letter of the best answer based on the information given.

 START

1. For what field might the new knowledge about polio be most useful?
   (A) Statistics
   (B) Medicine
   (C) Education
   (D) History

2. What will the man probably do as a result of this conversation?
   (A) Take the course next semester
   (B) Speak to the Spanish teacher
   (C) Sign up for Spanish
   (D) Take Italian

3. Why might Jean Muir have given so much attention to her staff?
   (A) So her business could continue after her death
   (B) So her collection could not be plagiarized
   (C) So her collections could be sold quickly
   (D) So her staff could take over the training

4. To what group of university students might this talk have been given?
   (A) Political science majors
   (B) Education majors
   (C) English majors
   (D) Art majors

 STOP

Answers to Exercise L39 are on page 511.

Exercise L40   ***Inferring reasons***

Sometimes information is mentioned within a talk for a particular reason, such as to demonstrate a point. Sometimes the entire talk will be given to illustrate a particular point. Listen to the following talk. Answer the question following the talk.

Example   You will hear: *Snow is a fantastic insulator. Ask any Eskimo. However, the extraordinary efficiency of snow as an insulator makes it difficult to find a person buried in an avalanche.*
   (narrator)   *Why does the speaker mention Eskimos?*

   You will write: <u>*Because an Eskimo would be an authority on snow.*</u>

Eskimos live in a snowy climate. Therefore, they would know a lot about the properties of snow.

 START

1. _____

2. _____

3. _____

4. _____   STOP

Answers to Exercise L40 are on page 511.

CHECK YOUR PROGRESS

Check your progress in understanding inferences in conversations or talks (Exercises L38–L40) by completing the following mini-test. This exercise uses a format similar to that used in Part B of the Listening Section of the Computer-Based TOEFL® Test. If you are unfamiliar with how to answer questions on the Computer-Based TOEFL® Test, see the Tutorial on pages 17–22.

Exercise L41   Mini-test

Listen to the conversation or talk, and the questions about it. Then select the letter of the best answer choice.

Now get ready to listen.

 START

Now get ready to answer the questions.

1. Why does the speaker mention fires?
   (A) To illustrate how unsafe wooden houses are
   (B) To show other ways in which synthetic materials are dangerous
   (C) To let people know about the toxic fumes when using natural alternatives
   (D) To demonstrate what happens when cadmium is added to paint

2. What would be an example of a natural building material?
   (A) Stone walls
   (B) Aluminum door frames
   (C) Linoleum flooring
   (D) Plywood paneling

3. What might the listeners do as a result of this talk?
   (A) Tear down their houses
   (B) Buy older homes
   (C) Build new houses
   (D) Modify their homes

Now get ready to answer the questions.

4. When would this conversation most likely take place?
   (A) Before finals week
   (B) At the beginning of the term
   (C) Before summer vacation
   (D) During a tour of the library

5. What would most likely be found at a library reserve desk?
   (A) The latest romance novel
   (B) The required course textbooks
   (C) All the reference books
   (D) An out-of-print book

6. What can be inferred about the articles?
   (A) They can't be taken out of the library.
   (B) They're out of print.
   (C) They have an asterisk.
   (D) They must be read before the following class.

Now get ready to listen.

Now get ready to answer the questions.

7. Why does the speaker mention aspirin bottles?
   (A) To demonstrate the continuing process of invention
   (B) To illustrate failures
   (C) To show how inventions can cause fatalities
   (D) To show that you can't satisfy everybody all the time

8. What might happen as a result of this talk?
   (A) A new bottle cap may be invented.
   (B) Some new approaches to medicine may be discussed.
   (C) A debate about the characteristics of inventors may take place.
   (D) The group may become dissatisfied with inventors.

9. How does the speaker close the talk?
   (A) By opening the floor to questions
   (B) By suggesting a break
   (C) By giving some hints
   (D) By involving the audience

Now get ready to listen.

Now get ready to answer the questions.

10. What are the people listening to the speaker probably interested in?
    (A) Collecting garbage
    (B) Making orange juice
    (C) Robbing graves
    (D) Learning about cultures

11. Why does the speaker mention orange peels?
    (A) To demonstrate what can be learned from them
    (B) To show how to find out how much orange juice a family drinks
    (C) To encourage people to make their own juice
    (D) To demonstrate how studying something organic is preferable

12. What would most likely be found in a Stone Age garbage dump?
    (A) Rotten orange peels
    (B) Broken stone tools
    (C) Torn grass clothing
    (D) Discarded animal skins

13. Why does the speaker regret that most garbage is organic?
    (A) Because our world is being filled with garbage
    (B) Because it is disgusting to sift through
    (C) Because its disintegration leaves no clues about its cultural origins
    (D) Because its preservation is limited to the Arctic Circle

 STOP

Answers to Exercise L41 are on page 511.

Exercise L42   ***Listening Section Practice Test***

When you have completed the Listening exercises from Part A and Part B as recommended on the Diagnostic Test, test your skills by taking this Listening Practice Test, which corresponds to the Listening Section of Test 2 on the CD-ROM that accompanies this book. Alternatively, you can take the test on the pages that follow.

During the Listening Section of the actual Computer-Based TOEFL® Test, you may not go back to check your work or change your answers. Maintain the same test conditions now that would be experienced during the real test.

Answers to Exercise L42 are on page 511.

The script for this exercise starts on page 580.

 START

LISTENING

Time – approximately 60 minutes

This section measures your ability to understand spoken English. There are fifty questions in this section. The listening material and questions about it will be presented only one time. You may not take notes.

Part A

In this part, you will hear short conversations between two people. Each conversation is followed by a question about it. Each question in this part has four answer choices. Choose the best answer to each question. Answer the questions on the basis of what is <u>stated</u> or <u>implied</u> by the speakers.

 Now we will begin Part A with the first conversation.

1. What does the woman mean?
   (A) Peter couldn't work because he injured his arm.
   (B) Peter really didn't want to help.
   (C) The woman hurt Peter.
   (D) The woman had to take Peter to the hospital.

2. What does the man imply?
   (A) His class will finish in a minute.
   (B) He thinks class will end too soon.
   (C) He would like classes to be over sooner.
   (D) He thinks the week after next is very early.

3. What did Robert do?
   (A) He elected the student body president.
   (B) He assured students that he would help with housing troubles.
   (C) He caused the students to have difficulties with rent.
   (D) He assisted students having trouble finding living accommodations.

4. What does the woman say about Jane?
   (A) She has problems with math.
   (B) She doesn't mind failing.
   (C) She's good at solving math problems.
   (D) She isn't careful in her work.

5. What does the man mean?
   (A) He would like to take a photograph.
   (B) The woman can't take the picture.
   (C) He can't give the woman the camera.
   (D) The woman forgot to buy film.

6. What does the woman imply?
   (A) He should have read the textbooks.
   (B) He probably did his homework.
   (C) He isn't a very serious student.
   (D) He might have failed the test.

7. What does the man mean?
   (A) He could meet her halfway.
   (B) He could lend her the money.
   (C) They could make part of the journey.
   (D) They could share the cost.

8. What does the woman mean?
   (A) The man is blind.
   (B) It's snowing very hard.
   (C) She doesn't know if it's snowing.
   (D) She can't get across the street to the Student Union.

9. What does the woman mean?
   (A) The testing ended last week.
   (B) They haven't had an exam in over
       a week.
   (C) They'll be finished taking the tests
       in two weeks.
   (D) The testing will take over two weeks.

10. What does the man say about Sue?
    (A) She enrolled in a short German-language
        course.
    (B) She had a bad accident while driving
        in Germany.
    (C) She met a German in her math course.
    (D) She is going to take a short trip
        to Germany.

11. What does the woman mean?
    (A) Margaret was sorry that Dr. Morris
        mislaid his paper.
    (B) Margaret should say she's sorry for having
        mislaid the paper.
    (C) Margaret made a better apology than
        Dr. Morris did.
    (D) Margaret apologized to Dr. Morris
        for the mislaid paper.

12. What does the man imply?
    (A) He doesn't want to return the book yet.
    (B) He wants the book the woman borrowed
        by next week.
    (C) He can't lend the woman the book
        until next week.
    (D) He has already given the book to
        the woman.

13. What does the woman mean?
    (A) Jason moved backward, not forward,
        in the line.
    (B) Jason knows the part extremely well.
    (C) Jason lined up with his back toward
        the memorial.
    (D) Jason moved behind the line.

14. What does the woman mean?
    (A) It's time to leave the show.
    (B) They could go see the show.
    (C) They could meet there at noon.
    (D) There's no time to design a costume.

15. What does the woman mean?
    (A) Botany is an easier course.
    (B) Botany is easy, but zoology is not.
    (C) She could do as well in botany as in zoology.
    (D) She would prefer studying zoology.

16. What does the woman mean?
    (A) She is going to the library later.
    (B) She isn't going to the library today.
    (C) She is going to take a lunch break.
    (D) She is going to go to the library before lunch.

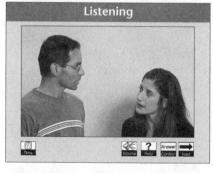

17. What does the woman mean?
    (A) The man's schedule could be worse.
    (B) Evening classes are better.
    (C) It is unfortunate that he has a ten-o'clock class.
    (D) She was correct about his schedule.

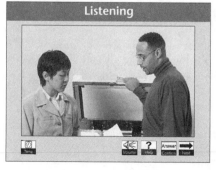

18. Why has the man come to the library?
    (A) To annoy the students
    (B) To study the photocopies
    (C) To fix the photocopier
    (D) To work for a week

This is the end of Part A.
Go on to Part B.

Part B

In this part, there are several talks and conversations. Each talk or conversation is followed by several questions. The conversations and talks are about a variety of topics. You do not need special knowledge of the topics to answer the questions correctly. Rather, you should answer each question on the basis of what is <u>stated</u> or <u>implied</u> in the conversation or talk. You may not take notes.

 Now we will begin Part B with the first conversation.

19. What are the two people discussing?
    (A) The arrangements for meeting each other
    (B) The best place and time to catch a taxi
    (C) The professor of an archaeology class
    (D) The importance of reserving theater tickets early

20. Why does the woman think the man might be late?
    (A) His professor has stopped him after class before.
    (B) He is in the habit of showing up late.
    (C) He might not be able to get a taxi.
    (D) His class sometimes gets out late.

21. What does the woman intend to do in the afternoon?
    (A) Reserve the tickets
    (B) Call the taxi
    (C) Pick up the tickets
    (D) Meet the man

22. What is the man's problem?
    (A) His studies keep him from attending sports events.
    (B) He doesn't have enough money to meet expenses.
    (C) He wants to get a part-time job at the concession stands.
    (D) His part-time job interferes with his studies.

23. What does the woman suggest he do?
    (A) Buy used books from the library
    (B) Try the library on University Avenue
    (C) Take time off to play sports
    (D) Work part-time at university events

24. What will the man probably do?
    (A) Buy used books
    (B) Go to the sports events
    (C) See a concert for free
    (D) Apply for a job

Now get ready to listen.

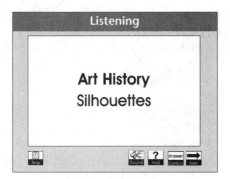

Now get ready to answer the questions.

25. What were silhouettes originally called?
    (A) Shadows
    (B) Profiles
    (C) Shades
    (D) Curiosities

28. Why are the discussed art forms known as silhouettes?
    (A) They were inexpensive.
    (B) They were mistaken for junk.
    (C) They were curiosities.
    (D) They were from the eighteenth century.

26. What is NOT mentioned as one of the materials artists transferred portraits onto?
    (A) Ivory
    (B) Clay
    (C) Porcelain
    (D) Glass

29. Select the picture that is an example of a silhouette.

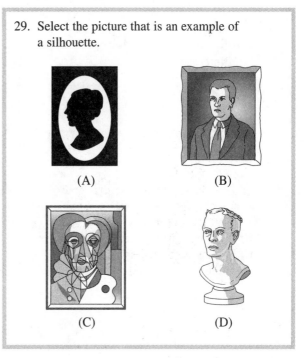

27. Who was Étienne de Silhouette?
    (A) The artist who invented shadow portraits
    (B) The man who paid a lot of money for a shadow painting
    (C) A French finance minister who was known for his stinginess
    (D) The man whose profile was the most infamous

Now get ready to answer the questions.

30. What are the people mainly discussing?
    (A) The man's major
    (B) The man's work-study duties
    (C) The reproduction of paramecia
    (D) The lab equipment

31. In what department is the professor probably working?
    (A) Biology
    (B) Zoology
    (C) Chemistry
    (D) Physics

32. What will the man's job be?
    (A) Counting paramecia
    (B) Watching paramecia reproduce
    (C) Timing paramecia speeds
    (D) Filling in forms about time

33. Why might it be important that the man come in at the same time daily?
    (A) The lab can be left open at that time.
    (B) Another professor must be in the lab.
    (C) It's necessary for analyzing the speed of reproduction.
    (D) The forms must be turned in to the office before it closes.

34. The professor briefly explains a process. Summarize the process by putting the events in order.

    Write the letter of each sentence in the space where it belongs. Use each sentence only once.

    A   A convenient time must be arranged for the student to come.
    B   A form must be filled out and turned in.
    C   The paramecia must be counted.
    D   The statistics must be fed into the computer.

1	
2	
3	
4	

Now get ready to listen.

Now get ready to answer the questions.

35. What is the talk mainly about?
    (A) A devastating war
    (B) The invasion of Martians
    (C) The public reaction to a media broadcast
    (D) A hoax planned by the media

36. According to the professor, what is true about the broadcast?

    Choose 2 answers.

    A George Orson Welles produced the radio play.
    B H. G. Wells wrote the radio script.
    C The radio play was produced in Grovers Mill, New Jersey.
    D The broadcast was convincing and realistic.

37. What can be said about the event?
    (A) It took place on Halloween Eve in 1898.
    (B) It had a widespread effect in the United States.
    (C) It began in England.
    (D) It made Orson Welles famous.

38. Why were people convinced of the invasion?
    (A) People trusted Orson Welles.
    (B) All regions of the United States were exposed.
    (C) Real places were referred to in realistic special bulletins.
    (D) Americans are genuinely frightened by Martians.

39. The professor explains a sequence of events. Summarize the sequence of events by putting the events in order.

    Write the letter of each sentence in the space where it belongs. Use each sentence only once.

    A H. G. Wells wrote *The War of the Worlds*.
    B The audience's reaction to the broadcast became well known.
    C A dramatic play was performed on radio.
    D Some Americans tried to flee the invasion.

1	
2	
3	
4	

40. What is the ironic twist the professor mentions?
    (A) The original play created mass panic.
    (B) The media may have misled the public about the extent of the panic.
    (C) Sociologists have demonstrated the influence of media on society.
    (D) Americans were influenced by the media.

Now get ready to listen.

Now get ready to answer the questions.

41. What is the discussion mainly about?
   (A) The thinning of the ozone layer
   (B) International convention agreements
   (C) The eradication of CFCs
   (D) General information about CFCs

42. According to the professor, how do CFCs get into the atmosphere?
   (A) They are a chemical reaction caused by ultraviolet rays.
   (B) They migrate from the stratosphere.
   (C) They are in the DNA of humans and plants.
   (D) They are released through some products and processes.

43. Why does the professor mention hair sprays and polishes?
   (A) To give examples of products that are put into aerosol containers
   (B) To show what kind of products are being phased out
   (C) To give an analogy of how CFCs are dispersed
   (D) To illustrate that products containing CFCs are unimportant

44. The professor briefly explains a process. Summarize the process by putting the events in order.

   Write the letter of each sentence in the space where it belongs. Use each sentence only once.

   A | Artificial chemicals called CFCs are used in the production of many goods.
   B | Oxygen combines with CFCs, causing the depletion of the ozone layer.
   C | Ultraviolet light is able to reach the Earth's surface and damage DNA.
   D | The use of products containing CFCs allows CFCs to enter the atmosphere.

1	
2	
3	
4	

45. Why is the professor cautious in her prediction of the future?
   (A) She is not certain everyone will comply with the international agreements.
   (B) She doesn't think the CFCs will disperse without some assistance.
   (C) She doesn't believe the ozone layer can recover from the environmental abuse.
   (D) She doesn't know if alternatives to CFCs are acceptable.

Now get ready to listen.

Now get ready to answer the questions.

46. What is the talk mainly about?
    (A) Juvenile crime
    (B) Criminal statistics concerning young people
    (C) Criminal rehabilitation of youth
    (D) Juvenile justice system reform

47. What resulted from the basic legal principle that children are different from adults?
    (A) Juvenile offenders received individualized treatment.
    (B) Children were made vulnerable.
    (C) The justice system was overhauled.
    (D) The justice system was subjected to a rational examination.

48. Why is the professor concerned about reforms to the juvenile justice system?
    (A) The reforms might fail to rehabilitate offenders.
    (B) Juvenile criminal offenses might continue to increase.
    (C) Juvenile criminals might be treated as adult criminals.
    (D) The reforms might not be tough enough.

49. What do the three key areas of research examine?

Write the letter of each phrase in the space where it belongs. Use each phrase only once.

A Risk evaluation
B Susceptibility to change
C Accountability

Juvenile's understanding of criminal behavior	Juvenile's likelihood of committing crimes	Juvenile's likelihood of modifying behavior
1.	2.	3.

50. What does the professor recommend?

Choose 2 answers.

A Debating issues with different juvenile offenders
B Spreading knowledge among professionals and the community
C Dismantling the whole juvenile justice system
D Conducting more research in relevant fields

This is the end of the Listening Section Practice Test.
Turn off your cassette or audio CD player now.

SECTION
·2·
STRUCTURE

The Structure Section of the Computer-Based TOEFL® Test measures your ability to understand the structures of standard written English. This section consists of two kinds of questions.

Complete the Sentence

In complete-the-sentence questions, you must decide which of the four choices best completes the sentence. Although all four answers may be grammatically correct when read by themselves, only one is grammatically correct in the context of the sentence. Therefore, you should spend your time analyzing the type of structure needed to make a grammatically correct sentence. When you have chosen an answer, click on the oval next to the answer of your choice. After you choose your answer, you must click on the **Next** icon. You are given the opportunity to check your answer and then click on the **Answer Confirm** icon. You must confirm your answer in order to go on to the next item.

Identify the Error

In identify-the-error questions, each sentence has four underlined words or phrases. One of the underlined choices contains an error or omission. The error is always one of the underlined words or phrases. Therefore, you should spend your time analyzing parts of the sentence. You must decide which one is incorrect and click on your choice. The word or phrase you click on will darken. You do not need to correct the error, so after you choose your answer, click on the **Next** icon. You are given the opportunity to check your answer and then click on the **Answer Confirm** icon. You must confirm your answer in order to go on to the next item.

STRATEGIES TO USE FOR THE STRUCTURE SECTION

1. Remember that you are looking for standard written English.

The language and topics in this section will be more formal than the conversational language used in the Listening Section. The topics frequently relate to academic subjects. You do not have to know about these subjects to answer the questions correctly.

2. Remember to change tactics.

In complete-the-sentence questions, you are looking for the one correct answer to complete the sentence. In identify-the-error questions, you are looking for the one answer that is wrong. The question types are presented alternately.

3. Answer every item.

You cannot go on to the next question until you have answered and confirmed the question that you are on. If you try to do so, you will lose time when the computer "error" message comes up to tell you that you must answer the question. If you do not know an answer, eliminate those answers you know are incorrect and then take a guess from the remaining choices.

4. Check your answer.

Since you cannot go back and change your answer, be sure you have clicked on the answer you want before you click on the Answer Confirm icon.

5. Pay attention to time.

Look frequently at the question number and the amount of time you have remaining. Be sure you are pacing yourself well in order to complete all the questions. Time management is important because your score will depend on the number of items correctly answered within the time allotted.

STRATEGIES TO USE FOR COMPLETE-THE-SENTENCE QUESTIONS

1. Read the incomplete sentence first.

Examine the sentence and decide what is needed to complete it.

2. Read all choices.

Once you have decided what is needed to complete the sentence, read all the choices. More than one of the choices may contain the structure you are looking for. Examine those choices to determine which one completes the sentence correctly.

3. Use your time wisely.

Do not look for mistakes within the answers. Most answers are grammatically correct by themselves. However, only one answer is correct when it is placed in the sentence.

STRATEGIES TO USE FOR IDENTIFY-THE-ERROR QUESTIONS

1. Read the complete sentence.

If you cannot identify the incorrect word or phrase after you read the sentence, look at each underlined word. Think about its position in the sentence and what may be incorrect about it.

2. Remember that the error will always be _underlined_.

Do not look for errors in the other parts of the sentence. Look at the rest of the sentence for clues to help you find the error.

3. Do not correct the sentence.

You do not have to correct the sentence. Therefore, do not lose time thinking about how to correct it. Once you have chosen which answer contains the error, go on to the next item.

PRACTICE WITH NOUNS

Ask yourself these questions when checking nouns.

1. *What kind of noun is it? Is it count or noncount?*

A *count noun* refers to people or things that can be counted. You can put a number before this kind of noun. If the noun refers to one person or thing, it needs to be in the singular form. If it refers to more than one person or thing, it needs to be in the plural form.

    one desk   three desks   one book   fifty books

A *noncount noun* refers to general things such as qualities, substances, or topics. Noncount nouns cannot be counted and have only a singular form.

    food   air   money   intelligence

Noncount nouns can become count nouns when they are used to indicate types.

    the wines of California
    the fruits of the Northwest

2. *Is there a quantifier with the noun that can be used to identify the nature of the noun?*

A *quantifier* is a word that indicates an amount or a quantity.

(A) Some quantifiers are used with both plural count nouns and noncount nouns.

    all   any   enough   a lot of   plenty of
    more   most   some   lots of

Examples   I have **enough** money to buy the watch. (noncount)
I have **enough** sandwiches for everyone. (count)

(B) Some quantifiers are used only with noncount nouns.

    a little   much

Examples   There's **a little** milk.
There's not **much** sugar.

(C) Some quantifiers are used only with plural count nouns.

    both   many   a few   several

Examples   I took **both** apples.
We saw **several** movies.

(D) Some quantifiers are used only with singular count nouns.

    another   each   every

Examples   Joe wanted **another** piece of pie.
Every child in the contest received a ribbon.

3. *Is the form of the noun correct?*

Noncount nouns only have a singular form. Most count nouns have a singular form and a plural form. The plural form for most nouns has an *-s* or *-es* ending. However, there are other singular and plural patterns.

(A) Some nouns form their plurals with a vowel change or an ending change.

Singular	Plural
foot	feet
goose	geese
tooth	teeth
mouse	mice
louse	lice
man	men
woman	women

(B) Some nouns form their plurals by changing a consonant before adding *-s* or *-es*.

Singular	Plural
wolf	wolves
leaf	leaves
wife	wives
knife	knives

(C) Some nouns form their plurals by adding an ending.

Singular	Plural
child	children
ox	oxen

(D) Some nouns have the same plural and singular form. These nouns frequently refer to animals or fish. However, there are exceptions.

bison	fish	series	offspring
deer	salmon	species	spacecraft
sheep	trout	corps	

Examples   One **fish** is on the plate.
Two **fish** are in the pan.

(E) When a noun is used as an adjective, it takes a singular form.

We are leaving for two **weeks**. (noun)
We are going on a two-**week** vacation. (adjective)

(F) *Collective nouns* refer to an entire group. When a collective noun indicates a period of time, a sum of money, or a measurement, it takes a singular verb.

Two weeks is enough time to finish the contract.
Ten dollars is all I have.
Seven pounds is an average weight for a newborn.

(G) Some nouns end in *-s* but are actually singular and take singular verbs.

Academic subjects: mathematics, politics, physics, economics, civics, statistics
Physics is Professor Brown's specialty.

Diseases: measles, mumps, herpes
Measles is usually contracted during childhood.

4. Is the noun used in a noun position?

Nouns are used in the following positions:

As subjects	An **engineer** designed the bridge.
As complements	My sister is an **engineer**.

As objects	I saw the **engineer**.
	Eric lent the book to the **engineer**.
	Jan walked past the **engineer**.

5. Is the correct form of the word used?

The form of a word depends on its position in the sentence. (See Practice with Word Forms on page 213.) Notice how the word "invitation" changes form.

Noun form	The **invitation** to Jerry's wedding has arrived.
Verb form	Susan **invited** us to dinner on Sunday.
Adjective form	The hot chocolate looked very **inviting**.
Adverb form	The man smiled **invitingly** as he opened the door.

Use Exercises S1–S5 to develop your skills in identifying nouns.

Exercise S1 Identifying count and noncount nouns

Write "C" if the underlined noun is a count noun, and "N" if it is a noncount noun.

Examples __N__ I studied <u>mathematics</u> with Professor Crane.

__C__ We caught three <u>fish</u> for dinner.

You should write "N" in the first blank because "mathematics" is a noncount noun. You should write "C" in the second blank because "fish" is a count noun in this sentence.

1. _____ <u>Rayon</u> can be mixed with cotton to strengthen the fabric.

2. _____ The <u>glass</u> in the window was cracked.

3. _____ Forty <u>children</u> were involved in the language-development study.

4. _____ The <u>news</u> concerning the student election was very positive.

5. _____ Thomas dropped a <u>test tube</u> on the classroom floor.

6. _____ The <u>information</u> gained from the experiment was significant.

7. _____ There was a <u>hair</u> on the microscope lens.

8. _____ Bananas and pineapples were once considered exotic <u>fruits</u>.

Extended practice: Some of the underlined nouns in these sentences can be either count or noncount. Identify those nouns and write your own sentences using them in both ways.

Answers to Exercise S1 are on page 513.

Exercise S2 Reviewing plural and singular forms

Write the correct form of the plural or singular word.

Examples	**Singular**	**Plural**
	foot	*feet*
	ox	oxen

Singular	Plural
1. person	_____
2. _____	lives
3. _____	series
4. _____	teeth
5. _____	children
6. man	_____
7. _____	sheep
8. leaf	_____
9. mouse	_____
10. goose	_____

Answers to Exercise S2 are on page 513.

Exercise S3　　*Locating and checking plurals and singulars*

Some of the following sentences contain a noun error. Circle the incorrect nouns.

Example　　Many traditional attitudes and (value) seem to be disappearing under the pressure of global media.

You should circle "value" because the word "many" indicates that there is more than one value disappearing.

1. Ultrasound bounces sound wave off the internal structure of the body.
2. Public lands in many parts of the West may be overgrazed as cattle, sheep, and wildlives compete for forage.
3. A landslide at a mining site uncovered a brownish yellow stone that yielded 650 gram of gold.
4. Lorenzo Ruiz, the first Filipino saints, was born about 1600 in Binondo to a Chinese father and a Tagalog mother.
5. America was discovered and inhabited thousands of years before the Europeans arrived.
6. For two century, Madrid's Plaza Mayor has served as the city's chief forum.
7. Putting radio collars on bears helps scientists to gather important informations concerning the bears' movements.
8. When a hive becomes overcrowded, a swarm of bees will search for a new home.

Extended practice: Correct the nouns that you have identified as incorrect.

Answers to Exercise S3 are on page 513.

Exercise S4   ***Checking noun forms***

Write the correct form of the underlined word. Some underlined words use the correct noun form.

Example   Captain Scott was an <u>exploration</u> of the Antarctic.

explorer
_____

You should write "explorer" in the space because it is the noun form that is used for people (see item 5 on page 167 and item 3 on page 165).

1. The <u>furnishings</u> of George Washington's house provide an insight into the social and domestic life on the estate.

   _____

2. A <u>colonization</u> was established in Jamestown in 1607.

   _____

3. A <u>disturb</u> will cause a seal to move her pups.

   _____

4. The <u>existence</u> of methane in the atmosphere is what gives Uranus its blue-green color.

   _____

5. A late spring <u>freeze</u> may kill all the new leaves on the trees.

   _____

6. The <u>landing</u> of the Allied troops at Normandy took place on June 6, 1944.

   _____

7. The <u>important</u> of children's play is reflected in their behavior.

   _____

8. Inside a forest, the <u>active</u> is constant.

   _____

9. The earliest <u>arrive</u> in Wyoming had to wade across the North Platte River.

   _____

10. When the Red Cross brings aid to victims in disaster areas, the <u>situate</u> improves.

   _____

Answers to Exercise S4 are on page 514.

Exercise S5   **Checking nouns**

Look at the underlined nouns in each sentence. Circle the noun that is incorrect.

Example   The art of calligraphy has been passed from one generation to another
(generations) over the centuries.

You should circle "generations" because the word "another" is used only with singular nouns (see item 2D on page 165).

1. A goal of the Young Politicians of America is to provide young citizen with the opportunity to participate in government.

2. Many highly paid executives owe their success to motivated rather than to brilliance.

3. Scientists have managed to clone that kind of protein genes, but only as an exercise in basic research.

4. The most renowned of America's metalworker, Samuel Yellin, designed the ironwork for the New York Federal Reserve Bank building.

5. The research project looked at the importance of childrens as consumers of fashion.

6. Curious animals by nature, calf learn about their environment by first sniffing objects and then licking them.

7. Although small-claims courts use very simplified procedures, a person unfamiliar with law may need some advices with a complicated case.

8. One series of grammar book that was used in the experimental class was written by the students themselves.

Extended practice: Write the correct form of the nouns you have circled.

Answers to Exercise S5 are on page 514.

PRACTICE WITH ARTICLES AND DEMONSTRATIVES

Ask yourself these questions when checking articles ("a," "an," "the") and demonstratives ("this," "these," "that," "those").

1. Is the indefinite article ("a" or "an") used correctly?

(A) "A" is used before a consonant sound, and "an" is used before a vowel sound.

(B) The letter "u" can have a consonant or vowel sound.

    a university   BUT   an umbrella

(C) The letter "h" is sometimes not pronounced.

    a horse   BUT   an hour

2. Should an indefinite article be used?

Use "a" or "an"

(A) before singular count nouns when the noun is mentioned for the first time.

    I see **a house**.

(B) when the singular form is used to make a general statement about all people or things of that type (see item 3B on page 166).

    A concert pianist spends many hours practicing. (All concert pianists spend many hours practicing.)

(C) in expressions of price, speed, and ratio.

    60 miles **an** hour   four times **a** day

"A" or "an" are not used

(D) before plural nouns.

    Flowers were growing along the riverbank.

(E) before noncount nouns.

    I wanted advice.

3. Should the definite article ("the") be used?

"The" is used

(A) before a noun that has already been mentioned.

    I saw a man. **The** man was wearing a hat.

or when it is clear in the situation which thing or person is referred to.

    The books on the shelf are first editions.

    I went to **the** bank. (a particular bank)

(B) before a singular noun that refers to a species or group.

    The tiger lives in Asia. (Tigers, as a species, live in Asia.)

(C) before adjectives used as nouns.

    The children collected money to donate to the institution for **the** deaf.
    ("the deaf" = deaf people)

(D) when there is only one of something.

    The sun shone down on the earth.

    This is **the** best horse in the race.

(E) before a body part in a prepositional phrase that belongs to the object
in the sentence.

    Someone hit me on **the** head. ("Me" is the object. Thus, it is my head that was hit.)

or a body part in a prepositional phrase that belongs to the subject of a passive sentence.

    I was hit on **the** head. ("I" is the subject of the passive sentence. Therefore, it is my head
    that was hit.)

Note: A possessive adjective, rather than the article "the," is usually used with body parts.

    I hit **my** head. ("I" is neither the object of this sentence nor the subject of a passive sentence.
    Therefore, a possessive adjective is used.)

(F) Some proper names use "the"; others do not.

"The" is usually used with canals, deserts, forests, oceans, rivers, seas, and *plural*
islands, lakes, and mountains.

    the Suez Canal   the Black Forest
    the Hawaiian Islands   the Atlantic Ocean

"The" is not usually used with planets and *singular* islands, lakes, mountains, and parks.

    Mars   Central Park   Lake Michigan
    Venus   Fiji Island   Mount Rushmore

(G) "The" is usually used when the name of a country or state includes the word "of," the type of government, or a plural form.

> the Republic of Ireland
> the United Kingdom
> the Philippines

(H) "The" is *not* usually used with

the names of other countries and states.

Japan	Brazil	Germany

the names of continents.

Africa	Asia	Europe

the names of cities.

Chicago	Mexico City	Hong Kong

4. Which article, if any, should be used?

(A) The expression "*a* number of" means "several" or "many" and takes a plural verb. The expression "*the* number of" refers to the group and takes a singular verb.

> **A large number of** tourists *get* lost because of that sign.
> **The number of** lost tourists *has* increased recently.

(B) The following nouns do not always take an article:

prison	school	college
church	bed	home
court	jail	sea

Look at how the meaning changes.

Example   bed

No article: Jack went to bed. (= Jack went to sleep. "Bed" refers to the general idea of sleep.)

With "the":   Jack went to **the** bed. (Jack walked over to a particular bed. The bed is referred to as a specific object. He may or may not have lain down and gone to sleep.)

With "a":   Jack bought **a** bed. (Jack purchased an object called a bed.)

(C) Articles are not used with possessive adjectives ("my," "your," etc.); possessive pronouns ("mine," "yours," etc.); or demonstratives ("this," "that," "these," and "those").

> This is **my** coat. Where's **yours**?
> **That** watch is broken.

Note: In the following question, the demonstrative "this" is not used as part of the noun phrase "the book."

> Is **this** the book you wanted?

"This" is the subject of the sentence. "The book" is the complement of the sentence. They are beside each other because of the subject/auxiliary inversion in the question form. They are not used together as a single phrase (see item 1 on page 207).

(D) Noncount nouns are used without an article to refer to something in general. Sometimes an article is used to show a specific meaning.

> People all over the world want **peace**. (= peace in general)
> The **peace** was broken by a group of passing children. ("The peace" refers to peace at a specific time and place.)
> The imparting of **knowledge** was the job of the elders in the community. (= knowledge in general)
> I have a **knowledge** of computers. (= a specific type of knowledge)

5. Are the demonstratives ("this," "that," "these," and "those") used correctly?

(A) The demonstrative adjectives and pronouns are for objects near the speaker.

> this (singular)   these (plural)

and for objects far away from the speaker.

> that (singular)   those (plural)

(B) Demonstratives are the only adjectives that agree in number with their nouns.

> **That hat** is nice.
> **Those hats** are nice.

(C) When there is the idea of selection, the pronoun "one" (or "ones") often follows the demonstrative.

> I want a book. I'll get this (one).

If the demonstrative is followed by an adjective, "one" (or "ones") *must* be used.

> I want a book. I'll get this **big** one.

Use Exercises S6–S10 to develop your skills in identifying articles and demonstratives.

Exercise S6   ***Identifying the need for articles***

Write the correct article ("a," "an," or "the"). If no article is needed, write Ø.

Example   An advanced free-trade zone is currently under development in _the_ United Arab Emirates.

You should write "the" in the blank because the name of the country includes its type of government.

1. The Babylonians were the first to divide a day into twenty-four hours, _____ hour into sixty minutes, and a minute into sixty seconds.

2. Of the approximately twenty thousand meteorites discovered on Earth, only thirteen have been identified as originating from _____ Mars.

3. In many countries there is an ongoing debate about whether, and in what way, early childhood education can prepare children for _____ school.

4. Robin Hood supposedly stole from _____ rich.

5. _____ untold number of people perished while attempting to cross Death Valley.

6. Venice is _____ only city in the world completely free of the automobile.

Answers to Exercise S6 are on page 514.

Exercise S7   *Checking articles*

If the underlined article is used incorrectly, cross it out and write the correct article.

Example   ~~A~~ island in the Pacific Ocean was used for the experiment. ___An___

You should write "an" in the blank because "island" begins with a vowel sound.

1. Countless tourists throng to <u>the</u> Greek islands. _____

2. <u>The</u> tomato originated in Central America. _____

3. The steam engine was developed in <u>an</u> eighteenth century. _____

4. <u>The</u> Russia has a very diverse culture. _____

5. <u>A</u> university education is a requirement for many highly paid positions. _____

6. Bacteria exist everywhere in <u>the</u> nature. _____

> Answers to Exercise S7 are on page 514.

Exercise S8   *Checking demonstratives*

Circle the letter of the demonstrative that correctly completes the sentence.

Example   ____ books are the ones I bought at the auction.
    (A) This
    ((B)) These

You should circle letter (B) because the demonstrative must agree in number with its noun. The plural "these" is used with the plural noun "books."

1. It was reported that interest rates would be cut, and _____ news lifted the stock market.
    (A) that
    (B) those

2. The dodo was first sighted around 1600 on Mauritius, but unfortunately _____ bird became extinct eighty years later.
    (A) this
    (B) these

3. _____ fish tastes best when baked in butter.
    (A) This
    (B) These

4. _____ physics courses offered at night school are mainly for non-science majors.
    (A) That
    (B) Those

5. Only in the park are _____ buffalo protected.
    (A) that
    (B) those

6. _____ two rings here on my left hand belonged to my great-grandmother.
    (A) Those
    (B) These

> Answers to Exercise S8 are on page 514.

Exercise S9   *Correcting articles and demonstratives*

Correct any sentence that contains an error in the underlined phrase.

Examples   Going to school for the first time can be traumatic. _____

                 Elderly sometimes need special care.   *The elderly* _____

The first sentence is correct. For the second sentence you should write "The" before the word "elderly" because "the" is needed when an adjective is used as a noun. "The elderly" means "elderly people."

1. Those brick house is the nicer of the two.

     _____

2. Staff evaluation procedures are completed at least twice the year.

     _____

3. Arched roofs were built for a first time twenty-five hundred years ago.

     _____

4. Postwar women had more opportunities to find the work than they had had in the prewar days.

     _____

5. The general always listened to advice from his staff.

     _____

6. Since beginning of the age of computers, technological advances have increased tenfold.

     _____

7. Jackson Pollock's freer techniques raised painting to new levels of the improvisation.

     _____

8. The boy took his sister by the hand.

     _____

Answers to Exercise S9 are on page 514.

Exercise S10   *Locating and checking articles and demonstratives*

Underline all the articles and demonstratives in the following sentences. Then circle any that have been used incorrectly.

Example   Ⓐlemon originated in ⓣⓗⓔ China and spread south to the Malaysian Islands and west to India.

You should underline and circle "A" before "lemon" (see item 3B, page 171) and "the" before "China" (see item 3H, page 172). You should underline "the" before "Malaysian" (see item 3F, page 171).

1. That dissertations have to be completed within a four-year time limit.

2. The good Dr. Sneider began his first year at Arizona State University after having been appointed a associate professor.

3. At a height of the tourist season, the small seaside community boasts a population of 15,000.

4. Since the beginning the research, Dr. Ahmedi has collected seventy different kinds of plant rocks.

5. In a famous book by Daniel Defoe, the hero, Robinson Crusoe, spent twenty years on a island.

6. Those child's computer was installed with added features for the blind.

7. The climbers on the trail admired the majesty of the Mount Everest.

8. The kangaroo travels at speeds up to twenty miles the hour by jumping on the powerful hind legs.

Answers to Exercise S10 are on page 514.

PRACTICE WITH PRONOUNS AND POSSESSIVE ADJECTIVES

Ask yourself these questions when checking pronouns and possessive adjectives.

1. Is the word in its correct form?

Subject Pronoun	Object Pronoun	Possessive Adjective	Possessive Pronoun	Reflexive Pronoun
I	me	my	mine	myself
you	you	your	yours	yourself
he	him	his	his	himself
she	her	her	hers	herself
it	it	its	–	itself
we	us	our	ours	ourselves
you	you	your	yours	yourselves
they	them	their	theirs	themselves

Examples   When you see the African lions in the park, you see them in their true environment.

Both instances of "you" are in the subject position. The pronoun "them" is the object pronoun and refers to the lions. "Their" is in the possessive adjective form because the environment discussed in the sentence is that of the lions.

2. Is a possessive pronoun or adjective used to refer to parts of the body?

Possessive pronouns or adjectives are usually used with reference to parts of the body. (For exceptions, see Practice with Articles and Demonstratives, item 3E, page 171.)

Examples   She put the shawl over **her** shoulder.
She lifted the boy and put the shawl over **his** shoulder.
She put a red hat on **her** head and a green one on **his**.

3. Does the pronoun or possessive adjective agree with the word it refers to?

Example   The little girl put on **her** hat, and the little boy put on **his**.

If the hat the girl put on belongs to the girl, the possessive adjective must agree with the word "girl." If the hat the boy put on belongs to the boy, the possessive pronoun must agree with the word "boy." If something in the sentence indicates that the hats they put on belong to someone else, agreement must be made between the possessive pronoun or adjective and that other person.

Use Exercises S11–S15 to develop your skills with pronouns and possessive adjectives.

Exercise S11   **Locating pronouns and possessive adjectives**

Circle the pronouns and possessive adjectives in the following sentences.

Example   When the boy grabbed the lizard,(its)tail broke off in(his)hand.

1. In 1978, Maxie Anderson and his two partners made the first crossing of the Atlantic Ocean in their hot-air balloon.

2. When Caesar and his troops invaded Britain, they anchored their transports above what they erroneously thought was the high tidemark.

3. Botanists themselves are so worried that the pollution problem may be irreversible in many areas that they are organizing their own monitoring programs.

4. The fame of Edgar Allan Poe rests on his short stories as well as on his poetry.

5. The Dutch artist Rembrandt van Rijn painted portraits of himself throughout his working life.

6. The island itself didn't become accessible to us until the late 1940s.

7. When attacking their prey, eagles reach out with their talons.

8. The deceptive look of a sinkhole is part of its danger as well as its fascination.

Answers to Exercise S11 are on page 514.

Exercise S12   **Checking pronoun and possessive adjective forms**

If the underlined word is incorrect, write its correct form.

Example   We prepared the supper by <u>ourself</u>.

_____*ourselves*_____

"Our" refers to more than one person. Therefore, "self" should be in the plural form.

1. Sometimes forest rangers tranquilize grizzly bears and attach transmitters to <u>them</u> necks.

_____

2. While tide pools can survive natural assaults, <u>their</u> are defenseless against humans.

_____

3. You and your brother need to take time to prepare <u>yourself</u> for the long journey.

_____

4. The larvae metamorphose into miniature versions of <u>their</u> adult form.

    _____

5. These minute insects – twenty of <u>they</u> could fit on a pinhead – drift on wind currents.

    _____

6. Using packing crates and sheet metal, the displaced families made <u>itself</u> a home.

    _____

7. <u>His</u> is a future dictated by poverty and hardship.

    _____

8. When elk migrate in the winter, it may take <u>their</u> days to reach the lower regions.

    _____

> Answers to Exercise S12 are on page 515.

Exercise S13   *Identifying referents*

Write the word that the underlined pronoun or possessive adjective refers to.

Example   He put the roast on the table and began to eat <u>it</u>.

        it _____*roast*_____

The pronoun "it" refers to "roast."

1. Vikings buried <u>their</u> chief with <u>his</u> boat, complete with <u>his</u> supplies.

    their _____   his _____   his _____

2. When President Abraham Lincoln met Harriet Beecher Stowe, writer of the novel about slavery called *Uncle Tom's Cabin,* <u>he</u> reputedly called <u>her</u> "the little lady who started the Civil War."

    he _____   her _____

3. People once thought the word "abracadabra" had mystical powers, so <u>they</u> wore <u>it</u> inscribed on amulets as a good-luck charm.

    they _____   it _____

4. There are no restrictions on debates in the English House of Lords, so if <u>its</u> members think something is important, <u>they</u> will talk <u>it</u> through until <u>they</u> are satisfied.

    its _____   they _____

    it _____   they _____

5. The dean expressed <u>his</u> support for setting up a private university provided <u>it</u> was supervised by the Department of Education.

    his _____   it _____

6. <u>This</u> was the place where the Roman ship had sunk with <u>its</u> cargo of stone.

    This _____   its _____

7. To pass <u>his</u> time away in jail, Charles d'Orléans smuggled out rhyming love letters to <u>his</u> wife, and <u>this</u> may have been the beginning of the custom of sending valentine cards to loved ones.

his ＿＿＿＿＿＿   his ＿＿＿＿＿＿   this ＿＿＿＿＿＿

8. During a drying time of six to eight weeks, the nutmeg shrinks away from <u>its</u> hard seed coat until the kernels rattle in <u>their</u> shell when shaken.

its ＿＿＿＿＿＿ ,   their ＿＿＿＿＿＿

Answers to Exercise S13 on page 515.

Exercise S14   *Checking for agreement*

If the underlined word does not agree with its referent, write the correct word.

Example   The dog bit <u>themselves</u> on the tail.

itself

1. The importance of the Chaco Canyon archaeological site is that <u>they</u> reveals insights into a whole civilization.

2. We know the risks and we are quite happy to take <u>us</u>.

3. The ancient Tayronas distinguished <u>themselves</u> as craftsmen working in gold, clay, and stone.

4. The gun was beautifully engraved, making <u>their</u> value close to twenty thousand dollars.

5. At Victor Harbor, South Australia, people can park <u>their</u> cars and walk to the coast to see over twenty different species of whales and dolphins.

6. When trawling for crab, he took several books so that he could study <u>it</u> during the long hours.

7. Millet's *The Gleaners* depicts peasants filling <u>her</u> aprons with leftover grain.

8. So numerous are the family's properties that the duchess cannot name <u>it</u> all.

Answers to Exercise S14 are on page 515.

Exercise S15   *Completing sentences*

Circle the letter of the answer that correctly completes the sentence.

1. To understand ancient Egypt, scholars study its hieroglyphics and try to interpret ＿＿＿ .
(A) it
(B) them
(C) itself
(D) themselves

2. The dialect that is spoken in Olimbos is so old that many of ＿＿＿ words date back to the time of Homer.
(A) its
(B) his
(C) hers
(D) theirs

3. One of the side effects of growing older is the tendency of one's idols to fall from _____ pedestals.
   (A) they
   (B) them
   (C) their
   (D) themselves

4. As the bare mountains turned green, the people found _____ looking forward to spring.
   (A) they
   (B) them
   (C) their
   (D) themselves

5. The police academy trains _____ dogs to fetch things on command.
   (A) its
   (B) his
   (C) hers
   (D) theirs

6. The Italian dramatist and poet Ugo Betti was a judge who gained literary recognition late in _____ life.
   (A) him
   (B) his
   (C) their
   (D them

7. The prickly pear anchors _____ on rocky, barren slopes and grows to about three meters high.
   (A) it
   (B) itself
   (C) their
   (D) themselves

8. New chemicals are not always tested to determine if _____ will cause cancer or genetic mutations.
   (A) it
   (B) she
   (C) he
   (D) they

Answers to Exercise S15 are on page 515.

CHECK YOUR PROGRESS

There are two types of questions in the Structure Section of the Computer-Based TOEFL® Test. The first type of question consists of incomplete sentences. Beneath each sentence there are four words or phrases. You will select the one word that best completes the sentence. The computer screen will look like this.

Structure
<u>Directions</u>: Click on the one word or phrase that best completes the sentence.

John Le Carré _____ for his novels concerning espionage.
- ○ famous
- ○ has fame
- ○ is famous
- ○ famed

| Time | | Help | Answer Confirm | Next |

To answer this question, you would click on the oval next to the words "is famous" because this is the only choice that correctly completes the sentence. The oval you click on will become dark. To change your answer, click on another oval. When you are sure of your answer, click on the ⬛Next⬛ icon. Check your answer and then click on the ⬛Answer Confirm⬛ icon.

The second type of question consists of a sentence with four underlined words or phrases. You will select the one underlined word or phrase that must be changed for the sentence to be correct.

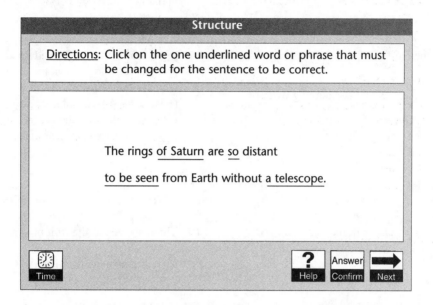

To answer this question, you would click on the word "so" because this word must be changed to "too" in order for the sentence to be correct. When you click on an underlined word or phrase, it will become highlighted. To change your answer, click on another underlined word or phrase. When you are sure of your answer, click on the ⬛Next⬛ icon. Check your answer and then click on the ⬛Answer Confirm⬛ icon.

Check your progress in using the skills you have been practicing in Exercises S1–S15 by completing the following mini-test. This exercise uses a format similar to that used in the Structure Section of the Computer-Based TOEFL® Test. If you are unfamiliar with how to answer questions on the Computer-Based TOEFL® Test, see the Tutorial on pages 22–23.

Exercise S16   Mini-test

Select the letter of the correct answer.

1. Crickets rub _____ together to make their chirping sound.
    (A) their legs
    (B) the legs
    (C) its legs
    (D) one's legs

2. <u>Progressive</u> for <u>its</u> time, Constantinople offered
    　　A　　　　B

    free medical services and <u>care</u> for <u>a</u> destitute.
    　　　　　　　　　　　　　C　　　D

3. Divers earn _____ living by retrieving money
   thrown into the river by pilgrims.
   (A) they
   (B) their
   (C) them
   (D) themselves

4. Oil <u>strikes</u> on the North Slope in <u>the</u> Alaska
         A   B

   provided the fuel to drive <u>its</u> economic <u>growth.</u>
                                C   D

5. Totem poles provide eloquent records of a
   tribe's lineage and _____ history.
   (A) its
   (B) his
   (C) her
   (D) their

6. <u>The</u> sale of pet <u>turtles</u> was banned because of
    A   B

   the disease risk <u>they</u> posed to young <u>child.</u>
                     C   D

7. When the limestone just below the ground
   surface dissolves, _____ collapses
   and forms ponds.
   (A) a land
   (B) the land
   (C) the lands
   (D) lands

8. <u>Inevitably</u> scholars disagree on an <u>authenticity</u>
       A   B
   of objects whose <u>origins</u> are <u>unknown.</u>
                      C   D

9. _____ called galaxiids feed on algae
   and mosses that grow in the warm waters.
   (A) A small Australian fishes
   (B) Small Australian fish
   (C) A small Australian fish
   (D) The small Australian fishes

10. Three species of <u>the</u> fruit <u>bat</u> have been found
                                A   B

    to <u>have</u> a primatelike visual <u>systems.</u>
         C   D

11. Solon H. Borglum's sculptures of horses show
    _____ one of the finest equestrian artists
    in the history of art.
    (A) him to be
    (B) he to be
    (C) his be
    (D) he be

12. Although Emily Dickinson wrote some of

    <u>the</u> most haunting lines of American <u>poetry,</u>
    A   B
    only seven of her poems <u>were</u> published during
                                        C

    <u>their</u> lifetime.
     D

13. _____ connect the word "happiness" with the symbols for white, silk, and tree.
    (A) Many Chinese person
    (B) Much Chineses
    (C) Many Chinese
    (D) Much Chinese people

14. Conservationists <u>hope</u> that <u>someday</u> captive
                    A   B
    wildlife <u>populations</u> will be reestablished
              C
    in <u>a</u> wild.
       D

15. Dogs that are trained to lead _____ must be loyal, intelligent, and calm.
    (A) a blind
    (B) the blind
    (C) blinds
    (D) blind

16. The local hot <u>springs</u> now serve as <u>a</u> bathhouse
                 A   B
    for <u>them</u> tranquil little <u>town.</u>
        C   D

17. Dr. August Raspet was a researcher and designer of _____ of the flying bicycle.
    (A) sailplanes and inventors
    (B) sailplane and inventor
    (C) sailplanes and inventor
    (D) sailplane and inventors

18. The <u>scars</u> of <u>the</u> earthquake remain in the
         A   B
    naked <u>rock</u>, and stunted trees mark <u>their</u>
          C   D
    fault line.

19. Barcelona was a stronghold of _____ during the Spanish Civil War.
    (A) the anti-Franco Republican forces
    (B) an anti-Franco Republican forces
    (C) a anti-Franco Republican forces
    (D) that anti-Franco Republican forces

20. Aeronautical <u>historian</u> have concluded that
                  A
    the Frenchman Clement Ader made a short
    <u>B</u>
    <u>leap</u> but never a sustained <u>flight.</u>
      C   D

Answers to Exercise S16 are on page 515.

PRACTICE WITH SUBJECTS

Ask yourself these questions when checking subjects.

1. Does the sentence contain a subject?

All complete sentences contain a subject. The command form, in which the subject is understood, is an exception (for example, "Do your homework.").

(A) The subject may consist of one or more nouns.

Birds fly.
Birds and bats fly.

(B) The subject may consist of a *phrase* (a group of words that includes the subject noun and words that modify it).

_____ **SUBJECT PHRASE** _____
The first Persian **carpet** I bought was very expensive.

The subject noun is "carpet." In general, the entire subject phrase can be replaced by a pronoun. In this case:

It was very expensive.

(C) Various structures may be used for subjects.

Noun	The **clover** smells sweet.
Pronoun	**It** is a new bookcase.
Clause (contains noun + verb)	**What they found** surprised me.
Gerund (-ing *forms*)	**Swimming** is good exercise.
Gerund phrase	**Working ten years in the mine** was enough.
Infinitive (to + verb)	**To sleep in** is a luxury.
Infinitive phrase	**To be able to read** is very important.

(D) Several different clause structures can be used for subjects.

Wh- structures:

Where we go depends on the job opportunities.

Yes/no structures:

Whether it rains or not doesn't matter.

"The fact that" structures ("the fact" is frequently omitted in these structures):

The fact that he survived the accident is a miracle.
That he survived the accident is a miracle.

2. Is there an unnecessary subject pronoun?

A subject noun or phrase and the pronoun that could replace it cannot be used in the same sentence.

Correct	**A ball** is a toy.	**A ball and a bat** are in the yard.
	It is a toy.	**They** are in the yard.
Incorrect	**A ball** <u>it</u> is a toy.	
	A ball and a bat <u>they</u> are in the yard.	

3. *Does the subject agree with the verb?*

Examples

S   **V**

Susie is working.

_____ **S** _____ **V**

Susie, Bill, and Albert are working.

The subject (S) and the verb (V) must agree in person and number. Note the following subject-verb agreement rules.

(A) A prepositional phrase does not affect the verb.

S   **V**

The houses **on that street** are for sale.

S   **V**

The house **with the broken steps** is for sale.

(B) The following expressions do not affect the verb.

accompanied by	as well as
along with	in addition to
among	together with

S   **V**

Jim, **together with Tom**, is going fishing.

_____ **S** _____   **V**

Jim and Linda, **along with Tom and Sally**, are going fishing.

(C) Subjects joined by "and" or "both . . . and . . ." take a plural verb.

Both Jill **and** Lydia *are* leaving town.

(D) When "several," "many," "both," and "few" are used as pronouns, they take a plural verb.

Several *have* already left the party.

(E) When the following phrases are used, the verb agrees with the subject that is closer to the verb in the sentence.

either . . . or
neither . . . nor
not only . . . but also

Neither my sister **nor** my brothers *want* to work in an office.
Neither my brothers **nor** my sister *wants* to work in an office.

(F) The expression "a number of" (meaning "several") is plural. The expression "the number of" is singular.

A number of items *have* been deleted.
The number of deleted items *is* small.

(G) When a word indicating nationality refers to a language, it is singular. When it refers to the people, it is plural.

Japanese *was* a difficult language for me to learn.
The Japanese *are* very industrious people.

(H) When clauses, infinitives, or gerunds are used as subjects, they usually take a singular verb.

> **What it takes** *is* lots of courage.
> **What those boys need** *is* a good hot meal.
> **To fly in space** *is* her dream.
> **Learning a new skill** *is* very satisfying.

4. Have "it" and "there" been used correctly?

(A) Sometimes a speaker wants to focus on the type of information that is expressed by an adjective. Since an adjective (ADJ) cannot be used in a subject position, the word "it" is used as the subject.

> **S   V   ADJ**
> **It** was windy and the rain beat down.

Sometimes a speaker wants to emphasize a noun and its relative clause. The speaker uses "it" in the subject position followed by the verb "be."

> **S   V _____ CLAUSE _____**
> **It** was Tom who broke the window.

Sometimes a speaker wants to say that something exists or wants to mention the presence of something. The word "there" is used as the subject, and the verb agrees with the noun or noun phrase (N PHR).

> **S   V   _N PHR_**
> **There** were six men in the boat.

(B) "It" can be used to refer to a previously stated topic. "It" can also be used to fill the subject position (see item 4A).

> **It** was warm in the house and I was afraid the milk might spoil, so I put **it** into the refrigerator.

The first "it" is used as the subject. The second "it" refers to the milk.

(C) "There" can be an adverb that tells where something is. "There" can also be used to fill the subject position (see item 4A).

> **There** are three bottles of orange juice over **there** by the sink.

The first "there" is used to fill the subject position and indicates that three bottles exist. The second "there" is an adverb which indicates where the bottles are.

Use Exercises S17–S23 to develop your skills in identifying and using subjects.

Exercise S17   *Focusing on subjects*

Underline the complete subject of the sentence and circle the subject noun (the noun that agrees with the verb).

Examples   Port (cities) are often the distribution centers for a country.

The beautiful, large, green (parrots) with the tuft of red plumage on their heads are on sale.

(Glass) and (alabaster) are both used to let light into some of the traditional Yemeni houses.

1. Until the mid-1950s, fishermen in the Northwest thought the eagles' gorging during annual salmon runs depleted stocks.

2. The Sami, along with many other indigenous peoples, have never had a sovereign state of their own.

3. Pictured on the one-dollar stamp is St. John's Cathedral.

4. Birds, mammals, reptiles, and fish that are not hunted, fished, or trapped need protection too.

5. Since nitrogen is a characteristic and relatively constant component of protein, scientists can measure protein by measuring nitrogen.

6. Far too many preservation programs in too many states rely on unstable voluntary donations.

7. When a tornado sweeps through a city, it causes a narrow band of total destruction.

8. Pesticide residues in livestock are largely the result of pesticide contamination in the general environment.

Answers to Exercise S17 are on page 516.

Exercise S18   *Locating subjects*

Underline the complete subjects of the following sentences.

Example   <u>Jogging</u> is an exercise that stimulates cardiovascular performance.

1. How wildlife has adapted to life along the road systems is being scrutinized by environmentalists.

2. To be among 200-foot-high towering rocks is an exhilarating experience.

3. Very early in the experiment, isolating the insects became necessary.

4. What happened at the Versailles Conference in 1919 resulted in treaties that have long since been the subject of contentious analysis, opinion, and debate.

5. Whispering in class not only prevents the whisperers from understanding the lesson but also bothers those who are trying to hear the class lecture.

6. In fashion, to create and produce new combinations of line and color takes real flair.

7. What caused the most damage to Michelangelo's works in the Sistine Chapel was a gluelike substance spread over the frescoes early in the sixteenth century.

8. Rolling dice, buying property, and accumulating play-money are the essential features of the board game Monopoly®.

Answers to Exercise S18 are on page 516.

Exercise S19   *Checking subject–verb agreement*

Write "C" (correct) if the subject agrees with the verb. Write "I" (incorrect) if the subject does not agree with the verb.

Examples   <u>*C*</u> An important goal was to increase tourism.

<u>*I*</u> The houses is open to the public.

In the first sentence, the subject "goal" agrees with the verb "was." In the second sentence, the subject "houses" does not agree with the verb "is."

1. _____ Deer are frequently seen in meadows at dusk.

2. _____ Physics provide an important background to the study of engineering.

3. _____ On old sailing vessels, neither the crew nor the captain was immune to scurvy.

4. _____ Nowadays, crossing Puget Sound in ferries are fast and convenient.

5. _____ Each river and ravine create an obstacle in the cross-country race.

6. _____ The U.S. president, together with cabinet members, exercise executive power.

7. _____ Four weeks is the amount of time concrete takes to reach its full strength.

8. _____ Metaphor and simile in literature reveals truth by suggesting new connections between disparate images.

Extended practice: Correct the sentences in the preceding exercise that have subject-verb agreement errors.

Answers to Exercise S19 are on page 516.

Exercise S20   *Choosing the correct subject*

All of the following statements need a subject. Circle the letter of the correct subject from the four possible choices.

Example   _____ are becoming endangered because their natural habitat is being lost.
(A) That animals
(B) Animals
(C) To be animals
(D) Being animals

You should circle (B) because the sentence needs a simple subject that agrees with the plural verb.

1. _____ takes eight years after sowing.
   (A) The nutmeg yields fruit
   (B) That the nutmeg yields fruit
   (C) For the nutmeg to yield fruit
   (D) To the nutmeg's yielding fruit

2. _____ has been used as a perfume for centuries.
   (A) To use lavender
   (B) That the lavender
   (C) Lavender
   (D) For the lavender

3. _____ shortens and thickens the muscles on either side of the jaw.
   (A) The teeth clenching
   (B) Clenching the teeth
   (C) That clenching the teeth
   (D) The teeth clenched

4. Even though 26 percent of California residents do not speak English in their homes, only _____ do not speak English at all.
   (A) that 6 percent of them
   (B) those of the 6 percent
   (C) to the 6 percent of them
   (D) 6 percent of them

5. _____ started as a modern sport in India at the same time that it did in Europe.
   (A) To ski
   (B) That skiing
   (C) Ski
   (D) Skiing

6. _____ was caused by a cow's kicking over a lantern has been told to American schoolchildren for several generations.
   (A) That the Great Chicago Fire
   (B) The Great Chicago Fire
   (C) To burn in the Great Chicago Fire
   (D) Burning in the Great Chicago Fire

7. _____ are effective means of communication.
   (A) Theater, music, dance, folk tales, and puppetry
   (B) That theater, music, dance, folk tales, and puppetry
   (C) To use theater, music, dance, folk tales, and puppetry
   (D) Using theater, music, dance, folk tales, and puppetry

8. When China's dramatic economic reforms began to encourage private enterprise, _____ began to set up a variety of businesses immediately.
   (A) that entrepreneurs
   (B) to be an entrepreneur
   (C) entrepreneur
   (D) entrepreneurs

9. _____ are worthy of protection moved English Heritage historians into action against developers.
   (A) Some buildings in and around Fleet Street
   (B) That some buildings in and around Fleet Street
   (C) Some buildings that are in and around Fleet Street
   (D) To build in and around Fleet Street

10. _____ makes the mountain-patrol team's job interesting and fulfilling.
    (A) Climbers and trekkers in distress are assisted
    (B) Assisting climbers and trekkers in distress
    (C) Assistance is given to climbers and trekkers that are in distress
    (D) Climbers and trekkers in distress

Answers to Exercise S20 are on page 516.

Exercise S21   *Understanding "it"*

If the underlined "it" refers to another word in the passage, write the word it refers to. If the underlined "it" does not refer to another word in the passage, write its accompanying adjective or noun.

Examples   I went into the dark house. <u>It</u> was very difficult to see anything.

difficult

I started a fire in the fireplace. <u>It</u> was burning slowly.

fire

In the first passage, "it" does not refer to another word; therefore, you should write the accompanying adjective "difficult" in the blank. In the second passage, "it" refers to the noun "fire"; therefore, you should write "fire" in the blank.

1. The castle of Neuschwanstein is one of many fanciful castles Ludwig II of Bavaria had built. <u>It</u> was to be the ultimate castle for a private kingdom.

   _____

2. Ross Island, rich in scenic beauty with old buildings and monuments of historical value, was a British headquarters. <u>It</u> is now a tourist attraction.

   _____

3. The gorilla is essentially a peaceful creature. <u>It</u> is true that the gorilla will fight, but only in life-threatening situations.

   _____

4. Noticing strange animal behavior might be a way to predict future earthquakes. <u>It</u> is a common belief that animals can sense environmental disturbances up to several days before the onset of a tremor.

   _____

5. Scientists must be willing to change their position when confronted with new and conflicting data. <u>It</u> is this openness to change that allows scientific progress to be made.

   _____

6. Coronary heart disease is sometimes referred to as the twentieth-century epidemic. <u>It</u> has been responsible for a third of all deaths among males and a quarter of all deaths among females in the United States.

   _____

7. Some people think chiropractors are quacks. But <u>it</u> is indisputable that many have gained benefits from chiropractic treatment.

   _____

8. Stuttering is a communication disorder involving the rate and rhythm of speech. <u>It</u> may have psychological or environmental causes.

   _____

Answers to Exercise S21 are on page 517.

Exercise S22   **Understanding "there"**

If the underlined "there" refers to the existence of something, write what exists. If the underlined "there" is used to refer to a place, write the name of the place.

Examples   I can see the books <u>there</u> on the table.

   _on the table_____

   <u>There</u> were six literature books and two history books.

   six literature books and two history books

In the first sentence, "there" refers to a place – on the table. In the second sentence, "there" refers to the existence of six literature books and two history books.

1. Almost all the mass of the universe is contained in superclusters of galaxies. <u>There</u> can be hundreds of thousands of galaxies in just one supercluster.

    _____

2. During the Second World War, water in England was rationed due to a shortage. In the bathtubs at Buckingham Palace, <u>there</u> were lines marking the limit allowed.

    _____

3. A rare foal was recently born at Cricket St. Thomas Wildlife Park. <u>There</u> they breed the smallest miniature ponies in the world.

    _____

4. When telephones were first invented, many business owners refused to have them installed in their offices. <u>There</u> were messenger services that they believed to be more efficient.

    _____

5. It is not uncommon for Americans to retire to homes in the southern states. <u>There</u> they find the climate more to their satisfaction.

    _____

6. In Europe, water companies keep live trout in special troughs to monitor water pollution. Special sensors <u>there</u> can detect high levels of pollution through the trout's gill movements.

    _____

Answers to Exercise S22 are on page 517.

Exercise S23   *Checking "there" and "it"*

Circle the letter of the word or phrase that correctly completes the sentence.

Example   _____ two kinds of decorative art.
     (A) It is
     (B) There are
     (C) There
     (D) It

You should circle (B) because "there are" indicates the existence of two kinds of decorative art. The verb "is" in (A) does not agree with the plural "two kinds," and the answers in (C) and (D) do not include a verb to complete the sentence.

1. _____ not until the invention of the camera that artists correctly painted horses racing.
    (A) There was
    (B) It was
    (C) There
    (D) It

2. Once a crocodile has seized an animal, _____ drags the prey beneath the surface of the water.
    (A) it
    (B) it is
    (C) there
    (D) there is

3. _____, in the center of old San'a, many of the city's houses – some ten centuries old – will collapse if restoration isn't started soon.
   (A) There are
   (B) It is
   (C) There
   (D) It

4. Nowadays, people in most countries use money because _____ impossible to carry on trade in the modern world without it.
   (A) it
   (B) there
   (C) there is
   (D) it is

5. In the city center, _____ noisy market stalls set in a maze of winding alleys.
   (A) it
   (B) it is
   (C) there
   (D) there are

6. In the United States, _____ a growing demand for foreign cuisine.
   (A) there is
   (B) it is
   (C) it
   (D) there

7. Our feeling for beauty is inspired by the harmonious arrangement of order and disorder as _____ occurs in nature.
   (A) it is
   (B) there
   (C) there is
   (D) it

8. _____ high technology and traditional industries in the Oulu region of Finland.
   (A) There
   (B) There are
   (C) It is
   (D) It

Answers to Exercise S23 are on page 517.

CHECK YOUR PROGRESS

Check your progress in using the skills you have been practicing in Exercises S17–S23 by completing the following mini-test. This exercise uses a format similar to that used in the Structure Section of the Computer-Based TOEFL® Test. If you are unfamiliar with how to answer questions on the Computer-Based TOEFL® Test, see the Tutorial on pages 22–23.

Exercise S24   Mini-test

Select the letter of the correct answer.

1. _____ are phosphorescent in the dark intrigues many people.
   (A) That certain species of centipedes
   (B) Certain species of centipedes
   (C) There are certain species of centipedes
   (D) It is certain species of centipedes

2. <u>Ironworking</u> probably spread to <u>a</u> rest of Africa
        A   B
   <u>via</u> the Meroitic <u>civilization</u>.
    C   D

3. _____ from the leaves of the rare weeping tree even though the sky may be cloudless.
(A) Great drops of water dripping
(B) Great drops of water drip
(C) Water dripping in great drops
(D) That great drops of water are dripping

8. The ships now <u>lying</u> at the bottom of Abukir
                A
Bay <u>was</u> rumored to be <u>carrying</u> treasures
    B   C
taken <u>from</u> Malta.
     D

4. <u>Some</u> of the most <u>influential</u> Middle Eastern
  A   B
newspapers, *The Pyramids*, was <u>established</u>
                        C
in Egypt <u>in</u> 1875.
        D

9. _____ that produced the famous *Crab nebula*, which is a favorite among astronomers.
(A) That it was a supernova
(B) It was a supernova
(C) A supernova
(D) There a supernova

5. _____ is a tiny sea animal that looks like a shrimp.
(A) It is the krill
(B) There is the krill
(C) The krill
(D) That the krill

10. Trade relations between Egypt and Africa

<u>began</u> in 1460 B.C.E. <u>when</u> Queen Hatshepsut
  A   B
sent <u>hers</u> ships to the country of Punt, <u>today's</u>
     C   D
Somalia.

6. <u>The</u> number of battles were <u>fought</u> <u>between</u>
  A   B   C
the <u>fleets</u> of Nelson and Napoleon.
    D

11. _____ mixed with a base such as egg yolk was the exclusive medium for painting panels in the Middle Ages.
(A) Finely ground pigments
(B) It is a finely ground pigment
(C) A finely ground pigment
(D) That a finely ground pigment

7. _____ in the frozen wastes of Antarctica takes special equipment.
(A) Survive
(B) It is survival
(C) That survival
(D) To survive

12. Ever since the <u>early</u> Greeks began the serious
                A
<u>contemplation</u> of natural things, <u>there</u> have
     B   C
existed two different emphases in thinking

about <u>universe</u>.
      D

13. _____ toward animated cartoons with war-related topics has come under criticism from such groups as the National Coalition against Television Violence.
(A) It is the trend
(B) Trends
(C) That the trend
(D) The trend

14. The Freedom of Information Act, passed by
                                        A
the U.S. Congress in 1966, gives U.S. citizen
                            B   C
the right of access to public records.
                D

15. Today _____ the single largest organized industry in India.
(A) the cotton textile industry is
(B) it is the cotton textile industry
(C) the cotton textile industry
(D) there is the cotton textile industry

16. The beautiful of Cyprus, with its pine-covered
        A   B
mountains, sandy beaches, historical

monuments, and picturesque villages,
                    C
is legendary.
D

17. _____ of the *Rubáiyát of Omar Khayyám* earned Edward FitzGerald fame.
(A) It is translating
(B) His translation
(C) Its being translated
(D) In his translation

18. The anthropologist is interested not in the
        A   B
actions of an individual, but in the social
    C
significant of these actions.
    D

19. When we put on thick woolen clothing, _____ in the woolen loops that protects us from the cold.
(A) it is the air
(B) that the air
(C) the air
(D) there is the air

20. Having lived there for long period, the French
                    A   B
writer Stendhal knew Italy well.
                C   D

Answers to Exercise S24 are on page 518.

PRACTICE WITH VERBS

Ask yourself these questions when checking verbs.

1. Does the sentence contain a verb?

The verb may consist of a single word, or a main verb and one or more auxiliary words (aux-words).

(A) A verb can indicate a state of being (what the subject is) or a location.

> Betty **is** intelligent.
> Robin and Donald **are** doctors.
> Mickey **is** at work.

(B) A verb can indicate what the subject is like or what it becomes.

> That child **seems** frightened.
> The book **had become** obsolete.

(C) A verb can indicate an action (what the subject is doing).

> The students **will finish** in time.
> My neighbor **has bought** a new car.

2. Does the verb agree with the subject?

Verbs must agree in number and person with the subject. (See agreement rules in Practice with Subjects, item 3, page 185.)

3. Is the verb tense correct?

Verbs indicate a point in time or period of time in the past, present, or future.

Tense	Used for	Example sentences
SIMPLE PRESENT	(A) a present state of affairs (B) a general fact (C) habitual actions (D) future timetables	(A) My sister **lives** in Washington. (B) The sun **rises** in the east. (C) I **listen** to the radio in the mornings. (D) My flight **leaves** at 10:00.
PRESENT CONTINUOUS	(A) a specific action that is occurring (B) a general activity that takes place over a period of time (C) future arrangements	(A) Andrew **is watching** TV (right now). (B) My sister **is living** in Washington. Sue's condition **is improving**. These days, I**'m taking** it easy. (C) I**'m inviting** Emma to the party on Friday.
SIMPLE PAST	(A) an action or a state that began and ended at a particular time in the past (B) an action that occurred over a period of time but was completed in the past (C) an activity that took place regularly in the past	(A) The mail **came** early this morning. I **was** shy in high school. (B) Dad **worked** in advertising for ten years. (C) We **jogged** every morning before class.

Tense	Used for	Example sentences
PAST CONTINUOUS	(A) ongoing actions that were interrupted	(A) I **was sewing** when the telephone rang. While I **was sewing**, the telephone rang.
	(B) a continuous state or repeated action in the past	(B) She **was looking** very ill. I **was meeting** lots of people at that time.
	(C) events planned in the past	(C) Nancy **was leaving** for Chicago but had to make a last-minute cancellation.
FUTURE (*going to*)	(A) expressing a future intent based on a decision made in the past	(A) Jim **is going to bring** his sister tonight.
	(B) predicting an event that is likely to happen in the future	(B) You **'re going to pass** the test. Don't worry.
	(C) predicting an event that is likely to happen based on the present conditions	(C) I don't feel well. I**'m going to faint**.
FUTURE (*will*)	(A) making a decision at the time of speaking	(A) I**'ll call** you after lunch.
	(B) predicting an event that is likely to happen in the future	(B) You **will pass** the test. Don't worry.
	(C) indicating willingness to do something	(C) If I don't feel better soon, I **will go** to the doctor.
FUTURE CONTINUOUS	(A) an action that will be ongoing at a particular time in the future	(A) At noon tomorrow, I**'ll be taking** the children to their piano lessons.
	(B) future actions that have already been decided	(B) I**'ll be wearing** my black evening dress to the dinner.
PRESENT PERFECT	(A) an action or a state that happened at an unspecified time	(A) He **has been** ill. I'm sorry. I **have forgotten** your name.
	(B) an action that has recently occurred	(B) He**'s** just **gone** to sleep.
	(C) an action that began in the past and continues up to the present (often used with "for" or "since")	(C) Judy **has lived** in Maine all her life. I**'ve been** here since Monday. He**'s known** her for two weeks.
	(D) an action that happened repeatedly before now	(D) We **have flown** across the Pacific four times. I**'ve failed** my driver's test twice.

Tense	Used for	Example sentences
PRESENT PERFECT CONTINUOUS	(A) an action that began in the past and has just recently ended (B) an action that began in the past and continues in the present (C) an action repeated over a period of time in the past and continuing in the present (D) a general action recently in progress (no particular time is mentioned)	(A) **Have** you **been raking** the lawn? There are leaves all over your shoes. (B) Laura **has been studying** for two hours. (C) Simon **has been smoking** since he was thirteen. (D) **I've been thinking** about going to college next year.
PAST PERFECT	(A) a past action that occurred before another past action (B) an action that was expected to occur in the past	(A) Tom **had left** hours before we got there. (B) I **had hoped** to know about the job before now.
PAST PERFECT CONTINUOUS	(A) a continuous action that occurred before another past action (B) a continuous action that was expected to occur in the past	(A) They **had been playing** tennis before the storm broke. His eyes hurt because he **had been reading** for eight hours. (B) I **had been expecting** his change in attitude.
FUTURE PERFECT	an action that will be completed before a particular time in the future	By next July, my parents **will have been married** for fifty years.
FUTURE PERFECT CONTINUOUS	an action emphasizing the length of time that has occurred before a specific time in the future	By May, my father **will have been working** at the same job for thirty years.

4. Are the modals used correctly?

Modals are always followed by the base form of a verb. They indicate mood or attitude.

can	had better	may	must	shall	will
could	have to	might	ought to	should	would

We **can** leave after 2:30. (= We are able to leave. . . .)

We **could** leave after 2:30. (This is a possibility.)
may
might

We **had better** leave after 2:30. (This is advisable.)
    ought to
    should

We **have to** leave in the morning. (This is a necessity.)
    must

We **shall** leave in the morning. (This is an intention.)
    will

We **would** leave every morning at 8:30. (This is a past habit.)

Modals have many meanings. Here are some special meanings you should know.

Must

I'm completely lost. I **must** have taken a wrong turn at the traffic light.
That man **must** be the new president.

In these sentences, "must" is used to show that an assumption is being made. When the assumption concerns a past action, it is always followed by "have."

Cannot/Could Not

You **can't** be hungry. We just ate!
He **couldn't** have taken the book. I had it with me.

In these sentences "can't" and "couldn't" indicate impossibility.

5. Is the passive or active form of the verb used correctly?

An active sentence focuses on the person or thing doing the action. A passive sentence focuses on the person or thing affected by the action.

Examples   The tower was built at the turn of the century. (Someone built the tower.)
        Rebecca had been given the assignment. (Someone gave the assignment to Rebecca.)

The passive voice is formed by the verb "be" in the appropriate tense followed by the past participle of the verb.

Examples

	Active	Passive
Present	My brother **washes** our car every weekend.	Our car **is washed** every weekend.
Present continuous	My brother **is washing** our car.	Our car **is being washed**.
Simple past	My brother **washed** our car yesterday.	Our car **was washed** yesterday.
Past perfect	My brother **had** just **washed** our car before it rained.	Our car **had** just **been washed** before it rained.

6. Is the verb in the correct word order?

(A) The following aux-words (helping words) are used in yes/no questions and *Wh-* questions.

AUX-WORDS					
Present	**Past**	**Present**	**Past**	**Present**	**Past**
will	would	have/has	had	is/am/are	was/were
can	could	do/does	did	shall	should
may	might				
must					

Examples   Where **did** Andy buy his camera?
Should I mention the problems involved?

(B) The negative is formed by adding the word "not" or the ending *-n't* after the first aux-word.

> I **cannot** go home.
> We **had not** gone to the shop.
> They **aren't** going with us.

(C) The verbs "do," "have," and "will" should not be confused with the aux-words "do," "have," and "will."

Verbs	**Aux-words**
I **do** my homework right after class.	**Do** you take the bus?
The Adamses still **have** an electric typewriter.	They **have** worked for us for many years.
My grandfather **willed** us his fortune.	I **will** bring my suit to the convention.

7. Is the verb in the correct form?

(A) A verb may be confused with other forms of the same word. Notice how the word "mechanize" changes form.

Verb form	The owners are going to **mechanize** the factory.
Noun form	The **mechanization** of the factory will take place in the near future.
Adjective form	**Mechanical** devices will be installed to do the work.
Adverb form	They are going to hire **mechanically** minded personnel.

(B) Verb forms may be confused with other verb forms.

Although the regular past tense uses an *-ed* ending, there are many irregular forms in English. It is important to know the past forms and past participle forms of irregular verbs for the Computer-Based TOEFL® Test.

> I walk**ed** to the library. (regular)
> I **came** back by bus. (irregular)

8. Are infinitives used correctly?

An infinitive is a verbal formed with "to" and the base form of the verb. It can be used as a noun, an adverb, or an adjective.

> **To eat** is a necessity. (noun)
> I came home **to change**. (adverb)
> He always has money **to spend**. (adjective)

(A) Some of the verbs that can be followed by an infinitive are:

afford	consent	hope	prepare	swear
agree	decide	intend	pretend	threaten
appear	demand	learn	promise	tend
arrange	deserve	manage	refuse	try
ask	desire	mean	regret	volunteer
attempt	expect	need	seem	wait
beg	fail	offer	struggle	want
care	forget	plan	strive	wish
claim	hesitate			

Examples   We *agreed* **to go** to the movies.
Emma couldn't *afford* **to buy** the ring.
Terry *volunteered* **to work** on the committee.

(B) Some of the adjectives that can be followed by an infinitive are:

anxious	difficult	hard	ready
boring	eager	pleased	strange
common	easy	prepared	usual
dangerous	good		

Examples   I am *anxious* **to hear** from him.
We were *ready* **to leave** before the end of the movie.
It is *dangerous* **to smoke** near gasoline.

(C) Some of the verbs that can be followed by a noun or pronoun and an infinitive are:

advise	convince	force	order	teach
allow	dare	hire	permit	tell
ask	encourage	instruct	persuade	urge
beg	expect	invite	remind	want
cause	forbid	need	require	warn
challenge				

Examples   He *advised* **me to buy** a newer car.
I *persuaded* **my father to lend** me the money.
I *needed* **the course to graduate.**

9. Are gerunds used correctly?

A gerund is formed by adding *-ing* to the base form of the verb. It is used as a noun.

Examples   **Swimming** is healthy for you. (subject)
You should try **studying** more. (object)
He was suspected of **cheating**. (object of the preposition)

(A) Some of the verbs that can be followed by a gerund are:

admit	deny	postpone	resist
advise	discuss	practice	resume
anticipate	enjoy	quit	risk
appreciate	finish	recall	suggest
avoid	keep	recommend	tolerate
can't help	mention	regret	try
consider	mind	report	understand
delay	miss	resent	

Examples   We *appreciated* his **giving** us the car.
I *finished* **writing** the report.
Lou *enjoys* **playing** tennis on weekends.

(B) Some of the two- and three-word verbs that can be followed by gerunds are:

aid in	depend on	put off
approve of	give up	rely on
be better off	insist on	succeed in
call for	keep on	think about
confess to	look forward to	think of
count on	object to	worry about

Examples You can *count on* his **being** there.
I *keep on* **forgetting** her name.
Sam *confessed to* **eating** all the cookies.

(C) Some of the adjectives + prepositions that can be followed by gerunds are:

accustomed to	intent on
afraid of	interested in
capable of	successful in
fond of	tired of

Examples Sue is *accustomed to* **working** long hours.
Edward is *interested in* **becoming** an artist.
I am *afraid of* **catching** another cold.

(D) Some of the nouns + prepositions that can be followed by gerunds are:

choice of	method of/for
excuse for	possibility of
intention of	reason for

Examples I have no *intention of* **driving** to Nevada.
Sean had a good *excuse for* **arriving** late.
There is a *possibility of* **flying** to Cyprus.

10. Are the infinitives and gerunds interchangeable?

(A) Some of the verbs that can be followed by either an infinitive or gerund without a difference in meaning are:

begin	dread	love
can't stand	hate	prefer
continue	like	start

Examples I *hate* **to go** shopping.
I *hate* **going** shopping.

(B) Some of the verbs that can be followed by either an infinitive or gerund but with a difference in meaning are:

forget	remember	stop

Examples I *stopped* **to buy** tomatoes. (I stopped at the store and bought tomatoes.)
I *stopped* **buying** tomatoes. (I no longer buy tomatoes.)

11. Are adjectives that are formed from verbs used correctly?

The adjective takes the present participle form when describing the "actor" and the past participle form when describing the "receiver."

Examples

The teacher	bores	the student.
(the actor)	(the action)	(the acted upon)

The teacher is do**ing** the action. Therefore, the teacher is bor**ing**.

> The **boring** teacher put the student to sleep.

The student is act**ed** upon. Therefore, the student is bor**ed**.

> The **bored** student was sleeping in class.

Some other verbs used as adjectives are:

amaze	depress	exhaust	satisfy
amuse	disgust	fascinate	shock
annoy	embarrass	frighten	terrify
astonish	excite	horrify	worry
confuse			

Use Exercises S25–S31 to develop your skills in identifying and using verbs.

Exercise S25   **Focusing on verbs**

Underline the complete verb in the independent clause. (See Practice with Clauses, page 230, for information about clauses.)

Example   The unassembled and conveniently packed furniture <u>can be carried</u> home by customers.

You should underline "can be carried" because this is the verb (passive voice).

1. Stuntmen and stuntwomen fall from great heights, use assorted weaponry, and negotiate burning obstacles.

2. Seasonal heavy swells and stiff winds in the Indian Ocean cause problems for even experienced crews.

3. The average temperature at the North Pole remains fairly constant at about –30 degrees Fahrenheit, and blizzards reduce visibilities to near zero for days on end.

4. The dry, eroded landscape dotted with cactus plants has made southern Spain an ideal location for filming Westerns.

5. Fingerprints might have proved that the suspect was at the scene of the crime.

6. Edwin Hubble's observations showed that the universe is expanding.

7. Industrial robots grasp and manipulate objects that are too dangerous for humans to handle.

8. What help refugees get is usually financed through government funds and donations from charitable organizations.

Answers to Exercise S25 are on page 519.

Exercise S26   ***Recognizing the passive and active voices***

Write "A" if the sentence is in the active voice and "P" if the sentence is in the passive voice.

Examples   __*A*__ Flanders borders the sea and is mostly flat plain with sandy beaches.

__*P*__ When the Eiffel Tower was first built, it was considered a monstrosity.

1. _____ Many cities' authorities have changed downtown areas to pedestrian zones because the traffic situation has become so troublesome.

2. _____ A century after his death, Horatio Alger Jr. is still associated with poor, hardworking boys who achieve success.

3. _____ The Romans used a cement made of lime and volcanic ash.

4. _____ Customers everywhere are demanding goods tailored to their own needs but sold at mass-production prices.

5. _____ J. Paul Getty, once the richest American, was buried near the Getty Museum in Malibu.

6. _____ Dickens had not finished writing his novel *The Mystery of Edwin Drood* at the time of his death.

7. _____ Fast-food restaurants have been established in almost every country in the world.

8. _____ The International Space Station is being designed, built, and equipped under the supervision of scientists from many nations.

Answers to Exercise S26 are on page 519.

Exercise S27   ***Checking verb tenses***

If the underlined verb tense is incorrect, write the correct tense in the blank.

Example   The nervous system is being comprised of the central and the peripheral nervous systems.

is comprised _____

1. Suburbs harbor an extraordinary variety of birds, insects, plants, and animals since urban sprawl began.

_____

2. Aerial photography will recently and unexpectedly revealed many historical sites.

_____

3. Electricity using superconductivity can travel farther with greater efficiency.

_____

4. Navigational errors have been now almost a thing of the past.

_____

5. Today neurochips are being designed for processing many tracks at once.

_____

6. In the future, we <u>may have been measuring</u> movements on the earth's crust that are undetectable today.

   _____

7. Mice with disorders similar to human diseases <u>have been grown</u> from genetically engineered mouse cells.

   _____

8. The desolate, ruined city of Merv <u>is dominated</u> by the mausoleum of Sanjar the Great.

   _____

Answers to Exercise S27 are on page 519.

Exercise S28   *Checking subject-verb agreement*

Write "C" (correct) if the verb agrees with the subject. Write "I" (incorrect) if the verb does not agree with the subject.

Example   __*I*__ Tropical fish is popular pets.

You should write "I" in the space because "fish" is plural in this sentence. The plural form "are" should be used instead if "is."

1. _____ The difference between the living conditions in the countryside and in towns has been eliminated.

2. _____ A reorganization of the brain cells occurs during adolescence.

3. _____ The radiation levels from a computer display terminal is well below presently accepted standards of exposure.

4. _____ Mathematics are important for those students studying physics.

5. _____ Pollution, together with water erosion, is taking its toll on the buildings.

6. _____ The execution of exquisite decoration and the effective use of space, light, and water contributes to the Alhambra's unique beauty.

7. _____ That species of butterfly are often seen in many parts of North and South America.

Extended practice: Correct the sentences that you have identified as incorrect.

Answers to Exercise S28 are on page 519.

Exercise S29   *Checking verb forms*

If the underlined verb in the following sentences is incorrect, write the correct form.

Example   Yesterday I <u>begin</u> a new book.

   *began*_____

You should write "began" in the space because "yesterday" indicates that the past tense verb form should be used.

1. The word "comet" <u>comes</u> from the Greek adjective *kometes*, which means "wearing long hair."

   _____

2. The mythical hero Orpheus once <u>haunted</u> the pine forests of the legendary Rhodopes.

   _____

3. Alpine meadows <u>be</u> a tranquil sight.

   _____

4. The content of fluorine in mineral water <u>make</u> it an excellent prophylactic agent against tooth decay.

   _____

5. Odysseus and his companions <u>longed</u> to return to their native Ithaca.

   _____

6. International, political, and cultural conferences <u>are holding</u> throughout the year at the Birmingham International Convention Center.

   _____

7. At the foot of the Tetons <u>lie</u> the oldest mountain resort in Wyoming.

   _____

8. The main street of this Saar village <u>dates</u> back over three thousand years.

   _____

Answers to Exercise S29 are on page 520.

Exercise S30   ***Checking infinitives and gerunds***

Circle the letter of the word or phrase that correctly completes the sentence.

Example   The professor mentioned _____ to Africa to collect a rare species of butterfly.
    (A) to travel
    (B) traveling

1. The English Heritage members attempt _____ castles and other ancient buildings in England.
   (A) to maintain
   (B) maintaining

2. Christopher Columbus persuaded the Spanish monarchs, Isabel and Fernando, _____ his expeditions to the Caribbean.
   (A) to finance
   (B) financing

3. Swimmers should avoid _____ ocean areas contaminated by red tide organisms.
   (A) to enter
   (B) entering

4. During drought periods in forested areas, officials require residents _____ outdoor burning until significant amounts of rainfall occur.
   (A) to postpone
   (B) postponing

5. Remote sensing from orbiting instruments helped explorers _____ the lost city of Ubar.
   (A) to find
   (B) finding

6. Aleksandr Pushkin managed _____ great stories despite being surrounded by spies and censored by the czar.
   (A) to write
   (B) writing

7. Because of financial restrictions, some schools cannot contemplate _____ abreast of advances in modern technology.
   (A) to stay
   (B) staying

8. Peace activist Baroness Bertha von Suttner encouraged Alfred Nobel _____ a prize for peace.
   (A) to establish
   (B) establishing

Answers to Exercise S30 are on page 520.

Exercise S31   *Completing the sentence*

Circle the letter of the verb that correctly completes the sentence.

Example   Quantum physics _____ into question the very foundations of our
traditional world view.
(A) calling
(B) call
(C) calls
(D) had been called

1. In 1970, the Canadian scientist
George Kell _____ that warm water
freezes more quickly than cold water.
(A) proved
(B) proving
(C) proves
(D) prove

2. The rebuilding of the Inca capital Cuzco
was _____ in the 1460s.
(A) begun
(B) beginning
(C) began
(D) begin

3. Only through diplomatic means can
a formal agreement be _____.
(A) reach
(B) to reach
(C) reaching
(D) reached

4. Hollywood film producers have
been regularly _____ tens of millions
of dollars for a single movie.
(A) budgeted
(B) budgeting
(C) budgets
(D) budget

5. The film-processing company has _____
a means of developing the 62-year-old
film that might solve the mystery.
(A) devising
(B) devised
(C) been devised
(D) devise

6. Platinum _____ a rare and valuable
metal, white in color, and – next to silver
and gold – the easiest to shape.
(A) is
(B) was
(C) has been
(D) be

7. A great deal of thought has _____ into
the designing of a concert hall.
(A) went
(B) going
(C) to go
(D) been gone

8. The healthful properties of fiber
have _____ for years.
(A) known
(B) be knowing
(C) knew
(D) been known

9. The vessel that sank may _____ the gold
and jewels from the dowry of
Catherine of Aragon.
(A) carry
(B) be carried
(C) have to carry
(D) have been carrying

10. Galileo _____ his first telescope in 1609.
(A) builds
(B) built
(C) building
(D) were built

Answers to Exercise S31 are on page 520.

PRACTICE WITH SUBJECT/AUX-WORD INVERSIONS

The order of the subject and the auxiliary word (aux-word) or verb can be changed for various reasons. Ask yourself these questions when checking changes in word order.

1. Has the word order been changed to make a question?

(A) In a statement, the subject is followed by the verb.

S   AUX   V

She has seen the Grand Canyon.

___ S ___ V

The boxes are on the table.

(B) In a question, the subject follows the aux-word or verb.

AUX   S   V

Have you seen the Grand Canyon?

V ___ S ___

Where are the boxes?

(C) An aux-word is used in a question except when the main verb is "be." An aux-word can be understood or used in a statement.

Do you live in a small town?   ("Do" is the aux-word.)
I live in a small town.   ("Do" is understood.)
I do live in a small town.   ("Do" can be used in statements for emphasis.)

2. Has the word order been changed to avoid repetition?

Examples

Jane works at Spencer Motors, and Bill works at Spencer Motors.
Jane works at Spencer Motors and **so does Bill**.

Jane isn't working on Saturday, and Bill isn't working on Saturday.
Jane isn't working on Saturday and **neither is Bill**.

3. Has the word order been changed because the statement begins with a prepositional phrase of location?

Example

___S___   V

Austin, Texas, lies at the edge of the Hill Country.

V   ___S___

At the edge of the Hill Country **lies Austin, Texas**.

4. Has the word order been changed because the conditional "if" has been omitted?

Example   **If I had gone** to the post office, I would have bought stamps.
Had I gone to the post office, I would have bought stamps.

5. Has the word order been changed because the statement begins with a negative word or phrase?

The words and phrases in the box on the next page are followed by a change in word order when they begin a sentence or an independent clause.

hardly ever	on no account
neither	only (when followed by an adverbial)
never	only by
no sooner . . . than	only in this way
nor	only then
not often	rarely
not once	scarcely
not only . . . as well	scarcely . . . when
not only . . . but also	seldom
not until	so
nowhere	under no circumstances

Examples

>   **S**   **V**
> **Mary** *not only* **works** at the post office, *but* she *also* works at the grocery store.

>   **AUX** **S** **V**
> *Not only* **does Mary work** at the post office, *but* she *also* works at the grocery store.

> **S**   **V**
> **Max** *never* **bought** another motorcycle again.

>   **AUX** **S** **V**
> *Never* again **did Max buy** another motorcycle.

>   **S**   **AUX** **V**
> Mark won't like that bread, and **he won't like** that cheese.

>   **AUX** **S** **V**
> Mark won't like that bread *nor* **will he like** that cheese.

Use Exercises S32–S35 to develop your skills in identifying word-order changes you may encounter on the Computer-Based TOEFL® Test.

Exercise S32   ***Identifying words and phrases that cause a change in word order***

Underline the word or phrase in each sentence that causes a change in word order.

Example   <u>Seldom</u> does Amanda buy a newspaper.

You should underline "seldom" because it has a negative meaning, which causes a change in word order when it comes at the beginning of a sentence or before an independent clause.

1. Rarely are people given permission to return to homes contaminated during a toxic waste accident.

2. On no account should front seat passengers travel without wearing seat belts.

3. Only if an individual is a natural-born United States citizen can he or she be elected president.

4. Not until the early nineteenth century was the modern notion of the atom formulated.

5. Not only was Michelangelo an artist and architect, but a poet as well.

6. No sooner had the Tower of Pisa been completed than its lean became obvious.

7. Nowhere have archaeologists found more Egyptian artifacts than in King Tutankhamen's tomb.

8. So incredible were explorer John Colter's descriptions of the Yellowstone area that people didn't believe in its existence.

Answers to Exercise S32 are on page 520.

Exercise S33   **Locating inversions**

Underline and label the subject, aux-word, and verb that have been inverted in each sentence.

                                       AUX _____ **S** _____ **V**

Example   Only once every seventy-six years <u>does Halley's Comet appear</u> in the sky.

1. Had Napoleon succeeded in his dream of conquering Europe, the map of the continent would look very different today.

2. Only under unusual circumstances are federal officials impeached.

3. Coffee contains caffeine and so does tea.

4. Not until a person has had a medical checkup should he or she start an exercise program.

5. Only when an institute is given funding will it be able to undertake research programs.

6. The potato is not indigenous to Europe and neither is the tomato.

7. Should a medical crisis occur, call the emergency services.

8. On Easter Island remain the mysterious giant stone heads carved by a forgotten civilization.

Answers to Exercise S33 are on page 520.

Exercise S34   **Correcting word order**

Rewrite the sentence if the word order is incorrect.

Example   Not often a Rembrandt is stolen.

     Not often is a Rembrandt stolen.

1. Wherever the blame lies, the elimination of the passenger pigeon was a shocking event.

2. Not only before exercising one should stretch but after exercising as well.

3. North of Winona, Minnesota, lies Lake City, which is considered the official "birthplace" of waterskiing.

4. Driving through downtown Houston during rush hour is difficult, as is parking there.

5. A dry, cold climate is not suitable for beautiful skin, and neither a hot climate is.

6. Only in 1865 were antiseptics first used.

_____

7. Not only swallows build their nests inside farm buildings, but do sparrows as well.

_____

8. Should you be bitten or stung by a venomous creature, you must seek medical assistance immediately.

_____

Answers to Exercise S34 are on page 520.

Exercise S35   **Completing the sentence**

Circle the letter of the answer that correctly completes the sentence.

Example   _____ once in his racing career did the horse Man o'War lose a race.
    (A) Scarcely
    (B) Only

You should circle (B) because "only" used with the word "once" indicates "one time" and no more.

1. _____ after years of planning do large-scale civil engineering projects get underway.
    (A) Seldom
    (B) Only

2. _____ has linguistic creativity been as pronounced as in Elizabethan England.
    (A) Only by
    (B) Never

3. _____ had the first Pilgrims landed than they were approached by the Native American Tisquantum speaking fluent English.
    (A) No sooner
    (B) Nowhere

4. _____ should a young child be allowed to play with fireworks without adult supervision.
    (A) Under no circumstances
    (B) No sooner than

5. _____ have playing cards been used for card games but also for fortune-telling.
    (A) Not as much
    (B) Not only

6. _____ will the emperor penguin leave its nest before the chick hatches.
    (A) Not once
    (B) Not until

7. _____ intensive research can a vaccine for new viruses be found.
    (A) Only when
    (B) Only through

8. _____ are the autumn colors so splendid as in New England.
    (A) Only
    (B) Nowhere

Answers to Exercise S35 are on page 520.

CHECK YOUR PROGRESS

Check your progress in using the skills you have been practicing in Exercises S25–S35 by completing the following mini-test. This exercise uses a format similar to that used in the Structure Section of the Computer-Based TOEFL® Test. If you are unfamiliar with how to answer questions on the Computer-Based TOEFL® Test, see the Tutorial on pages 22–23.

Exercise S36   Mini-test

Select the letter of the correct answer.

1. Samuel Pepys's *Diary* _____ eyewitness descriptions of the Great Plague and the Great Fire of London.
   (A) was contained
   (B) has been containing
   (C) contains
   (D) is containing

2. The first wagon train on the Oregon Trail
          A   B
   setting out from Independence, Missouri,
      C   D
   in 1841.

3. The sulky, a horse-drawn carriage, _____ to have been invented in the early nineteenth century by an English physician.
   (A) believed
   (B) was believing
   (C) is believed
   (D) is believing

4. Small animals can survival the desert heat
                         A
   by finding shade during the daytime.
      B   C   D

5. _____ the water clear but also prevent the river from overflowing.
   (A) Not only the hippo's eating habits keep
   (B) Keep not only the hippo's eating habits
   (C) The hippo's eating habits not only keep
   (D) Not only keep the hippo's eating habits

6. The term "Punchinello" refer to a clown
          A   B
   in Italian puppet shows.
   C   D

7. Not until 1865 _____ the first antiseptic treatment on a compound fracture.
   (A) when Joseph Lister tried
   (B) when did Joseph Lister try
   (C) did Joseph Lister try
   (D) that Joseph Lister tried

8. One out of every eight balloons in the world
      A   B   C
   are launched at Albuquerque, New Mexico.
      D

9. At each end of the tube _____, one which
    gathers light and one which magnifies
    the image.
    (A) are two lenses there
    (B) two lenses are
    (C) are two lenses
    (D) two lenses are there

14. As road traffic increases, <u>elevated</u> highways
                                    A
    <u>were built</u> to help solve <u>the</u> problem
          B   C
    of traffic <u>jams</u>.
                D

10. <u>Many</u> American novelists, <u>such as</u> Gore Vidal,
     A   B
    <u>resides</u> in <u>other</u> countries.
       C   D

15. Putrefaction _____ by bacteria and not by
    a chemical process.
    (A) to be caused
    (B) causing
    (C) caused
    (D) is caused

11. When _____ into the Colorado wilderness,
    no one could have predicted how popular
    the animal would become.
    (A) llamas first bring
    (B) were llamas first brought
    (C) first bringing llamas
    (D) llamas were first brought

16. The challenge of <u>reaching</u> <u>unexplored</u> places
                         A   B
    has <u>motivated</u> us <u>undertaking</u> space flights.
          C   D

12. The very obvious differences <u>among</u> the
                                   A
    various <u>cultures</u> discussed <u>is</u> at most <u>skin-deep</u>.
              B   C   D

17. West of Newport _____, one of the many
    mansions surrounded by acres of gardens.
    (A) where the Aston stately home stands
    (B) the stately home stands of Aston
    (C) the stately home of Aston stands
    (D) stands the stately Aston home

13. Noise pollution generally receives less attention
    than _____ air pollution.
    (A) does
    (B) it does
    (C) over
    (D) it does over

18. Lack of <u>exercise</u> and overindulgence in
               A
    high-fat diets have <u>long known</u> to <u>be</u> factors
                            B   C
    in heart <u>attacks</u>.
                D

19. In the Sonora Desert, the daytime temperatures _____ to 50 degrees Celsius.
    (A) rise
    (B) rising
    (C) to rise
    (D) risen

20. Only if packages are labeled properly,
    　　　　　　　　　　　　A
    sufferers will be able to avoid severe
    　　　　B　　　　　　　C
    allergic reactions.
    　　　D

Answers to Exercise S36 are on page 521.

PRACTICE WITH WORD FORMS

Ask yourself these questions when checking word forms.

1. Is the word a noun, a verb, an adjective, or an adverb?

A word may have one or more related forms. Notice how the word "decide" changes form.

Noun	The **decision** was made months ago.
Verb	We **decided** to move to a larger house.
Adjective	His **decisive** action brought order to the meeting.
Adverb	She acted very **decisively**.

2. Is the word in its correct position?

(A) Nouns are in the following positions (see Practice with Nouns, item 4, page 165):

As subject	The **doctor** came immediately.
As complement	My mother is a **doctor**.
As objects	We saw the **doctor**.
	The nurse gave the file to the **doctor**.
	The nurse stood beside the **doctor**.

(B) Verbs are used to express the action of the subject (see Practice with Verbs, item 1, page 195). Remember that verbs must agree in number and person with the subject.

Linda and Jan **jog** around the lake every day.
Paul **has rented** a tuxedo.

(C) Adjectives are words that modify (describe) the noun.

Adjectives have only one form, which is used with singular and plural nouns. With the exception of "this" / "these," "that" / "those," adjectives have no singular or plural form.

The **heavy** book was difficult for the **little** boy to carry.
The **old** man was carrying a **brown paper** sack.

To check if a word is an adjective, the question "What kind of?" can be asked.

I was **sad** because I lost my **lace** handkerchief.

"What kind of person was I?" – Sad. "What kind of handkerchief was it?" – Lace. Therefore, "sad" and "lace" are adjectives.

(D) Adverbs modify verbs, adjectives, and other adverbs. Like adjectives, adverbs have no singular or plural form.

              V   **ADV**

The soldier fought **bravely**.

         ADV **ADJ**

I am **very** fond of toffee.

          ADV   **ADV**

Jack ran **very swiftly**.

To check if a word is an adverb, the questions "How?" "When?" "Where?" and "How often?" can be asked.

The boy skipped **happily** along the road.

"How did the boy skip?" – Happily. Therefore, "happily" is an adverb.

I went **outside**.

"Where did I go?" – Outside. Therefore, "outside" is an adverb.

Adverbs can be used in many different positions in the sentence.

Frequently I eat out.
I **frequently** eat out.
I eat out **frequently**.

Most adverbs are formed by adding -*ly* to the adjective form.

Examples

          ADJ   **ADJ**

He was a **brave** soldier.   She is a **competent** truck driver.

          ADV   **ADV**

He fought **bravely**.   She drives trucks **competently**.

Some adverbs and adjectives have the same form.

deep	hard	late	low
early	high	leisurely	much
far	kindly	little	near
fast			

The adverb forms "highly," "lowly," "deeply," "nearly," "hardly," and "lately" exist, but they have different meanings from the adverb form without -*ly*.

Examples

          ADV

The seagull soared **high** above the rocks. ("*Where* did the seagull fly?" – A long way above the rocks.)

          ADV

The people spoke **highly** of their governor. ("*How* did the people speak?" – Favorably, or with praise.)

The adverbs "warmly," "hotly," "coolly," "coldly," "presently," "shortly," "scarcely," and "barely" have different meanings from their adjective forms.

Examples

> **ADJ**
> It was a **hot** day. (The temperature was high.)

> **ADV**
> They debated the issue **hotly**. (They showed strong emotions during the debate.)

3. Is the word form correct for its position in the sentence? Use the word endings (suffixes) to help identify the word forms.

The employ**er**'s enthusi**asm** infect**ed** all the employ**ees** equal**ly**.

-er, -or, and *-ee* are endings used for people.
-ism and *-asm* are endings used for nouns.
-ed is an ending for verbs and adjectives.
-ly is an ending for most adverbs and some adjectives.

Look at the following chart for endings that can help you identify word forms.

Nouns	Verbs	Adjectives	Adverbs
-acy (-cy)			
-age			
-al		-al (-ial, -ical)	
-ance (-ence)			
-ant (-ent)		-ant (-ent)	
-ate	-ate	-ate	
-ation			
-dom			
-ee			
-eer			
-en	-en	-en	
-er (-or)			
-ese		-ese	
-ess (-tress)			
-ful		-ful	
-hood			
-ian (-an)		-ian	
-ia			
-ic (-ics)		-ic	
-id			
-ide			
-in (-ine)			
-ing	-ing	-ing	
-ion			
-ism			
-ist			
-ite			
-ity			
-let (-lette)			
-ling			
-ment			
-ness			

-ocracy -ry (-ary, -ery) -ship -ster -tion (-sion) -tive -y (-ie)	-ed -er -ify -ize	-y -ed -er -able (-ible) -ile -ish -ive (-ative, -itive) -less -like -ly -ous (-eous, -ious)	-ly -ward -wise

Use Exercises S37–S42 to develop your skills in identifying the correct word forms and their positions.

Exercise S37   *Identifying suffixes*

Identify the following as a noun (N), a verb (V), an adjective (ADJ), or an adverb (ADV) by the word ending.

Example   __N__ department

You should write "N" in the space because the ending *-ment* indicates a noun.

1. _____ perfectionist
2. _____ energetic
3. _____ childhood
4. _____ fantasize
5. _____ graceful
6. _____ eagerly
7. _____ allowance
8. _____ suitable

9. _____ ability
10. _____ hasten
11. _____ sponsorship
12. _____ jovial
13. _____ commemorate
14. _____ publicly
15. _____ happiness

Answers to Exercise S37 are on page 521.

Exercise S38   *Identifying functions*

Identify the underlined word as a noun (N), a verb (V), an adjective (ADJ), or an adverb (ADV). Use word endings as clues.

Example   __N__ Anger was voiced against the installation of nuclear missiles.

1. _____ The Portuguese used to trade <u>extensively</u> with Bahrain in centuries past.

2. _____ The *Sojourner Rover*'s <u>successful</u> maneuvers on the Martian surface were watched by television viewers and Internet users around the world.

3. _____ Diseases such as malaria still <u>threaten</u> the lives of millions of people.

4. _____ The number of children per <u>household</u> has been steadily declining.

5. _____ From the <u>practical</u> point of view, one map system is as good as another.

6. _____ Marie Curie was the first <u>scientist</u> to win two Nobel Prizes in science.

7. _____ New technology has allowed us to <u>computerize</u> many educational programs.

8. _____ The streets of desert towns were <u>purposely</u> made narrow to provide the maximum amount of shade.

9. _____ Company managers are concerned by their staff's <u>private</u> use of the Internet during working hours.

10. _____ In 1887, John Styth Pemberton sold his invention, "Coca-Cola," for the <u>extremely</u> small sum of $283.29.

Extended practice: Write as many forms as possible for the underlined words. Then use them in sentences.

Answers to Exercise S38 are on page 522.

Exercise S39   *Checking noun forms*

If the underlined word is not in its noun form, write the noun form.

Example   In 238 B.C.E. the Seleucids were eclipsed by a nomadic Central Asian <u>tribal</u>, the Parthians.

_____tribe_____

1. Social interaction involves both verbal and nonverbal forms of <u>interaction</u>.

_____

2. The <u>restore</u> of Michelangelo's Sistine Chapel frescoes was completed several years ago.

_____

3. In 1975, the Ames test implicated <u>peroxide</u> in hair dyes as a cancer agent.

_____

4. Worshipers find <u>tranquil</u> in the great naves of medieval cathedrals.

_____

5. A royal wedding is the cause of media <u>exciting</u> around the world.

_____

6. The introduction of new <u>various</u> of apples and other crops has increased yields on many farms.

_____

7. Lack of transportation is a major <u>impede</u> to development in remote areas.

   _____

8. <u>Smoke</u> that escapes from a burning cigarette can be unpleasant for bystanders.

   _____

9. <u>Immigrated</u> from a wide variety of countries have given the United States cultural diversity.

   _____

10. Acts of vandalism are frequently blamed on low <u>employed</u> rates among youth.

    _____

Answers to Exercise S39 are on page 522.

Exercise S40   **Checking verb forms**

If the underlined word is not in its verb form, write the verb form.

1. Roaches <u>tolerant</u> and even thrive in climatic extremes.

   _____

2. Many farmers <u>fertilize</u> their crops with fish emulsion and cattle manure.

   _____

3. Each year bees <u>pollinate</u> several billion dollars' worth of bee-dependent crops.

   _____

4. Thirty centuries ago Phoenicians were the first to <u>establishment</u> colonies on the coast of modern-day Tunisia.

   _____

5. Maxwell's four equations neatly <u>summarize</u> the behavior of electric and magnetic fields.

   _____

6. In folktales the wolf usually <u>symbols</u> greed and rapacity.

   _____

7. Genetic factors alone cannot <u>explanation</u> criminal tendencies.

   _____

8. Lake Tahoe provides year-round recreation for those who <u>patronize</u> its facilities.

   _____

9. Many cultures still dramatically <u>verbal</u> their pasts in song.

   _____

10. Public appreciation of a new building can <u>reverse</u> radically within a few years.

_____

Answers to Exercise S40 are on page 522.

Exercise S41   *Checking adjective forms*

If the underlined word is not in its adjective form, write the adjective form.

1. Studies of newborn infants show that some <u>perceptual</u> processes, such as depth perception, may be inherited.

_____

2. Child development specialists have noted that <u>cooperate</u> games encourage self-esteem in young children.

_____

3. In the theocracy that evolved in Tibet, religious and <u>administrative</u> power centered in one person.

_____

4. The Musin-Puskin collection features many rare and unknown works of <u>historically</u> interest.

_____

5. A person's mental health can be improved by exposure to <u>beauty</u> surroundings.

_____

6. Butch Cassidy was an outlaw <u>fame</u> for robbing trains.

_____

7. The <u>deerlike</u> figures found in the Grand Canyon were made from willow shoots and have been dated as far back as 2100 B.C.E.

_____

8. The giant parade balloons seen in the <u>tradition</u> Macy's Thanksgiving Day Parade take about six months to design and <u>make</u>.

_____

9. Techniques such as <u>aerial</u> stereographic photography yield most of the detail on a map.

_____

10. The Isle of Man has over twenty Viking <u>bury</u> mounds built on its coastal ridges.

_____

Answers to Exercise S41 are on page 522.

Exercise S42   ***Checking adverb forms***

If the underlined word is not in its adverb form, write the adverb form.

1. Pesticides are necessary to maintain high crop yields because of a decreasing acreage of arable land and a <u>steadily</u> expanding population.

_____

2. Millions of dollars are donated <u>year</u> to the Red Cross to aid people in disaster-struck areas.

_____

3. Scientists can observe a chemical's effect in rats and <u>reasonable</u> expect a similar effect in humans.

_____

4. In communes, the land and products are <u>collective</u> owned.

_____

5. The <u>mildly</u> paranoid person may lead a relatively normal life.

_____

6. In early American colonial settlements, secular education was <u>virtual</u> nonexistent.

_____

7. While <u>undeniable</u> appealing, burros have also been destructive.

_____

8. Dolphins, whales, and many other sea creatures use <u>highly</u> sophisticated navigation systems.

_____

9. On November 25, 1872, something dreadful happened on board the brigantine *Mary Celeste*, causing all crew members to <u>hasty</u> abandon ship.

_____

10. Mass strandings of whales occur repeatedly on the same shores but <u>seldom</u> during heavy seas.

_____

Answers to Exercise S42 are on page 522.

PRACTICE WITH WORD CHOICES

The following words are frequently seen on the Computer-Based TOEFL® Test.

and, or, but
either . . . or, neither . . . nor, both . . . and

so, as, such as
too, enough, so
many, much, few, little
like, alike, unlike
another, the other, the others, other, others

Ask yourself the following questions when you encounter these words.

1. Have the words "and," "or," and "but" been used correctly?

(A) "And" joins two or more words, phrases, or clauses of similar value or equal importance.

> We went swimming **and** boating.
> We looked in the house **and** around the yard for the lost necklace.
> We booked the flight, **and** we picked up the tickets the same day.

When "and" joins two equal subjects, the verb must be plural.

> Swimming **and** boating *are* fun.

(B) "Or" joins two or more words, phrases, or clauses that contain the idea of a choice.

> We could go swimming **or** boating.
> We could look in the house **or** around the yard for the lost necklace.
> We could book the flight now, **or** we could wait until tomorrow.

(C) "But" shows a contrast between two or more words, phrases, or clauses.

> We went swimming **but** not boating.
> We didn't look in the house **but** around the yard for the lost necklace.
> We booked the flight, **but** we haven't picked up the tickets.

2. Have the words "either . . . or," "neither . . . nor," and "both . . . and" been used correctly?

(A) "Either" is used with "or" to express alternatives.

> We can **either** go to the park **or** stay home and watch TV.

(B) "Neither" is used with "nor" to express negative alternatives.

> He **neither** called **nor** came to visit me. (He didn't call, and he didn't visit me.)

(C) "Both" is used with "and" to combine two words, phrases, or clauses.

> He had **both** the time **and** the patience to be a good parent.

3. Have the words "so," "as," and "such as" been used correctly?

(A) "So" can connect two independent clauses. It means "therefore" or "as a result."

> She was hungry, **so** she ate early.

(B) "As" can be used to introduce an adverb clause. It can mean "while," "like," "because," "the way," or "since."

> **As** I understood it, Max was the winner. ("The way I understood it . . .")
> It began to snow **as** I was walking. ("It began to snow while I was walking.")

(C) "Such as" is used to introduce examples.

> He likes to wear casual clothes, **such as** a T-shirt and blue jeans.

4.   *Have the words "too," "enough," and "so" been used correctly?*

(A)   "Too" means more than necessary. It precedes an adjective or adverb.

> The food was **too** cold to eat.
> He ran **too** slowly to win the race.

(B)   "Enough" means a sufficient amount or number. It follows an adjective or adverb.

> The day was warm **enough** for a picnic.
> The girl swam fast **enough** to save her friend.

(C)   "So" can be used in adverb clauses of cause/result before adverbs and adjectives. (The use of "that" in the examples below is optional.)

> The rain fell **so** hard (that) the river overflowed.
> The boy ate **so** many cookies (that) he got a stomachache.

5.   *Have the words "many," "much," "few," and "little" been used correctly?*

(A)   "Many" and "few" are used with count nouns.

> **Few** cities are as crowded as Tokyo.

(B)   "Much" and "little" are used with noncount nouns.

> They have made **little** progress on the contract.

6.   *Have the words "like," "alike," and "unlike" been used correctly?*

(A)   When "like" is a preposition followed by an object, it means "similar."

> **Like** my father, I am an architect. ("My father is an architect, and I am one, too.")

(B)   "Unlike" is a preposition followed by an object and means "not similar."

> **Unlike** my mother, her mother has a full-time job. ("Her mother has a full-time job, but my mother does not.")

(C)   "Alike" can be an adverb meaning "equally" or an adjective meaning "similar."

> *As an adverb*   The tuition increase was opposed by students and teachers **alike**.
> *As an adjective*   My brother and sister are **alike** in many ways.

7.   *Have the words "another," "the other," "other," "the others," and "others" been used correctly?*

(A)   "Another" + a singular noun means "one more."

> I want **another** peach.
> I want **another** one.

(B)   "Another" means "one more."

> I've just eaten a peach, but I want **another**.

(C)   "The other" + a singular noun means "the last of the group being discussed."

> We bought three peaches. My brother and I each ate one. We left **the other** peach on the table.

(D)   "The other" + a plural noun means "the rest of the group."

> This peach is rotten, but **the other** peaches in the box are good.

(E)   "The other" + a noncount noun means "all the rest."

> We put the oranges in a bowl and stored **the other** fruit in the refrigerator.

(F) "The other" means "the remaining one of two."

I had two peaches. I ate one and put **the other** in a bowl.

(G) "Other" + a plural noun means "more of the group being discussed."

There are **other** peaches in the box.

(H) "Other" + a noncount noun means "more of the group."

There is **other** fruit besides peaches in the box.

(I) "Others" means "different members of a group."

There are many types of peaches in the market. Some are from California, but **others** are not.

(J) "The others" means "the rest of the different members of a group."

These peaches are from Florida. **The others** are not.

8. Have any of the following words been used incorrectly?

> able/enable
> accept/except
> after/afterwards
> among/between
> amount/number/quantity
> aside/beside/besides
> big/great
> do/make
> for/since
> good/well
> listen/hear
> live/life/alive
> people/person
> rather/rather than
> say/tell
> see/watch/look at
> separate/apart
> some/somewhat/somewhere

Check your dictionary to find the differences in the preceding list. Add more words as you find them in your studies.

Use Exercises S43–S50 to develop your skills in identifying the correct word choice.

Exercise S43   **Checking "and," "or," and "but"**

If the underlined word is used incorrectly, write the correction in the space.

Example   Eggs can be boiled <u>or</u> then peeled. *and*

1. All <u>but</u> two of the states in the United States are part of a contiguous landmass. _____

2. For North Africans, couscous is both a staple food <u>or</u> a part of their cultural identity. _____

3. New types of tomatoes have been developed that can resist high <u>but</u> low temperatures. _____

4. Istanbul is a city that spans two world cultures – the Oriental <u>and</u> the Occidental. _____

5. A fir, <u>or</u> pine, is most commonly used for the traditional Christmas tree. _____

6. Land provides people not only with food and clothing, <u>and</u> houses and buildings as well. _____

7. Educational sites on the Internet provide more opportunities for students <u>but</u> teachers alike. _____

8. America was probably not discovered by Columbus <u>and</u> by Vikings. _____

Answers to Exercise S43 are on page 522.

Exercise S44   **Checking "either . . . or," "neither . . . nor," and "both . . . and"**

If the underlined word is used incorrectly, write the correction in the space.

1. Antiochus I claimed descent from <u>both</u> Alexander the Great and the Persian monarch King Darius. _____

2. Neither the Mormon Trail <u>or</u> the Oregon Trail was easy to follow. _____

3. Goats provide both milk for cheese <u>or</u> wool for clothing. _____

4. When search parties failed to find the missing heir, Michael Rockefeller, authorities declared that he had <u>both</u> drowned or been eaten by sharks. _____

5. People think of voodoo as either an obscure ritual <u>nor</u> pure superstition. _____

6. In 1927, critics gave bad reviews to Buster Keaton's film *The General*, which is now regarded as both a classic <u>or</u> the best work of a cinematic genius. _____

7. Entrepreneurs who do a lot of traveling need <u>neither</u> a first-rate assistant and good time-management skills. _____

8. <u>Either</u> Anne Bonny nor Mary Read chose to live conventional female lifestyles, but became pirates instead. _____

Answers to Exercise S44 are on page 522.

Exercise S45   **Checking "so," "as," and "such as"**

If the underlined word or words are used incorrectly, write the correction in the space.

1. There are remains of Rajput art and architecture, <u>as</u> the cusped arches and traces of painting on the ceiling. _____

2. <u>As</u> Einstein suggested eighty years ago, space can vibrate. _____

3. Whiskers are very sensitive, <u>so</u> animals can use them to avoid obstacles in the dark. _____

4. <u>Such as</u> rockets zoom around in space, technicians track their progress on computer terminals. _____

5. Organisms respond to stimuli <u>so</u> pressure, light, and temperature. _____

6. During the period of the American Revolution, colonists took part in subversive acts, <u>such as</u> the Boston Tea Party. _____

7. The hormone androvine acts <u>so</u> a painkiller and is six times as strong as morphine.
_____

8. During a heart attack, the blood flow to the heart is blocked, <u>such as</u> the cells of the heart muscle die from the lack of oxygen. _____

Answers to Exercise S45 are on page 522.

Exercise S46   Checking "too," "enough," and "so"

If the underlined word is used incorrectly, write the correction in the space.

1. The West was <u>so</u> dry, the wood shrank on the wagons. _____

2. The grip of the Venus's-flytrap is <u>too</u> tight that an insect cannot escape from the leaf. _____

3. Napoleon Bonaparte calculated that the three pyramids at Giza contained <u>enough</u> stone to build a high wall around the entire boundary of France. _____

4. The walls of ancient cities had to be robust <u>so</u> to withstand assaults from powerful siege weapons. _____

5. What made porphyry, a beautiful fine-grained building stone, <u>too</u> valuable for the Romans was that they knew of only one place to quarry it. _____

6. According to conservationists, not <u>enough</u> is being done to save endangered species. _____

7. Unfortunately, <u>enough</u> many mail deliverers are still bitten by dogs. _____

8. If incubating eggs become <u>enough</u> warm, the chicks will not hatch. _____

Answers to Exercise S46 are on page 522.

Exercise S47   Checking "many," "much," "few," and "little"

If the underlined word is used incorrectly, write the correction in the space.

1. Intergalactic adventures are what <u>many</u> of today's animation consists of.
_____

2. <u>Little</u> scientists doubt the existence of an ozone hole over the polar regions.
_____

3. Yachting attracts <u>many</u> of the world's most famous and wealthy people.
_____

4. George Cadbury provided a pleasant housing estate for his chocolate factory workers, <u>much</u> of whom had previously lived in appalling conditions. _____

5. The rhinoceros has <u>few</u> natural enemies. _____

6. The artist Vincent van Gogh received <u>little</u> recognition during his lifetime.

_____

7. Heavy fines and jail sentences have made <u>few</u> difference in preventing poaching in many game reserves. _____

8. Tropical fish and songbirds give <u>many</u> pleasure to people who need to relax.

_____

Answers to Exercise S47 are on page 522.

Exercise S48   ***Checking "like," "alike," and "unlike"***

If the underlined word is used incorrectly, write the correction in the space.

1. The Cannes Film Festival exists, <u>like</u> most film festivals, for the purpose of awarding prizes. _____

2. Identical twins are <u>like</u> in many ways and are often difficult to tell apart.

_____

3. The harpsichord is a keyboard instrument <u>alike</u> the piano. _____

4. The Topkapi Palace encompasses the forms of grand monuments and of vernacular styles <u>like</u>. _____

5. Occasionally dolphins, <u>like</u> whales, get stranded on beaches. _____

6. <u>Like</u> automobiles, which use a four-stroke engine, motorcycles use a two-stroke engine. _____

7. Many sailing techniques of today and those of centuries past are <u>alike</u>.

_____

8. <u>Unlike</u> the coyote, which hunts in packs, the fox prefers to hunt alone.

_____

Answers to Exercise S48 are on page 522.

Exercise S49   ***Checking "another," "the other," "other," "the others," and "others"***

If the underlined word or words are used incorrectly, write the correction in the space.

1. Security threads, watermarks, tiny hidden print, and <u>another</u> hard-to-copy features are incorporated into paper money. _____

2. One of Mars's two moons is called Phobos, and <u>other</u> is called Deimos.

   _____

3. Like most of <u>the other</u> language skills, reading requires practice. _____

4. Roller coasters, gyro drops, and <u>other</u> exciting amusement park rides maintain their popularity with the thrill-seeking public. _____

5. Breathing into a paper bag is yet <u>others</u> cure for the hiccups. _____

6. Wool, as well as certain <u>other</u> fabrics, can cause skin irritation. _____

7. Some artists use traditional designs while <u>another</u> use more modern themes.

   _____

8. Historians believe that the charges against Nikolai Bukharin and <u>another</u> old Bolsheviks were fraudulent. _____

Answers to Exercise S49 are on page 522.

Exercise S50   *Checking frequently confused words*

Circle the underlined word that correctly completes the sentence.

Example   Disney World has many robots that look (alive)/life.

You should circle "alive" because an adjective is needed. "Alive" is an adjective, whereas "life" is a noun.

1. Walls that are smooth and flat <u>able/enable</u> sound to bounce back as an echo.

2. In California's Grand Kinetic Racers Challenge, the first sculpture-vehicle to fall <u>separate/apart</u> wins a special booby prize.

3. New security features make paper money <u>some/somewhat</u> harder to counterfeit.

4. Satellites have made communication with distant <u>person/people</u> fast and efficient.

5. A great <u>number/amount</u> of buffalo were shot from train windows in nineteenth-century America.

6. Humans <u>have done/have made</u> great advances in technology at the expense of the environment.

7. The American national symbol, the bald eagle, is <u>live/alive</u> and thriving in Alaska.

8. Prudent savers regularly set <u>aside/beside</u> a percentage of their paychecks.

9. The Mayans' <u>observance/observation</u> of the heavenly bodies helped them make an accurate calendar.

10. The Rocky Mountains boast a large <u>number/quantity</u> of peaks over ten thousand feet high.

Answers to Exercise S50 are on page 522.

CHECK YOUR PROGRESS

Check your progress in using the skills you have been practicing in Exercises S37–S50 by completing the following mini-test. This exercise uses a format similar to that used in the Structure Section of the Computer-Based TOEFL® Test. If you are unfamiliar with how to answer questions on the Computer-Based TOEFL® Test, see the Tutorial on pages 22–23.

Exercise S51   Mini-test

Select the letter of the correct answer.

1. The earliest references to Jericho so a city
        A   B
   date back several thousand years.
    C   D

2. In medieval times helmets were _____ and varied in shape from reign to reign.
   (A) most of metal
   (B) the most of metal
   (C) mostly of metal
   (D) the most metal

3. Much unknown plants and animals are
    A
   disappearing as the tropical forests
           B   C
   are destroyed.
      D

4. Blowing out birthday candles is an ancient test to see if a growing child is _____ to blow out a greater number each year.
   (A) enough strong
   (B) stronger enough
   (C) enough stronger
   (D) strong enough

5. Wooden grows more slowly
    A   B   C
   in summer and is darker.
               D

6. While searching for gold, the Spanish found the Grand Canyon _____.
   (A) be an impassable barrier
   (B) was an impassably barrier
   (C) an impassably barrier
   (D) to be an impassable barrier

7. Cloudy recorded in time lapses moved
    A   B
   counterclockwise faster than the planet rotated.
        C   D

8. _____, weapons and stable gear were placed upon the grave.
   (A) In ancient Greek traditional
   (B) In ancient Greek tradition
   (C) In ancient traditional Greek
   (D) In tradition ancient Greek

9. The figure known as the Long Man of

   Wilmington was $\underset{A}{\underline{\text{carved}}}$ on a $\underset{B}{\underline{\text{hillside}}}$

   $\underset{C}{\underline{\text{enough}}}$ that it could be seen from $\underset{D}{\underline{\text{a}}}$

   distance of several miles.

10. Transplanting organs _____ has proved easier
    than transplanting muscles.
    (A) such hearts and kidneys
    (B) as such hearts and kidneys as
    (C) so such hearts and kidneys
    (D) such as hearts and kidneys

11. The grenade is a small bomb $\underset{A}{\underline{\text{done}}}$ to be

    thrown by $\underset{B}{\underline{\text{hand}}}$ $\underset{C}{\underline{\text{or}}}$ shot from $\underset{D}{\underline{\text{a}}}$ modified rifle.

12. There is not enough room in zoos to house
    _____ subspecies that need preserving.
    (A) all the others
    (B) all another
    (C) all the other
    (D) all others

13. The $\underset{A}{\underline{\text{high}}}$ cost of testing new pesticides

    $\underset{B}{\underline{\text{inevitably}}}$ discourages the $\underset{C}{\underline{\text{develop}}}$ of viruses,

    protozoa, bacteria, and $\underset{D}{\underline{\text{molds}}}$ for pest control.

14. The glider uses gravity to _____ and updrafts
    of air to gain altitude.
    (A) keeping flying
    (B) keep flying
    (C) keeps flying
    (D) kept flying

15. $\underset{A}{\underline{\text{Unlike}}}$ a tractor $\underset{B}{\underline{\text{is}}}$, a mule $\underset{C}{\underline{\text{won't turn}}}$ over

    on a steep hillside $\underset{D}{\underline{\text{and}}}$ crush the driver.

16. _____ is not uncommon in elderly people who
    stand up suddenly.
    (A) Fainting
    (B) Faint
    (C) Faints
    (D) The faint

17. The rattlesnake $\underset{A}{\underline{\text{coils}}}$ up to $\underset{B}{\underline{\text{able}}}$ itself

    to $\underset{C}{\underline{\text{spring}}}$ forward and strike its $\underset{D}{\underline{\text{victim}}}$.

18. Common laws are rules based on _____ or
    long usage and are usually not recorded
    as laws.
    (A) customarily
    (B) customary
    (C) customize
    (D) custom

19. A <u>baby</u> elephant <u>sucks</u> its trunk <u>alike</u>
      A   B   C

     a human baby sucks its <u>thumb</u>.
                           D

20. Birds that breed on high cliffs have pear-shaped eggs that roll in a tight circle, making them _____ less likely to roll off the cliff.
(A) somewhere
(B) sometimes
(C) something
(D) somewhat

Answers to Exercise S51 are on page 522.

PRACTICE WITH CLAUSES

A clause is a group of words that contains a subject and a verb. Ask yourself these questions when checking clauses.

1. Is the clause independent?

Independent clauses are complete sentences. They contain a subject and verb. Three different types of sentences contain independent clauses.

(A) Simple sentences

Simple sentences are made up of one independent clause.

      S V
The cat ran.

                S   **V**
Last night the fat, black cat swiftly ran under the speeding blue sports car.

(B) Compound sentences

Compound sentences are made up of two (or sometimes more) independent clauses that are joined by a conjunction such as "and," "but," "or," "nor," and "yet."

      S V   **S V**
The cat ran **and** the dog chased it.

     S   **V**   **S ___ V ___**
Kelly wanted to take the geometry course, **but** it was offered at the same time as her biochemistry lab.

     S ___ V ___   **S ___ V ___**
We could trade in our old car, **or** we could keep it as a second car.

(C) Complex sentences

Complex sentences are made up of one or more independent clauses and one or more dependent clauses. (A dependent clause is an incomplete sentence. It needs to be connected to an independent clause. See item 2 on page 231.)

            DEPENDENT
     S **_ CLAUSE _** **V**
The cat that I saw ran.

S _ **DEPENDENT CLAUSE** _   **V**

Last night the fat, black cat that I saw in the street swiftly ran under the speeding

_____ **DEPENDENT CLAUSE** _____

blue sports car as the big shaggy dog chased after it.

2. *Is the clause dependent?*

Dependent clauses have a subject and a verb, but they do not form complete sentences. They must be connected to an independent clause. Look at the following dependent clauses.

> that I saw
> as the dog played with it

Both of the clauses have a subject and a verb. However, they are not complete sentences.

> The TV program **that I saw** was interesting.

The sentence above is complete. The dependent clause "that I saw" has been connected to the independent clause "The TV program was interesting." The dependent clause gives further information; in this example, it says who saw the TV program.

> The toy was torn to pieces **as the dog played with it**.

The sentence above is complete. The dependent clause "as the dog played with it" has been connected to the independent clause "The toy was torn to pieces." The dependent clause gives additional information; in this example, it says *who* tore apart the toy (the dog) and *how* the toy was torn apart (the dog played with it).

There are three kinds of dependent clauses: noun clauses, adjective clauses, and adverb clauses. (For more information see Practice with Noun Clauses, page 233; Practice with Adjective Clauses, page 240; and Practice with Adverb Clauses, page 253.)

(A) Noun clauses, like nouns, can be used in any noun position (see Practice with Nouns, page 165).

Subject	**Who does the work** is not important.
Object	I didn't see **what they did**.
Object of the preposition	I don't understand the implications of **what he said**.

(B) Adjective clauses, like adjectives, are used to describe a noun (see Practice with Word Forms, item 2C, page 213).

> The car **that is blue** is mine.
> Sam wrote the paper **that caused the controversy**.

(C) Adverb clauses are used in the same way as an adverb (see Practice with Word Forms, item 2D, page 214). Generally, adverb clauses can appear at either end of the sentence without changing the meaning of the sentence. When an adverb clause begins the sentence, it is usually set off by a comma.

> **When I leave**, I'll take the papers.
> I'll take the papers **when I leave**.

Use Exercises S52–S53 to develop your skills in clause recognition.

Exercise S52   ***Recognizing complete simple sentences***

Write "I" if the clause is independent (a complete sentence). Write "D" if the clause is dependent (an incomplete sentence).

Examples   _D_ The eagle spreading its wings.

_I_ The rain came suddenly.

1. _____ Swimming is an invigorating sport.
2. _____ Acupuncture's start in China.
3. _____ Lightning striking a hut can kill the people inside.
4. _____ A hormone in the body called androvine.
5. _____ It has been discovered.
6. _____ To be happy is a common personal goal.
7. _____ At the foot of the peak workers using bulldozers.
8. _____ What a good idea the committee presented.

Extended practice: Correct the incomplete sentences in this exercise.

Answers to Exercise S52 are on page 523.

Exercise S53   ***Recognizing complete complex sentences***

Write "C" in the space if the sentence is complete. Write "I" if the sentence is incorrect because of missing information.

Examples   _C_ The people who lived in the wilderness of the Yukon had to be self-sufficient.

_I_ The lighthouse that had burned down no longer warning sailors of the rocks.

The second sentence cannot be understood because the verb of the independent clause is missing.

1. _____ The report on the oil spill from the Exxon Valdez oil tanker made it clear that the disaster severely damaged the region's vulnerable ecosystem.
2. _____ As British scientist Sir Gilbert Walker sorted through world weather records, he noticed that when barometric pressure rises on the east side of the Pacific, it usually falls on the west side.
3. _____ Lightning produced in cumulonimbus clouds, which occur in thunderstorms.
4. _____ The hard part is to locate the answer on the map with a gadget called a reticle.
5. _____ Slang words that are related to a specific activity and are immediately understood.
6. _____ While large numbers of eagles have long nested in national parks, only recently the birds generating outside curiosity.
7. _____ Studies into the effects of music suggest that it can serve as a type of drug which regulates behavior.
8. _____ The most convincing evidence that female chimpanzees in Tanzania use the aspilia plant for medicinal purposes.

Extended practice: Correct the incomplete sentences in this exercise.

Answers to Exercise S53 are on page 523.

PRACTICE WITH NOUN CLAUSES

Ask yourself the following questions about noun clauses.

1. *Is the clause a noun clause?*

A noun clause has a subject and a verb. It is introduced by a clause marker (see item 2 that follows) and can be used in exactly the same way as a noun. Compare the following uses of nouns and noun clauses.

As subjects	Sam's **jokes** are very funny. (noun)
	What Sam says is very funny. (noun clause)
As objects	The man told us the **address**. (noun)
	The man told us **where he lived**. (noun clause)
As objects of the preposition	I wasn't asked about the **party**. (noun)
	I wasn't asked about **who was invited**. (noun clause)

2. *Is the correct clause marker used?*

A clause marker *introduces* a clause.

Noun clause markers	Examples
"That" indicates a fact.	I knew **that** he had to go.
"What" focuses on a fact.	Everyone was surprised at **what** he brought for the picnic.
"When" indicates a time.	He told us **when** the plane would arrive.
"Where" indicates a place.	**Where** they are going on their honeymoon is a secret.
"Why" indicates a reason.	She wouldn't say **why** he left so early.
"Who" indicates a person.	**Who** sent the letter is a mystery to me.
"How many" indicates a quantity.	I've lost count of **how many** times I've broken my glasses.
"How much" indicates an amount.	He wasn't paying attention to **how much** he ate.
"How" indicates a manner.	He showed us **how** he was going to win the race.
"Which" indicates a choice.	I didn't know **which** book I was supposed to read.
"Whether" indicates two or more alternatives.	I didn't know **whether** I should bring my bike or leave it at home.
"Whose" indicates possession.	I never found out **whose** car was parked outside our house.
"Whom" indicates a person.	Sue didn't know to **whom** he was engaged.
"If" indicates alternatives.	I didn't know **if** I should bring my bike.

When used as clause markers, "if" and "whether" are interchangeable.

3. *Is the clause marker missing?*

Wh- words used as clause markers cannot be left out of the sentence. "That" can sometimes be left out.

(A) "That" cannot be left out if the noun clause is the subject of the sentence.

Subject position   **That he passed** is a miracle.

(B) "That" can be left out if the noun clause is the object of the sentence.

> *Object position*   Janet noticed **that the window was broken**.

This sentence is also correct without the word "that":

> Janet noticed **the window was broken**.

4. Is there a subject and a verb in the noun clause?

The noun clause must have a subject and a verb to be complete.

$$\text{S} \quad \text{V}$$

One additional feature of the car is **that it has push-button windows**.

$$\text{S} \quad \text{V}$$

What was in the box surprised everyone.

5. Does the noun clause complete the independent clause?

If the noun clause is used in the subject position, there must be a verb in the independent clause.

$$\underline{\quad\quad} \text{S} \underline{\quad\quad} \quad \text{V}$$

That he might fall worries me.

If the noun clause is used in the object position, there must be a subject and a verb in the independent clause.

$$\text{S} \quad \text{V} \underline{\quad} \text{OBJECT} \underline{\quad}$$

Sam knew **what he had to do**.

6. Does the verb tense in the noun clause agree with the verb tense in the independent clause?

> *Correct*   Last week Alfred asked where we were going.

"Last week" indicates that the action of asking took place in the past. The verb tense "were going" indicates that the action of going could have occurred at any point in time after Alfred asked the question.

> *Correct*   Last week Alfred asked where we had gone.

"Last week" indicates that the action of asking took place in the past. The verb tense "had gone" indicates that the action of going occurred before Alfred asked the question.

> *Incorrect*   Last week Alfred asked where we will go.

The verb tense "will go" (future) in the noun clause does not agree with the verb tense "asked" (past) in the independent clause.

Use Exercises S54–S59 to develop your skills in identifying noun clauses.

Exercise S54   *Identifying noun clauses*

Circle the words that identify the following phrases.

Examples   that book was very interesting

> (noun clause)/(independent clause)

that the book was on the table

> (noun clause)/ independent clause

where is the book

> noun clause /(independent clause)

You should circle both "noun clause" and "independent clause" in the first example because the phrase could be either a noun clause or an independent clause. You should circle "noun clause" in the second example because the phrase is a noun clause and needs to be in the noun position of an independent clause. You should circle "independent clause" in the third example because the phrase is an independent clause in the question form.

1. that he is a good actor
   noun clause/independent clause

2. whichever program you prefer
   noun clause/independent clause

3. that crisis happened only a few years ago
   noun clause/independent clause

4. who is he
   noun clause/independent clause

5. whose house is across the street
   noun clause/independent clause

6. where she lives
   noun clause/independent clause

7. when are you going
   noun clause/independent clause

8. that picture was in the library
   noun clause/independent clause

> *Answers to Exercise S54 are on page 523.*

Exercise S55   *Identifying noun clause functions*

Underline the noun clause. Write "S" in the space if the noun clause is the subject and "O" if the clause is the object.

Examples   _S_ That most fast-food meals are high in fat has become an increasing concern.

   _O_ It is easy to understand why fast-food restaurants are so popular.

1. _____ How the buildings are constructed to keep their inhabitants cool is one of the most striking aspects of traditional Bahraini architecture.

2. _____ What many doctors advise is a vacation away from the hustle and bustle of urban life.

3. _____ When the city of Rome was actually founded is a matter of dispute among historians.

4. _____ Marie Curie showed that a woman can be as good a scientist as a man can be.

5. _____ The psychologist Abraham Maslow argued that all human beings have five levels of needs.

6. _____ In nonverbal communication, what gestures mean in one particular culture may be very different in another culture, thus causing misunderstandings.

7. _____ Volcanologists announce when an eruption is imminent so that people can be evacuated from the threatened area.

8. _____ That old cities lose their charm in their zeal to modernize is a common perception.

> *Answers to Exercise S55 are on page 523.*

Exercise S56   ***Locating subjects and verbs in independent clauses***

Locate the subject and verb of the independent clause. Underline the verb and circle the complete subject.

Example   (That lightning is electrical in nature) <u>was suggested</u> by Benjamin Franklin.

1. That rent-control laws may inhibit landlords from repairing properties is unfortunate but true.

2. Studies of newborn infants show that some perceptual processes, such as depth perception, may be inherited.

3. How glass is blown in a cylinder was demonstrated at the Stuart Crystal Factory.

4. A top architect lamented that cultural uniqueness has been replaced by international sameness.

5. Why consumers hesitated to buy the controversial digital audiotape players is a subject the article ignored.

6. Whom the late Dr. Bishopstone left his fortune to will be revealed this afternoon.

7. Major studies have indicated that there may be a causal link between televised violence and aggressive behavior by viewers.

8. What the manufacturer does to syrup results in one of three basic kinds of candy.

Answers to Exercise S56 are on page 523.

Exercise S57   ***Locating subjects and verbs in noun clauses***

Locate the subject and verb of the noun clause. Underline the verb and circle the subject.

Example   One of the characteristics of leather is that (it) <u>has</u> a fibrous structure.

1. Whose design is ultimately chosen for major civic projects is often a matter of controversy.

2. Herbal-medicine companies stress that no alcohol or chemicals are included in their formulas.

3. In 590 B.C.E. the Greek traveler Solon learned from Egyptian historians how a disaster had struck the island of Thera.

4. That many nonsmokers find the odor of cigarettes objectionable surprises many smokers.

5. How radioactive antibodies can help locate tumors was discussed at the conference.

6. A leading professor of tropical medicine said that far too little is being done to fight malaria.

7. That the poverty action group was set up in the 1970s was a sign of public awareness during that decade.

8. How witch doctors cure some illnesses still mystifies physicians today.

Extended practice: Locate the subject and verb in the independent clauses in Exercise S56 and the subject and verb in the noun clauses in Exercise S57.

Answers to Exercise S57 are on page 524.

Exercise S58   ***Checking verbs in noun clauses***

If the verb in the noun clause is used incorrectly, cross it out and write the correct form.

Example   Mary wondered what the extent of the destruction ~~will~~ *would* be.

1. In 1776, the U.S. Congress resolved that the authority of the British crown will be suppressed.

2. The orders to General J. Pershing were that he was to capture Mexico's revolutionary leader, Pancho Villa.

3. Apprentices sometimes fear that they might not have been able to master the intricacies of their chosen craft.

4. That the rather large President Taft will get stuck in a White House bathtub was an incentive for the installation of an oversized tub.

5. What we will already learn about tornadoes has contributed to reducing the casualty rates.

6. East Coker is where the Anglo-American poet T. S. Eliot was buried in 1965.

7. That Thomas Hardy used real locations in his novels is disguised by his having altered place names.

8. Before the flight of Sputnik, many people believed that space exploration is impossible.

Answers to Exercise S58 are on page 524.

Exercise S59   *Choosing correct clause markers*

Circle the letter of the clause marker that correctly completes the sentence.

Example   _____ raiding for camels was a significant part of Bedouin life was documented in Wilfred Thesiger's *Arabian Sands*.
(A) That
(B) Which
(C) What
(D) Where

You should circle (A) because "that" is the clause marker indicating a fact.

1. Bracewell told the people _____ effect a drought would have on the Great Plains.
   (A) that
   (B) how
   (C) what
   (D) then

2. The thieves knew precisely _____ the collection of priceless jewels was hidden.
   (A) where
   (B) then
   (C) who
   (D) what

3. _____ adults come to night classes eager to learn has been the experience of most adult-education teachers.
   (A) That
   (B) When
   (C) Where
   (D) Which

4. Just _____ created the fantastic jade masterpiece is unknown.
   (A) whether
   (B) why
   (C) who
   (D) by whom

5. Reports have recommended _____ colleges should prize good teaching as well as good research.
   (A) not only
   (B) both
   (C) that
   (D) where

6. Every four years the International Olympic Committee selects _____ city will hold the next games.
   (A) those
   (B) which
   (C) that
   (D) both

7. Beauty-contest coaches teach the contestants _____ they should walk, sit, and even apply makeup.
   - (A) what
   - (B) which
   - (C) then
   - (D) how

8. Political researchers have explained _____ female candidates have a difficult time raising campaign money.
   - (A) which reasons
   - (B) because
   - (C) the result
   - (D) why

Answers to Exercise S59 are on page 524.

CHECK YOUR PROGRESS

Check your progress in using the skills you have been practicing in Exercises S52–S59 by completing the following mini-test. This exercise uses a format similar to that used in the Structure Section of the Computer-Based TOEFL® Test. If you are unfamiliar with how to answer questions on the Computer-Based TOEFL® Test, see the Tutorial on pages 22–23.

Exercise S60   Mini-test

Select the letter of the correct answer.

1. _____ Freud and Marx were motivated primarily by compassionate concern for suffering humanity is elaborated upon in Fromm's biography.
   - (A) Both are
   - (B) What both
   - (C) Both
   - (D) That both

2. An understanding of the salesperson does
         A   B
   to get the potential buyer to make a purchase
               C
   can be helpful protection for dealing with
    D
   manipulative sales techniques.

3. Scientists have speculated that the destruction of Earth's ozone layer would _____ us to damaging ultraviolet rays.
   - (A) exposed
   - (B) have been exposed
   - (C) expose
   - (D) have been exposing

4. The study of how people use and perceive
         A   B
   their social and personal space be called
    C   D
   proxemics.

5. _____ Latin speakers originally borrowed the word "caupo," meaning "merchant," from Germanic speakers or vice versa is not clear.
   - (A) Then
   - (B) Whether
   - (C) Because
   - (D) Which

6. By studying London's mortality rates,
     A   B
   John Graunt showed however patterns
            C
   of sickness indicated a correlation between
        D
   illness, diet, and lifestyles.

7. The problem facing most tourists is _____ among so many possibilities.
   (A) what should they see
   (B) what they should see
   (C) should they see what
   (D) they should see what

8. Fuel cells <u>convert</u> hydrogen into electricity
              A
   so <u>that</u> what <u>come</u> out of the exhaust pipe
      B   C
   <u>is</u> not smoke but warm water vapor.
   D

9. That acne _____ by daily consumption of zinc-sulfate tablets gives patients much encouragement.
   (A) has been controlled
   (B) controlled
   (C) will have been controlled
   (D) had controlled

10. Astronomer Edwin Powell Hubble proved

    <u>when</u> other galaxies exist <u>beyond</u> Earth's own
     A   B
    galaxy and <u>that</u> galaxies are constantly moving
            C
    away from one <u>another</u>.
               D

11. One of the less well-known treasures of Paris is _____ Parisians call "La Mosquée d'Islam."
    (A) that
    (B) what
    (C) why
    (D) where

12. The clothes <u>that</u> you <u>choose</u> <u>tell an</u> observer
             A   B   C
    a great deal <u>about it</u> who you are.
              D

13. _____ patients should try to reduce needless office visits for colds and minor respiratory illnesses.
    (A) Doctors that agree
    (B) Doctors agree that
    (C) Doctors agreeing that
    (D) That doctors agree

14. A famous trial lawyer once noted <u>that</u> jury
                              A
    members seldom convicted a <u>person they</u> liked
                             B
    nor <u>acquit</u> one <u>they</u> disliked.
      C   D

15. Differences among environmental groups illustrate _____ a broad range of philosophies and tactics.
    (A) that is
    (B) that is there
    (C) that there
    (D) that there is

16. <u>That</u> workers <u>involved</u> in the decision-making
     A   B
    process <u>approach</u> their tasks with more
            C
    enthusiasm <u>have</u> been documented.
              D

17. Science has not yet made a machine that can learn _____ a young child can learn in a few days – how to tie a pair of shoes.
    (A) where
    (B) what
    (C) which
    (D) when

18. Eric Erikson's theory of development claims

    <u>who</u> individuals encounter <u>a</u> series of conflicts
    A   B
    <u>that</u> need to be <u>resolved</u> for healthy personality
    C   D
    development.

19. _____ a herd of horses on Assateague Island.
    (A) The pirate Blackbeard reputedly left
    (B) The pirate Blackbeard reputedly leaving
    (C) Had the pirate Blackbeard reputedly left
    (D) No sooner did the pirate Blackbeard reputedly leave

20. Amelia Earhart, <u>whose</u> mother was the first
    A
    woman to climb Pike's Peak, Colorado,

    <u>believed</u> fervently that <u>woman</u> had as much
    B   C
    right to fly as men <u>did</u>.
    D

Answers to Exercise S60 are on page 524.

PRACTICE WITH ADJECTIVE CLAUSES

Ask yourself the following questions about adjective clauses.

1. Is the clause an adjective clause?

An adjective clause has a subject and a verb. It is a dependent clause because it does not form a complete sentence. It is used like an adjective to describe, identify, or give more information about nouns and indefinite pronouns such as "someone," "anyone," and "everything."

NOUN _____ **ADJ CLAUSE** _____
The **house** that has the green shutters is for sale.

NOUN _____ **ADJ CLAUSE** _____
The **woman** whose son won the award was out of town.

PRONOUN _____ **ADJ CLAUSE** _____
Anybody who finishes the test early can leave.

NOUN __ **ADJ CLAUSE** __
Sam's **uncle**, who is very rich, came for a visit.

2. Is the correct clause marker used?

The adjective clause is introduced by the clause markers "that" or a *Wh-* word. The clause marker refers to the noun or pronoun it follows.

(A) The most common clause markers are the relative pronouns: "who," "whom," "which," "whose," and "that."

"Who" and "whom" are used to refer to people.

The man **who** saw the child works nearby. ("Who" refers to the man.)
The man **whom** we saw works nearby. ("Whom" refers to the man.)

"Who" is used in the subject position of a clause, and "whom" is used in the object position. However, you will not be tested on the difference between "who" and "whom" on the Computer-Based TOEFL® Test.

"Which" is used to refer to things.

The watch, **which** I lost, was not valuable. ("Which" refers to the watch.)

"That" can be used to refer to either people or things.

The man **that** was hired lives in the blue house. ("That" refers to the man.)
The vase **that** I bought was handmade. ("That" refers to the vase.)

"Whose" is used to refer to the person or thing that possesses something.

The woman **whose** car broke down needs a ride. ("Whose" refers to the woman. She owns the car.)

(B) Clause markers "where," "when," and "whereby" can also be used to introduce an adjective clause.

"Where" is used to refer to a location or the name of a location.

The school **where** I met my husband is now closed. ("Where" refers to the location – the school.)

"When" is used to refer to a time.

That was the year **when** we moved to Alaska. ("When" refers to the year.)

"Whereby" is used to refer to words indicating an agreement.

They made a deal **whereby** she would pay for the expenses and he would complete the work by Saturday. ("Whereby" refers to the deal.)

(C) Sometimes the adjective clause is used with a preposition. In conversational English the preposition usually goes at the end of the clause, but in formal and written English it goes at the beginning.

Informal	He asked questions that there were no answers **for**.
Formal	He asked questions **for** which there were no answers.
Informal	Mac was the man whom Linda was referring **to**.
Formal	Mac was the man **to** whom Linda was referring.

3. Is the clause marker in the correct position?

(A) Within the adjective clause, relative pronouns are used in the same positions as a noun.

S   V   __ OBJ __

As subject   The woman **who** wrote the book has just left.

OBJ S V

As object   The woman **whom** I saw was in a hurry.

OBJ OF
PREP S V

As object of the preposition   The woman to **whom** I owe my good fortune lives nearby.

(B) The clause markers "where," "when," and "whereby" take an adverb position.

ADV S   V   ___ OBJ ___

The store **where** I bought my camera is having a sale.

4.   *Is the clause marker missing?*

(A) If the relative pronoun is the subject of the adjective clause, it cannot be omitted.

S   V

The man **who** quit forgot his papers.

(B) If the relative pronoun is the object of the adjective clause, it can be omitted.

OBJ   S   V

The picture **that** I wanted had been sold.
The picture I wanted had been sold.

(C) If the relative pronoun is the object of the preposition in the adjective clause, it can be omitted, and the preposition goes to the end of the clause.

OBJ OF
PREP   S   V

The man for **whom** I work gave me a bonus.

S   V   PREP

The man I work for has given me a raise.

(D) The relative pronoun "whose" cannot be omitted.

The man **whose** opinion we respect teaches at the local community college.

(E) The clause marker "when" can be omitted.

That was the year **when** the miners were on strike.
That was the year the miners were on strike.

(F) "Where" and "whereby" cannot be omitted.

That's the room **where** I was born.
The factory devised a system **whereby** we could get more overtime work.

5.   *Does the adjective clause have a subject and a verb?*

The adjective clause must have a subject and a verb to be complete.

S   V

The music **that we heard** was composed by Bach.

S   V

The music **that was played** made me sad.

6.   *Is the independent clause that contains the adjective clause complete?*

The independent clause must have a subject and a verb.

S   V

Last night on TV we watched a clown **who could juggle bowling balls**.

S   V

The clown **who juggled bowling balls** was very funny.

7.   *Does the verb of the adjective clause agree with the verb in the independent clause?*

Although the tenses of the adjective clause may vary, they must be logical. In both of the following sentences, the verb in the adjective clause is in the past tense and the verb in the independent clause is in the present continuous tense. However, the first sentence is correct and the second one is nonsensical.

Correct   The man who sang at the concert last night is sitting over there.
Incorrect   The dog that was killed is wagging its tail.

In the second sentence, it is illogical for a dog to have been killed in the past and to be wagging its tail now.

Use Exercises S61–S66 to develop your skills with adjective clauses.

Exercise S61   ***Locating clause markers***

Circle the clause markers in the following sentences.

Example   The storks (that) stop at the lagoon on their way north are protected.

1. One of the German officers who attended the meeting was Field Marshal Erwin Rommel.

2. Agriculture relies on water, which may be scarce at times.

3. A museum curator, who was determined to read the label at every exhibit, spent five full days at the museum.

4. In the Colosseum in ancient Rome, hoists lifted cages to a level where the animals could enter the arena up a ramp.

5. Many English villages have churches that date back to Norman times or before.

6. As a person talks, he or she provides clues that serve as the basis for continued interaction.

7. The only U.S. president whom the people did not choose in a national election was President Ford.

8. The largest mosaic in the world is in Mexico City, where Juan O'Gorman's work covers 1,000 square meters of the walls in the university's library.

Answers to Exercise S61 are on page 525.

Exercise S62   ***Locating adjective clauses***

Underline the adjective clause and circle the word in the independent clause that it refers to.

Example   The number of (families) that owned TV sets grew dramatically during the 1950s.

1. The date on which Romulus founded Rome is generally considered to be 753 B.C.E.

2. Chekhov's calling *The Seagull* a comedy is a description that has puzzled playgoers, directors, and even critics.

3. Those who are reluctant to ask for clarification about a job requirement may regret it later.

4. The common hedgehog, which has outlived the mammoth and the saber-toothed tiger, is now threatened by traffic.

5. Shakespeare wrote plays people have enjoyed for four centuries.

6. Walt Disney was a man whose creations still bring happiness to many children.

7. An added attraction to many zoos is an enclosure where children can interact with young farm animals.

8. A balance between nature and the needs of human beings, which will safeguard succeeding generations, is what humanity should strive for.

Answers to Exercise S62 are on page 525.

Exercise S63   *Checking clause markers*

Write "C" if the correct clause marker has been used. Write "IC" if an incorrect clause marker has been used.

Example   _IC_   People <u>which</u> love car racing always enjoy the Indianapolis 500.

You should write "IC" in the space because the relative pronoun "who" refers to people.

1. _____ California's San Joaquin Valley, <u>where</u> has lured settlers throughout the years, is rimmed by beautiful mountains.

2. _____ Edward Kazarian, <u>which</u> is a master of making miniatures, uses microscopes and diamond-tipped tools to create figures the size of the head of a pin.

3. _____ Elvis Presley, <u>who</u> has been called the "king of rock and roll," made his first record, privately, in 1953.

4. _____ Vast oil spills <u>that</u> contaminate coastal areas cost huge sums to clean up.

5. _____ People <u>whose</u> are in charge of ticket reservations warn travelers to book early during the high seasons.

6. _____ Using low doses of antibiotics <u>that</u> don't kill bacteria only helps them develop their resistance.

7. _____ The last city of the Pyu civilization, <u>who</u> flourished from the ninth to first centuries B.C.E., lies about 160 miles from Rangoon, Burma.

8. _____ Anna Freud, <u>when</u> was the daughter of Sigmund Freud, was an eminent psychoanalyst as well.

Extended practice: Write the correct clause marker for the items that were incorrect.

Answers to Exercise S63 are on page 525.

Exercise S64   *Choosing correct clause markers*

Circle the letter of the word that correctly introduces the adjective clause.

Example   A species of tomato _____ is adapted to harsh climatic conditions has been developed.
  (A) what
  (B) where
  (C) that
  (D) who

The word being referred to is "tomato." You should circle (C) because "that" is the clause marker that can refer to either a person or a thing.

1. New Orleans is a city _____ older traditions can still be seen.
   (A) those
   (B) that
   (C) which
   (D) where

2. The preservation of ancient sites and historical buildings is a job _____ requires a person ready to fight a long battle.
   (A) whose
   (B) which
   (C) whom
   (D) where

3. Monteverdi, _____ works were mainly written on commission for the private theaters of wealthy Italian nobility, wrote his final opera in 1642.
   - (A) which
   - (B) who
   - (C) whom
   - (D) whose

4. Crossing Death Valley, _____ temperatures reach well above 110 degrees Fahrenheit, was a nearly insurmountable task for the early pioneers.
   - (A) which
   - (B) where
   - (C) that
   - (D) those

5. Marine excavation is a race against time, the sea, and the looters _____ want history's treasures for themselves.
   - (A) which
   - (B) who
   - (C) whose
   - (D) those

6. Those for _____ skiing is an obsession would find life in the Snowy Mountains to their liking.
   - (A) which
   - (B) were
   - (C) whom
   - (D) whose

7. T. A. Watson's business involved building models for inventors _____ had ideas but lacked the means or skills to execute them.
   - (A) who
   - (B) when
   - (C) whose
   - (D) to whom

8. Glaucoma, _____ is often called tunnel vision, happens when a buildup of pressure in the eye gradually shrinks the field of vision.
   - (A) where
   - (B) why
   - (C) which
   - (D) when

Answers to Exercise S64 are on page 525.

Exercise S65   *Locating subjects and verbs in adjective clauses*

Circle the complete subject and underline the verb of the adjective clause.

Example   Rosa Parks is famous as the black woman (who) refused to give up her bus seat for a white man.

The adjective clause is "who refused to give up her bus seat for a white man."

1. Anne Boleyn, who was the second wife of King Henry VIII, was beheaded at the age of 29.

2. Many words that people use daily have origins in other countries and cultures.

3. By the end of the tenth century, paper had supplanted papyrus, which had been used uninterruptedly in Egypt for four millennia.

4. Botulism spores, which bees carry from certain kinds of plants, have been found in jars of honey.

5. Locusts breed in remote desert areas where they go unnoticed.

6. Collapsed stars can form a black hole, which is matter so dense that its gravity sucks in even light.

7. Those people whom doctors have found to carry the sickle-cell gene are less susceptible to malaria.

8. Sharks, whose appetites are notorious, have acquired a taste for the cables that carry international telephone calls.

Extended practice: Write "S" above the subject and "V" above the verb of the independent clauses in the above sentences.

Answers to Exercise S65 are on page 525.

Exercise S66   *Checking verbs in adjective clauses*

If the verb in the adjective clause is used incorrectly, cross it out and write the correct form.

Example   Science-fiction writers have depicted future technologies that

have become
~~will become~~ reality.

The verb "have depicted" indicates that the act of depicting took place before now. Therefore, the verb in the adjective clause should also be in the perfect tense.

1. Bicyclists pedal through the countryside during a weeklong ride that is holding every summer in Iowa.

2. In 1918, Charles Strite invented the timer that turns off the toaster when the bread is toasted.

3. It is Earth's magnetic field that made a compass work.

4. A vending machine is a kind of robot that automatically gave out candy or other items when money is inserted.

5. Hans Christian Oersted, the man who made the electric motor possible, was a Danish scientist.

6. A laser cane, which the blind find useful, sends out beams that detecting obstacles.

7. For the foreign buyers to whom Canada supplying furs, the industry has never been healthier.

8. Lucid dreamers are those people who recognize when they are dreaming and thus controlling the plot of their dreams.

Answers to Exercise S66 are on page 526.

PRACTICE WITH REDUCED ADJECTIVE CLAUSES

Adjective clauses can be reduced to phrases. Unlike a clause, a *phrase* is a group of words that does *not* contain a subject and a verb. Ask yourself the following questions concerning adjective phrases.

1. Is the phrase a reduced adjective clause?

An adjective clause can often be reduced to an adjective phrase when the relative pronoun of the adjective clause is the *subject* of the clause. Study the following examples to see how the clause is reduced. Note that the clause marker and the aux-words and/or "be" verbs are omitted. The main verb change depends on the voice (active or passive).

(A) Active voice:

The man **who is driving** has a new car.   (clause)
The man **driving** has a new car.   (phrase)
The writer published a book **that contains illustrations**.   (clause)
The writer published a book **containing illustrations**.   (phrase)

(B) Passive voice:

The magazine ad, **which was printed in *Shoppers' Weekly***, showed
      the city skyline.   (clause)
The magazine ad **printed in *Shoppers' Weekly*** showed the city skyline.   (phrase)
The ideas **that had been presented in the previous meeting** were
      discussed.   (clause)
The ideas **presented in the previous meeting** were discussed.   (phrase)

(C) Subject + *to be* + adjective:

The man **who is responsible** said the underground water had a high salt content.   (clause)
The man **responsible** said the underground water had a high salt content.   (phrase)

(D) Subject + *to be* + noun:

Her name, **which is Lou Ann**, contains easy sounds for the deaf to pronounce.   (clause)
Her name, **Lou Ann**, contains easy sounds for the deaf to pronounce.   (phrase)

(E) Subject + *to be* + prepositional phrase:

The books **that are on the table** belong to Emma.   (clause)
The books **on the table** belong to Emma.   (phrase)

2. Is the verb form in the phrase correct?

The *-ing* form is used for the active voice, and the *-ed* form is used for the passive voice.

(A) A verb that is used to indicate a permanent characteristic uses the *-ing* form.

Present
The window that **overlooks** the yard is broken.
The window **overlooking** the yard is broken.

Past
The window that **overlooked** the yard was broken.
The window **overlooking** the yard was broken.

(B) A verb that is used to indicate an ongoing activity uses the *-ing* form.

Present continuous
The detective who **is investigating** the case has found an important clue.
The detective **investigating** the case has found an important clue.

Past continuous
The detective who **was investigating** the case has found an important clue.
The detective **investigating** the case has found an important clue.

(C) A verb that is used in the passive uses the *-ed* form (the past participle).

The woman that **was invited** to join the club declined.
The woman **invited** to join the club declined.

Remember that the past participle forms of many verbs are irregular.

He buys rugs that **are made** in Turkey.
He buys rugs **made** in Turkey.
The house that **has been built** in the forest doesn't have electricity.
The house **built** in the forest doesn't have electricity.

3. Is the phrase correct?

(A) When the clause marker is in the object position, it cannot be reduced to an adjective phrase.

Correct   The books **that I checked out of the library** are due today.
Incorrect   The books checking out of the library are due today.

The adjective clause cannot be shortened to "checking out of the library" because the subject "books" is not the subject for the verb "check." Books cannot "check" themselves out.

(B) The adjective clause beginning with "whose" cannot be reduced without a change in meaning.

> The woman **whose son is blocking the entrance** works upstairs.
> The woman **blocking the entrance** works upstairs.

Although the second sentence is grammatically correct, it does not mean the same as the first sentence. In the first sentence, the son is blocking the entrance. In the second sentence, the woman is blocking the entrance.

(C) The adjective clause beginning with a clause marker that takes the adverb position cannot be reduced to an adjective phrase.

> *Correct*   The time **when Andrew arrived** was inconvenient.
> *Incorrect* The time arriving was inconvenient.

"The time arriving was inconvenient" is incorrect because the time did not arrive, Andrew did.

> *Correct*   The house **where we grew up** was torn down.
> *Incorrect* The house growing up was torn down.

"The house growing up was torn down" is incorrect because the house did not grow up, we did.

Use Exercises S67–S70 to develop your skills with reduced adjective clauses.

Exercise S67   *Locating adjective phrases*

Underline the adjective phrase in each of the following sentences.

Example   People <u>living in a foreign country</u> may suffer culture shock.

"Living in a foreign country" is shortened from the adjective clause "who are living in a foreign country."

1. Passengers suffering from the heat on warm summer days should close the windows if the air-conditioning is to work effectively.

2. Bookworms can browse through or buy from a large selection of the literature on display at book festivals.

3. The fifteenth-century mystery plays first revived in 1951 in York are performed every four years at St. Mary's Abbey.

4. Leaflets giving full details of the layout of museums are usually available at the information desk.

5. The tough palm fiber used in street-sweeping machines is piassava.

6. Corporations discouraging casual appearance in their employees do so to promote a specific image.

7. For towns in remote areas, the airplane is the only means of external communication.

8. In ancient Greece, a person lucky enough to be wealthy and male could join a birthday club composed exclusively of men born on the same day.

Extended practice: Change the phrases into adjective clauses.

Answers to Exercise S67 are on page 526.

Exercise S68   *Identifying adjective phrases and clauses*

Underline the adjective phrase and/or clause in each of the following sentences. Then write "C" if the sentence contains an adjective clause or "P" if it contains an adjective phrase. If it contains both, write "P/C."

Examples   <u>C</u>   The bone <u>that he broke</u> was the clavicle.

       <u>P</u>   Helen Keller became a role model for all people <u>trying to overcome severe obstacles</u>.

      <u>P/C</u>   The world's first jigsaw puzzles, <u>which appeared in the 1760s</u>, were cut-up maps <u>intended to help children learn geography</u>.

In the first sentence, "that he broke" is a clause because it has a subject and a verb.

In the second sentence, "trying to overcome severe obstacles" is a phrase (reduced from the clause "who were trying to overcome severe obstacles.")

In the last sentence, "which appeared in the 1760s" is a clause, and "intended to help children learn geography" is a phrase.

1. _____   The cultural revolution, which historians call the Renaissance, has left a remarkable legacy in Italy.

2. _____   The track leading into the ancient city of Petra follows a mile-long canyon that ends in front of an impressive temple carved out of the sandstone cliffs.

3. _____   About 55 percent of those exiled to Siberia in czarist Russia were not sentenced by judicial process.

4. _____   The Romans recognized the need for a canal linking the southwestern corner of France to the Mediterranean.

5. _____   Identical twins who have been raised apart have shown amazing similarities on physical, intelligence, and behavioral tests.

6. _____   The highest ruins found in the Andes have yet to be properly examined because of their inaccessibility.

7. _____   Strong winds flowing over weaker ones can cause tornadoes.

8. _____   Gray whales migrate 5,000 miles from Arctic waters to bays in Baja California, where they give birth to their calves.

Answers to Exercise S68 are on page 526.

Exercise S69   *Recognizing whether or not clauses can be reduced*

If the adjective clause can be reduced without a change in meaning, write the changes that are necessary to do so.

Examples   George Washington, ~~who was~~ the first president of the United States, lived at Mount Vernon.

          Mount Vernon, where George Washington lived, is in the state of Virginia.

The clause in the first sentence can be reduced because the relative pronoun is the subject of the clause. The clause in the second sentence cannot be reduced because "George Washington," the subject of the clause, is not a relative pronoun and does not refer to "Mount Vernon."

1. The letter "M" may have originated as a hieroglyphic symbol that represented the crests of waves and meant "water."

2. There are still people who are dying from diseases that are preventable and controllable.

3. Before the age of steam, hemp, which was used for ropes on ships, was an important commodity.

4. The island of South Georgia, where half the world's population of southern elephant seals come to breed, is one of the most remote places on earth.

5. The film *The Jazz Singer* was produced many years ago, when the talking movie industry was still in its infancy.

6. Rings, which were probably invented by the Egyptians, were an easy way to display authority.

7. Wind that is deflected down the face of tall buildings causes gusty, swirling winds in the streets.

8. Pain is the body's warning signal that calls attention to a potentially harmful condition.

Answers to Exercise S69 are on page 526.

Exercise S70 **Checking verb forms**

If any verb form in an adjective phrase is incorrect, cross it out and write the correct form above the verb.

meaning
Example   The word "Minnesota," ~~means~~ many lakes, is another example of a Native

found
American word ~~finding~~ in American English.

1. Ambroise Paré, knowing as the father of modern surgery, brought medicine out of the Dark Ages.

2. Each child enter school for the first time is individually screened.

3. Natural oils taken from the rose and the jasmine flower are valuable ingredients of perfume.

4. Scissors, a Bronze Age invention remained basically unchanged to this day, consist of two blades linked by a C-shaped spring.

5. People protesting the destruction of old forests sometimes chain themselves to the trees marked to be cut down.

6. Butterfly wings have iridescent scales consist of thin, interlaced layers.

7. Glacier National Park is impressive with its mountain peaks are towering over splendid lakes.

8. Medicine finding in bathroom cabinets should be thrown out if the expiration date has passed.

Answers to Exercise S70 are on page 526.

CHECK YOUR PROGRESS

Check your progress in using the skills you have been practicing in Exercises S61–S70 by completing the following mini-test. This exercise uses a format similar to that used in the Structure Section of the Computer-Based TOEFL® Test. If you are unfamiliar with how to answer questions on the Computer-Based TOEFL® Test, see the Tutorial on pages 22–23.

Exercise S71   Mini-test

Select the letter of the correct answer.

---

1. A loudspeaker is an instrument _____
   electrical energy into sound energy.
   (A) that
   (B) who is transforming
   (C) transformed
   (D) that transforms

---

2. Paella, <u>which</u> <u>was</u> a traditional Valencian <u>dish</u>,
          A   B   C
   is made of rice, chicken, and <u>seafood</u>.
                                    D

---

3. Researchers may be able to find and monitor
   San Andreas Fault lines _____ since 1857
   or earlier.
   (A) where have not slipped
   (B) have not slipped
   (C) that have not slipped
   (D) have not been slipping

---

4. The caterpillar <u>shedding</u> old skin and encloses
                       A
   <u>itself</u> in a pupa from <u>which it</u> later emerges,
     B   C
   <u>transformed into</u> a butterfly.
         D

---

5. _____ found in New Zealand were brought
   there by homesick immigrants.
   (A) The hedgehogs which
   (B) The hedgehogs
   (C) Where the hedgehogs
   (D) The hedgehogs are

---

6. The stringy, slimy formations <u>discovered</u> <u>hang</u>
                                      A   B
   from the walls in a Mexican cave <u>are</u> colonies
                                       C
   of live bacteria <u>that</u> eat sulfur and drip acid.
                       D

---

7. Nantucket _____ a little island 20 miles off
   Cape Cod, Massachusetts.
   (A) which is
   (B) where
   (C) is
   (D) it is

---

8. Iufaa's tomb, <u>which</u> untouched for 2,500 years,
                    A
   is among the few Egyptian tombs found
   B
   <u>undisturbed</u> by robbers <u>since the tomb</u>
        C   D
   of King Tut was discovered in 1922.

---

9. The woolly musk ox, _____, survives on
   Ellesmere Island.
   (A) once hunted almost to extinction
   (B) hunted almost once to extinction
   (C) almost hunted once to extinction
   (D) hunted almost to once extinction

---

10. Extra wheels <u>attach</u> beside and <u>below</u> the rail
                    A   B
    keep roller-coaster cars on track <u>whether</u> they
                                         C
    are right-side up, upside down, or <u>sideways</u>.
                                          D

11. North Carolina _____ because of its production
    of tar, turpentine, and pitch.
    (A) called the Tar Heel State
    (B) it is called the Tar Heel State
    (C) which the Tar Heel State is called
    (D) is called the Tar Heel State

16. In ancient Greece, that ordinary people
                          A
    were allowed to participate in government,
         B
    any male citizen eighteen or older could vote.
                    C   D

12. Experts in aerodynamics study the placement
                                    A
    of dimples on golf balls to create balls that
                              B
    they fly in specific ways when hit.
     C   D

17. After $116 million had been spent, the
    Supreme Court stopped construction of the
    dam on the Little Tennessee River because
    of a little fish, _____ .
    (A) the famous endangered snail darter
    (B) it was the famous endangered snail darter
    (C) being the famous endangered snail darter
    (D) which the famous endangered snail darter

13. The Cherokee Indians, _____ west on the Trail
    of Tears in the late 1830s, were originally
    from the Appalachian Mountains.
    (A) forcing
    (B) forced
    (C) had forced
    (D) are forced

18. Crazy Horse's vision of a painted rider

    galloping through a storm was seen as a sign
      A
    that he will become a great warrior leading
     B   C   D
    his people into battle.

14. The Seeing-Eye Puppy-Raising Program places
                                            A
    future guide dogs with volunteers where start
                                      B
    preparing the puppies for the job ahead.
     C   D

19. The black moths _____ have become
    genetically more tolerant of pollution.
    (A) survive in industrial areas
    (B) survived in industrial areas
    (C) survival in industrial areas
    (D) surviving in industrial areas

15. The many people _____ must be willing to
    commute a long distance to work.
    (A) wished to live in rural areas
    (B) wished they lived in rural areas
    (C) those wishing to live in rural areas
    (D) who wish to live in rural areas

20. Windmills are making a comeback in Denmark,
                            A
    where centuries ago the people of this
     B
    windswept country use wind power to pump
     C   D
    water and grind grain.

Answers to Exercise S71 are on page 526.

PRACTICE WITH ADVERB CLAUSES

Ask yourself the following questions about adverb clauses.

1. Is the clause an adverb clause?

An adverb clause is a dependent clause (incomplete sentence) with a subject and a verb. It may occur at the beginning of a sentence before the independent clause or at the end of the sentence after the independent clause. When it occurs at the beginning, it is frequently separated from the independent clause by a comma.

> **Even though Ted knew the material**, he failed the exam.
> Ted failed the exam **even though he knew the material**.

2. Is the correct clause marker used?

The following clause markers are some of the more common ones used to introduce an adverb clause.

(A) Clause markers indicating time:

after	by the time	until
as	now that	when
as long as	once	whenever
as soon as	since	while
before		

Examples

> The people danced **as** the music played.
> We worked **as long as** we could.

(B) Clause markers indicating concessions:

although	even though	though
as much as	except that	whereas
despite the fact that	in spite of the fact that	while
even if	not that	

Examples

> Jim goes hiking, **despite the fact that** he has asthma.
> Jenny's smile is an important aspect of her personality, **even if** she doesn't realize it.

(C) Clause markers indicating cause and effect (reason):

as	in case	so
because	since	

Examples

> We should take a first-aid kit **in case** there is an accident.
> **Since** Max seldom talks about himself, I didn't know he liked classical ballet.

(D) Clause markers indicating results:

so that	so . . . that	such . . . that

Examples

The lock on my suitcase broke **so that** all my belongings fell onto the conveyor belt.
The traffic was **so** heavy **that** we arrived an hour late.
She got **such a** shock **that** she dropped the tray.

(E) Clause markers indicating purpose:

in order that	so	so that

Examples

He wrote that memo **in order that** there would be no misunderstandings.
I bought the book **so that** I could read on the flight.

(F) Clause markers indicating manner:

as	as if	as though	just as	like

Examples

Betty looks **as if** something is wrong.
The wind was cold yesterday **just as** it had been all week long.

(G) Clause markers indicating place:

where	wherever	everywhere

Examples

Wherever I looked, I found fingerprints.
Everywhere he went, people admired him.

(H) Clause markers indicating conditions:

even if	if	only if	provided	unless

Examples

We can go camping with Bill **provided** we bring our own equipment.
Lucy can't attend the meeting **unless** she finds a baby-sitter.

3. Is the clause marker missing?

(A) An adverb clause must begin with a clause marker.

When Sam arrives, we'll open the gifts.
I want to leave now **so** I'll get home early.

(B) If the aux-word or verb in a conditional clause is "should," "were," or "had," it is sometimes put at the beginning of the clause and the clause marker "if" is omitted.

If he had planned on going, he would have let us know.
Had he planned on going, he would have let us know.

4. *Is there a subject and a verb in the adverb clause?*

S   V

Mike wears glasses, **whereas his brother wears contact lenses**.

S   V

Whenever Ralph drinks cold water, he gets a toothache.

5. *Is the adverb clause used with an independent clause?*

INDEPENDENT
____ **CLAUSE** _____ _____ **ADV CLAUSE** _____

Lenny can't work until the cast is off his foot.

_ **ADV CLAUSE** _ _____ **INDEPENDENT CLAUSE** ____

After he leaves, we'll bring in the lawn chairs.

6. *Is the verb of the adverb clause used correctly?*

In most adverb clauses, the verb has the same tense as the verb in the independent clause. The following cases are exceptions.

(A) Clauses of time:

If the time refers to something that will happen, you use a present tense.

As soon as I **find** my car keys, we'll leave.

(B) Clauses of reason:

If the clause of reason introduced by the markers "in case" or "just in case" refers to a possible future situation, the reason clause is in the simple present tense.

I'm bringing my umbrella in case it **rains**.

(C) Clauses of purpose:

If the verb in the independent clause is in the present tense or in the present perfect tense, one of the modals "can," "may," "will," or "shall" is usually used.

I want to learn typing so that I **can type** my own essays.

If the verb in the independent clause is in the past tense, one of the modals "could," "might," "would," or "should" is usually used.

Margo wrote the items on a list so that we **would remember** everything.

(D) Clauses of condition:

If the sentence concerns a common occurrence, the simple present tense or the present continuous tense is used in both the adverb clause and the independent clause.

If someone **speaks** to Lily, she **turns** red.

If the sentence concerns a common occurrence in the past, the simple past tense or the past continuous tense is used in the adverb clause, and the simple past and a modal are used in the independent clause.

He **couldn't sleep** unless he **got** a lot of exercise.

If the sentence concerns a possible situation in the present, the simple present tense or the present perfect tense is used in the adverb clause and a modal is used in the independent clause.

If you **don't believe** me, you **can ask** Mike.
If you **haven't had** this kind of cookie, we **should get** some for you to try.

If the sentence concerns a possible future occurrence, the simple present tense is used in the adverb clause and the simple future tense is used in the independent clause.

> If he **goes**, I **will go** too.

Notice these more formal ways of expressing a possible future occurrence.

> If he **should go**, I **would go** too.
> If he **were to go**, I **would go** too.

If the sentence concerns an unlikely situation, the simple past tense is used in the adverb clause and "would," "should," or "might" is used in the independent clause.

> If I **asked** for another raise, my boss **would fire** me.

If the sentence concerns something that might have happened in the past but did not happen, the past perfect tense is used in the adverb clause, and "would have," "could have," "should have," or "might have" is used in the independent clause.

> If I **had realized** the danger at that time, I **would have taken** more precautions.

Use Exercises S72–S76 to develop your skills in identifying adverb clauses.

Exercise S72   ***Locating adverb clauses***

Underline the adverb clauses in the following sentences.

Example   By the time the Privacy Act became law, the Freedom of Information Act had been in use for eight years.

"By the time the Privacy Act became law" relates to when the Freedom of Information Act came into use.

1. The Romans built raised sidewalks of stone in Pompeii so that pedestrians would not get their feet muddy.

2. Although the existence of germs was verified in about 1600, scientists did not prove the connection between germs and diseases until the mid-nineteenth century.

3. If you should step on a stingray, it will whip its tail into your foot or calf.

4. Even though there was a campaign against smoking, tobacco farmers had not yet felt its effect.

5. Many people see the robin's homecoming as a sign that winter is nearly over because it is one of the first birds to return north.

6. Sun-dried clay returns to its malleable state when wet, whereas fired clay does not.

7. When an Easterner in 1886 described St. Paul, Minnesota, as another Siberia, the people responded by holding a winter carnival.

8. Since the search to find and document sites of Native American cave paintings was first begun, more than two hundred have come to light.

Answers to Exercise S72 are on page 527.

Exercise S73   ***Identifying adverb clauses***

If the sentence contains an adverb clause, underline the clause.

Examples   After his troops entered Moscow, Napoleon sent peace proposals to Czar Alexander.

Napoleon believed that the capture of Moscow meant the war was over.

In the first sentence, "after his troops entered Moscow" is an adverb clause indicating when Napoleon sent peace proposals. There is no adverb clause in the second sentence.

1. The word "moon" is an ancient word related to "month."

2. Even though it contains no fish, Mono Lake teems with brine shrimp.

3. As traders mill about in the New York Stock Exchange, information is flashed instantly on exchange tickers and display boards around the world.

4. An incredible 800,000 feeding birds were counted on Negit Island in one day.

5. Using computers in schools not only speeds the rate of learning but also frees the teacher to explain new concepts.

6. Aphrodisias continued as a Byzantine center until violent earthquakes and invasions brought its prosperity to an end.

7. Smoke from blazing fires often forces firefighters to retreat.

8. To combat damaging impurities that have penetrated their surface, marble sculptures can be placed into tubs of water and soaked for up to a month.

Answers to Exercise S73 are on page 527.

Exercise S74   *Locating subjects and verbs of adverb clauses*

Locate the subject and verb of the adverb clause. Underline the verb and circle the complete subject.

Example   Antiochus was overthrown by Rome around 34 B.C.E. after (he) apparently used some of his funds to support a local rebellion backed by the Persians.

You should circle "he" and underline "used" because they are the subject and verb of the adverb clause "after he apparently used some of his funds to support a local rebellion backed by the Persians."

1. Although monitoring earthquakes is a complex problem, seismologists are making considerable advances.

2. More than one hundred pandas starved to death when one of the species of bamboo on which they feed died out.

3. Since oceans cover so much of Earth's surface, it is natural to explore them for future resources.

4. Even though the Chinese sage Confucius lived 2,500 years ago, his teachings still profoundly influence daily life in China.

5. Mother Teresa was awarded the Nobel Peace Prize because she devoted her life to caring for poor people.

6. While the world population continues to grow, natural resources remain finite.

7. Although some Inuit still migrate using dogsleds, many now make the trek with snowmobiles.

8. Because the ice crystals from which they form are usually hexagonal, snowflakes often have six sides.

Extended practice: Locate the subject and verb of the independent clause in these sentences.

Answers to Exercise S74 are on page 528.

Exercise S75   ***Checking verb tenses and forms***

Check the verb tense and verb form of the adverb clause. If it is incorrect, cross it out and write the correct form above.

encountered

Example   Even though the team of scientists ~~encounter~~ snow and strong winds, they continued their excavation.

The verb in the adverb clause must be in the past tense for the action to agree in time with the verb "continued."

1. As dusk settling, fireflies begin to signal.

2. If the Italian authorities hadn't took measures to control the smuggling of national treasures, many Roman artifacts would have been lost.

3. Sixteenth-century mariners called Bermuda the "Isle of Devils" partly because breeding seabirds are making horrid sounds in the night.

4. As the numbers of shellfish diminished in the shallow waters, divers were forced to dive deeper.

5. NASA does not quarantine space crews since returning astronauts have carried no harmful agents or living organisms.

6. Whenever we blamed someone else for our own shortcomings, we are being unfair to them and to ourselves.

7. While students practice doctoring a plastic automated mannequin, instructors can use a computer to vary the mannequin's reactions.

8. When a key on a pipe organ pressed, a series of levers opens the hole in the pipe and air is pumped through.

Answers to Exercise S75 are on page 528.

Exercise S76   ***Choosing correct clause markers***

Circle the letter of the clause marker that correctly completes the sentence.

Example   The little terrier dog, Bobby, spent fourteen years on his master's tombstone in Greyfriar's churchyard _____ it were waiting for the old shepherd's return.
(A) as though
(B) even though
(C) although
(D) though

"As though" indicates a manner and correctly completes the sentence. (B), (C), and (D) all indicate concession.

1. _____ the mutineers seized command of the *Bounty,* they cast off Captain Bligh and eighteen other crewmen in an open wooden boat.
(A) Then
(B) As if
(C) In fact
(D) After

2. The county of Kent is known as the "Garden of England" _____ it yields a bountiful harvest of fruits and vegetables.
(A) although
(B) because
(C) so that
(D) such as

3. Seat belt laws were introduced _____ traffic fatalities would be reduced.
   (A) so that
   (B) then
   (C) when
   (D) as if

4. _____ a Mexican piñata is broken, children scramble to collect the treats that spill out of it.
   (A) As soon as
   (B) So that
   (C) As if
   (D) Such as

5. The great stone city Angkor flourished for six centuries _____ it fell in 1431 and lay prey to the jungle for four long centuries.
   (A) as soon as
   (B) because
   (C) until
   (D) so that

6. The most modern ladders cannot reach above seven stories, _____ firefighters must enter skyscrapers dressed in suits designed to supply oxygen and reflect heat.
   (A) before
   (B) so
   (C) as
   (D) until

7. _____ Kublai Khan's archers destroyed the Burmese war elephants, he shattered the elephant cavalry's myth of invincibility.
   (A) Although
   (B) Until
   (C) When
   (D) So that

8. _____ many governments disapprove, cultivation of the opium poppy thrives.
   (A) As if
   (B) Until
   (C) So that
   (D) Even though

> *Answers to Exercise S76 are on page 528.*

PRACTICE WITH REDUCED ADVERB CLAUSES

Some adverb clauses can be reduced to phrases without the meaning being changed. Ask yourself the following questions concerning adverb phrases. Remember: A clause contains a subject and a verb, but a phrase does not.

1. Is the phrase a reduced adverb clause?

An adverb clause can be reduced to an adverb phrase only when the subject of the independent clause is the same as the subject of the adverb clause. Notice how the following adverb clauses change to phrases.

(A) Time sequences: "after," "before," "once," "since," "until," "when," and "while"

⌐—— **SAME SUBJECT** ——⌐

Clause	**After they sang two songs**, they did a dance.
Phrase	**After singing two songs**, they did a dance.
Clause	**Before he answered the phone**, he grabbed a pencil and notepad.
Phrase	**Before answering the phone**, he grabbed a pencil and notepad.
Clause	**Once he had been challenged to play tennis**, Tim wouldn't stop practicing.
Phrase	**Once challenged to play tennis**, Tim wouldn't stop practicing.
Clause	**Since she finished studying at the university**, Ellen has gone on to become a successful designer.
Phrase	**Since studying at the university**, Ellen has gone on to become a successful designer.

Clause	We worked on the project **until we finished it**.
Phrase	We worked on the project **until finishing it**.
Clause	**When she is working on a car**, Jan always works overtime.
Phrase	**When working on a car**, Jan always works overtime.
Clause	**While George was in London**, he wrote daily.
Phrase	**While in London**, George wrote daily.

(B) Reason: "because"

When a clause introduced by "because" is reduced, "because" is omitted and the verb changes form.

Clause	**Because she had always been interested in sports**, Linda became an avid supporter of the team.
Phrase	**Having always been interested in sports**, Linda became an avid supporter of the team.

(C) Clauses of concession: "although," "despite," "in spite of," "though," and "while"

Clause	**Although he was hurt**, Jack managed to smile.
Phrase	**Although hurt**, Jack managed to smile.
Clause	**Despite the fact that she was ill**, Lisa went on stage.
Phrase	**Despite being ill**, Lisa went on stage.
Clause	**In spite of the fact that she works long hours**, Joan spends a lot of time with her family.
Phrase	**In spite of working long hours**, Joan spends a lot of time with her family.
Clause	**Though I am capable of making cakes**, I prefer to bake cookies.
Phrase	**Though capable of making cakes**, I prefer to bake cookies.
Clause	**While I am fond of Jeff**, I don't want to marry him.
Phrase	**While fond of Jeff**, I don't want to marry him.

2. Is the verb form in the clause correct?

(A) Active voice:

Present tense	**When I work**, I forget to eat. **When working**, I forget to eat.
Past tense	**While he was studying**, he heard the explosion. **While studying**, he heard the explosion.
Perfect tenses	**After he had finished the book**, he put it on the table. **After finishing the book**, he put it on the table. *or* **After having finished the book**, he put it on the table.

(B) Passive voice:

Present tense	The building will be used as a convention center **when it is completed**. **When completed**, the building will be used as a convention center.
Past tense	**When the boy was told to go to bed**, he began to cry. **When told to go to bed**, the boy began to cry.
Perfect tenses	**Because the house has been remodeled**, it will fetch more on the market. **Having been remodeled**, the house will fetch more on the market.

3. Is the phrase correct?

(A) When the subject of the adverb clause and the subject of the independent clause are not the same, the clause cannot be reduced.

Same subject:

Clause	Since **she** graduated, **she** has become an engineer.
Phrase	Since graduating, she has become an engineer.

Different subjects:

Clause	After **she** graduated, **her parents** retired. (= The daughter graduated, then her parents retired.)
Phrase	After graduating, her parents retired. (= Her parents graduated, then her parents retired.)

(Reducing the adverb clause changes the meaning.)

(B) Some adverb clauses, such as those beginning with "as" or "as soon as," cannot be reduced.

Correct	As he was walking, he kept stopping to look at the flowers.
Incorrect	As walking, he kept stopping to look at the flowers.

Use Exercises S77–S80 to develop your skills with reduced adverb clauses.

Exercise S77   Identifying adverb phrases and clauses

Write "C" if the sentence contains an adverb clause. Write "P" if the sentence contains an adverb phrase.

Examples   _P_   After graduating in 1902, the writer James Joyce moved to Paris and worked as a journalist.

  _C_   Because brine-shrimp eggs are almost indestructible, they can be frozen, dried, or exposed to toxic chemicals and still survive.

1. _____ Thor Heyerdahl sailed west across the Pacific in a balsa-wood raft until he reached Polynesia.

2. _____ While staying at the Greyfield Inn, tourists can visit the ruins of Dungeness, the most famous Carnegie mansion.

3. _____ Before migrating whales head for Baja California's lagoons, they feed on krill in the Arctic waters.

4. _____ When creating creatures for movies, computer-graphic animators start by scanning film footage of real animals into computers.

5. _____ Cowboys train their horses to neck-rein because holding the reins in one hand frees the other hand for roping.

6. _____ After harpooning walruses, hunters may drag the carcasses to camp for butchering.

7. _____ Before Disneyland's opening in 1955, Anaheim was a pastoral community of citrus groves.

8. _____ After having convinced himself that the Hudson was only a river and not the Northwest Passage, Henry Hudson sailed back south.

Answers to Exercise S77 are on page 528.

Exercise S78   **Recognizing clauses that can be reduced**

If the sentence contains an adverb clause that can be reduced, write the changes necessary to reduce it.

Examples   When ~~a cowboy is~~ working on the range, ~~he~~ goes for a long period of time without seeing his family. →
When working on the range, a cowboy goes for a long period of time without seeing his family.

The most recent glaciation on Mount Kilimanjaro occurred between 1400 and 1700, when the Northern Hemisphere was in the grip of the Little Ice Age. (Adverb clause cannot be reduced.)

1. Although some people prefer white eggs to brown, the contents are identical.

2. In winter, the Magdalen Islands are almost as isolated as when Cartier first discovered them.

3. While Amelia Earhart was attempting to fly around the world, she mysteriously disappeared without a trace.

4. After they end their larval period, the worms suddenly grow sluggish and enter the stage of metamorphosing into adults.

5. By the time newcomers to the United States had passed through the immigration center on Ellis Island, they had been screened for certain contagious diseases.

6. While knowledge about the brain is growing, many riddles of the thought process remain unsolved.

7. When they built Hadrian's Wall, the Romans also erected towers about every mile.

8. The Hussites had fled persecution in central Europe and Russia before they came to settle in the United States.

Answers to Exercise S78 are on page 528.

Exercise S79   **Checking verb forms**

If the verb form of the adverb phrase is incorrect, cross it out and write the correction.

Example   *going*
Before ~~having gone~~ on a long-distance hike, hikers should soak their feet in cold salty water to toughen the skin.

1. George Gershwin gathered motifs for his folk opera *Porgy and Bess* while lived in Charleston.

2. Since discovering the double helix structure of DNA, geneticists have made great advances in the knowledge of life at a molecular level.

3. Having first domesticated for milk production, sheep were then used for wool.

4. When immersed in liquid oxygen, a magnet's pulling power is intensified.

5. After spin its web using sticky silk threads, a spider retreats via a walkway of dry silk threads.

6. Architects must take noise levels into consideration before designing an auditorium.

7. Since been eradicated, the smallpox virus is found only in laboratories.

8. After attached themselves to a ship's hull, barnacles and algae create friction that impedes the ship's movements.

Answers to Exercise S79 are on page 528.

Exercise S80   *Choosing correct clause markers*

Circle the letter of the clause marker that correctly completes the sentence.

Example   Astronauts must follow a strenuous exercise program _____ living in a weightless environment.
(A) as though
(B) as soon as
(C) while
(D) so that

"While" indicates that two actions are occurring at the same time: following a strenuous exercise program and living in a weightless environment.

1. _____ capable of walking upright, apelike Australopithecus did so only for short periods of time.
(A) As if
(B) Though
(C) Until
(D) Because

2. _____ erupting in May 1980, Mount Saint Helens continued erupting intermittently throughout the following year.
(A) After
(B) Such as
(C) Since
(D) As if

3. _____ having seized their prey with their mouths, pythons swiftly coil themselves around it and suffocate it.
(A) Until
(B) Because
(C) Since
(D) After

4. _____ running, grizzly bears are capable of attaining speeds of 35 miles an hour.
(A) So that
(B) When
(C) Though
(D) So

5. _____ making a person ill enough to warrant hospitalization, poison ivy does not kill.
(A) As soon as
(B) Since
(C) While
(D) So that

6. _____ declaring the area useless, Daniel Webster could not have foretold how irrigation would make California's Imperial Valley bloom.
(A) Because
(B) When
(C) Though
(D) So that

7. _____ plowing a field, an Issyk farmer uncovered a rich burial site containing an ancient nomad buried in a suit of gold.
(A) As though
(B) While
(C) Since
(D) Until

8. _____ publicly executed in 1536 for making what his enemies considered a false translation of the Bible, William Tyndale had, in fact, written a version that became the foundation of subsequent English versions.
(A) As if
(B) After
(C) When
(D) Although

Answers to Exercise S80 are on page 529.

CHECK YOUR PROGRESS

Check your progress in using the skills you have been practicing in Exercises S72–S80 by completing the following mini-test. This exercise uses a format similar to that used in the Structure Section of the Computer-Based TOEFL® Test. If you are unfamiliar with how to answer questions on the Computer-Based TOEFL® Test, see the Tutorial on pages 22–23.

Exercise S81   Mini-test

Select the letter of the correct answer.

1. _____, their small size and the thin soil make them easy prey to a hiker's heel.
   (A) Alpine flowers, which can resist wind, cold, and snow
   (B) When alpine flowers can resist wind, cold, and snow
   (C) While alpine flowers can resist wind, cold, and snow
   (D) Alpine flowers resisting wind, cold, and snow

2. The fashion of decorating hats with feathers
                               A
   declined because too many birds slaughtered
              B   C
   for their feathers.
         D

3. _____ with strong flippers, seals gracefully glide through the sea.
   (A) Paddle and steer
   (B) It is paddling and steering
   (C) That they paddle and steer
   (D) Paddling and steering

4. While drained a lake below a roller coaster
     A   B
   in Blackpool, England, workers found hundreds
                             C
   of sets of false teeth lost by screaming
                     D
   passengers.

5. _____ pandas eat bamboo almost exclusively, they are also carnivorous.
   (A) Not only
   (B) Until
   (C) As soon as
   (D) Although

6. Whereas they are harvested, cranberries
     A
   are dropped down a chute that has a series
         B
   of barriers which fresh berries bounce over
              C
   and bruised or rotten berries do not.
         D

7. Although _____ a country illegally is risky, the illegal immigrant who finds work may believe the risk worthwhile.
   (A) when entering
   (B) he enters
   (C) entering
   (D) having entered

8. U.S. currency may be copied for noncriminal
                 A
   purposes only the copy is one-sided and
           B   C
   significantly different in size.
           D

9. The Andean condor glides on air currents and doesn't flap its wings _____ it must do so to reach updrafts.
   (A) because
   (B) until
   (C) that
   (D) as if

10. Although the hunting of foxes from horseback is
                A   B
    a valid form of pest control has come under
                   C
    attack.
     D

11. _____ to England remain strong, the Channel Islanders are exempt from most British taxes.
    (A) Although their ties
    (B) Although tied
    (C) Before their ties
    (D) Tied

12. Before beginning of the race, Formula One
                  A
    drivers get their cars nearer to race temperature
           B   C
    by undertaking a formation lap.
       D

13. When competing in a demolition derby, _____ until their cars are completely demolished.
    (A) that drivers continue
    (B) drivers must continue
    (C) drivers continuing
    (D) although drivers must continue

14. Before a major league baseball game
     A
    beginning, the umpires rub the baseballs with
     B
    special mud that roughens the ball's surface
             C
    to give pitchers a better grip.
     D

15. _____ governments point with pride to increasing mechanization in agriculture, power from humans and animals still produces a significant portion of the world's food.
    (A) Since
    (B) Because
    (C) So that
    (D) While

16. Before a skunk squirts an unpleasant spray
                   A
    from glands under its tail, after it will stamp
                   B   C
    its feet and hiss a warning.
          D

17. There were few settlements along the North Carolina coast _____ many problems for seafarers.
    (A) because the offshore barrier posed
    (B) before posing the offshore barrier
    (C) while posing the offshore barrier
    (D) that the offshore barrier had posed

18. Researchers have found that people who use
                   A   B
    hand movements when talking appearing freer,
               C   D
    more open, and more honest to an audience.

19. _____ of the tranquilizer, scientists tag and record details about each animal.
    (A) While under the effect deer
    (B) While being under effect the deer
    (C) While deer are under the effect
    (D) While deer under the effect

20. People <u>outdoors</u> for long periods of <u>time need</u>
            A   B
    to protect themselves so <u>that avoid</u> the harmful
                                 C
    <u>effects</u> of too much sun.
      D

Answers to Exercise S81 are on page 529.

PRACTICE WITH COMPARING

Ask yourself the following questions about comparatives and superlatives.

1. Is the comparative or superlative form correct?

(A) One-syllable adjectives and adverbs form their comparative and superlative forms by adding *-er* and *-est* to the base.

Base	Comparative	Superlative
small	smaller	smallest
fast	faster	fastest

> This ring is **smaller** than that ring.
> It is the **smallest** one in the box.

Note: The superlative structure includes "the." The comparative structure includes "the" only when the comparative takes a noun position (for example, "I like **the smaller** of the two").

(B) Two-syllable adjectives and adverbs ending in *-er, -y,* or *-ly* add *-er* and *-est* to the base form.

Base	Comparative	Superlative
clever	cleverer	cleverest
happy	happier	happiest
early	earlier	earliest

(C) Some two-syllable adjectives and adverbs and all those with three or more syllables use "more" and "most" with the base form.

Base	Comparative	Superlative
joyful	more joyful	most joyful
intelligent	more intelligent	most intelligent
happily	more happily	most happily

(D) Irregular comparatives and superlatives are as follows:

Base	Comparative	Superlative
good (ADJ)	better	best
well (ADV)	better	best
bad (ADJ)	worse	worst
badly (ADV)	worse	worst
little (ADJ & ADV)	less	least
many (ADJ)	more	most
much (ADJ & ADV)	more	most
far (ADJ & ADV)	farther	farthest
	further	furthest
late (ADV)	later	last, latest
old (ADJ)	older	oldest
	elder	eldest

(E) The comparative form "less" and the superlative form "least" are used with adjectives and adverbs to indicate that something does not have as much of a quality as what it is being compared to.

> I have become **less** anxious about the project.
> This is the **least** popular of the perfumes.

2. Is the comparative or superlative used correctly?

(A) Comparatives and superlatives can be used to modify a noun.

> A **harder** exam would discourage the students.
> The **taller** boy won the wrestling match.
> The **earliest** time I can come is ten o'clock.

(B) Comparatives and superlatives can be used after a verb.

> We need to be **more** understanding.
> The black horse is the **fastest**.

(C) Some structures using comparatives take the word "than." (*Note:* The words "the" and "than" are not used together in a comparative structure.)

Before nouns	Jackie is **more active than** her brother.
Before phrases	Last year the test results were **better than** in previous years.
Before clauses	He is **taller than** I thought he was.

(D) The superlative is used in the following structures.

With prepositions	The first step is **the most** important of all.
	He has **the worst** temper in the world.
With clauses	That book is **the best** I'm likely to find.
	That is **the most convincing** movie I've ever seen.

3. Is the expression of equality or inequality used correctly?

Expressions of equality or inequality can be made using the base form of the adjective or adverb with "as . . . as," "not as . . . as," or "not so . . . as."

> Jim is **as clever as** Nancy, but he doesn't work **as hard as** she does.
> I am just **as good** a typist **as** Bobby is.

4. Is the parallel comparison used correctly?

When a two-clause sentence begins with a comparative, the second clause also begins with a comparative.

> **The more encouragement** Edna got, **the harder** she tried to succeed.

Use Exercises S82–S87 to develop your skills in identifying comparisons.

Exercise S82   Locating phrases

Underline the comparatives, superlatives, and expressions of equality and inequality in the following sentences.

Example   Mount Everest is the highest mountain in the world.

You should underline "the highest" because this phrase is a superlative comparing Mount Everest with all the mountains in the world.

1. The largest known gathering of bald eagles anywhere is on the Chilkat River.

2. Settlers from Europe brought with them smallpox, which aided the conquest of the Americas by killing as much as half the native population.

3. As recently as the 1930s, Yemen was inaccessible to travelers.

4. The increasing popularity of tennis and bigger crowds meant that a grandstand had to be built at Wimbledon in 1880.

5. Of all salmon species, the king salmon is the rarest.

6. Once the world's largest church, Hagia Sophia is now a museum.

7. The more technical today's world becomes, the more compatible with both humans and machines language needs to be.

8. Rough, woven washcloths rub off dirt as well as sponges do.

> *Answers to Exercise S82 are on page 530.*

Exercise S83   Identifying kinds of phrases

Write "C" if the underlined phrase is a comparative, "S" if the phrase is a superlative, and "E" if the phrase is an expression of equality or inequality.

Example   __*E*__ Today as many as ten thousand crocodiles thrive in the warm waters of Lake Nasser.

1. _____ Lower prices have forced people in the fishing industry to seek fish other than salmon.

2. _____ The port of Mocha gave its name to what is possibly the most distinctive coffee in the world.

3. _____ Attempts to abolish the face cards from playing cards have proved as unsuccessful as trying to abolish royal figures from the game of chess.

4. _____ The oldest known dam, an engineering wonder of the ancient world, lies near Marib, once the home of the Queen of Sheba.

5. _____ Perhaps the most coveted prize of them all is the Nobel Peace Prize.

6. _____ More pioneers walked across the continent than rode in wagons or on horses.

7. _____ The Mexico earthquake of 1985 was <u>far worse than</u> that of 1979.

8. _____ Mice aren't really <u>as</u> <u>attracted</u> to cheese <u>as</u> they are to grains.

Answers to Exercise S83 are on page 530.

Exercise S84   *Checking comparatives*

Circle any comparative that is used incorrectly.

Example   Northern Mexico generally receives (the less rain than) does central Mexico.

You should circle "the less rain than" because the words "the" and "than" are not used together in a comparative structure.

1. More often than not, a honking goose frightens off strangers best than a barking dog.

2. Australia is the flatter and drier of all the continents.

3. Iowa produces the more feed corn than any other state.

4. The calmer of the two horses was more suitable for amateur riders.

5. The eastern side of the British Isles has a drier climate.

6. Both the épée and foil are descendants of the dueling sword, but the épée is heavier of the two fencing weapons.

7. The history of the United States as a nation spans less time than most major Chinese dynasties.

8. The fast of the two main styles of cross-country skiing is the Nordic skate style.

Extended practice: Rewrite the incorrect sentences using the correct form of the comparative.

Answers to Exercise S84 are on page 530.

Exercise S85   *Checking parallel comparatives*

Circle any parallel comparative that is used incorrectly.

Example   The more advances and improvements are made in technology, the more convenient (than) the banking transactions become.

1. The more populated the area becomes, the more noise one has to contend with.

2. The finer the particles, the better they bond when compacted.

3. The more the world's grasslands are overgrazed, the fast they become deserts.

4. Longer buildings are left standing empty, the harder they are to restore.

5. The lower the temperature and longer the cooking time used for a baked potato, the crunchier and tough the skin will be.

6. The further west the Native Americans were driven, the harder they fought to secure their lands.

7. The more the quest for security pushed the arms race forward, the greater the insecurity became.

8. The more development that takes place on the island, the less likelier the native wildlife will survive.

Extended practice: Rewrite the incorrect sentences using the correct form of the parallel comparative.

Answers to Exercise S85 are on page 530.

Exercise S86   **Checking superlatives**

Circle any superlative that is used incorrectly.

Example   One of (the difficultest) tasks we have to perform as listeners is concentration.

You should circle "the difficultest" because the correct superlative is "the most difficult."

1. Turkey's the largest city, Istanbul, played a central role in history as Constantinople, the capital of the Byzantine Empire.

2. Only the hardiest should attempt to scale Mount Everest.

3. The water in Half-Moon Bay is the bluest of blues.

4. Blown in from deserts to the north and west, China's loess deposits are the world's greater.

5. The most early set of cards found in Italy is the tarot deck.

6. Once one of the southernmost towns of biblical Palestine, Beersheba contains a well believed to have been dug by Abraham.

7. The *George W. Wells*, a six-masted schooner, was a largest sailing ship lost on the East Coast.

8. The world's longest-running sports competition began at Olympia in 776 B.C.E.

Extended practice: Rewrite the incorrect sentences using the correct form of the superlative.

Answers to Exercise S86 are on page 530.

Exercise S87   **Checking expressions of equality and inequality**

Circle any expression of equality and inequality that is used incorrectly.

Example   The Aztec emperor Moctezuma supposedly drank (too much as) fifty cups of chocolate a day.

You should circle "too much as" because the correct expression of equality is "as many as."

1. Every year many pounds of peanuts are grown as sweet potatoes in the fertile soil of the tidewater region.

2. As adaptable as wolves were, they were not able to survive human encroachment into the Rocky Mountains as well as coyotes.

3. Not as many people take advantage of public transport in the United States they used to.

4. Although the drought was as not severe as the previous one, its effect was more damaging.

5. Henry David Thoreau wanted to be as far from the noise of the crowded city as possible.

6. Though St. Paul is not as larger as Minneapolis, it shares the fame of being one of the "Twin Cities."

7. Elephants can siphon up their trunks as much as a gallon and a half of water before spraying it into their mouths.

8. Not as popular a sport as downhill skiing, cross-country skiing has its attractions.

Extended practice: Rewrite the incorrect sentences using the correct form of the expression of equality or inequality.

Answers to Exercise S87 are on page 530.

PRACTICE WITH PARALLEL STRUCTURES

Many sentences present information in a list or series. The list or series may consist of two or more parts that have the same grammatical function. This listing is known as parallel structure.

Ask yourself the following questions about parallel structures.

1. Do the parts in the list have the same grammatical form?

Notice how the words in the following sentences are parallel.

Nouns	The children played on the **swings, slides,** and **seesaw.**
Gerunds	**Reading, writing,** and **calculating** are important skills to learn.
Infinitives	After her accident, Emma had to learn how **to speak, to walk,** and **to write** again.
Verbs	We will **run, swim,** and **play** at the beach.
Adjectives	Betty is **short, chubby,** and **vivacious.**
Adverbs	This car runs **efficiently, quietly,** and **dependably.**
Subjects	**Vendors selling postcards, artists drawing on the pavement,** and **folk singers strumming guitars** can all be seen at the summer festival in the park.
Phrases	For all her years **of triumph and tragedy, of glory and ruin, of hope and despair,** the actress was still able to draw a crowd.
Clauses	The creation of a map is a compromise of **what needs to be shown, what can be shown in terms of map design,** and **what we would like to include.**

2. Are the parallel parts joined correctly?

Parallel structures may be joined by the following words or phrases.

and	both . . . and
but	not only . . . but also
or	either . . . or
nor	neither . . . nor

3. Are any necessary words missing from the parallel parts?

Study the following sentences.

Incorrect	The eagle swooped down, caught the rabbit, and brought back to its nest.
Correct	The eagle swooped down, caught the rabbit, and brought it back to its nest.

The verb "swoop" does not take an object. The verb "caught" has the object "rabbit." The verb "brought" must have an object. The pronoun "it" in the corrected sentence refers to "the rabbit."

Use Exercises S88–S90 to develop your skills in identifying parallel structures.

Exercise S88 *Locating parallels*

Underline the parallels in the following sentences.

Example   For millennia, Chinese aristocrats have been buried with the finest <u>scrolls,</u> <u>ceramic figurines,</u> and <u>religious icons</u> that surrounded them in life.

1. In the Welsh hills one can almost imagine the presence of gnomes, sprites, and elves.

2. Warm ocean conditions, regulation of foreign catches within the U.S. 200-mile limit, and international agreements reducing fishing fleets have played a part in saving the pink salmon from extinction.

3. Silk has been woven into luxurious tapestries, rugs, clothes, and accessories for some four thousand years.

4. A remarkable system of aqueducts, cisterns, and drains provided water and sanitation for the old city.

5. Pesticides protect us from insects, weeds, disease, and hunger, but some pose a risk of cancer, birth defects, genetic mutations, and sterility.

6. Lashed by storms, violated by opportunists plundering its resources, and struggling against today's economic pressures, Pennsylvania has endured.

7. Tenth-century Córdoba boasted more than one thousand mosques and at least eight hundred public bathhouses.

8. The grottoes have been a den for thieves, a hideout for guerrillas, and a tomb for unwary explorers.

Answers to Exercise S88 are on page 531.

Exercise S89   **Checking for parallels**

Write "Y" (for "Yes") if the sentence contains a parallel structure. Write "N" (for "No") if the sentence contains no parallel structure.

Example   ___N___ Learning how to snowboard can be tricky at first.

1. _____   Undisturbed by the pesticide, resistant insects can breed, multiply, and injure crops.

2. _____   The Welsh eisteddfods are an ancient tradition full of pageantry, ritual, and fanfare.

3. _____   Exploring Chesapeake Bay in 1608 for gold, Captain John Smith discovered instead a pathway for settlers.

4. _____   Hungry for freedom and land, the Swedes, Dutch, and English settled the Delaware Valley.

5. _____   The Philadelphia Museum of Art has a community program of public murals, free art instruction, and special exhibitions.

6. _____   You can see the Amish on Iowan country roads, driving their traditional horse-drawn carriages.

7. _____   The paint used is a mixture of pollen, cornmeal, and ground-up stones.

8. _____   The power to reward or to punish becomes significant in family, labor, or legal disputes.

Answers to Exercise S89 are on page 531.

Exercise S90   **Checking parallels**

Circle any incorrect parallels in the following sentences.

Example   In a preschool, children sometimes join hands, sing songs, and (are playing) circle games.

You should circle "are playing" because the present continuous tense of the verb is not parallel to the simple present tense of the other verbs in the sentence.

1. On the stones of the Sacra Via, patricians and plebeians bargained, elected officials, heard speeches, and were paying homage to pagan gods.

2. Following Charles V's death, the Louvre reverted to its former uses as a fortress, a prison, an arsenal, and a treasure house.

3. The towering pinnacles of Bryce Canyon, the eroded valleys of the Grand Canyon, and across Death Valley are sights the tourist will always remember.

4. The money raised goes directly to schooling for the children, teaching survival skills to women, and most importantly medical supplies.

5. The farmer explained which kinds of apples are used for cider, how they are processed, and the small bitter apples make the best cider.

6. Orphaned hawk chicks have been raised on a diet of liquidized mice, dog food, fish, proteins, and vitamins.

7. The Dartmoor sheep produces quality fleece, is comparatively prolific, and has lambs that fatten readily.

8. Filming a wild animal in its habitat requires meticulous preparation, unending patience, and, at times, one must be courageous.

Extended practice: Rewrite the incorrect sentences using the correct parallel structure.

Answers to Exercise S90 are on page 531.

PRACTICE WITH PREPOSITIONAL PHRASES

Ask yourself the following questions about prepositional phrases.

1. Is the phrase correct?

The prepositional phrase consists of a preposition and an object. The object is a noun or pronoun.

PREP   OBJ
into the house

PREP OBJ
above it

The noun can have modifiers.

PREP   OBJ
into the old broken-down house

2. Is the phrase in the correct position?

(A) Prepositional phrases that are used as adverbs can take various positions.

The city park is just **around the corner**.
Just **around the corner** is the city park.

"Around the corner" answers the question "Where is the city park?" and, therefore, is used like an adverb. (See Practice with Adverb Clauses, page 253.)

(B) Prepositional phrases that are used as adjectives *follow* the noun they describe.

NOUN _____ PREP PHRASE _____

I walked into the house **with the sagging porch**.

"With the sagging porch" describes the house and therefore is used like an adjective.

3. Is the correct preposition used to introduce the phrase?

(A) Some of the words and phrases that are commonly used as prepositions are:

about	behind	in	through
above	below	in spite of	throughout
across	beneath	into	till
after	beside	like/unlike	to
against	between	near	toward
along	beyond	of	under
among	by	off	until
around	despite	on	up
as	down	out	upon
at	during	out of	with
because of	for	over	within
before	from	since	without

(B) Some of the words that are used as prepositions can be used in other ways. To check whether a prepositional phrase is being used, look for a preposition and an object.

___PREP___ __ OBJ __

Because of the time, we had to leave.

CLAUSE
MARKER _ CLAUSE _

Because it was late, we had to leave.

PREP   __ OBJ __

We wrote the correction **above the error**.

ADV

Study the sentences **above**.

PREP _____ OBJ _____

We climbed **up the spiral staircase**.

PHRASAL
VERB*

We had to **get up** early.

*A phrasal verb is a verb + one or two other words that give the verb a different meaning. "Get" means "obtain," whereas "get up" means "arise."

(C) Some prepositions have several meanings.

I hung the picture **on** the wall.	(upon)
I bought a book **on** philosophy.	(about)
I called her **on** the phone.	(using)
I worked **on** the research committee.	(with)

Use Exercises S91–S94 to develop your skills in identifying prepositions.

Exercise S91 *Identifying prepositional phrases*

Write "Y" (for "Yes") if the phrase is a prepositional phrase. Write "N" (for "No") if the phrase is not a prepositional phrase.

Example   _N_   to go home

   _Y_   to the store

You should write "N" in the first space because "go" indicates that the phrase is an infinitive phrase. You should write "Y" in the second space because this prepositional phrase has the preposition "to" + the article "the" and the object "store."

1. _____ because of the promise

2. _____ by walking

3. _____ to bring the paper

4. _____ in the summertime

5. _____ because they left

6. _____ between the houses

7. _____ for drawing the plans

8. _____ during the evening

Answers to Exercise S91 are on page 531.

Exercise S92 *Locating prepositional phrases*

Underline the prepositional phrases in the following sentences.

Example   In a palm-shaded beach house south of Bombay, Professor Salim Ali battled against time and illness to complete his ten-volume handbook of the birds of India and Pakistan.

1. In the aftermath of the explosion, people worked night and day to clear the area.

2. The Outer Banks of North Carolina are a series of barrier islands stabilized by vegetation and made up entirely of sand, without the foundation of rock that anchors most islands.

3. Improved knowledge of soil properties and use of innovative building techniques has reduced casualties during earthquakes.

4. Researchers in the field of neurophysiology have claimed that damage centered in part of the right-brain hemisphere impairs one's ability to express emotion.

5. John Wesley Hyatt discovered plastics by accident while cooking up a recipe for making the billiard ball.

6. When buying property, it is a wise idea to consult a lawyer about the various legal aspects.

7. Only one man reached the mainland after escaping from the island prison of Alcatraz in San Francisco Bay, but he was apprehended by police within minutes of swimming ashore.

8. The picnic evolved in Europe as a pastime of the upper classes, whose outings would be attended by the bustle of servants.

Answers to Exercise S92 are on page 531.

Exercise S93 ***Identifying correct prepositions***

Circle the letter of the preposition that correctly completes the sentence.

Example   Information _____ bird-banding fills huge gaps in our knowledge of bird behavior and migration.
(A) by
(B) from
(C) with
(D) during

You should circle (B) because "from" indicates "the source of the information."

1. Wilbur Wright flew his airplane _____ France in 1909.
   (A) on
   (B) upon
   (C) until
   (D) over

2. Clay incense burners _____ effigy lids were excavated near Becan.
   (A) out
   (B) since
   (C) with
   (D) before

3. Mount Rainier towers nearly three miles _____ sea level.
   (A) up
   (B) at
   (C) along
   (D) above

4. Meriwether Lewis and William Clark made their epic journey across North America in the years 1804 _____ 1806.
   (A) to
   (B) between
   (C) over
   (D) for

5. While _____ a visit to Georgia, Eli Whitney learned of the need for a machine that could clean cotton.
   (A) of
   (B) on
   (C) above
   (D) for

6. It is claimed that the FBI director J. Edgar Hoover didn't want anyone to walk _____ his shadow.
   (A) to
   (B) at
   (C) of
   (D) in

7. China's first emperor was buried surrounded by 7,000 life-sized clay figures of soldiers standing in battle formation, along _____ life-sized ceramic chariots and horses.
   (A) behind
   (B) beside
   (C) with
   (D) after

8. The troposphere, the part of the atmosphere we live in, extends from sea level _____ 15 kilometers above sea level.
   (A) across from
   (B) up to
   (C) out from
   (D) out of

Answers to Exercise S93 are on page 531.

Exercise S94 ***Identifying correct phrases***

Circle the letter of the phrase that correctly completes the sentence.

Example   The man moved awkwardly _____ of a cane.
(A) with the aid
(B) while the aiding

1. _____ of his rule, Ataturk introduced significant changes to the Turkish people's way of life.
   (A) As the years
   (B) Through the years

2. The Mississippi region is _____ astonishingly diverse people.
   (A) full of
   (B) entirely filled

3. Doctors anticipate _____ will bring a revolution in surgical techniques.
   (A) that the twenty-first century
   (B) from the twenty-first century

4. _____ their complex structures, trilobites are ideal for studying small evolutionary changes.
   (A) Because
   (B) Because of

5. No animal sheds tears when in trouble or pain _____ the large, gentle marine mammal called the dugong.
   (A) except that
   (B) except for

6. In Europe the tradition _____ persisted well into the fourteenth and fifteenth centuries.
   (A) spring fertility celebrations was
   (B) of spring fertility celebrations

7. The degradation of plant and animal populations underscores the need _____ towards the ecosphere.
   (A) for a new attitude
   (B) being a new attitude

8. A prehistoric cairn is a pile of stones raised as a landmark or memorial and is usually erected _____.
   (A) over a burial site
   (B) that was a burial site

Answers to Exercise S94 are on page 531.

PRACTICE WITH REDUNDANCIES

Ask yourself the following question about repeated information.

Have words that repeat unnecessary information been used?

(A) When two words have essentially the same meaning, use one or the other, but not both.

Correct	It was **very** important. It was **extremely** important.
Incorrect	It was very, extremely important.

Because "very" and "extremely" have essentially the same meaning, they should not be used together.

Correct	Money is required for research to **advance**. Money is required for research to move **forward**.
Incorrect	Money is required for research to advance forward.

The word "advance" indicates "going forward." Therefore, the word "forward" is unnecessary.

(B) In general, avoid these combinations:

advance forward	repeat again
join together	reread again
new innovations	return back
only unique	revert back
proceed forward	same identical
progress forward	sufficient enough

Use Exercises S95–S96 to develop your skills in identifying redundancies.

Exercise S95   *Checking phrases*

If the following phrases are redundant, cross out "and" and the second word.

Examples   established ~~and founded~~

salt and pepper

In the first example, you should cross out "and founded" because "established" means "founded." In the second example, you should leave "salt and pepper" as it is because "salt" is different from "pepper."

1. enlarged and grew

2. wounded and injured

3. small and single

4. sneeze and cough

5. long and slender

6. protect and guard

7. divide and conquer

8. original and first

Answers to Exercise S95 are on page 532.

Exercise S96   *Identifying redundancies*

If there are any redundancies in the following sentences, cross them out.

Example   The tourist industry has expanded ~~and grown larger~~ in recent years.

1. Scientists who spend years studying jaguars rarely see these shy, timid creatures.

2. Drastic measures are often necessary and needed to stop famines.

3. Labels should include the information that allows shoppers to compare the ingredients and contents of the food they are buying.

4. Illnesses caused by viruses and bacteria may lower the level of vitamins in the bloodstream.

5. Heavy consumption of alcohol and drinking a lot of wine may interfere with the body's utilization of folic acid.

6. Both overeating and skipping meals can cause adverse effects.

7. Montreal is the charming and enchanting old capital city of Quebec.

8. A 1,300-year-old Byzantine ship and another old, ancient vessel have been retrieved from watery graves.

Answers to Exercise S96 are on page 532.

CHECK YOUR PROGRESS

Check your progress in using the skills you have been practicing in Exercises S82–S96 by completing the following mini-test. This exercise uses a format similar to that used in the Structure Section of the Computer-Based TOEFL®Test. If you are unfamiliar with how to answer questions on the Computer-Based TOEFL®Test, see the Tutorial on pages 22–23.

Exercise S97   Mini-test

Select the letter of the correct answer.

1. More advances have been made in
    technology in the last one hundred years
    _____ in all the rest of human history.
    (A) than
    (B) as
    (C) and
    (D) as well as

2. The main routes <u>used</u> by the pony express
                        A
    <u>were</u> equipped with <u>stops</u> providing stables,
     B   C
    lodging, and <u>eating</u>.
                   D

3. Bryce Canyon is 56 square miles of badlands,
    towering pinnacles, and _____.
    (A) it has eroded forms that are grotesque
    (B) forming grotesque erosion
    (C) grotesque eroded forms
    (D) there are grotesque forms of erosion

4. Married women are <u>twice</u> <u>so</u> likely as married
                          A   B
    <u>men</u> to <u>be depressed</u>.
     C   D

5. The shrinking range poses _____ to Africa's
    elephants.
    (A) a graver threat that is long-term
    (B) long-term the gravest threat
    (C) the gravest long-term threat
    (D) a long-term threat graver

6. <u>The</u> seemingly endless attacks of mosquitoes,
     A
    <u>fly</u>, and other pests can <u>ruin</u> an
     B   C
    otherwise enjoyable <u>outing</u> in the woods.
                          D

7. _____ in astronomy, the discovery of Uranus
    was by accident.
    (A) It was like many finds
    (B) Like many finds
    (C) Alike many finds
    (D) Many alike finds

8. Carnivals, <u>with</u> spectacular parades, masked
                 A
    balls, mock ceremonials, and street <u>dancing</u>,
                                          B
    usually last <u>for</u> a week or more <u>than</u> before
                  C   D
    Mardi Gras itself.

9. _____, the condor in Peru is threatened by the
    rapid encroachment of humans.
    (A) As isolated as its few remaining habitats
        may be
    (B) As its few remaining isolated habitats may be
    (C) May its few remaining habitats be
        as isolated
    (D) Its few remaining habitats may be as
        isolated as

10. Finland is <u>heaviest</u> <u>forested</u> and contains
                 A   B
    thousands <u>of</u> lakes, numerous rivers, and
                C
    <u>extensive</u> areas of marshland.
     D

11. _____, Mozart had already written his first composition.
    (A) His age was six
    (B) By the age of six
    (C) He was six
    (D) Six years old

12. Purple has always been considered the color

    of royalty <u>because</u> historically it was
    <u>A</u>   <u>B</u>
    the <u>harder</u> color <u>to</u> manufacture.
         <u>C</u>   <u>D</u>

13. Julius Caesar did not conquer Britain but instead stayed a few weeks, took some hostages, and _____.
    (A) before returning to Boulogne
    (B) he returned to Boulogne
    (C) then to Boulogne
    (D) returned to Boulogne

14. <u>No</u> structural style spread <u>as</u> rapidly and
    <u>A</u>   <u>B</u>
    <u>as</u> <u>wide</u> as the Gothic.
    <u>C</u> <u>D</u>

15. Today shire horses are seen more and more in their traditional role _____ workhorses.
    (A) alike
    (B) as
    (C) like
    (D) as if

16. <u>On</u> twelve-person <u>juries there</u> is <u>not much</u>
    <u>A</u>   <u>B</u>   <u>C</u>
    vocal participation as <u>on</u> six-person juries.
                 <u>D</u>

17. The Viking Ship Museum houses _____ ever recovered.
    (A) three finest funeral ships
    (B) the finest three funeral ships
    (C) the three finest funeral ships
    (D) the three funeral finest ships

18. Wearing high heels <u>too much</u> has immobilized
                   <u>A</u>
    women and resulted <u>in</u> their suffering from
                   <u>B</u>
    bunions, corns, <u>twisted</u> ankles, spinal
               <u>C</u>
    deformities, and <u>shorten</u> calf muscles.
              <u>D</u>

19. The Searight collection _____ of the Middle East by European artists covers work done in the past two centuries.
    (A) of some six thousand drawings and paintings
    (B) about six thousand drawings and paintings
    (C) some six thousand drawings and paintings big
    (D) about six thousand drawings and paintings in all

20. The Roman emperor Caligula set up

    <u>and established</u> a temple <u>with</u> a life-sized
       <u>A</u>   <u>B</u>
    golden statue <u>of</u> himself that was dressed
              <u>C</u>
    each day <u>in the same way</u> he was.
             <u>D</u>

Answers to Exercise S97 are on page 532.

Exercise S98   ***Structure Section Practice Test***

When you have completed the Structure exercises as recommended on the Diagnostic Test, test your skills by taking this Structure Practice Test, which corresponds to the Structure Section of Test 2 on the CD-ROM that accompanies this book. Alternatively, you can take the test on the pages that follow.

During the Structure Section of the actual Computer-Based TOEFL® Test, you may not go back to check your work or change your answers. Maintain the same test conditions now that would be experienced during the real test.

Answers to Exercise S98 are on page 533.

STRUCTURE
Time – 15 minutes

This section measures your ability to understand the structures of standard written English. There are twenty questions in this section. There are two types of questions.

The first type of question consists of incomplete sentences. Beneath each sentence there are four words or phrases. You will select the one word or phrase that best completes the sentence.

Example:

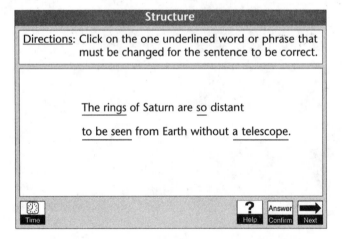

The second type of question consists of a sentence with four underlined words or phrases. You will select the one underlined word or phrase that must be changed for the sentence to be correct.

Example:

Now begin working on the Structure questions.

1. Deep in the Rio Bec area of Mexico's Yucatán Peninsula _____.
   (A) does a 1,250-year-old pyramid lie
   (B) a 1,250-year-old pyramid lie
   (C) is a 1,250-year-old pyramid lying
   (D) lies a 1,250-year-old pyramid

2. Motoring authorities <u>credit</u> mandatory
                                   A
   seat-belt laws for the <u>reduces</u> <u>in</u> traffic
                                 B   C
   <u>fatalities.</u>
    D

3. The Pacific Crest Trail is America's _____.
   (A) longest footpath
   (B) the long footpath
   (C) footpath the longest one
   (D) the longest footpath

4. Vancouver, British Columbia, <u>was named after</u>
                                       A   B
   the man <u>which</u> explored the <u>area</u> in 1792.
              C   D

5. _____ almost every major city in the world.
   (A) Air pollution that now afflicts
   (B) Not only does air pollution now afflict
   (C) Air pollution now afflicts
   (D) Air pollution what now afflicts

6. Belgian chocolate is <u>considered</u> by <u>many</u> to be
                               A   B
   <u>more</u> finer than any <u>other</u> in the world.
      C   D

7. Today, "carpet" refers to floor coverings that
   reach from wall to wall, _____ "rug" refers to
   a piece of material that covers only one section
   of the floor.
   (A) therefore
   (B) whereas
   (C) in as much as
   (D) among

8. It <u>is well-known</u> fact <u>that</u> camels can <u>go</u> for
          A   B   C
   extended periods <u>without</u> water.
                        D

9. The triple function of Bodiam Castle's moat
   was to be defensive, to be decorative,
   and _____.
   (A) to double the impression of impregnability
   (B) to be double the impression
       of impregnability
   (C) double the impression of impregnability
   (D) for doubling the impression
       of impregnability

10. The artists John Constable and Thomas

    Gainsborough <u>were born</u> <u>at</u> a <u>few</u> miles
                      A   B   C
    of each <u>other</u>.
               D

11. _____ is that a chicken stands up to lay its eggs.
    (A) Many people don't realize
    (B) It is that many people don't realize
    (C) Because many people don't realize
    (D) What many people don't realize

12. Sunlight <u>can be used</u> to generate electricity by
                  A
    means of cells <u>containing</u> substances that emit
                       B
    electrons <u>that</u> bombarded <u>with</u> photons.
                 C   D

13. _____ before the stork chick moves even six inches in the nest.
   (A) Just over five months is
   (B) It takes just over five months
   (C) When just five months are over
   (D) That it takes just over five months

14. The capital of Yemen is situating 2,190 meters
      A   B   C
   above sea level.
     D

15. Thor Heyerdahl, _____ from Peru in a frail balsa craft, attempted to prove his theory of South American migration to Polynesia.
   (A) set sail
   (B) has set sail
   (C) he set sail
   (D) setting sail

16. The psychological school of behaviorism
      A   B
   it was founded by J. B. Watson.
    C   D

17. Napoleon III eventually landed in England _____.
   (A) not only as a dethroned exile
   (B) but only as a dethroned exile
   (C) but a dethroned exile
   (D) but being only a dethroned exile

18. The discovery of gold in 1849 brought
       A   B   C
   California nationwide attentive.
                      D

19. Jacob Lawrence is considered by many critics _____.
   (A) to be the foremost African-American artist
   (B) the foremost African-American artist is
   (C) foremost African-American artist
   (D) is the foremost African-American artist

20. The Kerma civilization was some of the
            A   B
   earliest indigenous African tribal groups.
     C   D

This is the end of the Structure Section Practice Test.

SECTION ·3· READING

The Reading Section of the Computer-Based TOEFL® Test measures your ability to understand academic written English. It contains passages and questions about each passage. These questions include both vocabulary and reading comprehension questions. All the information needed to answer the comprehension questions is stated or implied in the passages.

This section is not computer-adaptive. This means that the computer will not choose a set of questions for you, so you can skip questions and return to them later. Read the entire passage and answer each question, or skip questions by clicking on the Next icon. If you want to go back, click on the Prev icon. The allotted time ranges from 70–90 minutes and the number of questions ranges from 44–60. The total number of questions in the section and the number of the item you are answering will be displayed on the computer screen. There is also a clock icon on the screen showing the number of minutes and seconds you have left. This display can be turned on or off, except during the last five minutes of your allotted time, when it will remain on.

STRATEGIES TO USE FOR BUILDING READING FLUENCY

1. Read extensively.

The more you read, the better you become at reading. Read on a variety of topics in order to build your vocabulary. The larger the vocabulary you have, the less time you will have to spend trying to understand words in context and the more time you will have for accurate reading.

2. Read challenging material.

Read material that challenges you. If you always read things that are easy for you, you will not develop your ability to read more difficult material.

3. Read materials related to topics commonly used on the Computer-Based TOEFL® Test.

A large proportion of the passages seen on the Computer-Based TOEFL® Test concern topics of science and technology. The social sciences are the second most common reading topics. A smaller proportion of the passages concern the humanities. Choose your reading material accordingly.

4. Read the material critically.

Think about what you are reading. Ask yourself what the reading is about. Ask yourself how the writer defends the ideas presented.

5. Increase formal and academic vocabulary.

Use the following strategies to build your vocabulary.

STRATEGIES TO USE FOR BUILDING VOCABULARY

1. *Read extensively.*

The kind of vocabulary that you will encounter on the Computer-Based TOEFL® Test is formal and academic. Read as much as you can – particularly newspapers, magazine articles, and encyclopedia entries that are academic in nature. By reading this type of material, you will encounter the kind of words that will be useful for you to learn.

When you are reading, try to guess the meaning of unknown words from the context. To do this, use other words in the sentence or passage as clues that show you the meaning of unfamiliar words. If you still are not certain, look the word up in your dictionary and check if your guess was correct.

2. *Use notecards.*

When you come across a word you do not know, first write it on a notecard and then look it up in a dictionary. On the back of the notecard write down its meaning and any other information that will help you to learn the word.

Increase your vocabulary by studying your notecards. Write sentences using the new words. Try to add at least three new words with their synonyms (words that mean the same) and antonyms (words that mean the opposite) to your vocabulary every day.

3. *Use a dictionary.*

Invest in a good English dictionary. Dictionaries vary greatly. A good dictionary will have more information than just meanings. Look for a dictionary that includes the following information:

(A) The pronunciation of the word.
(B) Information on how the word is used grammatically. For example, is it a noun (n.), verb (v.), etc.?
(C) Clear meanings.
(D) An example of the word used in a sentence or phrase.
(E) Optional: The origins of words. This information may help you learn new words by giving you the meanings of the parts of the word (roots, prefixes, and suffixes).

4. *Learn roots, prefixes, and suffixes.*

Prefixes and suffixes are additions at the beginning and end of a root word to modify its meaning. A knowledge of these additions will help you expand your vocabulary.

A. A *root* is the base element of a word. For example:

"Pose" is a root meaning "put."

B. A *prefix* is a word element that is placed before a root. Adding a prefix to a root changes the meaning. For example:

1. *ex-* is a prefix meaning "out" or "from."

"Expose" (prefix + root) means to uncover, disclose, or reveal (to "put out").

When the tide went out, the shipwreck was **exposed**.

2. *im-* is a prefix meaning "in," "on," "into," "toward," or "against."

"Impose" (prefix + root) means to place upon.

The government is debating the possibility of **imposing** yet another tax.

C. A *suffix* is a word element that is placed after a root. It, too, changes the meaning of a root. For example:

1. *-tion* is a suffix that indicates a noun form.

An "imposition" (prefix + root + suffix) is a state of affairs in which someone or something inflicts (imposes) on someone a set of conditions that needs to be met.

> It was an **imposition** to ask him to go miles out of his way to pick up your package.

2. *-ure* is another suffix that indicates a noun form.

"Exposure" (prefix + root + suffix) is the state of being in a position where something is revealed to you or you reveal something.

> The **exposure** to a constant high level of noise in the factory affected his hearing.

5. Use a thesaurus.

It is easier to remember a word if you know related words. A thesaurus is a good source for finding words that are related. It may also list expressions that the words are used in.

To use a thesaurus, you look up the word you want in the index at the back. The index entry is followed by one or more words with page references, all of which are in some way related to the word you are looking up (although they are not necessarily synonyms). A number following each reference will direct you to a section that contains lists of further related words. Use your dictionary to find the precise meaning for any word you are unsure of.

6. Use a dictionary of synonyms and antonyms.

A dictionary of synonyms and antonyms is useful because it lists both words that mean the same and words that mean the opposite. Expand your vocabulary by adding words that mean the opposite to your vocabulary list.

7. Make word diagrams.

It is easier for some people to remember related words if they use symbols, diagrams, or "word maps." Here are a few examples.

This is a word map for adjectives that mean the same as "strange."

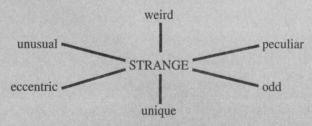

Here is a word chart for professions:

Concerning money	Helping people	Working with machinery
economist banker stock broker	social worker therapist counselor	engineer mechanic

Here is a way to write words and their opposites: poor ≠ rich
destitute ≠ affluent
indigent ≠ wealthy

By showing relationships between words, it is often easier to remember new vocabulary.

8. Make good use of your free time.

People spend a lot of time waiting. Keep your notecards with you. The next time you are waiting for a bus, sitting in a doctor's office, or standing in a line, get out your cards and review your words.

STRATEGIES TO USE FOR READING

1. Read the complete passage.

The reading passages are too long to fit on one computer screen. The scroll bar lets you move the passage up and down the screen. If you try to go on to the questions without scrolling down to the end of the passage, you will get a computer "error" message informing you that you can't go on until you have read the entire passage.

2. Read the question and the information carefully.

Some items consist of a question and answer choices. Other items consist of only a question. The answer choices are in the passage. Some items include added information such as arrows showing you which paragraph contains the answer. Some items include added instructions such as "scroll down to see all the answer choices."

3. Use context clues to understand the passage.

Even native speakers do not always understand all the vocabulary words used in the passages. Instead, they use clues from other words in the sentence or passage to determine the meaning of unfamiliar words.

Although context clues will not always help you to answer questions on particular vocabulary items, using them will help you understand the passage in general.

4. Read the passage even if you are familiar with the topic.

Sometimes you will find a passage about a topic you are familiar with. However, you should read the passage anyway. It might contain new information concerning the topic or concepts that conflict with your ideas about the topic.

5. Try to answer each question as you come to it.

Since the Reading Section is not computer-adaptive, you can skip difficult questions and return to them later. However, to return to a previous question you must click back through all the questions between the one you skipped and the one you are currently on. It is best to answer all the questions in a set and go back only if you realize that you have answered one incorrectly. In this way you avoid the possibility of forgetting that you skipped a question, and you avoid losing time in going back to a previous question.

6. Use your time wisely.

Every section has a time limit, so pacing yourself in order to make good progress is essential. You can use your time wisely in the following ways:

(A) Be familiar with the types of questions and directions in the test so you don't have to use your time in trying to understand what to do.

(B) Pay attention to the number of questions that are displayed on the computer screen and the amount of time remaining on the clock icon, which you can show and hide. Pace yourself according to the time and number of questions you have left.

(C) Be familiar with scrolling techniques and reading material on a computer screen.

(D) Be sure to read the complete passage. If you don't scroll down, a computer "error" message will appear on your screen and instruct you to do this. You must click off the box and go back to the passage. This procedure takes time that would be better used in reading and answering the questions.

(E) Be sure to go back to answer skipped questions before you proceed to the next passage. It is best to answer every question as you come to it, instead of skipping any. You are allowed to skip questions and go back at any time, but the further you continue in the test, the more time is lost in going back.

(F) Don't lose time thinking about something you don't know. Eliminate the answer choices you know are wrong and then decide which answer you think is best. Quickly go on to the next question.

PRACTICE WITH VOCABULARY

The vocabulary items consist of two types of questions: multiple-choice questions and questions that require you to click on a word or phrase in the passage.

In the multiple-choice questions, you are given a word that is highlighted in the passage and four different words from which to choose a word that is closest in meaning to the highlighted one. Sometimes you can understand the word by the way it is used in the passage and sometimes you cannot. The four answer choices are not in context, and therefore, you have to recognize these words in order to answer the question correctly.

In the click-on questions, you are given a word that is highlighted in the passage and you are to choose another word within a **bold section** of the passage that means the same as the highlighted word. You can understand the words by the way they are used in the passage.

It may be possible to guess the meaning of a word from the context. For example, consider this sentence:

Timothy **scowled** when he saw the dent in his new car.

We can guess that Timothy is upset when he notices a dent in his new car. Although we can't know the *exact* meaning of "scowl" from the context, we can guess that it is a way of showing displeasure. We might further guess that most people show they are upset by their facial expression. Thus, we have arrived at a definition of "scowl": a facial expression that shows displeasure.

It's not always possible to get a clue to the meaning of a word from the context. For example, consider this sentence:

Timothy **scowled** when he saw Aunt Agatha.

Unless we know what Timothy's opinion of Aunt Agatha is, we cannot guess the meaning of "scowled" here. However, other sentences in the passage might indicate what his opinion is, and these could give a clue to the meaning.

Timothy **scowled** when he saw Aunt Agatha. Whenever she came to visit, pleasant family conversations turned into angry family feuds.

We can now guess that Timothy might be upset about Aunt Agatha's visit because of the way she disrupts family conversations. His being upset might be indicated by his facial expression or body posture.

Sometimes two words that mean the same are used within a passage.

> A **scowl** came over Timothy's face when he saw his Aunt Agatha. Whenever she came to visit, pleasant family conversations turned into angry family feuds. His frown deepened when he noticed that she was carrying an overnight bag.

We can guess from this passage that a "scowl" is a facial expression. The situation indicates that it is probably a disagreeable look. The word "deepened," meaning to become deeper, indicates that this unpleasant facial feature has intensified. The use of this comparison indicates that a "scowl" and a "frown" are close in meaning.

Improving your skills in understanding words through context and increasing your vocabulary in general will help you succeed in the Reading Section of the Computer-Based TOEFL® Test. Use Reading Exercises R1–R3 to practice your vocabulary skills.

Exercise R1   ***Understanding words in context***

Look at the underlined word and write its meaning on the line.

Example I   A <u>cutlass</u> is a short, curved sword.

sword
_____

You should write "sword" as the meaning of "cutlass" because the definition of "cutlass" is included in the sentence.

Read the paragraph and circle the letter of the word or phrase that completes the sentence.

Example II   In law, a nuisance is an act that has no legal justification and which interferes with the safety or comfort of other people. Public nuisances, those which are injurious to the community, may be prosecuted as crimes.

A public nuisance is

(A) a protective law
(B) an injurious act
(C) a legal justification
(D) a safety precaution

You should circle (B) because a "nuisance" is an act which interferes with the safety of others, that is, an injurious act.

USING THE VERB "TO BE"

The object following the verb "to be" is frequently used to identify the subject.

Example   A <u>salmon</u> is a fish.

The meaning of "salmon" is identified by the word "fish."

1. <u>Hypoxia</u> is an illness caused by a deficiency of oxygen in the tissues of the body.

_____

2. A <u>porcupine</u> is a large climbing rodent that is covered with sharp spines for defense.

_____

3. The <u>atom</u> is the smallest part of a chemical element that can exist and still have the properties of the element.

_____

4. The Celtic religion centered on the worship of a pantheon of nature deities. Their religious ceremonies included animal sacrifices and various forms of magic. Druids were the priests who led the people in this highly ritualistic worship.

Druids were

     (A) deities
     (B) ceremonies
     (C) sacrifices
     (D) priests

5. Waste that has been made useful is said to have been recycled. Empty bottles can be returned and used again. Other things that can be recycled are paper, plastic, and metals. Besides the esthetic value of recycling, there are many environmental reasons to do so.

Recycled material is

     (A) strewn garbage
     (B) common waste materials
     (C) paper, glass, and coffee
     (D) reused waste

6. Both the Rocky Mountains in North America and the Swiss Alps in Europe have high peaks that challenge the most skilled of mountain climbers. As these climbers ascend the steep, rocky crevices, they may come across edelweiss. Although edelweiss is the Swiss national flower, it is also found in the Rocky Mountains. It grows wild near areas with year-round snow and can be recognized by its small, white, star-shaped blossoms.

Edelweiss is a

     (A) crevice
     (B) flower
     (C) star
     (D) peak

USING APPOSITIVES

A noun or noun group that follows a noun and is set off by commas is called an appositive. It identifies the noun it follows.

Example I   <u>Mercury</u>, **the silver-colored metal used in thermometers**, is usually in a liquid form.

The meaning of "mercury" is identified by its appositive, "the silver-colored metal used in thermometers."

By adding the words "which is/are" or "who is/are," you can test if the noun is an appositive.

Example II <u>Mercury</u>, **which is** the silver-colored metal used in thermometers, is usually in a liquid form.

7. <u>Pacemakers</u>, small electrical devices that stimulate the heart muscle, have saved many lives.

_____

8. Many residents of Hawaii used to believe that the volcano's flarings were tirades of their goddess, <u>Pele</u>.

_____

9. Studying <u>supernovas</u>, the catastrophic explosions of dying stars, may give answers to questions of modern cosmology.

_____

10. Seventeenth-century attempts to preserve anatomical specimens brought about modern embalming, the preservation of the body after death by artificial chemical means. The most common agent used today is formaldehyde, which is infused to replace body fluids.

Embalming is

    (A) death by a chemical means
    (B) the preservation of anatomical specimens
    (C) a common agent related to formaldehyde
    (D) the replacement of body chemicals

11. An extinct species of an animal or plant no longer has any living members. Many species have been recorded as having gone extinct in the twentieth century. However, occasionally a member of a species thought to be extinct is found. The coelacanth, a large-bodied, hollow-spined fish, was one such creature. This predecessor of the amphibians was considered extinct until 1938, when one was caught by a fisherman off the coast of South Africa.

A coelacanth is

    (A) an extinct creature
    (B) an amphibian
    (C) a predecessor
    (D) a fish

12. Samuel Finley Breese Morse spent twelve years perfecting his own version of André Ampère's idea for an electric telegraph. However, this inventor is best known for his Morse code, a system of telegraphic signals composed of dots and dashes. The dot represents a very brief depression of the telegraph key. The dash represents a depression three times as long as the dot. Different combinations of dots and dashes are used to code the alphabet, numerals, and some punctuation.

Morse code is a system of

    (A) telegraphic signals
    (B) telegraphic keys
    (C) telegraphic dots
    (D) telegraphic dashes

USING PUNCTUATION

Punctuation marks are sometimes used to set off a word that is being used to identify another word. Some of the punctuation marks you may see used in this way are:

commas	,	brackets	[ ]
dashes	–	single quotation marks	' '
parentheses	( )	double quotation marks	" "

Example   In laser printing, the greater the number of <u>dpi</u> (**dots per inch**), the higher the quality of the image produced.

The meaning of "dpi" is identified by the words in parentheses, "dots per inch."

13. The use of carved birds, "<u>decoys</u>," is not a new idea in hunting.

_____

14. If you are <u>ectomorphic</u> (the slender type), you are likely to be good in such sports as track, tennis, and basketball.

_____

15. A path to the chieftain's headquarters winds through ancient <u>petroglyphs</u> – inscriptions in stone.

_____

16. At the age of 19, Galileo discovered isochronism – the principle in which each oscillation of a pendulum takes the same time despite changes in amplitude.

Isochronism is

        (A) a principle
        (B) an oscillation
        (C) a pendulum
        (D) an amplitude

17. A composer indicates to a musician how a musical passage is to be played through the use of dynamic markings. The symbol for soft is p, whereas the one for loud is f. The intensity – loudness or softness – depends on the extent or amplitude of the vibrations made by the particular instrument being played.

Intensity is

        (A) dynamic markings
        (B) the symbol for soft and loud
        (C) the extent of the vibrations
        (D) loudness or softness

18. Oral history, the use of the tape recorder to capture memories of the past in private interviews, has become increasingly popular among professional historians. Studs Terkel is the best known of America's historians to use this method for recording historical events. He interviewed people about their experiences during important events such as the Great Depression and World War II.

Oral history is

        (A) private interviews
        (B) the recording of people's memories
        (C) experiences during important events
        (D) the history of tape recording

USING "OR"

A word or phrase is sometimes identified by a synonym following the word "or."

Example   The husky, or sled dog, of the North is a hardy breed.

The meaning of the word "husky" is identified by the words "sled dog" following the word "or."

19. Altitude, or the height above sea level, is a factor that determines climate.

_____

20. Vespers, or evening worship, can be heard at St. Matthew's Cathedral.

_____

21. In seagoing vessels, bulkheads, or internal walls, form watertight compartments and strengthen the overall structure.

_____

22. According to many psychologists, phobias, or irrational fears, represent or are symbolic of repressed anxiety. They are usually persistent, illogical, and intense. The most useful treatment has been through behavior-modification therapy.

A phobia is

    (A) a psychologist
    (B) a fear
    (C) a symbol
    (D) a treatment

23. Honeybees live in colonies of many thousand members. A typical colony has a queen that lays eggs; fertile males, or drones; and sexually undeveloped females called workers. The workers care for the queen and larvae, gather nectar, make and store honey, and protect the hive.

A drone is

    (A) an egg
    (B) a male bee
    (C) an undeveloped female
    (D) a worker

24. The nervous system of an animal is not a simple electrical circuit. When a signal gets to one end of a nerve cell, the cell sprays various molecules out for the next cell to pick up. The central nervous system of grasshoppers, fruit flies, and other insects includes both the brain and a chain of simpler segmental ganglia, or groups of nerve cells.

Ganglia are

    (A) nervous systems
    (B) electrical circuits
    (C) groups of nerve cells
    (D) the molecules the cells send out

USING EXAMPLES

A word or phrase is sometimes identified by examples. These terms often introduce examples:

as   for example   such as
like   for instance

Example I   Percussion instruments, **such as** drums, cymbals, and tambourines, were the preferred instruments in the study.

The meaning of "percussion instruments" is identified by the three examples: "drums," "cymbals," and "tambourines."

Sometimes the word or words used in the example can be identified by the word that is exemplified.

Example II   Everything we know about early humans **such as** Neanderthals is based on fossilized remains.

The meaning of "Neanderthals" is identified by the words that it is an example of: "early humans."

25. Such large fish as groupers and moray eels recognize the wrasse as a friend that will help them.

_____

26. Creatures such as the camel and the penguin are so highly specialized that they can only live in certain areas of the world.

_____

27. The sand absorbs enough moisture to support drought-resistant plants such as mesquite, as well as several species of grasses.

_____

28. Much can be done to halt the process of desertification. For example, an asphalt-like petroleum can be sprayed onto sand dunes, and seeds of trees and shrubs can then be planted. The oil stabilizes the sand and retains moisture, allowing vegetation to become established where the desert had previously taken over.

Desertification is

   (A) spraying oil onto sand dunes
   (B) the planting of trees and shrubs
   (C) the vegetation becoming established
   (D) the desert taking over an area

29. Of all the microelectronic devices that engineers have produced, the computer has the greatest potential impact on society. At the heart of every computer, there are microchips. Microchips consist of large collections of devices like the diode and transistor connected on a single piece ("chip") of silicon.

Diodes and transistors are

   (A) computer collections
   (B) microelectronic devices
   (C) silicon pieces
   (D) computer engineers

30. How complicated the preparations for a camping trip are depends on the duration of the trip as well as the isolation of the area in which the camper intends to be. If campers intend to stay at one of the many commercial campsites, most of their needs are provided for. However, if one desires to be far from civilization, choosing camping paraphernalia such as tents, sleeping bags, cooking implements, and other supplies should be done with care.

Paraphernalia is

    (A) equipment
    (B) food supplies
    (C) sleeping bags
    (D) campsites

USING CLAUSES

Adjective clauses sometimes identify words. They are introduced by these words:

| that | where | who |
| when | which | whom |

Example   Airships, **which** are cigar-shaped, steerable balloons, have many uses, such as filming, advertising, and entertainment.

The meaning of "airships" is identified by the adjective clause "which are cigar-shaped, steerable balloons."

31. Recent tests show that silver sulfadiazine, which is a compound used in the treatment of burns, can cure the most serious types of African sleeping sickness.

_____

32. Melody, which is the succession of sounds, takes on new interest when fit into a rhythmic pattern.

_____

33. The "O" in many Irish names comes from the Gaelic word "ua," which means "descended from."

_____

34. The Pueblo Indians are those who dwell in pueblos, a name derived from the Spanish word for "village." The pueblo is usually built against the face of a cliff and generally consists of connected houses rising in a series of receding terraces. The roof of one house is the yard or patio of the next house. The kiva, where Pueblo Indians hold their secret ceremonies, is entered by an opening in the roof.

A kiva is a

    (A) patio
    (B) ceremonial room
    (C) series of terraces
    (D) Pueblo Indian village

35. The coyote resembles a medium-sized dog with a pointed face, thick fur, and a black-tipped, bushy tail. Although its main diet consists of rabbits and other rodents, it is considered dangerous to livestock. Consequently, thousands are killed yearly. In recent years, nonlethal techniques, those that do not kill coyotes, have been developed to protect sheep and other livestock while allowing the coyote to remain in the wild.

Nonlethal techniques are those that

    (A) are dangerous to livestock
    (B) injure thousands of coyotes yearly
    (C) allow livestock to live in the wild
    (D) are not deadly to coyotes

36. The phenomenon of a mirage, which is an atmospheric optical illusion in which
an observer sees a nonexistent body of water, can be explained by two facts.
First, light rays are bent in passing between media of differing densities. Second,
the boundary between two such media acts as a mirror for rays of light coming
in at certain angles.

A mirage is

    (A) an illusion
    (B) a body of water
    (C) a medium acting as a mirror
    (D) the boundary between two media

USING REFERENTS

Referents are words that refer back to or forward to other words in the sentence or paragraph.

Example   The solar-powered batteries in the ERS-1 are expected to function for
at least two years, during which time this **satellite** will be able to gather
more information than any previous satellite.

The meaning of "ERS-l" is identified by its referent, "satellite."

37. The farmers were concerned about the growing number of boll weevils. An
infestation of these insects could destroy a cotton crop overnight.

_____

38. The groom struggled with his tuxedo. He wondered why he had to wear these kinds
of clothes to get married.

_____

39. Emma was told to put the sheets in the hamper, but she found the basket too full
of soiled clothes to fit the sheets in.

_____

40. Important officials visiting President Roosevelt were surprised by his menagerie
of pets. No previous president had filled the White House with such a variety
of animals.

A menagerie is a varied group of

    (A) officials
    (B) presidents
    (C) animals
    (D) staff members

41. At least fifty weed species fight off competitors by emitting toxins from their roots, leaves, or seeds. These poisons do their work in different ways, such as inhibiting germination of seeds and destroying photosynthesis abilities.

Toxins are

(A) roots
(B) leaves
(C) seeds
(D) poisons

42. The English longbowmen did not draw their bows but bent them by leaning on them with one arm and the upper part of their body. This method utilized the strength of the body instead of just the arm and gave the archers endurance to use the longbow longer.

A longbowman is

(A) an archer
(B) a bowing technique
(C) a method for utilizing the strength of the body
(D) a way to increase endurance for longer use of the longbow

USING CONTRASTS

Sometimes the meanings of words can be understood because they are in contrast to another word in the sentence. Some words that indicate a contrast are:

but	in contrast	or
despite	in spite of	unlike
however	instead	whereas

Example   The brief scenes in the movie focus on the boy's point of view, **whereas** the longer scenes depict the father's side.

"Brief" scenes are understood to be "short" scenes because they are in contrast to the "longer" scenes.

43. The bite of a garter snake, unlike that of the deadly cobra, is benign.

_____

44. The bluebonnet, the Texas state flower, thrives in dry, poor soil but dies in overly wet conditions.

_____

45. Despite proposed cutbacks in financial support for domestic students, assistance for foreign students studying and training in the United States is to be sharply increased.

_____

46. A unified field theory is one in which two forces, seemingly very different from each other, are shown to be basically identical. According to such a theory, unification will take place at various stages as the energy and temperature increase.

Identical is

(A) different
(B) unified
(C) equal
(D) level

47. The campanile is chiefly a medieval form of Italian architecture. Built in connection with a church or town hall, it served as a belfry, watch tower, and sometimes a civil monument. Unlike other bell towers that are attached to buildings, the campanile generally stands as a detached unit.

A campanile is

    (A) a church
    (B) a town hall
    (C) a tower
    (D) a unit

48. While the methods used at other learning institutions are based on the theory that children need a teacher, the Montessori method is based on the theory that a child will learn naturally if placed in an environment rich in learning materials to play with. These materials are suited to children's abilities and interests, and learning takes place as the child plays. Children following this method are autodidactic, and only when a child needs help does the teacher step in.

Autodidactic is

    (A) playful
    (B) self-taught
    (C) able to learn
    (D) dependent on teachers

USING OTHER WORDS IN THE SENTENCE

Other words in a sentence can sometimes help identify a word.

Example   In order to sip the <u>nectar</u> with its long tongue, the bee must dive into the flower and in so doing becomes dusted with the fine pollen grains from the anthers.

We can guess that "nectar" is the substance that bees collect from a flower because the bee must "sip . . . with its long tongue" and "dive into the flower." We can guess that "anther" is a part of the flower because the bee gets "dusted with the fine pollen grains from the anthers" when it dives into the flower.

49. The bright purple <u>gentian</u> grows wild in Colorado and blooms in late summer.

_____

50. While blowing air into the leather bag, the bagpipe player produces melodies by fingering the <u>chanter</u>.

_____

51. Unfortunately, the plant's hairs kill useful insects, but this problem can be <u>alleviated</u> by controlling the amount of hair.

_____

52. The much larger <u>hull</u> of the multidecked round ship allowed it to carry more supplies, more men, more guns, and more sails, all of which were necessary for long voyages of commerce and discovery.

A hull is a

    (A) storage place
    (B) deck
    (C) kind of sail
    (D) type of commerce

53. In the third century B.C.E., Ctesibuis, the Greek engineer and theorist, first exercised his inventive talents by making an adjustable mirror and then creating ingenious toys that could move under their own power.

Inventive is

    (A) regional
    (B) creative
    (C) flexible
    (D) effective

54. Vitamin D is called the sunshine vitamin because it is absorbed through bare skin. The body uses it to form strong bones, and therefore, it is essential for growing children. People who are not exposed to the sun can become deficient in vitamin D and may develop the bone disease rickets.

Deficient is

    (A) overexposed
    (B) infected
    (C) lacking
    (D) improved

Answers to Exercise R1 are on page 534.

Exercise R2   *Choosing the synonym*

Read the passages. Circle the letter of the word or phrase that is the best answer to the questions following each passage.

Example   The horse has played a little-known but very important role in the field of medicine. Horses were injected with toxins of diseases until their blood built up immunities. Then a serum was made from their blood. Serums to fight both diphtheria and tetanus were developed in this way.

The word "serum" in line 3 is closest in meaning to

    (A) ointment
    (B) antitoxin
    (C) blood
    (D) acid

According to the passage, horses were given toxins to which they became immune. The blood was made into serums, which acted as antitoxins against the toxins of diseases. Therefore, you should choose (B).

Questions 1–6

The fork, which did not become a standardized item in Europe until the eighteenth century, was almost unheard of in America. With the absence of forks, it can be assumed that colonists used a spoon instead. The knife was probably
Line held in the right hand, generally the preferred hand for manipulating utensils
(5) or tools. The spoon would have been held in the left hand with the concave part of the bowl facing downward. In this position, the diner would be more adept at securing a piece of meat against a plate while the cutting took place. Once the meat was cut, the down-turned spoon would not have been suitable for picking up the morsel. Probably the diner would have put the knife down and shifted
(10) the spoon to the right hand. This action would bring the spoon into the correct position for scooping up the bite of food. This practice of shifting utensils back

and forth between hands continued when the fork made its way to America
and replaced the spoon as the tool to secure the food being cut. The fork kept
Line the food against the plate more adequately, and its curving tines served the same
(15) function as the bowl of the spoon. The custom of shifting the fork from the left
hand to the right was no longer necessary, but people continued to use the style
that they were used to. This American style of handling eating utensils persists
to this day.

1. The word "utensils" in line 4 is closest in meaning to
   (A) gadgets
   (B) cutlery
   (C) hammers
   (D) weapons

2. The word "adept" in line 6 is closest in meaning to
   (A) cultivated
   (B) agreeable
   (C) cumbersome
   (D) proficient

3. The word "morsel" in line 9 is closest in meaning to
   (A) piece
   (B) meat
   (C) food
   (D) spoon

4. The phrase "scooping up" in line 11 is closest in meaning to
   (A) packing up
   (B) hoisting up
   (C) messing up
   (D) picking up

5. The word "tines" in line 14 is closest in meaning to
   (A) handles
   (B) blades
   (C) prongs
   (D) bowls

6. The word "persists" in line 17 is closest in meaning to
   (A) prevails
   (B) operates
   (C) traces
   (D) impresses

Questions 7–12

When Jessye Norman's parents were knocking on the wall of their young
daughter's room as a signal for her to stop singing and to go to sleep, little did
they dream that this small child who seemed to have been born singing would
Line grow up to be an internationally renowned opera singer.
(5) It is not surprising that Jessye loved to sing. Music was an integral part of her
family's lifestyle. Although Jessye remembers her mother singing spirituals, it was
her grandmother who was always singing. Every hour of her day and every mood
was highlighted with a song that fit the occasion. As Jessye was growing up, her
piano-playing mother and trumpet- and trombone-playing brothers accompanied
(10) her when the family was called upon to provide special music for church services,
parent-teacher meetings, and ribbon-cutting ceremonies.

During her childhood, Jessye knew only three operatic numbers: one that she learned from a recording and two others – the only opera scores she could find
Line   at the local music store. Although singing was in her blood, it was not until she
(15)   attended Howard University that Jessye Norman took her first voice lesson, with Carolyn Grant, who recognized her talent and knew how to channel it. It was almost immediately after leaving the university in 1968, on her first visit to Europe, that Jessye won the singing prize in the International Music Competition of German Radio. The following year, she was invited to go to Berlin to perform
(20)   at the Deutsche Opera. Since that time, Jessye Norman has become a world superstar whose singular voice reaches audiences all over the world.

7. The word "renowned" in line 4 is closest in meaning to
    (A) infamous
    (B) celebrated
    (C) notorious
    (D) precocious

8. The word "integral" in line 5 is closest in meaning to
    (A) demanding
    (B) persistent
    (C) essential
    (D) intuitive

9. The word "highlighted" in line 8 is closest in meaning to
    (A) emphasized
    (B) contradicted
    (C) conveyed
    (D) belittled

10. The word "scores" in line 13 is closest in meaning to
    (A) points
    (B) experts
    (C) voice lessons
    (D) sheet music

11. The word "channel" in line 16 is closest in meaning to
    (A) station
    (B) irrigate
    (C) exploit
    (D) direct

12. The word "singular" in line 21 is closest in meaning to
    (A) flattering
    (B) exceptional
    (C) fluctuating
    (D) different

Questions 13–18

Many laws that have been passed in the various states of the United States over the years since their entrance into the Union are now out of date or seem ludicrous. For example, the laws in one state make it illegal for women to expose
Line   their ankles and for men to go without their guns. Obviously, these laws are
(5)   broken daily. With current trends in fashion, every woman who walks down

the street or goes to a beach or public swimming pool is committing a crime. While it was once considered of utmost importance that a man be armed and ready for action on the frontier, it is hardly necessary for a man to tote guns to work today.
Line However, a man without a gun is also technically breaking the law. On the other
(10) hand, another law makes it illegal to tether one's horse to the fence surrounding the capitol building. It is hard to imagine anyone riding a horse into the city and leaving it tied outside of the capitol building today. One would have to go to great lengths in order to break this law.

These outdated laws remain on the record because the time needed for state
(15) legislatures to debate the issues and make changes in the existing laws would keep the members from attending to more important current and relevant issues. It would be hard to calculate the cost to the taxpayers for these laws to be purged or updated. Consequently, it is likely that these laws will remain on the books.

13. The word "ludicrous" in line 3 is closest in meaning to
    (A) insipid
    (B) demeaning
    (C) ridiculous
    (D) incomprehensible

14. The word "expose" in line 3 is closest in meaning to
    (A) sprain
    (B) conceal
    (C) decorate
    (D) display

15. The word "tether" in line 10 is closest in meaning to
    (A) gallop
    (B) fasten
    (C) saddle
    (D) conduct

16. The word "debate" in line 15 is closest in meaning to
    (A) challenge
    (B) contemplate
    (C) discuss
    (D) overturn

17. The word "relevant" in line 16 is closest in meaning to
    (A) pertinent
    (B) fashionable
    (C) extraneous
    (D) inadequate

18. The word "purged" in line 17 is closest in meaning to
    (A) extracted
    (B) restored
    (C) remedied
    (D) amended

Answers to Exercise R2 are on page 534.

Exercise R3   ***Finding synonyms***

To answer some of the questions on the Computer-Based TOEFL® Test, you have to click on a word or phrase that is a synonym of a word highlighted in the passage. The computer screen will look like this.

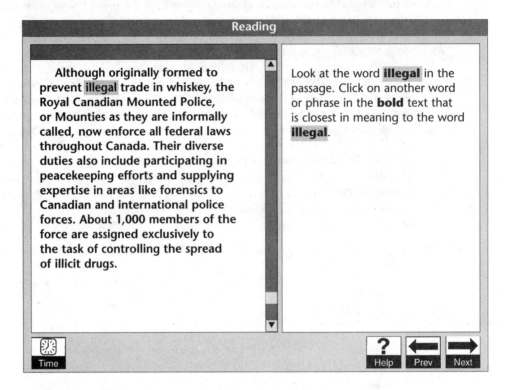

To answer this question, you would click on the word "illicit" because it is closest in meaning to the word "illegal." When you click on this word, it will darken to show which word you have chosen. If you change your mind, click on another word. When you are sure of your answer, click on Next to see the next question. There is no Answer Confirm icon in the Reading Section.

In the following exercise, each passage has a highlighted word within the **bold** print. Circle the word in the **bold** text that is closest in meaning to the highlighted word.

1. Astronomers have recently gained new knowledge of the behavior of galaxies. It has been discovered that spiral galaxies sometimes collide with each other. **The huge forces created in such a cosmic event can tug long trails of stars and create new ones from compressed gases. After repeated collisions galaxies may eventually merge, forming a single elliptical shape. Our own galaxy, the Milky Way, is on a collision course with the nearby Andromeda Galaxy. Hundreds of millions of years from now these two star systems may combine to form one giant configuration.**

2. **As long ago as the thirteenth century, Roger Bacon, the celebrated philosopher and Franciscan friar, postulated that humankind could fly with the aid of a large ball constructed of thin copper filled with air. Throughout the centuries other scientific dreamers hypothesized the construction of a variety of flying devices. Leonardo Da Vinci, in particular, studied aspects of flight and made sketches for flying machines.** It was not until 1783 that the first people, Pilatre de Rozier and the Marquis d'Arlandes, successfully took off from the ground, in a balloon designed by the Montgolfier brothers.

3. Christmas Island, discovered by Captain James Cook on Christmas Eve in 1777, was once populated by a wide variety of bird species. **In recent years, at least eighteen species of birds – a total of seventeen million birds – have been observed to leave or to perish on the island. It is suspected that the cause of the disappearance may be related to a cyclical weather phenomenon in the Pacific that alters wind patterns, salinity, and ocean currents. These conditions have resulted in higher water temperatures, which may have caused the fish and squid that the birds live on to die.**

4. **The historic centers of the sister cities of Savannah and Charleston have fortunately been saved from demolition or neglect and now attract tourists eager to view the gracious old houses. Of particular interest for the visitor is the exquisite decorative ironwork found throughout the older parts of both cities, especially on porch and stair railings and banisters. Both wrought and cast iron became popular there in the early 1800s, since fire was a constant threat and iron would not burn. Pig iron, which was used as ballast in ships coming from Europe to pick up cargoes of cotton, was bought cheaply, and a local industry producing beautiful ironwork developed.**

Answers to Exercise R3 are on page 534.

CHECK YOUR PROGRESS

Check your progress in understanding vocabulary (Exercises R1–R3) by completing the following mini-test. This exercise uses a format similar to that used in the Reading Section of the Computer-Based TOEFL® Test. If you are unfamiliar with how to answer questions on the Computer-Based TOEFL® Test, see the Tutorial on pages 24–28.

Exercise R4   ***Mini-test***

Select the correct answer.

Questions 1–4

The incorporation of broken-down scrap tires into asphalt to produce a blend suitable for the construction of road surfaces is becoming widespread. The resulting material, asphalt-rubber, has several advantages over customary road-building materials. It can be applied in a reduced thickness, and this means that less material has to be mined and transported to the road site. **Furthermore, roads constructed with this material require less maintenance than more conventional roads. Another benefit is the abatement of traffic noise, a serious issue in urban areas. Perhaps most important, the reduction and possible eventual elimination of waste tires with all their attendant environmental problems may one day become a reality.**

1. The word scrap is closest in meaning to
   (A) waste
   (B) old
   (C) rough
   (D) broken

2. Look at the word **reduction** in the passage. Select another word or phrase in the **bold** text that is closest in meaning to the word **reduction**.

The incorporation of broken-down scrap tires into asphalt to produce a blend suitable for the construction of road surfaces is becoming widespread. The resulting material, asphalt-rubber, has several advantages over customary road-building materials. It can be applied in a reduced thickness, and this means that less material has to be mined and transported to the road site. Furthermore, roads constructed with this material require less maintenance than more conventional roads. Another benefit is the abatement of traffic noise, a serious issue in urban areas. Perhaps most important, the reduction and possible eventual elimination of waste tires with all their attendant environmental problems may one day become a reality.

3. The word customary is closest in meaning to
(A) special
(B) unusual
(C) regular
(D) suitable

4. The word elimination is closest in meaning to
(A) revision
(B) fulfillment
(C) reduction
(D) eradication

Questions 5–8

Emily Dickinson had only a handful of her poems published during her lifetime, and so secretive was she about her writing that even her own family was not aware of her literary activities. Emily never married, and after the age of 30 she became increasingly reclusive, rarely venturing out of her family home in Amherst, Massachusetts. **She did, however, take a keen interest in contemporary culture and science and was a lively and prolific correspondent. Her poetic output was abundant and much concerned with the themes of religious conflict, nature, love, and death. Technically her poems show innovative use of rhyme and rhythm, and exhibit intense emotion concisely expressed. After her death in 1886, her sister, Lavinia, discovered her entire unpublished output, over seventeen hundred poems in all, concealed in drawers.** Four years after Emily's death a selection of these was published, and since then her reputation has grown immensely. Her poetry is now acclaimed throughout the world.

5. The word reclusive is closest in meaning to
(A) solitary
(B) distinct
(C) hostile
(D) lonely

6. Look at the word prolific in the passage. Select another word or phrase in the **bold** text that is closest in meaning to the word prolific.

Emily Dickinson had only a handful of her poems published during her lifetime, and so secretive was she about her writing that even her own family was not aware of her literary activities. Emily never married, and after the age of 30 she became increasingly reclusive, rarely venturing out of her family home in Amherst, Massachusetts. She did, however, take a keen interest in contemporary culture and science and was a lively and prolific correspondent. Her poetic output was abundant and much concerned with the themes of religious conflict, nature, love, and death. Technically her poems show innovative use of rhyme and rhythm, and exhibit intense emotion concisely expressed. After her death in 1886, her sister, Lavinia, discovered her entire unpublished output, over seventeen hundred poems in all, concealed in drawers. Four years after Emily's death a selection of these was published, and since then her reputation has grown immensely. Her poetry is now acclaimed throughout the world.

7. The word intense is closest in meaning to
   (A) focused
   (B) inhibited
   (C) weird
   (D) strong

8. The word concisely is closest in meaning to
   (A) accurately
   (B) cryptically
   (C) movingly
   (D) succinctly

Questions 9–12

In the last couple of decades marine researchers have observed that epidemic diseases are attacking a variety of sea creatures. Some of them are affecting rare species that are already at risk of extinction. For example, in the 1980s a mysterious epidemic struck a species of sea urchin in the Caribbean, wiping out over 90 percent of the population. **Later in the same decade harbor seals in the Baltic and North Seas succumbed to an unidentified affliction. The green sea turtle has expired in large numbers as a result of developing tumors, known as fibropapillomas, which eventually cover the creature and prevent it from seeing or eating.** Coral reefs and the species that inhabit them have also witnessed an explosion of new diseases. Most of these reported diseases are infections that have appeared recently or are increasing in incidence or geographic range. Some scientists infer that human activity is responsible for spreading these afflictions. Perhaps industrial pollution is weakening the immune systems of marine populations and making them more susceptible to pathogens.

9. Look at the word **succumbed** in the passage. Select another word or phrase in the **bold** text that is closest in meaning to the word **succumbed**.

10. The word afflictions is closest in meaning to
    (A) situations
    (B) toxins
    (C) diseases
    (D) seizures

In the last couple of decades marine researchers have observed that epidemic diseases are attacking a variety of sea creatures. Some of them are affecting rare species that are already at risk of extinction. For example, in the 1980s a mysterious epidemic struck a species of sea urchin in the Caribbean, wiping out over 90 percent of the population. Later in the same decade harbor seals in the Baltic and North Seas succumbed to an unidentified affliction. The green sea turtle has expired in large numbers as a result of developing tumors, known as fibropapillomas, which eventually cover the creature and prevent it from seeing or eating. Coral reefs and the species that inhabit them have also witnessed an explosion of new diseases. Most of these reported diseases are infections that have appeared recently or are increasing in incidence or geographic range. Some scientists infer that human activity is responsible for spreading these afflictions. Perhaps industrial pollution is weakening the immune systems of marine populations and making them more susceptible to pathogens.

11. The word incidence is closest in meaning to
  (A) rate of occurrence
  (B) degree of circumstance
  (C) degree of severity
  (D) rate of exposure

12. The word susceptible is closest in meaning to
  (A) attractive
  (B) heedful
  (C) perilous
  (D) vulnerable

Answers to Exercise R4 are on page 534.

PRACTICE WITH MAIN IDEAS

All well-written paragraphs have a main idea. The main idea is what the paragraph is about. Questions concerning the main idea may be phrased in different ways on the Computer-Based TOEFL® Test. Here are some examples:

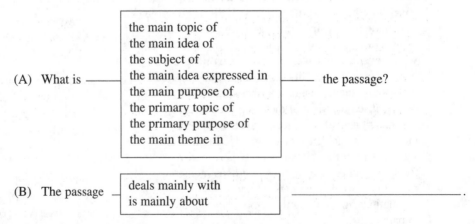

(A) What is ——
  the main topic of
  the main idea of
  the subject of
  the main idea expressed in
  the main purpose of
  the primary topic of
  the primary purpose of
  the main theme in
—— the passage?

(B) The passage
  deals mainly with
  is mainly about
————————————— .

(C) With what topic is the passage primarily concerned?

The topic of the passage is usually stated in the first sentence, although other positions are also possible. Read the following paragraph.

> The family heard the siren warning them that the tornado was coming. They hurried to the cellar. The roar of the tornado was deafening, and the children started crying. Suddenly it was silent. They waited awhile before they went outside to survey the damage.

In the preceding paragraph, the topic – the tornado – is stated in the first sentence. In the following paragraph, the main topic is stated in the last sentence.

> The family hurried to the cellar and waited. First, they heard the pounding of the hailstones. The wind became deafening, and the children started crying. Suddenly it was silent. They waited awhile before they ventured outside to see the damage the tornado had done.

Sometimes the topic is not stated in the passage at all but is implied, as in the following passage.

> The sky became dark and threatening. A funnel of dust began forming in the air and soon reached down to touch the ground. Debris was seen swirling around as everything was swallowed up, twisted, and then dropped.

Although "tornado" is not mentioned in the passage, it has been implied by the description ("a funnel of dust . . . in the air," "debris . . . swirling," "twisted").

Use Exercises R5–R7 to develop your skills in identifying the main ideas in reading passages.

Exercise R5   *Locating topics*

Read the following passages. Underline the word or words that give the "topic" of each passage. If the topic is implied, then write the topic in the space.

Example   Gilbert and Sullivan are best known for a series of operas that they collaborated on. Gilbert's humorous plots and paradoxes combined with Sullivan's music have made their operas unforgettable. Written in the nineteenth century, these operas maintain their popularity today.

You should underline "Gilbert and Sullivan" and "operas" because the passage is mainly about the operas that Gilbert and Sullivan wrote. You would leave the space empty because the topic is stated rather than implied.

1. The Japanese macaque is an endangered monkey. It inhabits an area farther north than any other primate except for humans. The Japanese call this animal the snow monkey because it can be found in the snowy regions of Japan. Ironically, some troops of macaques have been relocated to Texas to ensure their survival.

2. Originally, robots were found only in science fiction movies and books. Today, they have become science fact as technology has turned them into a feasible means of increasing productivity. The robot industries may still be in their infancy, but their products are no longer being ridiculed as an impossibility.

3. By nine o'clock in the morning, the streets are lined with people. Somewhere in the distance a band is heard playing a marching song. Shopkeepers are locking their doors and joining the crowds. Everyone is craning their necks to see how long it will be before the first float reaches them.

4. Parsley, a good source of iron and vitamins A, C, and E, is a common herb of the Mediterranean area. The ancient Greeks considered it sacred and therefore did not eat it. The Romans served it as a garnish and to improve the taste of food.

5. For thousands of years, desert dwellers have sheltered themselves in extremely functional buildings constructed of one of the most readily available, dependable, and inexpensive materials we know of. This ideal insulator, which absorbs heat during the day and slowly releases it at night, is mud.

6. Before World War II, Hay-on-Wye was a bustling little market town on the border of Wales and England. However, it became a dying town when Welsh agriculture declined, forcing many farmers off their land and to factory jobs in England. Today, Hay is flourishing again because of a flamboyant gentleman who has turned the town into the world's largest secondhand bookstore.

7. The Queens Children's Psychiatric Center on the eastern outskirts of New York is recruiting elderly men and women to work as foster grandparents for the children in the hospital. Even though these grandparents have no experience or training in dealing with emotionally disturbed children, they have lots of experience in being parents. It has been found that both foster grandparents and foster grandchildren benefit immensely from this relationship.

8. The koto is a traditional Japanese instrument originating in China. It is made by stretching thirteen strings of tightly coiled silk over an arched body of paulownia wood. The player plucks the strings to make the gentle zitherlike tones.

9. Parents are allowed at the starting gate only for the 6-and-under and the 5-and-under classes. Most of the bicycle racers in the 17-and-over expert classes have sponsors. Some of the racers even have an income.

10. Human beings are capable of thinking in two basic ways. Convergent thinking neatly and systematically tends toward an answer. Divergent thinking tends away from a center, perhaps in several directions at once, seeking avenues of inquiry rather than a particular destination. Scientists, on the whole, engage in convergent thinking, but it is divergent thinking that breaks with the past and leads to unpredictable conclusions.

Answers to Exercise R5 are on page 534.

Exercise R6   *Selecting a topic sentence*

In the following passages only the supporting ideas are given. The passages are followed by three possible topic sentences. Circle the letter of the sentence that would best introduce the passage.

Example   In Greek and Roman times, the cavalry was comprised of members of noble families. This distinction continued up to the Middle Ages. After the invention of gunpowder, this branch of the military service underwent great changes. With the development of heavy artillery and air forces, this service has almost disappeared.

(A) The cavalry has been displaced by armored regiments.
(B) Cavalry regiments still retain a mounted squadron for ceremonial duties.
(C) The cavalry is the part of an army consisting of troops that serve on horseback.

Both (A) and (B) discuss the cavalry situation of today. However, the passage discusses the cavalry from Greek and Roman times until today. Therefore, you should circle (C) because it introduces the topic – cavalry – by giving an explanation of what a cavalry is.

1. There appear to be tracks of young dinosaurs near tracks of older ones in the area. These dinosaur tracks are in sequences of eight to ten paces. They enable scientists to calculate the animals' weight, stride, and speed.
   (A) Important dinosaur tracks have been found in areas that were near ancient seas.
   (B) Some recently discovered tracks are giving important information about dinosaurs.
   (C) Dinosaurs may weigh as much as 10,000 pounds and be 23 feet tall.

2. This spider, named *Micromygale debliemma*, has only two eyes whereas most spiders have six or eight. Unlike most spiders, it does not have lungs but instead absorbs oxygen through its skin. Just three one-hundredths of an inch long, *M. debliemma* is one of the world's smallest spiders.
   (A) Scientists have discovered a spider that is remarkably different from any other known spider.
   (B) Scientists have discovered a spider that is the size of the head of a pin.
   (C) Scientists have discovered a spider that inhabits the coastal forested regions of Panama.

3. Trees can defend themselves against devouring insects by undergoing changes in the nutritional quality of their leaves. The leaves of nearby trees undergo the same changes in nutritional quality as do those attacked. It is hypothesized that trees emit chemical substances that transmit information to other trees concerning the attack.
   (A) Scientists believe that the nutritional quality of leaves causes chemical substances to transmit information.
   (B) Scientists believe that studies in tree communication could affect pest control programs.
   (C) Scientists believe that trees attacked by insects may communicate information to neighboring trees, which then take appropriate action.

4. It has an enameled surface decorated with elaborate designs, the outlines of which are formed by small bands of metal. The Byzantines excelled in making this kind of pottery. However, in the twentieth century, Japan and China have led in the production of cloisonné.
   (A) Cloisonné is a kind of fine pottery.
   (B) Pottery is fired in a kiln.
   (C) Fine pottery is made with a particular kind of clay.

5. Immunization can significantly reduce the microorganisms thought to cause cavities. The Federal Drug Administration needs to approve the vaccine before it can be sold to the public. Consequently, the vaccine will have to undergo a three-year trial period.
(A) A new cavity-preventing vaccine may soon be on the market.
(B) Vaccines given to animals can reduce tooth decay by 50 to 60 percent.
(C) The National Caries Program of the National Institute of Dental Research does research on immunizations.

6. Cirrus clouds are thin and delicate, whereas cumulus clouds look like cotton balls. Nimbus clouds are dark and ragged, and stratus clouds appear dull in color and cover the entire sky.
(A) A stratus cloud on the ground is called fog.
(B) There are four basic cloud types: cirrus, cumulus, nimbus, and stratus.
(C) It is possible to predict the weather by studying clouds.

7. For example, King William the First, better known as William the Conqueror, was the first Norman king of England. Perhaps the most famous English writer of all times was William Shakespeare. And who can forget the American hero of the West, Buffalo Bill (William) Cody?
(A) One of the most common boys' names in English is "William."
(B) "William" is not only a popular name today but was also the name of many famous people in the past.
(C) If your name is William, you have the same name as many other people.

8. Straw, which can absorb up to four times its weight in oil, can be thrown on the spill and then be burned. Oil can be broken up and sunk by either sand, talcum powder, or chalk. Under experimentation, some chemicals have been shown to disperse the spill into droplets, which microbes can then destroy.
(A) There are many ways in which oil spills in the sea can be dealt with.
(B) Contamination of the sea by oil spills is a critical problem.
(C) Wind and wave action can carry oil spills a great distance across the sea.

Answers to Exercise R6 are on page 535.

Exercise R7   *Checking the topic*

Each of the following passages is followed by a sentence that states a topic. If the stated topic is correct, go on to the next passage. If it is not correct, write the topic.

Example   The Pre-Raphaelite brotherhood was a school of artists formed in about 1848. The Pre-Raphaelites' ideal was absolute fidelity to nature. For a time, this school of thought greatly influenced art developments throughout Europe. However, within a decade the movement had disbanded.

The main topic of the passage is "the disbanding of the Pre-Raphaelite movement."

the Pre-Raphaelite movement
_____

The main topic of the passage is not the disbanding of the Pre-Raphaelite movement. Therefore, you would write the topic "the Pre-Raphaelite movement" in the space.

1. When a meteor collides with the Earth's atmosphere, the resulting friction causes the meteor to heat up and partially vaporize. Its entrance is seen as a brief flash of light and a luminous vapor trail that lasts for a few seconds. A meteor that reaches the Earth's surface is called a meteorite. Meteorites are extremely valuable to scientists because they are samples of actual cosmic material.

The main topic of the passage is "the vaporization of a meteor."

---

2. Because winning or losing a race in skiing can be a matter of a hundredth of a second, skiing equipment has undergone many changes. Even clothing has changed as skiers search for ways to increase speed. Now they wear one-piece suits that cling to their bodies in order to reduce wind resistance. Nothing is worn under these tight-fitting suits as anything extra may mean the loss of an important millisecond.

The main topic of this passage is "the changes in skiing equipment."

---

3. Addiction to cigarette smoking is basically an addiction to nicotine. Those who are attempting to overcome their addiction have found the most common cures ineffective. Switching to low-nicotine cigarettes simply causes problem smokers to smoke more. Cigarettes without any of this chemical substance are usually rejected because they don't satisfy smokers' needs. One aid, which some quitters have found effective, is a chewing gum containing nicotine, which allows them to stop without the unpleasant withdrawal symptoms. A newer version of the same kind of treatment provides a measured nicotine dose through an inhaler.

The main topic of this passage is "how smokers become addicted to nicotine."

---

4. Rice is the only major grain crop that is grown almost exclusively as human food. There has been a series of remarkable genetic advances that have made it possible to cultivate high-yield varieties that are resistant to disease and insect pests. Because rice constitutes half the diet of 1.6 billion people, and another 400 million people rely on it for between one-fourth and one-half of their diet, these advances have deterred disasters that otherwise would have left millions of people severely underfed.

This passage is mainly about world disasters.

---

5. While living in Germany with her family, Caroline Herschel was not allowed to learn anything other than useful household skills such as knitting. However, all this changed in 1772, when her astronomer brother, William, took her to live with him in England. He taught her mathematics, and she began to help him keep a record of his discoveries. The two of them would often stay up until dawn, gazing upward. Eventually, they built their own telescopes, which were even bigger and better than those at the Royal Observatory in Greenwich.

The passage is about the life of Caroline Herschel.

---

6. Two-thirds of China's vast territory is either mountainous or desert. Every spring, windstorms come raging out of the mountains and cross the great deserts gathering dust. A dense cloud of dust that is hundreds of miles wide forms. It is blown thousands of miles, traveling from the North Pacific to the Gulf of Alaska and from there moving south and then east. As the prevailing winds lose their velocity, dust particles fall from the cloud. It is believed that as much as 10 percent of the soil in Hawaii is composed of the dust particles collected from China's deserts and dispersed in the journey across the Pacific.

This passage is about the soil composition of Hawaii.

_____

7. Initially, underground homes are more expensive to build than conventional houses. In order to avoid a home resembling a dark, dank basement, much care and expense must be put into designing a home with well-placed windows and skylights that ensure brightness and fresh air. Also, expensive sophisticated waterproofing techniques need to be used to keep moisture out. However, in the long term, underground homes save the owner a great deal of money in heating and air-conditioning costs. Underground houses require much less energy because the soil temperature is relatively stable and the concrete walls can store the sun's heat and radiate it into the rooms at night.

The main topic of the passage is "the costs of an underground home."

_____

8. The potato, which is nutritious and tasty, is an important food for millions of people. Destruction of the potato crop by pests has resulted in famines. Plant researchers, studying the hundreds of varieties of potatoes, have uncovered a hairy wild variety of potato from Bolivia that emits a strong glue from the end of its hairs. This glue traps and kills insects. A new hairy potato was developed when researchers successfully crossed the common potato with the hairy potato. This new hybrid potato not only reduces aphid populations by 40 to 60 percent, but also emits a substance that checks the population of the Colorado potato beetle, one of the most destructive potato pests. Unfortunately, the hairs also trap beneficial insects. Plant researchers are currently trying to alleviate this problem by limiting the density of hairs.

The passage is about developments in the crossbreeding of potatoes.

_____

Answers to Exercise R7 are on page 535.

_____

CHECK YOUR PROGRESS

Check your progress in identifying the topic sentences (Exercises R5–R7) by completing the following mini-test. This exercise uses a format similar to that used in the Reading Section of the Computer-Based TOEFL® Test. If you are unfamiliar with how to answer questions on the Computer-Based TOEFL® Test, see the Tutorial on pages 24–28.

Exercise R8   Mini-test

Select the correct answer.

Between the late 1920s and 1950s, the Osborne Calendar Company produced a series of calendars featuring trains of the Pennsylvania Railroad. Up to three hundred thousand of these, featuring large, colorful scenes of trains at work, were published each year to hang in depots and shippers' offices along the lines of the famous railroad company. The scenes, mostly painted by one artist, Grif Teller, are now valuable collectibles.

1. What is the subject of this passage?
   (A) Trains at work
   (B) Calendars of the Pennsylvania Railroad trains
   (C) Valuable calendars
   (D) Grif Teller's paintings of trains

Yuzen dyeing is a Japanese art that produces a lavish, multicolored type of kimono design that dates from the seventeenth century. First, a pattern is sketched on a kimono of plain, undyed silk. The garment is then taken apart and the design carefully painted onto the fabric with a paste that prevents the fabric from absorbing dye. Next, dyes are brushed over the silk, their colors penetrating only the untreated areas. After the paste is rinsed out, the strips of silk are again sewed into the kimono. Elaborate embroidery often completes the decoration.

2. What is the main subject of this passage?
(A) Kimono design dating from the seventeenth century
(B) A description of Yuzen dyeing
(C) How kimonos are made
(D) The elaborate embroidery done on kimonos

The bioluminescent flashlight fish does not actually light up but has a saclike organ under each eye that contains luminous bacteria. Although the bacteria glow constantly, the fish can control the light by eye movements. The flashlight fish uses its lights to search for food in the dark depths. Upon finding the food, the fish blinks rapidly to signal its mates. If an intruder threatens, the fish can startle it by shining its light. Predators can be confused by the flashlight fish's flashing its light and abruptly changing directions.

3. What is the main idea of this passage?
(A) The flashlight fish uses its bioluminescence for different purposes.
(B) Bioluminescence can save the life of the flashlight fish.
(C) Bioluminescence in the flashlight fish is due to the luminous bacteria in the eye organs.
(D) Different fish use bioluminescence in different ways.

Cole Porter was never regarded in his lifetime as socially conscious. Society-conscious, yes; he was born rich and married richer, to Linda Lee Thomas, a wealthy divorcée. Songwriting made him a third fortune. He was not just rich and famous, he was famous for being rich. Though not a native New Yorker – he was a backcountry boy from Peru, Indiana – he and his work came to typify smart Manhattan society. His music was a highly personal mixture and had huge appeal. Porter, as an admiring contemporary remarked, made sophistication popular.

4. What is the subject of this passage?
(A) A socially conscious musician
(B) Becoming rich and famous
(C) The life of a songwriter
(D) Popularizing sophistication

The beaver's comical-looking flat tail, which is three-quarters of an inch thick, six or seven inches wide, and perhaps a foot long, is unique in the animal world. In the water, it serves as a rudder for swimming, and on land it props the beaver upright while the animal is cutting trees. It also serves as a radiator through which the heavily insulated beaver passes off excess body heat. The beaver uses its broad tail for an early warning system by slapping it against the water's surface, making a resounding whack that can be heard half a mile away.

5. What is the purpose of this passage?
   (A) To describe what the beaver's tail looks like to the reader
   (B) To inform the reader about the many uses of a beaver's tail
   (C) To give the reader a lesson in nature studies
   (D) To teach the reader how to use a beaver's tail

Tree rings have long been used to determine the ages of trees and to gauge past climatic conditions. New evidence adds considerable weight to the theory that tree rings also record earthquakes. The rings reflect the effects of earthquakes, such as tilting, the disruption of root systems, and breakage, as well as shifts in environments. Older trees and petrified trees may give information about earthquakes that took place hundreds and even thousands of years ago.

6. What is the main theme of this passage?
   (A) How earthquakes affect tree rings
   (B) How tree rings can be used to warn people of impending earthquakes
   (C) What information might be gained from studying tree rings
   (D) Why tree rings are used to determine tree ages, climatic conditions, and earthquakes

Answers to Exercise R8 are on page 535.

PRACTICE WITH UNDERSTANDING DETAILS AND RESTATEMENTS

In order to understand a reading passage, you need to be able to:

1. *Identify what the referents are referring to.*

   Instead of repeating the same words, writers use pronouns and short phrases to refer to these words. These are called "referents." They may refer back to a previously used word, phrase, or idea or anticipate a word, phrase, or idea that will follow.

Refer to the previous paragraph while looking at the following:

In the sentence **Instead of repeating the same words, writers use pronouns and short phrases to refer to these words,** these words refers to "the same words."

These in **These are called "referents,"** refers to "pronouns" and "short phrases."

They in **They may refer back to a previously used word, phrase, or idea or anticipate a word, phrase, or idea that will follow** refers to "referents."

All of the highlighted words are referents. Improving your understanding of referents will help you to follow the flow of ideas in reading passages, to answer specific referent questions, and to answer questions in general on the Computer-Based TOEFL® Test. (For more information, see Practice with Details, item 1, page 129.)

2. Follow the flow of ideas by paying attention to transitions and connectors.

The following list consists of transition words and connecting words that will help you to follow the flow of ideas.

Words that:

qualify	but, however, although, yet, except for
emphasize	surely, certainly, indeed, above all, most important
illustrate	for example, next, for instance, thus, such, such as
contrast	unlike, in contrast, whereas, on the other hand, instead
concede	although, yet, nevertheless, of course, after all
conclude	finally, in conclusion, at last, in summary, to sum up
add	in addition, also, moreover, then, first, second (etc.)
compare	similarly, like, in the same way, both, equally important
explain	now, in addition, furthermore, in fact, in this case, at this point
state a consequence	therefore, as a result, consequently, accordingly, otherwise

Using the clues from transition words and connecting words, as well as referents and other details in the passage, will help you to understand the reading passage, to answer questions requiring you to insert missing information, and to answer questions in general on the TOEFL® Test.

3. Concentrate on the details.

Numerous details are mentioned within a passage. Sometimes you must use this information to identify an illustration or to locate where in a paragraph or passage the information can be found. Sometimes you must use these details to identify information that has not been stated in the passage. Frequently, these details are stated in a different way in the TOEFL® Test questions and answer choices.

Improving your ability to recognize details from the passage that are stated in a different way in the questions and answers will help you find the information that you need to answer the questions.

Use Exercises R9–R20 to build your skills in understanding details and recognizing restatements in reading passages.

Exercise R9   *Locating referents*

Read the following statements. Find the referent for the underlined word or words and write it in the space. (For additional practice, see Exercise L31, page 131.)

Example   Because of <u>their</u> vitality and pervasiveness, some familiarity with Greek myth and legend is almost indispensable to a full appreciation of European culture.

their   *Greek myth and legend*

"Greek myth and legend" have "vitality and pervasiveness."

1. The first complete American dictionary of the English language was compiled in 1828 by the lawyer and lexicographer Noah Webster, <u>who</u> was particularly eager to show that American English was distinct from <u>that</u> spoken in Britain.

   who   _____

   that   _____

2. Under the ice, bubbles gather against the ice roof until <u>they</u> overflow and escape through the tide cracks.

   they   _____

3. Amnesty International consists of over nine hundred groups of individuals <u>who</u> work for the release of political prisoners incarcerated for <u>their</u> beliefs.

   who   _____

   their   _____

4. Seward's Folly is what people called Alaska when U.S. Secretary of State William Seward arranged to purchase <u>it</u> from Russia in 1867.

   it   _____

5. The Royal Canadian Mounted Police use horses and wear <u>their</u> famous red uniforms on ceremonial occasions.

   their   _____

6. Some psychiatrists believe that every person is surrounded by a force field that broadcasts <u>his</u> or <u>her</u> emotions to other people.

   his   _____

   her   _____

7. In 1863, <u>when</u> a Hungarian count recognized the potential of Californian soil and sun for growing wine grapes, <u>he</u> planted <u>the first European variety</u> <u>there</u> near the town of Sonoma.

   when   _____

   he   _____

   the first European variety   _____

   there   _____

8. Research in sensory deprivation has revealed that the human mind cannot operate normally unless <u>it</u> receives a constant succession of stimuli.

   it   _____

9. Novelist Willa Cather used the frontier life of the Nebraska prairie of her youth for her subject matter.

her _____

subject matter _____

10. Arctic people must not only defend themselves from the environment and wild animals, but they must also protect these natural resources.

themselves _____

they _____

these natural resources _____

Answers to Exercise R9 are on page 536.

Exercise R10   *Understanding referents*

Read each passage. Circle the letter of the correct answer to the question that follows each passage.

Example   Differences in the way men and women process language is of special interest to brain researchers. It has been known that aphasia – a kind of speech disorder – is more common in men than in women when the left side of the brain is damaged in an accident or after a stroke. However, women are more likely than men to suffer aphasia when the front part of the brain is damaged. This clearly indicates that the brains of men and women are organized differently in the way they process speech.

The word they in the passage refers to

(A) men
(B) women
(C) brains
(D) researchers

You should circle (C) because brains are organized differently in the way they process speech.

1. A mushroom found in New Jersey is more than three times as old as any previously discovered. Mushrooms are so fragile that they are seldom preserved for long. However, 90 million years ago this mushroom was surrounded by tree resin, which then solidified into amber. Bark fibers and leaves found in pieces of amber close by suggest that the mushroom was growing on the rotting remains of a cedar tree. Although tiny, only a few millimeters across, the New Jersey mushroom looks very similar to those belonging to the group of fungi that make up "fairy rings" found on lawns.

The phrase "fairy rings" in the passage refers to

(A) nearby pieces of amber
(B) the rotting remains of a cedar
(C) mushrooms trapped in amber
(D) a group of fungi

2. One of the most potentially explosive international problems is that of mass tourism. Of the more than six billion people in the world, an increasing number of them are determined to travel. Annually a vast number of travel-hungry tourists traipse around the globe, and thousands of perfect beaches, quaint villages, historic cities, and regions of exquisite natural beauty have fallen under developers' building schemes. Attempts to accommodate these people have led to the destruction of the very attractions that they have come to enjoy and have made daily living almost impossible for the local residents.

The phrase these people in the passage refers to

(A) people in the world
(B) tourists
(C) developers
(D) residents

3. Traditionally, America's fast-food companies have hired teenagers. While teenagers provide cheap labor, they are sometimes unreliable. Consequently, fast-food companies are looking into another source of cheap labor – the elderly. Older people are less likely to skip a day of work or quit without giving notice, but because they have not been brought up with computers, they view the high-tech fast-food counter with terror. Training centers are being opened in order to teach "mature workers" how to operate computerized cash registers, timed deep-fat fryers, and automatic drink-dispenser software. These students are put into classrooms with their peers and, since mental arithmetic is a thing of the past, are taught how to use a calculator.

The phrase These students in the passage refers to

(A) teenagers
(B) fast-food employers
(C) the elderly
(D) peers

4. The Bettmann Archive is a picture library that was founded in the 1930s by German immigrant Otto Bettmann. He arrived in New York City with two suitcases of photographs and opened a picture library, which he built into the biggest commercial operation of its kind in the world. Among the millions of photographs the archive contains are some of the most memorable images of the twentieth century: Marilyn Monroe standing by a street grate ventilating her skirt, Einstein sticking out his tongue, the Hindenburg exploding into flames. According to Bettmann, the archive's success was due to his unique filing system which he designed to suit journalistic needs. For example, the Mona Lisa was not filed under "Paintings" or "Leonardo da Vinci"; it was filed under "Smiling."

The word some in the passage refers to

(A) suitcases of photographs
(B) picture libraries
(C) commercial operations
(D) archive photographs

Answers to Exercise R10 are on page 536.

Exercise R11 **Finding the referent**

To answer some of the questions on the Computer-Based TOEFL® Test, you have to click on a word or phrase in the passage that the highlighted word refers to. The computer screen will look like this.

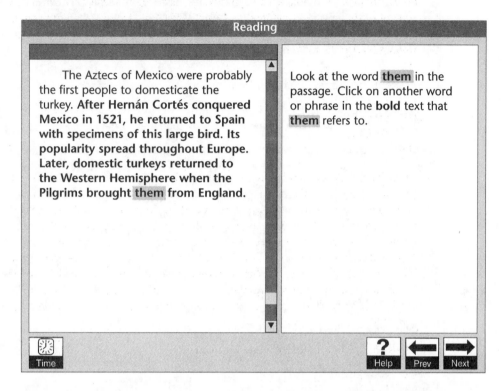

To answer this question, you would click on the word "turkeys" because them refers to the domestic turkeys brought by the Pilgrims. When you click on this word, it will darken to show which word you have chosen. When you are sure of your answer, click on Next to go on to the next question.

In the following exercise, each of the passages has a highlighted word within the **bold** print. Circle the word in the **bold** text that the highlighted word refers to.

1. People often assume that athletes are healthier and more attuned to their overall well-being than nonathletes. **However, two researchers who recently conducted a survey of college students reported that athletes are more likely than nonathletes to engage in behaviors that put their health at risk.**

2. **Scientists used to believe that animals scream to startle predators into loosening their grip. However, now some researchers have concluded that the piercing, far-reaching screams of animals are not warnings to kin or cries for help.** Recent studies indicate that these screams may be to attract other predators, which will give the prey a chance to escape during the ensuing struggle between predators.

3. When cartoonists take on the task of drawing real people, they do so by making a caricature. These kinds of cartoon drawings are frequently used to satirize well-known people. **Most famous people have several particular characteristics, such as facial features, body posture, or gestures, which are familiar to the general public. Cartoonists can cleverly exaggerate them to the point of ridiculousness.**

4. Satellites routinely relay pictures of desert areas. From these pictures, it can be determined where locusts are likely to breed. **With information on the locusts' breeding areas, agriculture officials can use pesticides to kill these insects before they become a menace. If not eradicated, a single swarm can devour 80,000 tons of corn a day – sustenance for half a million people for one year.**

Answers to Exercise R11 are on page 536.

Exercise R12   *Understanding transitions and connectors*

Complete these sentences by choosing the phrase or clause that would follow the underlined transition words or connectors. Circle the letter of the phrase or clause.

Example   Although potatoes are richer in food value than any other vegetable, they are not always a wise choice for a garden crop because they need a considerable amount of room. Consequently,

(A) they are the most common vegetable in a garden.
(B) people don't eat potatoes very much.
(C) they can be more economically grown on farms.
(D) farmers overcharge for their potatoes.

You should circle (C) because if potatoes are not a wise choice for a garden because of the amount of room they need, they could be grown on a farm more economically, since a farm does have adequate space.

1. Glass was precious to Egyptians, who used it interchangeably with gemstones, but
   (A) it is over 4,000 years old.
   (B) its novelty as an artist's material prevents its being taken seriously.
   (C) today it has come out of factories and into the workshops.
   (D) today it is so commonplace in everyday objects that it is seldom given a second thought.

2. Glimpses into the prenatal world via ultrasound imaging occasionally show behavior such as
   (A) the development of the central nervous system.
   (B) the sex of the baby-to-be.
   (C) a fetus sucking its thumb.
   (D) structures as small as the pupil of an eye of a second-trimester fetus.

3. Although the animals and plants that live in the world's various deserts come from different ancestral stocks,
   (A) they have solved their problems of survival differently.
   (B) none of them have adapted to the jungles.
   (C) they are from different deserts.
   (D) they resemble one another to a surprising degree.

4. Children dress up in witches' hats or goblin suits to play pranks when celebrating the ancient pagan holiday of Halloween. In contrast,
   (A) Thanksgiving is a traditional holiday.
   (B) Thanksgiving is always celebrated on the fourth Thursday of November.
   (C) families dress more formally and set elegant tables for the more serious occasion of Thanksgiving.
   (D) children enjoy Thanksgiving.

5. Everything from chairs and fishing poles to rope and paper can be made from bamboo. Equally important,

(A) this giant grass grows in warm climates.

(B) fresh spring bamboo shoots take longer to cook than winter ones.

(C) a variety of foods can be made from this giant grass.

(D) preserved bamboo shoots can be used in soups instead of fresh ones.

6. Earth satellites transmit telephone and television signals, relay information about weather patterns, and enable scientists to study the atmosphere. This information has helped people communicate ideas and expand their knowledge. In conclusion,

(A) satellites have enriched the lives of humankind.

(B) satellites are expensive to send into space and sometimes are difficult to maintain.

(C) a dish antenna can pick up 300 TV channels from satellites.

(D) satellites are placed in an orbital region around Earth called the geostationary belt.

7. In the 1940s, when many of today's astronauts hadn't even been born, comic-strip detective Dick Tracy fought crime in an atomic-powered space vehicle. In addition to that,

(A) many of today's astronauts have used a kind of atomic-powered space vehicle.

(B) he used lasers to process gold and a two-way wrist TV for communication.

(C) "Dick Tracy" was a very popular comic strip in the United States.

(D) astronauts used lasers to process gold and communicated on long-distance flights using two-way wrist TVs.

8. Until recently, chlamydial infections could be detected only by a complicated test that took up to seven days to complete and which was offered only at a few medical centers. As a result,

(A) up to 10 percent of all college students are afflicted with it.

(B) chlamydial infections were rarely diagnosed.

(C) chlamydial infections were treated promptly.

(D) doctors prescribe large doses of antibiotics to treat the infections.

9. Medical researchers have recently developed a nonsurgical method of treating heart disease that, in some cases,

(A) is just as effective as coronary bypass surgery but is much less expensive and disabling.

(B) can replace a clogged artery by the transplanting of a vein or artery from another part of the body.

(C) continues to be underused because coronary bypass operations are lucrative for hospitals and surgeons.

(D) requires opening up the chest and operating under local anesthesia.

10. Neurons, which cannot divide, are the basic cells of the brain. Glial cells, which can increase in number, provide support and nourishment to the neurons. It was hypothesized that if Einstein's brain had been more active in some areas, more glial cells would be found there. Indeed,

(A) scientists found that the physicist's brain contained more glial cells per neuron in all four areas, compared with the brains of eleven normal males.

(B) scientists' previous work had shown that animals put in environments that stimulate mental activity develop more glial cells per neuron.

(C) scientists examined sections of the upper front and lower rear of both hemispheres because these areas are involved in "higher" thinking.

(D) scientists found that even though there was evidence he had greater intellectual processing, it cannot be determined if Einstein was born with this or developed it later.

Answers to Exercise R12 are on page 536.

Exercise R13   *Inserting sentences*

To answer some questions on the Computer-Based TOEFL® Test, you have to click
on a square where a given sentence can be added. The computer screen will look like this.

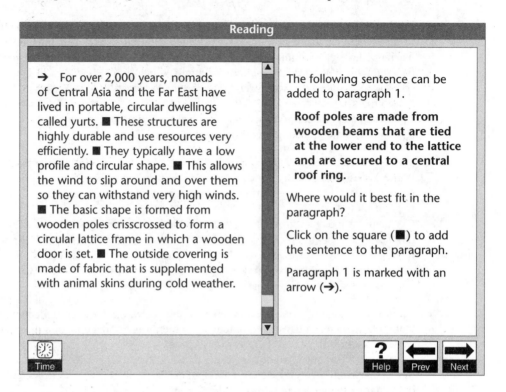

To answer this question, you would click on the box before the sentence "The outside
covering is made of fabric that is supplemented with animal skins during cold
weather." The sentence that can be inserted continues the discussion of the inside
structure (wooden poles and lattice). The following sentence then discusses the outside
covering of the structure. When you click on this box, the **bold** sentence will be
inserted. This gives you the opportunity to read it in context and decide if you have
inserted it in the best place. When you are sure of your answer, click on **Next** to go on
to the next question.

In each passage, select the numbered box where the **bold** sentence would best fit.

1. **Pragmatists believe that the test of any belief should be its practical
   consequences and that the truth of a proposition should be judged
   on how well it corresponds with experimental results.**

   [1] Pragmatism is essentially an American school of thought that has had few supporters
   elsewhere. [2] One of the first pragmatists, William James, wrote that it was impossible
   to discover the real world outside our senses and therefore we must concern ourselves
   primarily with human experience. [3] Because the world would be a worse place
   without a belief in human responsibility, morals, and the freedom of will, it was
   necessary, he considered, to believe in these concepts. [4] Another pragmatist, John
   Dewey, held that since truth is an instrument for solving problems, it must change
   as the problems it confronts change.

2. **The artists, who came to be called "the Eight" and were later dubbed "the Ashcan school," used vigorous brush strokes and dramatic lighting.**

[1] In the early years of the twentieth century the American art scene was dominated by painters who had established their reputations in the previous century. [2] There was a general intolerance both by critics and by the public of any deviation from the kind of work championed by academic institutions. [3] Acceptable art generally employed detailed realistic technique and focused on subject matter of historical or mythological scenes or sentimental landscapes. [4] In 1908 a group of artists organized an exhibition in a New York gallery that constituted a revolt against these current orthodoxies. [5] Their unconventional work often depicted the seamy side of urban life in settings such as backyards, saloons, dance halls, and theaters. Surprisingly, the show was a success, and for a time these artists enjoyed widespread popularity.

3. **In fact, a seed may require passage through the gut of the bird or animal before it can germinate.**

Seeds are dispersed to new sites by various means. Many, such as the dandelion or thistle, have fine tufts that allow them to be scattered by the action of the wind. [1] Some seeds such as the coconut can float and are dispersed by currents around the islands of the Pacific Ocean. [2] Other seeds have evolved ways of getting around through the activities of an intermediary animal. [3] This can happen in a number of different ways. For example, animals may devour the fruit containing seeds. [4] Sometimes a seed needs to be buried before it can germinate. This might happen when a hoarding animal such as a squirrel fails to return for its hidden meal. [5] Some seeds have sticky or spiky surfaces, often called burrs, which may catch on the coat of a passing animal and later drop off at a considerable distance from their origin.

4. **The Dutch in particular made considerable improvements and used windmills to pump water as well as to produce flour.**

The technique of using wind power to grind grain between stones to produce flour is ancient and was widely practiced. [1] Exactly where the first windmill was constructed is unknown although certainly the Persians ground corn over 2,000 years ago. [2] Tradition has it that the knowledge spread to the Middle East and from there to Northern Europe at the time of the Crusades. [3] The power of the wind replaced animal power in several regions of Europe where millwrights became highly skilled craftsmen and rapidly developed the technology. [4] In England the device became a ubiquitous feature of the landscape, and by 1400 there were ten thousand windmills concentrated in the southeast of the country, each capable of grinding 10,000 bushels of grain a week. Starting in the nineteenth century the mill started to decline in importance with the advent of steam power. [5] By the mid-twentieth century few working mills remained in use, but in recent years efforts have been made to restore and maintain these romantic souvenirs of a bygone age.

Answers to Exercise R13 are on page 537.

Exercise R14 *Identifying illustrations*

To answer some of the questions on the Computer-Based TOEFL® Test, you have to click on a picture that depicts what is described in the passage. The computer screen will look like this.

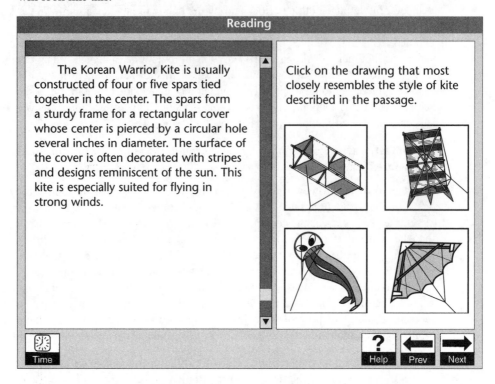

To answer this question, you would click on the picture in the upper right-hand corner. When you click on the picture, the box around it will become highlighted. When you are sure of your answer, click on Next to go on to the next question.

In the following exercise, circle the letter of the picture that is the correct answer to the question.

1. Early Greek columns were built in two main styles or orders, the Doric and the Ionic, named after Greek dialects. Of these two orders, the Ionic is the more slender, but is most notably different in the decoration of the capital that rests on top of the column. The Ionic is characterized by two pairs of prominent spiral scrolls, one on each side of the capital, which may have been inspired by curling leaves of foliage. Between the scrolls other ornamentation, such as an egg and dart pattern, were often carved for added embellishment.

Which one of the following pictures illustrates an Ionic column?

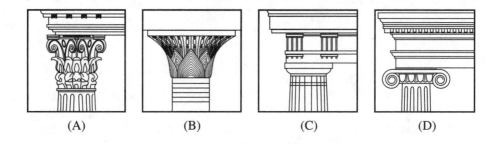

(A)   (B)   (C)   (D)

2. The earliest form of dueling was the clash of mounted knights armed with lances in medieval tournaments. These duels were often purely sporting affairs in which special nonlethal lances were used. They provided entertainment for the spectators and kept the knights in good condition for battle. In Elizabethan days, duels no longer took place on horseback, and the lance was exchanged for a sword and dagger. The sword was held in the right hand and used for attacking, while the dagger was held in the left hand and used for defense. Dueling with swords as a means to decide a point of honor later became obsolete with the invention of pistols. Pistols brought about a whole new set of rules and etiquette unique to that form of dueling.

Which one of the following pictures illustrates the equipment used in Elizabethan duels?

   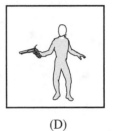

(A)   (B)   (C)   (D)

3. Playing marbles was supposedly popular in ancient Egypt, and it has yet to lose its popularity. There are several different games played with marbles, but the main object of all marble games is to hit a target by flicking a marble held between the forefinger and thumb. The best-known marble game is called "ringtaw." In this game, the players draw a circle on the ground. From a prearranged distance, they take turns shooting one of their marbles at marbles placed in the circle. The object is to knock as many marbles out of the circle as possible. In another game, "fortification," the marbles are placed in the center of a series of concentric circles marked on the ground. The players must knock marbles out of the center circle and into the adjacent circle. A marble is considered out when a player has knocked it through all the circles. A third popular game is one that uses holes instead of circles. In fact, this game is called "holes." Here, the players shoot their marbles into shallow holes dug in the ground.

Which one of the following pictures illustrates the layout of the most famous marble game?

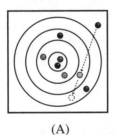 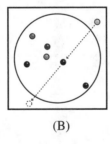 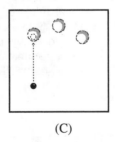 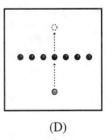

(A)   (B)   (C)   (D)

4. The homing instinct of pigeons has made them popular for the sport of pigeon racing. A young bird's training begins when it is about seven weeks old. This training consists of giving it short exercise flights, teaching it to recognize its owner's call, and teaching it to enter inside its cote, or home. The next phase of training is started when the bird is about four months old. The pigeon is taken short distances from its home and is then released. These flights are gradually extended from 3 miles to 100 miles as the bird's stamina increases. When the bird is ready, the owner may enter it in a race against other trained pigeons. The owners take their birds to a central meeting place where all the birds are tagged and released

simultaneously. A bird is not considered to be home until it has entered its cote and its owner has removed the tag and inserted it into a clock that records the bird's arrival time. Because owners live at varying distances from the release point, the first bird home may not be the fastest flier. The bird that makes the best time in flying the distance home is the winner.

Which one of the following graphs would best depict the training pattern for homing pigeons?

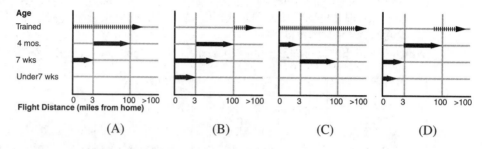

(A)   (B)   (C)   (D)

Answers to Exercise R14 are on page 537.

Exercise R15   *Identifying sentences*

To answer some of the questions on the Computer-Based TOEFL® Test, you have to click on a sentence in one of the paragraphs of the passage. The computer screen will look like this.

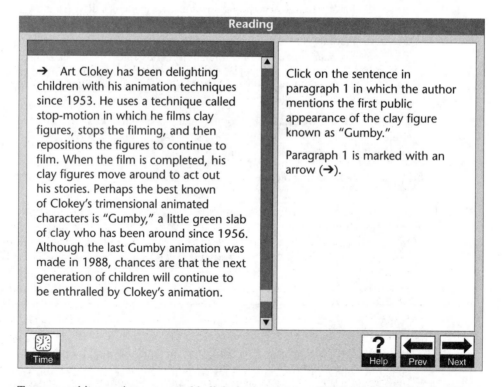

To answer this question, you would click on the sentence "Perhaps the best known of Clokey's trimensional animated characters is 'Gumby,' a little green slab of clay who has been around since 1956." This sentence gives the date in which Gumby was first seen by the public. When you click on this sentence, it will darken to show the sentence you have chosen. You can change your answer by clicking on another sentence. When you are sure of your answer, click on **Next** to go on to the next question.

In the following exercise, underline the sentence in the paragraph where the information asked for can be located.

1. Where in the passage does it discuss the second time the plan to bore a tunnel was proposed?

The plan to join the British Isles to the European continent by boring a tunnel under the sea between Dover, England, and Calais, France, was originally proposed in the second half of the nineteenth century. The bill authorizing the work was rejected in 1883. The plan was again proposed in 1930 by many enthusiastic supporters. The tunnel was to be the longest ever made and an engineering wonder. However, the estimated cost, the military risks, and the doubt as to the feasibility of construction led to the rejection of the proposal in June 1930. Finally, in the 1980s, the proposal was accepted and tunneling began.

2. Where in the passage are two types of molded cheeses discussed?

Cheese is made from the curd of milk. While there are literally thousands of varieties, which differ according to the method of preparation and quality of milk, they can be divided into three main classes. Soft cheeses are those with rinds and very soft creamy centers. Of these, Brie and Camembert are perhaps the most famous. Blue-veined cheeses have been injected with a penicillin mold, which creates the characteristic blue veins. Roquefort is perhaps the best known of the blue-veined cheeses. Pressed cheeses are those placed in a mold and firmly pressed. There are uncooked pressed cheeses, such as Cheddar, and cooked pressed cheeses, such as Gruyère.

3. Where in the passage does it imply that sweating can cause damage to a pearl?

If pearls are protected properly, they can last for centuries. One of the reasons a pearl loses its luster or cracks is due to the mineral constituent of the pearl being dissolved by weak acids. There are several kinds of acids that pearls may come in contact with. Human perspiration contains one such acid. Much of the cotton that pearls are wrapped in when not in use is treated with an acid. Another kind of acid that damages pearls is found in many modern cosmetics. Cosmetics seep into the string canal and may penetrate into the layers of the pearl and cause deterioration. The best protection to give a pearl to ensure its long life is having it cleaned and restrung at prescribed intervals.

4. Where in the passage does the author describe the traditional resort?

Sun City, South Africa; Disney World; and Sentosa Island are examples of the artificial, all-purpose holiday resort. These "tourism ghettoes," as they are referred to by seasoned travelers, isolate tourists from the real world and provide instead a sanitized package of pleasures. However much they are ridiculed and avoided by those looking for a cultural experience or seeking to study local fauna, they have proved their worth to those who are environmentally concerned with the welfare of the planet. Sun City, for example, was built on what had been useless scrubland, but now provides a haven for endangered or elusive wildlife. Unlike some vacation spots, such as beach resorts that have destroyed the beauty of the area and have put heavy burdens on the infrastructure of coastal villages not designed for a large influx of people, these resorts were carefully planned to accommodate large numbers of tourists. Incorporated in this planning is concern for the environment and for the local inhabitants. An artificial resort can gather into one compact area the best that the host country has to offer. Artificial lakes can attract birds that would not normally be seen. Trees can be planted to provide homes for animals and insects. Even species that have been wiped out in the wild could be reintroduced.

Answers to Exercise R15 are on page 537.

Exercise R16   *Identifying paragraphs*

To answer some of the questions on the Computer-Based TOEFL® Test, you have to click on a paragraph in the passage. You might have to scroll down to read the complete passage on the computer screen.

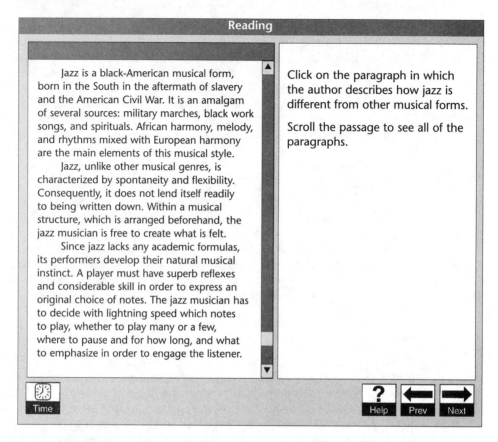

To answer this question, you would click on the paragraph that starts with the phrase "Jazz, unlike other musical genres, . . ." This is the paragraph where the author describes how jazz is different from other musical forms. When you click on this paragraph, it will darken to show the paragraph you have chosen. When you are sure of your answer, click on Next to go on to the next question.

In the following exercise, put a check [✔] by the paragraph in which the information asked for can be located.

1. Where in the passage does the author discuss the term used when a player does not score at all?

    The debt of lawn tennis to its French origins is illustrated in the unusual scoring system. This system probably stems from the habit of betting on individual points by the players or supporters. A game was worth one denier, so the points were worth the most convenient divisions of a denier. These were 15, 30, and 45 sous. In time, the latter became 40.

    "Deuce," when both players have reached 40 in a game, is a corruption of the French *à deux*, meaning both. This may refer to both players having the same score – or to the fact that a player will need to take both of the next two points to win. The term (as *dewce*) was first known in England in 1598.

    The word "love," which means nil, may well come from the French word *l'oeuf*, meaning egg. The explanation for the use of the word *l'oeuf* is said to be the similarity of the shape of an egg to a zero. Modern player slang for a 6-0 6-0 result is "egg and egg."

2. Where in the passage does the author define road rage?

In a recent survey, it was found that nine out of ten drivers admit to having felt intense anger toward other drivers at some time. Road rage seems to be on the increase, and this may be due to three main factors. First, there are more cars today competing for road space. People also are far more subject to time constraints. A person who must meet a time deadline, but is caught in a tangle of traffic, may feel increasingly frustrated. Soon this stress may result in an outburst of road rage ranging anywhere from pounding on the car horn to getting out of the car and attacking some other driver.

A second factor may be with the car itself. Three major responses to stress, which evolved in the brain long before thought, are fight, flight, or freeze. Of these responses, only one – fight – is available to the driver suddenly caught behind a dawdler in the fast lane.

Another explanation may be that people are not as courteous as they used to be. A person who is worried about getting to work on time, having the report ready for the afternoon mail, and meeting the boss while sneaking in late seems to forget how to be polite. Other drivers become the enemy and the car, a weapon.

3. Where in the passage does the author discuss an erosion of women's equal rights?

The American suffragettes finally won their battle when the right to vote in a democratic election was extended to women in 1919. Because of women's equal rights being harmed by discriminatory legislation, the Equal Rights Amendment was introduced in 1923. This was a time when the feminist symbolized a young generation of women. They were carefree, exuberant, and eager to break out of traditional roles and enjoy personal independence.

All this optimism came to an end during the Great Depression, an economic crisis precipitated by a stock market crash in 1929. At the depth of the Depression, over one-third of the labor force was unemployed.

As men lost their jobs, resentment toward women and the Equal Rights Amendment became widespread. Laws were passed that restricted women's rights. One such law was the married-person's clause. It prevented the civil service from hiring more than one member of a family. This law left many women unemployed. Following the same assumption that a man is the primary wage earner, many school boards fired married women. Even women in positions of power supported policies that worsened women's conditions rather than improved them.

At the same time that women were losing their rights, a propaganda campaign by social workers and public figures effectively convinced women that their responsibility was that of maintaining family morale. A strengthening of belief in traditional roles followed.

4. Where in the passage does the author discuss controlling people's beliefs through mistreatment?

We all know that people can and do influence each other. But the disturbing question is how far people's minds can be influenced against their own wills. There are three techniques that have been used in attempts to control other people's behavior.

One technique, subliminal perception, is frequently referred to as subception. This technique is based on the observation that people notice a great deal more than they consciously realize. This is not a new observation, but it has been given special attention since the results of an experiment in a New York movie theater were reported. In the experiment, an advertisement for ice cream was flashed onto the screen during the feature film. Apparently, the ad was shown for such a brief period that no one consciously saw the intrusion, yet ice-cream sales soared for the period of time the experiment continued.

Hypnosis is another technique that can be used for controlling people's minds. While in a deep trance, people can be told to do something at a specific time or at a certain signal. They can be told that they won't remember what has been said once out of the trance. This is called a post-hypnotic suggestion. It is still uncertain whether a subject can be made to carry out an action that otherwise would be unacceptable in that person's mind.

Yet another technique is called brainwashing. Brainwashing entails forcing people to believe something, usually something false, by continually telling them or showing them evidence that is supposedly true and preventing them from thinking about it properly or considering other evidence. Brainwashing can take extreme forms. For example, brainwashing can be done by first causing a complete breakdown of individuals through acts such as starving them, preventing them from sleeping, intimidating them, and keeping them in a state of constant fear. When the individuals lose their sense of reality, new ideas can be planted in their minds.

Answers to Exercise R16 are on page 537.

Exercise R17   *Understanding exceptions*

Read each passage. Circle the letter of the correct answer to the question that follows each passage.

Example   Today's readers look for knowledge and information through more than just an encyclopedia. Knowledge, information, data, and images race around the world in ever-increasing speed. With a quick press of a key on the computer keyboard, data from some of the great libraries in the world can be called onto a screen for immediate perusal.

The author mentions all of the following means of accessing information EXCEPT

    (A) encyclopedias
    (B) television
    (C) computers
    (D) libraries

The author's mention of a screen is in reference to a computer screen and not to a television screen. Therefore, the only means of accessing information not mentioned is television (B).

1. Whereas the scene of colonial North America was one of complex cultural negotiations and explosive interactions among Native Americans, Africans, and Europeans, history books have portrayed the settlement of North America as a unilinear push of Europeans into a virgin land. Although primary documentation – government reports, travel accounts, trade journals, all written from a European perspective – is literally filled with observations concerning Native American customs and beliefs, history books are more interested in outlining battles. Ethnohistorians, the scholars who blend anthropology's insights with historical research to produce a cultural understanding of the past, have been making advances in understanding the Native American perspective of European colonialization.

The author mentions all of the following as sources of primary documentation EXCEPT

    (A) government reports
    (B) travel accounts
    (C) trade journals
    (D) history books

2. Although Winslow Homer (1836–1910) is best known for his realistic watercolors of powerfully dramatic seascapes, he first won acclaim in the art world as an illustrator for the reportage of the American Civil War. This led to his illustrating texts of prose and poetry. His more than 160 drawings reached print as lithographs, wood engravings, and photomechanical cuts. Despite the skill and serious intent he invested in them, Homer's book illustrations made little impact during his lifetime. Even today, most of his illustrations are not discussed in the literature covering his work, and nearly all of them have been excluded from even the most comprehensive exhibitions of Homer's art.

The author mentions all of the following as types of work Homer did EXCEPT

(A) reportage
(B) lithographs
(C) watercolors
(D) illustrations

3. Almost all sports and outdoor leisure activities carry real risks. Swimmers are drowned, mountaineers fall, skiers are swept away by avalanches, and boxers are killed by a series of blows to the head. A person's skill or experience is no guarantee against disaster. In fact, the better an athlete is, the greater the desire to break records or succeed in doing something that has never been done before. Danger, which tests nerve, courage, and skill, is an essential element that adds thrill and enjoyment to the sport. Although those who organize sports formulate their rules in a way to minimize the risk of injury and to ensure that medical assistance is readily available, no amount of caution can alter basic facts: even the best-trained horse may panic; motorcycles give little protection in a crash; a hard-driven golf ball can go awry.

According to the passage, all of the following are risks in sports EXCEPT

(A) a fall
(B) a bicycle
(C) an accident
(D) an avalanche

4. Perhaps one of the most hazardous ways of making a living from the sea was diving for pearls. Only the most daring would risk their lives in this profession. The technique of pearl diving was simple. Divers attached themselves to ropes that were used to keep them in contact with an assistant on board the ship. Attached to a different rope were large weights that helped to speed the divers' descent and, hence, conserve their breath for searching the seabed. Also needed were nose clips, heavy gloves that provided protection for their hands against the sharp edges of the oyster shells, and a net in which they collected the oysters. These nets were slung around the divers' necks so as not to impede the usage of their hands. When the divers signaled their intention to surface, the assistant hauled them and their load of oysters up. The oysters were then opened and any pearls found were sifted through sieves and graded according to size and quality. Once a widely practiced profession, pearl diving has largely disappeared with the development of the cultured pearl.

The author mentions all of the following as the pearl divers' underwater activities EXCEPT

(A) the keeping in contact with an assistant on board
(B) the attachment of a heavy weight to conserve their breath
(C) the collection of oysters
(D) the opening of the oyster

5. Margaret Mitchell wrote only one novel, *Gone with the Wind*. It was published in 1936 and proved to be such a huge success that Mitchell's life was irrevocably altered. She lost all her privacy and lamented this fact constantly until her death in 1949. The novel, which has been translated into twenty-eight languages and has sold more copies than any other book except for the Bible, won the Pulitzer Prize in 1937. Not long afterward, the movie produced by David O. Selznick had its premiere in Atlanta in 1939. This movie holds the record of having been viewed more times than any other movie produced. Throughout her life, Mitchell denied that her main characters, Scarlett and Rhett, or any of her other characters were biographical in any way. She did have access to family correspondence dating from the 1850s to the 1880s, the time of the American Civil War. It seems natural that a woman with Margaret Mitchell's vivid imagination and historical awareness, and in possession of a collection of family correspondence that documents such a volatile era as that of a civil war, could weave a story that still enthralls.

The author of the passage gives all the relevant dates about Mitchell EXCEPT the date of

    (A) the family letters
    (B) her birth
    (C) the first showing of the movie
    (D) the first printing of the novel

Answers to Exercise R17 are on page 537.

Exercise R18   *Identifying if statements are the same or different*

Write "S" in the space if the two sentences mean the same. Write "D" in the space if they have different meanings.

Example   _D_   (A) A collection of fascinating tales called *The Arabian Nights* was introduced to Europe by the French scholar Antoine Galland.

                      (B) The French scholar Antoine Galland introduced to Europe a collection of fascinating tales that he called *The Arabian Nights*.

You should write "D" in the space because the sentences do not mean the same thing. The first sentence means that the scholar introduced the tales, whereas the second sentence means that the scholar both introduced and named the tales.

1. _____ (A) Scree, which abounds in the Rocky Mountains, has its origins in the ice ages.

       (B) The Rocky Mountains have a lot of scree, whose formation dates back to the ice ages.

2. _____ (A) The drum and flute music once heard in the streets has been replaced by noisy radios and cassette players.

       (B) Radios and cassette players are now heard in the streets, which once were filled by the sounds of drum and flute music.

3. _____ (A) Many reef organisms avoid dead-end caves, which lack the steady currents necessary for bringing a continuous food supply.

       (B) Dead-end caves don't have currents that bring in food supplies, so many reef organisms don't go there.

4. _____ (A) Instead of being overwhelmed by the hard life in Montana, Evelyn Cameron reveled in it.

       (B) Evelyn Cameron revealed how difficult life was in Montana.

5. _____ (A) Two theaters in Stratford-upon-Avon and two in London are regularly used by the Royal Shakespeare Company.

(B) The Royal Shakespeare Company regularly uses four theaters – two in Stratford-upon-Avon and two in London.

6. _____ (A) Police reconstruct scenes because people seem to recall things best when they are in the same physical situation.

(B) When people are in the same physical situation, they seem to remember better scenes than the ones police have reconstructed.

7. _____ (A) Despite the cold Alaskan temperatures, which freeze perspiration and breath in men's beards, cabin fever forces inhabitants to challenge the elements.

(B) The Alaskan inhabitants suffer from cabin fever, which causes perspiration and breath to freeze in men's beards.

8. _____ (A) Leather, when improperly handled and exposed to changeable temperatures, cracks easily.

(B) Leather cracks easily when it is handled incorrectly and is exposed to variable temperatures.

9. _____ (A) Despite the increasing pollution of their shorelines, oceans have become cleaner in the vast open-sea areas over the past decade.

(B) During the last ten years, pollution has been increasing along the coasts of the oceans and spreading to the once clean open-sea areas.

10. _____ (A) The Hitler diaries, the greatest known publishing fraud in history, were written by a man who copied material from Hitler's speeches and medical reports.

(B) By copying material from Hitler's speeches and medical reports, a man wrote the Hitler diaries, which became known as the greatest publishing fraud in history.

Answers to Exercise R18 are on page 537.

Exercise R19   *Identifying restatements*

Read the following statements. Circle the letter of the statement that has the same meaning as the given statement.

Example   The bulk of Kafka's writings was not published until after his early death from tuberculosis.

(A) It was not until after Kafka's early death from tuberculosis that the bulk of his writings was published.

(B) After the bulk of his writings was published, Kafka died an early death from tuberculosis.

(C) After Kafka had written the bulk of his published writings, he met with an early death from tuberculosis.

(D) An early death from tuberculosis kept Kafka from publishing the bulk of his writings.

You should circle (A) because this is the only sentence which contains the same information as the first sentence. First Kafka died, and then most of his writings were published.

1. Fainting is caused by a sudden drop in the normal blood supply to the brain.
   (A) The brain reacts to a drop in the normal blood supply by fainting.
   (B) Fainting occurs when the brain suddenly loses its normal blood supply.
   (C) Fainting happens when the brain drops its normal blood supply.
   (D) The brain faints when the normal blood supply drops.

2. Gorillas, which are vegetarians, have been observed to demonstrate gentle behavior toward small creatures in the wild.
   (A) Vegetarians have been observed to demonstrate gentle behavior toward gorillas and small creatures in the wild.
   (B) Only vegetarian gorillas have been observed as demonstrating gentle behavior toward small creatures in the wild.
   (C) Small creatures in the wild have been observed as behaving gently and demonstratively when near gorillas.
   (D) It has been observed in the wild that gorillas, by nature vegetarians, treat small animals gently.

3. In fighting forest fires, the initial attack crews dig a fire line, which varies in width depending on the strength and nature of the fire.
   (A) Initial attack crews dig a forest fire to vary the fire line's width.
   (B) Initial attack crews depend on the strength and nature of the fire to vary the fire line.
   (C) The width of the fire line, which the initial attack crews dig, varies according to the strength and nature of the fire.
   (D) In digging a fire line, the initial attack crews depend on fighting forest fires.

4. Medical quackery, which promises cures for all existing and even nonexisting diseases, has a powerful appeal even to the well educated.
   (A) Well-educated people in medicine promise to find powerful cures for diseases.
   (B) Even well-educated people are attracted to fake cures for diseases that may or may not exist.
   (C) Medical quackery promises the well educated a cure for diseases.
   (D) The medical profession has appealed to the well educated for funding to find cures for diseases.

5. A silver compound has been found to kill the parasitic protozoa that are carried by the dreaded tsetse fly and cause sleeping sickness.
   (A) The dreaded tsetse fly causes sleeping sickness and kills the parasitic protozoa used for finding silver compounds.
   (B) It has been found that the silver compound that is carried by the dreaded tsetse fly and causes sleeping sickness kills the parasitic protozoa.
   (C) Sleeping sickness, which is caused by the dreaded tsetse fly, has been found to kill the parasitic protozoa in silver compounds.
   (D) Parasitic protozoa that cause sleeping sickness and are carried by the dreaded tsetse fly can be killed with a silver compound.

6. While working as a postmaster at the University of Mississippi, William Faulkner submitted thirty-seven stories to magazines, six of which were accepted.
   (A) Of the thirty-seven stories that Faulkner wrote while working at the University of Mississippi as a postmaster, six became published in magazines.
   (B) Faulkner wrote six out of thirty-seven stories after accepting a job as postmaster at the University of Mississippi.
   (C) Faulkner published thirty-seven stories in magazines, six of which were accepted by the University of Mississippi.
   (D) The six accepted stories by Faulkner were about his job as a postmaster at the University of Mississippi.

7. The continental drift theory proposes that the earth's crustal plates are driven by a global system of convection currents in the hot magma below that behave like giant conveyor belts.
   (A) Theoretically, the earth's crustal plates behave like giant conveyor belts, driving the convection currents across the hot magma, which causes the continents to drift.
   (B) A global system of convection currents in the underlying hot magma acts as giant conveyor belts to drive the earth's crustal plates.
   (C) The continental drift theory suggests that global plates cover hot magma, which acts as a giant conveyor belt below the convection currents.
   (D) The continental drift theory is proposed by the earth's crustal plates, which drive a global system of convection currents in the hot magma below, behaving like giant conveyor belts.

8. Medical authorities have been reluctant to support the findings of some nutritionists that vitamin C given in large doses can prevent the common cold.
   (A) Medical authorities support the nutritionists' views about the value of vitamin C in preventing the common cold.
   (B) Nutritionists have found that medical authorities are not in favor of using vitamin C to prevent the common cold.
   (C) Some nutritionists have found that large doses of vitamin C can prevent the common cold, but this has not been completely accepted by medical authorities.
   (D) According to nutritionists and some medical authorities, the common cold can be prevented by giving large doses of vitamin C.

9. Female cowbirds, which cannot sing, are nonetheless able to teach songs to their young by responding to specific chirps and ignoring others.
   (A) Even though female cowbirds cannot sing, they teach their chicks to do so by responding to specific chirps and ignoring others.
   (B) Female cowbirds can neither sing nor teach songs to their babies by responding to certain chirps more than to others.
   (C) Female cowbirds, which cannot sing, have certain other birds teach their young to sing.
   (D) Female cowbirds, which cannot sing, unsuccessfully attempt to teach their young to sing by responding to other bird songs.

10. The conflict between those who wish to conserve a large area of unaltered and unimproved spaces and those who want the abolition of the last remnants of wilderness in the interest of industrial profit will not be resolved in the near future.
    (A) The people who desire to conserve a large area of untouched natural land and those who want to use all land for industrialization are in a conflict that will not have an immediate resolution.
    (B) The conflict over whether a large area of unaltered and unimproved space should be given over for industrial development and profit is of interest to those resolved to abolish the last remnants of wilderness.
    (C) Lawyers are profiting from the unresolved conflict between the people who wish to save the last remnants of wilderness and those who want to alter and improve the space for industry.
    (D) There is an unresolved conflict caused by people who wish to abolish industry and turn the spaces back into a natural wilderness state.

Answers to Exercise R19 are on page 537.

Exercise R20   *Locating restated information*

Underline the words or phrases in the passage that give the information that is restated in the sentence following the passage.

Example   The damp <u>British climate</u> may be infuriating to humans, but it's <u>ideal for plants</u>. The Gulf Stream flows across the Atlantic to warm the west coast of these Isles, which occupy the same latitudes as Newfoundland. Moisture-laden Atlantic winds bring almost <u>constant rain and mist</u>, so plants don't dry out.

The perfect weather conditions for plants to flourish are found in the wet British Isles.

You should underline "British climate" (weather conditions in the British Isles), "ideal for plants" (perfect for plants), and "constant rain and mist" (wet) because these are the words from the passage that are restated.

1. Europa, one of Jupiter's moons, is the only place in the solar system – outside of Earth – where enormous quantities of water are known to exist. Although this water is in ice form, there is a possibility that there is only a crust of ice with a liquid ocean underneath. Because of powerful thermal pulses caused by the tidal forces of Jupiter and the other moons, Europa may be the best place in the solar system for finding life forms.

   Europa's vast oceans are unequaled in the solar system, with one exception.

2. Using sophisticated instrumentation, lightning experts have learned that lightning travels at one-third the speed of light. A lightning bolt is five times hotter than the surface of the sun and can have ten times more power than the output of a large power company. A single discharge can actually contain twenty or more successive strokes, occurring too fast for the eye to separate. Some seem to stretch for 500 miles when observed from outer space.

   It is possible that a lightning bolt, which seems very large, is really a series of bolts.

3. Once porpoises reach speeds of 12 miles per hour, they leap out of the water to escape the pull of surface drag. At that point, leaping out of the water actually requires less energy than swimming. These leaps are most efficient at speeds of 40 miles per hour and greater.

   Porpoises conserve energy by traveling through the air, which creates less drag than water.

4. In the earliest stages of a star's formation – a process that takes some 10,000 years – the star is surrounded by an extremely dense layer of gas and dust. This matter eventually condenses and heats up to 1 million degrees and hotter, triggering a thermonuclear explosion. During the flare-up, strong winds blowing off the surface of the star disperse the surrounding dust and expose the newborn star to observers on Earth.

   People can see the birth of a star because of the strong winds that scatter the dust particles.

5. Perhaps the greatest navigators in history were the Vikings. Without compasses or other modern instruments, they explored Iceland, Greenland, and even crossed the Atlantic Ocean to the shores of North America. To find their way, they stayed close to shorelines or used the position of the sun to plot the latitude.

   The Vikings were expert sailors.

6. Since the first dolphin was trained by the United States Navy in 1965 to help divers in their underwater home, *Sealab II*, many other dolphins have been drafted into the Navy. Originally, dolphins were used as messengers or to answer calls for help. Today, dolphins do such dangerous and necessary work as locating explosives hidden in the sea and helping ships navigate safely in war zones.

   An important task for a dolphin is to find mines.

7. Saint Bernard dogs are large and shaggy animals. They were bred by Augustinian monks, who trained them to search for travelers lost in snowstorms or avalanches in the Alps. For hundreds of years, Saint Bernards served this purpose. But nowadays the journey across the Alps is on well-maintained road and tunnel systems, and the dogs are no longer needed.

   Saint Bernards aided travelers for centuries.

8. Every year in Japan, the competitions for the longest unpowered flights are held. Out on Lake Biwa, participants attempt to break records by flying their own inventions over the water without propeller or jet assistance. The would-be human birds glide until their craft meets its inevitable crash landing. A flotilla of small boats line the flight path waiting to rescue the pilot. In the first Japanese event, a world record of 88.53 meters was established. Since then, new records have been made every year.

   Participants fly in crafts they have designed themselves.

Answers to Exercise R20 are on page 538.

CHECK YOUR PROGRESS

Check your progress in understanding details and recognizing restatements (Exercises R9–R20) by completing the following mini-test. This exercise uses a format similar to that used in the Reading Section of the Computer-Based TOEFL® Test. If you are unfamiliar with how to answer questions on the Computer-Based TOEFL® Test, see the Tutorial on pages 24–28.

Exercise R21   *Mini-test*

Select the correct answer.

Questions 1–5

> **In the twentieth century, architects in large cities designed structures in a way that reduced noise and yet made living as comfortable as possible. They used such techniques as making walls hollow and filling this wall space with materials that absorb noise.** Thick carpets and heavy curtains were used to cover floors and windows. Air conditioners and furnaces were designed to filter air through soundproofing materials. However, after much time and effort had been spent in making buildings less noisy, it was discovered that people also reacted adversely to the lack of sound. Now architects are designing structures that reduce undesirable noise but retain the kind of noise that people seem to need.

1. Look at the word **They** in the passage. Select the word or phrase in the **bold** text that **They** refers to.

In the twentieth century, architects in large cities designed structures in a way that reduced noise and yet made living as comfortable as possible. They used such techniques as making walls hollow and filling this wall space with materials that absorb noise. Thick carpets and heavy curtains were used to cover floors and windows. Air conditioners and furnaces were designed to filter air through soundproofing materials. However, after much time and effort had been spent in making buildings less noisy, it was discovered that people also reacted adversely to the lack of sound. Now architects are designing structures that reduce undesirable noise but retain the kind of noise that people seem to need.

2. Which of the following is NOT mentioned as absorbing sound?
(A) Filled hollow walls
(B) Thick carpets and heavy curtains
(C) Air conditioners and furnaces
(D) Air filters

In the twentieth century, architects in large cities designed structures in a way that reduced noise and yet made living as comfortable as possible. They used such techniques as making walls hollow and filling this wall space with materials that absorb noise. Thick carpets and heavy curtains were used to cover floors and windows. Air conditioners and furnaces were designed to filter air through soundproofing materials. However, after much time and effort had been spent in making buildings less noisy, it was discovered that people also reacted adversely to the lack of sound. Now architects are designing structures that reduce undesirable noise but retain the kind of noise that people seem to need.

3. Architects are now designing
(A) new techniques of soundproofing
(B) the ideal noise
(C) structures with some noise
(D) adverse buildings

➜   1 In the twentieth century, architects in large cities designed structures in a way that reduced noise and yet made living as comfortable as possible. 2 They used such techniques as making walls hollow and filling this wall space with materials that absorb noise. 3 Thick carpets and heavy curtains were used to cover floors and windows. 4 Air conditioners and furnaces were designed to filter air through soundproofing materials. 5 However, after much time and effort had been spent in making buildings less noisy, it was discovered that people also reacted adversely to the lack of sound. 6 Now architects are designing structures that reduce undesirable noise but retain the kind of noise that people seem to need.

4. The following sentence can be added to paragraph 1.

A silent home can cause feelings of anxiety and isolation.

Where would it best fit in the paragraph?

Select the square (☐) that shows where the sentence should be added.

Paragraph 1 is marked with an arrow (➜).

In the twentieth century, architects in large cities designed structures in a way that reduced noise and yet made living as comfortable as possible. They used such techniques as making walls hollow and filling this wall space with materials that absorb noise. Thick carpets and heavy curtains were used to cover floors and windows. Air conditioners and furnaces were designed to filter air through soundproofing materials. However, after much time and effort had been spent in making buildings less noisy, it was discovered that people also reacted adversely to the lack of sound. Now architects are designing structures that reduce undesirable noise but retain the kind of noise that people seem to need.

5. According to the passage, people live most comfortably with
   (A) noisy furnaces
   (B) silence
   (C) hollow walls
   (D) certain noises

Questions 6–9

→ 1 The gambrel roof design has an enduring appeal to many builders and homeowners in America. 2 Originally a feature of Dutch colonial architectural style, the gambrel is a straight double-sloped roof joined at a central ridge. 3 The main distinguishing feature is that each roof side is broken into two planes with the lower slope inclined at a steeper pitch than the upper. 4 Sometimes the angle of the gambrel roof becomes shallower again at the eaves and projects over the wall of the house, giving a bell-shaped appearance in cross section. 5 The main advantage of the gambrel roof is that it creates a spacious interior on the upper floor of the house. 6 This spaciousness also makes the gambrel roof highly suitable for barn construction, since the upper floor can be used as a hayloft.

6. The following sentence can be added to paragraph 1.

   This makes it a perfect choice for a growing family.

   Where would it best fit in the paragraph?

   Select the square (□) that shows where the sentence should be added.

   Paragraph 1 is marked with an arrow (→).

The gambrel roof design has an enduring appeal to many builders and homeowners in America. Originally a feature of Dutch colonial architectural style, the gambrel is a straight double-sloped roof joined at a central ridge. The main distinguishing feature is that each roof side is broken into two planes with the lower slope inclined at a steeper pitch than the upper. Sometimes the angle of the gambrel roof becomes shallower again at the eaves and projects over the wall of the house, giving a bell-shaped appearance in cross section. The main advantage of the gambrel roof is that it creates a spacious interior on the upper floor of the house. This spaciousness also makes the gambrel roof highly suitable for barn construction, since the upper floor can be used as a hayloft.

7. According to the passage, all of the following may be features of the gambrel roof design EXCEPT
   (A) the double-sloped roof
   (B) the steep angle of the upper slope
   (C) the shallow angle at the eaves
   (D) the roof projecting over the walls

The gambrel roof design has an enduring appeal to many builders and homeowners in America. Originally a feature of Dutch colonial architectural style, the gambrel is a straight double-sloped roof joined at a central ridge. The main distinguishing feature is that each roof side is broken into two planes with the lower slope inclined at a steeper pitch than the upper. Sometimes the angle of the gambrel roof becomes shallower again at the eaves and projects over the wall of the house, giving a bell-shaped appearance in cross section. The main advantage of the gambrel roof is that it creates a spacious interior on the upper floor of the house. This spaciousness also makes the gambrel roof highly suitable for barn construction, since the upper floor can be used as a hayloft.

8. According to the passage, the gambrel roof design
   (A) was invented by the American Dutch
   (B) has been endured by builders and homeowners
   (C) was brought to America by Dutch settlers
   (D) is only appealing to American builders and homeowners

The gambrel roof design has an enduring appeal to many builders and homeowners in America. Originally a feature of Dutch colonial architectural style, the gambrel is a straight double-sloped roof joined at a central ridge. The main distinguishing feature is that each roof side is broken into two planes with the lower slope inclined at a steeper pitch than the upper. Sometimes the angle of the gambrel roof becomes shallower again at the eaves and projects over the wall of the house, giving a bell-shaped appearance in cross section. The main advantage of the gambrel roof is that it creates a spacious interior on the upper floor of the house. This spaciousness also makes the gambrel roof highly suitable for barn construction, since the upper floor can be used as a hayloft.

9. Select the picture that best illustrates the gambrel roof.

Questions 10–14

The 50-million-year-old fossils of an ancient whale found in the Himalayan foothills of Pakistan give strong evidence that modern whales are descended from a four-legged, land-dwelling animal. The fossils consist of part of the skull, some teeth, and the well-preserved middle ear of an animal that was 6 to 8 feet long, weighed 350 pounds, had a wolflike snout, and had two foot-long jaws with sharp, triangular teeth. It is the middle ear that suggests that the ancient whale lived on land. Analysis indicated that the animal had eardrums, which did not work in water and which modern whales have only in vestigial form. Furthermore, the right and left ear bones were not isolated from each other. The separation of these bones in marine whales enables them to detect the direction of underwater sounds.

10. The 50-million-year-old fossils found in Pakistan
    (A) are 6 to 8 feet long and 350 pounds in weight
    (B) are descended from a four-legged, land-dwelling animal
    (C) prove the Himalayan foothills were once underwater
    (D) include the middle ear of an ancient whale

The 50-million-year-old fossils of an ancient whale found in the Himalayan foothills of Pakistan give strong evidence that modern whales are descended from a four-legged, land-dwelling animal. The fossils consist of part of the skull, some teeth, and the well-preserved middle ear of an animal that was 6 to 8 feet long, weighed 350 pounds, had a wolflike snout, and had two foot-long jaws with sharp, triangular teeth. It is the middle ear that suggests that the ancient whale lived on land. Analysis indicated that the animal had eardrums, which did not work in water and which modern whales have only in vestigial form. Furthermore, the right and left ear bones were not isolated from each other. The separation of these bones in marine whales enables them to detect the direction of underwater sounds.

11. Whales with eardrums
    (A) would not be able to hear well in water
    (B) were marine creatures
    (C) could distinguish where underwater sounds originated
    (D) could not live on land

The 50-million-year-old fossils of an ancient whale found in the Himalayan foothills of Pakistan give strong evidence that modern whales are descended from a four-legged, land-dwelling animal. The fossils consist of part of the skull, some teeth, and the well-preserved middle ear of an animal that was 6 to 8 feet long, weighed 350 pounds, had a wolflike snout, and had two foot-long jaws with sharp, triangular teeth. It is the middle ear that suggests that the ancient whale lived on land. Analysis indicated that the animal had eardrums, which did not work in water and which modern whales have only in vestigial form. Furthermore, the right and left ear bones were not isolated from each other. The separation of these bones in marine whales enables them to detect the direction of underwater sounds.

12. A marine whale can recognize the source of a sound because
    (A) the right and left ear bones are isolated from each other
    (B) the middle ear is in a vestigial form
    (C) it lives underwater instead of on land
    (D) it has a well-preserved middle ear

The 50-million-year-old fossils of an ancient whale found in the Himalayan foothills of Pakistan give strong evidence that modern whales are descended from a four-legged, land-dwelling animal. The fossils consist of part of the skull, some teeth, and the well-preserved middle ear of an animal that was 6 to 8 feet long, weighed 350 pounds, had a wolflike snout, and had two foot-long jaws with sharp, triangular teeth. It is the middle ear that suggests that the ancient whale lived on land. **Analysis indicated that the animal had eardrums, which did not work in water and which modern whales have only in vestigial form. Furthermore, the right and left ear bones were not isolated from each other. The separation of these bones in marine whales enables them to detect the direction of underwater sounds.**

13. Look at the word **them** in the passage. Select another word or phrase in the **bold** text that **them** refers to.

→ 1 The 50-million-year-old fossils of an ancient whale found in the Himalayan foothills of Pakistan give strong evidence that modern whales are descended from a four-legged, land-dwelling animal. 2 The fossils consist of part of the skull, some teeth, and the well-preserved middle ear of an animal that was 6 to 8 feet long, weighed 350 pounds, had a wolflike snout, and had two foot-long jaws with sharp, triangular teeth. 3 It is the middle ear that suggests that the ancient whale lived on land. 4 Analysis indicated that the animal had eardrums, which did not work in water and which modern whales have only in vestigial form. 5 Furthermore, the right and left ear bones were not isolated from each other. 6 The separation of these bones in marine whales enables them to detect the direction of underwater sounds.

14. Select the number of the sentence in paragraph 1 in which the author describes the ancient whale.

Paragraph 1 is marked with an arrow (→).

Questions 15–18

A Stradivarius violin is unmatched in tonal quality and responds more quickly and easily to the touch than any other violin. Unfortunately, the secrets for making such a superb instrument were lost in 1737 with the death of Antonio Stradivari, the master craftsman who built them. Many attempts have been made to reproduce an instrument of such quality, but all have failed. It is believed that the secret lies in the wood that was used and the distinctive varnish, which ranges from orange to a deep reddish-brown color. Only around 650 Stradivarius violins are believed to be in existence today, and the price for such a rare instrument is well in the hundreds of thousands of dollars. Even a "cheap" Stradivarius costs around a quarter of a million dollars. It is not surprising that a Stradivarius is sought after by great violinists and musical-instrument collectors alike.

15. According to the passage, how many Stradivarius violins are there?
    (A) 1737
    (B) 650
    (C) 250,000
    (D) 100,000

A Stradivarius violin is unmatched in tonal quality and responds more quickly and easily to the touch than any other violin. Unfortunately, the secrets for making such a superb instrument were lost in 1737 with the death of Antonio Stradivari, the master craftsman who built them. Many attempts have been made to reproduce an instrument of such quality, but all have failed. It is believed that the secret lies in the wood that was used and the distinctive varnish, which ranges from orange to a deep reddish-brown color. Only around 650 Stradivarius violins are believed to be in existence today, and the price for such a rare instrument is well in the hundreds of thousands of dollars. Even a "cheap" Stradivarius costs around a quarter of a million dollars. It is not surprising that a Stradivarius is sought after by great violinists and musical-instrument collectors alike.

16. According to the passage, a Stradivarius that costs a quarter of a million dollars is
(A) the rarest kind
(B) the most expensive one
(C) a cheap reproduction
(D) an inexpensive one

A Stradivarius violin is unmatched in tonal quality and responds more quickly and easily to the touch than any other violin. Unfortunately, the secrets for making such a superb instrument were lost in 1737 with the death of Antonio Stradivari, the master craftsman who built them. Many attempts have been made to reproduce an instrument of such quality, but all have failed. It is believed that the secret lies in the wood that was used and the distinctive varnish, which ranges from orange to a deep reddish-brown color. Only around 650 Stradivarius violins are believed to be in existence today, and the price for such a rare instrument is well in the hundreds of thousands of dollars. Even a "cheap" Stradivarius costs around a quarter of a million dollars. It is not surprising that a Stradivarius is sought after by great violinists and musical-instrument collectors alike.

17. The main qualities of the Stradivarius are its
(A) age and number
(B) violinists and musical-instrument collectors
(C) tone and response
(D) orange to reddish-brown color

→ 1 A Stradivarius violin is unmatched in tonal quality and responds more quickly and easily to the touch than any other violin. 2 Unfortunately, the secrets for making such a superb instrument were lost in 1737 with the death of Antonio Stradivari, the master craftsman who built them. 3 Many attempts have been made to reproduce an instrument of such quality, but all have failed. 4 It is believed that the secret lies in the wood that was used and the distinctive varnish, which ranges from orange to a deep reddish-brown color. 5 Only around 650 Stradivarius violins are believed to be in existence today, and the price for such a rare instrument is well in the hundreds of thousands of dollars. 6 Even a "cheap" Stradivarius costs around a quarter of a million dollars. 7 It is not surprising that a Stradivarius is sought after by great violinists and musical-instrument collectors alike.

18. Select the number of the sentence in paragraph 1 in which the author talks about others trying to replicate the Stradivarius quality.

Paragraph 1 is marked with an arrow (→).

Questions 19–24

The most traditional American food may well be cornmeal. Cornmeal, as we know it today, began as a Native American staple. The Native Americans grew corn of six different colors – black, red, white, yellow, blue, and multicolored. They ground the corn kernels into cornmeal and mixed it with salt and water, then baked it. This recipe was introduced to the early colonists, who experimented with it and developed their own uses for cornmeal. Succotash (a meat stew with cornmeal added) and mush (leftover cornmeal porridge cut and fried) are two meals invented by early colonists.

Visitors can travel to the South and enjoy spoon bread, a smooth puddinglike dish, or to New England for johnnycakes, a kind of flat pancake. But probably the most common forms of cornmeal nationwide are cornbread, cornmeal muffins, and the "hush puppy" – a round ball of cornmeal batter that is fried in oil.

19. According to the passage, cornmeal was originally used by
   (A) the early colonists
   (B) the New Englanders
   (C) the Native Americans
   (D) the people in the South

The most traditional American food may well be cornmeal. Cornmeal, as we know it today, began as a Native American staple. **The Native Americans grew corn of six different colors – black, red, white, yellow, blue, and multicolored. They ground the corn kernels into cornmeal and mixed it with salt and water, then baked it. This recipe was introduced to the early colonists, who experimented with it and developed their own uses for cornmeal.** Succotash (a meat stew with cornmeal added) and mush (leftover cornmeal porridge cut and fried) are two meals invented by early colonists.

20. Look at the word **their** in the passage. Select another word or phrase in the **bold** text that **their** refers to.

The most traditional American food may well be cornmeal. Cornmeal, as we know it today, began as a Native American staple. The Native Americans grew corn of six different colors – black, red, white, yellow, blue, and multicolored. They ground the corn kernels into cornmeal and mixed it with salt and water, then baked it. This recipe was introduced to the early colonists, who experimented with it and developed their own uses for cornmeal. Succotash (a meat stew with cornmeal added) and mush (leftover cornmeal porridge cut and fried) are two meals invented by early colonists.

Visitors can travel to the South and enjoy spoon bread, a smooth puddinglike dish, or to New England for johnnycakes, a kind of flat pancake. But probably the most common forms of cornmeal nationwide are cornbread, cornmeal muffins, and the "hush puppy" – a round ball of cornmeal batter that is fried in oil.

21. According to the passage, mush is
    (A) a batter that is fried in oil
    (B) fried leftovers from a cornmeal dish
    (C) added to meat stew to make succotash
    (D) one of two meals developed by the Native Americans

The most traditional American food may well be cornmeal. Cornmeal, as we know it today, began as a Native American staple. The Native Americans grew corn of six different colors – black, red, white, yellow, blue, and multicolored. They ground the corn kernels into cornmeal and mixed it with salt and water, then baked it. This recipe was introduced to the early colonists, who experimented with it and developed their own uses for cornmeal. Succotash (a meat stew with cornmeal added) and mush (leftover cornmeal porridge cut and fried) are two meals invented by early colonists.

Visitors can travel to the South and enjoy spoon bread, a smooth puddinglike dish, or to New England for johnnycakes, a kind of flat pancake. But probably the most common forms of cornmeal nationwide are cornbread, cornmeal muffins, and the "hush puppy" – a round ball of cornmeal batter that is fried in oil.

22. According to the passage, common forms of cornmeal are
   (A) no longer popular
   (B) restricted to certain regions
   (C) found nationwide
   (D) multicolored

→ [1] The most traditional American food may well be cornmeal. [2] Cornmeal, as we know it today, began as a Native American staple. [3] The Native Americans grew corn of six different colors – black, red, white, yellow, blue, and multicolored. [4] They ground the corn kernels into cornmeal and mixed it with salt and water, then baked it. [5] This recipe was introduced to the early colonists, who experimented with it and developed their own uses for cornmeal. [6] Succotash (a meat stew with cornmeal added) and mush (leftover cornmeal porridge cut and fried) are two meals invented by early colonists.

Visitors can travel to the South and enjoy spoon bread, a smooth puddinglike dish, or to New England for johnnycakes, a kind of flat pancake. But probably the most common forms of cornmeal nationwide are cornbread, cornmeal muffins, and the "hush puppy" – a round ball of cornmeal batter that is fried in oil.

23. Select the number of the sentence in paragraph 1 in which the author tells the reader about two recipes that the colonists developed.

Paragraph 1 is marked with an arrow (→).

1 The most traditional American food may well be cornmeal. Cornmeal, as we know it today, began as a Native American. The Native Americans grew corn of six different colors – black, red, white, yellow, blue, and multicolored. They ground the corn kernels into cornmeal and mixed it with salt and water, then baked it. This recipe was introduced to the early colonists, who experimented with it and developed their own uses for cornmeal. Succotash (a meat stew with cornmeal added) and mush (leftover cornmeal porridge cut and fried) are two meals invented by early colonists.

2 Visitors can travel to the South and enjoy spoon bread, a smooth puddinglike dish, or to New England for johnnycakes, a kind of flat pancake. But probably the most common forms of cornmeal nationwide are cornbread, cornmeal muffins, and the "hush puppy" – a round ball of cornmeal batter that is fried in oil.

24. Select the number of the paragraph in which the author discusses regional differences in the uses of cornmeal.

Answers to Exercise R21 are on page 538.

PRACTICE WITH INFERENCES

When you read a passage, some details are not stated explicitly, but they can be understood from the other details that are stated. Read the following statement:

> Dr. Smitten and two other psychologists chose twenty-five children for their study: five from Campbell, ten from other multiracial schools in Miami, and the rest from multiracial schools in other cities in Florida.

The details stated are:

1. Dr. Smitten and two other psychologists chose twenty-five children for a study.
2. Five children were from Campbell.
3. Ten children were from other schools in Miami.
4. The rest were from schools in other Florida cities.

What is not stated but must be understood?

1. What kind of doctor is Dr. Smitten?
   You understand that Dr. Smitten is a psychologist because it can be inferred from the phrase "and two other psychologists."
2. How many psychologists were doing the study?
   You understand that three psychologists were doing the study because it can be inferred from the phrase "Dr. Smitten and two other psychologists."
3. What and where is Campbell?
   You understand that Campbell is a multiracial school in Miami because it can be inferred from the phrase "other multiracial schools in Miami."
4. What and where is Miami?
   You understand that Miami is a city in Florida because it can be inferred from the phrase "other cities in Florida."

5. How many children from other cities in Florida were chosen for the study?
   You understand that ten children came from other cities because it can be inferred from the phrase "chose twenty-five children, five from . . . , ten from. . . , and the rest from other cities."
6. What was the study probably about?
   You understand that the study was probably about some aspect of children in multiracial school environments because it can be inferred from the phrases "multiracial schools in Miami" and "multiracial schools in other cities" that "multiracial" was an important factor in choosing the children from those schools.

Some details are neither stated nor implied. Therefore, you cannot answer the following questions:

1. When did the study take place?
2. Why was the study done?
3. What were the results of the study?

On the TOEFL® Test, you will have to make inferences from the passages that you read. Sometimes you must use the information given to you in the passage to draw some conclusion about the topic. Practice making inferences and drawing conclusions in Exercises R22–R27.

Exercise R22   *Identifying inferences in statements*

Circle the letter of those inferences that can be made from the information given in the statement. There may be more than one possible inference.

Example   The lesser North American poets are more popular with children than major poets because they are direct and clear.
(A) Children have difficulty understanding major poets.
(B) Minor poets write poetry for children.
(C) There are fewer poets writing for children than writing for adults.
(D) Indirect and hidden meanings are used in the poetry of major poets.

You should circle (A) because it can be inferred that the poetry of major poets is difficult for children because, unlike that of minor poets, it is not direct and clear. You should not circle (B) because it cannot be inferred if either minor or major poets write for children, or (C) because "lesser" means "minor poets," not "fewer poets." You should circle (D) because it can be inferred that if children like the lesser poets because they write more directly and clearly, the major poets use indirect ways of expressing ideas and hide meanings by use of symbols.

1. Three of the published reports came from official investigations, but the other two came from private individuals.
   (A) Private individuals cannot submit reports for publication.
   (B) Only the three official reports were considered for publication.
   (C) Five reports were published.
   (D) Official investigations were made on private individuals.

2. The Institute of Anthropology plans to computerize archaeological data to help restore the Native American villages in Chaco Canyon.
   (A) The Chaco Canyon Native American villages were destroyed by European people.
   (B) The Institute of Anthropology collects information about Native American villages that are in ruins.
   (C) The Native Americans in Chaco Canyon have computers to help them store data.
   (D) Computers can be helpful to restore archaeological plans.

3. Some scientists believe that the African bees that have devastated the Latin American beekeeping industry will become gentler as they interbreed with the previously introduced European varieties.
   (A) European bees will not be advantageous to the Latin American beekeeping industry.
   (B) African bees are ferocious and destructive.
   (C) The Latin American beekeeping industry will become gentler as African bees and European bees interbreed.
   (D) African bees, as well as European bees, live in Latin America.

4. The need for a person to love and be loved is so pressing that when it is frustrated, the person will find a substitute, which can range from having a pet to collecting antiques.
   (A) Animal owners are people who think that nobody likes them.
   (B) A person who feels rejected may lavish an abnormal amount of affection upon a stray cat.
   (C) To show your love for someone, you should give that person a pet.
   (D) Collecting stamps can be a substitute for needed attention.

5. From the start of training to the finish of a race, the attention that endurance-race contestants give their horses to ensure their being in top condition for competing is more than these riders give to themselves.
   (A) To a contestant, the good condition of the horse is more important in winning an endurance race than the condition of the rider.
   (B) The riders in an endurance race like their horses better than they like themselves.
   (C) In order to win, the horses don't give themselves as much attention as the riders give to themselves.
   (D) After a race, endurance-race contestants give themselves more attention than they give their horses.

6. No partner helps the male pheasant-tailed jacana protect and nurture his chicks in their floating nest.
   (A) The female pheasant-tailed jacana does not take care of her babies.
   (B) The jacana is an aquatic bird.
   (C) The male pheasant-tailed jacana doesn't help to protect and nurture its partner.
   (D) The male pheasant-tailed jacana does not mate.

7. Elephants are slowly becoming trapped in isolated forest enclaves completely surrounded by land cleared for agriculture.
   (A) Hunters are trapping elephants in isolated forest enclaves to get their ivory tusks.
   (B) People are destroying the elephants' habitat to make farms.
   (C) Elephants would have to cross through farmland to migrate to different forests.
   (D) People are trapping elephants to use them for clearing land for agriculture.

8. To safeguard sunken ships from adventurers or thieves, ship salvagers keep the wrecks under constant surveillance by electronic and other means.
   (A) Thieves sunk the ships to steal the cargo.
   (B) Sunken ships contain things that are valuable.
   (C) Ship salvagers are usually caught before they steal anything because of safeguards.
   (D) There are various ways to guard sunken ships from pilferers.

9. A species of weeds known as the gopher plant has earned a new name – the gasoline plant – because it yields a milky latex containing hydrocarbons that can be refined into substitutes for crude oil and gasoline.
    (A) Some weeds have been renamed "gasoline plants" because their latex can be made into gasoline.
    (B) Gasoline refined from the gasoline plant will soon replace the need for gasoline from other sources.
    (C) Substitutes for crude oil and gasoline can come from hydrocarbons.
    (D) Milk contains hydrocarbons necessary for crude oil and gasoline substitutes.

10. Not yet profitably synthesized, morphine, a drug unsurpassed for controlling pain, is still being scraped from opium poppy heads as it was at least 5,000 years ago.
    (A) Morphine, a drug from the poppy plant, is no longer profitable to cultivate.
    (B) Cocaine is not as effective as morphine for stopping pain.
    (C) Morphine has been used for pain control for at least 5,000 years.
    (D) It is possible to make artificial morphine economically.

Answers to Exercise R22 are on page 539.

Exercise R23 **Locating inferred information**

Read the passages and the inferred statements that follow. Underline the part or parts of the passage from which the inference can be made.

Example Is it true that <u>crime</u> doesn't pay? Although it is impossible to report every <u>dollar that was generated into the U.S. economy by Watergate</u>, figures pointed at what could be termed a first-class growth industry. Fees, royalties, fines, bills, and other miscellaneous payments added up into the millions of dollars moving around in the U.S. economy.

It can be inferred that Watergate is the name for a crime that took place in the United States.

You should underline "crime" and "dollar that was generated into the U.S. economy by Watergate" because it can be inferred that Watergate was a crime or else it wouldn't have been cited in the discussion of how crime pays. The passage goes on to discuss how crime has paid by generating money into the U.S. economy.

1. Unlike other toads, the male golden toad is nearly voiceless. It attracts its mate by its unmistakable orange color. When the clouds are thick in the rain forest, usually in April and May, the male toads appear like flashing neon signals, which is as effective as croaking in luring females during the mating season.

    It can be inferred from this passage that most toads attract their mates by making sounds.

2. The great temple of Borobudur is a stepped pyramid of unmortared andesite and basalt volcanic stone, with a perimeter of 403 feet and standing 105 feet high. This holy place lay abandoned and forgotten for more than 800 years after a devastating earthquake and an eruption of one of the four surrounding volcanoes caused its population to flee in 1006. Besides earthquakes and volcanoes, torrential rains, encroaching tropical vegetation, and time have all taken their toll.

    It can be inferred from this passage that the temple of Borobudur is in ruins.

3. Some multiple sclerosis victims are experimenting with deadly snake venom to ease the pain and tiredness caused by their disease. First, the poison is milked from cobra, krait, and viper snakes. One part of it is then mixed to four thousand parts of a saline solution. Although medical authorities are skeptical of the treatment, those using it claim that the venom has startling healing qualities.

It can be inferred that snake venom for the treatment of multiple sclerosis has not yet been approved by doctors.

4. The cassowary, one of the world's largest and least known birds, grows to a height of 6 feet and a weight of 120 pounds. Its powerful legs, which it uses for defense, are fearful weapons because the inner toe of each foot is equipped with a sharp claw, 4 inches long. The cassowary has glossy black plumage, which hangs coarse and brushlike because it lacks the barbules that are needed to lock feathers into a flat vane. The naked neck is of iridescent blue on the sides and pink on the back. Its head is crowned by a leathery helmet that protects it when it is charging through the jungle.

   It can be inferred that the cassowary probably doesn't fly.

5. Prior to 1870, little stone decoration was done on New York buildings, except for churches and public buildings. With the arrival of artisans among the groups of European immigrants, architectural carving began to flourish. Architects would buy sculptures already done or show sketches of what they wanted carved. Away from the master carver, who dictated what was to be carved, the artisans created eclectic and uninhibited sculptures, which became integrated into a purely American style.

   It can be inferred from the passage that, in Europe, artisans did not carve what they wanted to carve.

6. The Society for Creative Anachronism is a nonprofit club that joins together people who enjoy reenacting life as it was lived before the 1700s. Members of both sexes not only learn the art of sword fighting in mock combat but learn a wide range of authentic medieval skills as well. These include such skills as armor making, equestrian arts, games, jewelry making, astrology, and magic. Since the first tournament held in 1966, in which a dozen fighters took part, the society has grown to some 5,000 members.

   It can be inferred from the passage that women members of the Society for Creative Anachronism fight in battles.

7. Computer-driven cameras, lights, and servomotors as well as lasers and tiny lens assemblies are just a few of the complex instruments that have brought to today's television viewers effective scientific informational films. Two crucial problems in such films are finding arresting visuals and creating special effects to illustrate complex scientific concepts. Computer-generated motion pictures allow the viewer to see the meaning of data and complex relationships instantly and are a new aid to human understanding of almost limitless power.

   It can be inferred from this passage that computers used in the film industry have enabled people to understand science better.

8. Fish rubbings and nature printing have been developing as art forms in North America over the past 40 years, although the techniques may date as far back as the time of early cave dwellers. To make a fish print, one should choose a very fresh fish with large rough scales and a flat body. Other needed materials are several brushes, including a fine brush for painting the eyes on the print, a thick waterbased ink, newspaper, modeling clay for supporting the fins, straight pins, and cloth or absorbent paper such as newsprint. Handmade paper is best, but it is more expensive and not recommended for beginners. The fish should be washed, dried, and laid out on the newspaper. A thin layer of ink should be brushed on in both directions. The paper is then placed over the fish and pressed carefully with the fingers, avoiding wrinkles or movement of the paper.

   It can be inferred from the passage that it takes practice to become proficient in using this technique.

9. Characteristics of tropical rain forests are high and steady levels of heat and moisture, as well as a wide variety of organisms. It is believed that two-thirds of all species live in the tropics, and half of those live in the tropical rain forests. Nowhere else, except perhaps in tropical coral reefs, is nature so great in its diversity of organisms and complex in its biological interaction.

It can be inferred from this passage that tropical coral reefs contain a wide variety of organisms.

10. Even though historians think that ice-skating has been a sport for the last 2,000 years, it is within the last five decades that skating has gained recognition as a form of art. Champion athletes combine new heights of athleticism with the elegance of dance in what is now called figure skating. Ice-skaters performing daring jumps in flamboyant costumes have brought ballet to the ice rink. Ice-skating is now seen as an exciting and innovative sport that has won millions of new admirers.

It can be inferred that ice-skaters are both athletes and artists.

Answers to Exercise R23 are on page 540.

Exercise R24   *Checking if a statement can be inferred*

Answer "Yes" or "No" to the question that follows each statement.

Example   Volunteers for organizations such as Save the Children make an extremely important personal contribution toward improving the daily lives of millions of children throughout the world.

Can it be inferred that Save the Children volunteers contribute a lot of money to aid children? ___No___

You should write "No" in the space because a "personal contribution" does not necessarily mean a monetary contribution. Volunteers may contribute time or a special personal skill that they have in order to aid children.

1. Each day, more and more communities discover that they have been living near dumps or on top of ground that has been contaminated by toxic chemicals.

Can it be inferred that communities aren't always told when and where toxic wastes are being disposed? _____

2. E. B. White's death, at 86, was cause for sadness in millions of homes.

Can it be inferred that E. B. White was famous? _____

3. Charles F. Richter helped devise a scale that is universally used to measure the magnitude of earthquakes.

Can it be inferred that the Richter scale was named for a devastating earthquake? _____

4. There is evidence that a global firestorm raged about the time the dinosaurs disappeared.

Can it be inferred that dinosaurs became extinct because of a global firestorm? _____

5. Of the twelve sulfite-associated deaths, one was caused by wine, one by beer, and one by hashed brown potatoes; the rest were linked to fresh fruits or vegetables.

Can it be inferred that nine people died from sulfite-contaminated fresh foods? _____

6. Early evaluation of data from *Vega I* showed that it encountered less dust than expected as it approached Halley's comet.

Can it be inferred that *Vega I* is an unidentified flying object, or "UFO"? _____

7. Quinolone, a recently discovered antibiotic, inhibits an enzyme that controls the way bacterial DNA unravels and rewinds when microbes reproduce.

Can it be inferred that quinolone will eventually replace all other antibiotics? _____

8. For people whose nerves have been damaged by illness or injuries, actions such as walking or grasping an object may be impossible.

Can it be inferred that the nervous system is important for muscle control? _____

Answers to Exercise R24 are on page 541.

Exercise R25 *Identifying inferences in paragraphs*

Read the passages and the statements that follow. Write "I" in the space if the statement is an inference. Write "R" if the statement is a restatement. Leave the space blank if the statement is neither an inference nor a restatement.

Example Francis Gary Powers survived when his high-flying reconnaissance aircraft was shot down over the Soviet Union in 1960. He was convicted of espionage after a trial in Moscow. Later, Powers was returned to the United States in exchange for Soviet spy Rudolf Abel. Powers was killed in a helicopter crash in California in 1977.

(A) __R__ Powers was found guilty of spying in the Soviet Union.

(B) __I__ Rudolf Abel was being held by the United States for spying.

(C) _____ Powers was killed during a reconnaissance mission.

You should write "R" for (A) because to be "convicted of espionage" means the same as to be "found guilty of spying." You should write "I" for (B) because Rudolf Abel must have been held by the United States if the Americans exchanged him for Powers. You should leave (C) blank because no information is given on why Powers was flying the helicopter (for example, for work or for recreation).

1. The MacArthur prizes, or "genius awards," are grants of money ranging from $128,000 to $300,000 given to individuals who show outstanding talents in their fields. According to a foundation spokesperson, this money frees geniuses from financial worries and allows them the time to devote themselves to creative thinking. The recipients of the MacArthur prizes are people who have already achieved considerable success. It may be asked whether they attained success despite the fact that they had to worry about money or because of it.

(A) _____ Someone who is not already known in his or her field will probably not be a recipient of the MacArthur prize.

(B) _____ Some people may become successful because they are worried about money.

(C) _____ Some individuals receive as much as $300,000 to think.

2. The CDC (Centers for Disease Control) is responsible for the research done in solving or attempting to solve medical mysteries. Teams of epidemiologists crisscross the country investigating outbreaks of disease. They ask questions, look for clues, and track down pieces of puzzles in a relentless pursuit to find answers that will bring about breakthroughs in the prevention or cure of serious diseases. The CDC rushes in to study epidemics because it is possible to quickly determine patterns and common links among the victims.

   (A) _____ The Centers for Disease Control is not always successful in its research of diseases.

   (B) _____ Epidemiologists travel across the nation to do their research.

   (C) _____ Because there are more victims when an epidemic strikes, more data can be collected to find answers to medical questions.

3. Astronomers have long believed that frozen gases and water account for up to 80 percent of a comet's mass. While observing Comet Bowell, astronomers were able to measure the amount of light this comet absorbed and reflected. On the basis of these observations, they determined that comets do indeed contain frozen water.

   (A) _____ Astronomers have proved the theory that comets contain frozen water.

   (B) _____ The ice content of other comets can be ascertained by measuring how much light they absorb and reflect.

   (C) _____ The name of the observed comet is Bowell.

4. Although most honeybees die in the field while gathering pollen, some bees die in the hives and must be removed in order to prevent the spread of disease and to keep the nest from filling up with corpses. These corpses emit a chemical that signals death. Most of the bees either ignore the corpses, poke at them, lick them, or inspect them. Usually within an hour, the bees that are in charge of removing dead bees grasp the corpses in their mandibles, pull them through the hive toward the entrance, then fly away and drop them as far as 400 feet from the hive.

   (A) _____ Dead bees cannot be left in the hive because they may make the other bees sick.

   (B) _____ The honeybees know there is a dead bee in the hive because of the death chemical that is emitted.

   (C) _____ In less than one hour, the dead bees have usually been removed from the hive.

5. The northern elephant seal, a 2,000-pound mammal, is making a dramatic comeback after being hunted to near extinction in the late nineteenth century. The seals that once thrived off the coast of California now receive protection from both the Mexican and United States governments. A contributing factor to their survival is the reduced demand for seal oil due to the availability of petroleum products.

   (A) _____ Products that were once made from seal oil are now made from petroleum.

   (B) _____ Petroleum is easier to obtain now than seal oil is.

   (C) _____ Northern elephant seals are now numerous.

6. Diverse in culture and language, the tenacious men and women who inhabit the world's harshest environment, the land above the Arctic Circle, probably descended from hunting societies pushed north from Central Asia by population pressure about 10,000 years ago. "Scarcity" is the word that best describes the Arctic ecosystem, where life-giving solar energy is in short supply. In the winter, the sun disappears for weeks or months depending on the latitude. Even during the months of prolonged sunlight, the slanted rays cannot thaw the frozen subsurface soil. But more than the severe cold, the lack of resources for food, clothing, and shelter defines the lifestyles that the Arctic peoples lead.

   (A) _____ Scarcity of food, clothing, and shelter influences Arctic living conditions more than the harsh climate does.

   (B) _____ Anthropologists are not completely certain about the ancestry of the Arctic peoples.

   (C) _____ The further north one is, the less sunshine there is.

7. Half of all the astronauts on space flights are afflicted with debilitating space sickness, an ailment akin to car sickness and marked by nausea and vomiting. It is believed that zero gravity and its effect on the inner ear and the flow of body fluids are the cause. Scientists are attempting to find a way to predict who is susceptible to the illness because it interferes with the important work that must be done efficiently during space missions.

   (A) _____ Scientists cannot tell whether an astronaut who suffers from car sickness will suffer from space sickness.

   (B) _____ Space sickness makes it difficult for afflicted astronauts to do their work.

   (C) _____ Space sickness and car sickness are related illnesses.

8. The white shark, which has acquired a reputation for mindless ferocity unequaled among terrestrial or aquatic predators, belongs to the family known as the mackerel shark. Nothing about this terrifying fish is predictable: not its behavior, range, or diet. Evidence from the remains of victims of shark attacks suggests that the white shark does not eat people.

   (A) _____ A white shark is a kind of mackerel shark.

   (B) _____ The white shark has gained a terrifying reputation because it attacks people.

   (C) _____ The white shark attacks its victims for reasons other than hunger.

9. Because they seem to be taking a measure with each looping stride, some caterpillars are called geometrids, or earth measurers. From this comes their common name, inchworms. This caterpillar grasps a twig with its back legs, extends itself forward, then draws its back end up to its front legs and repeats the sequence.

   (A) _____ The geometrid moves by stretching forward, then moving its back to its front, then repeating this process.

   (B) _____ Not all caterpillars are inchworms.

   (C) _____ All inchworms are earth measurers.

10. The Merlin is propelled by six compact engines, each encased in a separate duct. With no exposed blades, the craft is much safer to maneuver on the ground than either a helicopter or small plane. The Merlin takes off and hovers by blasting a column of air straight down and moves forward by directing some of that air backward with movable vanes behind each engine.

(A) _____ The Merlin is a kind of aircraft.

(B) _____ Exposed blades make some aircraft unsafe.

(C) _____ Production of the Merlin has not yet begun.

Answers to Exercise R25 are on page 541.

Exercise R26   *Making inferences*

To answer some of the questions on the Computer-Based TOEFL® Test, you have to make inferences about words or phrases in the passage. The computer screen will look like this.

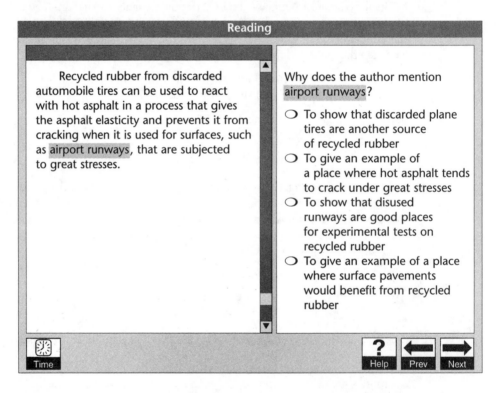

To answer this question, you would click on the last oval because the author uses airport runways as an example of highly stressed surfaces where the hot asphalt process would be beneficial. When you click on this oval, it will darken to show which choice you have made. When you are sure of your answer, click on **Next** to go on to the next question.

In the following exercise, circle the letter of the best answer choice based on the information given.

1. In the third and fourth centuries, the Germanic tribes of central Europe joined forces and plundered the crumbling Roman Empire. But they in turn became the victims of the Norse invasions of the eighth century. The Norsemen raided villages in every region. They killed the men, abducted the women and children, and then departed in their fast-sailing ships, leaving nothing but a few smoldering ruins.

   What does the author mean by the statement they in turn became the victims?
   (A) The Germanic tribes turned on the Norse invaders in the eighth century.
   (B) The Germanic tribes and the Norse invaders took turns in attacking the Roman Empire.
   (C) The Germanic tribes received the same treatment from the Norsemen as they had given the Roman Empire.
   (D) The Roman Empire was first plundered by the Germanic tribes in the third and fourth centuries and then by the Norsemen in the eighth century.

2. Erosion of America's farmland by wind and water has been a problem since settlers first put the prairies and grasslands under the plow in the nineteenth century. By the 1930s, more than 282 million acres of farmland were damaged by erosion. After forty years of conservation efforts, soil erosion has accelerated due to new demands placed on the land by heavy crop production. In the years ahead, soil erosion and the pollution problems it causes are likely to replace petroleum scarcity as the nation's most critical natural resource problem.

   Why does the author mention petroleum scarcity?
   (A) To show that petroleum scarcity will become the most critical natural resource problem
   (B) To prove that petroleum is causing heavy soil erosion and pollution problems
   (C) To indicate that soil erosion has caused humans to place new demands on heavy crop production
   (D) To emphasize the fact that soil erosion will become the most critical problem the nation faces

3. The quality of the graphics output on a computer printer is measured in dpi (dots per inch). Simply by changing the density of dots that make up each part of an image, the printer can produce graphics that look almost photographic. To understand how this works, consider how a black-and-white photograph shows the shades that, in real life, are colors. Each color is a different shade of gray. For graphics to be produced on the computer printer, a piece of software called a printer driver decides upon a dot pattern that will represent each color shade. These different patterns or textures each create an individual effect that your eye translates into gray shades. The closer you look at the image, however, the less lifelike it looks.

   Why does the author mention a black-and-white photograph?
   (A) To explain how a printer makes graphics
   (B) To compare the clarity of computer graphics to photographs
   (C) To emphasize the difference between colored graphics and black-and-white graphics
   (D) To convince the reader that dpi is preferable to photography

4. Endesha Ida Mae Holland became a playwright by a mere twist of fate. While studying at the University of Minnesota, Holland was consumed by activities other than academics. She helped start student groups dedicated to racial progress and black unity. Off campus, she formed an organization to get former prisoners back on their feet. So diverted, it took her nearly fifteen years to earn her bachelor's degree. When she found herself four credit hours short of a degree, she enrolled in an acting course, which she thought would be easy because of her experience on speaking tours. But by transposing two numbers, Holland had accidentally signed up for an advanced playwriting seminar. An author was born. Holland's latest play, *From the Mississippi Delta*, has been staged at major regional theaters in Chicago, Los Angeles, and Washington.

What does the author mean by stating Endesha Ida Mae Holland became a playwright by a mere twist of fate?
(A) It took nearly fifteen years to complete her bachelor's degree.
(B) An author was born.
(C) She didn't intend to take the playwriting seminar.
(D) She had experience on speaking tours.

Answers to Exercise R26 are on page 542.

Exercise R27   *Drawing conclusions*

Read the following statements and circle the letter of the best answer based on the information given.

Example   Few school curriculums include a unit on how to deal with bereavement and grief, and yet all students at some point in their lives suffer from losses through death and parting.

What topic would probably NOT be included in a unit on bereavement?
(A) How to write a letter of condolence
(B) What emotional stages are passed through in the healing process
(C) How to give support to a grieving friend
(D) What the leading causes of death are

Bereavement is the state of experiencing the death of a relative or friend. Since the leading causes of death are not relevant to the particular death that a person may have to deal with, you should circle (D).

1. Studies show that bike races in Mexico City, where air is 20 percent less dense than at sea level, tend to be 3 to 5 percent faster than at lower altitudes.

   In which area would a bike race probably be the slowest?
   (A) Along the coast
   (B) On an indoor track
   (C) On a high plateau
   (D) At the snowline of a volcano

2. Owners of famous and valuable paintings have recently been commissioning talented artists to paint copies of these art treasures to exhibit in their homes.

   What is the most likely reason an owner of a valuable painting might want to exhibit a copy instead of the original?
   (A) Because they need to trick the experts
   (B) Because they hope to foil would-be thieves
   (C) Because they want to encourage talented artists
   (D) Because they enjoy buying fake paintings

3. The Academy of Dog Training supplies law enforcement agencies with German shepherds that are trained to recognize the smell of marijuana and other drugs.

In which of the following places would these German shepherds most likely be used?
(A) At scenes of violent crimes
(B) Where burglaries have taken place
(C) At sports arenas
(D) At customs checks between borders

4. Schools based upon the philosophy of Rudolph Steiner are all coeducational, practice mixed-ability teaching, and discourage competition among children.

Which of the following activities would probably NOT be seen in a Steiner school?
(A) A class period devoted to the teaching of mathematics
(B) A game involving both boys and girls
(C) A poetry-writing contest
(D) A classroom of children reading at different levels

5. The microbiologist exposed bacteria to increasingly higher levels of cyanide until he had a type of bacteria that could destroy the cyanide that had been dumped into rivers by chemical plants.

In what way could this bacteria be useful?
(A) For saving the water life from toxic wastes
(B) For poisoning undesirable fish
(C) For cleaning swimming pools
(D) For increasing the cyanide in the chemical plants

Answers to Exercise R27 are on page 542.

CHECK YOUR PROGRESS

Check your progress with inference skills (Exercises R22–R27) by completing the following mini-test. This exercise uses a format similar to that used in the Reading Section of the Computer-Based TOEFL® Test. If you are unfamiliar with how to answer questions on the Computer-Based TOEFL® Test, see the Tutorial on pages 24–28.

Exercise R28   Mini-test

Select the correct answer.

Questions 1–4

The Malabar pied hornbill usually nests in the fruit trees that bear its food. The female enters a hole in the tree and molts. She and her mate seal the hollow with mud and dung, leaving a crack through which he feeds her. When the chicks hatch and her plumage returns, she breaks out, resealing the nest to guard the young, which emerge later.	1. The Malabar pied hornbill is probably a (A) chicken (B) seal (C) bird (D) bear

The Malabar pied hornbill usually nests in the fruit trees that bear its food. The female enters a hole in the tree and molts. She and her mate seal the hollow with mud and dung, leaving a crack through which he feeds her. When the chicks hatch and her plumage returns, she breaks out, resealing the nest to guard the young, which emerge later.

2. What can be said about the Malabar pied hornbill's nest?
   (A) It is lined with feathers.
   (B) It is so warm that the female Malabar pied hornbill loses its plumage.
   (C) The female Malabar pied hornbill breaks it up after molting.
   (D) Its cracks are covered by the feathers that the female Malabar pied hornbill plucks off itself.

The Malabar pied hornbill usually nests in the fruit trees that bear its food. The female enters a hole in the tree and molts. She and her mate seal the hollow with mud and dung, leaving a crack through which he feeds her. When the chicks hatch and her plumage returns, she breaks out, resealing the nest to guard the young, which emerge later.

3. Which of the following statements can be inferred?
   (A) The male is afraid of other males and, therefore, forces his mate into the nest and seals it.
   (B) The female is so involved in building her nest that she doesn't realize she's locked herself inside it.
   (C) The female purposely imprisons herself to lay her eggs.
   (D) The female has to keep the male from hurting the babies, so she encloses herself in the nest.

The Malabar pied hornbill usually nests in the fruit trees that bear its food. The female enters a hole in the tree and molts. She and her mate seal the hollow with mud and dung, leaving a crack through which he feeds her. When the chicks hatch and her plumage returns, she breaks out, resealing the nest to guard the young, which emerge later.

4. The male Malabar pied hornbill probably
   (A) feeds the eggs through a crack in the nest
   (B) doesn't help the female until she has enclosed herself in the nest
   (C) uses his plumage to guard the recently hatched chicks
   (D) doesn't hatch the eggs by keeping them warm with his own body

Questions 5–7

The Mississippi River and its tributaries form the world's fourth-longest river system. Two Canadian provinces and all or parts of thirty-one states in the United States have rivers that drain into the Mississippi. As the Mississippi River flows down to join the sea, it deposits sand, silt, and clay, building the delta seaward across Louisiana's shallow continental shelf. The delta marsh and its bays, lakes, and sounds provide shelter and nutrients for North America's most fertile marine nursery.

5. It can be inferred from the passage that
   (A) Canada has only two drainage areas in its provinces
   (B) there are thirty-one states in the United States
   (C) the thirty-one states mentioned have no other river systems to carry silt, sand, and clay
   (D) some of the silt deposited in the Louisiana delta is from Canada

---

The Mississippi River and its tributaries form the world's fourth-longest river system. Two Canadian provinces and all or parts of thirty-one states in the United States have rivers that drain into the Mississippi. As the Mississippi River flows down to join the sea, it deposits sand, silt, and clay, building the delta seaward across Louisiana's shallow continental shelf. The delta marsh and its bays, lakes, and sounds provide shelter and nutrients for North America's most fertile marine nursery.

6. It is probably true that
   (A) the delta system formed by the Mississippi River is very important for marine life
   (B) nurseries have been set up in the delta so that children can take part in aquatic sports in the bays, lakes, and sounds
   (C) the delta marshlands is an excellent area for medical people to study diseases caused by mosquitoes and other insects
   (D) the United States has established nurseries to provide shelter and food for migrating birds

---

The Mississippi River and its tributaries form the world's fourth-longest river system. Two Canadian provinces and all or parts of thirty-one states in the United States have rivers that drain into the Mississippi. As the Mississippi River flows down to join the sea, it deposits sand, silt, and clay, building the delta seaward across Louisiana's shallow continental shelf. The delta marsh and its bays, lakes, and sounds provide shelter and nutrients for North America's most fertile marine nursery.

7. It can be inferred from the passage that
   (A) the delta is being destroyed by the Mississippi River's depositing sand, silt, and clay
   (B) the geographic features of the delta are always changing
   (C) the sea movement is building a delta on the continental shelf at the mouth of the Mississippi
   (D) the river, delta, and sea all play an important role in building Louisiana's continental shelf

Questions 8–11

Time can be regarded as neither a biological nor a physical absolute but a cultural invention. Different cultures have differing perceptions about the passage of time. At opposing ends of the spectrum are the "monochronic," or linear, cultures and the "polychronic," or simultaneous, cultures. In monochronic societies, schedules and routines are primary. Monochronic societies tend to be more efficient and impartial. However, they may be blind to the humanity of their members. In polychronic societies, people take precedence over schedules. People are rarely alone, not even at home, and are usually dealing with several people at once. Time and schedules are not priorities.

8. It can be inferred from the passage that
   (A) people who are blind live in monochronic societies
   (B) it may be frustrating for monochronic and polychronic societies to deal with each other
   (C) monochronic cultures are concerned with schedules and linear cultures are concerned with people
   (D) in monochronic cultures, one person takes precedence over schedules, and in polychronic cultures, many people take precedence over schedules

Time can be regarded as neither a biological nor a physical absolute but a cultural invention. Different cultures have differing perceptions about the passage of time. At opposing ends of the spectrum are the "monochronic," or linear, cultures and the "polychronic," or simultaneous, cultures. In monochronic societies, schedules and routines are primary. Monochronic societies tend to be more efficient and impartial. However, they may be blind to the humanity of their members. In polychronic societies, people take precedence over schedules. People are rarely alone, not even at home, and are usually dealing with several people at once. Time and schedules are not priorities.

9. It is probably true that
   (A) in a polychronic society, a person will skip an appointment if a family member needs some help
   (B) in a monochronic society, a person will skip an appointment for a blind friend
   (C) in a polychronic society, a person will be on time for an appointment if the other person is from a monochronic society
   (D) in a monochronic society, people will look for any excuse in order to skip an appointment

Time can be regarded as neither a biological nor a physical absolute but a cultural invention. Different cultures have differing perceptions about the passage of time. At opposing ends of the spectrum are the "monochronic," or linear, cultures and the "polychronic," or simultaneous, cultures. In monochronic societies, schedules and routines are primary. Monochronic societies tend to be more efficient and impartial. However, they may be blind to the humanity of their members. In polychronic societies, people take precedence over schedules. People are rarely alone, not even at home, and are usually dealing with several people at once. Time and schedules are not priorities.

10. Why does the author use the terms linear and simultaneous?
    (A) To examine and compare monochronic and polychronic cultures
    (B) To introduce two more types of cultures
    (C) To define monochronic and polychronic cultures
    (D) To emphasize the different cultures

Time can be regarded as neither a biological nor a physical absolute but a cultural invention. Different cultures have differing perceptions about the passage of time. At opposing ends of the spectrum are the "monochronic," or linear, cultures and the "polychronic," or simultaneous, cultures. In monochronic societies, schedules and routines are primary. Monochronic societies tend to be more efficient and impartial. However, they may be blind to the humanity of their members. In polychronic societies, people take precedence over schedules. People are rarely alone, not even at home, and are usually dealing with several people at once. Time and schedules are not priorities.

11. It can be inferred from the passage that
    (A) there are other cultures that regard time differently from the way polychronic and monochronic cultures do
    (B) there are four different ways cultures regard time: monochronic, linear, polychronic, and simultaneous
    (C) a spectrum of time is not a culture's invention or a physical absolute
    (D) cultures invent biological and physical absolutes

Questions 12–14

An ultralight airplane is very different from a conventional airplane. It looks like a lawn chair with wings, weighs no more than 254 pounds, flies up to 60 miles an hour, and carries about 5 gallons of fuel. Most ultralights are sold as kits and take about 40 hours to assemble. Flying an ultralight is so easy that a pilot with no experience can fly one. Accidents are rarely fatal or even serious because the ultralight lands so slowly and gently and carries so little fuel. Some models now have parachutes attached, while others have parachute packs that pilots can wear.

12. Ultralights are powered by
    (A) an engine
    (B) human energy
    (C) remote control
    (D) solar energy

An ultralight airplane is very different from a conventional airplane. It looks like a lawn chair with wings, weighs no more than 254 pounds, flies up to 60 miles an hour, and carries about 5 gallons of fuel. Most ultralights are sold as kits and take about 40 hours to assemble. Flying an ultralight is so easy that a pilot with no experience can fly one. Accidents are rarely fatal or even serious because the ultralight lands so slowly and gently and carries so little fuel. Some models now have parachutes attached, while others have parachute packs that pilots can wear.

13. It is probably true that
    (A) an ultralight can be purchased at the airport
    (B) people can put their own ultralights together
    (C) people who fly ultralights have no experience
    (D) ultralight builders need to have training in aviation

An ultralight airplane is very different from a conventional airplane. It looks like a lawn chair with wings, weighs no more than 254 pounds, flies up to 60 miles an hour, and carries about 5 gallons of fuel. Most ultralights are sold as kits and take about 40 hours to assemble. Flying an ultralight is so easy that a pilot with no experience can fly one. Accidents are rarely fatal or even serious because the ultralight lands so slowly and gently and carries so little fuel. Some models now have parachutes attached, while others have parachute packs that pilots can wear.

14. It can be inferred from the passage that
    (A) accident statistics are inaccurate because ultralights are not registered at airports
    (B) fatal accidents are frequent because of the lack of experienced pilots
    (C) ultralight pilots can walk away from most of the accidents they are in
    (D) because of the frequency of fatal accidents, laws requiring parachutes have been enacted

Questions 15–18

Jacob Epstein's sculptures were the focus of much controversy during the sculptor's lifetime. Epstein was born in the United States of Russian-Jewish immigrants in 1880. He moved to Paris in his youth and later to England, where he eventually settled and took out British citizenship in 1907. His first major public commission, on a building in London, offended public taste because of the expressive distortion and nudity of the figures. In 1937, the Rhodesian government, which at that time owned the building, actually mutilated the sculptures to make them conform to public notions of decency. Many other of Epstein's monumental carvings received equally adverse criticism. While the general public denounced his work, many artists and critics praised it. They admired in particular the diversity of his work and noted the influence on it of primitive and ancient sculptural motifs from Africa and the Pacific. Today, Epstein's work has received the recognition it deserves, and Epstein is considered one of the major sculptors of the twentieth century.

15. Concerning Epstein's work, the tone of the article is
    (A) critical
    (B) derisive
    (C) amusing
    (D) admiring

Jacob Epstein's sculptures were the focus of much controversy during the sculptor's lifetime. Epstein was born in the United States of Russian-Jewish immigrants in 1880. He moved to Paris in his youth and later to England, where he eventually settled and took out British citizenship in 1907. His first major public commission, on a building in London, offended public taste because of the expressive distortion and nudity of the figures. In 1937, the Rhodesian government, which at that time owned the building, actually mutilated the sculptures to make them conform to public notions of decency. Many other of Epstein's monumental carvings received equally adverse criticism. While the general public denounced his work, many artists and critics praised it. They admired in particular the diversity of his work and noted the influence on it of primitive and ancient sculptural motifs from Africa and the Pacific. Today, Epstein's work has received the recognition it deserves, and Epstein is considered one of the major sculptors of the twentieth century.

16. Which of the following was most probably an important influence on Epstein's work?
    (A) Russian painting
    (B) Public tastes
    (C) The Rhodesian government
    (D) African carvings

Jacob Epstein's sculptures were the focus of much controversy during the sculptor's lifetime. Epstein was born in the United States of Russian-Jewish immigrants in 1880. He moved to Paris in his youth and later to England, where he eventually settled and took out British citizenship in 1907. His first major public commission, on a building in London, offended public taste because of the expressive distortion and nudity of the figures. In 1937, the Rhodesian government, which at that time owned the building, actually mutilated the sculptures to make them conform to public notions of decency. Many other of Epstein's monumental carvings received equally adverse criticism. While the general public denounced his work, many artists and critics praised it. They admired in particular the diversity of his work and noted the influence on it of primitive and ancient sculptural motifs from Africa and the Pacific. Today, Epstein's work has received the recognition it deserves, and Epstein is considered one of the major sculptors of the twentieth century.

17. Today, a newly erected Epstein sculpture would probably
    (A) be mutilated
    (B) conform to public opinions
    (C) be well received
    (D) be expressive

18. What does the author mean by the statement Many other of Epstein's monumental carvings received equally adverse criticism?
    (A) Many of Epstein's monuments have been defaced.
    (B) People have taken equal offense to other critical works of art.
    (C) Epstein's monuments are usually denounced for their nudity.
    (D) Other sculptures of Epstein's have elicited negative comments.

Answers to Exercise R28 are on page 542.

Exercise R29   **Reading Section Practice Test**

When you have completed the Reading exercises as recommended on the Diagnostic Test, test your skills by taking this final Reading Practice Test, which corresponds to the Reading Section of Test 2 on the CD-ROM that accompanies this book. Alternatively, you can take the test on the pages that follow.

During the Reading Section of the actual Computer-Based TOEFL® Test, you may go back and check your work or change your answers before time is called. Maintain the same test conditions now that would be experienced during the real test.

Answers to Exercise R29 are on page 544.

READING

Time – 80 minutes
(including the reading of the passages)

In this section, you will read several passages. Each passage is followed by ten to fifteen questions. There are fifty questions in this section. You should answer all questions following a passage on the basis of what is <u>stated</u> or <u>implied</u> in that passage. For each question, select or write the correct answer.

Now begin reading the first passage.

Questions 1–14

One of the foremost American entertainers of the first part of the twentieth century was a part-Cherokee Native American named Will Rogers (1879–1935). Rogers was born in territory that would later become the state of Oklahoma and spent much of his youth riding horses and mastering the use of the lariat. These skills were refined into an entertainment act based on fancy rope tricks interspersed with humorous anecdotes and witty remarks. Traveling widely as a vaudeville entertainer, Rogers had become a star act by 1915 with the Ziegfeld Follies, a famous stage show. In 1918 his stage skills led to a new career as a movie actor both in silent films and later in the "talkies."

In the early 1920s, Rogers embarked on another profession, this time as a journalist writing weekly newspaper columns that reached millions of people worldwide. Beginning in 1930 he also broadcast regular radio addresses. What distinguished his journalistic approach was his firsthand experience of ordinary people and places and a wry sense of humor, often debunking establishment figures and institutions. This poking fun at the serious side of life, combined with an optimistic homespun philosophy, gave him immense popular appeal. He became a national and international celebrity and acquired the unofficial status of a goodwill ambassador during his travels in Europe. He also had a strong philanthropic streak and devoted money and time to charitable causes.

Rogers also had a keen interest in flying. He often wrote about the development of aviation and made friends with trailblazing flyers such as Charles Lindbergh. Another pioneering aviator, Wiley Post, invited Rogers to join him in testing the viability of a commercial route between the United States and Asia. Tragically, both Rogers and Post were killed when their plane crashed in northern Alaska. Rogers's death was felt deeply throughout the United States and the public displays of mourning were heartfelt and widespread. The epitaph by his tomb is taken from one of his numerous quotable remarks and reminds us of the essential dignity of the man. It reads, "Never Met A Man I Didn't Like."

1. What is the passage mainly about?
   (A) The death of an ambassador
   (B) An epitaph to a remarkable person
   (C) An entertaining and accomplished man
   (D) The anecdotes of a humorous journalist

2. According to the passage, which of the following statements is true?
   (A) Rogers had Native-American blood.
   (B) Rogers told stories about his Native-American upbringing.
   (C) Rogers learned rope tricks from Native Americans.
   (D) Rogers portrayed Native Americans on film.

→ One of the foremost American entertainers of the first part of the twentieth century was a part-Cherokee Native American named Will Rogers (1879–1935). Rogers was born in territory that would later become the state of Oklahoma and spent much of his youth riding horses and mastering the use of the lariat. These skills were refined into an entertainment act based on fancy rope tricks interspersed with humorous anecdotes and witty remarks. Traveling widely as a vaudeville entertainer, Rogers had become a star act by 1915 with the Ziegfeld Follies, a famous stage show. In 1918 his stage skills led to a new career as a movie actor both in silent films and later in the "talkies."

3. The word anecdotes in paragraph 1 is closest in meaning to
   (A) tricks
   (B) stories
   (C) recalls
   (D) quips

Paragraph 1 is marked with an arrow (→).

→ [1] In the early 1920s, Rogers embarked on another profession, this time as a journalist writing weekly newspaper columns that reached millions of people worldwide. [2] Beginning in 1930 he also broadcast regular radio addresses. [3] What distinguished his journalistic approach was his firsthand experience of ordinary people and places and a wry sense of humor, often debunking establishment figures and institutions. [4] This poking fun at the serious side of life, combined with an optimistic homespun philosophy, gave him immense popular appeal. [5] He became a national and international celebrity and acquired the unofficial status of a goodwill ambassador during his travels in Europe. [6] He also had a strong philanthropic streak and devoted money and time to charitable causes.

4. Select the number of the sentence in paragraph 2 in which the author implies that the writing of some journalists was not humorous.

Paragraph 2 is marked with an arrow (→).

In the early 1920s, Rogers embarked on another profession, this time as a journalist writing weekly newspaper columns that reached millions of people worldwide. **Beginning in 1930 he also broadcast regular radio addresses. What distinguished his journalistic approach was his firsthand experience of ordinary people and places and a wry sense of humor, often debunking establishment figures and institutions. This poking fun at the serious side of life, combined with an optimistic homespun philosophy, gave him immense popular appeal. He became a national and international celebrity and acquired the unofficial status of a goodwill ambassador during his travels in Europe.** He also had a strong philanthropic streak and devoted money and time to charitable causes.

5. Look at the word **debunking** in the passage. Select another word or phrase in the **bold** text that is closest in meaning to the word **debunking**.

→ In the early 1920s, Rogers embarked on another profession, this time as a journalist writing weekly newspaper columns that reached millions of people worldwide. Beginning in 1930 he also broadcast regular radio addresses. What distinguished his journalistic approach was his firsthand experience of ordinary people and places and a wry sense of humor, often debunking establishment figures and institutions. This poking fun at the serious side of life, combined with an optimistic homespun philosophy, gave him immense popular appeal. He became a national and international celebrity and acquired the unofficial status of a goodwill ambassador during his travels in Europe. He also had a strong philanthropic streak and devoted money and time to charitable causes.

6. What does the author mean by a goodwill ambassador in paragraph 2?
   (A) Rogers worked in American embassies in European countries.
   (B) Rogers's homespun philosophy made him an international celebrity.
   (C) Rogers traveled the world projecting a kindly image of his country.
   (D) Rogers's immense popular appeal helped him to establish charitable institutions.

Paragraph 2 is marked with an arrow (→).

In the early 1920s, Rogers embarked on another profession, this time as a journalist writing weekly newspaper columns that reached millions of people worldwide. Beginning in 1930 he also broadcast regular radio addresses. ⬚1 What distinguished his journalistic approach was his firsthand experience of ordinary people and places and a wry sense of humor, often debunking establishment figures and institutions. ⬚2 This poking fun at the serious side of life, combined with an optimistic homespun philosophy, gave him immense popular appeal. ⬚3 He became a national and international celebrity and acquired the unofficial status of a goodwill ambassador during his travels in Europe. ⬚4 He also had a strong philanthropic streak and devoted money and time to charitable causes. ⬚5

7. The following sentence can be added to the paragraph.

Among his preferred causes was alleviating the plight of Native Americans and the needy victims of the Great Depression.

Where would it best fit in the paragraph?

Select the square (⬚) that shows where the sentence should be added.

→ In the early 1920s, Rogers embarked on another profession, this time as a journalist writing weekly newspaper columns that reached millions of people worldwide. Beginning in 1930 he also broadcast regular radio addresses. What distinguished his journalistic approach was his firsthand experience of ordinary people and places and a wry sense of humor, often debunking establishment figures and institutions. This poking fun at the serious side of life, combined with an optimistic homespun philosophy, gave him immense popular appeal. He became a national and international celebrity and acquired the unofficial status of a goodwill ambassador during his travels in Europe. He also had a strong philanthropic streak and devoted money and time to charitable causes.

8. Why does the author mention Rogers's philanthropic streak in paragraph 2?
   (A) To show Rogers's main preoccupation
   (B) To indicate how serious poverty was at the time
   (C) To outline Rogers's journalistic career
   (D) To emphasize the variety of his interests

Paragraph 2 is marked with an arrow (→).

In the early 1920s, Rogers embarked on another profession, this time as a journalist writing weekly newspaper columns that reached millions of people worldwide. Beginning in 1930 he also broadcast regular radio addresses. What distinguished his journalistic approach was his firsthand experience of ordinary people and places and a wry sense of humor, often debunking establishment figures and institutions. This poking fun at the serious side of life, combined with an optimistic homespun philosophy, gave him immense popular appeal. He became a national and international celebrity and acquired the unofficial status of a goodwill ambassador during his travels in Europe. He also had a strong philanthropic streak and devoted money and time to charitable causes.

9. According to the passage, which of the following is true of Rogers?
   (A) He was well known outside the United States.
   (B) His journalism was read especially by the establishment.
   (C) He did not enjoy making fun of serious issues.
   (D) His humor was not appreciated by many radio listeners.

Rogers also had a keen interest in flying. He often wrote about the development of aviation and made friends with trailblazing flyers such as Charles Lindbergh. Another pioneering aviator, Wiley Post, invited Rogers to join him in testing the viability of a commercial route between the United States and Asia. Tragically, both Rogers and Post were killed when their plane crashed in northern Alaska. Rogers's death was felt deeply throughout the United States and the public displays of mourning were heartfelt and widespread. The epitaph by his tomb is taken from one of his numerous quotable remarks and reminds us of the essential dignity of the man. It reads, "Never Met A Man I Didn't Like."

10. Look at the word **trailblazing** in the passage. Select another word or phrase in the **bold** text that is closest in meaning to the word **trailblazing**.

→ Rogers also had a keen interest in flying. He often wrote about the development of aviation and made friends with trailblazing flyers such as Charles Lindbergh. Another pioneering aviator, Wiley Post, invited Rogers to join him in testing the viability of a commercial route between the United States and Asia. Tragically, both Rogers and Post were killed when their plane crashed in northern Alaska. Rogers's death was felt deeply throughout the United States and the public displays of mourning were heartfelt and widespread. The epitaph by his tomb is taken from one of his numerous quotable remarks and reminds us of the essential dignity of the man. It reads, "Never Met A Man I Didn't Like."

11. The word viability in paragraph 3 is closest in meaning to
    (A) feasibility
    (B) conviction
    (C) importance
    (D) intensity

12. The word epitaph in paragraph 3 is closest in meaning to
    (A) homage
    (B) memoirs
    (C) mourning
    (D) inscription

Paragraph 3 is marked with an arrow (→).

One of the foremost American entertainers of the first part of the twentieth century was a part-Cherokee Native American named Will Rogers (1879–1935). Rogers was born in territory that would later become the state of Oklahoma and spent much of his youth riding horses and mastering the use of the lariat. These skills were refined into an entertainment act based on fancy rope tricks interspersed with humorous anecdotes and witty remarks. Traveling widely as a vaudeville entertainer, Rogers had become a star act by 1915 with the Ziegfeld Follies, a famous stage show. In 1918 his stage skills led to a new career as a movie actor both in silent films and later in the "talkies."

In the early 1920s, Rogers embarked on another profession, this time as a journalist writing weekly newspaper columns that reached millions of people worldwide. Beginning in 1930 he also broadcast regular radio addresses. What distinguished his journalistic approach was his firsthand experience of ordinary people and places and a wry sense of humor, often debunking establishment figures and institutions. This poking fun at the serious side of life, combined with an optimistic homespun philosophy, gave him immense popular appeal. He became a national and international celebrity and acquired the unofficial status of a goodwill ambassador during his travels in Europe. He also had a strong philanthropic streak and devoted money and time to charitable causes.

Rogers also had a keen interest in flying. He often wrote about the development of aviation and made friends with trailblazing flyers such as Charles Lindbergh. Another pioneering aviator, Wiley Post, invited Rogers to join him in testing the viability of a commercial route between the United States and Asia. **Tragically, both Rogers and Post were killed when their plane crashed in northern Alaska. Rogers's death was felt deeply throughout the United States and the public displays of mourning were heartfelt and widespread. The epitaph by his tomb is taken from one of his numerous quotable remarks and reminds us of the essential dignity of the man. It reads, "Never Met A Man I Didn't Like."**

13. Look at the word **It** in the passage. Select the word or phrase in the **bold** text that **It** refers to.

14. The author implies that Will Rogers was popular
    (A) only after he became a radio journalist
    (B) especially because of his charitable concerns
    (C) largely with establishment figures
    (D) throughout most of his career

Questions 15–27

The damming of river systems in the northwestern United States has had devastating effects on salmon. In the spring young salmon, called smolts, drift into rivers from smaller streams. They swim with the current downstream heading for the Pacific Ocean. Before the large-scale construction of dams, the young salmon used the strong flow from melting snows to get to the sea in between six and twenty days. It is necessary to do this because during these days the smolts' bodies undergo the physiological changes for adaptation to salt water.

Unfortunately, the current has become very slow due to the construction of numerous dams. Companies operating the dams also intentionally slow the current. They store the water from the melting snow until the winter, when more electric power is needed. The net result is that many of the young fish do not survive the now sixty-day trip to the sea. Consequently, there are fewer adult salmon to migrate back up the rivers for breeding. When it comes time for the salmon to return, they again face the problem of dams. As fewer adult salmon are able to get back to their cool upstream water, they fail to produce a sufficiently numerous new generation of salmon. This cycle could eventually lead to extinction of the fish.

Attempts are being made to transport the young salmon downriver by barge. However, many scientists think that this artificial method of getting the fish to the sea kills more than it saves. Another suggestion, recently proposed by environmentalists, is to increase the rate of water flow. This would be a partial solution to the declining salmon numbers. One method of doing this would call for releasing water from upstream reservoirs. This would speed up the downstream movement of the smolts.

Another method would be to reduce the water level in the reservoirs for a period in the spring when the smolts are migrating downstream. This would also increase the flow rate temporarily without requiring massive amounts of water and, thus, enable the young salmon to move downstream faster. Unfortunately, both of these proposals have met with criticism from the power companies.

15. Which of the following is the main topic of the passage?
    (A) The failure of adult salmon to reproduce
    (B) The importance of smolts returning upstream
    (C) The need for smolts to reach salt water quickly
    (D) The harm caused to salmon by river damming

→ The damming of river systems in the northwestern United States has had devastating effects on salmon. In the spring young salmon, called smolts, drift into rivers from smaller streams. They swim with the current downstream heading for the Pacific Ocean. Before the large-scale construction of dams, the young salmon used the strong flow from melting snows to get to the sea in between six and twenty days. It is necessary to do this because during these days the smolts' bodies undergo the physiological changes for adaptation to salt water.

16. In paragraph 1, the author suggests that
   (A) young salmon lose the ability to tolerate freshwater streams
   (B) salmon bodies are adversely affected by the cold melting snow
   (C) smolts are unable to swim in strong currents
   (D) large-scale dam construction causes the smolts to enter the sea too quickly

Paragraph 1 is marked with an arrow (→).

The damming of river systems in the northwestern United States has had devastating effects on salmon. **In the spring young salmon, called smolts, drift into rivers from smaller streams. They swim with the current downstream heading for the Pacific Ocean. Before the large-scale construction of dams, the young salmon used the strong flow from melting snows to get to the sea in between six and twenty days.** It is necessary to do this because during these days the smolts' bodies undergo the physiological changes for adaptation to salt water.

17. Look at the word **current** in the passage. Select another word or phrase in the **bold** text that is closest in meaning to the word **current**.

→ 1 The damming of river systems in the northwestern United States has had devastating effects on salmon. 2 In the spring young salmon, called smolts, drift into rivers from smaller streams. 3 They swim with the current downstream heading for the Pacific Ocean. 4 Before the large-scale construction of dams, the young salmon used the strong flow from melting snows to get to the sea in between six and twenty days. 5 It is necessary to do this because during these days the smolts' bodies undergo the physiological changes for adaptation to salt water.

18. Select the number of the sentence in paragraph 1 that explains how the smolts reached the sea previous to the damming of river systems.

Paragraph 1 is marked with an arrow (→).

→ Unfortunately, the current has become very slow due to the construction of numerous dams. ☐1 Companies operating the dams also intentionally slow the current. ☐2 They store the water from the melting snow until the winter, when more electric power is needed. ☐3 The net result is that many of the young fish do not survive the now sixty-day trip to the sea. Consequently, there are fewer adult salmon to migrate back up the rivers for breeding. ☐4 When it comes time for the salmon to return, they again face the problem of dams. As fewer adult salmon are able to get back to their cool upstream water, they fail to produce a sufficiently numerous new generation of salmon. ☐5 This cycle could eventually lead to extinction of the fish.

19. The following sentence can be added to paragraph 2.

This is also a time when they can charge higher prices for the electricity generated by the moving water.

Where would it best fit in the paragraph?

Select the square (☐) that shows where the sentence should be added.

Paragraph 2 is marked with an arrow (→).

Unfortunately, the current has become very slow due to the construction of numerous dams. Companies operating the dams also intentionally slow the current. They store the water from the melting snow until the winter, when more electric power is needed. The net result is that many of the young fish do not survive the now sixty-day trip to the sea. Consequently, there are fewer adult salmon to migrate back up the rivers for breeding. When it comes time for the salmon to return, they again face the problem of dams. As fewer adult salmon are able to get back to their cool upstream water, they fail to produce a sufficiently numerous new generation of salmon. This cycle could eventually lead to extinction of the fish.

20. Look at the word **They** in the passage. Select the word or phrase in the **bold** text that **They** refers to.

Unfortunately, the current has become very slow due to the construction of numerous dams. Companies operating the dams also intentionally slow the current. **They store the water from the melting snow until the winter, when more electric power is needed. The net result is that many of the young fish do not survive the now sixty-day trip to the sea. Consequently, there are fewer adult salmon to migrate back up the rivers for breeding. When it comes time for the salmon to return, they again face the problem of dams.** As fewer adult salmon are able to get back to their cool upstream water, they fail to produce a sufficiently numerous new generation of salmon. This cycle could eventually lead to extinction of the fish.

21. Look at the word **return** in the passage. Select another word or phrase in the **bold** text that is closest in meaning to the word **return**.

Attempts are being made to transport the young salmon downriver by barge. However, many scientists think that this artificial method of getting the fish to the sea kills more than it saves. Another suggestion, recently proposed by environmentalists, is to increase the rate of water flow. This would be a partial solution to the declining salmon numbers. One method of doing this would call for releasing water from upstream reservoirs. This would speed up the downstream movement of the smolts.

22. Look at the word it in the passage. Select the word or phrase in the **bold** text that it refers to.

➔ Attempts are being made to transport the young salmon downriver by barge. However, many scientists think that this artificial method of getting the fish to the sea kills more than it saves. Another suggestion, recently proposed by environmentalists, is to increase the rate of water flow. This would be a partial solution to the declining salmon numbers. One method of doing this would call for releasing water from upstream reservoirs. This would speed up the downstream movement of the smolts.

23. In paragraph 3, what does the author mean by the statement many scientists think that this artificial method of getting the fish to the sea kills more than it saves?
    (A) Saving fish is artificial.
    (B) More fish die when transported than would die otherwise.
    (C) Artificial methods of transportation save the lives of many fish.
    (D) The sea kills more fish than are saved by transportation.

Paragraph 3 is marked with an arrow (➔).

➔ Another method would be to reduce the water level in the reservoirs for a period in the spring when the smolts are migrating downstream. This would also increase the flow rate temporarily without requiring massive amounts of water and, thus, enable the young salmon to move downstream faster. Unfortunately, both of these proposals have met with criticism from the power companies.

24. The word proposals in paragraph 4 is closest in meaning to
    (A) invitations
    (B) propositions
    (C) assessments
    (D) endorsements

Paragraph 4 is marked with an arrow (➔).

1 The damming of river systems in the northwestern United States has had devastating effects on salmon. In the spring young salmon, called smolts, drift into rivers from smaller streams. They swim with the current downstream heading for the Pacific Ocean. Before the large-scale construction of dams, the young salmon used the strong flow from melting snows to get to the sea in between six and twenty days. It is necessary to do this because during these days the smolts' bodies undergo the physiological changes for adaptation to salt water.

2 Unfortunately, the current has become very slow due to the construction of numerous dams. Companies operating the dams also intentionally slow the current. They store the water from the melting snow until the winter, when more electric power is needed. The net result is that many of the young fish do not survive the now sixty-day trip to the sea. Consequently, there are fewer adult salmon to migrate back up the rivers for breeding. When it comes time for the salmon to return, they again face the problem of dams. As fewer adult salmon are able to get back to their cool upstream water, they fail to produce a sufficiently numerous new generation of salmon. This cycle could eventually lead to extinction of the fish.

3 Attempts are being made to transport the young salmon downriver by barge. However, many scientists think that this artificial method of getting the fish to the sea kills more than it saves. Another suggestion, recently proposed by environmentalists, is to increase the rate of water flow. This would be a partial solution to the declining salmon numbers. One method of doing this would call for releasing water from upstream reservoirs. This would speed up the downstream movement of the smolts.

4 Another method would be to reduce the water level in the reservoirs for a period in the spring when the smolts are migrating downstream. This would also increase the flow rate temporarily without requiring massive amounts of water and, thus, enable the young salmon to move downstream faster. Unfortunately, both of these proposals have met with criticism from the power companies.

25. The passage discusses all of the following methods of dealing with this problem EXCEPT
    (A) carrying the fish in boats
    (B) allowing water to be released from upstream reservoirs
    (C) dropping water levels in reservoirs
    (D) breeding salmon

26. With which of the following statements would the author most probably agree?
    (A) Controversy about the salmon issue is likely to continue.
    (B) A solution to the salmon problem will probably be found in the near future.
    (C) Salmon will become extinct within the next decade.
    (D) Selective breeding for longer physiological maturation is a possibility.

27. Select the number of the paragraph that best outlines the salmon's dilemma.

Questions 28–39

Psychologists have found that privately made resolutions are rarely followed, whereas a public commitment to achieve some goal, such as losing weight or giving up smoking, is likely to be much more effective. This is because the approval of others for reaching one's target is valued. In contrast, disapproval for failure can lead to feelings of shame.

Advertising agencies have designed studies bearing out the truth of this observation. In their research, a group of strangers was bombarded with information about the qualities of a particular product. They were then asked to either announce out loud or write down privately whether they intended to buy the product. It was later discovered that those who publicly declared their intention to buy were considerably more likely to do so than those who affirmed their intentions in private.

In another study, an experimenter claiming to represent a local utility company interviewed homeowners, telling them he was investigating ways in which energy consumption could be reduced. Half the subjects, randomly selected, were told that if they agreed to conserve energy, their names would be mentioned in an article published in the local newspaper; the remaining half were told their names would not be used. All those interviewed agreed to cooperate and signed a form either giving consent for their names to be used or stating that their names would not be used. Later in the year, the amount of gas consumed in each house was recorded. The owners who had agreed to their names being published had used significantly less gas than those who remained anonymous.

28. What is the main topic of this passage?
(A) The commitment to conserve energy
(B) The effectiveness of publicly stated commitments
(C) The results of studies done on advertising agencies
(D) The observations of the effects of advertising

→ Psychologists have found that privately made resolutions are rarely followed, whereas a public commitment to achieve some goal, such as losing weight or giving up smoking, is likely to be much more effective. This is because the approval of others for reaching one's target is valued. In contrast, disapproval for failure can lead to feelings of shame.

29. The word resolutions in paragraph 1 is closest in meaning to
(A) declarations
(B) explanations
(C) speculations
(D) persuasions

Paragraph 1 is marked with an arrow (→).

Psychologists have found that privately made resolutions are rarely followed, whereas a public commitment to achieve some goal, such as losing weight or giving up smoking, is likely to be much more effective. This is because the approval of others for reaching one's target is valued. In contrast, disapproval for failure can lead to feelings of shame.

30. Look at the word goal in the passage. Select another word or phrase in the **bold** text that is closest in meaning to the word goal.

→ Psychologists have found that privately made resolutions are rarely followed, whereas a public commitment to achieve some goal, such as losing weight or giving up smoking, is likely to be much more effective. This is because the approval of others for reaching one's target is valued. In contrast, disapproval for failure can lead to feelings of shame.

31. It can be inferred that all of the following help motivate a person to achieve a goal EXCEPT
   (A) a desire for approval
   (B) a fear of disapproval
   (C) a fear of failure
   (D) a sense of noncommitment

32. The word shame in paragraph 1 is closest in meaning to
   (A) anger
   (B) disgrace
   (C) humility
   (D) inadequacy

Paragraph 1 is marked with an arrow (→).

→ Advertising agencies have designed studies bearing out the truth of this observation. In their research, a group of strangers was bombarded with information about the qualities of a particular product. They were then asked to either announce out loud or write down privately whether they intended to buy the product. It was later discovered that those who publicly declared their intention to buy were considerably more likely to do so than those who affirmed their intentions in private.

33. Why were advertising agencies probably interested in conducting their study?
    (A) They wanted to introduce their people to more products.
    (B) They wanted to demonstrate the quality of their clients' products.
    (C) They wanted to know if people intended to purchase their clients' products.
    (D) They wanted to find the best way to get people to buy their clients' products.

34. The word bombarded in paragraph 2 is closest in meaning to
    (A) bombed
    (B) attacked
    (C) saturated
    (D) hampered

Paragraph 2 is marked with an arrow (→).

Advertising agencies have designed studies bearing out the truth of this observation. In their research, a group of strangers was bombarded with information about the qualities of a particular product. They were then asked to either announce out loud or write down privately whether they intended to buy the product. It was later discovered that those who publicly declared their intention to buy were considerably more likely to do so than those who affirmed their intentions in private.

35. Look at the word They in the passage. Select the word or phrase in the **bold** text that They refers to.

Psychologists have found that privately made resolutions are rarely followed, whereas a public commitment to achieve some goal, such as losing weight or giving up smoking, is likely to be much more effective. This is because the approval of others for reaching one's target is valued. In contrast, disapproval for failure can lead to feelings of shame.

Advertising agencies have designed studies bearing out the truth of this observation. In their research, a group of strangers was bombarded with information about the qualities of a particular product. They were then asked to either announce out loud or write down privately whether they intended to buy the product. It was later discovered that those who publicly declared their intention to buy were considerably more likely to do so than those who affirmed their intentions in private.

→ In another study, an experimenter claiming to represent a local utility company interviewed homeowners, telling them he was investigating ways in which energy consumption could be reduced. Half the subjects, randomly selected, were told that if they agreed to conserve energy, their names would be mentioned in an article published in the local newspaper; the remaining half were told their names would not be used. All those interviewed agreed to cooperate and signed a form either giving consent for their names to be used or stating that their names would not be used. **Later in the year, the amount of gas consumed in each house was recorded. The owners who had agreed to their names being published had used significantly less gas than those who remained anonymous.**

36. According to the passage, the anonymous subjects in the energy-consumption experiment
    (A) did not cooperate
    (B) did not sign a form
    (C) did not own their own house
    (D) used more gas than the other subjects

37. How did the experimenter in paragraph 3 find out how much gas the subjects used?
    (A) The amount was recorded.
    (B) The amount was stated in the contract.
    (C) The people published the amount.
    (D) The people were given a limited amount.

Paragraph 3 is marked with an arrow (→).

38. Look at the word consumed in the passage. Select another word or phrase in the **bold** text that is closest in meaning to the word consumed.

39. This passage supports which of the following conclusions?
    (A) Commitments made in private are more likely to fail.
    (B) Disapproval for failure makes people less willing to make public commitments.
    (C) Intentions announced out loud are more effective than those published in newspapers.
    (D) Well-informed people are more likely to publicly declare their intentions.

Questions 40–50

Research investigating what happens when people sleep has shown that they typically journey through five distinct levels or stages of sleep. Each level corresponds to changes in body temperature, respiration and body movements, and electroencephalograph (EEG) patterns. EEG patterns refer to the patterns of electrical activity in the brain as measured by a device called an electroencephalograph.

The first stage is a period of quiet sleep during which muscle tension decreases and the brain produces irregular, rapid waves. If woken at this time, a sleeper may jerk suddenly and deny having been asleep. In the second stage, breathing and the heart rate slow down and brain waves become larger. In the third and fourth stages, bodily functions decrease more and brain waves become even larger.

The deepest sleep occurs in the fourth stage and is very difficult to awaken from. This is considered a regenerative period, when the body repairs itself. In fact, during illness people may fall immediately into a deep sleep because infection-fighting antibodies are produced in greater numbers in this stage. After a period of time in Stage 4, a sleeper ascends back through each of the stages. He or she then enters a new stage that is sometimes known as Stage 5, even though it is, in a sense, higher than Stage 1.

The fifth stage is reached, judging by brain activity, when a person appears to be sleeping lightly as in Stage 1 but is very hard to rouse. Because of this, the stage is sometimes called "paradoxical sleep." During this stage, people exhibit what are known as rapid eye movements (REMs), and frequently their toes and facial muscles twitch, whereas the large muscles seem paralyzed. It is believed that during this stage most dreaming occurs. If something happens to awaken someone during this stage, the sleeper frequently recalls vivid dreams.

During the course of an eight-hour period, most people seem to pass through five or six cycles of sleep. In the earlier cycles, sleepers typically descend down to Stage 4. However, after several complete cycles earlier in the night, they do not reenter the deeper stages, but fluctuate between REM and Stage 2. As the end of the sleep period approaches, body temperature begins to rise and the breathing and heart rate normalize.

40. Which of the following would be a good title for this passage?
    (A) The paradoxes of sleep
    (B) The levels of EEG patterns
    (C) The regenerative stage of REM
    (D) The stages of sleep

→ Research investigating what happens when people sleep has shown that they typically journey through five distinct levels or stages of sleep. Each level corresponds to changes in body temperature, respiration and body movements, and electroencephalograph (EEG) patterns. EEG patterns refer to the patterns of electrical activity in the brain as measured by a device called an electroencephalograph.

41. What are the EEG patterns mentioned in paragraph 1?
    (A) Measured electrical brain activity
    (B) Devices called electroencephalographs
    (C) Monitored body changes
    (D) Modern technology used in sleep research

Paragraph 1 is marked with an arrow (→).

The first stage is a period of quiet sleep during which muscle tension decreases and the brain produces irregular, rapid waves. **If woken at this time, a sleeper may jerk suddenly and deny having been asleep. In the second stage, breathing and the heart rate slow down and brain waves become larger. In the third and fourth stages, bodily functions decrease more and brain waves become even larger.**

42. Look at the word **decrease** in the passage. Select another word or phrase in the **bold** text that is closest in meaning to the word **decrease**.

The deepest sleep occurs in the fourth stage and is very difficult to awaken from. **This is considered a regenerative period, when the body repairs itself. In fact, during illness people may fall immediately into a deep sleep because infection-fighting antibodies are produced in greater numbers in this stage.** After a period of time in Stage 4, a sleeper ascends back through each of the stages. He or she then enters a new stage that is sometimes known as Stage 5, even though it is, in a sense, higher than Stage 1.

43. Look at the word **period** in the passage. Select another word or phrase in the **bold** text that is closest in meaning to the word **period**.

The fifth stage is reached, judging by brain activity, when a person appears to be sleeping lightly as in Stage 1 but is very hard to **rouse**. Because of this, the stage is sometimes called "paradoxical sleep." During this stage, people exhibit what are known as rapid eye movements (REMs), and frequently their toes and facial muscles twitch, whereas the large muscles seem paralyzed. It is believed that during this stage most dreaming occurs. If something happens to awaken someone during this stage, the sleeper frequently recalls vivid dreams.

44. Look at the word **rouse** in the passage. Select another word or phrase in the **bold** text that is closest in meaning to the word **rouse**.

The fifth stage is reached, judging by brain activity, when a person appears to be sleeping lightly as in Stage 1 but is very hard to rouse. Because of this, the stage is sometimes called "paradoxical sleep." During this stage, people exhibit what are known as rapid eye movements (REMs), and frequently their toes and facial muscles twitch, whereas the large muscles seem paralyzed. It is believed that during this stage most dreaming occurs. If something happens to awaken someone during this stage, the sleeper frequently recalls vivid dreams.

45. What does the author mean by the statement Because of this, the stage is sometimes called "paradoxical sleep"?
    (A) It is a contradiction that Stages 1 and 5 are so similar in terms of depth of sleep.
    (B) The brain patterns of Stage 5 indicate a light sleep period, but the sleeper is not easily roused.
    (C) An inconsistency exists in that Stage 5 consists of a deeper sleep than Stage 4 but includes vivid dreams as in Stage 1.
    (D) The fact that Stage 1 does not include rapid eye movement and Stage 5 does is a paradox.

The fifth stage is reached, judging by brain activity, when a person appears to be sleeping lightly as in Stage 1, but is very hard to rouse. Because of this, the stage is sometimes called "paradoxical sleep." **During this stage, people exhibit what are known as rapid eye movements (REMs), and frequently their toes and facial muscles twitch, whereas the large muscles seem paralyzed. It is believed that during this stage most dreaming occurs. If something happens to awaken someone during this stage, the sleeper frequently recalls vivid dreams.**

46. Look at the word **their** in the passage. Select the word or phrase in the **bold** text that **their** refers to.

During the course of an eight-hour period, most people seem to pass through five or six cycles of sleep. **In the earlier cycles, sleepers typically descend down to Stage 4. However, after several complete cycles earlier in the night, they do not reenter the deeper stages, but fluctuate between REM and Stage 2. As the end of the sleep period approaches, body temperature begins to rise and the breathing and heart rate normalize.**

47. Look at the word **they** in the passage. Select another word or phrase in the **bold** text that **they** refers to.

48. Select the illustration that shows the pattern of cycles in a typical eight-hour period of sleep.

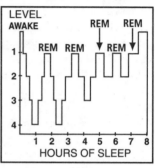

(A)

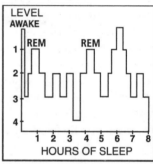

(B)

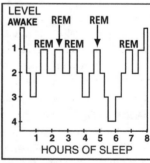

(C)

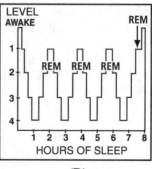

(D)

1 Research investigating what happens when people sleep has shown that they typically journey through five distinct levels or stages of sleep. Each level corresponds to changes in body temperature, respiration and body movements, and electroencephalograph (EEG) patterns. EEG patterns refer to the patterns of electrical activity in the brain as measured by a device called an electroencephalograph.

2 The first stage is a period of quiet sleep during which muscle tension decreases and the brain produces irregular, rapid waves. If woken at this time, a sleeper may jerk suddenly and deny having been asleep. In the second stage, breathing and the heart rate slow down and brain waves become larger. In the third and fourth stages, bodily functions decrease more and brain waves become even larger.

3 The deepest sleep occurs in the fourth stage and is very difficult to awaken from. This is considered a regenerative period – a time when the body repairs itself. In fact, during illness people may fall immediately into a deep sleep because infection-fighting antibodies are produced in greater numbers in this stage. After a period of time in Stage 4, a sleeper ascends back through each of the stages. He or she then enters a new stage that is sometimes known as Stage 5, even though it is, in a sense, higher than Stage 1.

4 The fifth stage is reached, judging by brain activity, when a person appears to be sleeping lightly as in Stage 1 but is very hard to rouse. Because of this, the stage is sometimes called "paradoxical sleep." During this stage, people exhibit what are known as rapid eye movements (REMs), and frequently their toes and facial muscles twitch, whereas the large muscles seem paralyzed. It is believed that during this stage most dreaming occurs. If something happens to awaken someone during this stage, the sleeper frequently recalls vivid dreams.

5 During the course of an eight-hour period, most people seem to pass through five or six cycles of sleep. In the earlier cycles, sleepers typically descend down to Stage 4. However, after several complete cycles earlier in the night, they do not reenter the deeper stages, but fluctuate between REM and Stage 2. As the end of the sleep period approaches, body temperature begins to rise and the breathing and heart rate normalize.

49. Select the number of the paragraph that discusses the healing properties of sleep.

Research investigating what happens when people sleep has shown that they typically journey through five distinct levels or stages of sleep. ☐1 Each level corresponds to changes in body temperature, respiration and body movements, and electroencephalograph (EEG) patterns. EEG patterns refer to the patterns of electrical activity in the brain as measured by a device called an electroencephalograph.

The first stage is a period of quiet sleep during which muscle tension decreases and the brain produces irregular, rapid waves. If woken at this time, a sleeper may jerk suddenly and deny having been asleep. In the second stage, breathing and the heart rate slow down and brain waves become larger. ☐2 In the third and fourth stages, bodily functions decrease more and brain waves become even larger.

The deepest sleep occurs in the fourth stage and is very difficult to awaken from. This is considered a regenerative period – a time when the body repairs itself. In fact, during illness people may fall immediately into a deep sleep because infection-fighting antibodies are produced in greater numbers in this stage. ☐3 After a period of time in Stage 4, a sleeper ascends back through each of the stages. He or she then enters a new stage that is sometimes known as Stage 5, even though it is, in a sense, higher than Stage 1.

The fifth stage is reached, judging by brain activity, when a person appears to be sleeping lightly as in Stage 1 but is very hard to rouse. ☐4 Because of this, the stage is sometimes called "paradoxical sleep." During this stage, people exhibit what are known as rapid eye movements (REMs), and frequently their toes and facial muscles twitch, whereas the large muscles seem paralyzed. It is believed that during this stage most dreaming occurs. If something happens to awaken someone during this stage, the sleeper frequently recalls vivid dreams.

During the course of an eight-hour period, most people seem to pass through five or six cycles of sleep. In the earlier cycles, sleepers typically descend down to Stage 4. However, after several complete cycles earlier in the night, they do not reenter the deeper stages, but fluctuate between REM and Stage 2. ☐5 As the end of the sleep period approaches, body temperature begins to rise and the breathing and heart rate normalize.

50. The following sentence can be added to the passage.

These stages form an overall pattern of quiescent periods and active periods.

Where would it best fit in the passage?

Select the square (☐) that shows where the sentence should be added.

This is the end of the Reading Section Practice Test.

SECTION ·4· WRITING

The Writing Section of the Computer-Based TOEFL® Test measures your ability to compose an essay in standard written English. You will have thirty minutes to write an essay in response to an assigned question. To answer the question you must do one or more of the following:

(A) Express and support an opinion.
(B) Choose and defend a point of view.
(C) Compare and contrast a topic.
(D) Present an argument.
(E) Persuade an audience.

Your essay will be scored on a scale of 1 to 6, with 6 being the highest score. There are no right or wrong answers to the questions. You are scored only on how well you have expressed yourself in addressing all parts of the question and how well you have organized and presented your ideas. Specific errors in grammar, punctuation, and spelling are counted against you when they affect the clarity of your essay.

STRATEGIES TO USE FOR BUILDING ESSAY-WRITING FLUENCY

1. Decide whether you are going to handwrite or type your essay.

In the Writing Section you can choose whether to write your essay by hand or type it on the computer. Only choose the computer if you are comfortable with typing on a keyboard with English characters. If you plan on typing your essay, write your practice essays on a computer. On the day of the test, if you choose the computer option, you will view the writing program on the tutorial. Once you have completed the tutorial, you will have another opportunity to choose between handwriting and typing your essay.

2. Practice writing essays.

Set aside regularly scheduled time periods to practice writing essays. Use the topics that are in this book or topics of your own to develop your writing fluency. Start writing down your ideas as soon as you have read the practice topic. Use the same strategies as are suggested in the following Strategies to Use for the Essay, both for writing practice essays and for the actual test.

3. Pay attention to time.

Time the essays that you write. Don't worry about the amount of time that it takes you to write your first essay. With each successive essay, try to decrease your time. In this way you can build up your writing fluency so that you can write your essay in the time allotted for the test.

STRATEGIES TO USE FOR THE ESSAY

1. Study the question carefully.

Be sure you understand what the question is asking. Consider some of the ways to address the question. You will be given paper to organize your thoughts whether you choose to type or handwrite your essay. Use this paper to quickly write down your ideas.

2. Organize your ideas with an outline.

Organize the ideas that you have written down into a logical progression by using a simple outline. Check your ideas to see that they answer the essay question. Then start typing your essay or use the official answer sheet for handwritten essays.

3. Budget your time so that you will be able to complete and correct your essay.

You have only thirty minutes to write your essay. Organize your time into the following slots: reading and thinking about the question, organizing your ideas with a simple outline form, writing the essay, and making minor corrections.

4. Use sentence structures and vocabulary you know to be correct.

You are more likely to make grammatical mistakes if you write long, complex sentences. In general, use sentence structures and vocabulary over which you have good command.

5. Don't waste time worrying about spelling, punctuation, and grammar.

Incorrect spelling, punctuation, and grammar will hurt your score if the errors make your essay difficult to understand. You should attempt to write your essay as correctly as possible, but don't waste time worrying whether or not each sentence is grammatical or each word is spelled correctly.

6. Don't waste time worrying about whether the evaluator agrees with your opinions and argument.

Your essay is evaluated on how you present your argument, not on whether the evaluator agrees with you. Be sure you have supported your argument well and have answered all parts of the question.

An essay is made up of several paragraphs. First, study paragraph form and structure in **Writing Paragraphs**, which follows. Then study essay form and structure in **Writing Essays** on pages 408–420.

WRITING PARAGRAPHS

PRACTICE WITH TOPIC SENTENCES

The topic sentence states the topic and a controlling idea concerning that topic. Look at the following example:

> People give many reasons for owning a car.

The topic of the sentence is "owning a car." The controlling idea is "reasons." All the supporting ideas in the paragraph should be "reasons for owning a car."

The following phrases, or ones similar to these, can be used in your topic sentence to express the controlling idea:

> the reasons for
> the causes of (the effects of)
> the steps for (the procedure for)
> the advantages of (the disadvantages of)
> the ways to (the methods of)
> the different sections (parts, kinds, types) of
> the characteristics (traits, qualities) of
> the problems of
> the precautions for
> the changes to

Exercise W1   *Looking at topic sentences*

Write a topic sentence for each of the following topics. Use one of the phrases above or one of your own for your controlling idea.

Example   catching colds

> *People can avoid catching colds by taking certain precautions.*

This topic sentence includes the topic "catching colds" and the controlling idea "taking precautions."

1. large cars

   _____

2. living in a remote area

   _____

3. studying abroad

   _____

4. accidents

   _____

5. airports

   _____

6. absenteeism

_____

7. taking exams

_____

8. computers

_____

9. rice

_____

10. camping

_____

Answers to Exercise W1 are on page 545.

Exercise W2   *Checking topic sentences*

Your topic sentence should tell the person who is reading your paragraph what the paragraph is about. Read the following paragraph and decide whether the topic sentence is strong or weak. (The topic sentence is underlined.)

> Baseball is a popular sport in the United States. There are two teams of nine players each. Players on one team take turns batting while the other team tries to put the batters out. The batter hits the ball and then tries to run around the bases and get "home" safely. The other team tries to put the batter out by catching the ball before it hits the ground, throwing the ball to the base before the batter gets there, or tagging the batter with the ball. The batter can stop at any one of the three bases if it is impossible to make it "home."

The topic sentence in the paragraph is weak because it tells us that "baseball is a popular sport," but the rest of the paragraph tells us how baseball is played. A stronger topic sentence would tell us, the readers, that the paragraph is going to describe how baseball is played. Here is a stronger topic sentence:

Baseball, a popular game in the United States, is played in the following way.

Now the reader knows that the paragraph will describe how baseball is played instead of where it is played, who plays it, or why it is popular.

Read the following paragraphs. The topic sentences are underlined. If the topic sentence is weak, rewrite it in the space provided.

1. Even though the procedures for enrolling in an American university vary according to each university, some steps are the same. First, you should contact the registration office of the university you want to attend to get the necessary forms and information concerning that particular university's entrance requirements. Then you must follow the steps outlined in its response. You will probably have to send copies of your high school diploma, get letters of recommendation, and write an essay on why you want to study at that particular university. You may have to achieve a certain score on the Computer-Based TOEFL® Test and have your scores forwarded to that university. Finally, you will have to contact the American embassy to start the procedures to obtain a student visa.

_____

_____

2. I like to go to the beach. I start the day by enjoying a refreshing swim. Then I walk along the beach and collect shells. Later you'll find me relaxing in the warm sunshine and making sand castles. Then I sleep for a while before I open the basket of food and drinks that I always bring with me.

_____

_____

3. Many students cannot afford a car. The city buses usually pass the university, so those students can get to class by bus. Many universities have a special shuttle bus that is provided for student transportation. Other students like to ride to class on bicycles. This is good exercise. Also, it is easier to find a space to leave a bicycle than to find a parking space for a car on a crowded university campus. Students who live close to campus or on campus can enjoy a leisurely walk to their classes.

_____

_____

Answers to Exercise W2 are on page 546.

Exercise W3   *Writing topic sentences*

The following paragraphs consist of supporting ideas. Read each paragraph and ask yourself what is being discussed or described (the topic) and how the topic is approached (the controlling idea). Then write a topic sentence for each paragraph in the space provided.

1. _____

_____

Pictures or posters on the wall make a dormitory room feel more like home. A rug on the floor beside the bed is a nice addition to an otherwise cold and hard floor. Besides textbooks, favorite books from home on the bookshelf and a photograph or two of the family on the desk also add a comforting touch to the impersonal dormitory room.

2. _____

_____

Students may study more effectively if they are in good physical condition. Since students tend to spend a lot of time in front of books, a physical education class forces them to take a break from studying. Also, in a physical education class, they can meet other students and make friends with people who enjoy the same sport. Another advantage is that students can learn a different sport that may not have been possible for them to learn before they came to the university.

3. _____

_____

First, the fast-food restaurant is good for people who must have a quick bite because of a busy schedule. Second, the food is inexpensive yet tasty. A person can eat an enjoyable meal out and stay within a limited budget. Finally, the food is usually consistent. For example, a cheeseburger from a well-known fast-food restaurant looks and tastes about the same no matter where in the world it is purchased. Consequently, buyers know exactly what they are getting.

Answers to Exercise W3 are on page 546.

PRACTICE WITH SUPPORTING IDEAS

Your topic sentence tells the reader what the paragraph will be about. The ideas stated in the rest of the paragraph should all refer to the given topic and the controlling idea. Look at the following example:

> There are many ways to eat peanut butter. You can spread it on a slice of bread like butter, or you can make it into a sandwich with jam. Peanut butter can be a major ingredient of very tasty cookies as well as cakes and candies. It is delicious in ice cream. Peanut butter was invented by George Washington Carver. My favorite way to eat peanut butter is to lick it off a spoon.

Our topic sentence tells the reader that we are discussing peanut butter. The controlling idea is "ways of eating it." All of the sentences should be about ways of eating peanut butter. Are they? No. The sentence "Peanut butter was invented by George Washington Carver" does not refer to ways of eating peanut butter.

Exercise W4   *Checking supporting ideas*

Look at the following excerpts from outlines. Circle the letter of the idea that does not support the topic.

1. I. Ways to get rid of hiccups
   A. breathe into a paper bag
   B. hold your breath to the count of ten
   C. have someone frighten you
   D. make an appointment with your adviser

2. I. Steps for planning a trip
   A. purchasing a map
   B. working late
   C. making an itinerary
   D. reserving a ticket

3. I. Reasons for car accidents
   A. fast driving
   B. drinking and driving
   C. not following traffic regulations
   D. giving signals

4. I. Advantages of small apartments
   A. good school facilities
   B. easy to clean
   C. cheaper to furnish
   D. relatively inexpensive

5. I. Characteristics of a good restaurant
   A. efficient waiters
   B. delicious food
   C. jacket and tie required
   D. pleasant atmosphere

Answers to Exercise W4 are on page 546.

Exercise W5   *Checking paragraphs for supporting ideas*

Read these paragraphs and cross out the one idea that doesn't support the topic sentence.

1. Working part-time while studying at a university has many advantages. If students can get a job in their area of study, they can gain valuable experience and put their knowledge to use immediately. The extra money they earn can be useful for meeting tuition fees and enjoying university activities. Also, they will have the satisfaction of having contributed to their own education. Students who need extra money can hold down a full-time job during their summer vacation.

2. Hobbies are important for many reasons. First, a hobby can be educational. For example, if the hobby is stamp collecting, the person can learn about the countries of the world and even some of their history. Second, engaging in the hobby can lead to meeting other people with the same interests. A person can also meet other people by going to parties. Third, a person's free time is being used in a positive way. The person has no time to be bored or get into mischief while engaged in the hobby. Finally, some hobbies can lead to a future job. A person who enjoys a hobby-related job is more satisfied with life.

3. There are several features of spoken English that make it difficult for me to understand. First, many words are not pronounced as they are spelled, so when I learn new words through reading, I sometimes don't understand them when they are spoken. Second, native speakers contract words and phrases. "What are you doing?" becomes "Whacha doin'?" In my opinion, people should write clearly. Third, native speakers have a wide range of accents. A British accent is very different from one from Texas. Fourth, there are lots of idioms and slang expressions. These expressions also differ depending on the area a speaker is from. Finally, there are sounds that don't exist in my language that do exist in English and vice versa. These sounds are difficult for me to distinguish.

Answers to Exercise W5 are on page 546.

Exercise W6   *Writing supporting ideas*

Use the topic sentences that you wrote for Exercise W1. Outline four supporting ideas.

Example   catching colds

      I. People can avoid catching colds by taking certain precautions.
        A. avoiding people with colds
        B. getting plenty of sleep
        C. eating nutritious food
        D. taking vitamin C

1. I. _____

    A. _____

    B. _____

    C. _____

    D. _____

2. I. _____

    A. _____

    B. _____

    C. _____

    D. _____

3. I. _____

   A. _____

   B. _____

   C. _____

   D. _____

4. I. _____

   A. _____

   B. _____

   C. _____

   D. _____

5. I. _____

   A. _____

   B. _____

   C. _____

   D. _____

6. I. _____

   A. _____

   B. _____

   C. _____

   D. _____

7. I. _____

   A. _____

   B. _____

   C. _____

   D. _____

8. I. _____

   A. _____

   B. _____

   C. _____

   D. _____

9. I. _____

   A. _____

   B. _____

   C. _____

   D. _____

10. I. _____

    A. _____

    B. _____

    C. _____

    D. _____

Answers to Exercise W6 are on page 546.

Exercise W7   *Writing supporting ideas in a paragraph*

On your own paper, write out the paragraphs you outlined in Exercise W6 by expanding your supporting ideas into complete sentences.

Example

Catching Colds

      People can avoid catching colds by taking certain precautions. Perhaps the most important precaution is to avoid people who already have a cold so that you are not exposed to their germs. You should also get plenty of sleep so that your resistance is strong. Eating nutritious food will ensure that you have the vitamins that can help fight cold germs. Finally, you could try taking vitamin C supplements, which may help prevent your catching a cold.

Extended practice: Use the sample outlines in the Answer Key for Exercise W6 to practice writing more paragraphs.

Answers to Exercise W7 are on page 547.

PRACTICE WITH DETAILS

To make a more fully developed paragraph, you need to add details to your supporting ideas. Your details can be *facts, examples, personal experiences,* or *descriptions.*

Look at this topic sentence:

    The Smithsonian Institution is worth visiting for a number of reasons.

The topic is "the Smithsonian Institution," and the controlling idea is "reasons for a visit."

Look at the following supporting ideas and details:

Supporting idea 1

    The Smithsonian Institution is composed of various museums that offer something for everyone.

Details – facts:

    These museums consist of the National Museum of History and Technology, the National Aeronautics and Space Museum, the National Collection of Fine Arts, the National Museum of Natural History, and several others.

Supporting idea 2

    A person can do more than just look at the exhibits.

Details – example:

For example, in the insect zoo at the National Museum of Natural History, anyone who so desires can handle some of the exhibits.

Supporting idea 3

The museums provide unforgettable experiences.

Details – personal experience:

In climbing through *Skylab* at the National Aeronautics and Space Museum, I was able to imagine what it would be like to be an astronaut in space.

Supporting idea 4

Movies shown at regular intervals aid in building an appreciation of our world.

Details – description:

In the National Aeronautics and Space Museum, there is a theater that has a large screen. When the movie is shown, it gives the viewer the feeling that he or she is in the movie itself, either floating above the earth in a hot-air balloon or hang gliding over cliffs.

Exercise W8   ***Adding details***

Write one sentence that adds a detail to each of the following ideas. Use facts, examples, personal experiences, or descriptions.

1. The capital city of my country is _____.

     _____

2. My favorite pastime is reading.

     _____

3. It is very important for me to score well on the Computer-Based TOEFL® Test.

     _____

4. A long vacation at the beach is a nice way to relax.

     _____

5. Habits such as smoking are hard to break.

     _____

6. Many bad traffic accidents could be prevented.

     _____

7. Modern architecture has its critics as well as its admirers.

     _____

8. The suburban mall has taken away a lot of business from city centers.

     _____

Answers to Exercise W8 are on page 547.

Exercise W9   ***Adding details to paragraphs***

Many paragraphs can be made better by adding details. Read the following paragraph.

> Although seat belts have been shown to save lives, people give a number of reasons for not using them. First, many people think they are a nuisance. Second, many people are lazy. Third, some people don't believe they will have an accident. Finally, some people are afraid the seat belt will trap them in their car. All of these reasons seem inadequate, since statistics show that wearing seat belts saves lives and prevents serious injuries.

The paragraph can be improved. Read the following questions.

(A) Why don't people like seat belts?
(B) In what way are people lazy?
(C) Why do people think they won't have an accident?
(D) Under what circumstances might people get trapped?

Asking and answering these kinds of questions will help strengthen the paragraph. Now read the paragraph with details. Notice how adding the answers to these questions has improved it.

> Although seat belts have been shown to save lives, people give a number of reasons for not using them. First, many people think they are a nuisance. They say the belt is uncomfortable and inhibits freedom of movement. Second, many people are lazy. For them it is too much trouble to put on and adjust a seat belt, especially if they are only going a short distance. Third, some people don't believe they will have an accident because they are careful and experienced drivers. They think they will be able to respond quickly to avoid a crash. Finally, some people are afraid the seat belt will trap them in their car. They feel that if they have an accident, they might not be able to get out of a car that is burning, or they might be unconscious and another person won't be able to get them out. All of these reasons seem inadequate, since statistics show that wearing seat belts saves lives and prevents serious injuries.

On your own paper, rewrite the following "weak" paragraphs by answering the questions and using those answers within the paragraph.

1. When you plant a tree, you are helping your environment in many ways. Your tree will provide a home and food for other creatures. It will hold the soil in place. It will provide shade in the summer. You can watch it grow and someday show your children, or even grandchildren, the tree you planted.
    (A) What kind of home would the tree provide?
    (B) What kind of food would the tree provide?
    (C) What kind of creatures might use the tree?
    (D) Why is holding the soil in place important?
    (E) Why is shade important?

2. Airplanes and helicopters can be used to save people's lives. Helicopters can be used for rescuing people in trouble. Planes can transport food and supplies when disasters strike. Both types of aircraft can transport people to hospitals in emergencies. Helicopters and airplanes can be used to provide medical services to people who live in remote areas.
    (A) In what situations do people need rescuing by helicopters?
    (B) What kinds of disasters might happen?
    (C) What kinds of emergencies may require transporting people to hospitals?
    (D) How can helicopters and airplanes be used to provide medical services to people in remote areas?

3. Studying in another country is advantageous in many ways. A student is exposed to a new culture. Sometimes he or she can learn a new language. Students can often have learning experiences not available in their own countries. A student may get the opportunity to study at a university where a leading expert in his or her field may be teaching.

   (A) How can exposure to a new culture be an advantage?

   (B) How can learning a new language be an advantage?

   (C) What kinds of experiences might a student have?

   (D) What are the benefits of studying under a leading expert?

Answers to Exercise W9 are on page 547.

Exercise W10   ***Further practice in adding details to paragraphs***

The following paragraphs are weak. They could be improved by adding details. On your own paper, write your own questions. Then make the paragraph stronger by inserting the answers to your questions.

1. Even though airplanes are fast and comfortable, I prefer to travel by car. When traveling by car, I can look at the scenery. Also, I can stop along the road. Sometimes I meet interesting people from the area I am traveling through. I can carry as much luggage as I want, and I don't worry about missing flights.

2. Wild animals should not be kept in captivity for many reasons. First, animals are often kept in poor and inhumane conditions. In addition, many suffer poor health from lack of exercise and indicate frustration and stress through their neurotic behavior. Also, some animals will not breed in captivity. Those animals that mate often do so with a related animal such as a sister or brother. In conclusion, money spent in the upkeep of zoos would be better spent in protecting natural habitats.

3. Good teachers should have the following qualities. First, they must know the material that they are teaching very well. Second, they should be able to explain their knowledge. Third, they must be patient and understanding. Last, they must be able to make the subject matter interesting to the students.

Extended practice: Add details to the paragraphs you wrote in Exercise W7.

Answers to Exercise W10 are on page 548.

PRACTICE WITH ORGANIZING AND WRITING PARAGRAPHS

Brainstorming means thinking of and writing down ideas concerning a topic. Ask yourself questions such as "Who?" "What?" "Where?" "When?" "Why?" and "How?" to get ideas about your topic. Write down any idea that comes into your head. Later you can go through your list and pick the ideas you want to write about. You will have to do this quickly when you write the TOEFL® Test essay. Practice first with simple topics, as in the following example.

Example

Topic: TV

Ideas

1. a TV set	11. makeup	21. private and public
2. programs	12. education	22. movies
3. sports	13. entertainment	23. actors and actresses
4. black-and-white	14. violence	24. camera operators
5. color	15. cable	25. soap operas
6. directors	16. public announcements	26. satellites
7. major studios	17. news	27. scriptwriters
8. cartoons	18. broadcaster	28. weather
9. schedules	19. technology	29. censorship
10. sound effects	20. commercials	30. documentaries

Exercise W11   *Brainstorming*

Take no more than two minutes to write as many ideas as you can about the following topic.

Topic: cars

1. _____	16. _____
2. _____	17. _____
3. _____	18. _____
4. _____	19. _____
5. _____	20. _____
6. _____	21. _____
7. _____	22. _____
8. _____	23. _____
9. _____	24. _____
10. _____	25. _____
11. _____	26. _____
12. _____	27. _____
13. _____	28. _____
14. _____	29. _____
15. _____	30. _____

Exercise W12   *Combining related ideas*

After you have listed your ideas in Exercise W11, group the related ideas together. For example, in the following list of ideas about the topic "TV,"

○   marks the ideas concerning programming,

□   marks the ideas concerning technology,

△   marks the ideas concerning people, and

◇   marks the ideas concerning informative programs.

Note that not all ideas have been used. Also, some ideas fit into two categories.

Example

☐ 1.	a TV set	◇ 16.	public announcements
○ 2.	programs	◇ 17.	news
○ 3.	sports	△ 18.	broadcaster
☐ 4.	black-and-white	☐ 19.	technology
☐ 5.	color	○ 20.	commercials
△ 6.	directors	21.	private and public
7.	major studios	○ 22.	movies
○ 8.	cartoons	△ 23.	actors and actresses
○ 9.	schedules	△ 24.	camera operators
☐ 10.	sound effects	○ 25.	soap operas
☐ 11.	makeup	☐ 26.	satellites
◇ 12.	education	△ 27.	scriptwriters
○ 13.	entertainment	◇ 28.	weather
○ 14.	violence	○ 29.	censorship
☐ 15.	cable	◇ 30.	documentaries

Look for related ideas about the topic "cars" in Exercise W11. Use the symbols to organize your ideas into related groups, as in the preceding example. Write how the ideas are related in the spaces that follow. (*Note:* You don't have to label every idea. Also, you may have fewer or more groups of related ideas than used in the example.)

○ _____

□ _____

△ _____

◇ _____

X _____

_____

Exercise W13   *Writing topic sentences*

Each group of related ideas that you have marked in Exercise W12 can be made into a paragraph. A topic sentence is needed to introduce the paragraph.

Look at the following topic sentences that cover the related ideas concerning the topic "TV" in Exercise W12.

Example   ◯ A large variety of programs can be seen on TV today.

▢ Modern technology plays an important part in today's TV broadcasting.

△ Many highly trained and skilled people are involved in making and presenting the programs we watch.

◇ The main purpose of many programs on TV is to bring the viewer up to date on important world or regional events.

Write topic sentences for your related ideas concerning "cars."

◯ _____

_____

▢ _____

_____

△ _____

_____

◇ _____

_____

X _____

_____

_____

_____

Exercise W14   *Outlining*

Write an outline to put your ideas from Exercises W12 and W13 in order. You may want to leave out some of the ideas or add more.

Example

   I. A large variety of programs can be seen on TV today.
     A. sports
     B. news
     C. children's programs
     D. educational programs
     E. movies
     F. soap operas

II. Modern technology plays an important part in today's TV broadcasting.
   A. satellites
   B. TV sets
   C. special effects

III. Many highly trained and skilled people are involved in making and presenting the programs we watch.
   A. directors
   B. actors and actresses
   C. camera operators
   D. costume designers
   E. hair stylists and makeup artists
   F. special effects experts

IV. The main purpose of many programs on TV is to bring the viewer up to date on important world or regional events.
   A. news
   B. public announcements
   C. weather

Write your outline about cars.

I. _____

   A. _____

   B. _____

   C. _____

   D. _____

II. _____

   A. _____

   B. _____

   C. _____

   D. _____

III. _____

   A. _____

   B. _____

   C. _____

   D. _____

IV. _____

   A. _____

   B. _____

   C. _____

   D. _____

V. _____

   A. _____

   B. _____

   C. _____

   D. _____

VI. _____

   A. _____

   B. _____

   C. _____

   D. _____

Exercise W15   *Adding details to the outline*

Add details to your outline about cars in Exercise W14. As you do this, you may decide to revise your outline in some way.

Example

I.   A large variety of programs can be seen on TV today.
   A. sports
      1. variety such as football, basketball
      2. day of week and time of day when shown
      3. Olympic games
   B. news
      1. local
      2. national
      3. international
   C. children's programs
      1. educational
      2. cartoons
   D. educational programs
      1. children
      2. university home study
      3. documentaries
   E. movies
      1. movies made for TV
      2. films shown on TV
      3. old movies
   F. soap operas
      1. variety
      2. time shown

Extended practice: Add details to all of your outlines from Exercise W6.

Exercise W16 *More brainstorming*

For each of the following topics, write at least twelve ideas. Then combine related ideas and make an outline. Do not spend more than five minutes on any topic.

1. books
2. education
3. space exploration
4. travel
5. holidays

Exercise W17 *Brainstorming for questions*

Read the following questions.

1. What things need to be considered before taking a long trip?
2. What are some of the advantages of large cars?
3. What factors should a student take into consideration when choosing a university?
4. What are some problems a person has to deal with when living with a roommate?
5. What are some of the disadvantages of having a job and being a student at the same time?

Use the steps in Exercises W11–W15 to write about the preceding five questions. First, brainstorm ideas about each question. Next, combine related ideas and write topic sentences. Then organize your ideas into an outline and add details. Your outlines do not have to be elaborate. Don't spend more than eight minutes on each question. Look at the following example first.

Example

What are some of the problems a working mother faces?

1. child care	◯ = children
2. sick children	☐ = extra expenses
3. exhaustion	△ = physical problems
4. raising children	◇ = work-related problems
5. worry and anxiety	
6. housework after job	
7. cost of transportation	
8. child-care expenses	
9. getting time off	
10. staying late at work	

I. The major problems a working mother faces concern her children.
   A. child care
      1. finding a reliable person to be at home with the child
      2. finding a day-care center where the child can go
   B. sick children
      1. special arrangements
      2. mother must skip work

C. raising children
   1. who is teaching mother's values
   2. how smaller children attend activities after school

II. Even though a mother is frequently forced into working for economic reasons, she soon discovers that there are added expenses.
   A. child-care expenses
   B. cost of transportation
      1. to work
      2. to day care
   C. clothes to work in

III. A working mother sometimes suffers physically.
   A. exhaustion
   B. worry and anxiety
      1. children's safety
      2. being a good parent
   C. extra work
      1. housework after job
      2. child care after job

IV. Women who have children sometimes face problems at work that don't affect other working women.
   A. can't stay late
      1. must pick up child
      2. must check up on child
   B. need extra time off
      1. care for newborns
      2. has ill child
      3. must attend school meetings

Exercise W18   *Writing paragraphs*

Write paragraphs for the topics you outlined in Exercises W16 and W17.

Example

Paragraph for I

    The major problems a working mother faces concern her children. She must either find a reliable person who will be loving toward the children or a good day-care center that the children can attend. If a child gets sick, the mother must make special arrangements for the child to be cared for at home, or she must stay home from work herself. While at work, the mother may worry about her children. She may wonder if they are safe, if they are learning the values she wants them to have, and if her absence is hurting them emotionally. She may also regret not being able to take them to after-school activities or participate in family activities with them.

WRITING ESSAYS

For the Writing Section, you will write an essay that covers a given topic.

The parts of an essay are much like the parts of a paragraph. The essay begins with an introductory paragraph that tells the reader what the essay is about, just as the topic sentence tells the reader what the paragraph is about. The body of the essay is made up of paragraphs that support the introduction, and the concluding paragraph completes the essay.

Study the following model essay.

Question

Some people believe that a mother should not work. Others argue against this. Consider the problems that a working mother faces. Do you believe a mother should work?

Essay

Introductory paragraph

Nowadays it is very common for mothers to work outside the home. Whether a woman should stay at home or join the workforce is debated by many people. Some argue that the family, especially small children, may be neglected. However, many women need to work because of economic reasons or want to work to maintain a career. I believe that every mother has the right to work, and the decision should be one that a woman makes on her own. But first she should carefully consider the many problems that she might encounter.

Supporting (developmental) paragraph I

The major problems a working mother faces concern her children. She must either find a reliable person who will be loving toward the children or a good day-care center that the children can attend. If a child gets sick, the mother must make special arrangements for the child to be cared for at home, or she must stay home from work herself. While at work, the mother may worry about her children. She may wonder if they are safe, if they are learning the values she wants them to have, and if her absence is hurting them emotionally. She may also regret not being able to take them to after-school activities or participate in family activities with them.

Supporting (developmental) paragraph II

Even though a mother is frequently forced into working for economic reasons, she soon discovers that there are added expenses. The biggest expense is child care. Another expense is transportation, which includes not only going to work but also getting her children to school or day care. This may include purchasing and maintaining a car. Yet another expense is clothing, such as a uniform or business suits to maintain a professional appearance.

Conclusion

After a mother takes into account all of the above problems and perhaps other problems unique to her situation, she must decide if a job outside the home is worth it. I believe that even though she faces major obstacles, these obstacles are not insurmountable. Many mothers do work and manage a family very successfully. In conclusion, it is a woman's right to make this choice, and only the woman herself should decide this matter.

Analysis

Introductory paragraph

Notice that the essay has an introductory paragraph that states the general topic "working mothers." It addresses the question directly and shows both sides of the argument. It states the author's opinion that every mother has the right to work and that the decision to work should be a mother's choice. It then tells the reader that the essay will focus on a controlling idea – the problems that a woman must first consider before making this decision. The sentence containing the controlling idea of an essay is called the *thesis statement*. The thesis statement is usually the last sentence of the introductory paragraph.

Second paragraph

The second paragraph in this essay is the first supporting paragraph of the body of the essay. It is the first *developmental paragraph*. It supports the controlling idea of "problems" that was identified in the introduction. The topic sentence (the first sentence) of this paragraph states the idea of "problems concerning children." All the sentences in this paragraph describe either a problem concerning children or a detail explaining a problem concerning children.

Third paragraph

The third paragraph, or second developmental paragraph, in this essay also supports the controlling idea – problems – that was identified in the introduction. The topic sentence of this paragraph states the idea of "problems of added expenses." All the sentences in this paragraph describe either an added expense or a detail explaining the added expense.

Conclusion

The last paragraph in this essay is the *conclusion*. The conclusion restates the topic of working mothers. Again, the controlling idea of problems that face a working mother is repeated. Also, the opinion that it should be a woman's choice is restated. All of these restatements use words that are different from those used in the first paragraph. The last statement is the concluding statement. It completes the essay.

PRACTICE WITH INTRODUCTIONS

To write an introduction for the Writing Section essay, follow these steps. First, introduce the topic in general. Then narrow the topic down to focus more on the question. Restate the question in your own words and in statement form. The concluding statement of the introduction is the thesis statement and indicates the controlling idea of the essay. Study the following writing topic and its introduction.

Question

Living in an apartment instead of a university dormitory has advantages and disadvantages. Discuss some of the advantages and disadvantages of apartment living, and then defend your preference.

Introduction

When a person decides to enter a university away from home, he or she must also consider living accommodations. Although most universities offer student dormitories, students frequently opt to live in an apartment. While there are many advantages to apartment living, there are also many disadvantages. Before a student decides to live in an apartment, all the aspects of that kind of accommodation should be reviewed.

1. The first sentence introduces the general topic of university living accommodations.

When a person decides to enter a university away from home, he or she must also consider **living accommodations**.

2. The second sentence narrows the topic down to apartment living.

> Although most universities offer student dormitories, students frequently opt to live in **an apartment**.

3. The third sentence restates the specific question.

> While there are many **advantages** to apartment living, there are also many **disadvantages**.

4. The fourth sentence is the thesis statement. It gives the controlling idea of the essay.

> Before a student decides to live in an apartment, **all the aspects** of that kind of accommodation should be reviewed.

In the following introduction, the writer restates the topic and gives the controlling idea of the essay.

An alternative introduction

> When students decide to enter a university away from home, they must also consider living accommodations. After considering the advantages and disadvantages of living in an apartment, I would prefer to live in a dormitory.

Things to remember when writing an introduction for the Writing Section essay:

1. Make sure you have an introduction.

Sometimes writers start the essay with the first developmental paragraph. However, you need at least a brief introduction so that your reader will know what you are writing about.

2. Keep your introductory paragraph simple.

A good introduction strengthens your essay. However, it is better to use your time writing the developmental paragraphs than spending too much time on the introductory paragraph.

3. Check that your introductory paragraph is aimed toward answering the question.

Your thesis statement tells your reader what you are going to write about. Your developmental paragraphs give support to your thesis statement. If you support a thesis statement that is not aimed toward answering the question, you may not get credit for your essay.

Exercise W19 **Rewriting introductions**

The following student-written introductory paragraphs are weak. Some of them don't state the problem. Some don't include a thesis statement. Others try to put all the information that will be discussed in the body or developmental paragraphs of the essay into the introduction.

Rewrite these essay introductions using the steps outlined above.

1. *Question:* In your opinion, what is the most dangerous threat the world faces today? Discuss some reasons for its existence. Give some possible ways of preventing its occurrence.

   Weak introduction: War is the most dangerous threat. Everyone in the world fears it. We must try to avoid it.

2. *Question:* Modern technology has brought about changes in the roles of men and women. Discuss some of these changes. Do you think these changes have been beneficial?

   Weak introduction: There are more changes in the roles of men and women due to technological development in recent times than in the past. This has changed our society.

3. *Question:* Advances in technology and science have solved many problems. However, they have also created new problems. Discuss some of the new problems caused by technological advances and give your opinion on how they should be dealt with.

Weak introduction: Nowadays, we have many great advantages in our society that came from technology and science. For that reason, we must protect our lives by taking care of the dangerous problems advanced technology has caused.

PRACTICE WITH DEVELOPMENTAL PARAGRAPHS

To write the body of an essay, follow the steps used in Exercises W1–W18. The body of your essay should consist of at least two developmental paragraphs. Each developmental paragraph should have a topic sentence that supports the controlling idea mentioned in the thesis statement of your introduction. All the ideas in each paragraph should support their topic sentence.

Study the following developmental paragraphs of the essay about apartment living (see page 409 for the introductory paragraph).

> Living in an apartment has many advantages. First, students can choose to live in a quiet neighborhood. A quiet neighborhood is conducive to studying. Away from the distractions of campus life, students can be more serious about their studies. Second, apartment life allows students to be more independent. For example, they can cook whatever they want to eat and have their meals whenever they want them. Third, students can often find apartments that are cheaper than the fee for room and board in a dormitory.
>
> However, living in an apartment also has disadvantages. Being away from campus life can make students feel isolated. Another disadvantage is that apartments close to campus are usually expensive, and those farther away are not within walking distance. Therefore, transportation must be considered. Finally, students who live in apartments must cook their own meals, shop for food, perhaps carry their clothes to a self-service laundry, and clean their entire apartment – not just their room.
>
> Even though there are many advantages to apartment living, I would prefer to live in the university dormitory for the following reasons. First, I will be new at the university and meeting people will be easier in a dormitory setting. Second, I won't have to worry about purchasing and cooking food or cleaning up afterward. Consequently, I will have more time for my studies. Finally, I will be within walking distance of my classes and the university library.

The first developmental paragraph in the body of the essay addresses the question of advantages. The second developmental paragraph addresses the question of disadvantages. The third developmental paragraph defends the writer's preference.

Exercise W20 *Writing developmental paragraphs*

Write the developmental paragraphs for the introductions that you rewrote in Exercise W19.

Exercise W21 *Comparing and contrasting*

When answering an essay question, you may need to compare and contrast some information. Look at the following question.

Question: Both living in an apartment and living in a university dormitory have advantages and disadvantages. Compare these two kinds of living accommodations and defend your preference.

To compare and contrast, you may want to use some of the following words and phrases.

Words used for comparing

alike, like	identical	equivalent
similar, similarities	also	resembles
just as	likewise	corresponds to
the same	comparable to	by the same token

Words used for contrasting

unlike	more than, less than, fewer than
different, differences	is different from, differs from
in contrast	worse, better
whereas	conversely
but	on the other hand

To brainstorm for a developmental paragraph that compares and contrasts, list the ideas that are similar and those that are different.

Similarities	*Differences*
1. places to live	1. kitchen facilities
2. may need to share	2. space
3. housing rules	3. privacy
	4. rent

There are two ways you can approach writing this essay.

1. You can discuss apartment and dormitory similarities in one developmental paragraph and apartment and dormitory differences in another developmental paragraph.

   or

2. You can discuss only apartments in one paragraph and only dormitories in the next paragraph.

Study the following developmental paragraph on the question concerning apartments and dormitories.

> Apartments and dormitories are similar in several ways. First, they are both living accommodations that provide a student with a place to sleep, bathe, and keep belongings. They are also alike in that they require living with or near another person. An apartment is usually in a building that houses other people as well. Frequently the person renting the apartment has a roommate to share the expenses. Similarly, in a dormitory, there are many rooms, and students either share rooms or live next door to each other. Another similarity is that both apartments and dormitories have certain rules by which people must abide.

This paragraph uses the first type of development and discusses similarities. Write the second developmental paragraph and discuss the differences between apartments and dormitories. (You can use the list of differences above as a guide.)

Extended practice: Write two developmental paragraphs for this essay question using the second type of development. Discuss only apartments in one paragraph and only dormitories in the other paragraph.

PRACTICE WITH CONCLUSIONS

So far you have practiced writing the introduction (which restates the problem and states the controlling idea) and writing the body (which discusses the problem). To end the essay, you need to write a concluding paragraph.

For the essay question, your concluding paragraph will:

1. Restate the thesis statement.
2. Restate the topic sentences from the developmental paragraphs.
3. State your opinion or preference, make a prediction, or give a solution.
4. Conclude with a statement that sums up the essay.

Look at the essay question in Exercise W21 again and read the following conclusion.

Conclusion

> In conclusion, living in an apartment has both advantages and disadvantages. One advantage is having independence and all that this freedom entails. Its disadvantages include possible isolation, extra expenses, and responsibilities. For a new student at a university, the advantages of dormitory living outweigh those of apartment living and, therefore, I would prefer living on campus to living in an apartment.

In the following conclusion, the writer restates the topic and makes a concluding statement.

An alternative conclusion

> In conclusion, it is important for students to carefully consider where they are going to live. For me, living on campus is more advantageous than living in an apartment.

Things to remember when writing a conclusion for the Writing Section essay:

1. Make sure you have a conclusion.

Sometimes writers don't complete the essay with a concluding paragraph. However, it is important to have a conclusion. Without one, it may be difficult for the reader to know whether you have completed your essay or run out of time.

2. Keep your concluding paragraph simple.

A good conclusion strengthens your essay. However, it is better to use your time writing the developmental paragraphs than spending too much time on the concluding paragraph.

3. Check that your concluding paragraph completes the essay.

Your concluding statement tells your reader that you are finished. Be careful not to include new ideas in your conclusion, which could make your reader think you are going to be discussing something else.

Exercise W22   Rewriting conclusions

The following student-written conclusions go with the essays you began writing in Exercise W19. These conclusions are weak. Some do not give a solution, prediction, reason, or opinion. Others have a topic sentence but do not support it.

Rewrite the following weak concluding paragraphs so that they are relevant to your introduction and developmental paragraphs from Exercises W19 and W20. You will then have three complete essays.

1. In summary, there must be a solution to any threat in the world, but a possible solution for this problem is difficult to find. Indeed, there is one possible solution, and that is all people must become pacifists, but it is doubtful that will happen.

2. To summarize, technological development has given us a new and better lifestyle, and I hope that it will remain so.

3. For all these problems we must find a solution. They can destroy our lives by killing us and making our lives boring. Our lives depend on progress, so we cannot stop it. But at the same time, we cannot kill ourselves by avoiding finding a solution.

Answers to Exercises W19, W20, and W22 are on page 548.

PRACTICE WITH ANALYZING ESSAYS

Read the following checklist. You will not have time to rewrite your essay during the test. Therefore, keep this list in mind as you write your outline and essay.

1. Is there an introductory paragraph?
2. Does the introductory paragraph restate the question?
3. Does the introductory paragraph have a thesis statement (a controlling idea)?

4. Does each paragraph have a clear topic sentence?
5. Do the topic sentences of the developmental paragraphs support the thesis statement?
6. Do the ideas in each developmental paragraph support its topic sentence?
7. Are the details (examples, facts, descriptions, personal experiences) clear?

8. Is there a concluding paragraph?
9. Does the concluding paragraph give the impression that the essay is complete?

10. Does the essay answer all parts of the question?
11. Have the grammar and spelling been corrected? (Incorrect grammar, spelling, punctuation, and word usage count against you if the errors lead to a lack of clarity. Your essay will be clearer if you correct as many of these errors as you can find in the limited time that you have.)

Exercise W23   *Analyzing essays*

Practice analyzing essays by reading the following student-written essays and answering "yes" or "no" to each of the eleven questions in the preceding checklist.

Question A

Both large cars and small cars have their advantages and disadvantages. Write about some of these advantages and disadvantages. State which type of car you prefer and why.

Essay

Both large and small cars have their advantages and disadvantages.

First, large cars have many advantages. For example, many people can be carried inside the car. Also, large cars are stronger in bad accidents, and they are very good for big families. About the disadvantages. Large cars cannot get through small streets, and they use a lot of gas to start and run.

Second, small cars also have advantages and disadvantages. About the advantages. You can drive the small car any place. Small car uses less gas and many people call them economical. The last advantage is that the small car is good for the small family like a father, mother, and one child. About the disadvantages of small cars. The small car is not strong if someone has a bad accident. Moreover, small cars cannot go very fast because of their size.

For all this I like small cars.

Question B

In your opinion, what is one of the major problems in the world today? Discuss some reasons for its existence. Give some possible solutions.

Essay

Every day on the radio, on TV, and in the newspapers, we hear, see, or read about many problems in the world. Because of this we must think about these problems. We must also try to find a solution for them. Our lives depend on this. For example, there are pollution problems.

Air pollution is the first kind. It mostly comes from fumes released from cars, airplanes, and trains. Also, factories dump waste anywhere, even in the city where many people are living. Public safety does not concern the factory owners, who must know that people don't want to live in pollution that is dangerous for their health. Nobody in this world wants to breathe dirty air.

The second pollution problem is sea pollution. Many people earn their living from fishing in the sea, and the fish they catch feed many people. Their lives depend on the fish. But the sea has become so polluted from oil spills and factory wastes that the fish are dying. This pollution is not only killing the fish, but is also affecting those people who depend on the sea for food.

Seldom do you find a place nowadays that is not polluted. This problem is growing more difficult every day. We must find a good solution that makes the world a better place to live. A good way to keep these dangerous fumes away from the people must be found. Also, programs about pollution should be shown on TV. When people understand the bad effect of pollution on the human body, maybe they will stop doing those things that make the air or the sea polluted. Also, we should plant trees, which are very useful for the land. In conclusion, I hope we can find a solution for every kind of pollution in the world.

Extended practice: Rewrite the preceding essays and improve them.

Answers to Exercise W23 are on page 549.

Exercise W24   *Scoring essays*

Give the following student essays a score: 6 is for essays that indicate strong writing abilities, 5 indicates average writing abilities, and 4 indicates minimal writing abilities. Scores of 3, 2, or 1 indicate a lack of writing abilities. Compare the score you gave the essays with the possible Writing Section score given in the Answer Key. Read the analysis of the essays to understand the given score.

Question: Some people claim that reading novels is a waste of time. They say that reading nonfictional works is more beneficial. Do you agree? Support your opinion.

1. Score _____

The main point is whether it is better to read fiction or nonfictional. The questions about this depends on the people who read. I am going to talk about both people.

The people who read the novels like to emphasize with the characters in the book. They can feel what to be another people. They can do things like traveling to the moon in their imagines during the read.

On the other hand, the people who read the nonfictional novels like to learn about facts. For these people, it solves problems and make them happy.

As you can see, I have discussed both novels and nonfictional works. Because of the above mentioned things both novels and nonfictional work is very important in our living.

2. Score _____

Some people claim that reading nonfictional works is beneficial whereas reading novels is a waste of time. Those who think this way do not realize the importance of the novel. The fictional world affects mankind in several ways.

When people read a novel, they are entering into a new world. Frequently, the story takes place in a real part of the world at a particular time in history. The reader then learns about this place and time. Also, the reader learns new words or about something unfamiliar. For example, someone who lives in the mountains might learn ship terms and how to sail a schooner.

Reading also stimulates the imagination. In our complex society, we need people who can find ways of solving problems. People who have been reading a lot of fiction have developed good imaginations. They can use their imaginations creatively to solve problems in ways that other people could never dream of.

Sometimes novels can change world events. For example, Harriet Beecher Stowe's antislavery novel may have helped end slavery in the United States. Sometimes novels can help us see things in a different way. *Animal Farm* may have influenced many readers about communism.

In conclusion, reading novels is not a waste of time. It provides readers with many satisfying hours that teaches them about life, stretches their imaginations, and focuses their minds on today's problems. Reading novels is and should always be an important activity for the people in the world.

3. Score _____

I think that reading novels is not a waste of time. In many years ago, people can't read. Therefore, grandfathers told their little boy about the stories. That is how knowledge about things that happen. For example, Helen of Troy. In these days, our grandfather don't tell stories. Most people in the life know how to read. We read the stories that in before times grandfathers say them. We can read about many adventures. People who don't want to read novels are not having a big adventure.

4. Score _____

I agree with the people who claim that reading novels is a waste of time. It is silly to spend the time reading about things that never can happen or that are not real such as science fiction is. But nonfictional works are beneficial.

There are many demands on our living these days. We must know about a lot of math and science. We must know more about computers and computer technology. Also, it is important to learn about other people and cultures. These are real things that we learn about them from nonfictional books.

People used to read novels for entertainment. We do not need to read fiction any more because of the television set. Now when people need to relax themselves, they can watch TV or go to the movies.

In conclusion, we need to read nonfictional works to improve our mental. Novels are no longer needed because things that are not real, we can see on TV. Therefore, reading nonfictional books is the more beneficial.

5. Score _____

Nowadays people read nonfictional works is better. Because it gave technology. Also, gave too much information the many things in the world. People need know too much nowadays can have a good life.

6. Score _____

Nonfictional works refer to those books that are informative. Novels are books that tell a story. Sometimes the story is completely made up. Sometimes it has real facts inside it. Reading either kind of book is beneficial.

Nonfictional works are not a waste of time. They are beneficial because they teach us things about our world. The things they teach us may be interesting information such as the history of our city. Sometimes the information is necessary for our lives such as a book on first-aid techniques.

Novels are not a waste of time either. They are beneficial because they help us enjoy our lives. We can do things vicariously with the people in the book that we would never experience in real life. Sometimes true events in history are more interesting because of the viewpoint of the fictional character in the story.

Since learning about life is necessary and since both kinds of books help us understand our world better, we should read both kinds of books. Therefore, the people who claim that reading novels is a waste of time are wrong about that. But they are right that reading nonfictional books is beneficial.

Answers to Exercise W24 are on page 549.

PRACTICE WITH ANSWERING ESSAY QUESTIONS

Now that you have studied all the parts of an essay and have analyzed problems in other students' essays, review the steps used for writing essays that answer essay questions.

Step 1: Read the question carefully.

Ask yourself questions. (What is the question *about*? What is it asking me to *do*?) Underline and number the key parts of the question.

Question   Violent TV programs have been blamed for causing crime rates to rise in

many cities. But many people do not agree that violence is related to

TV viewing. Discuss the possible reasons for both opinions. Give your

1

opinion as to whether or not violent programs should be taken off the air.

2

The question is about TV violence. It asks me to

1. Discuss reasons for both opinions:
   A. opinion that TV violence is bad
   B. opinion that TV violence is acceptable

2. Give my own opinion.

Step 2: Brainstorm.

In eight minutes or less, write down your ideas, group them into related ideas, and write a thesis statement and a *modified* outline. Compare the following complete outline and modified outline.

Example of a complete outline

I. Introduction
   A. state general topic
   B. restate question
   C. give thesis statement – reasons for both sides

II. Body
   A. crime related to violent TV programs
      1. children imitate what they see
         a. learn unacceptable values
         b. copy behavior
      2. heroes are frequently violent
      3. gives ideas for crimes
   B. crime not related to violent TV programs
      1. crime related to social pressures
         a. unemployment
         b. homelessness

    2. aggressive feelings vicariously released

    3. parental guidance more influential

    4. frequently bad consequences of violence shown

III. Conclusion

    A. my opinion

        1. shouldn't be censored

           a. people enjoy it

           b. change station

           c. turn off

        2. censorship questions

           a. who decides?

           b. what else may they censor?

        3. concluding statement

Example of modified outline

T.S. (thesis statement) reasons support both

    A. why crime related to TV

        imitate

        violent heroes

        gives ideas

    B. why crime not related to TV

        social pressures – joblessness, homelessness

        rids aggression

        parental influence

        bad consequences

conclude with opinion

        no censor – enjoyment, change, or turn off

        censor – who decides what

C.S. (concluding statement) need evidence

Step 3: Check if the topic sentences will support the thesis statement.

According to the preceding outlines, the thesis statement will introduce the essay with reasons for both sides of the question.

Topic sentence A indicates that the paragraph will discuss one side of the question – "reasons crime is related to TV." This sentence supports the thesis statement.

Topic sentence B indicates that the paragraph will discuss the other side of the question – "reasons crime is not related to TV." This sentence supports the thesis statement.

Step 4: Check if all supporting ideas relate to the topic.

According to the preceding outlines, the first topic sentence will discuss "reasons crime is related to TV." The supporting ideas – children imitate what is seen, heroes sometimes violent, and give ideas for crimes – support the argument that TV and crime are related.

The second topic sentence will discuss "reasons crime is not related to TV." The supporting ideas – social pressures, rids aggression, parental influence, and bad consequences – support the argument that TV and crime are not related.

Step 5: Add more details if necessary.

Step 6: Put ideas in a logical order if necessary.

Step 7: Write the introduction.

Keep in mind the checklist on page 414. You will not have time to rewrite your essay, so be certain your introduction is clear.

> The crime rate in many cities is rising alarmingly. Some people have the idea that violent TV programs are the cause of real crime. However, many others disagree that TV violence can be blamed for this rise. Both sides of the question of whether TV may or may not be to blame are supported by good reasons.

Step 8: Write the body.

Keep in mind the checklist on page 414. You will not have time to rewrite your essay, so be certain the paragraphs support the thesis statement.

> Those who believe that violent TV programs cause crime give many reasons. First, many viewers are children who have not formed a strong understanding of right and wrong. They imitate what they see. If a person on TV gets what he or she wants by stealing it, a child may copy this behavior. Thus, the child has learned unacceptable values. Second, many heroes in today's programs achieve their goals by violent means. Unfortunately, viewers might use similar means to achieve their objectives. Finally, people get ideas about how to commit crimes from watching TV.
>
> Other people argue that violent programs have no relation to the rise in crime rates. First, they claim that social factors, such as unemployment and homelessness, are to blame. Second, some argue that watching violence on TV is an acceptable way to reduce aggressive feelings. In other words, people may become less aggressive through viewing criminal and violent scenes. Third, even though children learn by imitation, their parents are the most influential models. Finally, the villains are usually punished for their crimes.

Step 9: Write the conclusion.

Keep in mind the checklist on page 414. You will not have time to rewrite your essay, so be certain your conclusion completes the essay.

> Whether or not violent programs are a factor in the rising crime rate, I am against their removal for the following reasons. First, some people enjoy them, and those who don't can change channels or turn their TVs off. Second, I disagree with other people deciding what I should watch. If violent programs can be censored, perhaps other programs that may be important for our well-being will also be censored. In conclusion, even though I am not fond of violent programs, I am against their removal until conclusive evidence proves that viewing violence creates violence.

Step 10: Read over the essay.

Make any minor corrections in spelling and grammar that will make your essay clearer. Remember, you will not have time to make major changes.

Exercise W25   *Practice writing essays*

When you write the essay for the Writing Section of the Computer-Based TOEFL® Test, you may write it by hand or on the computer. If you choose to write on the computer, the screen will look like this.

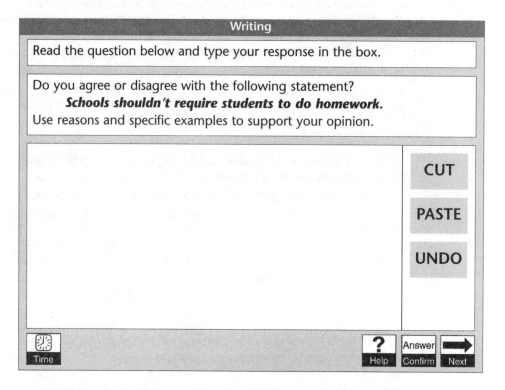

The directions and the question are at the top of the screen. You will write your essay in the blank space below the question. For more information on writing your essay by computer, see pages 29–34.

Write an essay for each of the following topics. Try to state and support your opinion.

1. Compare and contrast the advantages of city living and country living. Defend your preference.

2. Do you agree or disagree with the following statement? *The best teacher is one who is very knowledgeable about the subject matter.* Use reasons and specific examples to support your opinion.

3. "A universal language should replace all languages." Discuss the advantages and disadvantages of a universal language.

4. Do you agree or disagree with the following statement? *Students learn better when they are not threatened with possible failure.* Use reasons and specific examples to support your opinion.

5. Do you agree or disagree with the following statement? *The private car has brought more harm to the planet than benefits.* Use reasons and specific examples to support your opinion.

6. Many people believe that parents are too permissive with their children nowadays. Do you agree that this is a problem? Defend your answer.

7. Do you agree or disagree with the following statement? *The best things in life are free.* Use reasons and specific examples to support your opinion.

8. Drug abuse has become a major social problem in many parts of the world. Discuss the consequences of drug abuse and ways to deal with the problem.

CHECK YOUR PROGRESS

Exercise W26   *Mini-test*

Check your progress in using the skills that you have been practicing in Exercises W1–W25 by completing the following mini-test. This exercise presents a format that is similar to that used in the Writing Section of the Computer-Based TOEFL® Test. If you are unfamiliar with how to answer questions on the Computer-Based TOEFL® Test, see the Tutorial on pages 29–34.

Directions: Write an essay on a separate sheet of paper.

Billions of dollars go into space exploration projects every year. Some people feel that this money should be used to solve problems on Earth. Discuss reasons supporting both opinions. State and support your opinion.

Exercise W27   *Writing Section Practice Test*

When you have completed the exercises in the Writing Section, test your skills by taking this Writing Section Practice Test, which corresponds to the Writing Section of Test 2 on the CD-ROM that accompanies this book. Alternatively, you can take the test on the pages that follow.

On the day you take the actual test, you will have a choice of handwriting your essay or using a typewriter or a computer. If you are not familiar with using the computer to answer this question, see the Tutorial on pages 29–34.

WRITING

Time – 30 minutes

Read the essay question carefully.

Think before you write. Making notes may help you to organize your essay. It is important to write only on the topic you are given.

Check your work. Allow a few minutes before time is up to read over your essay and make changes.

You have thirty minutes to complete the essay. On the real test, if you continue to write, it will be considered cheating.

Set your clock or watch for thirty minutes.

Now get ready to begin.

Directions: Read the question below and write an essay on a separate sheet of paper.

Compare and contrast your way of life with that of your parents. Which way of life do you think would be more satisfying to future generations?

Use reasons and specific examples to support your opinion.

NOTES

Use this space for essay notes only. On the day of the Computer-Based TOEFL® Test, work done on the worksheet will not be scored.

This is the end of the Writing Section Test.

PRACTICE
·TESTS·

There are two complete Practice Tests in this section. Take these tests as if you were taking an actual Computer-Based TOEFL® Test. If you are unsure of Computer-Based TOEFL® Test procedures, read the instructions on pages 11–12 of the Introduction to this book.

The two Practice Tests on the following pages of this book correspond to Tests 3 and 4 on the CD-ROM that accompanies this book.

Taking the Practice Tests on the Computer

If you have access to computer equipment on which to use the CD-ROM, it is suggested that you take the Practice Tests (Tests 3 and 4) on the computer. This will allow you to experience a close approximation of the actual Computer-Based TOEFL® Test. The CD-ROM in this book presents three additional practice tests (Tests 5, 6, and 7), along with the Diagnostic Test (Test 1) and the Section Tests that appear at the end of the Listening, Structure, Reading, and Writing Sections of this book (combined to form Test 2). This gives you a total of seven tests on the CD-ROM that you can use to prepare for the Computer-Based TOEFL® Test.

   Before taking a test on the computer, arrange to have a quiet place where you will not be disturbed for the duration of the test. Each test will take approximately three hours.

   The CD-ROM will pace you through the test, and it will provide you with an approximate score. After you have finished the test, you can see a list of the questions that you answered incorrectly. If you review the questions, you will be referred to a section of the book that will help you answer questions of this type. For example, you may see: See Exercises L1–L8.

   During the Listening and Structure Sections of the actual Computer-Based TOEFL® Test, you may not go back to check your work or change your answers. However, you may go back to review your work in the Reading Section before time is called.

Taking the Practice Tests with the Book

If you do not have access to a computer, take the tests that follow in this book. The presentation of the questions in the book is similar to the way they will look on the computer screen. Before taking one of the tests, make the following preparations:

1. Arrange to have a quiet room where you will not be disturbed for the duration of the test. The test will take approximately three hours.
2. Bring the following items: a cassette or CD player; the cassette or CD that contains the Practice Tests; two sharpened black-lead pencils with erasers; and a watch, a clock, or a timer.
3. Bring extra paper if you do not want to write in the book. You will also need paper on which to write your essay.

   When you have completed the test, check your answers against the Answer Key. The Answer Key for Practice Test 1 starts on page 550; the Answer Key for Practice Test 2 starts on page 554. If you marked a wrong answer, the Answer Key will tell you which exercises in the book will help you improve in that area. For example, you may see: See Exercises L1–L8.

LISTENING

Time – approximately 60 minutes

This section measures your ability to understand spoken English. There are fifty questions in this section. The listening material and questions about it will be presented only one time. You may not take notes.

Part A

In this part, you will hear short conversations between two people. Each conversation is followed by a question about it. Each question in this part has four answer choices. Choose the best answer to each question. Answer the questions on the basis of what is <u>stated</u> or <u>implied</u> by the speakers.

 Now we will begin Part A with the first conversation.

1. What was Bob going to do?
   (A) Pick up something for a student
   (B) Loan a student his truck
   (C) Get a form for financial aid
   (D) Borrow money in a hurry

2. What does the man say about the scenery?
   (A) A carpenter built it according to the Drama Club's design.
   (B) The club members built it after getting advice.
   (C) The club members made it from a carpenter's design.
   (D) A carpenter had it designed for the Drama Club.

3. What does the woman mean?
   (A) Nobody knows where Elm Street is.
   (B) Nobody can find Elm Street.
   (C) There's no one to get directions from.
   (D) They've seen only one street that may be Elm Street.

4. What did the man say about the poll?
   (A) It was taken in the union.
   (B) The results are displayed
       on the bulletin board.
   (C) The poll was postponed.
   (D) The union board members passed
       the results on.

5. What does the woman imply?
   (A) She had to eat breakfast too early.
   (B) She can't have breakfast at this time
       of day.
   (C) She is always hungry at this time.
   (D) She missed her breakfast.

6. What does the man mean?
   (A) He's looking forward to seeing Gloria's
       presentation.
   (B) He'll miss the presentation to meet Gloria.
   (C) He doesn't want to hear another
       presentation.
   (D) He doesn't want Gloria to miss
       the program.

7. What does the man imply about
   Professor Wilson?
   (A) He always gives old quizzes.
   (B) He doesn't have a policy about exams.
   (C) He usually gives tests on Mondays.
   (D) He doesn't usually give exams.

8. What are the people discussing?
   (A) Going on a date
   (B) Having a good time
   (C) Working on an assignment
   (D) Meeting next week

9. What does the man mean?
    (A) He only has to do one problem.
    (B) He's finished one list of problems.
    (C) He has more problems to do.
    (D) He has just written a list of his problems.

10. What does the woman imply?
    (A) She'd like to go along.
    (B) There is a toll fee along the way.
    (C) The walk will take all evening.
    (D) She knows of a place to buy some rolls.

11. What does the woman say about Mary?
    (A) She is packing to go.
    (B) She is playing music.
    (C) She is practicing moves.
    (D) She is studying Plato.

12. What does the woman mean?
    (A) She's accustomed to a lot of work.
    (B) She doesn't attend evening classes anymore.
    (C) She usually has too much studying to do.
    (D) She has to study part-time.

13. What does the woman mean?
    (A) She has already had the callus removed.
    (B) She hasn't been to the infirmary yet.
    (C) She saw a doctor four weeks ago.
    (D) She has canceled her appointment.

14. What does the woman mean?
    (A) She has to revise the script.
    (B) She has to lengthen the communication.
    (C) She completed the assignment long ago.
    (D) She's already given the script to an editor.

15. What does the man mean?
    (A) He's going to set up his own business.
    (B) He intends to pay attention to his own business.
    (C) He plans to help the woman with her business.
    (D) He regrets that he has annoyed the woman.

16. What does the man mean?
    (A) He didn't have much fun selling T-shirts.
    (B) A lot of people sold more T-shirts than he did.
    (C) He didn't collect as much money as the woman.
    (D) They didn't make as much money as they had hoped.

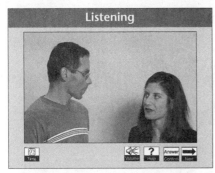

17. What does the man mean?
    (A) They forgot to charge their breakfast.
    (B) They must pay an extra charge for breakfast.
    (C) They aren't served breakfast at the hotel.
    (D) They don't have to pay for breakfast at the hotel.

18. Why was the man confused about the date for the midterm exam?
    (A) He missed an announcement.
    (B) He wrote the date incorrectly.
    (C) He confused the date with his dentist appointment.
    (D) He changed to Professor Peters's class.

This is the end of Part A.
Go on to Part B.

Part B

In this part, there are several talks and conversations. Each talk or conversation is followed by several questions. The conversations and talks are about a variety of topics. You do not need special knowledge of the topics to answer the questions correctly. Rather, you should answer each question on the basis of what is <u>stated</u> or <u>implied</u> in the conversation or talk. You may not take notes.

 Now we will begin Part B with the first conversation.

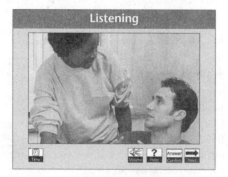

19. Why is the woman critical of the man's reading material?
    (A) She doesn't think it is intellectually stimulating.
    (B) She thinks that he is wasting the teacher's time.
    (C) She wonders why he isn't reading classics by Walt Disney.
    (D) She believes he is acting superior.

20. What does the man imply about his American popular culture course?
    (A) It is more important than studying famous American authors.
    (B) It requires more studying than the woman's course.
    (C) It is one aspect of the women's studies course.
    (D) It covers many different aspects of American culture.

21. What is one of the assignments the man has to do in the course?
    (A) Study the events that influenced comic-book writers
    (B) Read a large number of Walt Disney classics
    (C) Write an analysis of important historical events
    (D) Do a survey of contemporary American literature

22. What is the student's problem?
    (A) His registration has been canceled.
    (B) His emergency loan will be late.
    (C) He doesn't understand the application form.
    (D) He can't pay his university tuition fees.

23. Why wasn't the student's loan ready?
    (A) He hadn't signed the form.
    (B) The loan office was late in processing his loan.
    (C) His loan was not approved.
    (D) His application was late.

24. What can the student do in order to complete his registration?

Choose 2 answers.

A   Cancel his student loan
B   Take out an emergency loan
C   Pay his tuition with an emergency loan
D   Apply to pay late tuition fees

25. The woman briefly explains a process. Summarize the process by putting the events in order.

Write the letter of each event in the space where it belongs. Use each event only once.

A   He should take the form to Mr. Schultz.
B   He should use the student loan to pay back the emergency loan.
C   He should complete the registration procedures.
D   He should complete an emergency loan application.

1	
2	
3	
4	

26. When will the student be able to complete his registration?
    (A) After he gets his student loan
    (B) After he pays back his emergency loan
    (C) The same day he's granted an emergency loan
    (D) Before he returns the application on September 20

27. What will the student probably do immediately?
    (A) Take out a student loan
    (B) Take out an emergency loan
    (C) Drop out of the university
    (D) Pick up a part-time job

Now get ready to listen.

Now get ready to answer the questions.

28. What is the talk mainly about?
    (A) The first skyscrapers in America
    (B) The English Arts and Crafts Movement's influence on American architects
    (C) The Prairie School of Architecture
    (D) Oriental motifs in American architecture

29. What can be said about the nature of Prairie School architecture?

    Choose 2 answers.

    [A] It was expressed mainly in large public buildings.
    [B] It tried to harmonize with nature.
    [C] It was from midwestern America with no foreign influences.
    [D] It was mainly concerned with domestic living spaces.

30. Select the building that could be classified as an example of the Prairie School style.

(A)

(B)

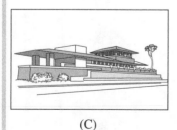

(C)

(D)

31. According to the professor, how did the Prairie School architect make living space more compatible with human needs?

    Choose 2 answers.

    [A] Through the inclusion of vertical windows
    [B] By abolishing closed interior corners
    [C] By decreasing the number of separate rooms
    [D] Through the use of elaborate ornamentation

32. Why does the professor mention traditional Japanese houses?
    (A) To contrast Japanese architectural design with the Prairie School design
    (B) To show the relationship between Japanese use of space and overall ornamentation
    (C) To give an example of how turned-up roof edges don't blend in with the horizontal lines of the flat prairies
    (D) To show how Oriental themes influenced Prairie School designs

Now get ready to listen.

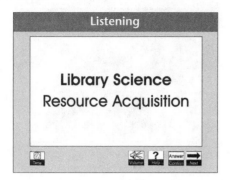 

Now get ready to answer the questions.

33. What is the main idea of the talk?
    (A) How to use the library
    (B) How libraries purchase materials
    (C) How libraries meet users' needs
    (D) How libraries use modern technology

36. According to the talk, what can students do
    if they can't find a book in the library?
    (A) Purchase it at the bookstore
    (B) Borrow it from the professor
    (C) Contact the publisher
    (D) Have the librarian do a computer search

34. What can be inferred from the talk?
    (A) Libraries have limited funds and space.
    (B) Libraries must purchase more books.
    (C) Libraries contain everything the user needs.
    (D) Libraries are no longer needed by students
        and professors.

37. The professor briefly explains the steps that a
    library user would follow to obtain materials.
    Put the steps in order.

    > Write the letter of each phrase in the space
    > where it belongs. Use each phrase only once.

    A A user would check if the library has copies
       of the needed materials.
    B A user would return the materials to the
       library to be sent back to the original library.
    C A user would search the computer system
       for other libraries that have the needed
       material.
    D A user would use the interlibrary loan
       system to order the materials.

35. How do librarians decide what to purchase?
    (A) They use the interlibrary loan system.
    (B) Professors make suggestions.
    (C) They contact other libraries.
    (D) They buy everything in print.

1	
2	
3	
4	

Now get ready to listen.

Now get ready to answer the questions.

38. What is the main topic of this lecture?
    (A) A successful scheme for lending money to entrepreneurs
    (B) The problems faced by entrepreneurs in securing the money needed to set up a business
    (C) The reason banks do not lend money to small-scale entrepreneurs
    (D) A policy that scrutinizes moneylenders who attach overly high interest rates to their loans

40. According to the professor, why did Mohammed Yunus found the Grameen Bank?
    (A) To help the poor work themselves out of poverty
    (B) To prove to traditional banks that poor people are good risks
    (C) To show that people should have collateral before being given a loan
    (D) To put informal moneylenders out of business

39. The professor briefly explains a traditional cycle of borrowing. Put the steps of the cycle in order.

    Write the letter of each sentence in the space where it belongs. Use each sentence only once.

    A The entrepreneur borrows money with a high interest rate from a moneylender.
    B The entrepreneur must borrow more money in order to pay back the loan.
    C The entrepreneur gets caught in a cycle of borrowing money to pay back loans.
    D The small-scale entrepreneur has no money to start and run a business.

1	
2	
3	
4	

41. What problem facing small-scale entrepreneurs does the professor discuss?
    (A) A cycle of debt
    (B) Loans that are too small
    (C) Low interest rates
    (D) A complicated loan repayment system

42. How can the success of the microenterprise scheme be judged?

    Choose 2 answers.

    A By the strength of the friendships within peer groups
    B By the high repayment rate
    C By the loans that are short-term and small
    D By the high percentage of borrowers who are running successful businesses

43. According to the professor, how is the Grameen Bank different from traditional banks?

    Choose 2 answers.

    A It lends money to people who have nothing to use as a guarantee of repayment.

    B It trains groups of borrowers so they can manage businesses successfully.

    C It attaches exorbitant interest rates to the loan.

    D It traps the borrower in a cycle of poverty from which there is no escape.

44. Who would be most likely to receive a loan from the Grameen Bank?
    (A) A moneylender wanting to loan money to the poor
    (B) A poor person wanting to run a small business
    (C) A student wanting to attend a university
    (D) A person wanting to borrow large sums of money

Now get ready to listen.

Physical Education
Jumping in Sports

Now get ready to answer the questions.

45. What is the class discussion mainly about?
    (A) The largest and strongest muscles in the body
    (B) The sports that require different kinds of jumping skills
    (C) The reasons arms are important in sports that involve jumping
    (D) The importance of training and practice needed for sports that involve jumping

46. Why does the professor bring up the topic of arm muscles in a discussion about jumping?
    (A) To emphasize the fact that arm muscles are not specific muscles used in jumping
    (B) To compare large muscle movement with small muscle movement
    (C) To criticize athletes for neglecting the development of their arm muscles
    (D) To focus on the importance of developing arm muscles when training for jumping skills

47. The professor mentions volleyball as an example of which of the following?
    (A) A team sport
    (B) A sport having a variety of jumps
    (C) A sport that uses arm muscles
    (D) A low-risk sport

48. According to the professor, what can an athlete do to improve efficiency of movement?

    Choose 2 answers.

    A Apply the pattern with greater speed

    B Perform the movement with less effort

    C Repeat the movement regularly

    D Ingrain the pattern of movement into the subconscious

49. What is probably true about training methods to improve jumping in different sports?
    (A) Athletes involved in jump-specific sports need to perfect skills for all kinds of jumps.
    (B) Athletes involved in sports requiring many kinds of jumps need to train longer.
    (C) Training methods are different depending on the types of jumping skills required.
    (D) Training for jumping should only concentrate on the body's largest and strongest muscles.

50. Based on the discussion, classify the training requirements for the sports that are illustrated.

    Write the letter of each phrase in the space where it belongs. Use each phrase only once.

    A   A sport that requires training for the same kind of jump
    B   A sport that requires training for a variety of jumps
    C   A sport in which arm muscle training cannot be neglected

1.

2.

3.

This is the end of the Listening Section.
Turn off your cassette or audio CD player now.

Go on to the Structure Section.

STRUCTURE

Time – 15 minutes

This section measures your ability to understand the structures of standard written English. There are twenty questions in this section. There are two types of questions.

The first type of question consists of incomplete sentences. Beneath each sentence there are four words or phrases. You will select the one word or phrase that best completes the sentence.

Example:

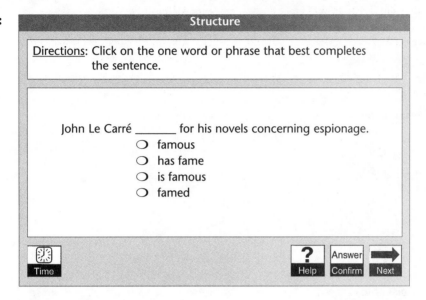

The second type of question consists of a sentence with four underlined words or phrases. You will select the one underlined word or phrase that must be changed for the sentence to be correct.

Example:

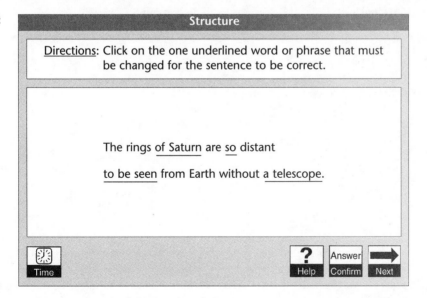

Now begin working on the Structure questions.

---

1. It is now known that Saturn _____ not the only planet in our solar system with rings.
   (A) which
   (B) be
   (C) so
   (D) is

---

2. It was not <u>until</u> 1937 <u>when</u> the southernmost
        A   B

   source of <u>the</u> Nile River <u>was discovered</u>.
             C   D

---

3. _____ is essential for the plant life of the Amazon basin.
   (A) It is an adequate rainfall
   (B) Though an adequate rainfall
   (C) Adequate rainfall
   (D) Although an adequate rainfall

---

4. Platinum is a <u>rare</u> and <u>value</u> metal, white
                  A   B

   <u>in color</u>, and <u>easy</u> to work.
      C   D

---

5. The Mediterranean monk seal is distinguished from the more familiar gray seal by _____.
   (A) is a size
   (B) its size
   (C) is its size
   (D) is size

---

6. <u>During</u> the two centuries <u>between</u> Herschel
      A   B

   and *Voyager*, <u>relatively</u> little <u>learned</u>
                   C   D

   about the planet Uranus.

---

7. The Himalayas are the _____.
   (A) height of world extensive ranges
   (B) ranges of the most extensive world
   (C) world's most extensive ranges
   (D) extensive ranges of the world

---

8. <u>Some</u> conservationists <u>attempt to save</u>
      A   B

   rare domestic farm <u>animal</u>, <u>such as the</u>
                       C   D

   Tamworth pig.

---

9. Anthony Burgess, _____ as a novelist, was originally a student of music.
   (A) because of being famous
   (B) who achieved fame
   (C) who because he was famous
   (D) he achieved fame

---

10. The head proctor tells the students when they

    should <u>begin</u> the exam, how long <u>they have</u>
            A   B

    to complete it, and what <u>the procedures</u> are
                              C

    for <u>turning in</u>.
        D

11. Not until Edward Jenner developed the first anti-smallpox serum in 1796 _____ against this terrible disease.
    (A) protection was
    (B) protection was given
    (C) it was protected
    (D) was there protection

16. Before 1992, Bobby Fischer had not <u>played</u>
                                         A

    in <u>other</u> chess tournament <u>since</u> winning
       B   C

    the Chess World Championship <u>in</u> 1972.
                                        D

12. Estimates <u>about</u> scientists <u>suggest</u> that only one
              A   B

    percent of the world's <u>extinct</u> animals and
                          C

    plants have been <u>identified</u>.
                      D

17. The smallest _____, paradoxically, explored by the largest machines.
    (A) particles in the universe
    (B) particles in the universe are
    (C) particles that are in the universe
    (D) particles in the universe have

13. Early sailors, _____ sometimes in uncharted seas, faced many hazards in reaching their destination.
    (A) navigating
    (B) were navigated
    (C) navigate
    (D) and navigates

18. <u>Perhaps was</u> his defiance against <u>his</u> parents'
         A   B

    attitude <u>that led</u> Salvatore Ferragamo
               C

    to fame <u>as the</u> shoemaker for the world's
              D

    most famous women.

14. The <u>oceans</u> contain many <u>forms</u> of life that
         A   B

    <u>has</u> not <u>yet</u> been discovered.
     C   D

19. Not only are reindeer used for their hides and milk _____.
    (A) as well as pulling sleighs
    (B) but they pull sleighs
    (C) but for pulling sleighs as well
    (D) also to pull sleighs

15. _____ first three years of the war with Germany and Austria-Hungary left 1.8 million Russian soldiers dead.
    (A) The
    (B) In the
    (C) It was the
    (D) When the

20. The United Nations Organization maintains

    <u>what</u> water will be <u>at</u> the heart of <u>many</u> future
     A   B   C

    international <u>disputes</u>.
                  D

This is the end of the Structure Section.
Go on to the Reading Section.

READING

Time – 80 minutes
(including the reading of the passages)

In this section, you will read several passages. Each passage is followed by ten to fifteen questions. There are fifty questions in this section. You should answer all questions following a passage on the basis of what is stated or implied in that passage. For each question, select or write the correct answer.

Now begin reading the first passage.

Questions 1–11

Nature has always provided a stimulus for inventive minds. Early flying machines clearly were an attempt to emulate the freedom of birds. Architects and engineers have often consciously modeled buildings on forms found in nature. A more recent example of the inspiration given by nature is the invention of Velcro®. The inventor of this now common fastening device noticed that small burrs attached to his dog's coat grasped the hairs by means of tiny hooks. This led him to invent a synthetic fabric whose surfaces mimic the clasping properties of this natural seedpod.

Animals and plants have evolved solutions to the kinds of problems that often interest engineers and designers. Much current research in material science is concerned with actively examining the natural world, especially at the molecular level, for inspiration to develop materials with novel properties. This relatively new field of study is sometimes known as biomimetics, since it consciously attempts to mimic nature.

Researchers have investigated several interesting areas. For example, they have studied how the molecular structure of antler bone contributes to its amazing toughness, how the skin structure of a worm contributes to its ability to crawl, how the sea cucumber softens its skeleton and changes shape so that it can squeeze through tiny gaps in rocks, or what gives wood its high resistance to impact. These investigations have led to several breakthroughs in the development of composite materials with remarkable properties.

Predictions for future inventions that may be developed from these lines of research include so-called smart structures that design and repair themselves in a similar way to a variety of processes in the natural world. For example, engineers have envisaged bridges that would detect areas heavily stressed by vehicle movement or wind. The bridge structure would then automatically add or move material to the weak areas until the stress is reduced. The same principle might be used to repair damaged buildings. Other new materials that have been imagined are substances that would copy photosynthesis in green plants in order to create new energy sources. The potential impact of biomimetic research is so great that the twenty-first century may come to be known as the "Age of Materials."

1. The passage is concerned with
   (A) future research into the uses of Velcro®
   (B) the effect of the Age of Materials on nature
   (C) the development of products based on nature
   (D) problems that preoccupy designers and engineers

2. Why does the author mention Velcro®?
   (A) To complain that burrs attach themselves to his dog's coat
   (B) To show how a natural structure inspired a useful invention
   (C) To suggest the use of Velcro® as a means of fastening objects
   (D) To give an example of tiny hooklike structures in synthetic fabric

Nature has always provided a stimulus for inventive minds. **Early flying machines clearly were an attempt to emulate the freedom of birds. Architects and engineers have often consciously modeled buildings on forms found in nature. A more recent example of the inspiration given by nature is the invention of Velcro®. The inventor of this now common fastening device noticed that small burrs attached to his dog's coat grasped the hairs by means of tiny hooks. This led him to invent a synthetic fabric whose surfaces mimic the clasping properties of this natural seedpod.**

3. Look at the word emulate in the passage. Select another word or phrase in the **bold** text that is closest in meaning to the word emulate.

Nature has always provided a stimulus for inventive minds. Early flying machines clearly were an attempt to emulate the freedom of birds. Architects and engineers have often consciously modeled buildings on forms found in nature. **A more recent example of the inspiration given by nature is the invention of Velcro®. The inventor of this now common fastening device noticed that small burrs attached to his dog's coat grasped the hairs by means of tiny hooks. This led him to invent a synthetic fabric whose surfaces mimic the clasping properties of this natural seedpod.**

4. Look at the word him in the passage. Select the word or phrase in the **bold** text that him refers to.

→ Animals and plants have evolved solutions to the kinds of problems that often interest engineers and designers. Much current research in material science is concerned with actively examining the natural world, especially at the molecular level, for inspiration to develop materials with novel properties. This relatively new field of study is sometimes known as biomimetics, since it consciously attempts to mimic nature.

5. The word novel in paragraph 2 is closest in meaning to
   (A) unique
   (B) familiar
   (C) fictitious
   (D) legendary

Paragraph 2 is marked with an arrow (→).

→ Predictions for future inventions that may be developed from these lines of research include so-called smart structures that design and repair themselves in a similar way to a variety of processes in the natural world. For example, engineers have envisaged bridges that would detect areas heavily stressed by vehicle movement or wind. The bridge structure would then automatically add or move material to the weak areas until the stress is reduced. The same principle might be used to repair damaged buildings. Other new materials that have been imagined are substances that would copy photosynthesis in green plants in order to create new energy sources. The potential impact of biomimetic research is so great that the twenty-first century may come to be known as the "Age of Materials."

6. With which of the following statements about investigations in biomimetics would the author most likely agree?
   (A) Biomimetics is not promising.
   (B) Biomimetics may lead to the development of new creatures.
   (C) Biomimetics may lead to useful inventions.
   (D) Biomimetics has provided the new material for smart structures.

7. Why does the author use the term smart in paragraph 4?
   (A) To compare the intelligence of structures with that of nature
   (B) To stress the analogy of the structures to fashion
   (C) To emphasize the self-directed nature of some processes
   (D) To satirize the processes in the natural world

Paragraph 4 is marked with an arrow (→).

Predictions for future inventions that may be developed from these lines of research include so-called smart structures that design and repair themselves in a similar way to a variety of processes in the natural world. **For example, engineers have envisaged bridges that would detect areas heavily stressed by vehicle movement or wind. The bridge structure would then automatically add or move material to the weak areas until the stress is reduced. The same principle might be used to repair damaged buildings. Other new materials that have been imagined are substances that would copy photosynthesis in green plants in order to create new energy sources.** The potential impact of biomimetic research is so great that the twenty-first century may come to be known as the "Age of Materials."

8. Look at the word envisaged in the passage. Select another word or phrase in the **bold** text that is closest in meaning to the word envisaged.

[1] Nature has always provided a stimulus for inventive minds. Early flying machines clearly were an attempt to emulate the freedom of birds. Architects and engineers have often consciously modeled buildings on forms found in nature. A more recent example of the inspiration given by nature is the invention of Velcro®. The inventor of this now common fastening device noticed that small burrs attached to his dog's coat grasped the hairs by means of tiny hooks. This led him to invent a synthetic fabric whose surfaces mimic the clasping properties of this natural seedpod.

[2] Animals and plants have evolved solutions to the kinds of problems that often interest engineers and designers. Much current research in material science is concerned with actively examining the natural world, especially at the molecular level, for inspiration to develop materials with novel properties. This relatively new field of study is sometimes known as biomimetics, since it consciously attempts to mimic nature.

[3] Researchers have investigated several interesting areas. For example, they have studied how the molecular structure of antler bone contributes to its amazing toughness, how the skin structure of a worm contributes to its ability to crawl, how the sea cucumber softens its skeleton and changes shape so that it can squeeze through tiny gaps in rocks, or what gives wood its high resistance to impact. These investigations have led to several breakthroughs in the development of composite materials with remarkable properties.

[4] Predictions for future inventions that may be developed from these lines of research include so-called smart structures that design and repair themselves in a similar way to a variety of processes in the natural world. For example, engineers have envisaged bridges that would detect areas heavily stressed by vehicle movement or wind. The bridge structure would then automatically add or move material to the weak areas until the stress is reduced. The same principle might be used to repair damaged buildings. Other new materials that have been imagined are substances that would copy photosynthesis in green plants in order to create new energy sources. The potential impact of biomimetic research is so great that the twenty-first century may come to be known as the "Age of Materials."

9. Which of the following would NOT be a useful biomimetic product?
   (A) Tomatoes mimicking the structures that give sea cucumbers the ability to squeeze through cracks
   (B) Bulletproof jackets mimicking the structures that give wood its resistance to impact
   (C) Glass in windshields mimicking the structures that give antler bone its toughness
   (D) Cables mimicking the structures that give spiderwebs their flexibility and tensile strength

10. According to the author, what would be the advantage of a product that mimics photosynthesis?
    (A) It could be used to create green plants.
    (B) It could help to meet future energy needs.
    (C) It could be an aid in repairing green areas.
    (D) It could form the basis of twenty-first century materials.

11. Select the number of the paragraph in the passage that explains the reason for the term "biomimetics."

Questions 12–26

Diamond value is based on four characteristics: carat, color, clarity, and cut. The size of a diamond is measured by carat weight. There are 100 points in a carat and 142 carats in an ounce. Each point above 1 carat is more valuable than each one below 1 carat. In other words, a stone that weighs more than 1 carat is more valuable per point than a stone that is smaller than 1 carat.

The scale used for rating color begins with D, which means the gem is absolutely colorless and, therefore, the most valuable. E and F are almost colorless. All three are good for investment purposes. A stone rated between G and J is good for jewelry. Beyond J the stones take on a slightly yellowish color, which gets deeper as the grade declines.

The clarity of a stone is determined by its lack of carbon spots, inner flaws, and surface blemishes. While most of these are invisible to the unaided eye, they do affect the diamond's brilliance. For jewelry, a diamond rated VVS1 (very, very slight imperfections) is as close to flawless as one will find. After that the scale goes to VVS2, VS1, VS2, SI1, SI2, I1, I2, and so on.

The final characteristic is cut. When shaped – whether round, oval, emerald, marquise, pear, or heart – the diamond should be faceted so that light is directed into the depths of the prism and then reflected outward again. A well-cut diamond will separate the light into different colors when the light is reflected. Only stones of similar shape should have their reflective qualities compared, as some shapes are more reflective than others. The round shape is the most reflective.

12. The passage is mainly about
    (A) the cost of diamonds
    (B) qualities affecting diamond values
    (C) how to judge an expensive diamond
    (D) buying diamonds for jewelry

Diamond value is based on four characteristics: carat, color, clarity, and cut. The size of a diamond is measured by carat weight. There are 100 points in a carat and 142 carats in an ounce. Each point above 1 carat is more valuable than each one below 1 carat. In other words, a stone that weighs more than 1 carat is more valuable per point than a stone that is smaller than 1 carat.

13. Look at the word one in the passage. Select the word or phrase in the **bold** text that one refers to.

14. With which of the following statements about a one-carat diamond would the author agree?
    (A) It has 100 points.
    (B) It weighs an ounce.
    (C) It costs twice as much as a smaller one.
    (D) It has the same quality as a half-carat diamond.

→ The scale used for rating color begins with D, which means the gem is absolutely colorless and, therefore, the most valuable. E and F are almost colorless. All three are good for investment purposes. A stone rated between G and J is good for jewelry. Beyond J the stones take on a slightly yellowish color, which gets deeper as the grade declines.

15. The word absolutely in paragraph 2 is closest in meaning to
    (A) actually
    (B) positively
    (C) greatly
    (D) completely

Paragraph 2 is marked with an arrow (→).

The scale used for rating color begins with D, which means the gem is absolutely colorless and, therefore, the most valuable. E and F are almost colorless. All three are good for investment purposes. A stone rated between G and J is good for jewelry. Beyond J the stones take on a slightly yellowish color, which gets deeper as the grade declines.

16. Look at the word stone in the passage. Select another word or phrase in the **bold** text that is closest in meaning to the word stone.

17. With which of the following letters might the author rate a stone that has no color at all?
    (A) A
    (B) Z
    (C) D
    (D) J

→ [1] The clarity of a stone is determined by its lack of carbon spots, inner flaws, and surface blemishes. [2] While most of these are invisible to the unaided eye, they do affect the diamond's brilliance. [3] For jewelry, a diamond rated VVS1 (very, very slight imperfections) is as close to flawless as one will find. [4] After that the scale goes to VVS2, VS1, VS2, SI1, SI2, I1, I2, and so on.

18. Select the number of the sentence in paragraph 3 where the author discusses a nearly perfect diamond.

Paragraph 3 is marked with an arrow (→).

19. With which of the following statements about the clarity of a stone would the author most probably agree?
    (A) It is invisible to the unaided eye.
    (B) It affects the diamond's brilliance.
    (C) It has spots, flaws, and blemishes.
    (D) It is determined by imperfections.

→ The clarity of a stone is determined by its lack of carbon spots, inner flaws, and surface blemishes. While most of these are invisible to the unaided eye, they do affect the diamond's brilliance. For jewelry, a diamond rated VVS1 (very, very slight imperfections) is as close to flawless as one will find. After that the scale goes to VVS2, VS1, VS2, SI1, SI2, I1, I2, and so on.

20. The word flawless in paragraph 3 is closest in meaning to
    (A) unblemished
    (B) unsaturated
    (C) unrefined
    (D) unbruised

Paragraph 3 is marked with an arrow (→).

→ [1] The clarity of a stone is determined by its lack of carbon spots, inner flaws, and surface blemishes. [2] While most of these are invisible to the unaided eye, they do affect the diamond's brilliance. [3] For jewelry, a diamond rated VVS1 (very, very slight imperfections) is as close to flawless as one will find. [4] After that the scale goes to VVS2, VS1, VS2, SI1, SI2, I1, I2, and so on.

21. Select the number of the sentence in paragraph 3 that outlines the factors associated with brilliance.

Paragraph 3 is marked with an arrow (→).

→ The final characteristic is cut. When shaped – whether round, oval, emerald, marquise, pear, or heart – the diamond should be faceted so that light is directed into the depths of the prism and then reflected outward again. A well-cut diamond will separate the light into different colors when the light is reflected. Only stones of similar shape should have their reflective qualities compared, as some shapes are more reflective than others. The round shape is the most reflective.

22. In paragraph 4, the author states that diamonds reflect
    (A) the prism
    (B) the depths
    (C) facets
    (D) light

Paragraph 4 is marked with an arrow (→).

23. Why does the author suggest only comparing two diamonds of the same shape?
    (A) Because they will have the same value
    (B) Because they can be compared for reflective quality
    (C) Because they can be compared for weight
    (D) Because they will be equally brilliant

→ The final characteristic is cut. When shaped – whether round, oval, emerald, marquise, pear, or heart – the diamond should be faceted so that light is directed into the depths of the prism and then reflected outward again. A well-cut diamond will separate the light into different colors when the light is reflected. Only stones of similar shape should have their reflective qualities compared, as some shapes are more reflective than others. The round shape is the most reflective.

24. The word faceted in paragraph 4 is closest in meaning to
    (A) split
    (B) turned
    (C) cut
    (D) set

Paragraph 4 is marked with an arrow (→).

25. Select the drawing that represents the shape of the most sparkling diamond cut.

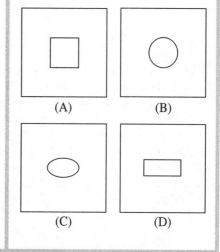

(A)   (B)

(C)   (D)

Diamond value is based on four characteristics: carat, color, clarity, and cut. The size of a diamond is measured by carat weight. There are 100 points in a carat and 142 carats in an ounce. Each point above 1 carat is more valuable than each one below 1 carat. ☐1 In other words, a stone that weighs more than 1 carat is more valuable per point than a stone that is smaller than 1 carat.

The scale used for rating color begins with D, which means the gem is absolutely colorless and, therefore, the most valuable. E and F are almost colorless. All three are good for investment purposes. ☐2 A stone rated between G and J is good for jewelry. ☐3 Beyond J the stones take on a slightly yellowish color, which gets deeper as the grade declines.

The clarity of a stone is determined by its lack of carbon spots, inner flaws, and surface blemishes. While most of these are invisible to the unaided eye, they do affect the diamond's brilliance. ☐4 For jewelry, a diamond rated VVS1 (very, very slight imperfections) is as close to flawless as one will find. ☐5 After that the scale goes to VVS2, VS1, VS2, SI1, SI2, I1, I2, and so on.

The final characteristic is cut. When shaped – whether round, oval, emerald, marquise, pear, or heart – the diamond should be faceted so that light is directed into the depths of the prism and then reflected outward again. A well-cut diamond will separate the light into different colors when the light is reflected. ☐6 Only stones of similar shape should have their reflective qualities compared, as some shapes are more reflective than others. The round shape is the most reflective.

26. The following sentence can be added to the passage.

In contrast, a nearly flawless diamond that is not professionally cut will not acquire its full reflective potential, and thus, its value may be diminished.

Where would it best fit in the passage?

Select the square (☐) that shows where the sentence should be added.

Questions 27–38

People who suffer from excessive drowsiness during the daytime may be victims of a condition known as "narcolepsy." Although most people may feel sleepy while watching TV or after eating a meal, narcoleptics may fall asleep at unusual or embarrassing times. They may doze while eating, talking, taking a shower, or even driving a car. Victims can be affected in one of two ways. Most narcoleptics have several sleeping periods during each day with alert periods in between. A minority of others feel drowsy almost all the time and are alert for only brief intervals. Many people with this condition also suffer from cataplexy – a form of muscular paralysis that can range from a mild weakness at the knees to complete immobility affecting the entire body. This condition lasts from a few seconds to several minutes and is often set off by intense emotions.

No reliable data exist showing how many people have narcolepsy. Some estimates put the number as high as three hundred thousand in the United States alone. Researchers suggest that the problem may stem from the immune system's reacting abnormally to the brain's chemical processes. Further studies have shown a link between narcolepsy and a number of genes, although it is quite possible for an individual to have these genes and not develop the disease. There are also cases of twins where one member has narcolepsy but the other does not. Thus, an explanation based on genetics alone is not adequate.

There is currently no cure for narcolepsy, so sufferers of this condition can only have their symptoms treated through a combination of counseling and drugs. The available drugs can help control the worst of the symptoms, but their administration has unwanted side effects such as increased blood pressure and heart rate and, sometimes, even increased sleepiness. It is clear that improved medications need to be developed.

27. What is the main topic of this passage?
    (A) Aspects of narcolepsy
    (B) Causes of narcolepsy
    (C) Treatment of narcolepsy
    (D) Development of narcolepsy

28. Narcolepsy is a condition in which people
    (A) doze after eating a meal
    (B) have unusual brain chemistry
    (C) only sleep in the day
    (D) doze at unusual times

29. A person is most likely to be narcoleptic if he or she falls asleep while
    (A) watching a movie
    (B) eating at a restaurant
    (C) lying on the beach
    (D) taking a long airplane trip

People who suffer from excessive drowsiness during the daytime may be victims of a condition known as "narcolepsy." **Although most people may feel sleepy while watching TV or after eating a meal, narcoleptics may fall asleep at unusual or embarrassing times. They may doze while eating, talking, taking a shower, or even driving a car. Victims can be affected in one of two ways. Most narcoleptics have several sleeping periods during each day with alert periods in between. A minority of others feel drowsy almost all the time and are alert for only brief intervals.** Many people with this condition also suffer from cataplexy – a form of muscular paralysis that can range from a mild weakness at the knees to complete immobility affecting the entire body. This condition lasts from a few seconds to several minutes and is often set off by intense emotions.

30. Look at the word **intervals** in the passage. Select another word or phrase in the **bold** text that is closest in meaning to the word **intervals**.

→ People who suffer from excessive drowsiness during the daytime may be victims of a condition known as "narcolepsy." Although most people may feel sleepy while watching TV or after eating a meal, narcoleptics may fall asleep at unusual or embarrassing times. They may doze while eating, talking, taking a shower, or even driving a car. Victims can be affected in one of two ways. Most narcoleptics have several sleeping periods during each day with alert periods in between. A minority of others feel drowsy almost all the time and are alert for only brief intervals. Many people with this condition also suffer from cataplexy – a form of muscular paralysis that can range from a mild weakness at the knees to complete immobility affecting the entire body. This condition lasts from a few seconds to several minutes and is often set off by intense emotions.

31. The word alert in paragraph 1 is closest in meaning to
    (A) tired
    (B) awake
    (C) alarmed
    (D) informed

Paragraph 1 is marked with an arrow (→).

People who suffer from excessive drowsiness during the daytime may be victims of a condition known as "narcolepsy." Although most people may feel sleepy while watching TV or after eating a meal, narcoleptics may fall asleep at unusual or embarrassing times. They may doze while eating, talking, taking a shower, or even driving a car. Victims can be affected in one of two ways. Most narcoleptics have several sleeping periods during each day with alert periods in between. **A minority of others feel drowsy almost all the time and are alert for only brief intervals. Many people with this condition also suffer from cataplexy – a form of muscular paralysis that can range from a mild weakness at the knees to complete immobility affecting the entire body. This condition lasts from a few seconds to several minutes and is often set off by intense emotions.**

32. Look at the word **paralysis** in the passage. Select another word or phrase in the **bold** text that is closest in meaning to the word **paralysis**.

33. The passage implies that narcolepsy
    (A) is an imaginary problem
    (B) can be a serious disorder
    (C) is easily cured
    (D) is really laziness

→ No reliable data exist showing how many people have narcolepsy. Some estimates put the number as high as three hundred thousand in the United States alone. Researchers suggest that the problem may stem from the immune system's reacting abnormally to the brain's chemical processes. Further studies have shown a link between narcolepsy and a number of genes, although it is quite possible for an individual to have these genes and not develop the disease. There are also cases of twins where one member has narcolepsy but the other does not. Thus, an explanation based on genetics alone is not adequate.

34. According to the information in paragraph 2, it can be said that
    (A) most people are narcoleptics sometimes
    (B) narcoleptics are drug addicts
    (C) narcolepsy is a very rare condition
    (D) the number of narcoleptics is unknown

Paragraph 2 is marked with an arrow (→).

→   No reliable data exist showing how many people have narcolepsy. [1] Some estimates put the number as high as three hundred thousand in the United States alone. [2] Researchers suggest that the problem may stem from the immune system's reacting abnormally to the brain's chemical processes. [3] Further studies have shown a link between narcolepsy and a number of genes, although it is quite possible for an individual to have these genes and not develop the disease. [4] There are also cases of twins where one member has narcolepsy but the other does not. Thus, an explanation based on genetics alone is not adequate.

35. The following sentence can be added to paragraph 2.

Unfortunately, there is also little knowledge about the causes of this illness.

Where would it best fit in the paragraph?

Select the square (☐) that shows where the sentence should be added.

Paragraph 2 is marked with an arrow (→).

→ [1] No reliable data exist showing how many people have narcolepsy. [2] Some estimates put the number as high as three hundred thousand in the United States alone. [3] Researchers suggest that the problem may stem from the immune system's reacting abnormally to the brain's chemical processes. [4] Further studies have shown a link between narcolepsy and a number of genes, although it is quite possible for an individual to have these genes and not develop the disease. [5] There are also cases of twins where one member has narcolepsy but the other does not. [6] Thus, an explanation based on genetics alone is not adequate.

36. Select the number of the sentence in paragraph 2 where the author mentions the possible cause of narcolepsy.

Paragraph 2 is marked with an arrow (→).

There is currently no cure for narcolepsy, so sufferers of this condition can only have their symptoms treated through a combination of counseling and drugs. The available drugs can help control the worst of the symptoms, but their administration has unwanted side effects such as increased blood pressure and heart rate and, sometimes, even increased sleepiness. It is clear that improved medications need to be developed.

37. Look at the word their in the passage. Select another word or phrase in the **bold** text that their refers to.

38. Which of the following statements about narcolepsy is NOT true?
   (A) Doctors treat symptoms rather than causes.
   (B) The causes of narcolepsy have not been found yet.
   (C) Narcolepsy affects people in two basic ways.
   (D) Narcolepsy can be cured through counseling and drugs.

Questions 39–50

In the eleventh century, people noticed that if a small hole were put in one wall of a darkened room, then light coming through the aperture would make a faint picture of the scene outside on the opposite wall of the room. A room like this was called a camera obscura. Artists later used a box to create a camera obscura, with a lens in its opening to make the picture clearer. But it was not possible to preserve the image that was produced in the box.

In 1727, Johann Heinrich Schulze mixed chalk, silver, and nitric acid in a bottle. He found that when the mixture was subjected to light, it became darker. In 1826, Joseph Nicéphore Niépce put some paper dipped in a light-sensitive chemical into his camera obscura, which he left exposed in a window. The result was probably the first permanent photographic image.

The image Niépce made was a negative, a picture where all the white parts are black and all the black parts are white. Later, Louis Daguerre found a way to reverse the black and white parts to make positive prints. But when he looked at the pictures in the light, the chemicals continued to react and the pictures went dark. In 1837, he found a way to fix the image. These images are known as daguerreotypes.

Many developments of photographic equipment were made in the nineteenth century. Glass plates coated with light-sensitive chemicals were used to produce clear, sharp, positive prints on paper. In the 1870s, George Eastman proposed using rolls of paper film, coated with chemicals, to replace glass plates. Then, in 1888, Eastman began manufacturing the Kodak® camera, the first "modern" lightweight camera that people could carry and use.

During the twentieth century, many technological improvements were made. One of the most important was color film. Color film is made from layers of chemicals that are sensitive to red, green, and blue light, from which all other colors can be made. Despite the fact that the space age has witnessed the creation of an array of technological marvels, even the ability to take photographs of distant galaxies from above the Earth's atmosphere via orbiting satellites, the basic principles of photography have not changed since Niépce took his first fuzzy negative pictures.

39. The passage is mainly about
    (A) the development of the camera obscura
    (B) how the camera obscura was invented
    (C) the history of photographic technology
    (D) the time period during which the first camera was developed

40. The first camera obscura can be described as nothing more than
    (A) a dark room in which an image was projected onto a wall
    (B) a preserved image of a dark room projected in a box
    (C) a box with a lens, which projected an image onto a wall in a dark room
    (D) a hole in a wall into which a lens could be inserted to project an image

→ In the eleventh century, people noticed that if a small hole were put in one wall of a darkened room, then light coming through the aperture would make a faint picture of the scene outside on the opposite wall of the room. A room like this was called a camera obscura. Artists later used a box to create a camera obscura, with a lens in its opening to make the picture clearer. But it was not possible to preserve the image that was produced in the box.

41. The word preserve in paragraph 1 is closest in meaning to
    (A) retain
    (B) retreat
    (C) defend
    (D) remedy

Paragraph 1 is marked with an arrow (→).

In the eleventh century, people noticed that if a small hole were put in one wall of a darkened room, then light coming through the aperture would make a faint picture of the scene outside on the opposite wall of the room. A room like this was called a camera obscura. Artists later used a box to create a camera obscura, with a lens in its opening to make the picture clearer. But it was not possible to preserve the image that was produced in the box.

42. Look at the word aperture in the passage. Select another word or phrase in the **bold** text that is closest in meaning to the word aperture.

43. Select the drawing that illustrates an example of the first camera obscura.

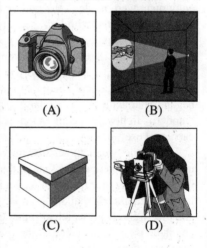

(A)   (B)

(C)   (D)

In the eleventh century, people noticed that if a small hole were put in one wall of a darkened room, then light coming through the aperture would make a faint picture of the scene outside on the opposite wall of the room. A room like this was called a camera obscura. Artists later used a box to create a camera obscura, with a lens in its opening to make the picture clearer. But it was not possible to preserve the image that was produced in the box.

→ In 1727, Johann Heinrich Schulze mixed chalk, silver, and nitric acid in a bottle. **He found that when the mixture was subjected to light, it became darker. In 1826, Joseph Nicéphore Niépce put some paper dipped in a light-sensitive chemical into his camera obscura, which he left exposed in a window. The result was probably the first permanent photographic image.**

The image Niépce made was a negative, a picture where all the white parts are black and all the black parts are white. Later, Louis Daguerre found a way to reverse the black and white parts to make positive prints. But when he looked at the pictures in the light, the chemicals continued to react and the pictures went dark. In 1837, he found a way to fix the image. These images are known as daguerreotypes.

Many developments of photographic equipment were made in the nineteenth century. Glass plates coated with light-sensitive chemicals were used to produce clear, sharp, positive prints on paper. In the 1870s, George Eastman proposed using rolls of paper film, coated with chemicals, to replace glass plates. Then, in 1888, Eastman began manufacturing the Kodak® camera, the first "modern" lightweight camera that people could carry and use.

During the twentieth century, many technological improvements were made. One of the most important was color film. Color film is made from layers of chemicals that are sensitive to red, green, and blue light, from which all other colors can be made. Despite the fact that the space age has witnessed the creation of an array of technological marvels, even the ability to take photographs of distant galaxies from above the Earth's atmosphere via orbiting satellites, the basic principles of photography have not changed since Niépce took his first fuzzy negative pictures.

44. Look at the word exposed in paragraph 2. Select another word or phrase in the **bold** text that is closest in meaning to the word exposed.

Paragraph 2 is marked with an arrow (→).

45. According to the passage, which of the following is most likely true?
    (A) In an attempt to preserve the image, artists added a lens to the camera obscura.
    (B) Johann Heinrich Schulze and Joseph Nicéphore Niépce collaborated in order to make the first permanent picture.
    (C) Johann Heinrich Schulze used Joseph Nicéphore Niépce's light-sensitive chemical to make his image permanent.
    (D) In the original camera obscura, people could observe on their wall a scene taking place on the outside of the room.

46. Which of the following people is NOT mentioned as working with photographic images?
    (A) Johann Heinrich Schulze
    (B) Joseph Nicéphore Niépce
    (C) Louis Daguerre
    (D) George Eastman

47. According to the passage, what problem did Daguerre encounter?
    (A) His pictures were all negative images.
    (B) He could not find a way to make positive images.
    (C) His positive images would darken.
    (D) He could not reverse the fixed image.

During the twentieth century, many technological improvements were made. One of the most important was color film. Color film is made from layers of chemicals that are sensitive to red, green, and blue light, from which all other colors can be made. Despite the fact that the space age has witnessed the creation of an array of technological marvels, even the ability to take photographs of distant galaxies from above the Earth's atmosphere via orbiting satellites, the basic principles of photography have not changed since Niépce took his first fuzzy negative pictures.

48. Look at the word **One** in the passage. Select the word or phrase in the **bold** text that **One** refers to.

[1] In the eleventh century, people noticed that if a small hole were put in one wall of a darkened room, then light coming through the aperture would make a faint picture of the scene outside on the opposite wall of the room. A room like this was called a camera obscura. Artists later used a box to create a camera obscura, with a lens in its opening to make the picture clearer. But it was not possible to preserve the image that was produced in the box.

[2] In 1727, Johann Heinrich Schulze mixed chalk, silver, and nitric acid in a bottle. He found that when the mixture was subjected to light, it became darker. In 1826, Joseph Nicéphore Niépce put some paper dipped in a light-sensitive chemical into his camera obscura, which he left exposed in a window. The result was probably the first permanent photographic image.

[3] The image Niépce made was a negative, a picture where all the white parts are black and all the black parts are white. Later, Louis Daguerre found a way to reverse the black and white parts to make positive prints. But when he looked at the pictures in the light, the chemicals continued to react and the pictures went dark. In 1837, he found a way to fix the image. These images are known as daguerreotypes.

49. Select the number of the paragraph in which the author compares present-day methods with those of the past.

50. Which of the following statements would the author probably agree with?
    (A) The Kodak® camera was the first portable camera to be developed.
    (B) Eastman was responsible for the development of color film.
    (C) Photographs of the earth from space are taken using a camera obscura.
    (D) Daguerreotypes were not effective permanent photographic images.

Read the rest of the passage on the next page.

4 Many developments of photographic equipment were made in the nineteenth century. Glass plates coated with light-sensitive chemicals were used to produce clear, sharp, positive prints on paper. In the 1870s, George Eastman proposed using rolls of paper film, coated with chemicals, to replace glass plates. Then, in 1888, Eastman began manufacturing the Kodak® camera, the first "modern" lightweight camera that people could carry and use.

5 During the twentieth century, many technological improvements were made. One of the most important was color film. Color film is made from layers of chemicals that are sensitive to red, green, and blue light, from which all other colors can be made. Despite the fact that the space age has witnessed the creation of an array of technological marvels, even the ability to take photographs of distant galaxies from above the Earth's atmosphere via orbiting satellites, the basic principles of photography have not changed since Niépce took his first fuzzy negative pictures.

This is the end of the Reading Section.

Go on to the Writing Section.

WRITING
Time – 30 minutes

Read the essay question carefully.

Think before you write. Making notes may help you to organize your essay. It is important to write only on the topic you are given.

Check your work. Allow a few minutes before time is up to read over your essay and make changes.

You have thirty minutes to complete the essay. On the real test, if you continue to write, it will be considered cheating.

Set your clock or watch for thirty minutes.
Now get ready to begin.

Directions: Read the question below and write an essay on a separate sheet of paper.

Do you agree or disagree with the following statement?

> *The nation-state is an outmoded institution and should be replaced with a world government.*

Use reasons and specific examples to support your opinion.

NOTES

Use this space for essay notes only. On the day of the Computer-Based TOEFL® Test, work done on the worksheet will not be scored.

This is the end of the Writing Section.

PRACTICE TEST 2
LISTENING
Time – approximately 60 minutes

This section measures your ability to understand spoken English. There are fifty questions in this section. The listening material and questions about it will be presented only one time. You may not take notes.

Part A

In this part, you will hear short conversations between two people. Each conversation is followed by a question about it. Each question in this part has four answer choices. Choose the best answer to each question. Answer the questions on the basis of what is <u>stated</u> or <u>implied</u> by the speakers.

 Now we will begin Part A with the first conversation.

1. What does the man mean?
   (A) The students asked people to make the props.
   (B) The students asked people to buy the props.
   (C) The students asked people to post the props.
   (D) The students asked people to contribute the props.

2. What does the man mean?
   (A) He couldn't get a ticket.
   (B) He bought a ticket weeks ago.
   (C) He reserved a ticket for tomorrow.
   (D) The concert has been canceled.

3. What does the woman mean?
   (A) Nancy will want to write her own notes.
   (B) She can't imagine Nancy writing notes.
   (C) She doesn't want to lend her notes to Nancy.
   (D) She thinks Nancy won't be able to read his notes.

4. What does the man mean?
   (A) Jennifer must learn those facts in order to graduate.
   (B) Jennifer must accept not being able to graduate.
   (C) Jennifer has faced many problems this spring.
   (D) Jennifer has to look for a spring.

5. What does the woman mean?
   (A) She set the flowers in the pail.
   (B) She bought the light-blue writing paper.
   (C) She had to water the flowers.
   (D) She got the blue flowers behind the station.

6. What does the man mean?
   (A) He is indifferent about the chemistry class.
   (B) He doesn't mind the chemistry class.
   (C) He isn't careful in chemistry class.
   (D) He doesn't like his chemistry class.

7. What does the woman mean?
   (A) Susie paid her the last week before Christmas.
   (B) Susie gave her the Christmas bonus.
   (C) Susie returned the money about two weeks ago.
   (D) Susie was going to pay her last week.

8. What did the man do?
   (A) He called for the string.
   (B) He cut his finger.
   (C) He fingered the tie.
   (D) He remembered the box.

9. What does the woman mean?
   (A) People are cheerful when they return from the stadium.
   (B) The stadium is so close that the spectators can be heard.
   (C) The noise from the stadium is too loud.
   (D) The stadium has clouds over it on most days.

10. What does the woman say about Jane?
    (A) There's nothing certain about Jane's success.
    (B) Jane's determination has nothing to do with her success.
    (C) Jane certainly is determined to be successful.
    (D) Jane's success has never been determined for certain.

11. What does the woman say about Mary?
    (A) Mary only passed this test because she scored higher than the others.
    (B) Mary's score was barely enough to pass.
    (C) Only on this test was Mary's score high enough.
    (D) Mary was the only one to pass the test.

12. What does the woman ask the man to do?
    (A) See if the paper that has come is hers
    (B) Check out the newspaper in the lobby
    (C) Use a check to buy her a newspaper
    (D) Find out whether or not her paper has arrived

13. What does the man suggest the woman do?
    (A) Extend her working hours
    (B) Meet with Dr. Joyce
    (C) Ask for more time
    (D) Get in line

14. What had the woman assumed about the flyers?
    (A) They hadn't yet been printed.
    (B) They weren't supposed to be handed out.
    (C) They had been given out already.
    (D) They hadn't passed inspection.

15. What does the woman imply?
    (A) Diane has already typed the essay.
    (B) Diane wouldn't do a good job.
    (C) Diane needs to do her work.
    (D) Diane doesn't really want to type
        the essay.

16. What does the woman imply about Rhoda?
    (A) She might look nice in turquoise.
    (B) She probably never wears necklaces.
    (C) She probably doesn't like jewelry.
    (D) She might not want a bracelet.

17. According to the woman, who does the
    best acting?
    (A) Carson
    (B) Angela
    (C) Terry
    (D) Nancy

18. What is the man's concern?
    (A) His friend has a very serious illness.
    (B) He has contaminated his professor's
        computer.
    (C) His friend's illness is contagious.
    (D) He forgot to check if his paper was
        on the diskette.

This is the end of Part A.
Go on to Part B.

Part B

In this part, there are several talks and conversations. Each talk or conversation is followed by several questions. The conversations and talks are about a variety of topics. You do not need special knowledge of the topics to answer the questions correctly. Rather, you should answer each question on the basis of what is <u>stated</u> or <u>implied</u> in the conversation or talk. You may not take notes.

 Now we will begin Part B with the first conversation.

19. What is the woman's problem?
    (A) She has lost her enthusiasm.
    (B) She feels differently about her course of study.
    (C) She has to drop some courses.
    (D) She hasn't done anything exciting for a semester.

20. What will the woman probably do?
    (A) Change her class schedule
    (B) Drop out of the university
    (C) Add another required course
    (D) Have fun instead of studying

22. What does the man say about history classes?
    (A) He finds them rather absorbing.
    (B) He dislikes them.
    (C) He has never taken one of Professor Lewis's classes.
    (D) He gets too involved with them.

21. What are the people discussing?
    (A) The period surrounding the Revolutionary War
    (B) Professor Lewis's American history class
    (C) How boring the first day of classes is
    (D) How to add and drop courses

23. What does the woman encourage the man to do?
    (A) Take Professor Lewis's course
    (B) Go to the movies
    (C) Drop other electives
    (D) Change his major

Now get ready to listen.

Now get ready to answer the questions.

24. What is the lecture about?
    (A) Facts about saffron
    (B) How important saffron is
    (C) How saffron is produced
    (D) The cost of saffron

26. What reason is given for saffron being known as the "king of spices"?
    (A) It is produced in Spain.
    (B) The finest variety comes from La Mancha.
    (C) It is one of the world's most prized foodstuffs.
    (D) It is obtained from the *Crocus sativus*.

25. Which part of this plant is used to produce saffron?

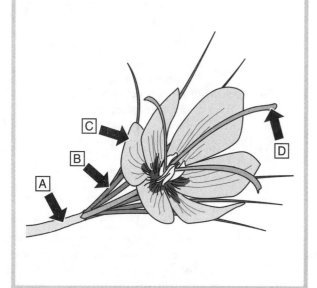

27. Besides Spain, which countries produce a significant amount of saffron?
    (A) India and Iran
    (B) Saudi Arabia and Bahrain
    (C) The United States and Italy
    (D) Middle Eastern countries and France

28. Which country is the biggest consumer of saffron?
    (A) Saudi Arabia
    (B) Bahrain
    (C) Spain
    (D) India

29. What is the relationship between the man and the woman?
    (A) They are strangers.
    (B) They are acquaintances.
    (C) They are members of a family.
    (D) They are in the same university class.

30. What does the woman want to know?
    (A) Which bus goes to the Music Complex
    (B) Where the Recreation Center Bus stops
    (C) What bus the man is taking
    (D) Where the Family Housing Bus goes

31. What can be inferred from the conversation?
    (A) The woman is going toward the Recreation Center.
    (B) The man is going to the Music Complex.
    (C) The woman enjoys sports.
    (D) The man is married.

32. How can the woman recognize the bus she wants?
    (A) It stops around the corner from the bookstore.
    (B) It will be at the stop in twenty minutes.
    (C) The Family Housing Bus comes before her bus.
    (D) It will have the letters "RC" above the windshield.

33. What can be said about the woman?
    (A) She usually walks to the Recreation Center.
    (B) She has an expensive car.
    (C) She doesn't drive during rush hour.
    (D) She's not used to taking the University Shuttle Bus.

Now get ready to listen.

Now get ready to answer the questions.

34. What is the lecture mainly about?
    - (A) What kinds of fossils can be recovered
    - (B) How fossils are scattered
    - (C) What prohibits fossilization
    - (D) What makes finding fossils relatively rare

35. What circumstances causing death will most likely ensure fossilization of an animal?

    Choose 2 answers.

    - A Being eaten by other animals
    - B Drowning
    - C Quick burial in a sandstorm
    - D Death by starvation

36. Why does the professor mention hyenas?
    - (A) To give an example of the type of animal found in the mountains
    - (B) To illustrate how animal bones reach the river bottom
    - (C) To name a type of animal that has been found fossilized
    - (D) To give an example of an animal that eats animal remains

37. What is the professor's attitude toward finding animal fossils?
    - (A) Optimistic about finding the fossils needed to complete the fossil record
    - (B) Realistic about the number of fossilized animals that can be found
    - (C) Confident about the possibility of finding fossils before they are exposed
    - (D) Concerned about the number of fossils that are washed away

38. The professor briefly explains a process. Summarize the process by putting the events in order.

    Write the letter of each sentence in the space where it belongs. Use each sentence only once.

    - A Erosion must eventually occur.
    - B A knowledgeable person must recognize the fossil.
    - C Layers of soil must be deposited over the carcass for a long period of time.
    - D The animal's death must occur in a situation where it will be buried quickly.

1	
2	
3	
4	

Now get ready to listen.

Now get ready to answer the questions.

39. What are the people discussing?
    (A) Illegal trading in weapons and drugs
    (B) The destruction of a country's national heritage
    (C) The development of electronic networks
    (D) Measures to control illicit trafficking of art treasures

40. Why does the professor mention the trade in weapons and drugs?
    (A) To illustrate how big the problem of illegal art trade is
    (B) To lecture against the use of drugs
    (C) To criticize the effectiveness of the International Police Organization
    (D) To explain how the black-market trade works

41. What does the professor say about electronic surveillance?
    (A) Some owners can't afford surveillance.
    (B) Many thieves are clever enough to steal objects under surveillance.
    (C) Some treasures aren't worth the expense.
    (D) Many governments don't care about the depletion of their treasures.

42. For which of the following pieces would the use of electronic surveillance be impractical?
    (A) A carving attached to the roof eaves of an old palace
    (B) A fountain in the middle of a busy city center
    (C) A painting in the storage room of a museum
    (D) A statue along a remote road

43. Which problem in policing the trade in national treasures was discussed?
    (A) The buyers are wealthy enough to pay officials to be quiet.
    (B) People are afraid to turn in information about the criminals.
    (C) The original owner cannot describe the property accurately.
    (D) The criminals change the work of art so it is unrecognizable.

44. What does the professor say about inventories of cultural properties?

    Choose 2 answers.

    A They are only useful if the information is widely available.
    B They could be used by criminals to find valuable treasures.
    C They would be useful for police as well as customs agencies and insurance companies.
    D They would help tourists from innocently getting involved in the black market.

Now get ready to listen.

Now get ready to answer the questions.

45. What is the lecture mainly about?
    (A) The relationship between music and screen action
    (B) The beginning of filmmaking
    (C) The development of film music
    (D) The importance of background music

46. The professor mentions three different composers. How does the music discussed in the lecture relate to the composers mentioned?

    Write the letter of each name in the space where it belongs. Use each name only once.

    A Camille Saint-Saëns
    B Max Steiner
    C Mendelssohn

Composed music, but not for film	Composed music for a French film
1.	2.

Composed music for soundtracks
3.

47. The professor briefly explains a process. Summarize the process by putting the events in order.

    Write the letter of each sentence in the space where it belongs. Use each sentence only once.

    A Music is heard, but without a visible means of production.
    B Music is performed by musicians in the movie theater.
    C Music is performed by musicians within the movie itself.
    D Music is underscoring the dialogue.

1	
2	
3	
4	

48. Why does the professor mention Mendelssohn's "Wedding March"?
    (A) To illustrate what kind of music was available in catalogs
    (B) To show how people might be confused if they could not see where the music was coming from
    (C) To give an example of music written specifically for a particular film
    (D) To highlight the kind of music that a player could improvise

49. According to the professor, in what ways
    was Max Steiner a pioneer of film scoring?

    Choose 2 answers.

    A He conducted music for films.
    B He experimented with background music.
    C He composed music to be played
       during dialogues.
    D He wrote the sophisticated music of today.

50. What event probably had the most influence
    on film music?
    (A) Camille Saint-Saëns's composition
        in 1908 of music for a specific film
    (B) The catalogs of music for specific
        dramatic purposes in the early 1910s
    (C) The synchronization of sound
        and image in 1922
    (D) The experiments with background
        music for film in the early 1930s

This is the end of the Listening Section.
Turn off your cassette or audio CD player now.

Go on to the Structure Section.

STRUCTURE

Time – 15 minutes

This section measures your ability to understand the structures of standard written English. There are twenty questions in this section. There are two types of questions.

The first type of question consists of incomplete sentences. Beneath each sentence there are four words or phrases. You will select the one word or phrase that best completes the sentence.

Example:

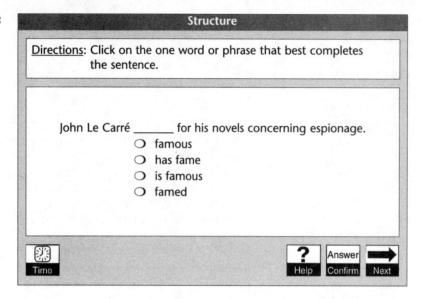

The second type of question consists of a sentence with four underlined words or phrases. You will select the one underlined word or phrase that must be changed for the sentence to be correct.

Example:

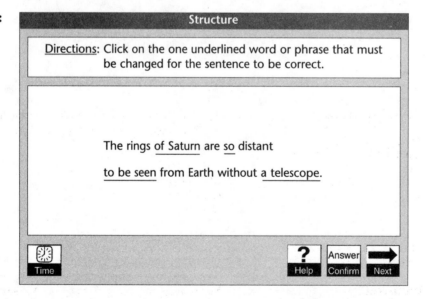

Now begin working on the Structure questions.

1. _____ infinitely large number of undiscovered galaxies.
   (A) An
   (B) There are an
   (C) From an
   (D) Since there are

2. For animals both humans, chewing helps
    A   B   C

   relieve tension.
   D

3. Square-rigged ships, _____ high speeds only when traveling with the trade winds, are not used commercially nowadays.
   (A) can attain
   (B) when attaining
   (C) they can attain
   (D) which can attain

4. An itch resulting when a nerve that can carry
             A   B

   pain is only slightly stimulated.
           C   D

5. By far, _____ of Saudi Arabia is oil.
   (A) it is the most important export
   (B) the most important export is
   (C) that is the most important export
   (D) the most important export

6. The whale's inexplicable predilection for
                    A

   beaching themselves is the second greatest
            B   C

   threat to its survival.
                    D

7. Yellowstone National Park's attractions include the famous Old Faithful geyser, vast forests, plentiful wildlife, and _____.
   (A) campgrounds are well maintained
   (B) campgrounds are maintained well
   (C) maintains campgrounds well
   (D) well-maintained campgrounds

8. America's first satellites exploded before it had
                    A   B

   risen three and a half feet off the ground.
   C   D

9. _____ the Dartmoor ewe and the Dumpy hen, the Tamworth pig is a rare breed of farm animal.
   (A) How
   (B) Like
   (C) The
   (D) Even

10. Most babies will grow up to be as cleverer
    A   B   C

    as their parents.
              D

11. _____ often serve as places of public
    entertainment and festivals, they can also
    be places where people can find peace and
    solitude.
    (A) Even though city parks
    (B) City parks
    (C) City parks that
    (D) There are city parks which

12. <u>Drying</u> food <u>by means</u> of solar energy
         A   B

    <u>is ancient</u> process <u>applied</u> wherever food
          C   D

    and climatic conditions make it possible.

13. _____ about genetic diseases has increased
    is welcome news.
    (A) That scientific knowledge
    (B) It was scientific knowledge
    (C) Though scientific knowledge
    (D) Scientific knowledge

14. Diane Arbus's <u>unusual</u> and controversial <u>work</u>
                      A   B

    includes <u>photograph</u> of celebrities of the <u>sixties</u>.
                  C   D

15. A fine tomb, _____, marks the grave of the
    poet Chaucer.
    (A) which in the fifteenth century was erecting
    (B) erected in the fifteenth century
    (C) erecting in the fifteenth century
    (D) being erected in the fifteenth century

16. It should not be <u>assume</u> that the <u>lower the</u>
                         A   B

    price, <u>the happier</u> the <u>buyer</u>.
                C   D

17. Not until about a century after Julius Caesar
    landed in Britain _____ actually conquer
    the island.
    (A) the Romans did
    (B) the Romans
    (C) Romans that
    (D) did the Romans

18. The Victorian constructions of Haight-Ashbury

    are <u>among</u> the <u>fewer</u> architectural <u>survivors</u>
           A   B   C

    of the San Francisco earthquake of <u>1906</u>.
                                          D

19. _____ perhaps the most awe inspiring among
    the great structures of the world.
    (A) The Great Wall of China
    (B) The Great Wall of China which is
    (C) The Great Wall of China is
    (D) That the Great Wall of China is

20. The <u>firing</u> of bricks and tiles <u>for use</u>
            A   B

    in the <u>build</u> industry requires large <u>amounts</u>
               C   D

    of fuel.

This is the end of the Structure Section.
Go on to the Reading Section.

READING

Time – 80 minutes
(including the reading of the passages)

In this section, you will read several passages. Each passage is followed by ten to fifteen questions. There are fifty questions in this section. You should answer all questions following a passage on the basis of what is <u>stated</u> or <u>implied</u> in that passage. For each question, select or write the correct answer.

Now begin reading the first passage.

Questions 1–11

Teotihuacán is the largest and most impressive urban archaeological site of ancient America, covering an area of roughly twenty square kilometers. The city was at one time thought to be the religious center of the Toltecs but is now believed to be a creation of an earlier civilization about whose origins little is known. The earliest artifacts from Teotihuacán date from over two thousand years ago, but the period of greatest expansion dates from A.D. 200 to A.D. 500. At its peak the city is estimated to have had a population of up to two hundred thousand inhabitants, with residential areas extending throughout the built-up area. Judging by regionally dispersed finds of the image of the rain god Tlaloc, of "thin orange wear" pottery, and of the characteristic architectural forms, the influence of Teotihuacán was widespread. It is not clear what caused the city's decline and eventual abandonment, but the evidence points to overpopulation, a depletion of resources, and the possible sacking by adversaries.

The primary axis of the city was the Avenue of the Dead, which extends for 2.5 kilometers through the center of the urban area, starting in the north at the Moon Plaza and continuing beyond the Great Compound complexes to the south. The avenue divided Teotihuacán into two sections with apartment compounds arranged on either side, often symmetrically, suggesting a highly planned layout from the earliest phases of construction.

The vast Pyramid of the Sun, located in the middle of the central zone, is the tallest and most dominant structure of Teotihuacán, with a height of 65 meters and a base covering approximately ten acres. At one time the edifice was surmounted by a temple. A cave located underneath the pyramid and possibly used for ritual activities hints at its religious importance. The Pyramids of the Moon and Feathered Serpent are other notable ceremonial sites nearby.

A particular feature of the architecture of many of the pyramidal platforms at this site is the series of sloping apron walls, known as *taluds*, interspersed with vertical panels – *tableros* – producing a steplike appearance. Originally all such structures would have been covered with a layer of stucco and then painted, often with pictures of animals and mythological creatures.

1. What is the passage mainly about?
   (A) The inhabitants of Teotihuacán
   (B) A large and ancient American city
   (C) Pyramid constructions of Teotihuacán
   (D) Life in an ancient American city

→ ⎡1⎤ Teotihuacán is the largest and most impressive urban archaeological site of ancient America, covering an area of roughly twenty square kilometers. ⎡2⎤ The city was at one time thought to be the religious center of the Toltecs but is now believed to be a creation of an earlier civilization about whose origins little is known. ⎡3⎤ The earliest artifacts from Teotihuacán date from over two thousand years ago, but the period of greatest expansion dates from A.D. 200 to A.D. 500. ⎡4⎤ At its peak the city is estimated to have had a population of up to two hundred thousand inhabitants, with residential areas extending throughout the built-up area. ⎡5⎤ Judging by regionally dispersed finds of the image of the rain god Tlaloc, of "thin orange wear" pottery, and of the characteristic architectural forms, the influence of Teotihuacán was widespread. ⎡6⎤ It is not clear what caused the city's decline and eventual abandonment, but the evidence points to overpopulation, a depletion of resources, and the possible sacking by adversaries.

2. Select the number of the sentence in paragraph 1 in which the founders of Teotihuacán are referred to.

Paragraph 1 is marked with an arrow (→).

→ Teotihuacán is the largest and most impressive urban archaeological site of ancient America, covering an area of roughly twenty square kilometers. The city was at one time thought to be the religious center of the Toltecs but is now believed to be a creation of an earlier civilization about whose origins little is known. The earliest artifacts from Teotihuacán date from over two thousand years ago, but the period of greatest expansion dates from A.D. 200 to A.D. 500. At its peak the city is estimated to have had a population of up to two hundred thousand inhabitants, with residential areas extending throughout the built-up area. Judging by regionally dispersed finds of the image of the rain god Tlaloc, of "thin orange wear" pottery, and of the characteristic architectural forms, the influence of Teotihuacán was widespread. It is not clear what caused the city's decline and eventual abandonment, but the evidence points to overpopulation, a depletion of resources, and the possible sacking by adversaries.

3. The word dispersed in paragraph 1 is closest in meaning to
   (A) displaced
   (B) produced
   (C) assembled
   (D) scattered

Paragraph 1 is marked with an arrow (→).

4. According to the passage, which of the following statements about the decline of Teotihuacán is known to be true?
   (A) The people migrated to another city.
   (B) The population of the city starved.
   (C) It was invaded by neighbors.
   (D) The cause of its decline is uncertain.

→ Teotihuacán is the largest and most impressive urban archaeological site of ancient America, covering an area of roughly twenty square kilometers. The city was at one time thought to be the religious center of the Toltecs but is now believed to be a creation of an earlier civilization about whose origins little is known. The earliest artifacts from Teotihuacán date from over two thousand years ago, but the period of greatest expansion dates from A.D. 200 to A.D. 500. At its peak the city is estimated to have had a population of up to two hundred thousand inhabitants, with residential areas extending throughout the built-up area. Judging by regionally dispersed finds of the image of the rain god Tlaloc, of "thin orange wear" pottery, and of the characteristic architectural forms, the influence of Teotihuacán was widespread. It is not clear what caused the city's decline and eventual abandonment, but the evidence points to overpopulation, a depletion of resources, and the possible sacking by adversaries.

The primary axis of the city was the Avenue of the Dead, which extends for 2.5 kilometers through the center of the urban area, starting in the north at the Moon Plaza and continuing beyond the Great Compound complexes to the south. The avenue divided Teotihuacán into two sections with apartment compounds arranged on either side, often symmetrically, suggesting a highly planned layout from the earliest phases of construction.

The vast Pyramid of the Sun, located in the middle of the central zone, is the tallest and most dominant structure of Teotihuacán, with a height of 65 meters and a base covering approximately ten acres. At one time the edifice was surmounted by a temple. A cave located underneath the pyramid and possibly used for ritual activities hints at its religious importance. The Pyramids of the Moon and Feathered Serpent are other notable ceremonial sites nearby.

A particular feature of the architecture of many of the pyramidal platforms at this site is the series of sloping apron walls, known as *taluds*, interspersed with vertical panels – *tableros* – producing a steplike appearance. Originally all such structures would have been covered with a layer of stucco and then painted, often with pictures of animals and mythological creatures.

5. The word adversaries in paragraph 1 is closest in meaning to
   (A) allies
   (B) rivals
   (C) civilians
   (D) attackers

Paragraph 1 is marked with an arrow (→).

6. All of the following are mentioned as having been found in the Teotihuacán area EXCEPT
   (A) market streets
   (B) religious artifacts
   (C) ceremonial structures
   (D) residential districts

7. Look at the phrase **urban area** in the passage. Select another word or phrase in the **bold** text that is closest in meaning to the phrase **urban area**.

The vast **Pyramid of the Sun, located in the middle of the central zone, is the tallest and most dominant structure of Teotihuacán, with a height of 65 meters and a base covering approximately ten acres. At one time the edifice was surmounted by a temple. A cave located underneath the pyramid and possibly used for ritual activities hints at its religious importance.** The Pyramids of the Moon and Feathered Serpent are other notable ceremonial sites nearby.

8. Look at the word **edifice** in the passage. Select another word or phrase in the **bold** text that is closest in meaning to the word **edifice**.

9. It can be inferred from the passage that the function of the Pyramid of the Sun was
   (A) military
   (B) residential
   (C) ceremonial
   (D) administrative

A particular feature of the architecture of many of the pyramidal platforms at this site is the series of sloping apron walls, known as *taluds*, interspersed with vertical panels – *tableros* – producing a steplike appearance. Originally all such structures would have been covered with a layer of stucco and then painted, often with pictures of animals and mythological creatures.

10. Select the illustration that shows the typical pyramid found at Teotihuacán.

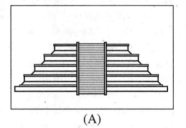

(A)

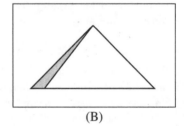

(B)

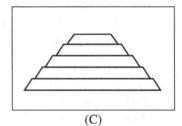

(C)

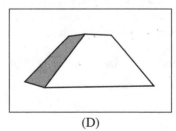

(D)

Teotihuacán is the largest and most impressive urban archaeological site of ancient America, covering an area of roughly twenty square kilometers. The city was at one time thought to be the religious center of the Toltecs but is now believed to be a creation of an earlier civilization about whose origins little is known. The earliest artifacts from Teotihuacán date from over two thousand years ago, but the period of greatest expansion dates from A.D. 200 to A.D. 500. At its peak the city is estimated to have had a population of up to two hundred thousand inhabitants, with residential areas extending throughout the built-up area. Judging by regionally dispersed finds of the image of the rain god Tlaloc, of "thin orange wear" pottery, and of the characteristic architectural forms, the influence of Teotihuacán was widespread. It is not clear what caused the city's decline and eventual abandonment, but the evidence points to overpopulation, a depletion of resources, and the possible sacking by adversaries.

The primary axis of the city was the Avenue of the Dead, which extends for 2.5 kilometers through the center of the urban area, starting in the north at the Moon Plaza and continuing beyond the Great Compound complexes to the south. The avenue divided Teotihuacán into two sections with apartment compounds arranged on either side, often symmetrically, suggesting a highly planned layout from the earliest phases of construction.

The vast Pyramid of the Sun, located in the middle of the central zone, is the tallest and most dominant structure of Teotihuacán, with a height of 65 meters and a base covering approximately ten acres. At one time the edifice was surmounted by a temple. A cave located underneath the pyramid and possibly used for ritual activities hints at its religious importance. The Pyramids of the Moon and Feathered Serpent are other notable ceremonial sites nearby.

A particular feature of the architecture of many of the pyramidal platforms at this site is the series of sloping apron walls, known as *taluds*, interspersed with vertical panels – *tableros* – producing a steplike appearance. Originally all such structures would have been covered with a layer of stucco and then painted, often with pictures of animals and mythological creatures.

11. In the passage, which of the following is NOT implied about the people who built Teotihuacán?
    (A) Their influence was extensive.
    (B) They worshipped several gods.
    (C) They were architecturally accomplished.
    (D) They were militarily aggressive.

Questions 12–25

Generations of American school children have been taught the story of how the Great Fire of Chicago of October 1871 was started by Daisy, a cow belonging to one Mrs. O'Leary. The cow, stabled in a barn behind Mrs. O'Leary's house, apparently kicked over a kerosene lamp, which set fire to hay and other combustible materials stored there. The blaze quickly spread, and fanned by a strong southwest wind and aided by intensely dry conditions, the conflagration engulfed and entirely destroyed more than three square miles of built-up area. Almost one hundred thousand people were left homeless, and about three hundred lost their lives. Property damage was estimated at two hundred million dollars, an immense sum in those days.

Soon after the fire, the O'Leary-cow story became an almost unchallenged truth and, over the years, took on the status of a modern-day myth – a staple ingredient in the fabric of American folklore. However, there are good reasons to believe that neither Mrs. O'Leary nor Daisy was culpable. First, a police reporter later claimed to have invented the whole story. Of course, this is not a conclusive refutation, but his reasoning was valid and his alternative suggestions credible. Furthermore, the testimony of one of the main witnesses, a neighbor called "Peg Leg" Sullivan, is now thought to be questionable. Some claim he invented the story to avoid censure, since he himself was not above suspicion and there were inconsistencies in his account. Other accusers have focused the blame on a variety of targets – some local boys smoking in the barn, a different neighbor, an unnamed terrorist organization, spontaneous combustion, and, most recently, an asteroid. This last theory gains credence from the fact that on the same night as the Chicago fire, neighboring states suffered more than a dozen major fires. One fire destroyed the entire town of Peshtigo, Wisconsin, with the loss of more than twelve hundred lives.

Whatever the real origin of the fire, the truth is that it was inevitable, given the near-drought conditions of the time and the fact that much of the city consisted of densely packed wooden shacks served by an undermanned fire department. It seems that Mrs. O'Leary and her cow were perhaps no more than convenient and vulnerable scapegoats on which a devastated populace could center its frustrations.

12. What would be a good title for the passage?
    (A) The Great Fire of Chicago
    (B) The Legend of Mrs. O'Leary's Cow
    (C) Daisy and Other Scapegoats
    (D) "Peg Leg" Sullivan's Testimony

Generations of American school children have been taught the story of how the Great Fire of Chicago of October 1871 was started by Daisy, a cow belonging to one Mrs. O'Leary. **The cow, stabled in a barn behind Mrs. O'Leary's house, apparently kicked over a kerosene lamp, which set fire to hay and other combustible materials stored there. The blaze quickly spread, and fanned by a strong southwest wind and aided by intensely dry conditions, the conflagration engulfed and entirely destroyed more than three square miles of built-up area.** Almost one hundred thousand people were left homeless, and about three hundred lost their lives. Property damage was estimated at two hundred million dollars, an immense sum in those days.

13. Look at the word **there** in the passage. Select the word or phrase in the **bold** text that **there** refers to.

Generations of American school children have been taught the story of how the Great Fire of Chicago of October 1871 was started by Daisy, a cow belonging to one Mrs. O'Leary. The cow, stabled in a barn behind Mrs. O'Leary's house, apparently kicked over a kerosene lamp, which set fire to hay and other combustible materials stored there. **The blaze quickly spread, and fanned by a strong southwest wind and aided by intensely dry conditions, the conflagration engulfed and entirely destroyed more than three square miles of built-up area. Almost one hundred thousand people were left homeless, and about three hundred lost their lives. Property damage was estimated at two hundred million dollars, an immense sum in those days.**

14. Look at the word **blaze** in the passage. Select another word or phrase in the **bold** text that is closest in meaning to the word **blaze**.

→ Generations of American school children have been taught the story of how the Great Fire of Chicago of October 1871 was started by Daisy, a cow belonging to one Mrs. O'Leary. The cow, stabled in a barn behind Mrs. O'Leary's house, apparently kicked over a kerosene lamp, which set fire to hay and other combustible materials stored there. The blaze quickly spread, and fanned by a strong southwest wind and aided by intensely dry conditions, the conflagration engulfed and entirely destroyed more than three square miles of built-up area. Almost one hundred thousand people were left homeless, and about three hundred lost their lives. Property damage was estimated at two hundred million dollars, an immense sum in those days.

15. The word fanned in paragraph 1 is closest in meaning to
   (A) intensified
   (B) irritated
   (C) cooled
   (D) funneled

Paragraph 1 is marked with an arrow (→).

→ Generations of American school children have been taught the story of how the Great Fire of Chicago of October 1871 was started by Daisy, a cow belonging to one Mrs. O'Leary. The cow, stabled in a barn behind Mrs. O'Leary's house, apparently kicked over a kerosene lamp, which set fire to hay and other combustible materials stored there. 1 The blaze quickly spread, and fanned by a strong southwest wind and aided by intensely dry conditions, the conflagration engulfed and entirely destroyed more than three square miles of built-up area. 2 Almost one hundred thousand people were left homeless, and about three hundred lost their lives. 3 Property damage was estimated at two hundred million dollars, an immense sum in those days. 4

16. The following sentence can be added to paragraph 1.

The fire was finally extinguished near midnight on the second day of devastation.

Where would it best fit in the paragraph?

Select the square (☐) that shows where the sentence should be added.

Paragraph 1 is marked with an arrow (➜).

→ Soon after the fire, the O'Leary-cow story became an almost unchallenged truth and, over the years, took on the status of a modern-day myth – a staple ingredient in the fabric of American folklore. However, there are good reasons to believe that neither Mrs. O'Leary nor Daisy was culpable. First, a police reporter later claimed to have invented the whole story. Of course, this is not a conclusive refutation, but his reasoning was valid and his alternative suggestions credible. Furthermore, the testimony of one of the main witnesses, a neighbor called "Peg Leg" Sullivan, is now thought to be questionable. Some claim he invented the story to avoid censure, since he himself was not above suspicion and there were inconsistencies in his account. Other accusers have focused the blame on a variety of targets – some local boys smoking in the barn, a different neighbor, an unnamed terrorist organization, spontaneous combustion, and, most recently, an asteroid. This last theory gains credence from the fact that on the same night as the Chicago fire, neighboring states suffered more than a dozen major fires. One fire destroyed the entire town of Peshtigo, Wisconsin, with the loss of more than twelve hundred lives.

17. Why does the author mention myth and folklore in paragraph 2?
    (A) To prove that cows do not start fires in barns
    (B) To convince the reader that the fire had never taken place
    (C) To ridicule the unreliable theories that abound in textbooks
    (D) To show the importance of the O'Leary-cow story in American culture

Paragraph 2 is marked with an arrow (➜).

18. What did "Peg Leg" Sullivan do?
    (A) Set the barn on fire
    (B) Accused some local boys
    (C) Gave a suspicious account
    (D) Made some believable alternative suggestions

Soon after the fire, the O'Leary-cow story became an almost unchallenged truth and, over the years, took on the status of a modern-day myth – a staple ingredient in the fabric of American folklore. However, there are good reasons to believe that neither Mrs. O'Leary nor Daisy was culpable. First, a police reporter later claimed to have invented the whole story. Of course, this is not a conclusive refutation, but his reasoning was valid and his alternative suggestions credible. **Furthermore, the testimony of one of the main witnesses, a neighbor called "Peg Leg" Sullivan, is now thought to be questionable. Some claim he invented the story to avoid censure, since he himself was not above suspicion and there were inconsistencies in his account. Other accusers have focused the blame on a variety of targets – some local boys smoking in the barn, a different neighbor, an unnamed terrorist organization, spontaneous combustion, and, most recently, an asteroid.** This last theory gains credence from the fact that on the same night as the Chicago fire, neighboring states suffered more than a dozen major fires. One fire destroyed the entire town of Peshtigo, Wisconsin, with the loss of more than twelve hundred lives.

19. Look at the word **censure** in the passage. Select the word or phrase in the **bold** text that is closest in meaning to the word **censure**.

20. Which of the following is NOT mentioned as a possible cause of the Great Fire of Chicago?
    (A) Mischievous boys
    (B) A stabled cow
    (C) A group of terrorists
    (D) A police reporter

→ 1 Soon after the fire, the O'Leary-cow story became an almost unchallenged truth and, over the years, took on the status of a modern-day myth – a staple ingredient in the fabric of American folklore. 2 However, there are good reasons to believe that neither Mrs. O'Leary nor Daisy was culpable. 3 First, a police reporter later claimed to have invented the whole story. 4 Of course, this is not a conclusive refutation, but his reasoning was valid and his alternative suggestions credible. 5 Furthermore, the testimony of one of the main witnesses, a neighbor called "Peg Leg" Sullivan, is now thought to be questionable. 6 Some claim he invented the story to avoid censure, since he himself was not above suspicion and there were inconsistencies in his account. 7 Other accusers have focused the blame on a variety of targets – some local boys smoking in the barn, a different neighbor, an unnamed terrorist organization, spontaneous combustion, and, most recently, an asteroid. 8 This last theory gains credence from the fact that on the same night as the Chicago fire, neighboring states suffered more than a dozen major fires. One fire destroyed the entire town of Peshtigo, Wisconsin, with the loss of more than twelve hundred lives.

21. Select the number of the sentence in paragraph 2 that gives support to a credible cause of the fire.

Paragraph 2 is marked with an arrow (→).

➜   Soon after the fire, the O'Leary-cow story became an almost unchallenged truth and, over the years, took on the status of a modern-day myth – a staple ingredient in the fabric of American folklore. However, there are good reasons to believe that neither Mrs. O'Leary nor Daisy was culpable. First, a police reporter later claimed to have invented the whole story. Of course, this is not a conclusive refutation, but his reasoning was valid and his alternative suggestions credible. Furthermore, the testimony of one of the main witnesses, a neighbor called "Peg Leg" Sullivan, is now thought to be questionable. Some claim he invented the story to avoid censure, since he himself was not above suspicion and there were inconsistencies in his account. Other accusers have focused the blame on a variety of targets – some local boys smoking in the barn, a different neighbor, an unnamed terrorist organization, spontaneous combustion, and, most recently, an asteroid. This last theory gains credence from the fact that on the same night as the Chicago fire, neighboring states suffered more than a dozen major fires. One fire destroyed the entire town of Peshtigo, Wisconsin, with the loss of more than twelve hundred lives.

22. Why does the author mention Peshtigo, Wisconsin, in paragraph 2?
(A) To give an example of another fire that occurred that night
(B) To question why there is not a story called the Great Fire of Peshtigo
(C) To show how organized terrorist groups were
(D) To compare the undermanned fire departments of both cities

Paragraph 2 is marked with an arrow (➜).

➜   Whatever the real origin of the fire, the truth is that it was inevitable, given the near-drought conditions of the time and the fact that much of the city consisted of densely packed wooden shacks served by an undermanned fire department. It seems that Mrs. O'Leary and her cow were perhaps no more than convenient and vulnerable scapegoats on which a devastated populace could center its frustrations.

23. The word shacks in paragraph 3 is closest in meaning to
(A) boxes
(B) huts
(C) platforms
(D) crates

Paragraph 3 is marked with an arrow (➜).

24. Which of the following is NOT mentioned as a reason that the fire was so devastating?
(A) The lack of rain
(B) Fire-prone building materials
(C) Too few firefighters
(D) A riotous populace

Generations of American school children have been taught the story of how the Great Fire of Chicago of October 1871 was started by Daisy, a cow belonging to one Mrs. O'Leary. The cow, stabled in a barn behind Mrs. O'Leary's house, apparently kicked over a kerosene lamp, which set fire to hay and other combustible materials stored there. The blaze quickly spread, and fanned by a strong southwest wind and aided by intensely dry conditions, the conflagration engulfed and entirely destroyed more than three square miles of built-up area. Almost one hundred thousand people were left homeless, and about three hundred lost their lives. Property damage was estimated at two hundred million dollars, an immense sum in those days.

Soon after the fire, the O'Leary-cow story became an almost unchallenged truth and, over the years, took on the status of a modern-day myth – a staple ingredient in the fabric of American folklore. However, there are good reasons to believe that neither Mrs. O'Leary nor Daisy was culpable. First, a police reporter later claimed to have invented the whole story. Of course, this is not a conclusive refutation, but his reasoning was valid and his alternative suggestions credible. Furthermore, the testimony of one of the main witnesses, a neighbor called "Peg Leg" Sullivan, is now thought to be questionable. Some claim he invented the story to avoid censure, since he himself was not above suspicion and there were inconsistencies in his account. Other accusers have focused the blame on a variety of targets – some local boys smoking in the barn, a different neighbor, an unnamed terrorist organization, spontaneous combustion, and, most recently, an asteroid. This last theory gains credence from the fact that on the same night as the Chicago fire, neighboring states suffered more than a dozen major fires. One fire destroyed the entire town of Peshtigo, Wisconsin, with the loss of more than twelve hundred lives.

Whatever the real origin of the fire, the truth is that it was inevitable, given the near-drought conditions of the time and the fact that much of the city consisted of densely packed wooden shacks served by an undermanned fire department. It seems that Mrs. O'Leary and her cow were perhaps no more than convenient and vulnerable scapegoats on which a devastated populace could center its frustrations.

25. Why is the fire known as the Great Fire of Chicago?
    (A) Because it was such a destructive fire
    (B) Because the O'Leary-cow story is a great story
    (C) Because the fire has become a staple ingredient of American folklore
    (D) Because American children are taught about it

Questions 26–38

→ On December 4, 1872, the brigantine *Mary Celeste*, carrying 1,700 barrels of crude alcohol en route from New York to Genoa, was found abandoned and drifting in the Atlantic Ocean between the Azores and Portugal. The crew of the *Dei Gratia*, the cargo ship that found the *Mary Celeste*, inspected her carefully and then sailed her to Gibraltar to collect the large salvage reward. Their report given at the inquiry suggests that the captain, his wife, his young daughter, and the seven-man crew had deserted the ship in a great hurry. The captain's bed was unmade, something unheard of in a well-run ship, which the *Mary Celeste* was known to be. The oilskin boots and pipes belonging to the crew had also been left, although the chronometer, sextant, and lifeboat were missing. The arrangement of the sails also suggested sudden abandonment. The cargo was intact, although some barrels had leaked and two of the hatches were not in place.

Several theories have been propounded to explain why those aboard left a perfectly seaworthy vessel to risk their lives in an open boat. It has been suggested that they were the victims of alien abduction or sea-monster attacks. Such outlandish notions are hardly credible. The idea that the ship was a victim of piracy can also be discounted, since the cargo and other valuables were untouched. Likewise, mutiny does not seem plausible, since the captain and first officer were known to be fair and experienced, the voyage was relatively short, and mutineers would probably have taken over the ship, not forsaken it.

A possible explanation is that some event made the captain fear for the safety of the ship. In fact, recently studied seismic records indicate that a violent earthquake, whose epicenter was on the seafloor in the region where the *Mary Celeste* was sailing, occurred some days before the ship's discovery. If the ship had been subjected to intense shocks caused by the quake, all aboard may have hastily abandoned ship to avoid what they imagined might be its imminent destruction from an explosion of the combustible cargo. A severed rope found dangling from the side of the *Mary Celeste* suggests that the evacuees trailed behind in the lifeboat, attached to the ship, waiting for the crisis to pass. Great waves may then have snapped the rope and capsized the smaller boat, whose occupants would have disappeared without a trace.

26. Which of the following is the main topic of paragraph 1?
    (A) The finding of the *Mary Celeste*
    (B) The salvaging of the *Mary Celeste*
    (C) The abandonment of the *Mary Celeste*
    (D) The fate of the *Mary Celeste*

Paragraph 1 is marked with an arrow (→).

→ ⎿1⏌ On December 4, 1872, the brigantine *Mary Celeste*, carrying 1,700 barrels of crude alcohol en route from New York to Genoa, was found abandoned and drifting in the Atlantic Ocean between the Azores and Portugal. ⎿2⏌ The crew of the *Dei Gratia*, the cargo ship that found the *Mary Celeste*, inspected her carefully and then sailed her to Gibraltar to collect the large salvage reward. ⎿3⏌ Their report given at the inquiry suggests that the captain, his wife, his young daughter, and the seven-man crew had deserted the ship in a great hurry. ⎿4⏌ The captain's bed was unmade, something unheard of in a well-run ship, which the *Mary Celeste* was known to be. ⎿5⏌ The oilskin boots and pipes belonging to the crew had also been left, although the chronometer, sextant, and lifeboat were missing. ⎿6⏌ The arrangement of the sails also suggested sudden abandonment. ⎿7⏌ The cargo was intact, although some barrels had leaked and two of the hatches were not in place.

27. Select the number of the sentence in paragraph 1 that indicates the crew of the *Dei Gratia* hoped to be compensated for bringing in the *Mary Celeste*.

Paragraph 1 is marked with an arrow (→).

On December 4, 1872, the brigantine *Mary Celeste*, carrying 1,700 barrels of crude alcohol en route from New York to Genoa, was found abandoned and drifting in the Atlantic Ocean between the Azores and Portugal. The crew of the *Dei Gratia*, the cargo ship that found the *Mary Celeste*, inspected her carefully and then sailed her to Gibraltar to collect the large salvage reward. Their report given at the inquiry suggests that the captain, his wife, his young daughter, and the seven-man crew had deserted the ship in a great hurry. The captain's bed was unmade, something unheard of in a well-run ship, which the *Mary Celeste* was known to be. The oilskin boots and pipes belonging to the crew had also been left, although the chronometer, sextant, and lifeboat were missing. The arrangement of the sails also suggested sudden abandonment. The cargo was intact, although some barrels had leaked and two of the hatches were not in place.

28. Look at the word **Their** in the passage. Select another word or phrase in the **bold** text that **Their** refers to.

On December 4, 1872, the brigantine *Mary Celeste*, carrying 1,700 barrels of crude alcohol en route from New York to Genoa, was found abandoned and drifting in the Atlantic Ocean between the Azores and Portugal. The crew of the *Dei Gratia*, the cargo ship that found the *Mary Celeste*, inspected her carefully and then sailed her to Gibraltar to collect the large salvage reward. Their report given at the inquiry suggests that the captain, his wife, his young daughter, and the seven-man crew had deserted the ship in a great hurry. The captain's bed was unmade, something unheard of in a well-run ship, which the *Mary Celeste* was known to be. The oilskin boots and pipes belonging to the crew had also been left, although the chronometer, sextant, and lifeboat were missing. The arrangement of the sails also suggested sudden abandonment. The cargo was intact, although some barrels had leaked and two of the hatches were not in place.

29. Look at the word **deserted** in the passage. Select another word or phrase in the **bold** text that is closest in meaning to the word **deserted** .

Several theories have been propounded to explain why those aboard left a perfectly seaworthy vessel to risk their lives in an open boat. It has been suggested that they were the victims of alien abduction or sea-monster attacks. Such outlandish notions are hardly credible. The idea that the ship was a victim of piracy can also be discounted, since the cargo and other valuables were untouched. Likewise, mutiny does not seem plausible, since the captain and first officer were known to be fair and experienced, the voyage was relatively short, and mutineers would probably have taken over the ship, not forsaken it.

30. Look at the word **propounded** in the passage. Select another word or phrase in the **bold** text that is closest in meaning to the word **propounded** .

Several theories have been propounded to explain why those aboard left a perfectly seaworthy vessel to risk their lives in an open boat. It has been suggested that they were the victims of alien abduction or sea-monster attacks. Such outlandish notions are hardly credible. The idea that the ship was a victim of piracy can also be discounted, since the cargo and other valuables were untouched. Likewise, mutiny does not seem plausible, since the captain and first officer were known to be fair and experienced, the voyage was relatively short, and mutineers would probably have taken over the ship, not forsaken it.

31. What does the author mean by outlandish notions?
    (A) It is odd that the mutineers would also abandon ship.
    (B) It is strange for a pirate not to take the cargo of a ship.
    (C) Mutinies do not occur when captains are fair and experienced.
    (D) Alien abductions and sea-monster attacks are unlikely explanations.

→ Several theories have been propounded to explain why those aboard left a perfectly seaworthy vessel to risk their lives in an open boat. It has been suggested that they were the victims of alien abduction or sea-monster attacks. Such outlandish notions are hardly credible. The idea that the ship was a victim of piracy can also be discounted, since the cargo and other valuables were untouched. Likewise, mutiny does not seem plausible, since the captain and first officer were known to be fair and experienced, the voyage was relatively short, and mutineers would probably have taken over the ship, not forsaken it.

32. What can be understood about the theories the author of the passage presents in paragraph 2?
    (A) Some were validated by the facts presented in the inquiry.
    (B) None explain the mystery satisfactorily.
    (C) None take into account the *Dei Gratia*'s part in the mystery.
    (D) Some are convincing, considering the outcome.

Paragraph 2 is marked with an arrow (→).

Several theories have been propounded to explain why those aboard left a perfectly seaworthy vessel to risk their lives in an open boat. It has been suggested that they were the victims of alien abduction or sea-monster attacks. **Such outlandish notions are hardly credible. The idea that the ship was a victim of piracy can also be discounted, since the cargo and other valuables were untouched. Likewise, mutiny does not seem plausible, since the captain and first officer were known to be fair and experienced, the voyage was relatively short, and mutineers would probably have taken over the ship, not forsaken it.**

33. Look at the word **plausible** in the passage. Select another word or phrase in the **bold** text that is closest in meaning to the word **plausible**.

A possible explanation is that some event made the captain fear for the safety of the ship. In fact, recently studied seismic records indicate that a violent earthquake, whose epicenter was on the seafloor in the region where the *Mary Celeste* was sailing, occurred some days before the ship's discovery. If the ship had been subjected to intense shocks caused by the quake, all aboard may have hastily abandoned ship to avoid what they imagined might be its imminent destruction from an explosion of the combustible cargo. A severed rope found dangling from the side of the *Mary Celeste* suggests that the evacuees trailed behind in the lifeboat, attached to the ship, waiting for the crisis to pass. Great waves may then have snapped the rope and capsized the smaller boat, whose occupants would have disappeared without a trace.

34. Look at the word **they** in the passage. Select another word or phrase in the **bold** text that **they** refers to.

→ A possible explanation is that some event made the captain fear for the safety of the ship. In fact, recently studied seismic records indicate that a violent earthquake, whose epicenter was on the seafloor in the region where the *Mary Celeste* was sailing, occurred some days before the ship's discovery. If the ship had been subjected to intense shocks caused by the quake, all aboard may have hastily abandoned ship to avoid what they imagined might be its imminent destruction from an explosion of the combustible cargo. A severed rope found dangling from the side of the *Mary Celeste* suggests that the evacuees trailed behind in the lifeboat, attached to the ship, waiting for the crisis to pass. Great waves may then have snapped the rope and capsized the smaller boat, whose occupants would have disappeared without a trace.

35. The word imminent in paragraph 3 is closest in meaning to
(A) impending
(B) atrocious
(C) inevitable
(D) prospective

Paragraph 3 is marked with an arrow (→).

→ A possible explanation is that some event made the captain fear for the safety of the ship. In fact, recently studied seismic records indicate that a violent earthquake, whose epicenter was on the seafloor in the region where the *Mary Celeste* was sailing, occurred some days before the ship's discovery. If the ship had been subjected to intense shocks caused by the quake, all aboard may have hastily abandoned ship to avoid what they imagined might be its imminent destruction from an explosion of the combustible cargo. A severed rope found dangling from the side of the *Mary Celeste* suggests that the evacuees trailed behind in the lifeboat, attached to the ship, waiting for the crisis to pass. Great waves may then have snapped the rope and capsized the smaller boat, whose occupants would have disappeared without a trace.

36. The word capsized in paragraph 3 is closest in meaning to
(A) detached
(B) splintered
(C) submerged
(D) overturned

Paragraph 3 is marked with an arrow (→).

→ A possible explanation is that some event made the captain fear for the safety of the ship. In fact, recently studied seismic records indicate that a violent earthquake, whose epicenter was on the seafloor in the region where the *Mary Celeste* was sailing, occurred some days before the ship's discovery. If the ship had been subjected to intense shocks caused by the quake, all aboard may have hastily abandoned ship to avoid what they imagined might be its imminent destruction from an explosion of the combustible cargo. A severed rope found dangling from the side of the *Mary Celeste* suggests that the evacuees trailed behind in the lifeboat, attached to the ship, waiting for the crisis to pass. Great waves may then have snapped the rope and capsized the smaller boat, whose occupants would have disappeared without a trace.

37. According to paragraph 3, what might the captain have been afraid of happening?
    (A) The ship's being torn apart by the intense shocks
    (B) The ship's being swallowed in the earthquake
    (C) The ship's catching fire because of the alcohol
    (D) The ship's keeling over because of the large waves

Paragraph 3 is marked with an arrow (→).

→ 1 A possible explanation is that some event made the captain fear for the safety of the ship. 2 In fact, recently studied seismic records indicate that a violent earthquake, whose epicenter was on the seafloor in the region where the *Mary Celeste* was sailing, occurred some days before the ship's discovery. 3 If the ship had been subjected to intense shocks caused by the quake, all aboard may have hastily abandoned ship to avoid what they imagined might be its imminent destruction from an explosion of the combustible cargo. 4 A severed rope found dangling from the side of the *Mary Celeste* suggests that the evacuees trailed behind in the lifeboat, attached to the ship, waiting for the crisis to pass. 5 Great waves may then have snapped the rope and capsized the smaller boat, whose occupants would have disappeared without a trace.

38. The following sentence can be added to paragraph 3.

The need to circulate air to prevent such a blast could explain why the crew left two hatches open.

Where would it best fit in the paragraph?

Select the square (□) that shows where the sentence should be added.

Paragraph 3 is marked with an arrow (→).

Questions 39–50

Every year about two million people visit Mount Rushmore, where the faces of four U.S. presidents were carved in granite by the sculptor Gutzon Borglum and his son. The creation of the Mount Rushmore monument took fourteen years – from 1927 to 1941 – and nearly a million dollars. These were times when money was difficult to come by and many people were jobless. To help him with this sculpture, Borglum hired laid-off workers from the closed-down mines in the Black Hills area. He taught these men to dynamite, drill, carve, and finish the granite as they were hanging in midair in his specially devised chairs, which had many safety features.

Borglum used dynamite to remove 90 percent of the 450,000 tons of rock from the mountain quickly and relatively inexpensively. His workmen became so skilled that they could blast to within four inches of the finished surface and grade the contours of the facial features. Borglum was proud of the fact that no workers were killed or severely injured during the years of blasting and carving the granite. Considering the workers regularly used dynamite and heavy equipment, this was a remarkable feat.

During the carving, many changes in the original design had to be made to keep the carved heads free of large fissures that were uncovered. However, not all the cracks could be avoided, so Borglum concocted a mixture of granite dust, white lead, and linseed oil to fill them.

Every winter, water from melting snow gets into the fissures and expands as it freezes, making the fissures bigger. Consequently, every autumn maintenance work is done to refill the cracks. To preserve this national monument for future generations, the repairers swing out in space over a 500-foot drop and fix the monument with the same mixture that Borglum used.

39. This passage is mainly about
(A) the visitors to the Mount Rushmore monument
(B) the faces at the Mount Rushmore monument
(C) the sculptor of the Mount Rushmore monument
(D) the creation of the Mount Rushmore monument

→ Every year about two million people visit Mount Rushmore, where the faces of four U.S. presidents were carved in granite by the sculptor Gutzon Borglum and his son. The creation of the Mount Rushmore monument took fourteen years – from 1927 to 1941 – and nearly a million dollars. These were times when money was difficult to come by and many people were jobless. To help him with this sculpture, Borglum hired laid-off workers from the closed-down mines in the Black Hills area. He taught these men to dynamite, drill, carve, and finish the granite as they were hanging in midair in his specially devised chairs, which had many safety features.

40. In paragraph 1, the author indicates that the men Borglum hired were
   (A) trained sculptors
   (B) laid-off stone carvers
   (C) Black Hills volunteers
   (D) unemployed miners

Paragraph 1 is marked with an arrow (→).

→ 1 Every year about two million people visit Mount Rushmore, where the faces of four U.S. presidents were carved in granite by the sculptor Gutzon Borglum and his son. 2 The creation of the Mount Rushmore monument took fourteen years – from 1927 to 1941 – and nearly a million dollars. 3 These were times when money was difficult to come by and many people were jobless. 4 To help him with this sculpture, Borglum hired laid-off workers from the closed-down mines in the Black Hills area. 5 He taught these men to dynamite, drill, carve, and finish the granite as they were hanging in midair in his specially devised chairs, which had many safety features.

41. Select the number of the sentence in paragraph 1 that explains how the artist protected his workmen.

Paragraph 1 is marked with an arrow (→).

→ Every year about two million people visit Mount Rushmore, where the faces of four U.S. presidents were carved in granite by the sculptor Gutzon Borglum and his son. The creation of the Mount Rushmore monument took fourteen years – from 1927 to 1941 – and nearly a million dollars. These were times when money was difficult to come by and many people were jobless. To help him with this sculpture, Borglum hired laid-off workers from the closed-down mines in the Black Hills area. He taught these men to dynamite, drill, carve, and finish the granite as they were hanging in midair in his specially devised chairs, which had many safety features.

42. The word devised in paragraph 1 is closest in meaning to
   (A) designed
   (B) described
   (C) scaffolded
   (D) elevated

Paragraph 1 is marked with an arrow (→).

During the carving, many changes in the original design had to be made to keep the carved heads free of large fissures that were uncovered. However, not all the cracks could be avoided, so Borglum concocted a mixture of granite dust, white lead, and linseed oil to fill them.

43. Look at the word fissures in the passage. Select another word or phrase in the **bold** text that is closest in meaning to the word fissures.

During the carving, many changes in the original design had to be made to keep the carved heads free of large fissures that were uncovered. However, not all the cracks could be avoided, so Borglum concocted a mixture of granite dust, white lead, and linseed oil to fill them.

44. What does the author mean by Borglum concocted a mixture of granite dust, white lead, and linseed oil to fill them?
    (A) Borglum's mixture for filling cracks was very expensive.
    (B) Borglum bought the mixture at the Black Hills mines.
    (C) The mixture was invented by the sculptor himself.
    (D) The mixture was discovered by the sculptor during carving.

→ Every winter, water from melting snow gets into the fissures and expands as it freezes, making the fissures bigger. Consequently, every autumn maintenance work is done to refill the cracks. To preserve this national monument for future generations, the repairers swing out in space over a 500-foot drop and fix the monument with the same mixture that Borglum used.

45. The word expands in paragraph 4 is closest in meaning to
    (A) dilutes
    (B) enlarges
    (C) sprouts
    (D) shrivels

Paragraph 4 is marked with an arrow (→).

Every winter, water from melting snow gets into the fissures and expands as **it** freezes, making the fissures bigger. Consequently, every autumn maintenance work is done to refill the cracks. To preserve this national monument for future generations, the repairers swing out in space over a 500-foot drop and fix the monument with the same mixture that Borglum used.

46. Look at the word **it** in the passage. Select another word or phrase in the **bold** text that **it** refers to.

47. Today, Mount Rushmore needs to be
    (A) protected from air pollution
    (B) polished for tourists
    (C) restored during the winter
    (D) repaired periodically

Every year about two million people visit Mount Rushmore, where the faces of four U.S. presidents were carved in granite by the sculptor Gutzon Borglum and his son. ☐1 The creation of the Mount Rushmore monument took fourteen years – from 1927 to 1941 – and nearly a million dollars. ☐2 These were times when money was difficult to come by and many people were jobless. To help him with this sculpture, Borglum hired laid-off workers from the closed-down mines in the Black Hills area. He taught these men to dynamite, drill, carve, and finish the granite as they were hanging in midair in his specially devised chairs, which had many safety features.

Borglum used dynamite to remove 90 percent of the 450,000 tons of rock from the mountain quickly and relatively inexpensively. ☐3 His workmen became so skilled that they could blast to within four inches of the finished surface and grade the contours of the facial features. Borglum was proud of the fact that no workers were killed or severely injured during the years of blasting and carving the granite. Considering the workers regularly used dynamite and heavy equipment, this was a remarkable feat.

During the carving, many changes in the original design had to be made to keep the carved heads free of large fissures that were uncovered. ☐4 However, not all the cracks could be avoided, so Borglum concocted a mixture of granite dust, white lead, and linseed oil to fill them.

Every winter, water from melting snow gets into the fissures and expands as it freezes, making the fissures bigger. ☐5 Consequently, every autumn maintenance work is done to refill the cracks. ☐6 To preserve this national monument for future generations, the repairers swing out in space over a 500-foot drop and fix the monument with the same mixture that Borglum used.

48. The following sentence can be added to the passage.

In the summer, the heat also adversely affects the fissures.

Where would it best fit in the passage?

Select the square (☐) that shows where the sentence should be added.

49. With which of the following statements would the author most probably agree?
    (A) The heads are not as originally planned.
    (B) The workers made mistakes when blasting.
    (C) The cracks caused serious injuries.
    (D) The designs had large fissures in them.

50. The passage discusses the following aspects of the creation of the Mount Rushmore carvings EXCEPT
    (A) where the people who worked on Mount Rushmore came from
    (B) why Borglum carved the heads of four U.S. presidents
    (C) how Borglum dealt with fissures that could not be avoided
    (D) when repairs to this national monument are made

**This is the end of the Reading Section.
Go on to the Writing Section.**

WRITING

Time – 30 minutes

Read the essay question carefully.

Think before you write. Making notes may help you to organize your essay. It is important to write only on the topic you are given.

Check your work. Allow a few minutes before time is up to read over your essay and make changes.

You have thirty minutes to complete the essay. On the real test, if you continue to write, it will be considered cheating.

Set your clock or watch for thirty minutes.

Now get ready to begin.

Directions: Read the question below and write an essay on a separate sheet of paper.

Some people wish to ban smoking in public places. Others don't agree. What is your opinion?

Use reasons and specific examples to support your opinion.

NOTES

Use this space for essay notes only. On the day of the Computer-Based TOEFL® Test, work done on the worksheet will not be scored.

This is the end of the Writing Section.

ANSWER
·KEYS·

When explanations are given for all possible answers to a question, an asterisk (*) will be used to indicate the correct answer.

DIAGNOSTIC TEST (p. 35, script on p. 559)

Note: If you answer an item incorrectly, complete the exercises following the letter you chose and those following the explanation of the correct answer.

Section 1 Listening

Part A

1. (A), (B), (D) See Exercises L1–L8.
   *(C) "Nice" means "kind," and a "gesture" is something someone does as a courtesy. See Exercises L1–L8.
2. (A), (B), (C) See Exercises L1–L8.
   *(D) "Chip in" means "to donate a small sum of money or amount of time to help someone." See Exercises L9–L11.
3. *(A) "Costs" refers to "price," "twice as much" means the same as "double," and "in the last three years" indicates "three years before now." See Exercises L13–L18.
   (B), (C), (D) See Exercises L13–L18.
4. (A), (B), (D) See Exercises L13–L18.
   *(C) "It doesn't seem possible" means "it's hard to believe." See Exercises L13–L18.
5. *(A) The expression "close call" is used when a person has had a narrow escape; he has just barely managed to pass the exam. See Exercises L9–L11.
   (B), (C), (D) See Exercises L1–L8.
6. (A), (B), (C) See Exercises L20–L24.
   *(D) The man's wanting to meet the woman at a well-known place (the Student Activities Center) and lead her to his house suggests that it is difficult to explain how to get to his house. See Exercises L20–L24.
7. (A), (B), (D) See Exercises L13–L18.
   *(C) When the man asks, "How long?" the woman replies, "At least that long" – meaning five years or more. See Exercises L13–L18.
8. (A) See Exercises L20–L24.
   *(B) The woman is responding to the man's inability to read the map by suggesting that they pull into a gas station. It can be inferred that this is to ask for directions. See Exercises L20–L24.

(C), (D) See Exercises L9–L11.
9. (A) See Exercises L5–L8.
   (B), (C) See Exercises L1–L4.
   *(D) A gym is a place to get exercise. Since Barbara is going to the gym, she's probably going to work out. See Exercises L20–L24.
10. (A), (C), (D) See Exercises L13–L18.
   *(B) The woman is surprised that an exam that took her "no time" to finish (that she finished quickly) took the man a long time to finish. See Exercises L13–L18.
11. (A), (B) See Exercises L20–L24.
   *(C) The woman's saying that there are maps of bus routes at the information desk indicates that he should get one there. See Exercises L20–L24.
   (D) See Exercises L5–L8.
12. *(A) The woman's saying that her sister wanted some practice implies that she let her sister cut her hair. See Exercises L20–L24.
   (B), (D) See Exercises L20–L24.
   (C) See Exercises L13–L18.
13. *(A) The expression "give a piece of one's mind" means "let someone know that one is angry about something that person has done." See Exercises L9–L11.
   (B) See Exercises L9–L11.
   (C), (D) See Exercises L1–L8.
14. (A) See Exercises L5–L8.
   (B) See Exercises L20–L24.
   *(C) In the man's opinion, Sue's ideas are too ambitious to put into action. See Exercises L20–L24.
   (D) See Exercises L1–L8.
15. *(A) "Couldn't have" indicates that something is contrary to expectation. The woman's intonation indicates surprise because she thinks it is impossible that Bob has completed the assignment and has already returned. See Exercises L1–L4 and L13–L18.
   (B) See Exercises L1–L4 and L13–L18.
   (C) See Exercises L20–L24.
   (D) See Exercises L1–L4.
16. (A), (B), (C) See Exercises L20–L24.
   *(D) The woman's desire for a place that is within commuting distance of the university indicates that she needs to go there often. See Exercises L20–L24.

17. (A) See Exercises L5–L8.
    (B) See Exercises L13–L18.
    (C) See Exercises L1–L4.
    *(D) To be "left speechless" means to be "unable to say anything in response." He was unable to speak because he was shocked by the accusations (charges that someone had done something wrong). See Exercises L9–L11.
18. (A) See Exercises L9–L11.
    (B), (C) See Exercises L20–L24.
    *(D) The woman is suggesting that the man get Ted's advice when buying a bicycle because Ted knows a lot about bicycles. See Exercises L20–L24.

Part B

19. (C) The conversation is mainly about arrangements for a time and place to meet so that the woman can give the man a ride downtown. See Exercises L26–L29.
20. (B) The woman states that she is going downtown to pick up her new contact lenses. See Exercises L31–L36.
21. (D) Although the woman suggests meeting in front of the gym, the man convinces her that the student parking lot is the best place to meet. See Exercises L31–L36.
22. (A) The woman says that she was unable to meet the deadline for her report. Her statement means she couldn't complete the assignment by the date it was due. See Exercises L31–L36.
23. (C) The woman says that Dr. Reed gave her some ideas (tips) on how to organize her material. See Exercises L31–L36.
24. (D) The man says he needs advice on that (organizing his material better), and the woman says she'll make a copy for him of the main points of what Dr. Reed said. See Exercises L31–L36.
25. (A) The man tells the woman that he's signing up for a class. See Exercises L26–L29.
26. (C) The man states that they'll return to campus to do the lab work. See Exercises L31–L36.
27. (B), (D) The man states that these courses can't be held during the academic year because students would miss too many of their other classes while away from campus for extended periods of time. He also states that unpredictable storms in spring and fall could make it difficult to do the fieldwork. See Exercises L31–L36.
28. (A) Buffalo bones and flint knives would not deteriorate over time and, therefore, would be the most likely to be found at a site. See Exercises L38–L40.
29. (A) The man's enthusiastic descriptions of the classes indicate that he thinks they are more interesting. See Exercises L38–L40.

30. (B) Although the painting is well known, the discussion is mainly about the problem of theft. The professor says the painting is favored by thieves and has been taken from the museum four times. See Exercises L26–L29.
31. (A) The professor says the painting has been "out on unauthorized loan for three years." "Unauthorized loan" is a humorous way of saying it was stolen. See Exercises L31–L36.
32. (D) Its small size makes it easy to conceal and take out of the museum. See Exercises L31–L36.
33. (D) The professor says that the painting is appraised at $5 million, but she doesn't know what a thief can sell it for. See Exercises L31–L36.
34. (D) It can be inferred that the small size of a vase would make it easier to steal than the other objects. See Exercises L38–L40.
35. (D) The talk briefly describes patterns of human migration throughout history. See Exercises L26–L29.
36. (B) The speaker states that people's abilities to make shelter and clothes and to control fire helped them survive. See Exercises L31–L36.
37. (B) The speaker explains that human migration involves taking over both unused land and occupied land. See Exercises L31–L36.
38. (C) The speaker ends the talk with the point that migration seems to be a fundamental human instinct. See Exercises L31–L36.
39.   1. (B); 2. (C); 3. (A); 4. (D) First humans left the grasslands of Africa and followed the migration of plants and animals affected by glacial cycles into Europe and Asia. Then they spread to Japan, Indonesia, and Australia. They crossed the Bering land bridge and spread down to the southern tip of South America. Humans continue to migrate. See Exercises L31–L36.
40. (B) London's works, family, and politics are all aspects of his life. See Exercises L26–L29.
41. (B) The professor states London chose the life of a writer to escape the prospect of becoming a factory worker. See Exercises L31–L36.
42. (C), (D) The professor states that London's adventurous life gave him the material to create imaginative literature. See Exercises L31–L36.
43. (C) The professor names this novel as the one that brought London lasting fame. See Exercises L38–L40.
44. (A), (B) The professor states that London's support for socialism was offset by his belief in individualism, and that although he supported women's rights, he dominated his own female family members. See Exercises L31–L36.
45.   1. (C); 2. (D); 3. (A); 4. (B) London's family moved to Oakland when he was young. He then held a variety of jobs. He decided to become a writer rather than do factory work. He got into ranching towards the end of his life. See Exercises L31–L36.

46. (D) The professor starts the talk with an explanation of the original Roanoke colonists and goes through the events that ended with the disappearance of the second set of colonists. See Exercises L26–L29.

47. (B), (D) The professor states that the fort was abandoned without a trace except for one clue – the word "Croatoan" was scratched onto an entrance post. See Exercises L31–L36.

48. (C) Since descendants of native people claim that these colonists are their ancestors, it is plausible that the colonists married into the native population. See Exercises L38–L40.

49. 1. (C); 2. (A); 3. (B) The professor states that the original settlers returned to England with some ships that were passing the settlement. The fifteen men whom the captain left to hold the fort were found dead, and 100 new settlers disappeared mysteriously. See Exercises L31–L36.

50. (C) Something that is enigmatic is mysterious. The disappearance of the settlement is a mystery. The word "enigmatic" is a synonym for "mysterious." See Exercises L38–L40.

Section 2 Structure

1. (B) A verb in the simple present tense, "fly," is needed to complete the sentence. See Exercises S25–S31.

2. (A) The nouns "predators" and "pollution" are used as subjects. Therefore, the word "disturbing" needs to be in the noun form "disturbances" to be a part of the parallel structure. See Exercises S37–S42 and S88–S90.

3. The adjective clause "that can be" is incomplete. A verb, "fitted," can complete the clause. "Together" tells how the parts fit.
   (A) See Exercises S52–S53.
   (B) See Exercises S11–S15 and S67–S70.
   *(C) See Exercises S25–S31.
   (D) See Exercises S25–S31.

4. (A) The superlative form "oldest" should be used because Soay sheep are being compared to all other breeds of sheep. See Exercises S82–S87.

5. (C) A verb is needed to complete the independent clause. "Alfred B. Nobel" identifies the Swedish scientist who "left money to be awarded." See Exercises S52–S53.

6. (B) The plural noun "villages" should be used. "Some" indicates that there is more than one village. See Exercises S1–S5.

7. An aux-word (auxiliary verb), "does," is needed to complete the sentence.
   (A), (C) See Exercises S11–S15 and S91–94.
   *(B) See Exercises S32–S35.
   (D) See Exercises S91–S94.

8. (A) An article is needed in the noun phrase "important element." The article "an" should be used because it precedes a vowel sound. See Exercises S6–S10.

9. "Like," meaning "similar to," is a preposition that indicates a comparison. Here there is a comparison between "porpoises and dolphins" and "whales."
   (A), (B) See Exercises S91–S94.
   *(C) See Exercises S91–S94.
   (D) See Exercises S72–S76.

10. (B) "Settlement" is a noun that refers to a place. The noun form "settlers" is used for people. See Exercises S37–S42.

11. The independent clause is complete, indicating that a clause or phrase is needed to fill in the blank. "Although" introduces the reduced adverb clause "founded many centuries earlier."
    (A), (B) See Exercises S52–S53.
    *(C) See Exercises S77–S80.
    (D) See Exercises S67–S70.

12. (D) "Which" is the object of the adjective clause and refers to "nutrients." The pronoun "them" cannot be used to fill the same position and therefore must be removed for the sentence to be correct. See Exercises S61–S66.

13. A subject and verb are needed to complete the sentence. The word "it" fills the subject position, and the verb "was" fills the verb position. An adverb, "while," is needed to introduce the adverb phrase "living in Birmingham, England."
    (A) See Exercises S52–S53 and S77–S80.
    (B), (D) See Exercises S72–S76.
    *(C) See Exercises S52–S53 and S77–S80.

14. (D) The possessive adjective "its" should be used instead of "their" because it refers to "Bactrian camel," which is used in the singular form indicating a class of animal. See Exercises S11–S15.

15. The verb in the passive voice "has never been determined" needs a subject that indicates what hasn't yet been determined. "Who built the stone circle" fills that position.
    *(A) See Exercises S54–S59.
    (B) See Exercises S54–S59.
    (C), (D) See Exercises S52–S53.

16. (D) The noun "outsider" should be in the plural form, "outsiders." The article "an" would have been included if there had been only one outsider who ruled Catalonia. See Exercises S1–S5.

17. An adjective clause or adjective phrase is needed to modify the noun "terms." The phrase "indicating the location of their discovery" describes what kind of terms.
    (A), (B), (C) See Exercises S61–S66.
    *(D) See Exercises S67–S70.

18. (B) The phrase "in the air" is redundant because "in the air" means the same as the word "aloft." The sentence should read, "Early balloonists remained aloft for relatively short periods." See Exercises S95–S96.

19. (A) An adverb clause is needed to complete the sentence. The word order for an adverb clause introduced by the clause marker "how" is: "how" + adjective + subject + verb. See Exercises S72–S76.

20. (D) "Simulations" is not being contrasted with "training." Therefore, the two nouns should be joined by the word "and." See Exercises S43–S50.

Section 3 Reading

1. (B) The passage discusses four different reasons why interviewing job applicants is an inadequate way to determine one's working ability. See Exercises R5–R7.

2. (D) A "hindrance" or an "interference" makes the completion of an activity more difficult. See Exercises R1–R3.

3. The word "they" refers to the other "characteristics" that will be judged as being better because of a noticeably good trait. See Exercises R9–R11.

4. (C) The author discusses how one good characteristic, such as dressing smartly, makes the interviewer think that other characteristics of the applicant are also good. See Exercises R9–R20.

5. (A) When something is "confirmed" or "verified," it is shown to be true. See Exercises R1–R3.

6. (B) The primacy effect is one in which the first impression is likely to endure. The interviewer spends the interviewing time trying to confirm this impression. See Exercises R9–R20.

7. (A) Something is "skewed" or "biased" when it is distorted by various factors. See Exercises R1–R3.

8. The predictor that appears to "accurately predict candidate suitability" most successfully is the applicant's cognitive ability. See Exercises R9–R11.

9. (D) The cognitive effect is not mentioned in the passage. See Exercises R9–R20.

10. [3] In paragraph 3, the author discusses the contrast effect in which one candidate is contrasted with a previous candidate. See Exercises R9–R20.

11. (C) The passage ends by introducing tests designed to measure cognitive ability. The next paragraphs would probably be about these tests. See Exercises R22–R27.

12. (C) The paragraphs are mainly about Thomas Young's classic double-slit experiment to illustrate the nature of light. See Exercises R5–R7

13. A "slit" is a long narrow opening or a type of "hole." See Exercises R1–R3.

14. The central "one" is the "band" in the center. See Exercises R9–R11.

15. (B) A single photon fired through two open slits builds a pattern that has a central band and alternating bands of light and darkness. See Exercises R9–R20.

16. "Each other" refers to each of the "waves of light" from the two slits. See Exercises R9–R11.

17. (D) The author describes waves in general to give the background information the reader needs to understand how one light wave interferes with the other light wave. See Exercises R22–R27.

18. When something "overlaps" something else, it covers a part of the other thing or "extends over" it. See Exercises R1–R3.

19. [5] When a crest overlaps a trough, they cancel each other out. See Exercises R9–R20.

20. "Photons" are "particles of light." See Exercises R1–R3.

21. (A) The author means that a single photon behaves in the same way that it would behave if there were other photons causing interference. See Exercises R22–R27.

22. (B) Since light beams consist of a constant stream of photons, they are not shone one at a time. See Exercises R9–R20.

23. (B) The author's statement that light behavior is fascinating and that an inanimate object appears to "know" something suggests that there are phenomena that are not completely understood. See Exercises R22–R27.

24. [1] The word "this" refers to an "experiment," since that is what could be replicated in a classroom setting. This sentence would probably follow the sentence introducing Thomas Young's classic double-slit experiment and would precede the sentences describing the experiment. See Exercises R9–R20.

25. [1] In paragraph 1, a light beam shone through a vertical slit on a screen and allowed to pass on to a second detecting screen builds up a pattern of a large illuminated area that fades into darkness at its edges. See Exercises R9–R20.

26. (D) The passage presents the results of various studies that have been undertaken concerning obesity. See Exercises R5–R7.

27. (C) According to the passage, 44 percent of people respond to stress by eating. See Exercises R22–R27.

28. (D) If someone "craves" something, he or she has a strong desire for it. See Exercises R1–R3.

29. (B) Because the lack of variety and flavor leaves heavy people dissatisfied, it can be inferred that eating a variety of food with strong flavors will satisfy them. See Exercises R22–R27.

30. (D) It is stated in the passage that "this [an increase in blood insulin] did not happen to average-weight people." See Exercises R9–R20.
31. (A) It is stated in the passage that "when people eat carbohydrates, the level of serotonin . . . rises [which] produces a sense of satiation, thereby eliminating their hunger." See Exercises R9–R27.
32. "When people" eat carbohydrates, their hunger subsides. See Exercises R9–R11.
33. When something "subsides," it becomes less intense. When something "rises," it becomes more intense. See Exercises R1–R3.
34. (C) It is stated that serotonin is a neurotransmitter that produces a sense of satiation, or feeling full. See Exercises R9–R20.
35. An exercise that is "strenuous" requires a lot of effort or energy. An exercise that is "mild" does not require a lot of effort or energy. See Exercises R1–R3.
36. (A) According to the passage, both strenuous exercise and looking at pictures of food increase the appetite of overweight people. Therefore, these activities would not be helpful. See Exercises R9–R20.
37. (A) A stroll is a relaxed walk and, therefore, the kind of mild exercise recommended. See Exercises R22–R27.
38. [3] In paragraph 3, the author states that carbohydrates raise the level of serotonin, and this increase produces a sense of being full. See Exercises R9–R20.
39. (B) The passage discusses the American Civil War battle that took place between the Confederate and Union forces at Gettysburg, Pennsylvania. See Exercises R5–R7.
40. (A) "Reinforcements" are additional troops sent to join an army to make it stronger. See Exercises R1–R3.
41. "The Union forces" formed defensive positions along Cemetery Ridge. See Exercises R9–R11.
42. [4] The phrase "these positions" refers to the "defensive positions" mentioned in the sentence that should precede this one, and the "remainder of Meade's forces" refers to those who came later to join the ones who "formed defensive positions." See Exercises R9–R20.
43. [2] The author states that the "Union forces were overpowered and were driven back to the south of Gettysburg." See Exercises R9–R20.
44. When a place is "stormed" by military troops, it is "attacked" suddenly with the intent of defeating the troops who are defending it. See Exercises R1–R3.
45. (D) When people "sustain" something, such as a number of casualties, they "suffer" or endure it. See Exercises R1–R3.
46. (A) Poor visibility was the reason the two hours of bombardment did not inflict much damage and, consequently, why the charge failed. See Exercises R22–R27.
47. (D) The Confederates' failure to invade the North was the point in the war that decided the outcome in the Union's favor. See Exercises R22–R27.
48. (C) The author does not discuss any instance of espionage (spying). See Exercises R9–R20.
49. (C) In paragraph 2, the passage states that the Confederate forces faced the Union positions in an arc from the west and north. Therefore, the Confederate attack known as Pickett's Charge originated from the northwest. See Exercises R9–R20.
50. (B) The author states that the battle is considered the single most important engagement of the Civil War. See Exercises R9–R20.

SECTION 1   LISTENING

Part A   Short conversations

Exercise L1 (p. 76, script on p. 562)
1. B (ship/sheep)   4. B (major/mayor)
2. A (bell/bill)   5. B (pan/pen)
3. A (clue/glue)

Exercise L2 (p. 77, script on p. 562)
1. Q   3. Q   5. S   7. S
2. S   4. S   6. Q   8. S

Exercise L3 (p. 77, script on p. 562)
1. right   4. hour   7. brakes   10. hole
2. feat   5. heir   8. won
3. wait   6. dye   9. loan

Exercise L4 (p. 78, script on p. 562)
1. A (meet, not meat)   4. B (weak, not week)
2. B (sail, not sale)   5. A (mail, not male)
3. B (cruise, not crews)

Exercise L5 (p. 78, script on p. 563)
1. A   3. C   5. D   7. D   9. A
2. C   4. A   6. B   8. D   10. C

Exercise L6 (p. 80, script on p. 563)
1. (A) "Light" in sentence (B) means "not heavy."
2. (A) "Strike" in sentence (B) means to "ignite."
3. (A) "Note" in sentence (B) means "a musical tone."
4. (B) A "spring" in sentence (A) is a "place where water comes up from the ground."
5. (A) "Exercise" in sentence (B) means to "do physical activities."

Exercise L7 (p. 80, script on p. 563)
1. A   2. B   3. A   4. A   5. B

Exercise L8 (p. 81, script on p. 563)
1. (A) "Weak" and "week" could be confused because they are pronounced the same.

*(B) "To be weak" means "to be lacking strength."

(C) "Timing" (the selection of a moment to do something) and "time" (duration) could be confused.

(D) "For" and "four" could be confused because they are pronounced the same.

2. *(A) "A coin" and "change" are terms for money.

(B) The similar sounds of "coin" and "join" could be confused.

(C) An engine is a kind of machine, but not the kind that would use a coin.

(D) The meanings of "change" (coins) and "change" (replace) could be confused.

3. (A) "Twice" means "two times" and "couple" means "two," but the similar sounds of "mistake" and "steak" could be confused.

(B) The similar sounds of "correcting" and "collecting" could be confused.

(C) The similar sounds of "proof" and "prove" as well as "mistake" and "state" could be confused.

*(D) "To proofread" something means "to look for mistakes;" "mistakes" are "errors."

4. (A) "Bored" and "board" could be confused because they are pronounced the same.

(B) "To serve on the board" means to be one of the directors.

(C) The meaning of "serve" (to cater for – something a waitress does when she brings food to customers) could be confused with "serve" (to perform official duties).

*(D) Since Carmen "serves" on the "board" (the committee) of directors, she is one of the directors.

5. (A) The similar sounds of "yolks" and "jokes" could be confused.

*(B) The expression "sink in" means "to come to an understanding gradually." The woman means that Ted understands the jokes after he has had time to think about them.

(C) Eggs have yolks (see A); the similar sounds of "sink" and "stink" could also be confused.

(D) The meanings of "sink in" (to come to an understanding gradually) and "sink" (a basin) could be confused.

Exercise L9 (p. 84, script on p. 563)

1. (B) "To one's heart's content" means "as much as one wants."

2. (A) "Beside oneself with worry" means "very worried."

3. (A) "To catch cold" means "to come down with an illness (a cold)."

4. (A) "To cross that bridge when I come to it" means "to take care of that situation when it arises" (usually at a later date).

5. (B) "To not lift a finger" means "to not help."

6. (A) Something that "makes one's hair stand on end" is something that is very frightening.

7. (B) "To have a crack at something" means "to have the opportunity to try doing something."

8. (A) "To put something off" means "to postpone it." The man says he can't put it off; therefore, he will have to register for the music course.

9. (A) "To ring a bell" means "to sound familiar." The woman has heard the name before, so she might know Cindy.

10. (B) "To be given the runaround" means "to be given incorrect information or evasive answers to a request."

11. (B) "To blow up" means "to suddenly lose one's temper."

12. (B) "To catch a ride" means "to get someone to take you somewhere in his or her vehicle."

13. (D) "To have money to burn" means "to have extra cash to spend."

14. (C) "To not know how to put something" means "to not know how to say the right words." The man is not sure how to tell the woman that he doesn't like her dress.

15. (A) "To cheer up" means "to make one feel better," and "good for a laugh" means "full of good humor."

16. (B) "To see someone off" means "to take someone who is leaving to the airport or station and say good-bye there." Ann will take the woman to the airport and say good-bye there.

17. (B) "To have something in one's head" means "to have a plan to do something or an idea about something."

18. (C) "To be getting on in years" means "to be aging." She is implying that her grandfather is too old to be teaching.

Exercise L10 (p. 86, script on p. 564)

1. (A) If you had to put up with the idea, you had to tolerate it.

(B) If you had to put the idea together, you had to compose it.

*(C) If you had to put the idea across, you had to make it understood (convey it).

(D) If you had to put away the idea, you had to store it or remove it.

2. *(A) If Rita helped Emma see the light, she helped her understand something.

(B) If Rita helped Emma see the light at the end of the tunnel, she helped her see the end of a difficult situation.

(C) If Rita helped Emma light up, she helped her to light a cigarette.

(D) If Rita helped Emma go out like a light, she helped her go to sleep quickly.

3. (A) If Stephen was in over his head, he was involved in something that was beyond his understanding.

(B) If Stephen was head over heels in love, he was very much in love.

*(C) If Stephen lost his head, he couldn't control himself and he panicked.

(D) If Stephen had a big head, he was conceited.

4. (A) If my brother is footing the bills, he is paying for everything.

(B) If my brother is on his toes, he's well prepared.

*(C) If my brother is pulling my leg, he's joking with me.

(D) If my brother is underfoot, he's getting in my way.

5. *(A) If I'm going to put that bicycle together, I'm going to take its parts and join them to make the bicycle; I'm going to assemble it.

(B) If I put that bicycle aside, I'm moving it out of the way.

(C) If I put that bicycle down, I'm laying it on the floor or ground.

(D) If I put that bicycle out, I'm taking it outside.

6. (A) If the romance tests the waters, it is a situation that will bring people's views and opinions to the surface.

(B) If the romance is a test case, it is one that establishes an important principle to be applied later.

(C) If the romance is put to the test, some new event will put a strain on it and, thus, give an indication of how strong the romance is.

*(D) If the romance stands the test of time, it is strong enough to last for a very long time.

7. (A) If she held something against her son, she didn't forgive him for one of his actions.

*(B) If she held onto her son, she wouldn't let go of him – she clung to him.

(C) If she got hold of her son, she contacted him by telephone or some other means of communication.

(D) If she held her son up, she either physically supported him or delayed him from doing something.

8. (A) If the children give me a run for my money, they force me to use all my skills to succeed with them.

(B) If the children make my blood run cold, they frighten me.

*(C) If the children run me ragged, they tire me – exhaust me.

(D) If the children put me in the running, they enter me into a contest.

9. *(A) In this sentence, "fall behind" means "fail to do something on time."

(B) "Fall asleep" means "go to sleep."

(C) "Fall in love" means "feel love for."

(D) "Fall apart" means "break down."

10. (A) "Weigh one's words" means "think carefully before speaking."

(B) "Gain weight" means "add pounds."

(C) "Throw one's weight around" means "use one's influence."

*(D) "Pull one's weight" means "do one's share of the work."

11. (A) "On the off chance" means "there's a small possibility."

*(B) "Stand a good chance" means "there's a good possibility of achieving success."

(C) "Chance upon something" means "accidentally find something."

(D) "Chance something" means "take a risk."

12. (A) "Call it a day" means "stop working for the day."

(B) "Call a halt to something" means "order somebody to stop doing something."

(C) "Call someone's bluff" means "test to see if someone is being serious about something."

*(D) "Call attention to something" means "point something out."

13. (A) "Turn the other cheek" means "ignore it when someone treats you badly."

(B) "Speak tongue-in-cheek" means "say something as a joke."

*(C) "Dance cheek to cheek" means "dance very closely."

(D) "Be cheeky" means "be disrespectful."

14. (A) "See the last of something" means "it will never be seen again."

*(B) "Seeing things" means "imagining things are present that aren't."

(C) "See one's way clear" means "decide to do something that one had not intended to do previously."

(D) "See the daylight" means "suddenly understand something or finish an overwhelming job."

15. *(A) "Throw cold water on something" means "discourage something."

(B) "Throw a party" means "have a party."

(C) "Throw in the towel" means "give up or stop trying."

(D) "Throw something away" means "get rid of something."

16. (A) "Might as well" means "see no reason not to do something."

(B) "Come off well" means "be successful."

*(C) "Leave well enough alone" means "don't tamper with what is already in good shape."

(D) "It's just as well" means "it's fortunate that it happened the way it did."

Exercise L11 (p. 88, script on p. 564)

1. (A) The expression "run into" can mean "meet unexpectedly" or "collide with." This meeting or collision took place in the mall, not in the parking lot.

(B) The expression "ran into" could be confused with "ran" (jogged).

*(C) The expression "run into" means "meet unexpectedly" in this sentence.

(D) The expression "run into" can mean "enter in a hurry." However, Sue did not run into the mall; she ran into Mary (that is, she met her unexpectedly).

2. (A) The expression "doesn't stand a chance" means "has no possibility of succeeding," so John will probably not win.

(B) The expression "does his best" (does the best job that he can do) could be confused with "has the best chance" (is the most likely).

*(C) "Does his best" means "does the best job that he can do" and "doesn't stand a chance" means "has no possibility of succeeding."

(D) The expression "doesn't stand a chance" (has no possibility of succeeding) could be confused with "can't stand" (cannot tolerate).

3. (A), (B), (D) "Run" in the expression "in the long run" (meaning "eventually") could be confused with "run" (jog); "work out" (resolve) could be confused with "work out" (which means "do physical exercises").

*(C) "In the long run" means "eventually," and "work out" means "resolve" or "turn out well."

4. (A) The expression "right away" (immediately) could be confused with "all right" (a good job).

(B) "Entrance" in the term "entrance exam" (an exam necessary to take in order to enter a university or college) could be confused with "entrance" (the door used to enter an area), and "right away" (immediately) could be confused with "on the right" (the right-hand side).

(C) The expression "right away" (immediately) could be confused with "right" (all correct).

*(D) "Notified" means "let someone know;" "mother and father" are "parents;" and "right away" means "immediately."

5. (A) The expression "on time" (punctual) could be confused with "time" (a specific point in time). Bill didn't take the test because he didn't have his identification card, not because of the time the test was held.

*(B) The expression "on time" means "not late;" however, the reason Bill didn't take the test was because he didn't have his identification card. His punctuality was not a factor.

(C) The expression "on time" (punctual) could be confused with "short time" (a small duration of time). "Check something out" could be confused with "take something."

(D) Bill could not have used his identification card to take the test because he had forgotten the card.

6. *(A) "Set up" means "get something ready" (organize it).

(B) The concession "stands" (where food is sold) could be confused with "stands" (where observers sit). "Set up" (get something ready) could be confused with "seat" (a place to sit).

(C) "Set up" (get something ready) could be confused with "upset" (unhappy). The noun "stand" (where food is sold) could be confused with the verb "stand" (remain on foot).

(D) "Set up" (get something ready) could be confused with "set" (a television set).

7. (A) "Miss" (make a mistake) could be confused with "miss" in the expression "missed the point" (see D).

(B) The expression "missed the point" (see D) is taken literally as "miss the point" (get the point wrong).

(C) "Miss" (fail to attend) could be confused with "miss" in the expression "missed the point" (see D).

*(D) The expression "missed the point" means "failed to understand the argument." The woman failed to understand the argument presented in the lecture.

8. (A) "Run" (move quickly) could be confused with "run" in the expression "run across something" (see C).

(B) The similar sounds of "panting" (breathing hard) and "pamphlet" (a small brochure) could be confused. "Run" (move quickly) could be confused with "run" in the expression "run across something" (see C).

*(C) The expression "run across something" means "find (discover) something by chance."

(D) "Cross" (annoyed) could be confused with "across" in the expression "run across something" (see C).

9. (A) The speakers are talking about their voting, not Mary's.

*(B) The expression "have what it takes" means "have the ability or skills to do something."

(C) The expressions "have what it takes" (see B) and "takes what one can" (tolerates as much as possible) could be confused.

(D) The original statement concerns "seriously" voting for Mary, not "seriousness" about elections.

10. *(A) "The go-ahead" is the approval to proceed.

(B), (D) "Ahead" (in advance) could be confused with "go-ahead" (see A).

(C) "Head" (leader) and "go" (leave) could be confused with "go-ahead" (see A).

11. (A) "Take something up" (pursue a new interest) is the opposite of "swearing off something" (decide not to do something anymore).

(B) The similar sounds of "sworn" and "has worn" could be confused.

*(C) The expression "swear off something" means "to decide against doing something, or give something up."

(D) The verb "swear" (use bad language) could be confused with the expression "swear off something" (see C).

12. (A) The expression "grasp at straws" means "try something with little chance of succeeding." The woman thinks it is too late to turn in the form.
   (B) The word "grasp" means "hold on to" something. The expression "grasp at straws" refers to holding on to something that is impossible.
   (C) The similar sounds of "form" and "farm" could be confused.
   *(D) The woman's use of the expression "grasp at straws" indicates that she thinks his applying for a loan will not be worthwhile because he is too late to be successful in getting one.

13. (A) The *woman* thinks that it would be difficult for Ruth to work and study at the same time.
   *(B) The man points out that Ruth would get good experience if she accepted the teaching assistantship.
   (C) The man is stating that Ruth would get good experience. He is not discussing whether she would be good as an assistant.
   (D) The man doesn't indicate how difficult he thinks Ruth's decision is.

14. (A) The meanings of "stumble" (trip over) and "stumble across" (discover by chance) could be confused.
   (B) The similar sounds of "tumble" and "stumble" could be confused.
   *(C) If the woman discovered the shop "by accident," she "stumbled across it."
   (D) The meaning of second-hand (used) and second hand (the measure on a watch that marks off seconds in time) could be confused.

Exercise L12 (p. 91, script on p. 565)
1. (A) "To climb stairs" could be confused with "to go climbing" (climb mountains).
   (B) The meanings of "flight" (an airplane trip) and "flight" (a set of stairs) could be confused.
   *(C) "The stairs" are made up of "steps."
   (D) The meanings of "fly" (to take an airplane trip) and "flight" (a set of stairs) could be confused.

2. (A) They are replacing glass in a picture frame, not replacing a picture.
   (B) The similar sounds of "glass" and "class" could be confused.
   (C) A painting can be called a picture and be put in a "frame," but the man is talking about the glass in the picture frame.
   *(D) In order to replace the glass, the people will have to buy some glass.

3. (A) The meanings of "spare" (an extra tire) and "spare" (anything extra) could be confused.
   (B) The meanings of "plug" (a device to put in the drain to stop the water from getting out) and "plugged-up" (stopped-up) could be confused.
   *(C) A sink has a drain, and "blocked" can mean "clogged."

   (D) The similar sounds of "sink" (a basin) and "stink" (an odor) could be confused.

4. (A) The expression "shut-eye" (sleep) could be confused with "closing one's eyes."
   *(B) "Get some shut-eye" means "get some sleep."
   (C) "Shut-eye" could be confused with "shut off" (turn off).
   (D) "Shut-eye" could be confused with "shut" (close).

5. (A) The similar sounds of "pack" and "back" could be confused.
   (B) "Back out of" (withdraw from an engagement) could be confused with "come back" (return).
   *(C) The expression "back out of" means "to withdraw from an engagement." The man doesn't want to go to the party.
   (D) "Back out of" could be confused with "out back" (in the yard behind the house).

6. *(A) The expression "make light of" means "to treat as unimportant." The woman thinks that the man is not being serious about his bad exam grade.
   (B) The meaning of "light" in the expression "make light of" (treat as unimportant) could be confused with "light" (not hard).
   (C) The meaning of "light" in the expression "make light of" could be confused with "light" (lamp).
   (D) The meaning of "light" in the expression "make light of" could be confused with "light" (not dark).

7. (A) The similar sounds of "'brush up" (to review) and "hush up" (keep silent) could be confused.
   (B) The similar sounds of "rush" (in a hurry) and "hush" (be quiet) could be confused.
   *(C) The expression "hush something up" means "keep others from finding out about something." The woman understands why the man doesn't want people to know (find out) about the experiment.
   (D) The woman is agreeing with the man that people should <u>not</u> know about the experiment.

8. (A) The meanings of "TV screen" (a TV monitor) and "screen out" (eliminate) could be confused.
   (B) The similar sounds of "screen" and "scream" could be confused.
   (C) The similar sounds of "screen" and "ice cream" could be confused.
   *(D) The expression "screen out" means "eliminate." Some people are not qualified for the experiment and cannot continue in it.

9. (A) The expression "stick around" (stay) could be confused with "sticky" (like glue).
   (B) The similar sounds of "stick" and "Rick" could be confused.
   (C) The expressions "stuck up" (have too high an opinion of oneself) and "stick around" could be confused.

*(D) The expression "stick around" means "stay." Neil usually stays after class has ended.

10. (A) The expressions "pass something out" (distribute) and "pass out" (lose consciousness) could be confused.

    *(B) The expression "pass out" means "lose consciousness." If someone passes out, they lose consciousness.

    (C) "Pass" (give a mark of adequate completion) and "pass out" (lose consciousness) could be confused.

    (D) "Past" and "passed" could be confused because they are pronounced the same.

11. (A) The meanings of "space" (room) and "space" (the region beyond the earth's atmosphere) could be confused.

    (B) The similar sounds of "class" and "glass" could be confused, as could the meanings of "backpack" and "back."

    *(C) The man wants to know if there is room in the backpack for a glass.

    (D) The man is not offering to carry the woman's pack, but rather he is asking if there is room in her pack for his glass so he won't have to carry it.

12. (A) A tailor doesn't clean clothing; he or she makes or alters clothing.

    *(B) The expression "take something in," in this case, means "make something smaller."

    (C) Although the jacket doesn't fit, it is not being returned to the store where it was bought. It is being taken to someone who can alter it.

    (D) Although a tailor may be asked to mend clothing, the problem is not that the jacket is torn but that it needs to be made smaller.

13. (A) The expression "tag along" (accompany) could be confused with "tag" (a label).

    (B) The expressions "tag along" (accompany) and "get along" (be friendly with) could be confused.

    (C) "A price" is put on a "tag" and attached to an article for sale. The meaning of "tag" (a label) could be confused with the expression "tag along" (accompany).

    *(D) The woman thought that the man did not want them to go (tag along) with him.

14. *(A) The expression "water something down" means "make something less difficult." The professor made his course easier, or simplified it.

    (B) The similar sounds of "course" and "horse" could be confused.

    (C) The university has changed its requirements, so the professor has changed aspects of his course to make it easier. He has not required a change to another course.

    (D) The professor has simplified his course because of the change in university requirements, but that doesn't mean he has dropped the requirements for this particular course.

15. (A) The meanings of "pool" (a billiard game) and "pool" (a swimming pool) could be confused.

    (B) The similar sounds of "cab" and "cap" could be confused.

    (C) The similar sounds of "cool" and "pool" as well as "car" and "cap" could be confused.

    *(D) The woman is getting her swimming cap to go to the pool with the man.

Exercise L13 (p. 97, script on p. 565)

1. (B) "No later than tomorrow" means "not after tomorrow."

2. (B) "Until" indicates that Tom was not studying before midnight but rather he began to study *at* midnight.

3. (A) "A couple" means "two."

4. (B) "Up to thirty" can mean thirty or nearly thirty, but not more than thirty.

5. (B) The comparison is between the amount of fog tonight and the usual amount of fog. Tonight the fog is heavier than it usually is.

6. (A) "A lot more books this semester" means the man bought fewer books last semester; in other words, he didn't buy as many last semester.

7. (B) "A couple of hours at least" means "a minimum of two, but probably more than two."

8. (B) The use of "either" implies that there are two examples. The people cannot understand either one of the two examples.

9. (A) The woman is not discussing the quality of the box, but the size of the box. She means that a big box is a better box for her purposes.

10. (B) "Quite a few" means "a large number," whereas "a few" means "not many."

11. (A) "At least a dozen" means "no fewer than a dozen (twelve) and maybe more than a dozen."

12. (C) The man disagrees with the woman about Kathy's spending "too much time" in the computer lab because he knows that Kathy has to meet a deadline.

13. (A) The expression "take five" means "take a short break (five minutes)." He thinks that she could work better after taking a rest.

14. (B) The phrase "to put in a couple of hours overtime" means "to work two hours more than the regular workload."

15. (D) The woman is quite certain that Sue is not back yet; therefore, the man could not have seen her.

Exercise L14 (p. 100, script on p. 566)

1. A	4. A	7. A	10. C	13. C
2. B	5. B	8. A	11. D	14. D
3. B	6. A	9. A	12. D	

Exercise L15 (p. 102, script on p. 566)

1. B	4. B	7. A	10. B	13. C
2. A	5. A	8. A	11. A	14. B
3. A	6. B	9. D	12. B	

Exercise L16 (p. 104, script on p. 567)

1. A	4. A	7. A	10. C	13. C
2. B	5. B	8. B	11. B	14. B
3. B	6. B	9. D	12. A	

Exercise L17 (p. 106, script on p. 567)

1. B	4. B	7. A	10. B	13. B
2. A	5. A	8. B	11. C	14. D
3. A	6. B	9. C	12. A	

Exercise L18 (p. 109, script on p. 568)

1. R	4. C	7. R	10. A	13. B
2. C	5. C	8. C	11. C	14. A
3. R	6. C	9. A	12. D	

Exercise L19 (p. 111, script on p. 568)

1. (A), (B) The man already has a car.
   (C) Whether or not he gives her a ride does not depend on his having a car but rather on when she must be on campus.
   *(D) The man implies that he will give the woman a ride if she is going at a convenient time for him.

2. *(A) "He almost didn't pass" means that while he came close to failing, he did pass and this is the stated reason for his being happy.
   (B) "Must not have passed" (probably didn't pass) could be confused with "almost didn't pass" (came close to failing, but didn't).
   (C) "Almost didn't pass" (came close to failing, but didn't) could be confused with "didn't pass" (failed).
   (D) "Almost didn't pass" means "barely passed;" therefore, he did <u>not</u> do very well.

3. (A) Tom, not the woman, is in the University Health Center.
   (B) She wants Tom to *receive* the card.
   *(C) The expression "can't make it" means "unable to do something" (in this case, get to the hospital).
   (D) "Make" in the expression "can't make it" could be confused with "make" (construct).

4. (A) "Stopped giving" (no longer give) could be confused with "quit taking" (no longer take).
   (B) It is not Mary who has quit (stopped attending); it is the woman who has stopped giving the class.
   (C) It is not Mary's class, but the woman's.
   *(D) The woman has postponed (delayed giving) her class, but only for a month. After a month, the class will resume.

5. *(A) The man's exclaiming "Have I!" means that "yes, he has gone over the results." The expression "you won't believe the statistics" indicates that the statistics are very surprising.
   (B) It's not that he "wouldn't go over" (examine) the statistics, but that he thinks the statistics are so surprising that the woman "wouldn't believe" them.
   (C) The expression "you won't believe them" is not to be taken literally. It means that the statistics are very surprising.

(D) "Have I!" is an exclamation meaning "Yes, I have."

6. (A) "Had to finish by Monday" (last Monday) could be confused with "will have finished by Monday" (next Monday).
   (B) "Finished last Monday" could be confused with "will have finished by Monday" (next Monday).
   *(C) "Will have finished by Monday" means that on Monday all her exams will be done.
   (D) "Finished by Monday" (a Monday in the past) could be confused with "will have finished by Monday" (next Monday).

7. (A) "She can't remember" means that she doesn't know if she signed the paper or not.
   (B) The similar sounds of "uniform" and "form," and the similar spellings of "sign" and "signal" could be confused.
   (C) The meanings of "sign" (to write one's name) and "sign" (a posted announcement) could be confused.
   *(D) "She forgot to sign" (write her name) means she didn't put her name on the form.

8. (A) Andy, not Dr. Roberts, gave the newsletter to Sue. There is no information concerning whose newsletter it was.
   *(B) Andy gave the newsletter to Sue. Dr. Roberts asked him to do this.
   (C) Andy did not give the newsletter to Dr. Roberts. Dr. Roberts gave it to him and he gave it to Sue. There is no information concerning whose newsletter it was.
   (D) Sue was given the newsletter at Dr. Roberts's request.

9. (A) "At least twenty-five guests" means "no fewer than twenty-five guests, and possibly more." Nothing is stated concerning what Jim wants.
   (B) "As many guests as possible" means "an unlimited number of guests." However, Bob gave Jim a limit of twenty-five names.
   *(C) "As many as twenty-five names" means "up to twenty-five and no more."
   (D) Nothing is stated concerning what Jim wants.

10. (A) David does have a serious problem (a serious disability).
    (B) "Never misses classes" means "always goes to classes," but "hardly ever makes it to classes" means "seldom goes to classes."
    (C) The meanings of "serious" (earnest about something) and "serious" (severe) could be confused.
    *(D) A "serious disability" suggests a "physical condition," and "not keep from" means "not prevent."

11. (A) It was the student who left the testing center, not the professor.
    *(B) The professor did not allow the student to come into the center because the student forgot to bring his identification card.

(C) We are not told that the student went to get his identification card, but that he left because he hadn't brought it.

(D) It was the student who forgot to bring his identification card, not the professor.

12. (A) "Put into"(insert) could be confused with "put in two hours" (spent two hours of time doing something).

(B) "Put in two hours" could be confused with "put in (returned) two books."

(C) The similar sounds of "walk" and "work" could be confused.

*(D) "A couple" means "two," and the idiom "to put in" means "to spend time."

13. (A) The woman doesn't want to talk. She wants to study.

(B) The woman doesn't want to go to the library; the man suggests she go there.

*(C) The woman is trying to study, but she is having difficulty because the man is talking too much.

(D) It is the man who wants the woman to go to the library to study. The woman doesn't say anything about getting a book.

14. (A) "To be used to" (to be accustomed to) could be confused with "used to do something" (a past habit).

*(B) "To be used to" means "to be accustomed to."

(C) Since Nancy isn't used to dancing so much, she may actually find it difficult to dance.

(D) "As much as" could be confused with "so much," and "used to" could be confused with "be used to" (see A).

15. (A), (D) "Should have (been) taken" (the action of taking the test was a desirable thing to do in the past, but it was not taken) could be confused with "must have been taken" (indicating a belief that the test was already taken sometime in the past).

*(B) "Was probably" means "must have been," and "harder than any other" means "the most difficult."

(C) "Must take" implies "to take in the future," but the spoken statement says "must have been," which implies that the action has already taken place.

Exercise L20 (p. 115, script on p. 569)

1. (A) The speaker needs to know who speaks Spanish.

2. (B) The negative question indicates that the speaker is expecting agreement with the opinion.

3. (B) The speaker would like a job and is requesting the opportunity to apply for one.

4. (A) The negative tag question indicates that the speaker is expecting the other person to agree.

5. (A) The speaker is advising the listener to go to a doctor.

6. (B) The speaker uses the words "I'm afraid" as a way to apologize.

7. (B) "To be supposed to" in the present tense indicates a responsibility or an obligation.

8. (A) The speaker uses the words "I'm really sorry" to indicate a feeling of regret.

Exercise L21 (p. 115, script on p. 569)

1. (A) The woman gives information to correct the man's mistake.

2. (B) The woman uses the expression "to be sick of" to mean that she is annoyed. She is making a complaint (stating what she finds unsatisfactory) about busywork (she feels it is not useful).

3. (B) The man's apology ("I'm sorry") and excuse ("I've got a headache") imply that he is refusing the invitation.

4. (B) The man says, "I don't know," not because he actually doesn't know if the lecture was interesting, but because he is politely disagreeing with the woman.

5. (B) The man is declining dessert by stating the reason he doesn't want any.

6. (A) The woman is explaining where the car keys can be found because she is agreeing to the man's request to use the car.

7. (B) The man criticizes the paintings by saying they look like a child's work. This indicates that he dislikes them. The woman disagrees with his opinion (she likes the paintings).

8. (A) The woman says, "Help yourself," meaning "You're welcome to take as many cookies as you want."

Exercise L22 (p. 116, script on p. 569)

1. (B) In this case, the expression "How about" is used informally to mean "Would you like."

(D) "What a good idea!" expresses the woman's opinion of having a cup of coffee. In other words, she would like one and is accepting the man's offer.

2. (B) The woman is describing an exam. She is making a complaint (stating what she found unsatisfactory) about it (its difficulty).

(D) The man uses the expression "cheer up" to try to help her feel better.

3. (A) The man is explaining the reason he wasn't in class. He is giving an excuse.

(D) Although "I'm sorry" can be used to introduce an apology, it is also used to express regret when you hear sad news. The woman is expressing her feelings of sympathy.

4. (B) When the man uses the expression "fit me in," he means "find a time to make an appointment" (arrange a time for a meeting).

(C) The woman wants to know if 11:45 is a convenient time for the man to come. She is suggesting a time.

5. (B) The woman uses the idiom "give me a hand" to ask for help in doing something.

(C) By using the word "which," the man is asking her whether she wants his left hand or his right hand. He is making a joke by taking her words "give me a hand" literally.

6. (A) The man's claim that he could teach better than the professor is a criticism of the professor's teaching abilities.

(C) "You sure could" indicates that the woman agrees that the man would be able to teach geology well.

7. (B) "I don't understand" and "mix-up" (a change in order, disorder) indicate that the man could be confused.

(C) The woman is advising the man (telling him what she thinks he should do). In this case, she thinks the man shouldn't worry (be concerned).

8. (A) The man's problem is that he needs to have his watch fixed.

(D) The woman suggests that he take it to the jewelry store where it can be fixed.

Exercise L23 (p. 117, script on p. 569)

1. (B) The man is suggesting they go get a drink. The woman rejects the suggestion by pointing out that they might miss the end of the game if they go. Because the woman strongly opposes leaving before the end, the man will probably wait.

2. (B) Although the woman doesn't say that she broke the glass, her mentioning a "crash" implies that she dropped or knocked over the glass of milk, and that's why it is no longer on the table.

3. (A) The woman is asking the man if she can come over for help. Therefore, the man is probably good at math.

4. (A) The man's surprise at the woman's statement about Chris's doing badly and his calling Chris a genius imply that Chris usually does very well on exams.

5. (B) Since Tim and Dave don't get along and Dave is definitely coming, the man probably won't invite Tim.

6. (B) Although the man says that the class will have started, the woman's response that he is being silly indicates that the man is worrying for no reason. In fact, the class will not have started when they arrive.

7. (B) If the man is encouraged by the fact that Linda got the job without experience, it is probably because he wants a similar job and doesn't have experience either.

8. (A) The man's saying "Nothing that you'd want to read" indicates that what he wrote would not interest the woman.

Exercise L24 (p. 118, script on p. 570)

1. (C) The woman's question "When have you ever seen me smoking?" indicates that she doesn't smoke.

2. (D) The hedge protects the classroom from wind and reduces the traffic noise. It also improves the appearance of the property.

3. (A) The man's reply indicates that the answer to the question is so obvious that the woman shouldn't have had to ask it.

4. (A) The man is responding to the woman's insult instead of to her request. This response gives no indication as to whether or not he will do what she has asked.

5. (C) The man's response implies that he does not want to go. He may not want to break (go off of) his diet, or perhaps he is using his diet as an excuse for not going.

6. (B) The man's response indicates that he was on the committee for a while, but he is not on the committee now.

7. (B) The man is suggesting that the woman use the computer to find the book that she needs.

8. (C) The woman's not seeing someone who had lived across the hall from her for a semester indicates that the person probably moved out.

Exercise L25 (p. 119, script on p. 570)

1. (A), (B) The meanings of "I'm afraid" (I'm frightened) and "I'm afraid" (an expression used to show regret or concern) could be confused.

*(C) The woman uses the phrase "I'm afraid" to show regret that she can't go with the man because she will be busy writing the report.

(D) The woman gives no indication of willingness to go out after the report has been written.

2. *(A) If the concert ends at 10:30 and they'll get home around twelve, then it takes them more than an hour to get home.

(B) The man is figuring the travel time according to the time the concert will end. He does not suggest that midnight is too late to get home.

(C), (D) The man makes a simple observation. It cannot be inferred from the conversation that the people feel 10:30 is too late for the concert to end or that twelve is too late to get home.

3. (A) If the man thought there was little to worry about, he would not be "*so* worried" about it.

*(B) If the exam will determine the man's future, it is very important to him.

(C) The woman calls the exam "little" meaning "unimportant," not "short."

(D) It cannot be inferred from the conversation that this is the man's first scholarship.

4. *(A) The man's response indicates that Dr. Mason's background explains why he had not been able to identify her accent.

(B) Dr. Mason is a native speaker, not just someone who speaks like one.

(C) He doesn't say he can't understand the accent, but rather he implies that he can't place the region it is from.

(D) The accent the people are discussing is a regional one, not a foreign one.

5. (A) The man's watch is missing.

(B), (D) See (C).

*(C) It can be inferred from the woman's saying "You've never seen me wearing a watch, have you?" that the woman doesn't own a watch.

6. (A) The words "correct-change-only light" could be confused with "light to change" regarding a traffic signal.

(B) Since the woman knew she didn't have the correct change, she must have known how much the drink cost.

*(C) The man's negative question is used to confirm his belief that the woman couldn't get a drink. Her response indicates why she couldn't get one – she didn't have the correct change (right coins).

(D) The machine was not out of order, but out of coins for change.

7. (A) He went to Bill's party the previous night, but he must have gone home at some point. At home, he had the bad night.

*(B) The man states that he "had a bad night" (wasn't able to sleep) because something didn't agree with him (made him unwell).

(C), (D) Something he ate or drank didn't agree with him (made him unwell).

8. (A) The man is talking about two people – the woman and himself – not about two movies.

(B) The words "how to make" could be confused with "that makes."

*(C) The man means that there are two people that don't like the movie – the woman doesn't like it and neither does he.

(D) The man is talking about two people – the woman and himself – not about a sequel to a movie.

9. (A) "Not know anything" could be confused with "not come up with anything."

*(B) The woman says, "No one (not one person in her group) has come up with (thought of) anything good (a good project) yet." This indicates that they have not decided what to do for the project yet.

(C) The group members' not deciding on a project does not imply they have postponed doing it.

(D) There is no indication that the group is being secretive about the project.

10. (A), (B) The man's telling the woman what he has to do indicates that he can't go with them to the museum.

(C) The man is meeting *his mother* at the airport.

*(D) The man will probably meet his mother at the airport to pick her up.

11. *(A) The woman's being certain that she would have slept through a speech on economics implies that she's not interested in the subject.

(B) There is nothing in the conversation to indicate that the woman would have slept during the speech because she didn't get enough sleep.

(C), (D) If the woman was certain it was very interesting and/or enjoyable, she would not have suggested that she would have slept through it.

12. (A) The statement "Sue might have to be there early" does not imply that Sue might have already left.

*(B) The woman can't give the man a ride to the theater, but she suggests that he could go with Sue whom she knows is going.

(C) The woman's response gives no indication that she is going to the theater herself.

(D) Sue is probably helping put makeup on the members of the cast in the play. There is no indication that the man could help Sue.

13. (A), (D) The man is checking out a book. This action indicates they are in a library, and not in a place where books and magazines are bought and sold.

(B) The woman is going to wait while the man gets the book out.

*(C) Since the woman is going to the magazine section, she is probably going to look at the magazines.

14. (A) See (B).

*(B) The fact that Sally's keys are still on the kitchen counter indicates that she hasn't left yet.

(C) There is no indication that the keys are car keys that she didn't take because she was walking, or house keys that she would need to take in any case.

(D) There is no indication that Sally forgot the meeting.

15. *(A) If they are "laying off" workers at the factory, they are discharging or firing them, not hiring them. Consequently, the woman wouldn't be able to get a job there.

(B) The workers are being "laid off" (discharged or fired), <u>not</u> "taking off."

(C) Since the woman doesn't say that *all* workers are being laid off, the factory will probably not be closing down.

(D) Since the man has suggested the woman work at the factory, it probably *is* an adequate place to work.

Part B Longer conversations and talks

Exercise L26 (p. 125, script on p. 571)

1. the United Kingdom (The speaker will probably go on to give more facts about the United Kingdom.)

2. the Award for Architecture (The speaker will probably continue his talk by giving more information about the award. He may discuss the qualities an architect must have in order to be considered for the award.)

3. patterns of Irish linen (The speaker will probably continue to talk about the patterns as he displays the Irish linen.)
4. figures carved in hillsides (The speaker will probably talk about specific human- and animal-shaped figures.)
5. other Germans attracted to Italy (The speaker has probably finished saying something about Goethe and now will talk about Goethe's contemporaries who also went to Italy.)
6. Professor Brown's talk on Balzac (The speaker has attended the talk and will probably discuss it.)

Exercise L27 (p. 125, script on p. 571)
1. (A) Although the discussion may develop into the uses of acupuncture in the West, the talk will probably concentrate on the practice of acupuncture.
   (B) The topic sentence concerns acupuncture in China five thousand years ago, not modern China.
   *(C) The talk has begun with the topic of the practice of acupuncture and will probably continue to discuss the development of acupuncture throughout the centuries.
   (D) There is no mention of arthritis or its cures.
2. (A) Although fabric is made up of threads called fibers, the fibers in the topic sentence concern those of the muscles.
   *(B) The talk begins with a description of muscles and will probably continue with more information about them.
   (C) Although muscle fiber is measured in millimeters, the talk will probably not continue with details about millimeters.
   (D) The length of muscle fiber is mentioned, but the talk will probably not continue with details about lengths in general.
3. (A) The talk mentions satellite-communications technology, not communications technology in general.
   (B) The challenges mentioned are those in education, not in communications.
   (C) The satellites are those of communications, not education.
   *(D) The talk will probably expand on the possibilities and challenges in education that satellites have opened up.
4. (A) This seminar covers a specific period of time in Spanish literature.
   (B) Although this is a Spanish course, it is a specific course.
   (C) Historical events are mentioned in the context of the period of time when the Golden Age Spanish literature flourished.
   *(D) The professor is probably explaining to the seminar class what the course will be about.

He will probably continue to give the students more information concerning Golden Age Spanish literature.
5. *(A) Because influenza is emphasized by its being discussed in the main clause, the speaker will probably talk more about its particular characteristics.
   (B), (C) The common cold may be compared to influenza, but the emphasis will probably be on influenza.
   (D) The speaker does not mention other diseases.
6. (A) It is not human protein but rather animal protein that is being introduced.
   (B) Only one cause of malnutrition will probably be discussed.
   (C) Only one world problem – malnutrition – is being introduced.
   *(D) The talk will probably discuss the lack of animal protein in the diet of some peoples and the malnutrition that it causes.

Exercise L28 (p. 126, script on p. 571)
1. yes (topic = magic squares)
2. no (topic = zoos)
3. no (topic = the Pony Express)
4. yes (topic = butterfly farm)
5. no (topic = gargoyles)

Exercise L29 (p. 127, script on p. 571)
1. development of a written system to describe dance movements
2. helping people lose weight
3. emigration to the New World
4. no official language in the United States

Exercise L30 (p. 127, script on p. 572)
1. (D) The woman asks the man about his job at the library. The man describes aspects of the job.
2. (C) The talk begins by introducing Buffalo Bill (William Cody) and his "Wild West Show." It goes on to discuss the performers in the show and those who saw the show.
3. (B) The talk begins by introducing a new musical form in America, called ragtime. It goes on to discuss important composers of ragtime and its becoming the most popular musical art form in America.
4. (A) The speaker introduces the proposed fine-arts building and then discusses various aspects of it.

Exercise L31 (p. 131, script on p. 572)
1. (A) elderly people
   (B) no home and no one to help
   (C) delegates'
2. (A) climb of Mount Everest
   (B) an alpine club
   (C) permits
3. (A) calculator that replaced the abacus

(B) calculator
(C) mechanical one
4. (A) Turkish Cultural Arts Exhibition
   (B) a lecture
   (C) traditional Turkish music

Exercise L32 (p. 132, script on p. 573)

1. (B) It is not that the people in Homer's time used words from the Kárpathos dialect, but that the Kárpathos dialect of today uses words from the time of Homer.
2. (A) It is not the first hot-air balloon, but the first hot-air balloon flight that was piloted by a person on board.
3. (B) It is not that the word for "beautiful bird" means "tail feather," but that "quetzal," which is the name of a beautiful bird, means "tail feather."
4. (B) It was not that the twenty-two men cut off the escape route, but that they secured the escape route.
5. (A) It wasn't the areas themselves that set up the centers; the centers were set up in the areas.
6. (B) It is not our past that has been revolutionized, but our concepts about our past that have been revolutionized.
7. (B) It is not that explorers were not able to locate the island in March 1783, but that the island was described in March 1783.
8. (A) It was not dolphins, whales, and dead fish that were spotted. This suggests that only the fish were dead. Dead fish, dolphins, and whales were spotted. This suggests that creatures from all three groups were dead. Also, the dead creatures were reported by the authorities. The actual spotting could have been either by the authorities or by other people.

Exercise L33 (p. 133, script on p. 573)
1. A, C   2. B, D   3. A, B   4. B, C

Exercise L34 (p. 134, script on p. 574)

1.	1. C	2.	1. D	3.	1. D	4.	1. A
	2. B		2. A		2. C		2. B
	3. A		3. C		3. A		3. D
	4. D		4. B		4. B		4. C

Exercise L35 (p. 136, script on p. 575)

1. B	5. D	8. B	11. B
2. C	6. B	9. C	12. A
3. A	7. C	10. A	13. C
4. A			

Exercise L36 (p. 139, script on p. 575)
1. D
2. C
3. B
4. A

Exercise L37 (p. 141, script on p. 576)

1. (A) The passage states that the Boston Tea Party was the first major act of defiance on the part of the American colonists.
2. (B) The "Boston Tea Party of 1773" means that 1773 is the date that the party took place.
3. (C) The colonists were defiant because the tax was imposed without their having a representative in the British Parliament to defend their interests ("taxation without representation").
4. (D) Prominent citizens dressed as Native Americans threw the cargo overboard.
5. 1–B The British Parliament was under King George III.
   2–A The American colonists defied the British rulers.
   3–C Disguised prominent citizens attended the Boston Tea Party.
6. (B) Although the man reported the car as stolen, the police officer had a record of its having been towed away.
7. (D) The man says he left his car on Oak Street, which is near the Geology Building.
8. (A) The woman suggests that the man make the call using her mobile phone.
9. 1–B The man left the car on the street near the Geology Building.
   2–D The car was towed away.
   3–C Oak Street was resurfaced.
   4–A The man reported the car missing.
10. (A) The speaker states that the societies faced with the problems of aging are the ones with a large aging population and a low birthrate.
11. (B) The speaker states that the aging populations need more medical attention.
12. (D) The speaker states that when the family or the individual cannot pay for "care," the financial burden falls on the state.
13. (C) This graph shows more older people and fewer younger people.
14. (B), (C) According to the talk, photographs preserved images in extraordinary detail and provided a perfect way to document historical events.
15. (A) The speaker says that nineteenth-century photographs make excellent records, but recent ones do not because technological advances make it possible to manipulate their images.
16. (B) The speaker states that it is increasingly difficult to use contemporary photographs as a reliable source of historical information.

Exercise L38 (p. 145, script on p. 577)

1. yes It has been new research that has brought doubt to Mata Hari's being a spy. Therefore, either a death sentence or prison sentence was probably given at the time of her trial.

2. yes The Manx is identified as the only domestic cat without a tail. This implies that there are wild cats without tails as well.

3. no The woman is showing interest in the man's experience, but there is no indication that she wants to build a mud house herself.

4. no A fossil is the remains of a prehistoric creature or organism.

5. yes The speaker's saying that further experiments need to be done before a decision is made concerning their use on humans indicates that humans have not yet undergone the operation.

Exercise L39 (p. 146, script on p. 578)
1. (B) Research into the recurrence of polio may give those involved in medicine new insights in how to treat the disease.

2. (D) The man will probably sign up to take Italian in order to complete his foreign language requirement.

3. (A) Jean Muir's working with her staff to prepare twenty years of materials suggests she wanted her fashion business to continue after her death.

4. (B) A way to motivate learners and encourage learning would be important for education majors.

Exercise L40 (p. 148, script on p. 578)
These are possible answers. Your answers may differ.
1. She's probably an art major.
2. To contrast the lasting enjoyment that children get from common objects with the short-term enjoyment that they get from high-tech toys.
3. He wants the students to take the opportunity to experience Spanish culture and language outside of the classroom.
4. Because there has been a violent incident on campus recently.

Exercise L41 (p. 149, script on p. 579)
1. (B) The toxic fumes, which have led to more fire-related deaths, are created when synthetic materials catch on fire. This is another danger of using synthetic materials in houses.

2. (A) Stone is a natural material. The other items are synthetic building materials or use synthetic materials in their processing.

3. (D) Most people cannot move from their homes very easily, but they can remove some of the synthetic materials in their homes and replace them with natural alternatives.

4. (B) The instructor would probably hand out the list of required readings at the beginning of the semester.

5. (D) An out-of-print book would not be available in a bookstore, so a professor might leave a personal copy at the reserve desk.

6. (A) Because the articles are on microfiche, which cannot be taken from the library, it can be inferred that the articles cannot be taken out.

7. (A) The speaker uses the example of the aspirin bottle to demonstrate that one invention often brings about another invention created to rectify a fault of the first one.

8. (A) The speaker asks for the audience to suggest ways to improve the aspirin bottle cap. They may come up with a good improvement.

9. (D) The speaker closes the talk by having the audience discuss their ideas.

10. (D) The people are listening to a talk about how anthropologists can use garbage to learn about cultures.

11. (A) The speaker uses the example of orange peels to demonstrate the various things that can be learned about a group of people by looking at what they discarded.

12. (B) A Stone Age person may have thrown away all of the stated items. However, the broken stone tools would most likely be the only objects that remain today.

13. (C) Since the organic materials that ancient cultures used disintegrated, they no longer exist and, therefore, cannot be studied. The speaker regrets that this information has been lost.

Exercise L42 (p. 151, script on p. 580)
Part A
1. (A), (C), (D) See Exercises L9–L11.
   *(B) The woman uses the expression "twist his arm" to imply that she had to pressure Peter to help because he didn't want to. His not wanting to help can also be understood from her saying, "It wasn't easy," in response to the man's question. See Exercises L9–L11.
2. (A), (D) See Exercises L13–L18.
   (B) See Exercises L9–L11.
   *(C) The man's use of the expression "That's not a minute too soon for me" implies "Classes cannot be over soon enough to please me." In other words, the man is extremely eager for classes to be over. See Exercises L9–L11.
3. (A), (C), (D) See Exercises L13–L18.
   *(B) Robert promised to help solve student problems that concerned housing. See Exercises L13–L18.
4. (A) See Exercises L13–L18.
   (B), (D) See Exercises L9–L11.
   *(C) If someone "has a head for something" (gains knowledge about something easily), that person is probably "good at it" (competent at doing it). See Exercises L9–L11.
5. (A) See Exercises L13–L18.
   *(B) The man regrets that there is no more film. Therefore, the woman can't take the picture. See Exercises L20–L24.

(C), (D) See Exercises L20–L24.
6. (A), (B), (D) See Exercises L20–L24.
   *(C) The woman lists several things that the man hadn't done but would have done if he had been serious about his studies. See Exercises L20–L24.
7. (A), (C) See Exercises L1–L8.
   (B) See Exercises L9–L11.
   *(D) The expression "go halves" means "share the cost." Because the woman does not have the money to buy gasoline for the trip, the man is suggesting that they share the cost of gas. Perhaps in that way she can afford the trip. See Exercises L9–L11.
8. (A), (D) See Exercises L20–L24.
   *(B) The woman means that there is so much snow falling that it is blocking the view of the Student Union. Therefore, it must be snowing very hard. See Exercises L20–L24.
   (C) See Exercises L1–L4.
9. (A), (B), (D) See Exercises L13–L18.
   *(C) The woman encourages the man by telling him that tests will be finished (be over) in two weeks (the week after next). See Exercises L13–L18.
10. *(A) Sue has signed up for a course (enrolled in a course). A crash course is a short course that is held for many hours over several days or weeks. In other words, it's intensive for a short period of time. See Exercises L9–L11.
    (B), (C), (D) See Exercises L1–L8.
11. (A), (C), (D) See Exercises L13–L18.
    *(B) The woman agrees with the man that since Margaret mislaid Dr. Morris's research paper, she should say she is sorry for doing that. See Exercises L13–L18.
12. *(A) The man's asking the woman if she can wait another week before he returns the book indicates that he wants to keep it for a longer time. See Exercises L13–L18.
    (B), (C), (D) See Exercises L13–L18.
13. (A), (C), (D) See Exercises L9–L11.
    *(B) Jason's "lines" are "his part of the script," and to memorize them "backwards and forwards" (thoroughly) means that he knows them extremely well. See Exercises L9–L11.
14. (A), (C) See Exercises L1–L8.
    *(B) The woman is suggesting that they go to the exhibition. See Exercises L20–L24.
    (D) See Exercises L20–L24.
15. (A), (B), (C) See Exercises L13–L18.
    *(D) The woman is indicating a preference for a different course (zoology) from the one the man is suggesting (botany). See Exercises L13–L18.
16. *(A) The woman means that she isn't going to the library now but that she is going to the library after lunch. See Exercises L13–L18.
    (B), (C), (D) See Exercises L13–L18.

17. *(A) The woman means that having a class in the afternoon is better than having one in the evening. Therefore, the man's schedule could be worse than it is. See Exercises L13–L18.
    (B), (C), (D) See Exercises L13–L18.
18. (A), (B), (D) See Exercises L20–L24.
    *(C) It can be inferred by the man's statement that he has come about the photocopier and by the woman's description of the problem that he has come to repair it. See Exercises L20–L24.

Part B
19. (A) The people are talking about a time and place to meet before going to the theater. See Exercises L26–L29.
20. (D) The woman states that the man's professor sometimes gets carried away (might be so enthusiastic about the lecture that he or she doesn't notice the time). This implies that the man might arrive at the meeting place late. See Exercises L38–L40.
21. (C) The woman offers to pick up the tickets early in order to save time. See Exercises L31–L36.
22. (B) The man states that he didn't have enough money to get all the required books. See Exercises L31–L36.
23. (D) Although the woman suggests buying used books and checking out books from the library, she also suggests that he take care of his financial problem by getting a part-time job. See Exercises L31–L36.
24. (D) The woman has given the man several reasons to apply for a job in order to meet his expenses. He sees the advantages of doing this and will probably try to get the part-time job the woman has recommended. See Exercises L38–L40.
25. (C) It is stated in the talk that these portraits were once called shades. See Exercises L31–L36.
26. (B) The mentioned materials are ivory, plaster, porcelain, and glass. Clay is not mentioned. See Exercises L31–L36.
27. (C) It is stated in the talk that Étienne de Silhouette was an eighteenth-century French finance minister who was infamous for his stringent economic policies. See Exercises L31–L36.
28. (A) Because the phrase "à la silhouette" meant "cheap," the term was used for this art form, which was inexpensive to produce. See Exercises L31–L36.
29. (A) A silhouette is described as the shadow of a sitter's profile captured on paper. See Exercises L31–L36.
30. (B) The man introduces himself as the person the work-study office sent. The woman then explains the job. See Exercises L26–L29.

31. (A) The professor offers to show the man "our lab," and the man asks if he will be working in the biology lab. This indicates that the professor is probably working in the Biology Department. See Exercises L38–L40.

32. (A) The woman states that they need him to count paramecia. See Exercises L31–L36.

33. (C) The paramecia probably need to be counted at regular intervals in order to ascertain the speed at which they are reproducing. See Exercises L38–L40.

34. 1. (A); 2. (C); 3. (B); 4. (D) First, the man must arrange a time to come to the biology lab. At the lab, he will count paramecia and write these numbers on a form that he will give to Nancy, who will enter the statistics into the computer. See Exercises L31–L36.

35. (C) The talk is mainly about the public's reaction to a radio play. See Exercises L26–L29.

36. (A), (D) The professor states that the radio play was produced by George Orson Welles and that it contained convincing sound effects and realistic special bulletins. See Exercises L31–L36.

37. (B) The professor states that the event is the most widely known delusion in United States, if not world, history. See Exercises L31–L36.

38. (C) The professor talks about the play being so realistically produced that people believed the events it portrayed were really happening. See Exercises L31–L36.

39. 1. (A); 2. (C); 3. (D); 4. (B) The original novel was published in 1898. The novel was adapted and broadcast on radio to Americans in 1938. Some of the audience believed the broadcast and tried to flee the invasion. This incident has become well known. See Exercises L31–L36.

40. (B) The professor argues that the media may have exaggerated the actual extent of the panic. This is ironic because the original panic was caused by the media itself. See Exercises L31–L36.

41. (D) The professor talks about many different aspects of chlorofluorocarbons (CFCs). See Exercises L26–L29.

42. (D) The professor states that CFCs are components of certain products and are produced in various manufacturing processes. See Exercises L31–L36.

43. (A) The professor gives hair sprays and polishes as examples of aerosol products containing CFCs. See Exercises L38–L40.

44. 1. (A); 2. (D); 3. (B); 4. (C) First, artificial chemicals called CFCs are used in products. The use of these products releases CFCs into the atmosphere, where they combine with the oxygen in the ozone. This combination depletes the ozone. This depletion allows ultraviolet light to damage DNA. See Exercises L31–L36.

45. (A) The professor states that because of economic reasons, some countries are not enthusiastic about phasing out the production of CFCs. See Exercises L31–L36.

46. (D) The speaker talks about the American justice system's needing to deal differently with children than it deals with adults and goes on to discuss reforming the system in a way that continues to protect children. See Exercises L26–L29.

47. (A) The professor states that the American justice system reflects the differences between children and adults, and it provides for these differences by individualizing the treatment of children. See Exercises L31–L36.

48. (C) The professor realizes that there is an increase in criminal offenses by juveniles. Nonetheless, he worries that juveniles who commit crimes may be treated as adult criminals. See Exercises L31–L36.

49. 1. (C), 2. (A), 3. (B) Accountability involves assessing how juveniles differ from adults in their understanding of criminal behavior. Risk evaluation involves determining the chances that a juvenile will commit an offense. Susceptibility to change involves assessing how likely it is that a juvenile may respond to treatment. See Exercises L31–L36.

50. (B), (D) The professor recommends that research into the key areas be based on a thorough understanding of the related fields of child and adolescent development and that this knowledge be spread among professionals and throughout the community. See Exercises L31–L36.

SECTION 2   STRUCTURE

Exercise S1 (p. 167)

1. N	3. C	5. C	7. C
2. N	4. N	6. N	8. C

Extended practice: The nouns in items 2, 7, and 8 can be either count or noncount.

Exercise S2 (p. 167)

1. people/persons	6. men
2. life	7. sheep
3. series	8. leaves
4. tooth	9. mice
5. child	10. geese

Exercise S3 (p. 168)

1. wave (The noun "wave" should be in its plural form, "waves." The article "a" is needed for "wave" to be in its singular form.)
2. wildlives ("Wildlife" is a noncount noun and has no plural form.)
3. gram (The plural form is needed: There are "650 grams of gold.")

4. saints ("Saints" should be in its singular form because there was only one – "first saint.")
5. This sentence is correct.
6. century ("Century" should be in its plural form: There are "two centuries.")
7. informations ("Information" is a noncount noun and takes the singular form.)
8. This sentence is correct.

Exercise S4 (p. 169)
1. This sentence is correct.
2. colony
3. disturbance
4. This sentence is correct.
5. This sentence is correct.
6. This sentence is correct.
7. importance
8. activity
9. arrival(s)
10. situation

Exercise S5 (p. 170)
1. "Citizen" should be in its plural form, "citizens."
2. "Motivation" is the correct noun form.
3. The use of "that kind" indicates that the noun "genes" should be in its singular form, "gene."
4. "Metalworker" should be in the plural form, "metalworkers," because there is a comparison between Yellin and all the other metalworkers in America.
5. "Children" is the plural form. An "s" should not be added.
6. The use of the plural verb "learn" and the pronoun "their" indicate that the noun "calf" should be in its plural form, "calves."
7. "Advice" does not have a plural form.
8. "Book" should be in its plural form, "books," because there are several books in a series.

Exercise S6 (p. 173)
1. an hour (see 1C, page 170)
2. Ø Mars (see 3F, page 171)
3. Ø school (see 4B, page 172)
4. the rich (see 3C, page 171)
5. An untold number (see 4A, page 172)
6. the only city (see 3D, page 171)

Exercise S7 (p. 174)
1. This article is correct. (see 3F, page 171)
2. This article is correct. (see 3B, page 171)
3. the eighteenth century (see 3D, page 171)
4. Ø Russia (see 3G and 3H, page 172)
5. This article is correct. (see 1B, page 170)
6. Ø nature (see 4D, page 173)

Exercise S8 (p. 174)
1. (A) See Practice with Nouns, 1, page 165.
2. (A) See Practice with Articles and Demonstratives, 5B, page 173.

3. (A) See Practice with Nouns, 3D, page 166.
4. (B) See Practice with Articles and Demonstratives, 5B, page 173.
5. (B) See Practice with Nouns, 3D, page 166.
6. (B) See Practice with Articles and Demonstratives, 5A, page 173.

Exercise S9 (p. 175)
1. That brick house (see 5B, page 173)
2. twice a year (see 2C, page 171)
3. for the first (see 3D, page 171)
4. to find work (see 4D, page 173)
5. This sentence is correct. (see 4D, page 173)
6. Since the beginning (see 3D, page 171)
7. of improvisation (see 4D, page 173)
8. This sentence is correct. (see 3E, page 171)

Exercise S10 (p. 175)
1. (That) dissertations have to be completed within a four-year time limit.
   "That" should be "Those" or "These" (see 5B, page 173); "a" is correct.
2. The good Dr. Sneider began his first year at Arizona State University after having been appointed (a) associate professor.
   "The" is correct ("the" can be used before adjectives preceding names for emphasis); "a" should be "an" (see 1A, page 170).
3. At (a) height of the tourist season, the small seaside community boasts a population of 15,000.
   The first "a" should be "the" (see 3D, page 171); the other articles are correct.
4. Since (the) beginning the research, Dr. Ahmedi has collected seventy different kinds of plant rocks.
   The first "the" is incorrect (an article is not used before a verb form); the second "the" is correct.
5. In a famous book by Daniel Defoe, the hero, Robinson Crusoe, spent twenty years on (a) island.
   The first two articles are correct; the last "a" should be "an" (see 1A, page 170).
6. (Those) child's computer was installed with added features for the blind.
   "Those" should be "That" (see 5B, page 173); "the" is correct.
7. The climbers on the trail admired the majesty of (the) Mount Everest.
   The first three articles are correct; the last "the" should be omitted (see 3F, page 171).
8. The kangaroo travels at speeds up to twenty miles (the) hour by jumping on (the) powerful hind legs.
   The first "the" is correct; the second "the" should be "an" (see 2C, page 171); the third "the" should be "its" (see 3E, page 171).

Exercise S11 (p. 177)
1. his, their
2. his, they, their, they
3. themselves, they, their
4. his, his
5. himself, his
6. itself, us
7. their, their
8. its, its

Exercise S12 (p. 177)

1. "Them" is an object pronoun that is used incorrectly in the possessive adjective position. "Their" is the correct form.
2. "Their" is a possessive adjective, but here it is used in the subject position. "They" is the correct form.
3. "Yourself" is a reflexive pronoun and is used in the correct position. However, "yourself" refers to only "you." "Yourselves" refers to "you and your brother" and is the correct pronoun to use.
4. "Their" is a possessive adjective and is used correctly. "Larvae" is the plural form of "larva." The verb "metamorphose" agrees with the plural form.
5. "They" is a subject pronoun, but here it is used in the object position. "Them" is the correct object of the preposition "of."
6. "Itself" refers to a thing. "Themselves" should be used to refer to the families.
7. "His" is a possessive pronoun used correctly in a noun position.
8. "Their" is a possessive adjective. However, "days" does not belong to anyone. The object pronoun "them" should be used in this position because the meaning is "it took days for them to reach the lower regions."

Exercise S13 (p. 178)

1. their: Vikings
   his: chief
   his: chief
2. he: Abraham Lincoln
   her: Harriet Beecher Stowe
3. they: people
   it: the word "abracadabra"
4. its: the English House of Lords
   they: members
   it: something
   they: members
5. his: the dean
   it: university
6. This: place
   its: ship
7. his: Charles d'Orléans
   his: Charles d'Orléans
   this: Charles d'Orléans smuggled out rhyming
      love letters to his wife
8. its: nutmeg
   their: kernels

Exercise S14 (p. 179)

1. "They" should refer to "site," which is singular. Therefore, the correct pronoun is "it."
2. "Us" should refer to "risks." Therefore, the correct pronoun is "them."
3. "Themselves" refers to the "Tayronas" and is used correctly.
4. "Their" should refer to "gun," which is singular. Therefore, the correct possessive adjective is "its."
5. "Their" refers to "people" and is correct.
6. "It" should refer to "books." Therefore, the correct pronoun is "them."
7. "Her" should refer to "peasants," which is plural. Therefore, the correct pronoun is "their."
8. "It" should refer to "properties," which is plural. Therefore, the correct pronoun is "them."

Exercise S15 (p. 179)

1. (B) The object pronoun "them" refers to "hieroglyphics."
2. (A) The possessive adjective "its" refers to "the dialect."
3. (C) The possessive adjective "their" refers to "idols."
4. (D) The reflexive pronoun "themselves" refers to "the people."
5. (A) The possessive adjective "its" refers to "the police academy."
6. (B) The possessive adjective "his" refers to "Ugo Betti."
7. (B) The reflexive pronoun "itself" refers to "the prickly pear."
8. (D) The subject pronoun "they" refers to "new chemicals."

Exercise S16 (p. 181)

1. (A) A possessive adjective is usually used with body parts. The word "crickets" is plural and would use the possessive adjective "their." (B) uses the article instead of the possessive adjective. (C) and (D) use the singular form of the possessive adjectives.
2. (D) "The" is used with adjectives that represent the group. "The destitute" means "destitute people."
3. (B) The possessive adjective "their" should be used to refer to "divers."
   (A), (B), (C) are personal pronouns that cannot take an adjective position.
4. (B) "The" is not used with the names of states.
5. (A) "Its" should be used as the possessive adjective referring to "tribe."
   (B), (C), and (D) are possessive adjectives that refer to a male or female person or plural people and things.
6. (D) "Children" is the plural form of "child." Turtles were a disease risk to more than one child.
7. (B) The verb "collapses" indicates that the singular form "land" should be used. Since the land refers to the specific land "ground surface," the article "the" is needed.
   (A) uses the incorrect article. (C) and (D) use the plural form of "land."
8. (B) "The" should be used before a noun when it is clear in the situation which thing is being referred to: the authenticity of objects.
9. (B) The noun "fish" can be either plural and singular. The verb "feed" indicates that the "fish" known as "galaxiids" is in the plural form.

(A) and (C) are incorrect because the article "a" is used with singular objects. (D) uses the word "fishes;" this plural form can only be used when more than one type of fish is being discussed.

10. (D) The singular form "system" should be used with the article "a."

11. (A) "Him" is used as the object pronoun for the verb "show." The infinitive phrase "to be" is used with this construction.
(B), (C), (D) do not use the object pronoun form.

12. (D) The possessive adjective "her" should be used with the noun "lifetime" to refer to "Emily Dickinson."

13. (C) "Chinese" has the same singular and plural form. "Many" is used with count nouns. (A) uses the singular word "person," which does not agree with the plural form of the verb "connect." (B), (D) use the word "much," which is used with noncount nouns. The "Chinese" can be counted.

14. (D) "The" is used with adjectives that represent a group. "The wild" means "wild areas."

15. (B) "The" is used with adjectives that represent a group. "The blind" means "blind people." (A) represents one blind person and therefore would need to be followed by the word "person" to be correct. (C) is incorrect because an adjective does not have a plural form. (D) is incorrect because an adjective that represents a group needs the article "the."

16. (C) "Them" is an object pronoun and cannot be used to show possession. Either the possessive adjective "their" referring to "the people" of the town, or the article "the" referring to that particular town could be used here.

17. (C) The plural form "sailplanes" is needed. A singular form would be indicated by the use of an article. The singular form "inventor" is used because Dr. Raspet can only be one inventor. (A) and (D) use the plural form "inventors" but Dr. Raspet cannot be more than one inventor. (B) uses the singular form "sailplane" but an article is missing for this to be correct.

18. (D) "Its" is the possessive adjective that should be used to refer to "rock."

19. (A) The plural noun "forces" indicates that either the article "the," indicating particular forces, or no article, indicating forces in general, would be correct.
(B) and (C) use an article for singular nouns, but "forces" is a plural noun. (D) uses the demonstrative "that," which is used for singular nouns.

20. (A) The verb "have" indicates that the plural form "historians" should be used.

Exercise S17 (p. 186)

1. "Fishermen in the Northwest" is the complete subject. The subject noun which agrees with the verb "thought" is "fishermen."

2. "The Sami" is the complete subject of the verb "have." The phrase "along with many other indigenous peoples" is not part of the subject and does not affect the verb.

3. The complete subject is "St. John's Cathedral." The subject noun which agrees with the verb "is" is "Cathedral." The word order of this sentence has been changed from "St. John's Cathedral is pictured on the one-dollar stamp."

4. The complete subject is "birds, mammals, reptiles, and fish that are not hunted, fished, or trapped." The subject nouns that agree with the verb "need" are "birds, mammals, reptiles, and fish."

5. "Scientists" is the complete subject of the verb "can measure."

6. The complete subject is "far too many preservation programs in too many states." The subject noun that agrees with the verb "rely" is "programs."

7. "It" is the complete subject of the verb "causes."

8. The complete subject is "pesticide residues in livestock." The subject noun that agrees with the verb "are" is "residues."

Exercise S18 (p. 187)

1. "How wildlife has adapted to life along the road systems" is a noun clause used as a subject.

2. "To be among 200-foot-high towering rocks" is an infinitive phrase used as a subject.

3. "Isolating the insects" is a gerund phrase used as a subject.

4. "What happened at the Versailles Conference in 1919" is a noun clause used as a subject.

5. "Whispering in class" is a gerund phrase used as a subject.

6. "To create and produce new combinations of line and color" is an infinitive phrase used as a subject.

7. "What caused the most damage to Michelangelo's works in the Sistine Chapel" is a noun clause used as a subject.

8. "Rolling dice, buying property, and accumulating play-money" are gerund phrases used as a plural subject.

Exercise S19 (p. 187)

1. C   See Practice with Nouns, 3D, page 166.
2. I   "Physics" is singular and takes the verb "is." See Practice with Nouns, 3G, page 166.
3. C   See Practice with Subjects, 3E, page 185.
4. I   The subject "crossing Puget Sound in ferries" is a gerund phrase and takes the singular verb "is." See Practice with Subjects, 3H, page 186.

5. I   "Each" indicates that all rivers and ravines are being discussed as individual units. Therefore, it takes the verb "creates." See Practice with Nouns, 2D, page 165.

6. I   The subject "president" is singular and takes the verb "exercises." See Practice with Subjects, 3B, page 185.

7. C   "Four weeks" is considered a single unit and takes the verb "is." See Practice with Nouns, 3F, page 166.

8. I   "Metaphor and simile" are two nouns that together make a plural subject, which takes the verb "reveal." See Practice with Subjects, 3C, page 185.

Exercise S20 (p. 188)

1. (C)   (C) has an infinitive with the subject preceded by "for." This structure can take a subject position.
        (A) is incorrect because it contains both a subject and a verb. (B) is incorrect because it implies that "the fact (that nutmeg yields fruit) takes eight years" rather than "it takes eight years for nutmeg to yield fruit." (D) is incorrect because it is a prepositional phrase, which cannot take the subject position.

2. (C)   The sentence needs a simple subject that agrees with the singular verb.
        (A) is an infinitive but is illogical because of the redundant verb "use." (B) is not a complete clause and, therefore, cannot be used as a subject. (D) is a prepositional phrase and cannot be used as a subject.

3. (B)   "Clenching the teeth" is a gerund phrase and can take the subject position.
        (A) and (D) are simple subjects, but are not logical because teeth do not clench themselves. Rather, something else (the jaw) clenches the teeth. (C) is not a complete clause and, therefore, cannot be used as a subject.

4. (D)   The sentence needs a simple subject that agrees with the verb "do."
        (A) is not a complete clause and, therefore, cannot be used as a subject. (B) is incorrect because it implies that 6 percent, rather than the stated 26 percent, is the total. (C) is a prepositional phrase and cannot be used as a subject.

5. (D)   The sentence needs a subject that is the name of the sport.
        (A), an infinitive, is not the name of the sport. (B) is not a complete clause and, therefore, cannot be used as a subject. (C) is a piece of equipment used in the sport.

6. (A)   (A) completes the clause that is used as a subject. (B) added to the sentence makes a complete independent clause, which cannot be used as a subject. Neither an infinitive phrase (C) nor a gerund phrase (D) can be used to complete the clause.

7. (A)   (A) is a list of nouns, which can be used as a plural subject and agrees with the plural verb "are."
        (B) is not a complete clause and, therefore, cannot be used as a subject. (C) and (D) use phrases that take a singular verb.

8. (D)   The sentence needs a simple subject.
        (A) is not a complete clause and, therefore, cannot be used as a subject. (B) is illogical because an infinitive phrase cannot perform an activity such as beginning to set up a business. (C) needs an article to be correct.

9. (B)   (B) completes the clause that is used as a subject.
        (A) or (C) added to the sentence makes a complete independent clause, which cannot be used as a subject. (D) is an infinitive phrase that when used as a subject takes a singular verb.

10. (B)   In (B) the gerund phrase is used as a subject and takes the singular verb "makes."
        (A) and (C) are independent clauses and, therefore, cannot be used as subjects. In (D) the subject "climbers and trekkers" is plural and needs a plural verb.

Exercise S21 (p. 189)

1. "It" refers to "the castle of Neuschwanstein."
2. "It" refers to "Ross Island."
3. true (ADJ)
4. belief (NOUN)
5. openness (NOUN)
6. "It" refers to "coronary heart disease."
7. indisputable (ADJ)
8. "It" refers to "stuttering."

Exercise S22 (p. 190)

1. hundreds of thousands of galaxies (EXISTENCE)
2. lines (EXISTENCE)
3. Cricket St. Thomas Wildlife Park (PLACE)
4. messenger services (EXISTENCE)
5. the southern states (PLACE)
6. special troughs (PLACE)

Exercise S23 (p. 191)

1. (B)   A subject and verb are needed to complete the sentence. (A) and (B) have subjects and verbs. However, since the incomplete sentence does not indicate the existence of something, (A) cannot complete the sentence. "It" in (B) is used at the beginning of the sentence to emphasize the object – the fact that the invention of the camera changed how artists painted horses.

2. (A)   Only a subject is needed to complete the sentence. (A) and (C) have only subjects. However, since the incomplete sentence does not contain a noun group that indicates existence, (C) does not complete the sentence. The pronoun "it," in (A) can be used as a subject to complete the sentence and can refer to "crocodile."

3. (C) The sentence is complete and cannot take another subject and verb as in (A) and (B) or a pronoun as in (D). However, the adverb "there" in (C) can be used to emphasize the place, "the center of old San'a."

4. (D) A subject and verb are needed to complete the sentence. Both (C) and (D) have subjects and verbs. The phrase "there is" in (C) needs to be followed by a noun. The phrase "it is" (D) can be followed by an adjective. "Impossible" is an adjective, so (D) completes the sentence.

5. (D) A subject and verb are needed to complete the sentence. (B) and (D) have subjects and verbs. However, the incomplete sentence contains a noun group which indicates existence (noisy market stalls), so only (D) can complete the sentence.

6. (A) A subject and verb are needed to complete the sentence. (A) and (B) have subjects and verbs. However, the incomplete sentence contains a noun group which indicates existence (a growing demand), so only (A) can complete the sentence.

7. (D) Only a subject is needed to complete this sentence. (B) and (D) have only subjects. However, the incomplete sentence does not contain a noun group that indicates existence, so (B) does not complete this sentence. The pronoun "it" in (D) can be used as a subject to complete the sentence and can refer to "arrangement."

8. (B) A subject and verb are needed to complete the sentence. (B) and (C) have subjects and verbs. However, the incomplete sentence contains a noun group that indicates existence (high technology and traditional industries), so only (B) can complete the sentence.

Exercise S24 (p. 192)

1. (A) "Intrigues" is the main verb, and "are" is the verb for a clause used as a subject. A subject is needed to complete the dependent clause. (B) added to the sentence makes a complete independent clause, which cannot be used as a subject. (C) and (D) have both a subject and a verb, so they cannot be used as subjects.

2. (B) The noun "rest" refers to the remaining areas of Africa. Therefore, the article "the" should be used.

3. (B) A subject and verb are needed to complete the sentence. (B) has both a subject, "drops," and a verb, "drip." (A) and (C) have no verbs. (D) is a clause that can be used as a subject but not as a verb.

4. (A) The singular form of the verb "was" and the name of one newspaper indicate that only one newspaper is being discussed. Therefore, the word "some" (meaning "more than one") should be changed to "one."

5. (C) A subject is needed to complete the sentence. (A) and (B) contain both a verb and a subject. (D) is an incomplete clause and, therefore, cannot be used as a subject.

6. (A) The article "a" should be used with "number of" to indicate several battles.

7. (D) Only a subject is needed to complete the sentence. (D) is an infinitive that can be used as a subject. (A) is a verb. (B) contains both a verb and a subject. (C) is an incomplete clause. It needs to be complete to be used as a subject.

8. (B) The plural subject "ships" indicates that the verb form "were" should be used.

9. (B) A subject and a verb are needed to complete the sentence. (B) has both a subject, "it," and a verb, "was." (A) is a clause that can only take the position of a subject in the sentence. (C) and (D) do not contain verbs.

10. (C) The possessive adjective "her" should be used with the noun "ships." The possessive pronoun "hers" cannot be used with a noun.

11. (C) A singular subject is needed to complete the sentence and agree with the singular verb "was." The plural subject "pigments" in (A) does not agree with the singular verb "was." (B) contains a subject and a verb. (D) is an incomplete clause that does not complete the subject.

12. (D) The article "the" is needed before the noun "universe" to indicate that only one universe is being discussed.

13. (D) A subject that agrees with the singular verb is needed to complete the sentence. (A) contains a verb. In (B) the subject is plural and does not agree with the singular verb "has." (C) is an incomplete clause and, therefore, cannot be used as a subject.

14. (C) The singular form "citizen" needs an article. The absence of an article before "U.S." indicates that the plural form "citizens" should be used.

15. (A) Both a subject and a verb are needed to complete the sentence. (C) does not contain a verb. In (B) and (D) the phrase "the cotton textile industry" takes the object position, but the sentence already has the object "the single largest organized industry in India."

16. (A) The article "the" and the prepositional phrase "of Cyprus" indicate that the noun form "beauty" should be used.

17. (B) A singular subject is needed to complete the sentence. (A) contains both a subject and a verb. Although (C) is a subject, it does not fit into the sentence because its verb "translated" cannot be modified by the prepositional phrase "of the *Rubáiyát of Omar Khayyám*." (D) is a prepositional phrase and cannot be used as a subject.

18. (D) The article "the" and the prepositional phrase "of these actions" indicate that the noun form "significance" should be used.

19. (A) A subject and verb is needed. (A) can complete the sentence with the subject "it," the verb "is," and a noun in the object position. The relative clause in the given sentence indicates the structure used to emphasize the noun and clause. (B) and (C) do not have verbs. (D) completes the sentence but is illogical because the article "the" indicates specific "air." However, air in general keeps out the cold.

20. (B) The singular count noun "period" needs an article. Either the article "a" should be used before "long period" or the plural form "periods" should be used.

Exercise S25 (p. 202)

1. "Fall," "use," and "negotiate" are all actions that the subject "stuntmen and stuntwomen" perform.
2. "Cause" is the present tense verb indicating the action of the plural subject "swells" and "winds."
3. This sentence has two independent clauses joined by "and." "Remains" is the present tense verb indicating the action of the subject "temperature," and "reduce" is the present tense verb indicating the action of the subject "blizzards."
4. "Has made" is the present perfect verb form indicating the action of the "landscape."
5. "Might have proved" is the verb of the independent clause and indicates the action of the subject "fingerprints."
6. "Showed" is the past tense verb of the independent clause and indicates the action of the "observations."
7. "Grasp" and "manipulate" are the verbs of the independent clause and indicate the actions of the subject "robots."
8. "Is financed" is the passive form of the present tense verb. The receiver of this action is the noun clause "what help refugees get."

Exercise S26 (p. 203)

1. A The "authorities" are doing the action of "changing downtown areas to pedestrian zones."
2. P "Horatio Alger Jr." is not doing the action of "associating." Others are "associating" him with poor, hardworking boys who achieve success.
3. A The "Romans" did the action of "using cement."
4. A The "customers are doing the action of "demanding goods."
5. P "J. Paul Getty" could not bury himself after he had died. Others did the action of "burying him."
6. A "Dickens" did not complete the action of "finishing his novel."
7. P The "restaurants" could not establish themselves. Others have done the action of "establishing them."

8. P The "International Space Station" could not design, build, and equip itself. Others did the actions.

Exercise S27 (p. 203)

1. The word "since" indicates that this is an action that began in the past and is continuing. Therefore, the verb should be in a present perfect tense. Either "have harbored" or "have been harboring" could be used correctly.
2. The word "recently" indicates a recent past action. Therefore, the verb should be either "has revealed" or "revealed."
3. The verb is used correctly. It indicates the electricity's present ability to travel.
4. The word "now" indicates that the verb should be in the present tense: "are."
5. The verb is used correctly. The word "today" indicates that a present tense should be used. "Are being designed" is in the present progressive tense and indicates that the action is ongoing.
6. The phrase "in the future" indicates that a future tense should be used. "May have been measuring" indicates possibility in an undefined past time. "May be measuring" would be correct.
7. The verb is used correctly. "Have been grown" is the passive voice of the present perfect and indicates that someone has done this action in an undefined past time.
8. The verb is used correctly. The action is taking place now. The verb is in the passive form because the mausoleum does the action of dominating the city.

Exercise S28 (p. 204)

1. C The verb "has been eliminated" agrees with the subject "difference." See Practice with Subjects, 3A, page 185.
2. C The verb "occurs" agrees with the subject "reorganization." See Practice with Subjects, 3A, page 185.
3. I The verb "is" should be "are" to agree with the plural subject "levels." See Practice with Subjects, 3A, page 185.
4. I The verb "are" should be "is" to agree with the singular subject "mathematics." See Practice with Nouns, 3G, page 166.
5. C The verb "is taking" agrees with the noncount noun "pollution." See Practice with Subjects, 3B, page 185.
6. I The verb "contributes" should be "contribute" to agree with the plural subject "execution and use." See Practice with Subjects, 3C, page 185.
7. I The verb "are seen" should be "is seen" to agree with the subject "species." The demonstrative "that" indicates that the singular form of the subject is being used. See Practice with Nouns, 3D, page 166, and Practice with Articles and Demonstratives, 5B, page 173.

Exercise S29 (p. 204)
1. "Comes" is correct.
2. "Haunted" is correct.
3. are
4. makes (or made)
5. "Longed" is correct.
6. are held (or are being held)
7. lies
8. "Dates" is correct.

Exercise S30 (p. 205)

If you have difficulty with any of these items, see Practice with Verbs, 8 and 9, pages 199–201.

1. A	3. B	5. A	7. B
2. A	4. A	6. A	8. A

Exercise S31 (p. 206)
1. (A) The phrase "in 1970" shows that a past tense is required.
    (C) and (D) are present tenses. (B) is an incomplete verb.
2. (A) Since the subject "rebuilding" cannot begin itself, the voice is passive. A past participle is needed: "begun."
    (C) and (D) are complete verbs. (B) is the continuous verb in the active voice.
3. (D) Since the agreement is reached by people, the voice is passive. A past participle is needed: "reached."
    (A) is the present tense. (B) is an infinitive. (C) is the continuous verb in the active voice.
4. (B) Since the subject "producers" is doing the action, the voice is active. The verb "be" (in this case, "have been") is used as an aux-word. It precedes a continuous verb in the active voice.
    (C) and (D) are complete verbs. (A) is the past participle for the passive voice.
5. (B) Since the subject "company" is doing the action, the voice is active. The aux-word "has" is used for the perfect tense.
    (A) is a continuous verb. (D) is a complete verb. (C) is the passive form.
6. (A) The sentence needs a complete verb.
    (D) is not a complete verb. (B) and (C) are complete verbs but are incorrect because they indicate that platinum is no longer rare and valuable (which is not true).
7. (C) "Has" indicates that a present perfect tense or an infinitive meaning "must have" is needed.
    (D) is in the passive voice, but "a great deal of thought" is doing the action. (A) and (B) are verb forms that cannot be used with "has."
8. (D) The verb "have" can indicate a perfect tense. The subject "properties" is not doing the action. Therefore, a passive voice is needed.
    (B) and (C) are not perfect tenses or passive forms. (A) is used for a perfect tense, but does not make a passive voice.

9. (D) The verb "sank" indicates that the action took place in the past. (D) indicates a past possibility. (A) indicates a present time. (B) indicates a present passive. (C) indicates a future time.
10. (B) The phrase "in 1609" indicates a past tense. (B) is a past tense in the active voice. (A) is a present tense. (C) is incomplete. (D) indicates a passive voice, but Galileo did the action of building.

Exercise S32 (p. 208)

1. Rarely	5. Not only . . . as well
2. On no account	6. No sooner . . . than
3. Only if	7. Nowhere
4. Not until	8. So

Exercise S33 (p. 209)

1.   **AUX   SUBJ   V**
     Had Napoleon succeeded
2.   **AUX ____ SUBJ ____   V**
     are federal officials impeached
3.   **AUX SUBJ**
     does tea
4.   **AUX   _ SUBJ _   V**
     should he or she start
5.   **AUX SUBJ _____ V _____**
     will it be able to undertake
6.   **V   SUBJ**
     is the tomato
7.   **AUX ____ SUBJ ____   V**
     Should a medical crisis occur
8.   **V _____ SUBJ _____**
     remain the mysterious giant stone heads

Exercise S34 (p. 209)
1. This sentence is correct.
2. Not only before exercising should one stretch . . . See Practice with Subject/Aux-Word Inversions, 5, page 207.
3. This sentence is correct.
4. This sentence is correct.
5. . . . neither is a hot climate. See Practice with Subject/Aux-Word Inversions, 2, page 207.
6. This sentence is correct.
7. Not only do swallows build their nests inside farm buildings, but sparrows do as well. See Practice with Subject/Aux-Word Inversions, 5, page 207.
8. This sentence is correct.

Exercise S35 (p. 210)
1. (B) "Only" in this sentence indicates that "no major projects" get underway until after years of planning.
2. (B) "Never" in this sentence indicates that linguistic creativity was most notable in Elizabethan England.
3. (A) "No sooner" means that "at the same time" and "not before" the Pilgrims landed, they were approached by Tisquantum.

4. (A) "Under no circumstances" means "never."

5. (B) "Not only" is used with "but also" to join two related ideas.

6. (A) "Not once" indicates that the penguin never leaves its nest before the chick hatches.

7. (B) "Through" is a preposition and needs to be followed by a noun. "Only" indicates that there is no other way that a vaccine can be found.

8. (B) "Nowhere" means "no other place" has such splendid autumn colors.

Exercise S36 (p. 211)

1. (C) "Contains" is a verb in the simple present tense. Since the book continues to exist, it still contains this information.
   (A) is a passive verb form. (B) and (D) are continuous forms, but the book always contains the descriptions.

2. (C) "Setting" is an incomplete verb. The date 1841 indicates a completed past action, so the verb should be in the simple past tense form "set."

3. (C) A verb is missing. Since the subject "sulky" cannot believe anything, a passive form is needed.
   (A), (B) and (D) are not passive verb forms.

4. (A) The verb form "survive" should be used after the modal "can."

5. (C) The words "but also" indicate that a "not only" phrase is needed. (C) uses the "not only" phrase after the subject, not at the beginning, so a subject/aux-word inversion is not needed.
   If the "not only" phrase begins the sentence as in (A) and (D), a subject/aux-word inversion should be used. (B) is incorrect because the verb "keep" should follow the subject "habits."

6. (B) The verb "refer" is in plural form and does not agree with the singular noun "the term." The correct form is "refers."

7. (C) A subject and verb are needed to complete the sentence. The phrase "not until" indicates that a subject/aux-word inversion is needed.
   (A) and (D) are clauses that cannot take a subject/verb position. (B) is the question form of an independent clause and cannot take a subject/verb position.

8. (D) The plural verb form "are" does not agree with the singular subject "one." The singular verb form "is" should be used.

9. (C) The prepositional phrase indicating place at the beginning of the sentence requires a subject/aux-word inversion.
   (A) has the inversion but includes the adverb "there," which is an unnecessary redundancy because the place is emphasized by the prepositional phrase at the beginning of the sentence. (B) and (D) do not have the required subject/aux-word inversion.

10. (C) The plural noun "novelists" needs the plural verb "reside."

11. (D) A subject and verb are needed to complete the dependent clause. Since llamas did not bring themselves, a passive form is necessary.
    (A) does not use the passive verb form. The word order in (B) is incorrect because no inversion is needed. (C) is an adverb phrase that cannot be used in a subject/verb position.

12. (C) The plural subject "differences" indicates that the plural verb "are" should be used.

13. (A) The blank before the subject "air pollution" indicates that the subject and aux-word have been inverted to avoid the repetition of the word "receives."
    (B) and (D) use "it" as a subject, which is redundant because "air pollution" is already the subject. (C) is a preposition and cannot take the aux-word position.

14. (B) The verb tense "were built" should be in a present tense form to agree in time with the verb "increases."

15. (D) A verb is needed to complete the sentence. The phrase "by bacteria" indicates the use of a passive form.
    (A) and (B) are not complete verbs. The verb in (C) is in the active form.

16. (D) The infinitive form "to undertake" should be used with the verb "has motivated."

17. (D) A subject and verb are needed to complete the sentence. The prepositional phrase of location at the beginning of the sentence indicates that a change in the word order of the subject and verb is needed.
    (A) is a dependent clause and cannot take a subject/verb position. (B) has incorrect word order. (C) is a subject and verb but it does not have the change in word order that is needed.

18. (B) The verb is incomplete. Since the subject "lack" and "overindulgence" cannot know anything, a passive form is needed. The verb phrase should be "have long been known to be."

19. (A) A verb is needed to complete the sentence. The verbs in (B) and (D) are incomplete. (C) is an infinitive form of the verb.

20. (B) The words "only if" affect the word order of the independent clause. The subject/aux-word inversion should be "will sufferers."

Exercise S37 (p. 216)

1. N	*(-ist)*	9. N	*(-ity)*
2. ADJ	*(-ic)*	10. V	*(-en)*
3. N	*(-hood)*	11. N	*(-ship)*
4. V	*(-ize)*	12. ADJ	*(-ial)*
5. ADJ	*(-ful)*	13. V	*(-ate)*
6. ADV	*(-ly)*	14. ADV	*(-ly)*
7. N	*(-ance)*	15. N	*(-ness)*
8. ADJ	*(-able)*		

Exercise S38 (p. 216)

1. ADV
2. ADJ
3. V
4. N
5. ADJ
6. N
7. V
8. ADV
9. ADJ
10. ADV

Exercise S39 (p. 217)

1. (correct)
2. restoration
3. (correct)
4. tranquility
5. excitement
6. varieties
7. impediment
8. (correct)
9. Immigrants
10. employment

Exercise S40 (p. 218)

1. tolerate
2. (correct)
3. (correct)
4. establish
5. (correct)
6. symbolizes
7. explain
8. (correct)
9. verbalize
10. (correct)

Exercise S41 (p. 219)

1. (correct)
2. cooperative
3. (correct)
4. historical
5. beautiful
6. famous
7. (correct)
8. traditional
9. (correct)
10. burial

Exercise S42 (p. 220)

1. (correct)
2. yearly
3. reasonably
4. collectively
5. (correct)
6. virtually
7. undeniably
8. (correct)
9. hastily
10. (correct)

Exercise S43 (p. 223)

1. (correct)
2. and
3. and/or
4. (correct)
5. (correct)
6. but
7. and
8. but/or

Exercise S44 (p. 224)

1. (correct)
2. nor
3. and
4. either
5. or
6. and
7. both
8. Neither

Exercise S45 (p. 224)

1. such as
2. (correct)
3. (correct)
4. As
5. such as
6. (correct)
7. as
8. so

Exercise S46 (p. 225)

1. (correct)
2. so
3. (correct)
4. enough
5. so
6. (correct)
7. too
8. too

Exercise S47 (p. 225)

1. much
2. Few
3. (correct)
4. many
5. (correct)
6. (correct)
7. little
8. much

Exercise S48 (p. 226)

1. (correct)
2. alike
3. like
4. alike
5. (correct)
6. Unlike
7. (correct)
8. (correct)

Exercise S49 (p. 226)

1. other
2. the other
3. (correct)
4. (correct)
5. another
6. (correct)
7. others
8. other

Exercise S50 (p. 227)

1. enable
   A verb is needed. "Enable" is a verb, whereas "able" is an adjective.
2. apart
   An adverb is needed. "Apart" is an adverb, whereas "separate" is an adjective or verb.
3. somewhat
   An adverb is needed. "Somewhat" is an adverb. "Some" is a quantifier – a word that indicates a quantity.
4. people
   A plural noun is needed. "People" is plural, whereas "person" is singular.
5. number
   "Number" is used with count nouns. "Buffalo" can be counted. "Amount" is used with noncount nouns.
6. have made
   The general meaning of "do" is connected with activity. The general meaning of "make" is to produce something that did not exist before.
7. alive
   An adjective is needed. Although both "alive" and "live" are adjectives, "live" must be used before a noun but "alive" cannot be used before a noun. It is always used after a verb.
8. aside
   "Aside" is used to indicate a movement. "Beside" is used to indicate a position.
9. observation
   "Observation" is the action of carefully watching someone or something. "Observance" is the practice of obeying or following a law or custom.
10. number
    "Number" is used with a count noun. "Peaks" can be counted. "Quantity" is used with a noncount noun.

Exercise S51 (p. 228)

1. (B) "So" cannot be used as a preposition. The correct word is "as."

2. (C) The adverb form "mostly" should be used to indicate that there was more metal than anything else used in helmets.
(A) uses the word "most" as a quantifier. (B) and (D) use the word "most" as the superlative form.

3. (A) "Much" is used with noncount nouns, but plants and animals can be counted. "Many" is the correct word.

4. (D) There is no comparison in this sentence. "Enough" should follow the word it modifies: "strong enough."
(A) uses an incorrect word order. (B) and (C) use the comparative form.

5. (A) The correct form in the subject position is "wood." "Wooden" is the adjective form.

6. (D) The verb in its infinitive form plus noun is used to describe the Grand Canyon. The adjective "impassable" should be used to modify the noun "barrier."
(A) uses the incorrect form of the verb "be."
(B) and (C) use the adverb form "impassably."

7. (A) The correct form in the subject position is "clouds." "Cloudy" is the adjective form.

8. (B) Since a prepositional phrase needs a noun, the noun form "tradition" should be used.
(A), (C), and (D) are missing a noun to complete the prepositional phrase. The word "Greek" in these phrases is used as an adjective. Greek can be a noun only when referring to people or the language.

9. (C) "Enough" follows an adjective or adverb. "Hillside" is a noun. "So" can follow a noun and is the correct word to introduce a "that" clause.

10. (D) "Hearts" and "kidneys" are examples of "organs." Examples are introduced by the words "such as."
(A) is missing the word "as" to complete the phrase "such as." (B) uses an expression of equality. (C) uses the clause marker "so."

11. (A) "Do" is generally used to indicate an activity. "Make" is generally used to indicate the production of something that did not exist before. In this case, "made" indicates that the grenade has been constructed.

12. (C) The adjective "other" should be used before the noun "subspecies."
(A) and (D) are noun forms. In (B) the word "another," which refers to "one," cannot be used with "all," a word that refers to more than one.

13. (C) "Develop" is the verb form. The article "the" indicates that the noun "development" should be used.

14. (B) "To" indicates that the infinitive form "to keep" should be used.
(A) contains the gerund form "flying," which would be used with the word "for." (C) and (D) are verb tense forms that could not be used in the infinitive position.

15. (B) A verb cannot be used in a prepositional phrase. Since "unlike a tractor" is a prepositional phrase, the verb "is" should be omitted from the sentence.

16. (A) The noun form "fainting" should be used in the subject position.
(B) and (C) are adjective or verb forms that cannot be used in a noun position. (D) is a noun, but refers to a group or class of people who are faint.

17. (B) "Able" is an adjective, but there is no noun for it to modify. The verb "enable" should be used to complete the infinitive form "to enable."

18. (D) The noun form "custom" should be used as the object of the preposition "on."
(A) is the adverb form, (B) is the adjective form, and (C) is the verb form.

19. (C) "Alike" is an adverb or adjective and cannot be used to introduce a clause. "Like" is the correct word to use.

20. (D) "Somewhat" is an adverb meaning "to some degree." To some degree the egg is less likely to roll off the cliff.
(A) refers to an unidentified place, (B) means occasionally, and (C) refers to an object.

Exercise S52 (p. 232)

1. I	3. I	5. I	7. D
2. D	4. D	6. I	8. I

Exercise S53 (p. 232)

1. C	3. I	5. I	7. C
2. C	4. C	6. I	8. I

Exercise S54 (p. 234)

1. noun clause
2. noun clause
3. noun clause/independent clause
4. independent clause
5. noun clause/independent clause
6. noun clause
7. independent clause
8. noun clause/independent clause

Exercise S55 (p. 235)

1. S   How the buildings are constructed to keep their inhabitants cool
2. S   What many doctors advise
3. S   When the city of Rome was actually founded
4. O   that a woman can be as good a scientist as a man can be
5. O   that all human beings have five levels of needs
6. S   what gestures mean in one particular culture
7. O   when an eruption is imminent
8. S   That old cities lose their charm in their zeal to modernize

Exercise S56 (p. 236)

1. That rent control laws may inhibit landlords from repairing properties is

2. (Studies of newborn infants) show
3. (How glass is blown in a cylinder) was demonstrated
4. (A top architect) lamented
5. (Why consumers hesitated to buy the controversial digital audiotape players) is
6. (Whom the late Dr. Bishopstone left his fortune to) will be revealed
7. (Major studies) have indicated
8. (What the manufacturer does to syrup) results

Exercise S57 (p. 236)

1. (Whose design) is ultimately chosen
2. (no alcohol or chemicals) are included
3. (a disaster) had struck
4. (many nonsmokers) find
5. (radioactive antibodies) can help locate
6. (far too little) is being done
7. (the poverty action group) was set up
8. (witch doctors) cure

Exercise S58 (p. 236)

1. In 1776, the U.S. Congress resolved that the
   would
   authority of the British crown ~~will~~ be suppressed.
   (The action in the independent clause took place in the past, in 1776, so the verb "will" should change to "would" in past reported speech.
2. This sentence is correct.
3. Apprentices sometimes fear that they might not
   be
   ~~have been~~ able to master the intricacies of their chosen craft.
   (Apprentices fear something now, so the verb in the noun clause should indicate either a present or future possibility.)
   got
4. That the rather large President Taft ~~will get~~ stuck in a White House bathtub was an incentive for the installation of an oversized tub.
   (The past tense "was" in the independent clause indicates that Taft's getting stuck happened in the past. Therefore, a past tense is needed in the noun clause.)
   have   learned
5. What we ~~will~~ already ~~learn~~ about tornadoes has contributed to reducing the casualty rates.
   (The word "already" indicates that the action took place in the recent past.)
6. This sentence is correct.
7. This sentence is correct.
8. Before the flight of Sputnik, many people believed
   was/would be
   that space exploration ~~is~~ impossible.
   (The past tense "believed" in the independent clause means that a past tense is needed in the noun clause as well.)

Exercise S59 (p. 237)

1. (C) "What" is used to focus on specific information.
2. (A) "Where" is used to indicate a place.
3. (A) "That" is used to indicate a fact.
4. (C) "Who" is used to indicate a person.
5. (C) "That" is used to indicate a fact.
6. (B) "Which" is used to specify an alternative.
7. (D) "How" is used to indicate the manner in which something is done.
8. (D) "Why" is used to indicate a reason.

Exercise S60 (p. 238)

1. (D) The noun clause needs a clause marker. The clause marker "that" completes the sentence by indicating a fact.
   (A) and (C) do not contain clause markers. In (B) the information indicated by the clause marker "what" is mentioned in the sentence and, therefore, is incorrect.
2. (A) The noun clause needs the noun clause marker "what" to introduce the clause "the sales person does to get the potential buyer to make a purchase."
3. (C) The verb in the noun clause is incomplete. The verb in (C) indicates a future action and completes the sentence.
   The verb form in (A) cannot be used with the aux-word "would." (B) and (D) indicate that the action has already occurred, but the verb in the independent clause indicates that the action is something that may occur in the future.
4. (D) The independent clause needs the complete verb "is called."
5. (B) The noun clause used as a subject needs a clause marker. "Whether" is a clause marker and indicates an alternative. Either Latin speakers borrowed the word "caupo" from Germanic speakers or Germanic speakers borrowed the word from Latin speakers.
   (A) and (C) are not noun-clause markers. In (D) the clause marker "which" indicates a choice. However, there is no choice between Latin speakers.
6. (C) The clause marker "how" should be used to introduce the noun clause.
7. (B) An object is needed to complete the sentence. A noun clause can take the object position.
   (A) uses the word order for a question. (C) and (D) do not use a clause marker to introduce the clause.
8. (C) The clause marker "what" is the subject of the noun clause and takes the singular verb form "comes."
9. (A) A verb is needed to complete the noun clause used as a subject. A passive voice is indicated by the phrase "by daily consumption."
   (B) and (D) are not in the passive voice. The future perfect in (C) indicates that the action has not taken place. However, the present tense verb "gives" indicates that the action has taken place.

10. (A) The noun clause marker "that" should be used to indicate the fact Hubble proved.
11. (B) A clause marker is needed to complete the sentence. "What" should be used to focus on the information concerning the treasure. (A) indicates a fact. (C) indicates a reason. (D) indicates a place.
12. (D) The object of the preposition "about" is the noun clause "who you are." The pronoun "it" cannot take the noun position already occupied by the noun clause.
13. (B) A subject and verb are needed to complete the sentence. The clause marker "that" should introduce the noun clause.
The clause marker does not introduce the clause in (A) and (D). In (C) the verb is incomplete.
14. (C) The verb form "acquitted" should be used in the noun clause so that it is parallel with the other simple past tense verbs in the clause.
15. (D) A subject, verb, and clause marker are needed to complete the sentence.
(A) does not have a subject. (B) is in question word order. (C) does not have a verb.
16. (D) The noun clause used as a subject of the independent clauses uses a singular verb form, "has."
17. (B) A clause marker is needed to complete the sentence. The clause marker "what" focuses on the specific thing – the act of tying shoes. In (A) "where" indicates a place. In (C) "which" indicates a choice. In (D) "when" indicates a time.
18. (A) The noun clause already has the subject "individuals" so "who" is incorrect. The clause marker "that" should introduce the noun clause.
19. (A) A subject and verb are needed to complete the sentence.
The verb in (B) is not complete. (C) and (D) are dependent-clause forms that cannot complete both a subject and verb position.
20. (C) The word "woman" should be in the plural form "women" so that it is parallel with "men." The singular form would need the article "a" or "the" to be correct.

Exercise S61 (p. 243)
1. who   3. who   5. that   7. whom
2. which   4. where   6. that   8. where

Exercise S62 (p. 243)
1. (date) on which Romulus founded Rome
2. (description) that has puzzled playgoers, directors, and even critics
3. (Those) who are reluctant to ask for clarification about a job requirement
4. (hedgehog) which has outlived the mammoth and the saber-toothed tiger
5. (plays) people have enjoyed for four centuries
6. (man) whose creations still bring happiness to many children

7. (enclosure) where children can interact with young farm animals
8. (balance) which will safeguard succeeding generations

Exercise S63 (p. 244)
1. IC "Which" can refer to a place when it is used in the subject position of the adjective clause. "Where" cannot fill a subject position.
2. IC "Who" refers to a person and is the correct pronoun in the subject position.
3. C
4. C
5. IC "Who" refers to a person and is the correct pronoun in the subject position.
6. C
7. IC "Which" is the correct pronoun referring to "civilization."
8. IC "Who" refers to a person and is the correct pronoun in the subject position.

Exercise S64 (p. 244)
1. (D) The missing clause marker refers to "city." (D) is the clause marker that refers to a location and takes the adverb position in the clause.
2. (B) The missing clause marker is the subject of the clause and refers to "job." (B) is the clause marker that refers to things and can be used in the subject position.
3. (D) The missing clause marker takes the possessive position before the noun "works" and refers to "Monteverdi." (D) is the clause marker that is used in clauses showing possession.
4. (B) The missing clause marker is in the adverb position of the clause and refers to a place, "Death Valley." (B) is the clause marker that takes an adverb position and refers to a place.
5. (B) The missing clause marker is the subject of the clause and refers to "looters." Looters are people. (B) is the clause marker that can be used in the subject position and refers to people.
6. (C) The missing clause marker is the object of the preposition "for" and refers to "those." "Those" refers to people who are obsessed with skiing. (C) is the clause marker that can take the object of the preposition position and refers to people.
7. (A) The missing clause marker is the subject of the clause and refers to "inventors." Inventors are people. (A) is the clause marker that takes the subject position and refers to people.
8. (C) The missing clause marker is the subject of the clause and refers to "glaucoma." (C) is the clause marker that can be used in the subject position and refers to a thing.

Exercise S65 (p. 245)
1. (who) was   5. (they) go
2. (people) use   6. (which) is
3. (which) had been used 7. (doctors) have found
4. (bees) carry   8. (whose appetites) are
                         (that) carry

Exercise S66 (p. 246)

1. Bicyclists pedal through the countryside during
   held
   a week-long ride that is ~~holding~~ every summer
   in Iowa.
2. This sentence is correct.
3. It is Earth's magnetic field that ~~made~~ a compass
   makes
   work.
4. A vending machine is a kind of robot salesperson
   gives
   that automatically ~~gave~~ out candy or other items
   when money is inserted.
5. This sentence is correct.
6. A laser cane, which the blind find useful, sends out
   detect
   beams that ~~detecting~~ obstacles.
7. For the foreign buyers to whom Canada ~~supplying~~
   supplies/is supplying
   furs, the industry has never been healthier.
8. Lucid dreamers are those people who recognize
   control/can control
   when they are dreaming and thus ~~controlling~~
   the plot of their dreams.

Exercise S67 (p. 248)

1. suffering from the heat on warm summer days
2. on display at book festivals
3. first revived in 1951 in York
4. giving full details of the layout of museums
5. used in street-sweeping machines
6. discouraging casual appearance in their employees
7. in remote areas
8. lucky enough to be wealthy and male; composed
   exclusively of men; born on the same day

Exercise S68 (p. 249)

1. C which historians call the Renaissance
2. P/C leading into the ancient city of Petra; that ends
   in front of an impressive temple; carved out
   of the sandstone cliffs
3. P exiled to Siberia in czarist Russia
4. P linking the southwestern corner of France
   to the Mediterranean
5. C who have been raised apart
6. P found in the Andes
7. P flowing over weaker ones
8. C where they give birth to their calves

Exercise S69 (p. 249)

1. The letter "M" may have originated as a hieroglyphic
   symbol representing the crests of waves and meaning
   "water."
2. There are still people dying from diseases that are
   preventable and controllable.
3. Before the age of steam, hemp, used for ropes on
   ships, was an important commodity.
4. No change is possible.
5. No change is possible.
6. Rings, probably invented by the Egyptians, were an
   easy way to display authority.

7. Wind deflected down the face of tall buildings
   causes gusty, swirling winds in the streets.
8. Pain is the body's warning signal calling attention
   to a potentially harmful condition.

Exercise S70 (p. 250)

1. Ambroise Paré, ~~knowing~~ as the father of modern
   known
   surgery, brought medicine out of the Dark Ages.
2. Each child ~~enter~~ school for the first time is
   entering
   individually screened.
3. This sentence is correct.
4. Scissors, a Bronze Age invention ~~remained~~ basically
   remaining
   unchanged to this day, consist of two blades linked
   by a C-shaped spring.
5. This sentence is correct.
6. Butterfly wings have iridescent scales ~~consist~~
   consisting
   of thin, interlaced layers.
7. Glacier National Park is impressive with its
   towering
   mountain peaks ~~are towering~~ over splendid lakes.
8. Medicine ~~finding~~ in bathroom cabinets should be
   found
   thrown out if the expiration date has passed.

Exercise S71 (p. 251)

1. (D) The adjective clause is missing a subject and a
   verb. "That transforms" has both a subject and
   a verb and completes the sentence.
   (A) is only the clause marker. (B) is a complete
   adjective clause but the clause marker
   "who" refers to a person instead of a thing –
   "instrument." (C) is the passive voice of an
   adjective phrase, but the instrument does not
   transform itself.
2. (B) The verb in the adjective clause should be in the
   present tense form "is" to be logical in meaning.
3. (C) An adjective clause or phrase is needed. (C) is
   a complete adjective clause.
   (A) is incorrect because the clause marker
   "where" cannot take the subject position.
   (B) and (D) are complete verbs that cannot take
   an adjective clause or phrase position.
4. (A) The words "and encloses" indicates that another
   verb is needed. "Shedding" should be "sheds"
   to be a parallel verb.
5. (B) A subject for the independent clause is needed.
   (B) completes the sentence with a noun that
   can be used in the subject position.
   (C) is an incomplete clause and cannot take
   the subject position. (D) contains a verb that is
   incorrect because the independent clause already
   has a verb. (A) has a subject but is incorrect
   because the clause marker "which" cannot
   be used with the verb "found" without the
   aux-word "are."

6. (B) The subject and verb of the independent clause are "formations" and "are." The adjective clauses that have been reduced are "that were discovered" and "that were hanging." The first clause is reduced to the passive form "discovered" and the second clause should be reduced to the active form "hanging."

7. (C) A simple verb "is" is needed.
(A) and (B) form adjective clauses, but complete the independent clause. (D) includes a subject that cannot take the subject position because "Nantucket" is in the subject position.

8. (A) The clause marker "which" should not be in the sentence. The word "untouched" is in the passive form of the verb indicating that the clause "which had been untouched for 2,500 years" has been reduced to the adjective phrase "untouched for 2,500 years."

9. (A) An adjective clause or phrase is needed. All four choices are adjective phrases. (A) completes the sentence with the correct word order. "Once" is an adverb indicating that the action of being "hunted" occurred in the past and "almost" is an adverb indicating how close "to extinction" the ox was.
The word order in (B), (C), and (D) is incorrect.

10. (A) The passive form "attached" should be used in the adjective phrase reduced from the adjective clause "that are attached."

11. (D) The passive verb form "is called" is needed to complete the independent clause.
(A) is the passive form for an adjective phrase. (B) is a complete independent clause. (C) is an adjective clause.

12. (C) The adjective clause marker "that" is in the subject position of the adjective clause. Therefore, the pronoun "they" cannot take the subject position of the adjective clause.

13. (B) An adjective clause or phrase is needed. The passive voice is indicated because someone forced the Cherokee Indians west.
(C) and (D) are verbs, not adjective clauses or phrases. The verb form in (A) indicates the active voice.

14. (B) The clause marker "who" or "that" should be used because volunteers are people.

15. (D) An adjective clause or phrase in the active voice is needed. The relative pronoun "who" in (D) is the clause marker introducing a clause that refers to "people."
(A) is an adjective phrase, but the verb form indicates a passive voice. (B) is not an adjective clause or phrase. The word "those" in (C) is not an adjective clause marker.

16. (A) The clause marker "where" should be used to refer to the place "ancient Greece."

17. (A) An adjective clause or phrase is needed. (A) is an adjective phrase, reduced from the clause "which was the famous endangered snaildarter." (B) is an independent clause. (C) is incorrect because the verb "is" is dropped when the adjective clause pattern "subject + to be + noun" is reduced. (D) is an incomplete adjective clause because the verb is missing.

18. (C) The verb in the adjective clause should be "would become" to agree with the verb "was seen" in the independent clause.

19. (D) An adjective clause or phrase in the active voice is needed. The active voice of the adjective phrase in (D) indicates that the moths are surviving.
(A) and (C) are not adjective clauses or phrases. The passive form in (B) is incorrect because the moths are doing the action of surviving.

20. (D) The verb in the adjective clause is in the present tense. It should be in the past tense "used" because the clause is about people centuries ago.

Exercise S72 (p. 256)
1. so that pedestrians would not get their feet muddy
2. Although the existence of germs was verified in about 1600
3. If you should step on a stingray
4. Even though there was a campaign against smoking
5. because it is one of the first birds to return north
6. whereas fired clay does not
7. When an Easterner in 1886 described St. Paul, Minnesota, as another Siberia
8. Since the search to find and document sites of Native American cave paintings was first begun

Exercise S73 (p. 256)
1. There is no adverb clause in this sentence. The adjective phrase "related to 'month'" describes the word "word."
2. Even though it contains no fish
3. As traders mill about in the New York Stock Exchange
4. There is no adverb clause. The prepositional phrases "on Negit Island" and "in one day" are used as adverbs to indicate place and time.
5. There is no adverb clause. This sentence has a gerund phrase used as a subject, and the phrase "not only. . . but also" is used to join the two verbs.
6. until violent earthquakes and invasions brought its prosperity to an end
7. There is no adverb clause. The prepositional phrase "from blazing fires" comes from a reduced adjective clause and describes the word "smoke."
8. There is no adverb clause. "To combat damaging impurities" is a phrase. "That have penetrated their surface" is an adjective clause describing the word "impurities."

Exercise S74 (p. 257)

1. (monitoring earthquakes) is
2. (one of the species of bamboo on which they feed) died out
3. (oceans) cover
4. (the Chinese sage Confucius) lived
5. (she) devoted
6. (the world population) continues
7. (some Inuit) migrate
8. (the ice crystals from which they form) are

Exercise S75 (p. 258)

1. As dusk ~~settling~~ *settles*, fireflies begin to signal.
2. If the Italian authorities hadn't ~~took~~ *taken* measures to control the smuggling of national treasures, many Roman artifacts would have been lost.
3. Sixteenth-century mariners called Bermuda the "Isle of Devils" partly because breeding seabirds ~~are making~~ *made* horrid sounds in the night.
4. This sentence is correct.
5. This sentence is correct.
6. Whenever we ~~blamed~~ *blame* someone else for our own shortcomings, we are being unfair to them and to ourselves.
7. This sentence is correct.
8. When a key on a pipe organ ~~pressed~~ *is pressed*, a series of levers opens the hole in the pipe and air is pumped through.

Exercise S76 (p. 258)

1. (D) A clause marker that indicates a time sequence is needed. "After" indicates that first the mutineers seized command of the ship, and then they cast off the captain and crew members.
2. (B) A clause marker that indicates a cause and effect (reason) is needed. "Because" introduces the reason the region is referred to as the "Garden of England."
3. (A) A clause marker that indicates a purpose is needed. "So that" introduces the purpose for seat belt laws.
4. (A) A clause marker that indicates time is needed. "As soon as" indicates that children scramble for treats immediately after a piñata is broken.
5. (C) A clause marker that indicates time is needed. "Until" indicates that the city flourished and then fell. (A) also indicates time, but "as soon as" introduces a time sequence of one action happening almost immediately after the other.
6. (B) A clause marker that indicates a cause and effect (reason) is needed. "So" introduces the reason firefighters must enter skyscrapers dressed in suits designed to supply oxygen and reflect heat.

7. (C) A clause marker that indicates a time sequence is needed. "When" indicates that the myth was shattered at the time the elephants were destroyed. (B) is incorrect because "until" indicates that the action occurred up to a point in time.
8. (D) A clause marker that indicates a concession is needed. "Even though" indicates that the thriving cultivation of the poppy is contrary to many governments' wishes.

Exercise S77 (p. 261)

1. C until he reached Polynesia
2. P While staying at the Greyfield Inn
3. C Before migrating whales head for Baja California's lagoons
4. P When creating creatures for movies
5. C because holding the reins in one hand frees the other hand for roping
6. P After harpooning walruses
7. P Before Disneyland's opening in 1955
8. P After having convinced himself that the Hudson was only a river and not the Northwest Passage

Exercise S78 (p. 262)

1. The adverb clause "although some people prefer white eggs to brown" cannot be reduced.
2. The adverb clause "when Cartier first discovered them" cannot be reduced.
3. While attempting to fly around the world, Amelia Earhart mysteriously disappeared without a trace.
4. After ending their larval period, the worms suddenly grow sluggish and enter the stage of metamorphosing into adults.
5. The adverb clause "by the time newcomers to the United States had passed through the immigration center on Ellis Island" cannot be reduced.
6. The adverb clause "While knowledge about the brain is growing" cannot be reduced.
7. When building Hadrian's Wall, the Romans also erected towers about every mile.
8. The Hussites had fled persecution in central Europe and Russia before coming to settle in the United States.

Exercise S79 (p. 262)

1. George Gershwin gathered motifs for his opera *Porgy and Bess* while ~~lived~~ *living* in Charleston.
2. This sentence is correct.
3. Having first *been* domesticated for production, sheep were then used for wool.
4. This sentence is correct.
5. After ~~spin~~ *spinning* its web using sticky silk threads, a spider retreats via a walkway of dry silk threads.
6. This sentence is correct.
   being

7. Since ~~been~~ eradicated, the smallpox virus is only found in laboratories.

8. After ~~attached~~ *attaching* themselves to a ship's hull, barnacles and algae create friction that impedes the ship's movements.

Exercise S80 (p. 263)

1. (B) A clause marker that indicates concession is needed. "Though" indicates the contrast between the Australopithecus's ability to walk and the fact that it only walked for short periods of time.

2. (A) A clause marker that indicates a time sequence is needed. "After" indicates that intermittent eruptions occurred following the first eruption in May 1980. (C) is incorrect because when a clause introduced by "since" is used, the verb in the independent clause is usually either in the present perfect or the past perfect.

3. (D) A clause marker that indicates a time sequence is needed. "After" indicates that first pythons seize their prey and then they coil themselves around the prey. (A) is incorrect because "until" suggests that pythons coil themselves around their prey up to the point of seizing it. (C) is illogical because it is used to indicate when a situation began.

4. (B) A clause marker that indicates a time sequence is needed. "When" indicates that at the time the bear is running, it can go 35 miles an hour.

5. (C) A clause marker that indicates a concession is needed. "While" indicates that poison ivy does not kill people, it just makes them very ill.

6. (B) A clause marker that indicates a time sequence is needed. "When" indicates that at the time Daniel Webster declared the area useless, it was not possible for him to know the importance of irrigation for the valley.

7. (B) A clause marker that indicates a time sequence is needed. "While" indicates that the farmer uncovered the burial during the time that he or she was plowing. (C) is incorrect because "since" indicates that the farmer uncovered the burial after plowing the field. (D) is incorrect because "until" indicates that the farmer uncovered the burial up to the point of time that he or she plowed the field.

8. (D) A clause marker that indicates a concession is needed. "Although" indicates that contrary to one's expectation that the Tyndale Bible would not be used, it has been used extensively.

Exercise S81 (p. 264)

1. (C) An adverb clause or phrase of concession is needed. The clause marker "while" in (C) indicates a contrast between the flower's strength and its fragility.

(A) and (D) are not adverb clauses or phrases. The clause marker "when" in (B) is illogical because the relationship between the clauses is not one of time.

2. (C) Someone has to slaughter the birds. Therefore, "slaughtered" should be in a passive form, "were being slaughtered" or "had been slaughtered."

3. (D) The independent clause is complete. Therefore, either a dependent clause or phrase is needed in the blank. (D) is an adverb phrase indicating how seals glide through the sea.

(A) has verbs that need a subject. The use of (B) makes a complete independent clause. (C) is a dependent clause that takes a subject position in an independent clause.

4. (B) The verb in the adverb phrase should be in the active voice "draining."

5. (D) A clause marker that indicates a concession is needed. (D) "Although" indicates a contrast between the pandas' eating bamboo and their being carnivorous.

(A) "Not only" is not a clause marker. (B) "Until" and (C) "As soon as" indicate a time sequence.

6. (A) "Whereas" indicates a contrast. This sentence is about a series of events. Cranberries are first harvested and then dropped down a chute. The correct adverb clause marker would be "after" or "as soon as."

7. (C) A subject for the adverb clause is needed. (C) is a gerund that can be used as the subject of the adverb clause.

(A) is incorrect because it includes an unnecessary clause marker "when." (B) is incorrect because it includes a verb, and there is already a verb in the clause. (D) is incorrect because it is the verb form for an adverb phrase.

8. (B) The clause marker "if" is missing from the phrase "only if."

9. (B) A clause marker that indicates a time sequence is needed. (B) "Until" indicates that the condor glides up to the point in time when it needs to flap its wings to reach updrafts.

(A) "Because" indicates a reason. (C) "That" is not a clause marker. (D) "As if" indicates a manner.

10. (C) "Has come" is the main verb and "is" is the verb for the dependent clause. The subject "it" is needed to complete the independent clause.

11. (A) A clause marker that indicates a concession and a subject for the adverb clause are needed. In (A) the noun "ties" fills the subject position, and the clause marker "although" indicates a contrast between keeping strong ties and being exempt from paying taxes.

In (B) the verb "tied" cannot take the subject position. (D) does not include a clause marker or a subject. (C) has a clause marker and subject, but the clause marker "before" is incorrect because the verb tense in the clause indicates that the actions occurred at the same time.

12. (A) The adverb clause "before they begin the race" would be reduced to the adverb phrase "before beginning the race. "Of" is not part of the clause. The gerund form "beginning" would need the article "the" in order for the phrase to be the prepositional phrase "before the beginning of the race."

13. (B) A subject and verb for the independent clause are needed.
    (A) is a noun clause and can only fill the subject position. (C) has an incomplete verb and, therefore, does not fill the verb position. (D) is an adverb clause and cannot fill a subject and verb position.

14. (B) The adverb clause should have the verb form "begins."

15. (D) A clause marker that indicates a concession is needed. (D) "While" indicates a contrast between the increase in mechanization and the fact that power from humans and animals still produces much of the world's food.
    (A) "Since" indicates a time sequence or cause and effect (reason). (B) "Because" indicates a cause and effect (reason). (C) "So that" indicates a purpose.

16. (B) A sentence cannot be made up of two dependent clauses. "After" should be deleted to make the second clause an independent clause.

17. (A) An adverb clause indicating a cause and effect (reason) is needed. (A) includes a clause marker, a subject, and a verb, and completes the sentence by giving the reason there were few settlements.
    (B) and (C) indicate a time sequence. (D) is a noun or adjective clause.

18. (D) The word "appearing" is not part of the adverb phrase "when talking," but rather it is the verb of the noun clause "that people appear."

19. (C) An adverb clause or phrase indicating a time sequence is needed.
    In (A) and (D) the verb is missing. In (B) the verb is incomplete and the subject is in the wrong position.

20. (C) The adverb clause introduced by "so that" cannot be reduced. A subject of the clause is needed.

Exercise S82 (p. 268)
1. The largest
2. as much as
3. As recently as
4. bigger

5. the rarest
6. the world's largest
7. the more technical; the more compatible
8. as well as

Exercise S83 (p. 268)

1. C	3. E	5. S	7. C
2. S	4. S	6. C	8. E

Exercise S84 (p. 269)
1. "Best than" is incorrect because two things are being compared.
2. "The flatter and drier" is incorrect because there are more than two continents.
3. "The more feed corn than" is incorrect because the words "the" and "than" are not used together in a comparative structure.
4. This sentence is correct.
5. This sentence is correct.
6. "Heavier" is incorrect because the word "the" is used with a comparative that takes a noun position.
7. This sentence is correct.
8. "Fast" is incorrect because it is not in the comparative form.

Exercise S85 (p. 269)
1. This sentence is correct.
2. This sentence is correct.
3. "The fast" is incorrect because "fast" is not in the comparative form.
4. "Longer" is incorrect because the word "the" is missing from the phrase.
5. "Tough" is incorrect because it is not in the comparative form.
6. This sentence is correct.
7. This sentence is correct.
8. "Likelier" is incorrect. The comparative form should be "less likely."

Exercise S86 (p. 270)
1. "The largest city" is incorrect because the word "the" should not be used with the possessive form "Turkey's."
2. This sentence is correct.
3. This sentence is correct.
4. "Greater" is incorrect because it is not in the superlative form.
5. "The most early" is incorrect because the word "most" should not be used with "early," and "early" should be in the superlative form.
6. This sentence is correct.
7. "A" is incorrect because the article "the" is used with the superlative.
8. This sentence is correct.

Exercise S87 (p. 270)
1. "Many pounds of peanuts are grown as sweet potatoes" is incorrect because the word "as" is missing from the beginning of the phrase.
2. This sentence is correct.

3. "Not as many people take advantage of public transport in the United States" is incorrect because the word "as" is missing from the end of the phrase.

4. "As not severe as" is incorrect because the word "not" should not be within the phrase.

5. This sentence is correct.

6. "As larger as" is incorrect because the comparative form "larger" should not be used in a phrase of equality.

7. This sentence is correct.

8. This sentence is correct.

Exercise S88 (p. 271)

1. gnomes, sprites, elves

2. Warm ocean conditions, regulation of foreign catches within the U.S. 200-mile limit, international agreements reducing fishing fleets

3. tapestries, rugs, clothes, accessories

4. aqueducts, cisterns, drains; water, sanitation

5. insects, weeds, disease, hunger; cancer, birth defects, genetic mutations, sterility

6. Lashed by storms, violated by opportunists plundering its resources, struggling against today's economic pressures

7. one thousand mosques, eight hundred public bathhouses

8. a den for thieves, a hideout for guerrillas, a tomb for unwary explorers

Exercise S89 (p. 272)

1. Y   breed, multiply, and injure crops

2. Y   pageantry, ritual, and fanfare

3. N

4. Y   freedom and land; Swedes, Dutch, and English

5. Y   public murals, free art instruction, and special exhibitions

6. N

7. Y   pollen, cornmeal, and ground-up stones

8. Y   to reward or to punish; in family, labor, or legal disputes

Exercise S90 (p. 272)

1. "Were paying homage to pagan gods" is incorrect because the verb is in the past continuous form and the other verbs are in the simple past form.

2. This sentence is correct.

3. "Across Death Valley" is incorrect because it is a prepositional phrase and the other phrases are subjects.

4. "Most importantly medical supplies" is incorrect because it is a noun phrase and the other phrases are gerund phrases.

5. "The small bitter apples make the best cider" is incorrect because it is an independent clause and the other clauses are noun clauses.

6. This sentence is correct.

7. This sentence is correct.

8. "One must be courageous" is incorrect because it is an independent clause and the other phrases are nouns.

Exercise S91 (p. 275)

1. Y   3. N   5. N   7. Y
2. Y   4. Y   6. Y   8. Y

Exercise S92 (p. 275)

1. In the aftermath, of the explosion

2. of North Carolina, of barrier islands, by vegetation, of sand, without the foundation, of rock

3. of soil properties, of innovative building techniques, during earthquakes

4. in the field, of neurophysiology, in part, of the right-brain hemisphere

5. by accident, for making the billiard ball

6. about the various legal aspects

7. from the island prison, of Alcatraz, in San Francisco Bay, by police, within minutes, of swimming ashore

8. in Europe, as a pastime, of the upper classes, by the bustle, of servants

Exercise S93 (p. 276)

1. (D) A preposition that indicates a movement toward or a movement above is needed. "Over" indicates a movement above or at a higher level.

2. (C) A preposition that indicates that two things accompany each other is needed. "With" indicates that the two objects were together.

3. (D) A preposition that indicates a position higher than another position is needed. "Above" indicates a position higher than another position. (A) is incorrect because "up" indicates movement toward a higher position. ("The climbers went up the mountain.")

4. (A) A preposition that indicates the movement of time from one year to another year is needed. "To" can be used to indicate movement and takes a position between the given years: "1804 to 1806."

5. (B) A preposition that indicates duration is needed. "On" indicates a duration, in this case "during the time of a visit to Georgia."

6. (D) A preposition that indicates a position is needed. In this sentence, "in" indicates a position within the shadow's area.

7. (C) A preposition that indicates that two things accompany each other is needed. "With" indicates that the two objects were together.

8. (B) A preposition that indicates a given point is needed. "Up to" indicates time or space to a given point and no further. In this case, the given point is 15 kilometers above sea level and no higher.

Exercise S94 (p. 276)

1. (A) "As" appears to be a clause marker, but there is no verb to complete a clause.

   *(B) "Through" indicates from one point in time to another point in time.

2. *(A) "Full" is the adjective describing the region and "of" is used in the sense of containing.

(B) "Filled" makes the sentence passive, so the preposition "with" is needed to complete the sentence correctly.

3. *(A) "That" is a clause marker, "the twenty-first century" is the subject of the clause, and "will bring" is the verb.

(B) The object of the preposition "from" is the noun "twenty-first century," which cannot also serve as the subject for the verb "will bring."

4. (A) "Because" is a clause marker, but there is no verb to complete the clause.

*(B) "Because of" is the preposition and "structures" is the object of the preposition.

5. (A) "That" is a clause marker, but there is no verb to complete the clause.

*(B) "For" is a preposition. The noun "mammal" completes the prepositional phrase.

6. (A) "Was" cannot be used because the sentence is not passive.

*(B) "Of" indicates the tradition pertains to the spring fertility celebrations.

7. *(A) "For" expresses the object or purpose of the need.

(B) "Being a new attitude" suggests a reduced adverbial clause, which would not fill the position of describing the noun "need."

8. *(A) "Over" indicates the position of the stones.

(B) "That" is a clause marker, but there is no position for a clause.

Exercise S95 (p. 278)

1. Cross out "and grew."
2. Cross out "and injured."
3. (correct)
4. (correct)
5. (correct)
6. Cross out "and guard."
7. (correct)
8. Cross out "and first."

Exercise S96 (p. 278)

1. Cross out "timid."
2. Cross out "and needed."
3. Cross out "and contents."
4. (correct)
5. Cross out "and drinking a lot of wine."
6. (correct)
7. Cross out "and enchanting."
8. Cross out "ancient."

Exercise S97 (p. 279)

1. (A) "Than" is the word used in comparatives. The advances in the last one hundred years are being compared to those in all the rest of history.
(B) is a preposition or adverb clause marker. (C) joins two words, phrases, or clauses of equal value, but there is a comparison here. (D) indicates equality, but "more" in the sentence indicates a comparison.

2. (D) The verb "eating" is not parallel to the nouns "stables" and "lodging." "Food" or "meals" would be a suitable noun.

3. (C) The list of nouns indicates that a parallel structure is needed. (C) is a noun with adjective modifiers.
In (B) the word "forming" is in a verb position. (A) and (D) are independent clauses.

4. (B) The adverb "likely" precedes the word "as." This indicates a comparison of equality. The word "as" should be used to complete the comparison-of-equality phrase. "So" can be used in a phrase of inequality, "not so likely as," but not in the phrase of equality.

5. (C) The choices indicate that a comparison is being made. (C) completes the sentence with the correct word order for the superlative form. (A) is ungrammatical because the adjective "long-term" cannot be modified by the prepositional phrase "to Africa's elephants." (B) is ungrammatical because of the incorrect word order. (D) is ungrammatical because a second threat is not mentioned.

6. (B) The plural form "flies" should be used to be parallel with the other plural forms "mosquitoes" and "pests."

7. (B) A phrase is needed. (B) is a prepositional phrase that can be used in an adverb position. (A) is an independent clause. (C) is ungrammatical because "alike" cannot be used as a preposition. (D) is ungrammatical because "alike" used as an adjective must follow the verb form of "be."

8. (D) "Than" should not be used with the word "more" because "more" is being used to indicate how many weeks the carnivals last, not to compare the carnivals with the Mardi Gras.

9. (A) An adverb clause or phrase is needed. (A) is an adverb clause; the complement of "may be" is the word "isolated."
(B) is an adverb clause but is incorrect because the verb "may be" needs a complement to complete the clause. (C) and (D) are not adverb clauses or phrases.

10. (A) Finland is not being compared to any other area so the word "heaviest" should not be in the superlative form, but in the adverb form "heavily."

11. (B) An adverb clause or phrase is needed. (B) is a prepositional phrase correctly used in the adverb position.
(A) and (C) are independent clauses. (D) is a noun phrase that must take a noun position.

12. (C) There are more than two colors so the word "harder" should be in the superlative form "hardest."

13. (D) A list of verbs + objects/complements in the sentence indicates that a verb + object/complement is needed to complete the parallel structure.

(A) is an adverb phrase. (B) is an independent clause. (C) is a prepositional phrase.

14. (D) The word "wide" should be in its adverb form "widely" to show how extensively the Gothic style spread and to be parallel with the first adverb form "rapidly."

15. (B) A preposition is needed. In (B) "as" is a preposition used to indicate the function of the horses.

    (A) and (D) are incorrect because "alike" and "as if" are not prepositions. In (C) "like" is a preposition which indicates a manner or comparison. However, the shire horses are not similar to workhorses, but are workhorses.

16. (C) The word "as" is needed to complete the inequality phrase. It should be "not as much vocal participation as."

17. (C) A noun object is needed. The word "ever" indicates that the noun is modified by a superlative. (C) uses the correct word order; article + number + superlative + a noun used as an adjective + a noun.

    (A) is incorrect because the article "the" is missing. (B) and (D) use an incorrect word order.

18. (D) The verb form "shorten" is not parallel with the adjective forms in the other phrases. The adjective form "shortened" should be used.

19. (A) A prepositional phrase modifying the noun "collection" is needed. In (A) the prepositional phrase "of some six thousand drawings and paintings" describes the collection.

    (C) is not a prepositional phrase. In (B) and (D), "about" is used to introduce the topic "six thousand drawings and paintings." However, the topic is the collection.

20. (A) The phrase "set up" and "established" mean the same and are therefore redundant. "And established" should be deleted.

Exercise S98 (p. 281)

1. The prepositional phrase which states location at the beginning of the sentence indicates that the subject (pyramid) and verb (lies) should be inverted.
   (A) See Exercises S32–S35.
   (B), (C) See Exercises S25–S31.
   *(D) See Exercises S32–S35.

2. (B) The noun form "reduction" should be used as the object of the preposition "for." See Exercises S37–S42.

3. After a possessive noun, the superlative form of the adjective, "longest," is not preceded by "the."
   *(A) See Exercises S1–S5 and S82–S87.
   (B), (C), (D) See Exercises S1–S5 and S82–S87.

4. (C) The relative pronoun "which" cannot refer to people. "Who" is the correct pronoun. See Exercises S61–S66.

5. A subject and a verb are needed to complete the sentence.
   (A), (D) See Exercises S61–S66.
   (B) See Exercises S32–S35.
   *(C) See Exercises S52–S53.

6. (C) The comparative word "more" should not be used with the comparative form "finer." See Exercises S82–S87.

7. The clause marker "whereas," indicating a contrast between "carpet" and "rug," is needed to complete the sentence.
   (A), (C) See Exercises S72–S76.
   *(B) See Exercises S72–S76.
   (D) See Exercises S91–S94.

8. (A) The article "a" is needed with the singular noun "fact." See Exercises S6–S10.

9. (A) The list of parallel adjectives in the sentence is in an infinitive phrase. The infinitive "to double" is parallel to the infinitive "to be." See Exercises S88–S90.

10. (B) The preposition "at" indicates a specific place. Its use here is illogical because there are two places. "Within" is the correct preposition and indicates being inside a certain area. See Exercises S91–S94.

11. A subject is needed. A noun clause taking the subject position needs a clause marker, such as "what."
    (A) See Exercises S52–S53.
    (B) See Exercises S54–S59.
    (C) See Exercises S72–S76.
    *(D) See Exercises S54–S59.

12. (C) The clause marker "when," instead of "that," should be used to show at what point substances emit electrons. See Exercises S77–S80.

13. An independent clause that includes a subject, verb, and object is needed to complete this sentence.
    (A) See Exercises S52–S53.
    *(B) See Exercises S52–S53.
    (C) See Exercises S72–S76.
    (D) See Exercises S54–S59.

14. (C) The capital cannot perform the action of situating. Therefore, the passive form of the verb "situated" is correct. See Exercises S25–S31.

15. An -ing verb form, "setting sail," is needed to complete the adjective phrase, which gives more information about the subject, Thor Heyerdahl.
    (A), (B) See Exercises S67–S70.
    (C) See Exercises S61–S66.
    *(D) See Exercises S67–S70.

16. (C) The subject of the sentence is "school." The pronoun "it" cannot be used to fill the same subject position. See Exercises S17–S23.

17. (B) The independent clause is complete. This indicates that a phrase that adds information could be used after it. The prepositional phrase "as a dethroned exile" defines Napoleon III's position in England. "But only" qualifies the phrase and connects it to the clause. See Exercises S91–S94.

18. (D) "Attentive" is the adjective form; however, the noun form "attention" should be used in the object position. See Exercises S37–S42.

19. (A) The verb that follows "considered" must be in the infinitive form. See Exercises S25–S31.

20. (B) The word "some" must be changed to "one." The word "civilization," which agrees with the singular verb "was," indicates that only one civilization is being discussed. See Exercises S43–S50.

SECTION 3   READING

Exercise R1 (p. 290)

1. an illness
2. a rodent
3. the smallest part of a chemical element
4. D
5. D
6. B
7. electrical devices
8. a goddess
9. explosions of dying stars
10. B
11. D
12. A
13. carved birds
14. having a slender body build
15. inscriptions (writings) in stone
16. A
17. D
18. B
19. height above sea level
20. evening worship
21. internal walls
22. B
23. B
24. C
25. large fish
26. animals
27. plants
28. D
29. B
30. A
31. a compound used for burns
32. the succession of sounds
33. descended from
34. B
35. D
36. A
37. insects
38. a kind of clothing
39. a basket
40. C
41. D
42. A
43. not deadly
44. flourishes, grows easily, does well
45. decreases
46. C
47. C
48. B
49. a flower
50. part of a bagpipe
51. stopped, lessened
52. A
53. B
54. C

Exercise R2 (p. 300)

1. B	7. B	13. C
2. D	8. C	14. D
3. A	9. A	15. B
4. D	10. D	16. C
5. C	11. D	17. A
6. A	12. B	18. A

Exercise R3 (p. 304)

1. merge
2. postulated
3. die
4. exquisite

Exercise R4 (p. 305)

1. (A) The words "scrap" and "waste" can refer to materials that are thrown out because they are damaged or no longer serve their purpose.
2. A "reduction" or "abatement" is a decrease in size, quantity, or amount.
3. (C) Something that is "customary" or "regular" is something that is usual or habitual.
4. (D) The words "elimination" and "eradication" refer to a complete removal or destruction of something.
5. (A) To be "reclusive" means to deliberately avoid other people, to be "solitary," or to be alone.
6. Something that is produced in "prolific" or "abundant" amounts is done in large quantities.
7. (D) When a feeling is "intense," we can also say it is very "strong."
8. (D) The words "concisely" and "succinctly" refer to something being said clearly, using few words.
9. When something has "succumbed" to a disease or has "expired," it has died.
10. (C) "Afflictions" and "diseases" refer to illnesses.
11. (A) The "incidence" of a disease is the number of cases that appear or the "rate of occurrence."
12. (D) To be "susceptible" or "vulnerable" means to be unprotected and open to the possibility of being harmed.

Exercise R5 (p. 309)

1. the Japanese macaque
2. robots
3. parade (This is implied by the phrases "streets lined with people," "shopkeepers locking their doors and joining the crowds," and "the first float.")

4. parsley
5. mud
6. Hay-on-Wye
7. foster grandparents
8. the koto
9. bicycle race (This is implied by the words "starting gate," "bicycle racers," "sponsors," and "racers.")
10. thinking

Exercise R6 (p. 311)
1. (B) The passage explains information derived from dinosaur tracks, and (B) states "recently discovered tracks are giving important information about dinosaurs."
   (A) gives details about the dinosaur tracks.
   (C) gives details about dinosaurs.
2. (A) The passage tells how the spider is different, and (A) states this spider is different from other spiders.
   (B) and (C) give details about the spider.
3. (C) The passage discusses how the trees communicate, and (C) states what scientists believe about trees communicating.
   (A) is a restatement of information in the passage.
   (B) could be inferred as a logical use of this information.
4. (A) The kind of pottery that is discussed in the passage is introduced in (A).
   (B) and (C) are details about pottery.
5. (A) The passage discusses the details of the vaccine, and (A) introduces the topic of a cavity-preventing vaccine.
   (B) is a detail about vaccines.
   (C) tells of the research.
6. (B) The passage discusses each type of cloud, and (B) states that there are four basic cloud types.
   (A) gives more information about stratus clouds.
   (C) could be the topic of the following paragraph.
7. (B) All the people mentioned in the passage are famous people from the past, and (B) states that the name William was the name of many famous people in the past.
   (A) and (C) may be details concerning the name William today.
8. (A) The passage discusses three ways to deal with oil spills, and (A) states that there are ways to deal with oil spills. (B) states only that oil spills are a problem. (C) tells how oil spills spread, but the passage does not discuss that problem.

Exercise R7 (p. 312)
1. a meteor's entrance into the Earth's atmosphere
2. This topic is correct.
3. ways smokers have tried to overcome nicotine addiction
4. rice as a food crop
5. This topic is correct.

6. the movement of dust from China's windstorms
7. This topic is correct.
8. This topic is correct.

Exercise R8 (p. 314)
1. (A) The subject is not trains at work, but calendars showing scenes of trains at work.
   *(B) The passage discusses calendars showing train scenes painted by Grif Teller.
   (C) The passage states that the scenes by Grif Teller are valuable. It does not discuss valuable calendars in general.
   (D) The passage is about the calendars that included Grif Teller's paintings.
2. (A) It is not the kimono design but the Yuzen dyeing that dates from the seventeenth century.
   *(B) The passage consists of a step-by-step description of Yuzen dyeing.
   (C) There is no information on how kimonos are made but rather on how the design is made on kimonos.
   (D) The elaborate embroidery is one detail in the passage.
3. *(A) The passage states the different ways a flashlight fish can use bioluminescence.
   (B) The way a flashlight fish saves its life is only one of the ways it uses bioluminescence.
   (C) How bioluminescence works is a detail introducing the main topic – its uses.
   (D) The flashlight fish is the only fish discussed in the passage.
4. (A) The passage states that the songwriter Cole Porter was not regarded as socially conscious in his lifetime.
   (B) Porter's being rich and famous is a detail.
   *(C) The passage contains various details of the life of the songwriter Cole Porter.
   (D) Porter's making sophistication popular is a detail.
5. (A) How the beaver's tail looks is only one detail in the passage.
   *(B) The passage discusses each of the uses that a beaver's tail has.
   (C) A lesson in nature studies is too broad a topic to be the main idea.
   (D) A reader cannot use a beaver's tail; only a beaver can use its tail.
6. (A) The passage is not about how earthquakes affect tree rings but how tree rings can be used to obtain information about earthquakes.
   (B) Once the tree has recorded an earthquake, it has already occurred and therefore cannot warn people of its coming.
   *(C) Although the passage doesn't explain how this information is gained, it lists the kind of information that can be gained from tree rings.
   (D) The passage tells us that tree rings can be used to obtain this information, but it does not explain why.

Exercise R9 (p. 318)

1. who: Noah Webster
   that: English
2. they: bubbles
3. who: individuals
   their: political prisoners
4. it: Alaska
5. their: Royal Canadian Mounted Police
6. his: every person
   her: every person
7. when: 1863
   he: a Hungarian count
   the first European variety: wine grapes
   there: California
8. it: the human mind
9. her: Willa Cather
   subject matter: frontier life
10. themselves: Arctic people
    they: Arctic people
    these natural resources: the environment
    and wild animals

Exercise R10 (p. 319)

1. D   2. B   3. C   4. D

Exercise R11 (p. 321)

1. athletes
2. predators
3. characteristics
4. insects (or locusts)

Exercise R12 (p. 322)

1. (D) "But" is used to qualify a statement. The statement concerning the value of glass in Egyptian times is qualified by (D) concerning the value of glass today.
   (A) is added information. (B) and (C) are not related to the fact that glass was valued in Egyptian times.

2. (C) "Such as" is used to introduce examples. An example of "behavior" is (C), sucking a thumb.
   (A) development, (B) the sex, and (D) structures are not examples of behavior.

3. (D) "Although" is used to qualify a statement. In (D) the fact that desert species are similar is qualified by the contrasting fact that their ancestry is different.
   (A) gives information that one might assume to be true. However, "although" indicates that the information is not as one might expect.
   In (B) the species' not adapting to jungles is not related to their coming from different ancestral stocks. (C) is a repetition of the phrase "the world's various deserts."

4. (C) "In contrast" is used to contrast statements. The informality of Halloween is contrasted with (C), the formality of Thanksgiving.
   (A) doesn't make a contrast but gives another example of a traditional holiday. (B) and (D) don't make contrasts but instead give information that is not related to the topic of Halloween.

5. (C) The main point of the statement is the uses of bamboo in general. "Equally important" introduces another way bamboo is used. In this case, (C), the food that can be made from bamboo and the items that can be made from bamboo are both important.
   In (A) the reason why the grass growing in warm climates is important is not clear.
   In (B) the longer cooking time seems to be more of a disadvantage than an aspect of equal importance. (D) does not relate to the importance of making something.

6. (A) "In conclusion" is used to indicate that something is true because the facts lead to this belief. All the facts about satellites lead to the belief that (A) the lives of humankind have been enriched by their existence.
   (B) The facts given do not lead to any conclusion about the difficulties of satellites.
   (C) The facts given do not lead to any conclusion about how many TV channels can be picked up. (D) The facts given do not lead to any conclusion about orbital placement.

7. (B) "In addition" is used to add more information. The lasers and two-way wrist TV in (B) are two additional items Dick Tracy used besides the atomic-powered space vehicle.
   (A) gives new information about today's astronauts, not added information about space items introduced in a comic strip.
   In (C) Dick Tracy's popularity is not an addition to his devices.
   (D) gives new information about space items of today's astronauts. These items are not an addition to items Dick Tracy used.

8. (B) "As a result" is used to show a consequence. The consequences of the infection's being difficult to detect is (B), that it was rarely diagnosed.
   (A) The number of students afflicted with the infection is not a result of its difficulty to detect. It is a result of the infection's spreading.
   (C) The fact that there were few centers that offered the test and the test took up to seven days to be completed suggests that the infection was not treated promptly and in many cases was not even diagnosed.
   (D) The doctors would not prescribe a medicine for the infection as a consequence of the infection's being difficult to detect.

9. (A) "In some cases" is used to explain. The information in (A) is used to give information that explains the advantages of the nonsurgical method of treating heart disease.
   In (B) the nonsurgical method cannot replace an artery.

In (C) the fact that coronary bypass operations are lucrative does not explain the nonsurgical method.

In (D) the fact that the chest is opened up indicates that this information does not relate to the "nonsurgical method."

10. (A) "Indeed" is used to emphasize a fact. In (A) the fact that Einstein's brain contained more glial cells than other people's brains is being emphasized.

(B) is added information concerning scientists' studies of brains.

(C) is added information concerning where scientists looked for glial cells.

(D) is a conclusion concerning the development of Einstein's intellectual processing.

Exercise R13 (p. 324)
1. 2
2. 5
3. 4
4. 4

Exercise R14 (p. 326)
1. D
2. C
3. B
4. A

Exercise R15 (p. 328)
1. The plan was again proposed in 1930 by many enthusiastic supporters.
2. There are uncooked pressed cheeses, such as Cheddar, and cooked pressed cheeses, such as Gruyère. (The noun "mold" can refer to a kind of fungus or it can refer to a container used to give something a particular shape. The verb "mold" means "to shape.")
3. Human perspiration contains one such acid.
4. . . . beach resorts that have destroyed the beauty of the area and have put heavy burdens on the infrastructure of coastal villages not designed for a large influx of people . . .

Exercise R16 (p. 330)
1. The word "love," which means nil, . . .
2. In a recent survey, . . . nine out of ten drivers admit to having felt intense anger toward other drivers at some time.
3. As men lost their jobs, . . .
4. Yet another technique is called brainwashing. Brainwashing entails forcing people . . .

Exercise R17 (p. 332)
1. D   2. A   3. B   4. D   5. B

Exercise R18 (p. 334)
1. S   3. S   5. S   7. D   9. D
2. S   4. D   6. D   8. S   10. S

Exercise R19 (p. 335)
1. *(B)
   (A) and (D) It is not the brain that faints.
   (C) It is not the brain that causes the drop in the blood supply.
2. *(D)
   (A) It is not vegetarians that treat gorillas and small animals gently, but gorillas that treat small animals gently.
   (B) All gorillas are vegetarians, not just some.
   (C) Gorillas have been observed behaving in a gentle manner, not the small creatures.
3. *(C)
   (A) The crews do not dig a fire; they dig a fire line.
   (B) It is not the fire that varies the fire line, but the crews who vary the fire line according to the strength and nature of the fire.
   (D) "Depend on" means "rely on." Crews do not rely on fighting fires to dig a line. The result of the fire line is determined by the strength and nature of the fire.
4. *(B)
   (A) It is not the well educated who promise cures, but the medical quacks.
   (C) All people are promised cures, not only the well educated.
   (D) It is not the medical profession that has appealed to the well educated, but the promise of cures that has appeal for even the well educated.
5. *(D)
   (A) It is not the tsetse fly that kills the parasitic protozoa, but the tsetse fly that carries the parasitic protozoa.
   (B) The tsetse fly carries the parasitic protozoa, not the silver compound.
   (C) Parasitic protozoa cause the sleeping sickness, not the tsetse fly.
6. *(A)
   (B) Six out of thirty-seven stories were published, not written.
   (C) Only six stories were published.
   (D) There is no information concerning the topic of the six accepted stories.
7. *(B)
   (A) It is the convection currents that behave like conveyor belts driving the plates, not the plates.
   (C) It is the convection currents that are in the hot magma and that behave as conveyor belts.
   (D) The earth's crustal plates cannot propose a theory.
8. *(C)
   (A) Medical authorities are reluctant to support the views.
   (B) This statement might be inferred, but it is not a restatement of the sentence that medical authorities are reluctant to support the nutritionists' findings.

(D) Medical authorities have not supported the findings that vitamin C may prevent the common cold.

9. *(A)

(B), (C), and (D) Female cowbirds can teach songs by responding to certain chirps.

10. *(A)

(B) The conflict is of interest not only to those who want to abolish the last remnants of wilderness but to those who want to save it as well.

(C) There is no information about lawyers' involvement in this conflict.

(D) The conflict is not about abolishing industry but about abolishing or maintaining wilderness areas.

Exercise R20 (p. 338)

1. Europa, one of Jupiter's moons, is the only place in the solar system (unequaled in the solar system) – outside of Earth (with one exception) – where enormous quantities of water (vast oceans) are known to exist . . .

2. . . . A single discharge (a lightning bolt) can actually (it is possible) contain twenty or more successive strokes (a series of bolts) . . . Some seem to stretch for 500 miles (which seems very large).

3. . . . they (porpoises) leap out of the water (travel through the air) to escape the pull of surface drag (air, which creates less drag than water). At that point, leaping out of the water (traveling through the air) actually requires less energy (conserve energy) than swimming . . .

4. . . . During the flare-up, strong winds blowing off the surface of the star disperse the surrounding dust (scatter the dust particles) and expose the newborn star (allow the birth of a star to be seen) to observers on Earth (people who see).

5. Perhaps the greatest navigators (expert sailors) in history were the Vikings (the Vikings were) . . .

6. . . . Today, dolphins do such dangerous and necessary work (important task) as locating explosives (find mines) hidden in the sea . . .

7. . . . trained them (Saint Bernards) to search for travelers lost in snowstorms or avalanches (aided travelers) in the Alps. For hundreds of years, (for centuries) Saint Bernards served this purpose (aided travelers) . . .

8. . . . Out on Lake Biwa, participants attempt to break records by flying (fly) their own inventions (crafts they have designed themselves) . . .

Exercise R21 (p. 339)

1. "Architects" use techniques to reduce noise.

2. (A) It is stated that filling wall space with materials absorbs noise.

(B) Using thick carpets and heavy curtains is an example of the techniques used to reduce noise.

(C) Air conditioners and furnaces were designed to filter air through soundproofing materials.

*(D) Air filters themselves are not mentioned in the passage.

3. (A) There is no mention of new techniques being designed.

(B) See (C).

*(C) Architects are designing structures that have the right kind of noise.

(D) Architects are designing buildings that are desirable, not adverse.

4. ⑥ A description of the symptoms people suffer when they are in a noiseless environment would follow the fact that people react adversely to the lack of sound.

5. (A) A noisy furnace is not stated as one of the noises people need.

(B) It is stated that people react adversely to the lack of sound.

(C) Hollow walls do not reduce noise unless they are filled.

*(D) It is stated that there is a "kind of noise that people seem to need."

6. ⑥ A sentence about the ideal house for a family would follow the fact that the roof creates a spacious interior on the upper floor of a house and precede the fact that this kind of roof is good for barns.

7. (A) It is stated that the gambrel roof is a straight double-sloped roof.

*(B) The angle of the lower slope is steep, not the upper slope.

(C) It is stated that the angle of the slope at the eaves sometimes becomes shallow again.

(D) It is stated that sometimes the roof projects over the wall of the house.

8. (A) This was a feature of the Dutch colonists' architectural style. It cannot be inferred that they invented it after arriving in America.

(B) It is the appeal that endures (continues).

* (C) This feature of Dutch colonial architectural style probably originated in Holland and was brought to America by the Dutch settlers.

(D) This feature may be appealing to people anywhere in the world.

9. Ⓐ This roof does not have a central ridge.

Ⓑ This roof is not double-sloped.

* Ⓒ This illustration depicts the double-sloped roof joined at a central ridge, the two planes with the lower slope being steeper, and the projection over the wall of the building.

Ⓓ This roof's upper slope is steeper than its lower slope.

10. (A) It is not the fossils that are 6 to 8 feet long and 350 pounds, but the animal itself.

(B) The fossils cannot be descended from an animal. They are the remains of one.

(C) It is not that the foothills were underwater, but that the whale was on land.

*(D) The first line of the passage states that the fossils are of an ancient whale. The second sentence states that "the fossils consist of . . . the well-preserved middle ear . . ."

11. *(A) The passage states that eardrums do not work in water.
(B) Marine means "of the sea." The presence of eardrums suggests that the ancient whales lived on land.
(C) Since eardrums do not work in water, whales with eardrums could not distinguish underwater sounds.
(D) It is their having eardrums that suggests that they did live on land.

12. *(A) It is stated in the passage that the separation of the right and left ear bones enables marine whales to detect the direction of underwater sounds.
(B) A middle ear suggests eardrums, which do not work in water.
(C) It is not because it lives underwater that a whale can hear.
(D) It is the fossils that have a well-preserved middle ear.

13. The separation of the right and left ear bones in marine whales enables "whales" to detect the direction of underwater sounds.

14. ☐2 The author describes the probable length and weight of the animal as well as the shape of its face and teeth.

15. (A) 1737 was the year that Stradivari died.
*(B) It is stated that "650" Stradivarius violins are believed to be in existence today.
(C) A quarter of a million dollars is how much a "cheap" Stradivarius costs.
(D) Hundreds of thousands is the approximate price of any Stradivarius.

16. (A) All Stradivarius violins are rare.
(B) A price is not given for the most expensive one.
(C) Cheap reproductions are not mentioned in the passage.
*(D) It is stated that a "cheap" Stradivarius costs a quarter of a million dollars.

17. (A) Age and number are not qualities, but reasons why they are expensive.
(B) Violinists and collectors are not qualities, but people who want them.
*(C) It is stated that the Stradivarius is unmatched in tonal quality and responds more quickly and easily than any other violin.
(D) The color is not a quality.

18. ☐3 The author states that attempts have been made to reproduce (replicate) a Stradivarius.

19. (A) Cornmeal was introduced to the early colonists by Native Americans.
(B) New England is mentioned only as a place where visitors can get johnnycakes.

*(C) It is stated that cornmeal began as a Native American staple.
(D) The people of the South are mentioned as using cornmeal to make spoon bread. Nothing is stated about their using it originally.

20. "Their own uses" refers to the colonists' uses for cornmeal.

21. (A) This is a description of a "hush puppy."
*(B) The passage mentions "mush (leftover cornmeal porridge cut and fried.)"
(C) Succotash is a dish in which cornmeal is added, not mush.
(D) Mush is one of two meals developed by the colonists.

22. (A) These forms would not be eaten nationwide if they were unpopular.
(B) The common forms are eaten nationwide, not restricted to regions.
*(C) The passage mentions "the most common forms of cornmeal nationwide."
(D) The corn the Native Americans grew was multicolored.

23. ☐6 The author names two recipes – succotash and mush – in the following sentence. **Succotash (a meat stew with cornmeal added) and mush (leftover cornmeal porridge cut and fried) are two meals invented by early colonists.**

24. ☐2 The author talks about regional differences in **Visitors can travel to the South . . . , or to New England . . . common forms of cornmeal nationwide . . .**

Exercise R22 (p. 350)
1. (A) Private individuals must be able to submit reports because two reports came from private individuals.
(B) The reports were already published. This is understood from the phrase "three of the published reports."
*(C) Three reports from official investigations and two from private individuals equals a total of five reports.
(D) There is no information given on what the investigations covered.

2. (A) No information is given concerning how the villages were destroyed.
*(B) Information must have been collected for the Institute of Anthropology to computerize it, and the villages must be in ruins if the plans are to restore them.
(C) It is not the Native Americans who have the computers to store data but the Institute of Anthropology.
(D) It is not the plans that need to be restored but the villages.

3. (A) This statement is contrary to the information given in the statement, which suggests that the European bees will make the African bees gentler. This may be an advantage.

*(B) If the bees have "devastated" the beekeeping industry, they must be destructive, and if it is believed that the interbreeding might make them "gentler," they must not be gentle now.

(C) The question of becoming gentler refers to the bees, not the industry.

*(D) Both kinds of bees must live in Latin America if they are interbreeding there.

4. (A) While people who think nobody likes them might own a pet, it cannot be inferred that all pet owners feel unloved.

*(B) This is one way a person frustrated in feeling love may express the need.

(C) Appropriate ways to show love cannot be inferred from the statement.

*(D) Collecting stamps could be one of the substitutes that a person frustrated by the need for love may choose.

5. *(A) If the condition of the rider were as important as the condition of the horse, the contestants would give as much attention to themselves as to their horses.

(B) It cannot be inferred that the riders like their horses better; they would probably give more attention to their horses in order to win the race.

(C) The statement does not concern the horses' giving attention to themselves but the riders' giving attention to the horses.

(D) What happens after a race is not mentioned. Race contestants may continue to give attention to their horses in preparation for the next race.

6. *(A) If "no partner" helps the male, then the female does not help him.

*(B) If the nest is floating, it must be on water, and this suggests that the jacana is an aquatic bird.

(C) The male protects and nurtures its chicks, but whether or not it protects its partner cannot be inferred. A partner probably doesn't need to be nurtured.

(D) Mating is not mentioned.

7. (A) Elephants are being trapped as a result of farmers' clearing land, not by hunters.

*(B) It can be inferred by the elephants' being trapped in forest enclaves that these must be their habitat, and these forests are being cleared away for agriculture or farming.

*(C) Since the land cleared of forests is being used for agriculture, these farms would have to be crossed for an elephant to reach another forest.

(D) People are not trapping elephants for use. The elephants are unintentionally being trapped through the process of making space for more cropland.

8. (A) Since it is sunken ships that are being safeguarded, it is understood that they were already sunken and not made to sink by thieves.

*(B) Sunken shops must contain something valuable for thieves to be interested in plundering them.

(C) It is not the salvagers who are caught but the salvagers who are trying to protect the ships from adventurers or thieves.

*(D) There must be more ways than electronic means to protect a ship because "other" means are also used.

9. *(A) The weeds known as gopher plants have been given the name (renamed) gasoline plant.

(B) Although gasoline can be refined from the gasoline plant, there is no mention of replacing other sources of gasoline.

*(C) The hydrocarbons in latex can be refined into substitutes for crude oil and gasoline. Therefore, hydrocarbons must contain something that can be made into a substitute for crude oil and gasoline.

(D) It is the "milky latex" that contains hydrocarbons. It cannot be inferred that milk contains hydrocarbons.

10. (A) Since morphine is still being scraped from the poppy plant and since it has not been profitably synthesized, it must still be profitable to cultivate.

*(B) If morphine is unsurpassed for controlling pain, it must be more effective than any other drug, including cocaine.

(C) Although morphine has been used for at least 5,000 years, it cannot be inferred that its use was for controlling pain.

(D) If morphine is not yet profitably synthesized, then artificial morphine cannot be made economically.

Exercise R23 (p. 352)

1. "Unlike other toads, the male golden toad is nearly voiceless"; "which is as effective as croaking in luring females during the mating season."

2. "Besides earthquakes and volcanos, torrential rains, encroaching tropical vegetation, and time have all taken their toll."

3. "medical authorities are skeptical of the treatment"

4. "powerful legs"; "lacks the barbules that are needed to lock feathers into a flat vane"; "head is crowned by a leathery helmet that protects it when it is charging through the jungle."

5. "Away from the master carver, who dictated what was to be carved . . ."

6. "Members of both sexes"; "learn the art of sword fighting in mock combat"

7. "Computer-generated motion pictures allow the viewer to see the meaning of data and complex relationships instantly and are a new aid to human understanding."

8. "not recommended for beginners"

9. "Nowhere else, except perhaps in tropical coral reefs, is nature so great in its diversity of organisms."

10. "Champion athletes combine new heights of athleticism with the elegance of dance."

Exercise R24 (p. 354)

1. Yes If communities are discovering that they are living near toxic waste dumps, then they must not have known it in the first place because no one told them.

2. Yes E. B. White must have been well known if his death was cause for sadness in millions of homes.

3. No The Richter scale was not named for an earthquake but for Charles F. Richter, the man who helped devise it.

4. No Although a firestorm may have caused the dinosaurs to disappear, it was not necessarily the cause of their disappearance. Some other catastrophe may have been responsible for the dinosaurs' extinction.

5. Yes There were twelve deaths and three were not linked to fresh fruits and vegetables. The rest (nine) were linked to fresh foods. The deaths were sulfite-associated and, therefore, the fresh foods must have been contaminated with sulfite.

6. No If data is being received from *Vega I* and if people had expected this object to encounter dust, it is not an "unidentified" object.

7. No Other antibiotics may still be useful for other kinds of illnesses.

8. Yes If actions such as walking and grasping may be impossible for those people who have had nerves damaged, then the nervous system must be important for muscle control.

Exercise R25 (p. 355)

1. (A) __I__ Individuals who have shown outstanding talents in a field must be known. Since these awards are given to such people, it can be inferred that those who are not already known will not receive an award.

   (B) __I__ The last sentence in the passage implies that some people might attain success because they worry about money.

   (C) __R__ Three hundred thousand dollars is the maximum amount of money given to individuals to allow them time to devote to creative "thinking."

2. (A) __I__ The phrase "attempting to solve" suggests that the CDC is not always successful.

   (B) __R__ "To crisscross the country" means "to travel back and forth across the nation."

   (C) __I__ If patterns and common links among the victims are found during epidemics, it can be inferred that it is through the extra data collected that the patterns emerge.

3. (A) __R__ On the basis of the amount of light absorbed and reflected, astronomers determined that comets contain frozen water.

   (B) __I__ It can be inferred that since the ice content in Comet Bowell was determined by measuring the light it absorbed and reflected, the ice content in other comets can also be determined.

   (C) __R__ The name given for the comet that astronomers were observing was Comet Bowell.

4. (A) __R__ "Must be removed" means "not left" and "prevent the spread of disease" means "stop other bees from being sick."

   (B) __R__ If the corpses emit a chemical that signals death, then the chemical that is emitted signals to the honeybees that a death has occurred.

   (C) __R__ "Within an hour" means "in less than one hour."

5. (A) __I__ If the availability of petroleum products is a factor in the reduced demand for seal oil, the implication is that products that were made from seal oil are now made from petroleum.

   (B) __I__ Because petroleum products are more available, we can infer that the petroleum to make those products is probably easier to obtain than seal oil.

   (C) _____ Although the northern elephant seal has made a dramatic comeback, there is no information concerning how numerous they are.

6. (A) __R__ More than the severe cold (the harsh climate), it's the lack (the scarcity) of resources for food, clothing, and shelter that defines (influences) the lifestyles (living conditions).

   (B) __I__ It can be inferred from the words "probably descended from" that their ancestry is not known for certain.

   (C) _____ One cannot make any inference from the information in this passage whether there is more or less sunshine the further north one is.

7. (A) __I__ If scientists could tell whether an astronaut who suffers from car sickness will suffer from space sickness, they would not be attempting to find a way to predict who was susceptible.

   (B) __R__ It (space sickness) interferes with (causes problems or makes difficult) the important work that must be done (work the astronauts do).

   (C) __R__ "Akin" means "related to."

8. (A) __R__ If a white shark belongs to the mackerel shark family, it is a kind of mackerel shark.

   (B) __I__ If the white shark did not attack people, it would not have a terrifying reputation.

   (C) __I__ If the shark does not eat people, as the evidence suggests, it must kill them for other reasons. Also, "mindless ferocity" implies that the shark attacks for no discernible reason.

9. (A) __R__ An inchworm is a geometrid. "Extends itself forward" means "stretching forward," "draws its back end up to its front legs" means

"moving its back to its front," and "repeats the sequence" means "repeating this process."

(B) __I__ If only some caterpillars are called earth measurers or inchworms, it can be inferred that not all caterpillars are inchworms.

(C) __R__ The caterpillars that are called geometrids, or earth measurers, are commonly named inchworms.

10. (A) __I__ The Merlin must be a kind of aircraft because it is compared with a helicopter or small plane and it "takes off and hovers."

(B) __I__ If the Merlin is safer than a helicopter or small plane because it has no exposed blades, it must be the exposed blades that make some aircraft unsafe.

(C) _____ There is no information given concerning the production of the Merlin. The passage could simply be describing the "design" or a "model" of the Merlin, not a Merlin that has actually been produced.

Exercise R26 (p. 358)

1. C   3. A
2. D   4. C

Exercise R27 (p. 360)

1. *(A) Along the coast would be at sea level, where the races must be slower if racing is faster at high altitudes.

(B) An indoor track could be in an area at sea level or at a higher altitude.

(C) and (D) A high plateau and the snowline of a volcano are both high-altitude areas, where the racing would be faster, not slower.

2. (A) While an owner may think it amusing to trick an expert, there would be no need for the owner to do so.

*(B) An owner could hang a copy of a valuable painting so that in the case of a theft, the real painting would not be taken.

(C) If owners want to encourage talented artists, they would do so through other means, such as buying an original work by those artists or encouraging them to paint something special.

(D) If owners enjoyed buying fake paintings, they would probably do this instead of spending a lot of money on valuable paintings.

3. (A), (B), and (C) These are all places where a law enforcement official could use a dog for detecting drugs, but only if he were suspicious that drugs were in use.

*(D) A law enforcement official would always be on the lookout for possible smuggling of drugs into a country and might, therefore, use such a trained dog.

4. (A) There is no information that implies that a Steiner school does not include academic subjects.

(B) A game that is not competitive could be played in a coeducational (boys and girls together) school.

*(C) A contest suggests a competition, and this kind of activity is discouraged in a Steiner school.

(D) A school that is practicing mixed-ability teaching is teaching children with different abilities; therefore, the children are probably at different levels.

5. *(A) If the bacteria can destroy the cyanide, a toxic waste dumped into rivers, then the bacteria can save the water life by getting rid of this poison.

(B) The bacteria destroy cyanide, not fish.

(C) Cyanide is not put into swimming pools; therefore, the bacteria would not serve a purpose there.

(D) The bacteria were exposed to increasing levels of cyanide. An increase of cyanide in the chemical plants is not desirable.

Exercise R28 (p. 361)

1. (A) The term "chicks" can refer to any baby bird, not just chickens.

(B) Seals do not build nests in trees.

*(C) The words "nests," "molts," "chicks," "hatch," and "plumage" all refer to birds.

(D) Bears do not build nests in trees.

2. *(A) Since the female molts (loses her feathers) inside the nest, the nest is probably lined with those feathers.

(B) The female probably loses her feathers in order to make the nest, not because the nest is too warm.

(C) After the female molts, she seals herself into the nest; she does not break it up.

(D) To lose feathers by molting is different from losing feathers by plucking them out. The female probably uses her feathers to make the nest warm. The passage states she uses mud and dung to seal the nest.

3. (A) There is no information to indicate that the male forces the female into the nest. Both birds seal the opening.

(B) If sealing the nest happened by accident, it would be exceptional rather than the typical behavior of the species.

*(C) The female probably seals herself in on purpose for laying her eggs and hatching the chicks.

(D) There is no information to indicate that the female is protecting her eggs from the male as opposed to other predators.

4. (A) The baby chicks can be fed, but eggs cannot.

(B) The male helps seal in the female.

(C) It is not plumage that keeps the chicks safe, but sealing the nest that keeps the chicks safe.

*(D) Since the male is outside of the sealed nest, he cannot hatch the eggs by keeping them warm.

5. (A) The rivers from two Canadian provinces drain into the Mississippi River. Drainage areas in Canada are not mentioned.

(B) Only thirty-one states out of all the states in the United States have rivers that drain into the Mississippi.

(C) If only parts of some states have rivers that drain into the Mississippi, there are probably other rivers in other parts of those states that drain elsewhere.

*(D) If the Mississippi extends to Canada and flows down to the sea carrying sand, silt, and clay, probably some of the silt the river is carrying comes from Canada.

6. *(A) Since the delta system provides shelter and nutrients for the continent's most fertile marine nursery, it must be very important to marine life.

(B) "Nursery" in the passage means a place where marine life grows, not a nursery for children.

(C) There is no information about diseases caused by mosquitoes and other insects in the passage.

(D) There is no information about the United States's establishing nurseries.

7. (A) It is not being destroyed but being built up.

*(B) If the delta is constantly being built up by the river deposits of sand, silt, and clay, it is probably always changing.

(C) It is not the sea movement but the river deposits that are building up the delta.

(D) The delta is being built on the continental shelf. The continental shelf is already there.

8. (A) Being blind to the humanity of their members does not mean that the people are actually blind.

*(B) It may be difficult for a person who is more concerned with schedules to deal with a person who is not so concerned and vice versa.

(C) Monochronic cultures are linear cultures.

(D) In monochronic cultures, schedules take precedence over all people; and in polychronic cultures, all people take precedence over schedules.

9. *(A) If people are more important than schedules, a person may skip an appointment to help another person.

(B) In a monochronic society, a person might be blind to the needs of a friend.

(C) A person from a polychronic society might be on time for an appointment with a person from a monochronic society only if no other person needs attention.

(D) Since schedules are important in a monochronic society, people will probably do everything possible to keep an appointment.

10. (A) In this sentence the author is defining, not examining the two different cultures.

(B) A monochronic culture is linear, and a polychronic culture is simultaneous.

*(C) These terms are used to further define monochronic and polychronic cultures.

(D) These terms are not terms used for emphasis here.

11. *(A) Since monochronic and polychronic cultures are at opposing ends of the spectrum, it can be inferred that there are other cultures between the two opposing ones.

(B) A monochronic culture is linear, and a polychronic culture is simultaneous.

(C) According to the passage, time can be regarded not as a physical absolute but as a cultural invention.

(D) It is not biological or physical absolutes that a culture invents, but a way to regard time.

12. *(A) The phrase "carries about 5 gallons of fuel" implies that ultralights have an engine that uses fuel.

(B) If human energy were used, then there would be no need for fuel.

(C) If an ultralight were powered by remote control, there would be no need for a pilot.

(D) No mention is made of solar energy in the passage.

13. (A) There is no information given as to where the kits can be bought.

*(B) If ultralights are sold as kits and take about 40 hours to assemble, people can probably buy their own kit and assemble it.

(C) Although a person without experience can fly an ultralight, it doesn't mean that people in general who fly ultralights have no experience.

(D) If a person can buy a kit and assemble it, there is probably no need to have training in aviation to do this.

14. (A) There is no information given as to whether or not ultralights are registered.

(B) "Rarely fatal" means that they are "not frequently fatal."

*(C) If an accident is rarely fatal or even serious, the pilots can probably walk away from most of the accidents.

(D) Fatal accidents rarely occur.

15. (A) The author does not discuss whether Epstein's sculpture is good or bad.

(B) The author does not ridicule or scorn Epstein's work.

(C) The author does not make any amusing comments.

*(D) The author states that artists and critics praised his works, that it now receives the recognition it deserves, and that Epstein is considered one of the major sculptors.

16. (A) Although Epstein had Russian parents, it cannot be inferred that Russian paintings influenced his work.

(B) Although the public tastes were offended, it cannot be inferred that he let their opinions influence him.

(C) It cannot be inferred that the Rhodesian government's dislike for the sculpture affected Epstein's future work.

*(D) It is stated in the passage that critics noted the "influence on it of primitive and ancient sculptural motifs from Africa."

17. (A) It is stated in the passage that today Epstein's work has received the recognition it deserves, and therefore, we can conclude that it wouldn't be mutilated.

 (B) It cannot be inferred that because the work has received recognition, it is because it conforms to public tastes. Perhaps public tastes have changed.

*(C) Because Epstein's work has received the recognition it deserves, it would probably be well received.

 (D) It is stated that Epstein's first commission was of expressive distortion. It cannot not be inferred that all his works are expressive.

18. (A) It is stated that one of Epstein's sculptures was mutilated. The author does not mean that others have been defaced.

 (B) This statement could include all artists' important works of art. The author is only discussing Epstein's works.

 (C) It is stated that the figures of one sculpture offended public tastes because of nudity. The author does not discuss why others have incited criticism.

*(D) The author means that other sculptures of Epstein's have been criticized.

Exercise R29 (p. 368)

1. (C) The passage is mainly about the accomplishments of Will Rogers, a man who started out in the entertainment industry and moved into journalism, where he become most widely known for his humorous approach. See Exercises R5–R7.

2. (A) According to the passage, Rogers was a part-Cherokee Native American. See Exercises R9–R20.

3. (B) An anecdote is an account, often humorous, of some interesting event. See Exercises R1–R3.

4. [3] Rogers's use of humor in his writing, which often debunked the establishment, is what made him different (distinguished him) from other journalists. See Exercises R22–R27.

5. When people "debunk" or "poke fun" at something, they ridicule it. See Exercises R1–R3.

6. (C) An ambassador is a person who represents the policies of one particular country while in another country. A goodwill ambassador is one who travels around projecting a good image of his or her country. See Exercises R22–R27.

7. [5] This sentence gives examples of Rogers's preferred causes and would follow the sentence that introduces his being devoted to charitable causes. See Exercises R9–R20.

8. (D) The author has outlined the diverse interests and occupations that Rogers had. His philanthropic streak is one of these. See Exercises R22–R27.

9. (A) According to the passage, Rogers was both a national and international celebrity. See Exercises R9–R20.

10. A "trailblazer" or "pioneer" explores something new. Aviation was a relatively new field in Rogers's time. See Exercises R1–R3.

11. (A) "Viability" refers to the "feasibility" of doing something. In other words, Rogers was interested in the practical possibility of the commercial route. See Exercises R1–R3.

12. (D) An "epitaph" is a short thought or message usually "inscribed" (an inscription) on a gravestone. See Exercises R1–R3.

13. "The epitaph" reads, "Never Met A Man I Didn't Like." See Exercises R9–R11.

14. (D) The passage indicates that Will Rogers achieved popularity and success in all his endeavors. See Exercises R22–R27.

15. (D) The passage is mainly about the ways dam construction is bringing about the extinction of salmon. See Exercises R5–R7.

16. (A) Smolts must get to the sea in between six and twenty days because their bodies undergo physiological changes allowing them to live in salt water. Therefore, they lose the ability to tolerate freshwater streams. See Exercises R22–R27.

17. The "current" is the continuous "flow" or movement of water in a particular direction. See Exercises R1–R3.

18. [4] It is stated that the salmon used the strong flow from melting snows to reach the sea. See Exercises R9–R20.

19. [3] The sentence that explains why the companies store water until the winter would be followed by a sentence giving another reason for the storage of water until the winter. See Exercises R9–R20.

20. "Companies" store the water. See Exercises R9–R11.

21. When the salmon "return" to the rivers from the sea, they "migrate back" up the rivers. See Exercises R1–R3.

22. "This artificial method" of getting the fish to the sea kills more than "it" (this artificial method) saves. See Exercises R9–R11.

23. (B) The author means that when fish are transported more of them die than when the fish try to get to the sea on their own. See Exercises R22–R27.

24. (B) A "proposal" is a "proposition" or formal statement put forward for discussion. See Exercises R1–R3.

25. (D) The author does not mention breeding salmon as a solution to the problem. See Exercises R9–R20.

26. (A) Since the proposals of scientists and environmentalists have met with criticism from the power companies, this issue is likely to be debated further. See Exercises R22–R27.

27. [2] Paragraph 2 discusses the problems facing salmon throughout their life cycles that could lead to their extinction. See Exercises R9–R20.

28. (B) The passage discusses several studies indicating that people who make a public commitment are more likely to achieve their goals. See Exercises R5–R7.

29. (A) When people make a "resolution," they declare their intentions (make a declaration). See Exercises R1–R3.

30. A "goal" is the "target" or objective that someone hopes to achieve. See Exercises R1–R3.

31. (D) The studies indicate that the people who do not commit themselves are less likely to succeed. See Exercises R22–R27.

32. (B) A feeling of "shame" or "disgrace" is a feeling that the good opinion and respect of others has been lost because one has not behaved in an acceptable way. See Exercises R1–R3.

33. (D) Advertising agencies' business is to help their clients sell the most products. Their studies were probably done for this reason. See Exercises R22–R27.

34. (C) When people are "bombarded" or "saturated" with information, they are given an overwhelming amount of it. See Exercises R1–R3.

35. The group of "strangers" was asked to announce out loud or write down their intentions. See Exercises R9–R11.

36. (D) The subjects who did not make a public commitment (who remained anonymous) cooperated but did not conserve as much gas. See Exercises R9–R20.

37. (A) The passage states that "the amount of gas consumed in each house was recorded." See Exercises R9–R20.

38. When something is "consumed," it is "used" or made use of by someone. See Exercises R1–R3.

39. (A) The passage cites several studies indicating that people who make their intentions known to others are more likely to succeed than those who keep their intentions private. See Exercises R22–R27.

40. (D) The passage discusses the five stages of sleep based on physiological changes. See Exercises R5–R7.

41. (A) EEG patterns are patterns of electrical activity in the brain measured by an electroencephalograph. See Exercises R9–R20.

42. When an activity "decreases," it occurs less often or "slows down." See Exercises R1–R3.

43. A length of time that an activity occurs is called a "period." This can also be referred to as a "stage" of that activity. See Exercises R1–R3.

44. To "rouse" people from sleep means to "awaken" them or make them stop sleeping. See Exercises R1–R3.

45. (B) The paradox (contradiction) is that in Stage 5, the brain patterns indicate the person is sleeping lightly (as in Stage 1), but in fact it is difficult to awaken him or her. See Exercises R22–R27.

46. "People" exhibit what are known as rapid eye movements, and frequently "their" toes and facial muscles twitch. See Exercises R9–R11.

47. "Sleepers" typically descend down to Stage 4. "They" do not reenter the deeper stages. See Exercises R9–R11.

48. (A) According to the passage most people pass through five or six cycles. After several cycles of descent down to Stage 4 and ascent to Stage 5 (REM), they then fluctuate between REM and Stage 2 for the rest of the period of sleep. See Exercises R9–R20.

49. [3] In paragraph 3, it is stated that Stage 4 is the regenerative period – a time when the body repairs itself. See Exercises R9–R20.

50. [1] This sentence helps to introduce the concept of stages. It would come before the description of the stages. See Exercises R9–R20.

SECTION 4 WRITING

Exercise W1 (p. 391)
Two examples are given for each item. The controlling idea is underlined. Your controlling ideas may be different.

1. Owning a large car has many advantages.
   The disadvantages of owning a large car are many.

2. The reason a person lives in a remote area may be one of the following.
   A person who lives in a remote area may face many problems.

3. Before applying to a foreign university, one should consider the disadvantages of studying abroad.
   The advantages of studying abroad outweigh the disadvantages.

4. Car accidents can be avoided or minimized if the driver takes certain precautions.
   Although a person thinks home is a safe place, many different kinds of accidents occur there.

5. An international airport is divided into different sections.
   There are several kinds of airports.

6. Teachers can list many reasons why students are absent from their classes.
   Absenteeism causes the employer many problems.

7. Taking exams is required of all students, and to do their best, students should use the following methods to prepare themselves.

One should follow these <u>procedures</u> when taking an exam.

8. Computers have brought many <u>changes</u> to our way of life.
    Many <u>educational games</u> can be played on computers.

9. Rice can be prepared in many <u>ways</u>.
    Rice can be put to many <u>uses</u>.

10. Preparing to go camping is easy when you organize your trip using these <u>steps</u>.
    Camping has changed in many <u>ways</u>.

Exercise W2 (p. 392)

The following topic sentences are examples. Your topic sentences may be different.

1. This is a strong topic sentence.

2. This is a weak topic sentence because the rest of the paragraph describes what the writer does when he or she goes to the beach. A better topic sentence would be: "Whenever I have the opportunity to go to the beach, I always follow the same routine."

3. This is a weak topic sentence because the rest of the paragraph describes the various ways students can get to class. A better topic sentence would be: "For the many students who cannot afford a car, there are several alternative ways of getting to class."

Exercise W3 (p. 393)

The following topic sentences are examples. Your topic sentences may be different.

1. A dormitory room is cold and impersonal until changes have been made to make it more inviting.

2. University students should take physical education classes as part of their degree program.

3. The fast-food restaurant has become popular for various reasons.

Exercise W4 (p. 394)

1. D   2. B   3. D   4. A   5. C

Exercise W5 (p. 395)

1. Students who need extra money can hold down a full-time job during their summer vacation.

2. A person can also meet other people by going to parties.

3. In my opinion, people should write clearly.

Note: The possible correct answers for Exercises W6–W25 are so varied that you might wish to discuss your answers with a fluent English speaker.

Exercise W6 (p. 395)

These supporting ideas are based on the examples given in the Answer Key for Exercise W1. Yours may be different.

1. I. <u>Disadvantages</u> of large cars
   A. expensive to buy
   B. expensive to maintain
   C. use more gasoline
   D. difficult to park

2. I. <u>Reasons</u> for living in a remote area
   A. get away from city noise
   B. live in unpolluted area
   C. remain where one has been born
   D. be closer to nature

3. I. <u>Disadvantages</u> of studying abroad
   A. far from family and friends
   B. difficulty in understanding a foreign language
   C. more expensive
   D. hard to get home in an emergency

4. I. <u>Kinds</u> of home accidents
   A. falls
   B. poisoning
   C. burns
   D. cuts

5. I. <u>Kinds</u> of airports
   A. international
   B. national
   C. rural
   D. private

6. I. <u>Problems</u> caused by absenteeism
   A. lost production
   B. missed deadlines
   C. mistakes made by substitutes
   D. expenses for training substitutes

7. I. <u>Methods</u> to prepare for taking exams
   A. study on a regular basis
   B. review appropriate material
   C. anticipate questions
   D. get a good night's sleep the night before

8. I. <u>Changes</u> brought by computers
   A. better telephone services
   B. information easier to obtain
   C. easier inventory procedures in businesses
   D. helpful in education

9. I. <u>Ways</u> to prepare rice
   A. steamed rice
   B. fried rice
   C. curried rice
   D. cold rice salad

10. I. <u>Steps</u> to organize a camping trip
    A. make list of necessary items to take
    B. get maps of area
    C. have car in good condition
    D. check weather report

Exercise W7 (p. 397)

These are examples. Your paragraphs will be different. Have a fluent English speaker check your paragraphs.

1. The disadvantages of owning a large car are many. First, they are much more expensive to buy. After having purchased a large car, the owner is then faced with the expense of maintaining it. It uses more gasoline than a small car. Also, it is frequently hard to find a parking place for large cars.

2. The reason a person lives in a remote area may be one of the following. Cities are usually very noisy,

and a person may want to get away from the noise. Another attraction of a remote area might be that it is unpolluted. If a person were born and raised in a remote area, he or she may want to remain in the place that is best known to him or her. Finally, some people like to be closer to nature, and this is easier away from a city.

3. Before applying to a foreign university, one should consider the disadvantages of studying abroad. First, a student may feel alone by being far from family and friends. Also, difficulty in understanding a foreign language can be very frustrating and can affect the student's grades. It can be very expensive to pay the costs of travel and housing in a different country. Finally, if there is an emergency at home, it is hard to get back in a hurry.

4. Although a person thinks home is a safe place, many different kinds of accidents occur there. Falls are perhaps the most common accident among both young children and older adults. Poisoning is a danger, especially if an adult leaves medicines or cleaning chemicals within the reach of a small child. Burns frequently occur in the kitchen area during meal preparation. Finally, people cut themselves when using kitchen knives, trimming equipment in the yard, and power tools in the workshop or garage.

5. There are several kinds of airports. From an international airport, flights go to other countries as well as to cities in the same country. A national airport usually only serves the cities within its nation. Rural airports usually link a town with a nearby national airport. Private airports are those on a military base or at a hospital. Also, individuals and companies can own their own private airports.

Exercise W8 (p. 398)

These are examples. Your answers may differ greatly.

1. It is the largest and most interesting city in the country.

2. I read on the bus on my way to class, while I'm waiting for my friends, and before I go to sleep.

3. The university that I want to attend requires that I get a good score.

4. The sound of the water along the shore calms one's nerves.

5. They can be both psychologically and physically addictive.

6. Had my brother been paying attention to the road instead of changing the CD in the CD player while he was driving, he wouldn't have crashed into the tree and broken his leg.

7. A building such as the Pompidou Centre in Paris has had as many people criticize its design as it has had people praise its modern features.

8. Many city centers are not bustling with shoppers anymore. Instead, the streets are empty except when workers are leaving or returning to their offices.

Exercise W9 (p. 399)

The following answers are only one way that you could add details. Your answers may be different.

1. When you plant a tree, you are helping your environment in many ways. Your tree will provide a home and food for other creatures. Birds may build nests in the branches. The flowers will provide nectar for insects, and the fruits or nuts may feed squirrels or other small animals. Your tree will hold the soil in place. This will help stop erosion. In addition, your tree will provide shade in the summer. This will give welcome relief on hot days. You can watch your tree grow and someday show your children, or even grandchildren, the tree you planted.

2. Airplanes and helicopters can be used to save people's lives. Helicopters can be used for rescuing people in trouble. For example, when a tall building is on fire, people sometimes escape to the roof, where a helicopter can pick them up. Passengers on a sinking ship could also be rescued by helicopter. Because planes can carry heavy loads, they are useful in transporting food and supplies when disasters strike. This is very important when there is an earthquake, flood, or drought. Both types of aircraft can transport people to hospitals in emergencies. Getting a victim of an accident or heart attack to a hospital quickly could save the person's life. Helicopters and airplanes can be used to deliver medical services to people who live in remote areas. They can also be used as a kind of ambulance service in cases where getting to the hospital by car would take too long.

3. Studying in another country is advantageous in many ways. A student is exposed to a new culture. This exposure teaches him or her about other people and other ways of thinking, which can promote friendships among countries. Sometimes students can learn a new language. This language may be beneficial for keeping up with research after the student has finished studying. Furthermore, students can often have learning experiences not available in their own countries. For example, an art history student studying in Rome would get to see works of art that can only be seen in Italian museums and churches. A student may also get the opportunity to study at a university where a leading expert in his or her field may be teaching. A leading expert can introduce the student to the most up-to-date findings of the top researchers in the field. Exposure to such valuable knowledge and insights into the field can aid the student in becoming an expert as well.

Exercise W10 (p. 400)

The following are possible questions to stimulate details.

1. What kind of scenery do you like?
   Why would you want to stop along the road?
   Where and when have you met interesting people on your travels?

How much luggage can you carry on airplanes?
Why don't you have to worry about missing flights?

2. What are the poor and inhumane conditions?
Why don't the animals get exercise?
What is an example of neurotic behavior?
Why is it a problem for animals not to breed?
Why is it a problem for animals to breed with a related animal?

3. Why is knowing the material important?
Why should teachers be able to explain their knowledge?
Why are patience and understanding important?
What should teachers do to show their patience and understanding?
How can teachers make the subject matter interesting?

Note: There is no Answer Key for Exercises W11–W18 and W21.

Exercises W19, W20, and W22 (pp. 410–413)
The following are completed student essays using the questions in W19. There are several other ways these essays could be written. As long as the arguments are well reasoned, it does not matter whether or not the examiner agrees with their content.

1. Our world today is faced with many major threats. The most dangerous threat of all is war. Everyone in the world fears the outbreak of a war, especially another world war in which nuclear weapons may be used. With the use of nuclear weapons there is the possibility of the destruction of our entire planet. Each war starts for a particular reason, but there are a number of steps countries can take to prevent its outbreak.

One main reason for war is a difference in ideology. For example, nations have engaged in struggles over the merits of communist and capitalist systems of government. They frequently aided other countries in wars in order to topple governments that have not agreed with their principles.

Land ownership is also a reason that countries declare wars on their neighbors. Frequently, these conflicts are economic in nature. For example, if oil is found on land in one country but that land can be claimed by another country for historical reasons, the country having historical ties to the land may declare war in order to recover the area containing oil. A landlocked country needing access to the sea may claim the territory between itself and the sea. When a border between two countries lies in an important food-growing area, it is also possible for war to break out. For example, if a border is formed by rivers, disputes over the water rights and the fertile land can turn into war.

To prevent the destruction of Earth in a nuclear catastrophe, countries should try to resolve their differences through international organizations such as the United Nations. All countries need to educate their citizens to be more tolerant of other ideologies. After all, no ideology is worth the annihilation of the planet. In addition, the countries that are better off need to give more assistance to those countries that suffer severe economic troubles so that economically devastated countries will not try to solve their problems through violence. In conclusion, there are solutions to the world's problems, and they should be put into practice now before it is too late.

2. For centuries, the roles of women and men in any particular country remained unchanged. However, modern technology has spread into most societies. This technology has made it possible for men and women to enter into new roles. Some of these changes in roles have been very beneficial.

The role of women has shifted from the homemaker and nurturer of the family to the outside working world. This change has widened women's point of view. Women can now better understand men and the problems they face every day in their jobs. Because women are more knowledgeable about the world, they are now more prepared to take on decision-making roles. Their solutions to problems may be very different from those of men.

Men's roles have changed dramatically as well. The world of business is no longer a man's world. Husbands find that with their wives helping to support the family, they themselves are helping to do many chores that were not considered "manly" before. Furthermore, in activities such as taking care of children, men have learned more nurturing habits. Men also no longer view women as helpless and mindless grown children, but rather as adults with decision-making abilities. Such experiences have helped men acquire a different, more positive attitude toward women and children.

In conclusion, these changes have been very beneficial. The two sexes are able to understand each other better and, therefore, can help each other as a team. However, as with all change, there are conflicts. Some men resent the intrusion of women into their domain, and some women resent being forced out of their homemaking role. With the rise of a new generation accustomed to these roles, these conflicts will eventually smooth themselves out for the benefit of all.

3. Nowadays, we have many conveniences in our society that have been brought about through technology and science. However, these same advancements in technology and science have caused some very dangerous problems. These problems won't go away easily because people don't want to give up the conveniences of a modern lifestyle. The most critical problems that should be dealt with immediately are those of pollution.

Pollution caused by chemicals is a very serious problem because it causes the loss of the ozone layer. Without our ozone, not only human beings but all plant and animal life are exposed to dangerous rays from the sun. Aerosol cans emit chemicals that break down our ozone layer. Refrigeration and air-conditioning systems and cars also have dangerous emissions.

Perhaps the most serious threat to the planet is the warming of the earth's atmosphere, primarily through carbon dioxide emissions. Many scientists think that the warming could be sufficient to melt the polar ice caps, thus raising the sea levels. This would mean that many parts of the world would be submerged below sea level.

There are other problems caused by pollution. Factories that make our modern conveniences emit poisonous gases into the air we breathe. The chemicals we use for cleaning and wastes from factories go into our water systems and pollute the water we drink and the fish we eat. They also kill much of the wildlife we depend on for food. Some of the pesticides we have sprayed on our crops have been found to be dangerous. This kind of pollution may stay in the ground for a very long period of time.

In conclusion, the problems created by pollution are growing daily. Because people do not want to change their lifestyles, we must invent a way to neutralize the pollutants we are putting into our environment. People need to be educated so they will stop damaging the planet. Furthermore, governments must take action to prevent individuals and companies from harming their environment.

Exercise W23 (p. 414)

Question A
1. no The introductory paragraph is incomplete.
2. no The restated problem should be different words, not in the same words as the question.
3. yes The thesis statement gives the controlling idea as *advantages and disadvantages* of small and large cars.
4. yes In the topic sentence of the first developmental paragraph, the topic is "large cars" and the controlling idea is "advantages." In the topic sentence of the second developmental paragraph, the topic is "small cars" and the controlling idea is "advantages and disadvantages."
5. no According to the first developmental paragraph, only *advantages* of large cars will be discussed in that paragraph.
6. no The first developmental paragraph discusses both advantages and disadvantages. This supports the thesis statement but not the topic sentence of the paragraph.
7. yes However, more details could be added. For example, how are large cars good for big

families? Why is strength important in a bad accident? Has the student had any experiences of crashes in big or small cars?
8. no The concluding paragraph is incomplete. The topic and controlling idea are not restated. It is not clear what "for this" refers to or why the student has this preference.
9. no A concluding statement should sum up the essay.
10. no The reasons the writer likes small cars are not included.
11. no There are some minor grammatical mistakes, which may cause confusion.

Question B
1. yes
2. yes
3. yes The controlling idea is "pollution problems."
4. yes
5. yes
6. no The statements "Public safety does not concern the factory owners, who must know that people don't want to live in pollution that is dangerous for their health," and "Nobody in this world wants to breathe dirty air" are irrelevant.
7. yes
8. yes
9. yes It gives solutions. However, it is weak. A better concluding statement might be "In conclusion, the pollution of our air and seas is a major problem. We must work together to solve it now."
10. yes
11. yes

Exercise W24 (p. 415)
1. Score 3 This essay demonstrates some development, but the writer focuses on people who read instead of supporting his or her agreement or disagreement with the given statement. There are insufficient details and a noticeably inappropriate choice of words or word forms (e.g., "emphasize," "imagines," "the read").
2. Score 6 This essay demonstrates competence in writing. It gives a thesis statement that all the paragraphs support. It uses details to illustrate ideas. There is unity, coherence, and progression. Syntactic variety and appropriate word choices are demonstrated.
3. Score 2 This essay contains serious errors in sentence structure. It states an opinion but does not give enough information to support that opinion. There are few details. The specifics are irrelevant (e.g., Helen of Troy).
4. Score 4 This paper demonstrates minimal competence. It lacks a strong thesis statement to give it direction. The first developmental paragraph supports the opinion that reading nonfictional works is beneficial. The second developmental paragraph supports (with only one detail) an implied opinion

that reading novels is no longer beneficial. That detail is unnecessarily repeated (TV has taken the place of the novel). There are a number of mistakes in syntax and usage.

5. Score 1   This is not an essay. There is no development of ideas. There are writing errors that make the meaning difficult to understand.

6. Score 5   This paper demonstrates a generally well-organized and well-developed essay. The paper shows unity, coherence, and progression. There are some grammatical errors, but they do not impede understanding. Although the essay is well developed, it does not have the details and the syntactic variety seen on a score 6 paper.

Note: There is no Answer Key for Exercises W25–W27.

PRACTICE TEST 1 (p. 424, script on p. 583)

Note: If you answer an item incorrectly, complete the exercises following the letter you chose and those following the explanation of the correct answer.

Section 1 Listening

Part A

1. (A) See Exercises L13–L18.
   (B) See Exercises L5–L8.
   *(C) He's getting an application form for a student loan (financial aid). See Exercises L13–L18.
   (D) See Exercises L20–L24.

2. (A), (C), (D) See Exercises L13–L18.
   *(B) The club members built the scenery after having a carpenter advise them on the design. See Exercises L13–L18.

3. (A), (D) See Exercises L13–L18.
   (B) See Exercises L20–L24.
   *(C) The expression "not a single soul" means "no one." See Exercises L9–L11.

4. (A) See Exercises L20–L24.
   *(B) "Posted" means "displayed." See Exercises L5–L8.
   (C), (D) See Exercises L5–L8 and L13–L18.

5. (A) See Exercises L13–L18.
   (B), (C) See Exercises L20–L24.
   *(D) The woman missed her breakfast because it was not ready before she had to leave. See Exercises L13–L18.

6. *(A) The man's not wanting to miss the presentation means that he wants to see it. See Exercises L20–L24.
   (B), (C), (D) See Exercises L13–L18.

7. (A), (D) See Exercises L20–L24.
   (B) See Exercises L1–L4.
   *(C) The fact that there's nothing new about his giving a quiz on Monday means he usually does this. See Exercises L20–L24.

8. (A), (B), (D) See Exercises L20–L24.

*(C) It can be inferred that the two people are studying together from the phrase "term project," and that they are arranging a time to discuss it. See Exercises L20–L24.

9. (A), (B), (D) See Exercises L13–L18.
   *(C) "Just one on a long list" means there are more problems to do. See Exercises L20–L24.

10. *(A) By expressing her pleasure, the woman shows that she wants to go with him. See Exercises L20–L24.
    (B), (D) See Exercise L1–L4.
    (C) See Exercises L20–L24.

11. (A), (C), (D) See Exercises L1–L4.
    *(B) When one is practicing a musical instrument, one is playing music. See Exercises L5–L8.

12. (A), (C), (D) See Exercises L13–L18.
    *(B) "Used to" means "doesn't anymore," and "it got to be too much" means that part-time studying and working full-time became more than she could do. This indicates that she no longer takes classes. See Exercises L13–L18.

13. (A), (C), See Exercises L13–L18.
    *(B) The woman has "put off" (postponed) her visit to the infirmary. See Exercises L9–L11.
    (D) See Exercises L20–L24.

14. *(A) The woman will be revising the script by editing it. See Exercises L13–L18.
    (B), (C) See Exercises L13–L18.
    (D) See Exercises L5–L8.

15. (A) See Exercises L5–L8.
    (B), (C) See Exercises L9–L11.
    *(D) The man apologizes to the woman for having annoyed her so much that she has told him to "mind his own business." See Exercises L9–L11.

16. (A), (B), (C) See Exercises L13–L18.
    *(D) The man is talking about the money they collected when he uses the words "not as much" and is comparing the realized quantity to how much they had hoped to collect. See Exercises L13–L18.

17. (A), (C), (D) See Exercises L13–L18.
    *(B) The charge does not include breakfast. Therefore, guests must pay extra for breakfast. See Exercises L13–L18.

18. *(A) The professor announced the change of dates during a class session that the man didn't attend because he had to go to the dentist. See Exercises L13–L18.
    (B), (C), (D) See Exercises L13–L18.

Part B

19. (A) The woman talks about her own reading of major works by important authors and criticizes the man for reading material he is too old for. This implies that she doesn't think he is reading intellectually stimulating books. See Exercises L38–L40.

20. (D) The man disagrees with the woman's criticism and tells her more about the course. His description indicates that the course covers many aspects of American culture. See Exercises L38–L40.

21. (A) The man states that he has to read a lot about the surrounding historical events that influenced the comic-book writers. See Exercises L31–L36.

22. (D) The man's concern about paying his fees can be understood from his question "How will I complete my registration?" and the statement "The registrar drops students if they don't pay their tuition fees." See Exercises L31–L36.

23. (D) The woman states that the application arrived after the deadline. See Exercises L31–L36.

24. (B), (C) The woman tells the man that he could take out an emergency loan and use it to pay his tuition fees. See Exercises L31–L36.

25. 1. (D), 2. (A), 3. (C), 4. (B) The woman explains that the man should complete the emergency-loan application form and take it to Mr. Schultz. After the man gets the emergency loan, he can complete the registration procedures. He can pay back the emergency loan when he gets his student loan. See Exercises L31–L36.

26. (C) The woman tells the man that he can get an emergency loan the same day he applies for one and then can complete his registration that day. See Exercises L31–L36.

27. (B) Since the student is worried about having the money to complete the registration procedures, he will probably take out an emergency loan. See Exercises L38–L40.

28. (C) The professor introduces the Prairie School of Architecture and talks about its formative influences and its guiding principles. See Exercises L26–L29.

29. (B), (D) The professor states that most of the effort of the Prairie School was devoted to domestic habitations and that the architects tried to relate the interiors to the surrounding landscape. See Exercises L31–L36.

30. (C) Prairie School architecture includes horizontal lines with projecting roofs and projecting terraces with plant boxes. See Exercises L31–L36.

31. (B), (C) The professor states that the number of rooms was reduced to open up living space and that closed interior corners were abolished to create a feeling of movement and freedom. This was an attempt to make living space more compatible with human living requirements. See Exercises L31–L36.

32. (D) The professor gives the turned-up roof edge of traditional Japanese houses as an example of the use of Oriental motifs. See Exercises L38–L40.

33. (C) The talk discusses three ways libraries meet users' needs. See Exercises L26–L29.

34. (A) If libraries had sufficient funds and space, they would not need to use microfilm, microfiche, and computers because they could purchase and house all materials. See Exercises L38–L40.

35. (B) It is stated in the talk that professors make recommendations for the purchase of books and journals. See Exercises L31–L36.

36. (D) It is stated that students can ask their librarian to do a computer search. See Exercises L31–L36.

37. 1. (A), 2. (C), 3. (D), 4. (B) First, the student should check the materials that his or her own library has available. If the library doesn't have the needed materials, a computer check could be run. When the materials are located at another library, they can be ordered. After the student is finished with the materials, they should be sent back to the lending library. See Exercises L31–L36.

38. (A) The professor talks about how the Grameen Bank successfully supported microenterprises by lending money to entrepreneurs. See Exercises L26–L29.

39. 1. (D), 2. (A), 3. (B), 4. (C) First, the entrepreneur wants to start a business. Since he or she has no money, he or she borrows it from a moneylender at a high interest rate. Then when the entrepreneur cannot pay back the high interest, he or she borrows more. This becomes a cycle that keeps the entrepreneur in poverty. See Exercises L31–L36.

40. (A) According to the professor, Mohammed Yunus founded the Grameen Bank with the goal of helping poor people escape from poverty by allowing them to borrow small amounts of money at reasonable interest rates. See Exercises L31–L36.

41. (A) The small-scale entrepreneur gets into a cycle of borrowing money to pay back loans with high interest rates. See Exercises L31–L36.

42. (B), (D) The professor states that the success of such schemes can be judged by the high loan-repayment rate and the high percentage of borrowers that have been able to work themselves out of poverty by running a business. See Exercises L31–L36.

43. (A), (B) The professor states that the Grameen Bank lends money to poor people who have no collateral (something used as a guarantee of repayment) and trains peer groups to manage business operations. See Exercises L31–L36.

44. (B) According to the professor, Mohammed Yunus founded the Grameen Bank with the purpose of lending small amounts of money to poor entrepreneurs. See Exercises L38–L40.

45. (D) The class is mainly discussing the importance of practicing jumping for different kinds of sports. See Exercises L26–L29.

46. (D) Since some athletes neglect this part of training, the professor wants to focus on its importance. See Exercises L38–L40.

47. (B) The professor states that a volleyball player may have to jump immediately after landing from a previous jump, depending on variety of situations. See Exercises L31–L36.

48. (C), (D) The professor states that an athlete has to repeat the motion thousands of times to ingrain its pattern into the subconscious memory of movement. See Exercises L31–L36.

49. (C) The professor talks about sports with a repertoire of jumps and those with a specific type of jump. It can be inferred that training methods vary according to the types of skills required. See Exercises L38–L40.

50.   1. (A), 2. (C), 3. (B) Jumping hurdles is a sport that requires the athlete to make the same kind of jump repeatedly. Pole vaulting is a sport that requires extensive use of arm muscles in the jump. Basketball is a sport that requires the player to make a variety of jumps. See Exercises L38–L40.

Section 2 Structure

1. A verb is needed to complete the noun clause. "Is" agrees with the subject "Saturn."
   (A), (C) See Exercises S61–S66.
   (B) See Exercises S25–S31.
   *(D) See Exercises S54–S59.

2. (B) The clause marker "that" should be used instead of "when" to introduce the noun clause because the emphasis is on the event – discovering the source of the Nile – and not the time. See Exercises S55–S60.

3. A simple subject is needed to complete the independent clause.
   (A) See Exercises S17–S23.
   (B), (D) See Exercises S72–S76.
   *(C) See Exercises S17–S23.

4. (B) "Value" is a noun. The adjective form "valuable" should be used to describe "what kind" of metal. See Exercises S37–S42.

5. The preposition "by" needs to be followed by a noun or noun phrase, "its size," to fill the object position.
   (A), (C), (D) See Exercises S91–S94.
   *(B) See Exercises S1–S5.

6. (D) The passive voice "was learned" should be used because people were learning about Uranus. See Exercises S25–S31.

7. (C) The Himalayas are one of many existing mountain ranges. "World's most extensive ranges" uses the correct word order and is logical. See Exercises S82–S87.

8. (C) An article would be used with the singular form "animal." The example "such as the Tamworth pig" indicates that the pig is just one animal of many the conservationists are attempting

to save. These points indicate that the plural noun "animals" should be used. See Exercises S1–S5.

9. (B) The adjective clause that identifies "Anthony Burgess" needs to be completed. "Who achieved fame" begins the clause. See Exercises S61–S66.

10. (D) When the phrasal verb "turn in" means "hand something in," it needs an object. The phrase should be "turning it in." The object "it" refers to the exam. See Exercises S11–S15.

11. (D) A subject, "there," and verb, "was," are needed to complete the sentence. The negative phrase "not until" indicates that the positions of the subject and aux-word or verb will be inverted. See Exercises S32–S35.

12. (A) The preposition "by" should be used instead of "about," because scientists ordinarily make these estimates. The estimates are not made about them. See Exercises S91–S94.

13. (A) An adjective clause or phrase is needed to give more information about "sailors." "Navigating sometimes in uncharted seas" is an adjective phrase. See Exercises S67–S70.

14. (C) The subject of the adjective clause "that" refers to "forms," a plural noun. Therefore, the verb of the clause should be the plural form "have." See Exercises S25–S31.

15. An article, "the," is needed to complete the noun phrase used as the subject.
   *(A) See Exercises S6–S10.
   (B) See Exercises S91–S94.
   (C) See Exercises S17–S23.
   (D) See Exercises S52–S53.

16. (B) "Other" is used with plural nouns. "Another" should be used with the singular noun "tournament." See Exercises S43–S50.

17. A subject and verb are needed to complete the sentence. The phrase "by the largest machines" indicates that the verb should be in the passive form – "are explored."
   (A) See Exercises S52–S53.
   *(B) See Exercises S52–S53.
   (C) See Exercises S61–S66.
   (D) See Exercises S25–S31.

18. (A) A subject is needed to complete the sentence. The word "it" should be used in the phrase "perhaps was" in order to complete the sentence – "perhaps it was." See Exercises S17–S23.

19. (C) "Not only" indicates that a phrase or clause introduced by "but" or "but also" is needed to complete the sentence. The prepositional phrase "for their hides and milk" indicates that a prepositional phrase, "for pulling sleighs," is needed to complete a parallel structure. See Exercises S88–S90 and S91–S94.

20. (A) When the object of a verb is a sentence, "that," not "what," introduces it. See Exercises S54–S59.

Section 3 Reading

1. (C) The passage discusses the natural world as a stimulus for inventions and goes on to discuss how structures in nature are used for the advancement of product development. See Exercises R5–R7.

2. (B) The author gives Velcro® as an example of a product that is based on a feature found in nature. See Exercises R9–R20.

3. When something "emulates" something else, it "mimics" that other thing or tries to be similar to it. See Exercises R1–R3.

4. This led "the inventor" to invent a synthetic fabric. See Exercises R9–R11.

5. (A) If something is "novel" or "unique," no other thing exactly like it exists. See Exercises R1–R3.

6. (C) Biomimetics is a branch of science in which structures of nature are applied to the development of useful inventions. See Exercises R22–R27.

7. (C) The author uses the term "smart" because structures that are able to design and repair themselves seem to have intelligence. See Exercises R22–R27.

8. When people "envisage" something, they form a mental picture of it or "imagine" it. See Exercises R1–R3.

9. (A) There would probably be no use for a tomato that could change its shape. See Exercises R22–R27.

10. (B) Photosynthesis is the process by which green plants turn sunlight into energy. A product that mimicked photosynthesis could be useful in supplying energy. See Exercises R9–R20.

11. ☐2 In paragraph 2, the author explains that this new field of study is called biomimetics because it attempts to mimic nature. See Exercises R9–R20.

12. (B) All the supporting ideas in the passage concern the qualities of diamonds that affect their value. See Exercises R5–R7.

13. Each point above 1 carat is more valuable than each "point" below 1 carat. See Exercises R9–R11.

14. (A) It is stated in the passage that "there are 100 points in a carat." See Exercises R9–R20.

15. (D) "Absolutely" or "completely" is used to emphasize the lack of color. See Exercises R1–R3.

16. "Stone" is another name for "gem." See Exercises R1–R3.

17. (C) It is stated that a D rating means the stone is absolutely colorless. See Exercises R9–R20.

18. ☐3 A nearly perfect diamond is one that "is as close to flawless as one will find." See Exercises R9–R20.

19. (D) Clarity is rated according to whether imperfections are present. See Exercises R9–R20.

20. (A) Something that is "flawless" or "unblemished" is in perfect condition. See Exercises R1–R3.

21. ☐1 The factors that affect the diamond's brilliance are "carbon spots, inner flaws, and surface blemishes." See Exercises R9–R20.

22. (D) It is stated in the passage that "a well-cut diamond will separate the light into different colors when the light is reflected." See Exercises R9–R20.

23. (B) It is stated that the reflective quality can only be compared between diamonds of the same shape. See Exercises R9–R20.

24. (C) To be "faceted" means to be "cut" in a way that leaves many faces. See Exercises R1–R3.

25. (B) It is stated in the passage that the round shape is the most reflective and thus sparkles more. See Exercises R9–R20.

26. ☐6 A sentence that describes unprofessionally cut diamonds would follow the one in the last paragraph that discusses well-cut diamonds. See Exercises R9–R20.

27. (A) The topic "aspects of narcolepsy" covers all the supporting ideas discussed in the passage. See Exercises R5–R7.

28. (D) It is stated that "narcoleptics may fall asleep at unusual or embarrassing times." See Exercises R9–R20.

29. (B) Only a person with narcolepsy would be likely to fall asleep while eating. See Exercises R22–R27.

30. The word "intervals" refers to "periods" of time that occur between other moments of time. See Exercises R1–R3.

31. (B) When someone is "alert," he or she is wide "awake" and ready to be active. See Exercises R1–R3.

32. When someone is suffering from "paralysis," they suffer from "immobility." In other words, they cannot move their muscles. See Exercises R1–R3.

33. (B) An illness that incapacitates a person while, for example, he or she is driving a car can be considered serious. See Exercises R22–R27.

34. (D) In the passage it is stated that there are "estimates" but "no reliable data" concerning the number of narcoleptics. See Exercises R9–R20.

35. ☐2 There are several sentences in the middle of the paragraph that discuss some possible causes of narcolepsy. A sentence that introduces the topic of causes would precede them. See Exercises R9–R20.

36. ☐3 The problem of narcolepsy may "stem from the immune system's reacting abnormally to the brain's chemical processes." This problem may or may not be genetic. See Exercises R9–R20.

37. The administration of the "drugs" has unwanted side effects. See Exercises R9–R11.

38. (D) It is stated that there currently is no cure for narcolepsy. See Exercises R9–R20.

39. (C) The author discusses the development of photography beginning with the camera obscura and ending with the photos taken from space today. See Exercises R5–R7.

40. (A) The first camera obscura was the natural phenomenon of light entering a hole in a wall and creating an image on the opposite wall. See Exercises R9–R20.

41. (A) When something is "preserved" or "retained," it is kept in its current state. See Exercises R1–R3.

42. An "aperture" is a "hole." See Exercises R1–R3.

43. (B) A room with a hole in one of its walls was first called a camera obscura. See Exercises R9–R20.

44. When something is "exposed" or "subjected" to something else, it is made to experience that thing. See Exercises R1–R3.

45. (D) If the scene outside the room is projected on one of its walls, the people in the room could watch what is taking place outside of the room. See Exercises R9–R20.

46. (A) Although Johann Heinrich Schulze discovered a mixture that became darker when subjected to light, the passage does not indicate that he was working on this mixture to produce photographic images. See Exercises R9–R20.

47. (C) Daguerre found a way to reverse the image to make positive prints, but at first he could not keep the images from getting darker. See Exercises R9–R20.

48. Color film is one of the most important "technological improvements." See Exercises R9–R11.

49. ⑤ The final sentence of the passage explains that the principles used today are no different from those used in Niepce's first photographs. See Exercises R9–R20.

50. (A) In the passage, the Kodak® camera is called the first lightweight camera that people could carry and use. See Exercises R9–R20.

PRACTICE TEST 2 (p. 457, script on p. 587)

Note: If you answer an item incorrectly, complete the exercises following the letter you chose and those following the explanation of the correct answer.

Section 1 Listening

Part A

1. (A), (B), (C) See Exercises L13–L18.
   *(D) "To contribute something" means "to give something to help others." People contributed, or donated, the props to help the students. See Exercises L13–L18.

2. *(A) "To be sold out" means "there are no tickets left because they were all sold." Consequently, he could not get a ticket. See Exercises L9–L11.
   (B), (C) See Exercises L13–L18.
   (D) See Exercises L9–L11.

3. (A), (B), (C) See Exercises L20–L24.
   *(D) The woman is criticizing the way the man writes. She doesn't think that Nancy will want the notes because his handwriting is hard to read. See Exercises L20–L24.

4. (A), (C) See Exercises L13–L18.
   *(B) The expression "face facts" means "accept facts." See Exercises L9–L11.
   (D) See Exercises L1–L8.

5. (A), (C), (D) See Exercises L1–L8.
   *(B) "Pale blue" means "light blue" and "stationery" means "writing paper." The expression "to settle for" means "to reconcile oneself to something." The woman bought the writing paper even though it wasn't exactly what she wanted. See Exercises L9–L11.

6. (A), (B), (C) See Exercises L9–L11.
   *(D) "To not care for something" means "to not like something." See Exercises L9–L11.

7. (A), (B), (D) See Exercises L13–L18.
   *(C) Last week was one week ago, and the week before that was two weeks ago. See Exercises L13–L18.

8. (A), (B) See Exercises L20–L24.
   (C) See Exercises L5–L8.
   *(D) It can be inferred that the man remembered the box because he answered "yes" when the woman asked him if he would have remembered it without her calling to remind him. See Exercises L20–L24.

9. (A), (D) See Exercises L1–L4.
   *(B) The woman's being able to hear the people at the stadium indicates that the stadium is near the house. See Exercises L20–L24.
   (C) See Exercises L20–L24.

10. (A), (B), (D) See Exercises L13–L18.
    *(C) "Certainly" means the same as "nothing is more certain," and "determined to be successful" refers to "determination to succeed." See Exercises L13–L18.

11. (A), (B), (C) See Exercises L13–L18.
    *(D) "Only Mary" means that "she was the only one." See Exercises L13–L18.

12. (A) See Exercises L13–L18.
    (B), (C) See Exercises L5–L8.
    *(D) The woman has asked the man to check (find out) if her paper has come (has arrived). See Exercises L13–L18.

13. (A) See Exercises L13–L18.
    (B) See Exercises L5–L8.
    *(C) "To ask for an extension" means "to ask for more time." See Exercises L13–L18.
    (D) See Exercises L1–L8.

14. *(A) The woman's question indicates she is surprised that the flyers have been printed. See Exercises L20–L24.
    (B), (C), (D) See Exercises L20–L24.

15. (A), (C) See Exercises L13–L18.
    *(B) The woman's asking the man if he has seen Diane's work as a response to his question indicates that she doesn't think Diane does good work. See Exercises L20–L24.
    (D) See Exercises L20–L24.

16. (A), (B), (C) See Exercises L20–L24.
    *(D) The woman's asking if the man is certain about Rhoda's preference suggests that she thinks Rhoda may not want a bracelet. See Exercises L20–L24.

17. (A), (B) See Exercises L13–L18.
    *(C) The woman states her opinion that Terry did a better job of acting. See Exercises L13–L18.
    (D) See Exercises L1–L8.

18. (A), (C), (D) See Exercises L20–L24.
    *(B) The man explains that he turned in his paper on a diskette that might be contaminated with a virus. The diskette could infect his professor's computer. See Exercises L20–L24.

Part B

19. (A) The woman's saying that she can't get excited about classes indicates that she has lost her enthusiasm. See Exercises L31–L36.

20. (A) The woman feels better after the man suggests dropping one class and adding a different one, so she will probably follow his suggestion and change her class schedule. See Exercises L38–L40.

21. (B) The man asks about the woman's first day of classes and she responds by telling him about her American history course. They continue discussing this class. See Exercises L26–L29.

22. (B) The man states that he never liked history. See Exercises L31–L36.

23. (A) The woman thinks that the man would like history if he took a course with Professor Lewis. See Exercises L31–L36.

24. (A) The talk is about saffron in general. Therefore, it includes many facts about saffron. See Exercises L26–L29.

25. (D) The stamen of the plant is described as three slender threads in the center of each flower, which are dried and used to produce saffron. See Exercises L31–L36.

26. (C) Saffron is referred to as the "king of spices" because it is one of the world's most prized and expensive foodstuffs. See Exercises L31–L36.

27. (A) In the lecture, it is stated that "India and Iran [are] the only other producers of note [of importance]." See Exercises L31–L36.

28. (C) It is stated in the lecture that "not only is Spain the largest producer of saffron, but it is also the largest consumer." See Exercises L31–L36.

29. (B) The woman uses the man's name. This indicates that they probably know each other. See Exercises L38–L40.

30. (B) It can be inferred that the woman wants to know where the Recreation Center Bus stop is because when the man tells her where the university buses stop, she asks how the Recreation Center Bus can be identified. See Exercises L38–L40.

31. (A) While it cannot be inferred that the woman is going directly to the Recreation Center, she is going in the vicinity of the center. Otherwise she wouldn't be taking that particular bus. See Exercises L38–L40.

32. (D) The man states that university buses have identifying letters. The Recreation Center Bus will have the letters "RC" above the windshield. See Exercises L31–L36.

33. (D) It can be inferred from the woman's ignorance of bus schedules, bus names, and bus stop locations that she is unaccustomed to taking university buses. See Exercises L38–L40.

34. (D) The professor begins the talk by stating that fossilization is a complicated process and continues by explaining the four conditions that must occur in order for fossils to be created and later found. It is not common that all four conditions are met; therefore, finding fossils is rare. See Exercises L26–L29.

35. (B), (C) The professor states that an animal has to be buried quickly and mentions several situations in which this could happen, such as drowning and being buried in a sandbar, and being buried in a sandstorm. See Exercises L31–L36.

36. (D) The professor gives these animals as an example of scavengers that reduce dead animals to bone chips. See Exercises L38–L40.

37. (B) The professor gives several reasons why fossilization is rare. This indicates her realistic attitude toward finding fossils. See Exercises L38–L40.

38. 1. (D), 2. (C), 3. (A), 4. (B) First, the animal must die and be buried quickly. The carcass must be buried for a long period of time. Before the fossil can be found, it must be exposed through erosion of the layers covering it. Then someone who would recognize it must find it before it is destroyed by the elements. See Exercises L31–L36.

39. (D) The professor introduces the problem of the theft of cultural antiquities and art. She goes on to discuss what measures can be taken against it. See Exercises L26–L29.

40. (A) The professor compares the illegal art trade to that of the illegal trade in weapons and drugs to show how great the problem has become. See Exercises L38–L40.

41. (A) The professor states that surveillance is not always affordable. See Exercises L31–L36.

42. (D) The professor states that surveillance is not a practical option in remote places. It would be

difficult to put a surveillance device on a statue along a remote road. See Exercises L38–L40.

43. (C) The professor states that original owners cannot always furnish an accurate description of their stolen property and, consequently, cannot prove ownership. See Exercises L31–L36.

44. (A), (C) The professor agrees with the man's point that inventories would only be useful if they were available for concerned organizations. The professor then gives examples of several organizations, such as the police, customs agencies, and insurance companies, that would find this information useful for stopping the illegal art trade. See Exercises L31–L36.

45. (C) The speaker introduces the topic of background music in film and talks about its development from its infancy to the experience it provides moviegoers today. See Exercises L26–L29.

46. 1. (C), 2. (A), 3. (B) Mendelssohn composed music before the advent of movies, Camille Saint-Saëns was the first person to compose music for a particular film, and Max Steiner was a pioneer in film scoring for sound tracks. See Exercises L31–L36.

47. 1. (B), 2. (C), 3. (A), 4. (D) Movie music was first performed by musicians who were playing along with the movie in the theater. When a system for synchronization was developed, music was performed by musicians within the movie itself. Music then could be heard without the viewer seeing where the music was coming from. Finally, music was added to underscore the dialogue. See Exercises L31–L36.

48. (A) The professor uses a composition of Mendelssohn's as an example of the type of music by famous composers that the catalogs offered musicians. See Exercises L38–L40.

49. (B), (C) The professor states that Max Steiner was the composer for the first film to experiment with background music without a visible means of production as well as for the first film to experiment with music underscoring dialogue. See Exercises L31–L36.

50. (C) None of the developments in film music could have taken place without the synchronization of sound and image developed in 1922. See Exercises L38–L40.

Section 2 Structure

1. A subject and a verb are needed to complete the sentence. Because the word "number" is singular, an article, in this case "an," is also needed.
   (A), (C) See Exercises S17–S23 and S25–S31.
   *(B) See Exercises S17–S23 and S25–S31.
   (D) See Exercises S72–S76.

2. (B) Instead of "both," "as well as" meaning "in addition to" should be used here. See Exercises S43–S50.

3. The adjective clause giving more information about "ships" needs to be completed. "Which can attain" begins the adjective clause.
   (A) See Exercises S67–S70.
   (B) See Exercises S61–S66 and S72–S76.
   (C) See Exercises S17–S23.
   *(D) See Exercises S61–S66.

4. (A) Because the action happens each time a nerve is stimulated, it is a recurring action. Therefore, the verb "resulting" should be in the present-tense form – "results." See Exercises S25–S31.

5. A subject is needed. The noun phrase "the most important export" completes the sentence.
   (A), (C) See Exercises S52–S53.
   (B) See Exercises S17–S23.
   *(D) See Exercises S1–S5 and S17–S23.

6. (B) The pronoun "itself" should be used in place of "themselves" to refer to the singular noun "whale." See Exercises S11–S15.

7. The list of nouns in the object position indicates that a parallel structure using a noun is needed to complete the sentence. "Well-maintained campgrounds" completes the list.
   (A), (B) See Exercises S52–S53.
   (C) See Exercises S88–S90.
   *(D) See Exercises S88–S90.

8. (A) The pronoun "it" refers to the noun "satellites." Because "it" is a singular form, the noun should also take the singular form, "satellite." See Exercises S1–S5.

9. A comparison is needed for the sentence to be logical. The word "like" indicates a comparison.
   (A), (D) See Exercises S72–S76.
   *(B) See Exercises S91–S94.
   (C) See Exercises S6–S10.

10. (C) Because the sentence expresses equality ("as . . . as"), the adjective form "clever" is correct. (Note that the correct comparative form for "clever" would be "more clever," not "cleverer.") See Exercises S82–S87.

11. A clause marker, "even though," and a subject, "city parks," are needed to complete the adverb clause.
   *(A) See Exercises S72–S76.
   (B), (D) See Exercises S52–S53.
   (C) See Exercises S61–S66.

12. (C) An article is needed with the singular noun "process." The article "an" should precede the adjective, because "ancient" begins with a vowel sound. See Exercises S6–S10.

13. A clause marker, "that," and a subject, "knowledge," for the verb "has increased" are needed to complete the noun clause that is used as a subject of the sentence.
   *(A) See Exercises S54–S59.
   (B), (D) See Exercises S54–S59.
   (C) See Exercises S52–S53.

14. (C) "Photograph" should be preceded by the article "a" if there is only one. The absence of "a" indicates that the plural form "photographs" should be used. See Exercises S1–S10.

15. The independent clause is a complete sentence. An adjective clause or phrase giving more information about the tomb is needed. The adjective clause "which was erected in the fifteenth century," can be reduced to "erected in the fifteenth century." The passive voice is needed because someone erected the tomb.
    (A), (D) See Exercises S25–S31.
    *(B) See Exercises S67–S70.
    (C) See Exercises S67–S70.

16. (A) The passive voice requires a past participle. The past participle of the verb "assume" is "assumed." See Exercises S25–S31.

17. A subject is needed to complete the independent clause. The use of the phrase "not until" at the beginning of the sentence indicates that the subject and an aux-word will be inverted. "Did the Romans" completes the sentence.
    (A), (B) See Exercises S32–S35.
    (C) See Exercises S61–S66.
    *(D) See Exercises S32–S35.

18. (B) Because the Victorian constructions are not being compared, the adjective form "few" should be used. See Exercises S37–S42 and S82–S87.

19. A subject, "The Great Wall of China," and a verb, "is," are needed to complete the sentence.
    (A) See Exercises S52–S53.
    (B) See Exercises S61–S66.
    *(C) See Exercises S52–S53.
    (D) See Exercises S54–S59.

20. (C) The adjective form "building" should be used to describe the kind of industry. See Exercises S37–S42.

Section 3 Reading

1. (B) Teotihuacán is a large and ancient city in the Americas. The passage discusses various aspects of the city. See Exercises R5–R7.

2. [2] It is stated that Teotihuacán is believed to be a creation of a civilization earlier than the Toltecs. Little is known about their origins. See Exercises R9–R20.

3. (D) When something is "dispersed," it is "scattered" or spread over a large area. See Exercises R1–R3.

4. (D) It is stated in the passage that it is not clear what caused the city's decline. See Exercises R9–R20.

5. (B) "Adversaries" or "rivals" are the people that one is competing with or fighting against. See Exercises R1–R3.

6. (A) There is no mention of market streets. See Exercises R9–R20.

7. An "urban area" is an area where a lot of people live and work. In other words, it is a "city." See Exercises R1–R3.

8. An "edifice" is a building or "structure" that is usually large and impressive. See Exercises R1–R3.

9. (C) The fact that the Pyramid of the Sun was at one time surmounted by a temple and had a cave underneath possibly used for ritual activities indicates that it probably had a ceremonial function. See Exercises R22–R27.

10. (A) The pyramids in Teotihuacán are described as having a series of sloping apron walls interspersed with vertical panels producing a steplike appearance. See Exercises R9–R20.

11. (D) There is nothing in the passage to indicate whether or not the people of Teotihuacán were militarily aggressive. See Exercises R22–R27.

12. (B) The first paragraph presents the story of how the Great Fire of Chicago was started by a cow, and although the author gives data about the fire, the events surrounding the legend are the main focus of the passage. See Exercises R5–R7.

13. The other combustible materials were stored in the barn. See Exercises R9–R11.

14. A "blaze" and a "conflagration" both refer to a large fire. See Exercises R1–R3.

15. (A) When a fire is "fanned," it burns more strongly or is "intensified." See Exercises R1–R3.

16. [2] A sentence about the extinguishing of the fire would probably come before sentences that discuss the aftermath of the fire. See Exercises R9–R20.

17. (D) The author considers the cow story as an important ingredient in the fabric of American folklore. See Exercises R22–R27.

18. (C) It is stated that Peg Leg's testimony was questionable because his account had inconsistencies and he himself could have been suspected. See Exercises R9–R20.

19. When people "censure" or "blame" someone, they show strong disapproval of what that person has done. See Exercises R1–R3.

20. (D) The author mentions the police reporter as a person who may have started the story, not as a person who may have started the fire. See Exercises R9–R20.

21. [8] The sentence "This last theory gains credence from the fact that on the same night as the Chicago fire, neighboring states suffered more than a dozen major fires" gives support to the theory that all the fires were caused by a natural phenomenon – asteroids. See Exercises R9–R20.

22. (A) Peshtigo, Wisconsin, is a town that was destroyed by fire on the same night that Chicago was. The author uses this town to support the asteroid theory. See Exercises R22–R27.

23. (B) A "shack" is a wooden "hut" used for living or storage purposes. See Exercises R1–R3.

24. (D) The populace was described as devastated, not as riotous. See Exercises R9–R20.

25. (A) The fire is known as the Great Fire of Chicago because of the number of people left homeless, the death toll, and the property damage caused. See Exercises R22–R27.

26. (A) The first paragraph discusses the finding of the *Mary Celeste* and details about her condition when found. See Exercises R5–R7.

27. [2] The crew brought the *Mary Celeste* to Gibraltar in order "to collect the large salvage reward." See Exercises R9–R20.

28. "The crew" of the *Dei Gratia* gave the report at the inquiry. See Exercises R9–R11.

29. When something is "deserted" or "abandoned," it is left unattended. See Exercises R1–R3.

30. When something is "propounded" or "suggested," it is put forward as a possibility. See Exercises R1–R3.

31. (D) The reference to alien abductions and sea-monster attacks as "outlandish notions" indicates that the author considers these explanations as highly improbable. See Exercises R22–R27.

32. (B) All of the theories that the author discusses in paragraph 2 are flawed. See Exercises R22–R27.

33. Something that is "plausible" or "credible" is something that can be believed to be true. See Exercises R1–R3.

34. "All aboard" the *Mary Celeste* imagined that the ship's cargo might explode. See Exercises R9–R11.

35. (A) Something that is "impending" or "imminent" is something that will happen soon. See Exercises R1–R3.

36. (D) When a boat is "capsized" or "overturned," it has rolled over in the water. See Exercises R1–R3.

37. (C) The cargo of crude alcohol was combustible, so the captain might have been afraid that it would explode into flames. See Exercises R9–R20.

38. [4] A sentence about leaving the hatches open to prevent a blast would come between the sentence that introduces the possibility of an explosion and the sentence that gives other details to support the explanation. See Exercises R9–R20.

39. (D) The passage is mainly about how Borglum created the Mount Rushmore monument. See Exercises R5–R7.

40. (D) The passage states that Borglum hired "laid-off workers from the closed-down mines." See Exercises R9–R20.

41. [5] The last sentence indicates that Borglum was careful to train his workmen and to use equipment with safety features. See Exercises R9–R20.

42. (A) When something is "devised" or "designed," it is invented and made for a particular use. See Exercises R1–R3.

43. (B) A "fissure" is a deep "crack." See Exercises R1–R3.

44. (C) The author means that Borglum himself invented the mixture to fill the cracks. See Exercises R9–R20.

45. (B) To "expand" or "enlarge" means to get bigger. See Exercises R1–R3.

46. The "water" expands as it freezes. See Exercises R9–R11.

47. (D) Mount Rushmore is repaired every autumn, or "periodically." See Exercises R9–R20.

48. [5] The sentence about the summer heat also affecting the fissures would come after the sentence about the effects of winter on the fissures. See Exercises R9–R20.

49. (A) The passage states that changes in the original design had to be made because of the cracks that were uncovered. Therefore, it can be inferred that the heads are not as originally planned. See Exercises R22–R27.

50. (B) The author concentrates on the work involved in making and maintaining the heads but does not mention why Borglum undertook this work. See Exercises R9–R20.

• SCRIPTS •

DIAGNOSTIC TEST

Section 1 Listening

Part A

Now we will begin Part A with the first conversation.

1. W: Tom offered to give us a lift to the University Theater since our car is in the shop.
   M: That was a nice gesture on Tom's part.
   What does the man mean?

2. M: What a great retirement present the biology class got for Dr. Winslow! It must have been expensive.
   W: It was, but we all chipped in for it.
   What does the woman mean?

3. M: I can't believe how much I spend for textbooks these days. Everything costs more.
   W: I know. The price of hardback books has doubled in the last three years.
   What does the woman mean?

4. M: I suppose Jack told you all about our field trip to the capital with our American government class.
   W: Yes, he did. And I can't believe you didn't visit the Supreme Court.
   What does the woman mean?

5. M: I got a sixty on the physics exam.
   W: What a close call!
   What does the woman imply?

6. W: Can you explain to me how to get to your house?
   M: It's better if I meet you in the parking lot in front of the Student Activities Center and lead you there.
   What does the man imply?

7. M: How long has Scott been writing his dissertation – five years?
   W: At least that long.
   What does the woman say about Scott?

8. M: I can't make heads or tails of this map.
   W: Let's pull into the next gas station.
   What does the woman mean?

9. M: Where are you headed, Barbara?
   W: To the gym.
   What does the woman imply?

10. M: I hardly had time to finish the exam.
    W: Really? I finished in no time.
    What does the woman mean?

11. M: Do you know which bus goes out to Rocky Heights?
    W: There are maps of bus routes at the information desk in the Student Union.
    What does the woman imply the man should do?

12. M: Hey, I like your haircut. Where did you have it done?
    W: At home. My sister wanted to get some practice.
    What does the woman imply?

13. M: Did Jill return your notes last night?
    W: No. And when I see her, I'm going to give her a piece of my mind.
    What does the woman mean?

14. W: Sue's ideas for her research project sound great, don't you agree?
    M: I think they're somewhat overambitious.
    What does the man mean?

15. M: Bob's back from the library.
    W: He couldn't have finished that assignment already.
    What does the woman mean?

16. M: What kind of house are you looking for?
    W: We'd like a small one in a quiet suburb that's within commuting distance of the university.
    M: The Los Altos district is quiet, and it's a five-minute walk to a bus route that passes directly by the main campus.
    What can be inferred about the woman?

17. W: I was surprised that you didn't say anything in your defense.
    M: I should have.
    W: Well, why didn't you? You had the chance.
    M: It's just that Dan's accusations left me speechless.
    What does the man mean?

18. M: Parking on campus is really difficult. I think I'm going to sell my car and get a bicycle.
    W: Why not take the bus? The service here is very good.
    M: It's not that good. Besides, riding bicycles is healthy, and they're cheap and easy to maintain.
    W: If you're going to get a bike, talk to Ted first. He's very knowledgeable about them.
    What does the woman mean?

Part B

Now we will begin Part B with the first conversation.

Listen to a conversation between two friends.

M: I need to buy Phil something for his birthday.

W: I'm going downtown to pick up my new contact lenses. Would you like a ride?

M: What time would you be going?

W: About one o'clock.

M: I have a fencing class then.

W: I can wait until later if you'd like.

M: Can you? That would be great. I get out of class at 1:50, but I'll have to shower afterwards. Would 2:30 be too late?

W: No problem. Shall I pick you up in front of the gym?

M: There's really no place to park there, and if I'm a little late, that could cause you problems. How about meeting me in the student parking lot behind the gym? I know it's a bit out of the way because of that one-way street, but it might be the safer bet.

W: That's fine. I'd rather drive a bit more than get a traffic ticket. They're really strict around here. So, I'll meet you about 2:30 in the student parking lot. See you later.

19. What is the main topic of the conversation?
20. Why does the woman want to go downtown?
21. Where are the people going to meet?

Listen to a conversation between two students.

W: I wasn't able to meet Dr. Reed's deadline for that report.

M: Have you been to see her about it?

W: Yes, I spoke to her yesterday.

M: Did she give you an extension?

W: No, she didn't, unfortunately, but she did give me some ideas on how to organize my material better so I'll be able to make the deadline for the next assignment.

M: I could use some advice on how to do that.

W: I can't remember all she said, but I jotted down the main points. I can make a copy for you.

M: Could you? I'd really appreciate that.

W: I'll give it to you tomorrow before class.

M: Thanks. See you tomorrow, then.

22. What happened to the woman?
23. What did Dr. Reed give the woman?
24. What does the man want?

Listen to a conversation between two students. They are discussing plans for the summer.

W: What are your plans for the summer?

M: I'm going to attend summer classes.

W: Summer classes? You're kidding. Aren't you burned out by the end of the term? Don't you need a holiday?

M: Not really. I don't carry a heavy class load during the year so I can hold down a part-time job. Then I take a summer class or two that I really enjoy to make up for it.

W: That sounds like a good idea, but I don't think I could stand taking classes year-round. So, what are you taking?

M: Geology 306. It's a special course that's offered only during the summer. I'm really looking forward to it. We're taking a two-week field trip out to Copper Mountain where we'll be collecting fossils and mapping the strata. Then we'll return to campus to do lab work on our finds.

W: That sounds fascinating. Why don't they offer it during the academic year?

M: Unfortunately, the department can't hold classes like these during the year because students are taking so many classes at the same time, they can't manage the field trips. Also, the weather in the fall and spring can be unpredictable. It would be hard to do the fieldwork in a snowstorm.

W: Well, that's true. What other classes have you taken during the summer sessions?

M: Well, I got university credit for digging on an archaeological site last year.

W: Oh? Where did you dig?

M: In Colorado. It was a buffalo-kill site. You know, one where the early Americans drove the animals off a cliff.

W: Did you find anything of interest?

M: Lots of broken stone tools used for butchering the buffalo.

W: You must have had a great time. I think I might consider taking some summer classes.

25. What is the man going to do during the summer?
26. What is NOT done at Copper Mountain?
27. According to the man, why can't some of the summer classes be held during the academic year?
28. What objects might be found at a buffalo-kill site?
29. What does the man imply about summer classes?

Listen to a conversation between a professor and a student. They are talking about a particular painting.

W: Did you hear on the news last night that a Rembrandt has just been returned to our city museum after being out on unauthorized loan for three years?

M: Yes, Dr. Matson. I saw the news last night and was wondering why that particular painting was stolen when there are so many valuable items in the museum.

W: Actually, that Rembrandt is favored by thieves. It's been taken four times in the last twenty years. The museum curators believe it may have something to do with its size – nine by eleven inches.

M: That would make it easier to steal and hide, wouldn't it? How valuable is the painting?

W: Well, it's been appraised at five million dollars, but I don't know what a thief can sell it for.

M: The painting is quite well known, isn't it? It seems that no one would want a stolen painting that's so easily recognized.

W: It seems that way, but the museum has had to take extra security precautions because of its popularity with thieves.

30. What are the people discussing?
31. How long had the painting been missing?
32. What reason is given for the painting's popularity among thieves?
33. What is the professor uncertain about?
34. Select the work of art below that thieves would be attracted to.

Listen to part of a lecture in an anthropology class. The professor is talking about human migration.

Although we don't think of ourselves as migratory in the way we do of other animal species, people have always been on the move. A few hundred thousand years ago, humans migrated from the savannahs of Africa and spread rapidly into present-day Europe and Asia. This migration coincided with successive cycles of glacial periods known as the "Ice Age," and it probably occurred as humans followed the advance and retreat of plants and animals. Humans survived the bitterly cold weather that prevailed in these regions due to their ability to make things, such as shelter and clothing, but, more importantly, due to their ability to control fire.

Later migrations took humans to Japan, on to Indonesia, and finally to Australia. They also migrated across the Bering land bridge into North America and spread quickly down to the southern tip of South America. Later movements brought people to the eastern part of the Canadian Arctic and to northern Greenland.

Human migration has not just involved taking over unused land. People have also invaded land occupied by other peoples through killing, displacing, or genetically mixing with the land's existing inhabitants. Looking at today's world, it is clear that we continue to do this. To sum up, migration seems to be a fundamental human instinct.

35. What is the purpose of the talk?
36. How did people survive the Ice Age in northern Europe and Asia?
37. What does the speaker say about the invasion of occupied land by human groups?
38. What does the speaker say about human migration?
39. The professor briefly explains a series of human migrations. Put the migrations in chronological order.

Listen to part of a lecture in an American literature class. The professor is talking about the writer Jack London.

Today I want to discuss the life of the writer Jack London. London was born in San Francisco in 1876. His mother was married to a disabled Civil War veteran called John London. The family moved around a lot when Jack was young and eventually settled in the city of Oakland. As a very young man, Jack worked at various jobs – some menial, but some adventurous. He sailed the Pacific, worked on a fish patrol to capture poachers, raided oyster farms, prospected for gold, and at one time joined an army of unemployed workers. He became acquainted with socialism and ran as a socialist candidate for mayor of Oakland, although he was unsuccessful.

Jack was always an avid reader and studied the works of many writers in order to learn to become a writer himself. In fact, he consciously chose the life of a writer in order to escape the unpleasant prospect of becoming a factory worker. The varied and adventurous life he led provided him with a wealth of material from which to create imaginative literature. At first, his submissions met with very little success. However, his disciplined approach eventually paid off and he gained international renown, with over fifty volumes of stories, novels, and essays to his name. His novel *The Call of the Wild* brought him lasting fame, and many of his short stories are considered classics. Other works of his critiqued capitalism, poverty, and alcoholism. At one point, he journeyed across the Pacific in a small boat; this trip provided the inspiration for stories about Polynesian culture.

London became one of the best-known public figures of his time. He used his fame to draw support for socialism, suffrage for women, and, later, prohibition of alcohol. However, his political and social views were considered inconsistent and self-contradictory. For example, his support for socialism was countered by a strong belief in individualism. He supported women's rights but dominated the female members of his family.

In his thirties, London tried his hand at agriculture. He pursued this interest with great energy at his ranch in California and introduced many practical innovations that were ahead of the times. During this period, he developed a kidney disease from which he eventually died in November 1916, at the age of 40.

40. What is the main topic of the professor's discussion?
41. Why did London become a writer?
42. According to the professor, where did London get his ideas for his publications?
43. Why does the professor mention London's novel *The Call of the Wild*?
44. According to the professor, in what ways was London inconsistent and self-contradictory?
45. The professor describes London's life chronologically. Summarize his life by putting the events in order.

Listen to a part of a lecture in an American history class. The professor is talking about the Lost Colony of Roanoke.

Some of you may have heard of the Lost Colony, the first English settlement on the North American continent, established in 1585 on Roanoke Island in what is now North Carolina.

The original settlers found the island swampy and inhospitable, and relations with the nearby Native Americans soon deteriorated. In June 1586, the original colonists, fearful and hungry, returned to England on some ships that were passing their settlement. Then, just three weeks later, ships sent from England and loaded with supplies arrived. Upon finding the colonists gone, the captain left fifteen men to hold the fort and left again for England.

A second group of colonists arrived in 1587 only to find that the holding force had been killed. The leader of this new group, aware that his settlers needed assistance and more supplies, sailed again to England, but his return voyage was delayed due to war between England and Spain. When relief vessels finally got back to Roanoke in 1590, the crew members found that the fort had been abandoned. Not a trace of the more than one hundred pioneers was left. Only one clue to their whereabouts was found. At the site of the fort the enigmatic word "Croatoan," the Native-American name for a nearby island, had been scratched on one of the entrance posts of the fort. Elsewhere on the island the search party found the first three letters of this same word carved on a tree. Perhaps the carver had been interrupted and hadn't had time to finish writing.

There has been much speculation about this enigmatic episode in early American history. It is generally believed that the unlucky colonists either starved or were killed. Some scholars claim that there were survivors and that they were adopted by the Native Americans, since the descendants of the indigenous people from this area still claim these colonists as their ancestors. But, whatever the fate of the Lost Colony, the story will always fascinate students of history.

46. What is the lecture mainly about?
47. According to the professor, what did the people on the relief vessels find in Roanoke?
48. Which of the following may explain what happened to the Roanoke settlers?
49. What happened to each of the three groups of people left at Roanoke?
50. Why does the professor refer to Roanoke as an enigmatic episode in early American history?

SECTION 1   LISTENING

Read the directions to each exercise. When you understand what to do, start the recording. You will hear the exercise title and then the question number. The directions and the example are not on the recording.

Start the recording when you see the 🎧 symbol and the word **START**. Stop or pause the recording when you see the 🎧 symbol and the word **STOP** or **PAUSE**.

Part A   Short conversations

Exercise L1   Identifying the correct sound

1. Did you see the sheep?
2. He gave me the bell.
3. I didn't have any clue.
4. The mayor was sitting at his desk.
5. Where did she put the pen?

Exercise L2   Recognizing questions and statements

1. Ann's from San Francisco?
2. What an impossible teacher!
3. Read anything good recently?
4. Can Tom ever cook!
5. What a terrible mistake that was!
6. Why should I?
7. He asked where the library was.
8. Is it ever raining hard!

Exercise L3   Identifying words that are pronounced the same but have different meanings

1. At the corner turn right.
2. It was a difficult feat to climb that mountain.
3. Please wait your turn.
4. It's one hour before the movie starts.
5. Bill is an heir to a fortune.
6. W: I want to dye my hair.
   M: Why do that? It's already a nice color.
7. M: My brakes failed on the freeway last night.
   W: That must have been very frightening.
8. W: Who won the motorcycle race?
   M: Albert Jackson did.
9. M: Did you have enough money for tuition and books?
   W: No, I had to take out a loan.
10. M: I've just torn a hole in my sweater.
    W: Too bad. Can it be fixed?

Exercise L4   Identifying the meaning of the word in the conversation

1. meet
   W: What time did you tell Ann we would meet her?
   M: At 6:00, in front of the main administration building.

2. sail
   M: Did Michael replace the torn sail on his boat?
   W: No, he thinks he can mend it.

3. cruise

   M: Sue is going on a cruise to the Bahamas.

   W: Is she? I wish I could go, too.

4. weak

   W: I felt very weak when I came home from the hospital.

   M: How long were you there?

5. mail

   M: Has the mail been delivered yet?

   W: Yes, but it was all junk.

Exercise L5   Identifying which meaning is correct

1. That's a very simple cake to make.
2. Rita pays a reasonable rate for room and board there.
3. Please don't kid me about such a serious matter.
4. That police officer's beat covers this entire neighborhood.
5. Nancy and I have a common interest in astronomy.
6. W: Where did Jack earn his degree?

   M: At Colorado State Teachers' College.
7. M: I thought your major was economics.

   W: It was. But I changed to international relations last semester.
8. W: Why are you getting rid of that easy chair?

   M: It has a broken spring.
9. M: Could you turn up the volume on the radio?

   W: That's as high as it can go.
10. M: Are you sure that it's a sound deal?

    W: Not really. You can't believe everything Tim says.

Exercise L6   Identifying multiple meanings

1. (A) New evidence came to light after the investigation.

   (B) Because of the heat, she wore a light summer dress.
2. (A) Did you read about the military strike in the newspaper?

   (B) These matches are damp and won't light when you strike them.
3. (A) Please note that the times for the concert have been changed.

   (B) Fred can sing the lowest note of anybody in the choir.
4. (A) There's a freshwater spring near the park.

   (B) The cat waited patiently to spring on the mouse.
5. (A) If you don't agree with the decision, you can exercise your rights to a new trial.

   (B) The doctor has advised me to exercise more and eat less.

Exercise L7   Matching words

1. (A) The pass through those mountains is treacherous.

   (B) Do you need a pass to get into the conference?
2. (A) Patty's just an ordinary-looking girl.

   (B) She was famous for being a just leader.
3. (A) Those chairs tip easily, so be careful.

   (B) She left the waiter a large tip.

4. (A) The angry protesters filed past the armed guards.

   (B) I filed down the rough edges of the wood.
5. (A) I wrote a check to pay for the furniture.

   (B) Put a check in front of the items you wish to order.

Exercise L8   Practice with conversations

1. W: You sure were sick for a long time.

   M: Yes, and I'm still very weak.

   What is the man's problem?
2. M: Do you have a coin for this machine?

   W: Sorry, I don't have any change at all.

   What does the woman mean?
3. M: I proofread that essay twice.

   W: Well, I still had to correct a couple of mistakes.

   What are the people doing?
4. M: Does Carmen still work for the University Computer Center?

   W: Oh, no. Now she serves on the board of directors at the Yacht Club.

   What does the woman mean?
5. M: Ted never understands my jokes.

   W: Yes, he does. It just takes a while for them to sink in.

   What does the woman say about Ted?

Exercise L9   Understanding idiomatic expressions

1. Now that Marsha is on the swim team, she can swim to her heart's content.
2. Jim was beside himself with worry about the political science exam.
3. Gordon catches colds easily.
4. My dissertation proposal may not be approved, but I'll cross that bridge when I come to it.
5. Sue didn't lift a finger during the student body government elections.
6. The movie playing in the Student Union Theater will make your hair stand on end.
7. M: I just can't uncork this bottle.

   W: Can I have a crack at it?

   What does the woman mean?
8. W: Are you going to sign up for Music 319?

   M: Well, I can't put it off any longer.

   What are the man's plans?
9. M: Do you know Cindy Wilson?

   W: That name rings a bell.

   What does the woman mean?
10. M: They sure gave me the runaround at registration.

    W: I know what you mean. That's happened to me.

    What happened to the man?
11. M: I heard that your chemistry instructor blew up in class.

    W: Yeah. None of us had done the assignment because we really hadn't understood it.

    What does the woman mean?
12. W: I won't be able to take you to campus tomorrow.

    M: That's all right. I can catch a ride with Gus.

What is the man going to do?

13. M: How would you like to go to the rock concert with me?
    W: Where did you get money to burn?
    What does the woman mean?

14. W: What do you think of my new dress?
    M: Well, I don't know how to put this. Let's just say the blue one suits you better.
    What does the man imply?

15. W: I think I failed my calculus midterm.
    M: Oh, it looks like you could do with some cheering up. How about inviting Mike over tonight?
    W: That's a good idea. He's always good for a laugh.
    What does the woman mean?

16. M: When are you heading home for spring break?
    W: My flight is at four o'clock on Friday.
    M: My geology midterm finishes at two. I could drive you to the airport if you need a lift.
    W: Thanks, but Ann is going to see me off.
    What does the woman mean?

17. M: Did you know that the university owns some camping facilities in the forest?
    W: No, I didn't. Is that where they do their summer research?
    M: Yes, it is. They also let students use the area when research is not taking place.
    W: That explains why Janet has it in her head to go camping.
    What does the woman say about Janet?

18. M: Is your grandfather still a professor in the Engineering Department?
    W: Of course. He just can't seem to give up teaching.
    M: You sound like you don't approve.
    W: Well, he really is getting on in years.
    What does the woman imply about her grandfather?

Exercise L10   Identifying the correct idiom or phrasal verb

1. It was hard to convey the idea.
2. Only Rita was able to help Emma understand.
3. Stephen panicked at the interview.
4. My brother is always teasing me.
5. Tonight I'm going to assemble that bicycle.
6. Do you think their romance will last?
7. The old woman clung to her son.
8. Those children exhaust me.
9. W: Why are you studying so hard these days?
   M: Because the class is five units ahead of me.
10. M: Why don't you ask Tim to join the committee?
    W: That's a good idea. He always does his share of the work.
11. M: Wendy may well win the election for student body president.
    W: She does have a good chance.
12. W: I was so embarrassed when the professor showed everyone my mistake.

    M: I'll bet that you won't make that mistake again.

13. M: Janet and Mike were dancing close together at Bill's party.
    W: Did you know that they're engaged?

14. W: I saw a snake in the kitchen.
    M: You just imagined it.

15. W: My roommate was really critical of my project.
    M: Don't let her discourage you.

16. M: I'm going to rewrite my essay.
    W: Again? Don't do that. It's fine the way it is.

Exercise L11   Identifying the correct meaning of expressions

1. Sue ran into Mary in the mall.
2. Even though John is doing his best, he doesn't stand a chance of winning the medal.
3. In the long run, things will work out for the best.
4. When Rebecca failed to pass the entrance exams, she notified her mother and father right away.
5. Even though Bill was on time to take the test, he couldn't because he had forgotten his identification card.
6. W: Why are you going to the game so early?
   M: I'm working and have to set up the concession stand.
   What is the man going to do?
7. W: Professor Martin's talk on ethics was very boring.
   M: You must have missed the point. It was fantastic.
   What does the man mean?
8. M: Where did you find out about this diet?
   W: I ran across it in a pamphlet in the doctor's office.
   What does the woman mean?
9. W: Are you seriously going to vote for Mary in the student body election?
   M: Well, I think she has what it takes.
   What does the man say about Mary?
10. W: Haven't you started your research yet?
    M: No, I still haven't been given the committee's go-ahead.
    What does the man mean?
11. W: Steve sure seems nervous these days.
    M: Since Professor Avery exhibited that diseased lung, Steve has sworn off smoking.
    W: That's good news. I hope he can keep it up.
    What has Steve done?
12. M: I was supposed to turn this form in at the student loan office last week.
    W: It's probably too late now, but you still have time to apply for the work-study program.
    M: I'm going to go ahead and turn in the form. Better late than never.
    W: Personally, I think you're grasping at straws.
    What does the woman mean?
13. W: Don't you think Ruth should accept the scholarship at Stanford University instead of the teaching assistantship at Yale?

M: Well, that's a decision she has to make
for herself.

W: I think it would be difficult to teach and study
at the same time.

M: Maybe, but she'll build up some useful
professional experience.

What does the man say about Ruth?

14. M: Where did you get that crazy watch?

W: Don't you like it? I got it from an interesting
second-hand shop I stumbled across.

M: I'd like to get one. Where is this place?

W: Just a few blocks from Main Street in the
direction of campus.

What happened to the woman?

Exercise L12   Mini-test

1. W: Let's take the stairs.
   M: Let's not. There are too many flights to climb.
   What does the man mean?

2. M: We need to replace the glass in that picture
   frame before we hang these pictures in the
   dormitory lobby.
   W: We can go to the framing shop and have it
   done now.
   What are the people discussing?

3. M: The University Housing plumber is here to fix
   the sink. Which one is blocked?
   W: The one in the spare bathroom.
   What are the people discussing?

4. W: I studied all night long.
   M: Why don't you go home and get some shut-eye?
   What does the man mean?

5. W: I really dread going to that dinner party
   to celebrate Sam's getting his Ph.D.
   M: Do you think we could back out of it gracefully?
   What does the man want to do?

6. W: You sure are making light of that bad exam
   grade in sociology.
   M: Well, I can't let it ruin my life.
   What can be inferred about the man?

7. M: Please don't let anyone know about the social
   science experiment.
   W: I understand why you want to hush it up.
   What does the woman mean?

8. W: Why do they insist on the test?
   M: To screen out those who shouldn't be
   in the experiment.
   What does the man mean?

9. W: Neil sure rushed off quickly.
   M: Hmm. He usually sticks around after our
   physical education class.
   What does the man say about Neil?

10. W: Professor Jenson passed out in class.
    M: Did they discover the reason for it?
    What can be inferred about Professor Jenson?

11. W: What are you doing with my backpack?
    M: I'm trying to see if there's space in it for
    this glass.
    What does the man want to do?

12. M: I need to have my jacket taken in.
    W: The tailor around the corner from the University
    Bookstore is very good.
    What needs to be done to the jacket?

13. W: What are you waiting for?
    M: Aren't you and Cindy ready to go to the
    University Bookstore with me?
    W: Oh, I thought you didn't want us to tag along.
    What does the woman mean?

14. M: Look at all the books I have to read for
    Professor Higgins's Elizabethan literature course.
    W: It isn't as much as I had to read when I took it.
    He has really watered down his course.
    M: Why did he do that?
    W: Because of some changes in university
    requirements.
    What has the instructor done?

15. M: They've just reopened the University Pool.
    W: Have you been to see it yet?
    M: No, I'm going to try it out now. Would you care
    to join me?
    W: Sure. Let me grab my cap.
    What are the people going to do?

Exercise L13   Practice with time, quantity,
and comparisons

1. Can you let me know no later than tomorrow who
   will be helping new students?

2. Tom didn't start studying until midnight.

3. Alice needs only a couple more credits to graduate.

4. Professor Merrill has written up to thirty articles
   on art history.

5. The fog is heavier than usual tonight.

6. M: I had to buy a lot more books this semester.
   W: You should have gone to the used-book store.

7. W: How much time did you spend preparing
   that speech?
   M: A couple of hours at least.

8. M: I don't understand either example.
   W: Neither do I.

9. M: What size box do you need for all those books?
   W: The bigger the better.

10. W: I couldn't get a student loan this semester.
    M: Quite a few students haven't been able
    to get loans.

11. M: It's going to take a lot of organization to get
    this project off the ground.
    W: Right. I think I need to buy at least a dozen
    file folders.
    What does the woman mean?

12. W: I think Kathy has spent too much time in the
    computer lab.

M: She has to finish that program before final exams start.
What does the man say about Kathy?

13. W: The more time I spend trying to sort out this math problem, the more confused I get.
M: Take five. Come back with a clearer head.
What does the man mean?

14. M: Tony hasn't been doing very well in his classes.
W: That's because he spends too much time working in that pizza place. Did you know it's open twenty-four hours a day?
M: Yeah. He didn't get back to the dorm until after 3:00 A.M. last night.
W: I heard that he put in a couple of hours' overtime.
What does the woman mean?

15. M: Why don't you ask Sue to help you type your essay?
W: Sue's spending the weekend with her parents.
M: I thought I saw her in the bookstore this morning.
W: It couldn't have been. Her roommate told me she wasn't due back until Monday.
What does the woman mean?

Exercise L14   Understanding causatives

1. W: Kathy got John to give her a ride.
Who needed a ride?

2. M: Vicky let Ann take the blame.
Who took the blame?

3. M: Mary made Dan leave the room.
Who left the room?

4. W: Nancy caused Jeff to have an accident.
Whose fault was the accident?

5. W: Did Joe cut those dead branches from the tree himself?
M: He got Fred to cut them because he doesn't like to climb ladders.
Who cut the dead branches?

6. M: Mike consulted Steve about his exam schedule.
W: I would have consulted Tom myself.
Who consulted Steve?

7. M: Ms. Jones admitted Mary into the testing center without an I.D.
W: I bet Dr. Welsh would have, too.
Who admitted the student?

8. W: Rebecca asked both Amy and Barbara to take her home.
M: Actually, Amy was the one who took her.
Who needed a ride home?

9. W: Did you get an application form for a student loan?
M: In fact, I had Jane pick one up for me this morning.
What does the man mean?

10. M: Tom finally got a plumber to fix that leaking pipe.
W: He called a plumber to do something I could do?
What does the woman imply?

11. W: That was a fantastic speech Rick gave.
M: Yes, but he got Marie to write it for him.
What does the man mean?

12. W: Do you know who is driving the archeology students out to the site?
M: Professor Johnson is taking most of them in the university van and Ellen is taking the rest.
W: Ellen? Her car is too small, and I know her mother wouldn't permit her to take the family car.
M: Well, you also know that Ellen has her father wrapped around her little finger.
What does the man imply?

13. W: I can tell that this rent dispute is really getting you down.
M: It is. I just may have go to the small-claims court to take care of it.
W: Personally, I would have Mrs. Jones, the student legal-aid adviser, handle it.
What does the woman mean?

14. M: Your paper looks very good, Mary. It just needs those few revisions we discussed.
W: Thank you, Dr. Thompson. I'll have the final draft back to you by next Friday.
M: Oh, I'll be in Chicago at the World Ecology Conference, so could you leave it with the department secretary? He'll see that I get it.
What does the man mean?

Exercise L15   Understanding negative meaning

1. I don't always catch the number 9 bus.

2. Motivation, not experience, often determines success.

3. Seldom have my suggestions been taken seriously.

4. There is barely enough bread for lunch.

5. W: I heard you had a little problem with the calculus exercises.
M: Are you joking? Never have I had so much trouble in my life.

6. W: I didn't see a single course I wanted to attend.
M: What are you going to do?

7. M: I've never seen Mark so tense about an exam.
W: I can understand why. It's an important one.

8. W: There was hardly enough equipment to go around.
M: You're lucky some students were absent.

9. M: You'll never guess what I did. I signed up to be a model for the art department.
W: Oh, no. You've got to be kidding.
What does the woman mean?

10. M: I think the fencing club will have the funds to sponsor the tournament.
W: Don't be so sure. Not everyone has paid their membership dues.
What does the woman imply?

11. W: Seldom has Robert gone to so much trouble to pass a course.
M: Well, he is on probation, you know.
What does the man mean?

12. W: Jim sure is a talented athlete, isn't he?
    M: You can say that again. He could have easily qualified for a position on the football team.
    W: I'll never understand why he isn't more interested in athletics.
    What does the woman imply?

13. M: I heard that Dan went to the department head about the animals in the science lab.
    W: Not only did Dan complain, but so did Maria.
    M: I think they're exaggerating the problem somewhat.
    What does the man mean?

14. W: I'd like to get a break from studying.
    M: Let's take the afternoon off and go to town. You can get some shopping done.
    W: I'd rather go to the mall or the farmer's market than go shopping downtown.
    M: Well, I definitely don't want to go to the mall.
    What will the man and woman probably do?

Exercise L16   Understanding modals

1. We'd better meet once a week to discuss our project.
2. Ben couldn't have heard the lecture.
3. I'd prefer that you not call me tomorrow.
4. Jill must have returned to the dorm.
5. M: Will you be attending the graduation ceremonies this year?
   W: Only if I graduate.
6. M: Did Jim call a plumber to fix the leaking faucet?
   W: That would have been a waste of money. It only needed a new washer.
7. M: You might get Professor Roth for biology.
   W: By the time I take that course, he will have retired.
8. W: We will have been married ten years on our next anniversary.
   M: How are you going to celebrate?
9. M: I think I've ironed out all the problems in my essay.
   W: You ought to go over it one more time just to be sure.
   What does the woman mean?
10. M: We really should get this engine overhauled before it breaks down again.
    W: Maybe we ought to trade the car in.
    What problem do the speakers have?
11. W: This literature assignment is the most frightening horror story I've ever read.
    M: Really? Judging by the book's cover, I would have thought it was another ridiculous romance.
    What does the man imply?
12. W: What are Lisa's plans for the summer vacation?
    M: Nothing special. She's going to stay home and help out at her parents' travel agency.
    W: All summer? With parents in the travel business, she could spend a few weeks anywhere in the world.
    What does the woman say about Lisa?

13. W: Are you still working on the history project?
    M: Yes, and the deadline for it is next Monday.
    W: You'll never finish on time unless you get Jerry's help.
    What does the woman mean?

14. W: I wish we had taken the bus instead of walking.
    M: You look really tired. Would you like to stop for a rest?
    W: No, let's keep going. We aren't that far from the campus now.
    What does the woman want to do?

Exercise L17   Identifying conditions

1. If Sarah had gotten the raise, she would have bought a car.
2. Mary wouldn't have gone to Spain if her mother hadn't been there.
3. I wouldn't be so nervous if I hadn't drunk so much coffee.
4. If Ted doesn't bring the sandwiches, Cindy will make some.
5. W: If you had come to the seminar, you would have met Helen Martin.
   M: She's the famous poet, isn't she?
6. M: If Sue gets another low grade, she'll be put on probation.
   W: She'd better start studying.
7. M: Marion would have attended the protest march if her father hadn't come for a visit.
   W: She should have brought him.
8. M: No matter how hard I try to solve this problem, I just can't seem to get it.
   W: If you took a walk to clear your mind, it might help.
9. W: What will we do if our science experiment doesn't work?
   M: We'll think about that if it happens.
   What does the man imply?
10. W: I wouldn't have studied so hard if I'd known the test only covered Unit 10.
    M: Now you don't have to study so hard for the final.
    What does the man mean?
11. W: I found these car keys in the student parking lot.
    M: If I were you, I'd turn them in to the campus security office. The owner can't drive home without them and will probably check there first.
    What does the man suggest the woman do?
12. W: Marvin writes such interesting stories in our creative writing course.
    M: Had Marvin had the money, he could have gone with Larry to the writers' workshop.
    W: The fees weren't that much, were they?
    M: No, in fact they were quite reasonable. Marvin is just very short of money until his loan comes through.

W: Larry could have offered to cover the charges for him. Marvin would have paid him back.
What does the woman imply about Larry?

13. M: I really am under a lot of pressure to turn this research paper in.
W: If you like, I could type it for you.
M: That would be great. If I could get it to you by Tuesday, could you have it typed by Wednesday?
W: That depends on how legibly you write.
What does the woman mean?

14. W: What are you doing?
M: I've decided to take sandwiches for lunch instead of eating at the university cafeteria.
W: That's a good way to save some money.
M: Would you get the jam out for me?
W: Sorry, but if this cupboard weren't so full, I could find it.
What does the woman mean?

Exercise L18   Identifying causes and results

1. It was such a difficult exam that Paul didn't finish it.
2. Since you're a math major, maybe you could help me with this equation.
3. Due to the heat, we stayed at home and watched TV.
4. The instructor didn't come, so we left the classroom.
5. M: As long as the movie at the student union is free, why don't we go there?
W: That's a good idea.
6. M: Since Monday is a national holiday, all the university offices will be closed.
W: Oh, I'd better go to the financial aid office now and pick up those application forms.
7. M: I went to the library because I needed to get some work done.
W: Did you finish everything?
8. M: My parents are going to call tonight, so I'm staying home.
W: Give them my regards.
9. W: There's some hot coffee, but I'd have to put on water for tea.
M: As long as the coffee is ready, I'll have that.
What does the man mean?
10. M: Why is the print exhibition being shown in the student union?
W: Oh, the art museum is closed for the summer for remodeling.
What does the woman mean?
11. M: Do you know what the matter is with Jeff? He's developed a bad stutter.
W: Don't worry. He got a part in the play, and he's really been getting into the role.
What does the woman say about Jeff?
12. M: I'm really glad you were able to come and see my new apartment. How do you like my lasagna?
W: Mmmm. I didn't realize you were such a good cook.

M: Now that I no longer live in the dormitory, I've had to learn how to fend for myself.
What does the man mean?

13. M: Linda said she was applying for work in the bookstore.
W: What happened to her job at the library?
M: That was a work-study position, and she's completed all her working hours.
W: So now she has to find a new job.
What happened to Linda?

14. W: Hasn't Alex finished his degree yet?
M: He has to complete at least another year of courses before he graduates.
W: Why is he taking so long? He can't have failed any classes.
M: Oh, he keeps changing his major and may even do so again.
W: I can't believe he hasn't chosen a major yet.
What can be said about Alex?

Exercise L19   Mini-test

1. W: Now that you have a new car, are you going to give me a ride to campus?
M: Well, that depends on when you have to be there.
What does the man mean?
2. M: Peter must be very happy to have passed the French exam.
W: Yes, but he almost didn't pass.
What does the woman say about Peter?
3. W: I can't make it to the University Health Center, so can you give Tom this get-well card?
M: Sure. Is there anything you want me to tell him?
What is the woman's problem?
4. M: Mary mentioned that you've stopped giving the aerobics class.
W: Yes, but only until next month.
What does the woman mean?
5. W: Have you been going over the computer results?
M: Have I! And you won't believe the statistics.
What does the man mean?
6. M: My last final is on Wednesday.
W: I will have finished my finals by Monday.
What does the woman mean?
7. W: Why was Julia called back to the student loan office?
M: She forgot to sign her application form.
What does the man say about Julia?
8. W: Didn't Dr. Roberts ask you to give Sue a copy of the newsletter?
M: Yes, but then he had Andy give it to her.
What does the man mean?
9. W: Do you know how many people have been invited to Bob's graduation reception?
M: Bob told Jim that he could put as many as twenty-five names on the guest list.
What does the man mean?

10. W: David is not only a good friend but an excellent student.
    M: I know. He never misses a day of classes, even though he has a serious disability.
    What does the man say about David?

11. W: Why did the professor make that student leave the testing center?
    M: Because he didn't bring his identification card with him.
    What does the man mean?

12. M: Does Rick ever do any studying?
    W: Well, I know he put in two hours at the library last night.
    What does the woman say about Rick?

13. W: Could you please stop making so much noise?
    M: Why don't you go to the library?
    W: I might have to. I can't get any studying done with all your talking.
    What does the woman want to do?

14. M: I'm sure glad you and Nancy could come.
    W: After the stress of final exams, it is nice to relax with friends.
    M: Yeah, but what's the matter with Nancy? Did she stay up all night studying for finals? She looks beat.
    W: Oh, she's just not used to dancing so much.
    What does the woman say about Nancy?

15. W: What did you think of that geology test?
    M: I read all the questions through and couldn't answer one of them with complete certainty.
    W: Neither could I. I thought I understood all the concepts, but then I could hardly struggle through the test.
    M: That's for sure. It must have been the most difficult test I've ever taken.
    What does the man mean?

Exercise L20   Identifying the purpose

1. Do you know anyone who can speak Spanish?
2. Don't you think Margo would be the best student senator?
3. I'd like to apply for the job you advertised in the student bulletin.
4. The administration office opens at eight o'clock, doesn't it?
5. You should see a doctor about that cough.
6. I'm afraid I can't meet you at the union after all.
7. We're supposed to have this project in by Monday.
8. I'm really sorry I didn't sign up for that class with Professor Oates.

Exercise L21   Understanding responses

1. M: I thought Bill's operation was scheduled for this morning.
   W: No, it was the day before yesterday, and it went so well that he's already been released from the hospital.

2. M: Professor Davis assigned another three books in class today.
   W: I sure am sick of his busywork.

3. W: How about going to the movies tonight?
   M: I'm sorry, I've got a headache.

4. W: That was a very interesting lecture Dr. Elliot gave, wasn't it?
   M: Oh, I don't know.

5. W: Shall we have dessert?
   M: I'm on a diet.

6. M: May I use the car to run down to campus?
   W: The keys are on the table.

7. M: The paintings in the exhibition look like the work of a child.
   W: Personally, I like them.

8. M: These cookies look fresh from the oven.
   W: Help yourself.

Exercise L22   Identifying what people are doing

1. M: How about a cup of coffee?
   W: What a good idea!

2. W: The chemistry exam was much more difficult than it should have been.
   M: Cheer up. You probably did all right.

3. M: I missed your class last week, Professor Blair, because my uncle died.
   W: I'm sorry to hear that.

4. M: Can you fit me in during the morning?
   W: Well, there's a cancellation at 11:45. Is that too late?

5. W: Would you give me a hand with these boxes?
   M: Which hand would you like?

6. M: I could teach geology better than Professor Stone. Don't you think so?
   W: You sure could.

7. M: I don't understand all this mix-up.
   W: Well, don't worry yourself about it.

8. M: My watch needs to be fixed.
   W: Why don't you take it to the jewelry store?

Exercise L23   Drawing conclusions

1. M: Let's go get a nice cold drink.
   W: And miss the final inning?

2. M: Where's the glass of milk I set on the table?
   W: Oh, didn't you hear that crash a little while ago?

3. M: I heard you were having a little trouble with the math assignment.
   W: No kidding! Could I come over for some help tonight?

4. W: I heard that Chris did poorly on his exams.
   M: Chris do poorly? You've got to be kidding. He's a genius.

5. W: Since Dave is bringing his friend, why don't you invite Tim?
   M: Tim and Dave don't get along.

6. M: The class will have started by the time we get there.
   W: Don't be silly. We aren't that late.

7. W: Until Linda started working at the shoe store, she didn't have any sales experience.
   M: That's encouraging. Maybe they'll hire me.
8. W: What have you written recently?
   M: Nothing that you'd want to read.

Exercise L24   Making inferences based on context

1. M: I wish you'd dump your ashtray when you've finished smoking.
   W: My ashtray? When have you ever seen me smoking?
   What does the woman imply?
2. M: That hedge outside the classroom building is very attractive.
   W: It's also useful. It serves as a windbreak, and it cuts down on the traffic noise.
   What does the woman imply?
3. W: Should we watch the movie or the football game?
   M: Need you ask?
   What does the man imply?
4. W: Can you move that monstrosity from my desk?
   M: You shouldn't call it that. I got a good grade for that sculpture.
   What does the man imply?
5. W: How about cake and ice cream at Sandy's Soda?
   M: And break my diet?
   What does the man imply?
6. W: Weren't you on the committee that organized the student debate?
   M: Only for a short time.
   What does the man imply?
7. W: I'm looking for a biography of T. E. Lawrence to check out.
   M: Our library is fully computerized. Just follow the instructions on the screen.
   What does the man imply the woman should do?
8. M: Does Anita still live across the hall from you?
   W: I haven't seen her in the dorm at all this semester.
   What does the woman imply?

Exercise L25   Mini-test

1. M: How about going out to eat this evening?
   W: I'm afraid I have to write this biology report.
   What does the woman mean?
2. W: The concert starts at 8:15 and ends at about 10:30.
   M: That means we'll be home around midnight.
   What does the man imply?
3. W: How can you be so worried about a little exam?
   M: Little? This exam could determine whether or not I get a scholarship.
   What does the man mean?
4. W: Dr. Mason's parents are from Texas, she was raised in Boston, and she did her doctoral studies in Chicago.
   M: That explains her interesting accent.
   What does the man imply?

5. M: I've misplaced my watch. Could you lend me yours for the afternoon?
   W: My watch? You've never seen me wearing a watch, have you?
   What does the woman imply?
6. M: Weren't you able to get a drink?
   W: The correct-change-only light was on.
   What does the woman imply?
7. W: You look bleary-eyed this morning.
   M: Yeah. I had a bad night. Something I had at Bill's party didn't agree with me.
   What does the man mean?
8. W: I don't like this movie very much.
   M: That makes two of us.
   What does the man mean?
9. M: What has your group decided to do for the sociology project?
   W: No one's come up with anything good yet.
   What does the woman mean?
10. W: You are joining us at the museum, aren't you?
    M: I have to meet my mother at the airport.
    What will the man probably do?
11. M: Dr. Spencer's speech on the economic structure of nineteenth-century New England was fascinating.
    W: I'm sure I would have slept through it.
    What does the woman imply?
12. M: Can you give me a ride to the University Theater tonight?
    W: I can't, but you might ask Sue. She's helping with makeup, so she might have to be there early.
    What does the woman mean?
13. W: It's almost time for the library to close. Are you ready to go?
    M: I have to check this book out, and then I'll be ready.
    W: I'll wait for you in the magazine section.
    What will the woman probably do?
14. M: Have you seen Sally around?
    W: I just got back from class and haven't seen anyone.
    M: We're supposed to meet Jack at noon in the Student Union to work on the intercultural communication project.
    W: Well, her keys are there on the kitchen counter.
    What does the woman imply about Sally?
15. M: How are you going to spend your summer break?
    W: I really need to get work to pay for next semester's tuition.
    M: Why don't you see if you could get a summer job at the factory?
    W: I heard they're laying off workers there.
    What does the woman mean?

Part B Longer conversations and talks

Exercise L26   Predicting the topic from the first statement

1. W: The United Kingdom is made up of four countries: England, Northern Ireland, Scotland, and Wales.

2. M: Architects from around the world vote for the one architect they believe should receive the Award for Architecture.

3. M: Let me show you samples of Irish linen to help you get a better idea of the various patterns.

4. W: There are a number of human- and animal-shaped figures carved in hillsides around the world.

5. M: Goethe was not the only German of his time to be attracted to Italy.

6. W: I attended Professor Brown's talk on Balzac last night.

Exercise L27   Identifying the topic from the first statement

1. W: The practice of acupuncture began in China about five thousand years ago.

2. M: Muscles are made of many fine fibers about twenty-five millimeters long.

3. M: A whole new world of possibilities and challenges in education has been opened up by satellite-communications technology.

4. W: We will be concentrating specifically on the Golden Age of Spanish literature in this seminar and the historical setting in which the literature flourished.

5. W: Although some of the signs and symptoms of the common cold are similar to those of influenza, influenza is a highly contagious, potentially life-threatening disease.

6. M: Lack of animal protein in the human diet is a serious cause of malnutrition in many parts of the world.

Exercise L28   Determining if the topic is stated in the first sentence of the passage

1. M: A magic square is a square-shaped arrangement of numbers. The numbers are arranged so that the horizontal, vertical, and diagonal groups of numbers all add up to the same figure. The largest magic square ever devised had 578,865 boxes.

2. W: The wealthy have kept their own private collections of animals for thousands of years. The first public zoo, however, was not opened until 1793, at the Jardin des Plantes in Paris. Zoos have not only protected endangered species but have also allowed people to see exotic animals without having to travel to distant countries.

3. W: In the mid-1800s, the Overland Mail stagecoach carried the mail across the American continent. Because this service was unsatisfactory, a freight company established a new service called the Pony Express. The Pony Express used relays of pony riders. These daring young riders made weekly treks across the rough and dangerous terrain between St. Joseph, Missouri, and Sacramento, California. Although very successful, the Pony Express was short-lived. After only sixteen months of service, it was replaced by the telegraph.

4. M: Penang, Malaysia, is the home of the world's largest butterfly farm. The farm is both a sanctuary and a breeding center for the two thousand recorded species of Malaysian butterflies, which are being driven away from populated areas by pollution and industrialization. Studies into tropical butterflies' habitat, diseases that attack caterpillars, and pest control are being conducted there, as is research into how the ecological balance would be affected if foreign butterflies were to be imported and bred on the farm.

5. W: Did you enjoy the architecture excursion to St. Martin's Cathedral?

   M: Yes, very much, Mrs. Macdonald. We appreciate your arranging that for us.

   W: Was there anything special that impressed you?

   M: I especially liked the gargoyles. Why did stoneworkers put those grotesque heads on cathedrals, anyway? To frighten away bad spirits?

   W: No, they're designed to catch the water that runs off the roof when it rains or the snow melts.

   M: I see. The water collects in the gargoyle's mouth and is spat out onto the street.

   W: That's right. That protects the walls from moisture dripping down and causing erosion. They were also a kind of joke.

   M: What do you mean?

   W: Those ugly faces represent the stoneworkers' friends.

   M: Really? I wonder if they stayed friends afterward.

Exercise L29   Identifying a change in topic

1. Folk dances have been passed on from one dancer to another over the years without the movements being written down. Since this system is not always very accurate, choreographers have invented ways of writing down the movements. At first, they drew little pictures under the music. Later, a new system that uses dots and lines to represent hands, feet, and heads was invented.

2. W: As nutritionists, we need to try to educate the general public about carbohydrates. For example, a lot of people think that eliminating

all starches from their daily meals will help them lose weight. However, carbohydrates provide important nutrients, so they should never be cut out. In fact, they actually help in the process of losing weight.

M: I understand the importance of carbohydrates, but how to they help in dieting, Dr. Parsons?

W: They take longer to digest, so you're not hungry for a longer period of time. Consequently, you eat less.

M: What should we suggest to our future patients or clients when they ask us for help in losing weight?

W: First, they should cut down on their intake of fats. Animal products contain large amounts of fat.

M: Are you suggesting that we try to convince people to become vegetarians?

W: Oh, no, not at all. Animal products provide much-needed protein. You should suggest that they just trim the fat off meat, broil it instead of frying it, and drink low-fat milk. In other words, we need to help people change their cooking habits as well as their eating habits.

3. M: It was during his search for a new route to India that Columbus reached America. Although he made his discovery in 1492, it took a little over a hundred years for people to finally settle in the New World. Some settlers hoped to escape from the problems of the Old World by emigrating to the New World. Reports that excellent crops could be produced in Virginia induced many more people to make the long journey. America was not the sought-after India, but it offered its settlers a new and, potentially, rich life.

4. W: Even though snatches of Spanish, French, Russian, Chinese, and a dozen other languages besides English can be heard on the streets of major cities in America, the vast majority of people living in the United States communicate in English. Therefore, the United States is considered an English-speaking country. The fact is, however, that no single language is recognized as an official language in the United States Constitution. Most state constitutions don't recognize an official language, although Nebraska made English its official language early in the twentieth century, and the constitution of Louisiana recognizes both English and French as official languages.

Exercise L30 Mini-test

1. Listen to part of a discussion between two friends.

W: How is your job at the university library working out?

M: Very well. I've been working in the acquisitions department.

W: What do you do there?

M: Log in new books. The best part of the job is opening the boxes of newly purchased books. It's like getting presents.

W: That does sound like fun.

M: Later I have to enter each book into the computer. I don't mind that so much, but I don't like having to paste the checkout sheet into the front cover.

What are the people discussing?

2. Listen to part of a lecture from a history class.

W: William Cody, more widely known as Buffalo Bill, was an American showman who founded the great "Wild West Show" in 1883. He traveled around Europe with other famous people, such as the sharpshooter Annie Oakley and Chief Sitting Bull to perform for many heads of state, like the czar of Russia and the king of England.

What is the talk mainly about?

3. Listen to part of a lecture from a music class.

M: Just before the turn of the twentieth century, a new musical form captivated America – ragtime. Although ragtime had its start in 1897 with William Krell's "Mississippi Rag," it was Scott Joplin who popularized the form with his "Maple Leaf Rag." John Philip Sousa began to feature rags in his band concerts in America and Europe. By the early 1900s, ragtime was the most popular musical art form in America.

What does the speaker mainly discuss?

4. Listen to part of a talk.

W: The proposed fine-arts building would serve the university's drama and music majors as well as its art majors. The building would contain several stages — a main stage for visiting groups and major productions and two smaller stages for experimental theater classes. For the music majors, a large concert hall and many practice rooms are planned. Finally, for the art majors, the building would provide an exhibition hall, with spaces for a permanent collection and space for students' temporary shows, as well as many workrooms and classrooms.

What is the main purpose of this talk?

Exercise L31 Understanding referents in a conversation or talk

1. M: Because of the breakdown of the traditional family in some countries, many elderly people have no home and no one to help them in an emergency. In order to address these problems, delegates to the United Nations Symposium on Population met to pool their ideas and make recommendations.

2. W: To climb Mount Everest is the dream of every mountaineer. In order for an alpine club to make this climb, it must apply to the Nepalese Tourism Ministry for a permit. Normally, these are granted to only a few groups each season.

3. M: The first machine to replace the abacus for calculating was invented by a French mathematician in 1642. In 1671, a German mathematician improved this calculator. Then, in the 1830s, an English mathematician devised another mechanical one that had most of the features of modern computers. This machine became outdated in 1946 when an American team developed the electronic computer.

4. M: I would like all of you to try to get to the Turkish Cultural Arts Exhibition at the Metropolitan Museum of Art.

   W: Do you know how long it will be on?

   M: Yes. From October 29 through November 18. The museum opening times are ten to five Tuesday through Saturday and twelve to five Sundays. The museum is closed on Mondays. There will be a number of events to complement the exhibition. These will include three lectures. I realize that you have busy schedules, but do try to attend at least one.

   W: Do you have the topics and dates of the lectures?

   M: No, I don't, but I'll let you know next week. Also, there will be an evening of traditional Turkish music.

   W: I would be very interested in that. Could you get more information on the music as well?

Exercise L32   Understanding restatements

1. The dialect spoken in Kárpathos is so old that many words date back to the time of Homer.

2. A Frenchman's twenty-five-minute flight in a hot-air balloon in 1783 was the first manned flight.

3. One of the most beautiful birds in the world, the quetzal, takes its name from the Aztec word meaning "tail feather."

4. Twenty-two men from Mao Tse-tung's Red Army had to storm the Luding Bridge after an all-night march to capture a needed escape route for Mao's forces.

5. Many relief centers were set up in the drought-stricken areas.

6. Recently discovered fossils have revolutionized our concept of the human past.

7. Recent explorers have been unable to locate the island that was vividly described in the captain's log in March 1783.

8. The executive secretary of the Protection of the Marine Environment Organization has reported that a large number of dead fish, dolphins, and whales have been spotted off the East Coast.

Exercise L33   Getting all the facts

1. M: I have arranged for our art appreciation class to meet at the art museum next week because it is having a special exhibition on fish rubbings.

   W: Fish rubbings? What are they? Do we have to touch a horrible, slimy fish?

   M: No. It's an ancient art form in which fish are used to make prints.

   W: Where was this practiced?

   M: I'm not sure. I think both in the Far East and by some native people in America.

   W: Will we have to make some of our own fish rubbings afterwards?

   M: That is up to you. I think that you will find fish rubbings very interesting and might like to try it yourself.

   What can be said about fish rubbings?

2. The world's heaviest gold coin is worth millions of dollars. Minted in the year 1613 in India, the name of its issuer, Mughal Emperor Jehangir, is stamped on the coin. Prior to the reign of this Muslim emperor, rulers in India obtained permission to mint coins from the caliph in Baghdad. However, Emperor Jehangir changed this tradition and started his own policy of issuing coins in his own name. It was during the time of the Mughal dynasty that many art forms were encouraged to flourish. Therefore, it is not surprising that the art of minting coins began and reached its peak of perfection during Emperor Jehangir's reign.

   What is true about Mughal Emperor Jehangir?

3. When microscopes are referred to, most people think of optical microscopes. These instruments were developed principally to meet the needs of the biological sciences. However, they are not useful for the metallurgist. Scientists who need to examine metal objects or metal structures use a metallurgical microscope. The observing and illuminating systems of a metallurgical microscope are mounted in a way that allows adjustment for accommodating large or awkwardly shaped specimens. Metallurgical microscopes are equipped with devices that provide the capacity to measure an object in the X, Y, and Z axes. Since metallurgical microscopes are frequently used in the field instead of in the laboratory, they must also be more durable.

   How is a metallurgical microscope different from an optical microscope?

4. W: Since people communicate mostly through speech, you can imagine that a defect in speaking or hearing abilities can be an enormous handicap. There are three conditions in which communication disorders can result. Do you have any ideas what these may be?

   M: Well, the obvious condition would be a physical one. For example, if someone's eardrum has been damaged because of an illness or injury, that person might not be able to hear. Being deaf or partially deaf not only affects the person's ability to hear, but also their speech sometimes is not clear, making it difficult for others to understand them.

W: That's right. If something goes wrong with the speech or hearing mechanisms, communication disorders can result. Yes, Sue.

W2: Some people are born with some sort of defect. I have a mentally handicapped cousin who can't speak very well.

W: We would classify that under the condition of abnormal functioning of the brain. People may be born with this condition or it can occur as a result of a stroke or a tumor.

M: Some people are emotionally upset. I read about a boy who just stopped speaking after he saw a terrible accident.

W: Good point. An unusual emotional or psychological problem can cause communication disorders. So communication disorders can result from something going wrong with the speech or hearing mechanisms, abnormal functioning of the brain, or an unusual emotional or psychological problem. Fortunately, most communication disorders can be improved with the help of a speech pathologist.

What is true about communication disorders?

Exercise L34 Organizing details

1. Victoria C. Woodhull is remembered for being the first woman candidate to run for the U.S. presidency, which she did in 1872 against Ulysses S. Grant. In fact, Woodhull had long been involved in many radical movements including spiritualism, utopian socialism, and women's rights. In 1868 she cofounded the first woman-owned brokerage firm and then two years later established an outspoken political journal which promoted a variety of extreme views. Although she lost the presidential election, she continued her political work for several decades but with less radical views and a quieter public profile.

The speaker gives a brief account of Victoria C. Woodhull's life. Summarize the events by putting them in order.

2. Fox hunting, the "blood sport" enjoyed by Great Britain's landed gentry for centuries, has come under much criticism. The activities of animal-rights campaigners such as the Hunt Saboteurs Association have brought media attention to an area that previously excited little interest. The methods some of the animal-rights campaigners have used to sabotage

the hunts have resulted in legal proceedings. Although the debate is still continuing, the sight of scores of horses, hounds, and red-coated riders setting off across the English countryside in search of a fox may be a thing of the past within a few years.

Put these statements about fox hunting in the correct order.

3. W: The coral reef is only fifty feet below us. I want you to first check all your diving equipment. Do you have a full oxygen tank? Is all your equipment functioning properly? Good. Now I want everyone to find a diving partner. Once you are in the water remember to stay together. You should always have someone with you who can signal for help in case of an emergency.

M: My diving partner is absent today. Is there anyone else who doesn't have someone?

W: There doesn't seem to be anyone without a partner so you can join Linda and Jeff. Now, stay together as we descend to the coral reef and follow me as I go along the reef. Try to identify the kinds of corals we looked at in class. I will give a signal when it is time to return to the boat. Remember that we must make our ascent slowly.

In which order should the diving teacher's instructions be carried out?

4. W: Professor Jackson, I was reading an article the other day that mentions a phenomenon called the "hundredth-monkey" phenomenon. It didn't explain the study, but I was curious to know more about it. Are you familiar with it?

M: Yes, I am. Supposedly, this study involved a group of monkeys inhabiting an island off the coast of Japan. The monkeys were shown how to eat sweet potatoes in a particular way, which was not typical of monkeys. Other monkeys living on the island began to copy this behavior, and soon a hundred monkeys were eating sweet potatoes in the new way. At this point, it is claimed that monkeys from another island about two hundred miles away began performing the new sweet-potato eating behavior. These monkeys had never had contact with the monkeys on the first island.

W: That is really intriguing. Why do you sound so skeptical?

M: Well, I haven't seen the study mentioned in a serious journal. I have only read about it in a popular science magazine that may not have investigated the origin of the research.

What is the order of events in the hundredth-monkey phenomenon study?

Exercise L35   Focusing on details
Questions 1–3
The answer to the question of which flying bird is the largest in the world depends on whether birds are measured by weight, wingspan, or wing area. The South African bustard is the heaviest. The average male weighs about 18 kilos. The bird with the longest wingspan is the albatross. The longest measured was 3.4 meters, but there are sure to be others with a span of 3.6 meters. The bird with the largest wings is the South American vulture, commonly called the condor.

Based on the professor's description of birds, answer the question about which flying bird is the largest.

Questions 4–7
A gear is a wheel, cylinder, or other machine element that has teeth around its edge. These teeth usually interlock with the teeth of another gear in order to transfer motion within a machine. As one gear turns, it moves the second gear in the opposite direction. The four most common gears are spur gears, worm gears, bevel gears, and the rack and pinion. A spur gear is a toothed wheel whose teeth are arranged around the outer diameter in the same plane as the wheel face. A worm gear consists of a continuous screw thread wrapped around a cylinder called a worm and a separate wheel whose teeth mesh with the worm. Bevel gears are comprised of two conical-shaped, toothed wheels, which intersect at 90 degrees. A rack and pinion is an arrangement of gears in which a wheel meshes with a straight-toothed element known as a rack.

Based on the professor's description of several gears, identify the following.

Questions 8–10
Since the seventh century, large bells have been cast for use in both religious and secular institutions. The largest bell in the world is in Moscow. This famous king of bells, the Emperor Bell, was cast in 1734 and weighs about 200 tons. The next largest bell, weighing 171 tons, is also located in Russia, near St. Petersburg. Great Paul, the bell at St. Paul's Cathedral in London, was cast in 1881, more than 150 years after the building was completed. Although Great Paul weighs a mere 17 tons, it is the largest bell in England. Perhaps the baby of famous bells, weighing only 2 tons, is the Liberty Bell in Philadelphia. Cast in 1751, the Liberty Bell was commissioned to commemorate the fiftieth anniversary of William Penn's charter, Pennsylvania's original constitution. The Liberty Bell was rung from the tower of Independence Hall on July 8, 1776, to summon Americans to hear the first public reading of the Declaration of Independence.

Based on the professor's discussion, identify the city where the following bells can be found.

Questions 11–13
Puppetry is an art form used for entertainment and education. It consists of a show in which puppets, figures made to represent humans and other creatures, authentic or mythical, are used to tell a story. Traditional puppets come in many forms. The most common type of puppet and the easiest to make and use is the hand puppet. This puppet is like a glove and is worn over the hand of the puppeteer. The puppeteer works the head and arms of the puppet by moving his or her fingers. Another common type of puppet is known as the marionette. The marionette looks much like a doll and has an elaborately jointed body that is controlled by strings. The puppeteer usually stands on a bridge over the stage and manipulates the marionette by pulling the strings. A third kind of puppet is the shadow puppet. These puppets are controlled by rods attached to their hands that the puppeteer manipulates from below the stage. The legs of the figure hang loosely allowing freedom of movement. The performance takes place behind a screen with the lighting such that the puppet casts a shadow.

Based on the professor's description, identify the following puppets.

Exercise L36   Using details
1. A stairway is comprised of various components fitting together to allow access from one floor of a building to another. The horizontal boards, which are the pieces actually stepped on, are called the treads. These should be sufficiently deep to enable users to place their feet comfortably without slipping. The vertical boards that meet each tread at right angles and that raise the stairway are called the risers. These can vary in height depending on architectural requirements. On many stairways the tread usually juts out a small amount over the riser and this feature is known as a nosing. Each end of the treads and risers is supported on an inclined structure called a stringer that runs flush with the sides of the staircase and, thus, presents a diagonal saw-toothed pattern when viewed from the side. For safety a stairway will usually have a handrail on one side surmounting vertical supports called balusters. Balusters and handrails together are known as banisters and these are firmly supported at the bottom and top of the stairs by heavy posts.

   While these features are common to most stairway types, the actual layout of the stairway will vary depending on space and esthetic considerations. If the stairway turns back on itself a total of 180 degrees, the landing, which is the flat area at the top of the stairs, will be twice the width of the stairs. If the stairs turn at right angles, the landing will be the width of the stairs. Perhaps the most elegant layout is called a spiral stairway. This structure usually rises around a central vertical post to which tapered treads are attached at their narrow end.

Identify the stringer in the stairway.

2. The pipe organ is actually a wind instrument whose main features are the keyboards, stops, pipes, and blower. Pipe organs usually consist of two types of keyboards: the manual keyboard, which is played with the hands, and the pedalboard – commonly called the pedals – played with the feet. Although most organs have two or three manual keyboards and a pedalboard, they can have any number of manual keyboards and do not always include pedals. Arranged on the console at the side of the manual keyboards are round knobs called stops. The organist selects the pipes that will sound by pulling out the stops. To provide the supply of air, the modern pipe organ has an electric blower. Air from the blower is directed to the selected pipes through a series of mechanical operations. When the stream of air passes the lip or reed of the organ pipes, a sound is produced in a similar way to what happens when a flutist blows air over the opening of a flute or an oboist blows air through a reed.

Identify the pipe organ's stops.

3. The bow and arrow have been used to secure food, protect people from enemies, and provide competitive games of skill since the dawn of civilization. Although archery is no longer a necessary skill for survival, it is becoming increasingly popular as a sport. Today's bows are much easier to handle than those of the past were, but the basic form has not changed. The bow is usually from five to six feet long and can be made of steel or laminated wood and fiberglass. The handle is at the center of the bow. This is where the archer grips the weapon. The bow tapers toward the tips, where there are notches that hold the bowstring. The central portion of the bowstring is called the serving. In the middle of the serving is the point, where the archer sets the end of his arrow before drawing it back and letting it fly.

Identify the serving on the bow.

4. Theaters of the Elizabethan period were open-air constructions in which poorer members of the audience, "the groundlings," stood in a space called "the pit" around three sides of a projecting rectangular platform which formed the main stage. Most of the perimeter of the building was comprised of covered, tiered galleries, and it is here that the wealthier members of the audience sat. A roof supported on two pillars projected from the back wall and covered part of the stage area. The main stage was hollow and could be accessed from below through trapdoors set in the floor. The main stage had a door on either side at the back, which gave

access to the dressing rooms. Between these doors was a small recess usually curtained off that could be used for extra stage space. Above this recess was a balcony sometimes used by musicians or, when necessary, by actors in a performance.

Identify the pit in the Elizabethan theater.

Exercise L37   Mini-test

Listen to a talk about the Boston Tea Party.

The Boston Tea Party of 1773 was not a tea party at all, but the first major act of defiance on the part of the American colonists against their British rulers. The British Parliament under King George III had imposed high taxes without representation on the British colonies. A party of prominent citizens disguised themselves as Native Americans and secretly boarded ships that were laden with tea. They then threw the entire cargo of tea overboard. This incident was a prelude to the American War of Independence and perhaps the beginning of a nation of coffee drinkers.

1. What was the Boston Tea Party?
2. According to the passage, when did the Boston Tea Party take place?
3. Why did the Boston Tea Party take place?
4. Who threw the cargo overboard?
5. Which person or group of people is identified in the boxes?

Listen to a discussion between two friends.

    M: I had a real scare about my car being stolen yesterday when I got back from our geology trip last weekend.

    W: You mean that old wreck you drive around? Nobody would want to steal that.

    M: Don't be so sure.

    W: Well, what happened?

    M: Well, I left it on Oak Street, near the Geology Building, so when we got back I wouldn't have to walk home.

    W: Let me guess. Oak Street was resurfaced on Saturday, so your car was probably towed away.

    M: That's right. How did you know?

    W: I passed Oak Street on my way to the library last Saturday. So what happened then?

    M: I reported my stolen car to the police. The officer at the desk checked the records, and sure enough, my car was listed as one that the City Roads Department had towed away. I had to leave home early for my eight-o'clock class, so I haven't had a chance to call Jim's Wrecker Service to pick it up yet.

    W: Why don't you use my mobile phone to call them right now?

    M: Oh, thank you. That would be helpful.

6. What has happened to the man's car?
7. Where did the man leave his car?

8. What does the woman suggest the man do?
9. In what order did the following events occur?

Listen to a lecture about aging.

The problem of aging is taking on new dimensions in many countries. Those societies that are faced with this problem are the ones with a large aging population and a low birthrate. They are finding that social security expenditure has become an excessive percentage of the national income. The aging populations need more medical attention at a time when those costs are skyrocketing. Furthermore, many elderly people can no longer look after themselves and need to be cared for. Frequently, neither they nor their families can pay for this intensive care. Thus, the financial burden falls on the state. Those countries where the problems associated with an aging population are most acute are actively seeking long-term solutions.

10. Which societies are faced with the problem of aging?
11. According to the talk, what do older people need?
12. According to the talk, what burden frequently falls on the state?
13. Which graph represents the age structure discussed in the talk?

Listen to a talk given by a photographer.

It used to be widely accepted that photographs provided a perfect way to document historical events. Photographs preserved the past for future generations who could look upon the very faces of the men and women who had made history. It seemed that a photographic image preserved in extraordinary detail the deeds of both the famous and the unknown masses. Thus, photographs were a source of information unequaled before the invention of photography. The close correspondence between the subject of the photograph and its photographic image makes photographs excellent records that can be used for any historical inquiry. Such is not the case with contemporary photographs. Technological advances in the field of photography in recent years have made it possible to manipulate and alter photographic images. This is done through a process known as electronic imaging. Electronic imaging has made it increasingly difficult to use contemporary photographs as a reliable source of historical information.

14. What did photographs use to provide?
15. According to the talk, nineteenth-century photographs may differ from contemporary photographs in which way?
16. What has electronic imaging done to contemporary photographs?

Exercise L38 Understanding inferences

1. W: At her trial, Mata Hari was dubbed the greatest spy of the First World War. Her French accusers brought eight charges of spying against her. However, new research suggests Mata Hari was not really a spy at all.

   Mata Hari was probably given a sentence for spying.

2. M: The Manx is the only domestic cat that doesn't have a tail. Legend has it that at the time of the Great Flood, the Manx cat was so late in getting to the Ark that Noah closed the door before it was completely inside and cut off its tail.

   There are probably some wild cats that don't have tails.

3. W: Dr. Lennon, I heard you took an interesting course in New Mexico last summer. What was it?

   M: It was a course on building mud houses.

   W: Are you joking?

   M: No. First, we studied about the styles of traditional adobe homes in different parts of the world. We learned the techniques of mixing sand and water. Then we dried the mud in molds and built a structure of our own.

   W: Is it true that adobe structures are cool during the day and warm at night?

   M: Yes, it is.

   The woman will probably sign up for the course.

4. W: A fossil that has been identified as history's largest flying seabird has recently been excavated in the United States. Extinct and previously unknown, this species had a wingspan of more than 18 feet and probably weighed close to 90 pounds. The albatross, which weighs up to 20 pounds and has a wingspan of 11 feet, is the largest living seabird today.

   There are probably many fossils of today's albatross in the United States.

5. M: The synovial membranes in the body produce fluids which lubricate the areas between the bones. They also keep the cartilage tissues in good condition. Can anyone tell me why it is important to keep the cartilage tissues in good condition?

   W: These tissues protect the ends of the bones by acting much like elastic shock absorbers.

   M: That's right. Now if the cartilage tissues are damaged, regeneration is slowed down or stopped.

   W: Can anything be done to recondition cartilage tissue?

   M: Experiments are being conducted to renew damaged cartilage by transplanting synovial membrane cells. So far, the results have been very encouraging, but further experiments need to be conducted before a decision can be made concerning their use on humans.

   The transplant operation of synovial membrane cells has probably not been done on humans.

Exercise L39   Drawing conclusions

1. Polio is a crippling disease that reached epidemic proportions during the 1950s. Unfortunately, many sufferers from that decade started experiencing a return of the symptoms thirty years later. The reason behind this recurrence is not yet understood, but it has given scientists new knowledge about the disease.

   For what field might the new knowledge about polio be most useful?

2. M: I would really like to get my foreign language requirements out of the way, but when I went to register for beginning Spanish, all the courses were filled. Do you have any suggestions, Dr. Abbot?

   W: Well, you could take a different language. The Italian teacher on our staff is excellent, and the classes are smaller, so there's more opportunity to practice speaking.

   M: I never thought of Italian. Thank you for the advice.

   What will the man probably do as a result of this conversation?

3. W: You were telling us about the famous fashion designer Jean Muir yesterday at the end of the class period. But we had to rush off. I know that it wasn't part of your lecture, but we thought it was interesting. Could you finish what you were saying about her discovery that she had terminal cancer and how she set about changing the way she managed her fashion business.

   M: Well, I was just saying that she concentrated her time and energy on four women who had worked for her over the years. She gradually increased their responsibilities and their training. Together they worked on both Muir's mainline collection and the studio collection using her original ideas and patterns. At the time of her death, she had left enough material for these women to produce collections for another twenty years.

   W: She really sounds like a woman who was passionate about design.

   Why might Jean Muir have given so much attention to her staff?

4. Two University of Alaska professors have devised a novel way of getting junior high school students interested in the economic history of their state. The professors have produced a 120-page comic book that traces the economic history of Alaska from the mid-eighteenth century until the granting of statehood in 1959. Most students seem to find the comic-book format ideal for learning a subject they would otherwise view as dull and uninteresting. The writers use fictional and historical characters to illustrate economic concepts and historical events, such as the hunting of whales and the Klondike gold rush of the 1890s. The response from students has been overwhelmingly enthusiastic, and their teachers also have welcomed the ease with which these students have grasped economic concepts taught in this way.

   To what group of university students might this talk have been given?

Exercise L40   Inferring reasons

1. W: I saw in the course catalog that the university is offering a batik class this semester. Is it still open?

   M: Do you have the course number?

   W: Three-oh-nine.

   M: Yes, it's open. It meets Monday, Wednesday, and Friday at nine o'clock.

   W: Do you know if it can be used to meet undergraduate course requirements for art majors?

   M: Yes, it fulfills course requirements for both art and home economics majors.

   W: Good. I'd like to register for it, please.

   Why does the woman ask if the course meets the requirements for art majors?

2. Sound-activated toys are just one example of how high technology has affected childhood experience. A sound-activated toy responds whenever the child talks to it. There is currently a doll on the market that has an extensive memory much like a personal computer. It has a soft face that looks alive because it moves when the doll speaks. Its eyes respond to light by blinking, its hands are sensitive to heat, and it has a voice-recognition facility that gives it the ability to respond to the child playing with it. Considering all the high technology that goes into making such expensive toys, it may be surprising to find that children become bored with the new toy after its novelty has worn off. Children seem to get the most lasting enjoyment from balls, ordinary sticks, and common cardboard boxes. Perhaps this is because these toys can be turned into anything the child's imaginative play needs, whereas a high-tech doll can never be anything else.

   Why does the speaker mention balls, sticks, and boxes?

3. Before we go over those sentences I asked you to translate for today, I want to announce that the Foreign Language Department has set up a foreign-film festival that will take place during the first two weeks of November. I'm especially excited about the Spanish-language films they were able to obtain. Besides two movies from Spain and three from Mexico, there are films representing producers from Chile, Argentina, Cuba, and . . . just a minute . . . ah, yes . . . there's a Puerto Rican film that takes

place among the New York City Puerto Rican population. These films will give you a wonderful opportunity to listen to regional accents. A schedule of all the movies has been posted outside the door of the Foreign Language Department office. I've typed up a list of the names, days, and times of just those in Spanish, which I'll pass out at the end of the hour. Now, I realize that some of these showings may conflict with your individual schedules, but please make every effort to get to as many movies as possible.

Why does the speaker encourage students to see the films?

4. I think you all know the reason I am here. First of all, I want to say I regret that violent crime has reached our campus, and until the perpetrator is caught, all of you need to take extra precautions. I don't mean to frighten any of you. Assault is still a rare occurrence here, and the chance of your becoming a victim is remote. However, as women, we need to be alert and cautious here or any other place we go. Try not to be out alone at night, and never use short cuts, such as unlit alleyways or routes across vacant lots. Walk facing the traffic so a car can't pull up behind you. You might consider buying a personal safety alarm. Some of you take night classes. If you don't have anyone to meet you after class, you should call campus security. They will send someone to pick you up from your classroom and escort you to your bus, car, or dormitory. At this point I would like to introduce Mr. Lang, who is going to demonstrate some ways to protect yourselves through body language and the best ways to conduct yourselves if you are confronted. He will also teach you some techniques to break someone's hold on you if it should become necessary.

Why is the speaker giving the talk at this time?

Exercise L41   Mini-test

Listen to an architect talk about hazards in the home.

It used to be that the safety of a house was judged simply by whether it stood up or not. However, during the twentieth century, people began to build houses with synthetic materials that have proved over time to endanger the health of the houses' occupants. Asbestos roofing sheets and paneling were found to cause lung cancer. Formaldehyde, used in insulating foams, synthetic resins, and glues in plywood, chipboard, and hardboard, causes damage to the nervous system and severe memory loss. Wood preservatives contain potent fungicides and insecticides. These cause cirrhosis of the liver, bone marrow atrophy, and nervous disorders. At one time, lead was the major ingredient in paint. When lead levels were restricted due to lead poisoning, paint technologists came up with more poisonous metals, such as cadmium, to add

to paints. The dangers of synthetic material are never more apparent than when a fire breaks out. Today more people are killed by toxic fumes in house fires than by fire itself.

For every synthetic material used in a home, there is a biological or natural counterpart. People can't very well tear down their houses and start from scratch. However, there are ways to recognize and safely remove some synthetic material and replace it with natural alternatives.

1. Why does the speaker mention fires?
2. What would be an example of a natural building material?
3. What might the listeners do as a result of this talk?

Listen to a conversation between a professor and a student.

M: Are there any questions concerning the required reading list I've just passed out?

W: Yes, I have one. I see that some of the book titles have an asterisk by them.

M: Yes. Those books are out of print and cannot be purchased, so I've put my personal copies on reserve at the library. You'll have to read them there.

W: OK. Also, I was wondering about the list of articles on the second page. I don't understand the numbers.

M: Oh. These articles are on microfiche. Have you ever used microfiche?

W: No, I'm afraid I haven't.

M: Give that number to the librarian at the reserve desk, and he'll give you a small folder containing the articles on microfiche. Then go to the room directly across from the desk where the microfiche machines are. There are pamphlets beside each machine explaining how to insert the microfiche. It's really very easy.

W: OK. Thank you.

M: Well, that's all for today. Now, be prepared to discuss the first reading for our next class.

4. When would this conversation most likely take place?
5. What would most likely be found at a library reserve desk?
6. What can be inferred about the articles?

Listen to a talk given by an inventor.

It has been said that "necessity is the mother of invention." This may be true in some cases, but most things that people need already exist. We inventors tend to be dissatisfied people. We see the drawbacks of products already in existence. Most people do. But while they grumble, an inventor starts to visualize solutions. He or she is swept away into a passion for remedying the problem. Not only are we dissatisfied, passionate problem solvers, we have to be extremely optimistic to persist through the inevitable failures. Inventors thrive on failures. Where most people give up, the inventor uses failures as stepping stones to new approaches and then to eventual success. I shouldn't say "success" because once the invention is completed, we often see another fault. Sometimes the invention brings about a change that requires another invention. Take an aspirin bottle, for example. Small children managed to get into aspirin bottles with sometimes fatal results, so the childproof bottle cap was invented. However, arthritis sufferers couldn't open the bottle to get their medicine. Then, the two-way cap was invented. The users can now choose the most convenient way to close the bottle. Problem solved? No. A small child and an arthritis sufferer could share the same household. What are we going to do about it? Let's toss some ideas around to get your inventor brains operating.

7. Why does the speaker mention aspirin bottles?
8. What might happen as a result of this talk?
9. How does the speaker close the talk?

Listen to a discussion about garbage dumps.

> M: One way cultural anthropologists can study a culture is by sifting through garbage dumps. Garbage is the remains of what a society used or threw away. Take, for example, an orange peel. What can I tell by looking at an orange peel?
> W: Well, you can possibly tell whether that orange was eaten or made into juice.
> M: OK. Let's assume that this pile of orange peels indicates they were squeezed to make juice. What information can I gain from that?
> W: You could count those peels and estimate the number of oranges used. Enough for two glasses may indicate a single person or a married couple. Enough for a couple of liters might indicate a family.
> M: Good. We can make even more assumptions. For example, what could we infer if there's enough for fifty people? What would a seasonal change in the number of peels indicate?
>
> As you can see, an analysis of what is discarded can help us map out patterns and give us insights into human behavior. Unfortunately – or fortunately, depending on one's point of view – much of what is thrown away is organic, so when we're sifting through, say, the garbage dump of a Paleolithic village, the remains are limited. Of course, there are places where artifacts are better preserved – areas with dry desert air, such as Egypt, for instance, or with freezing temperatures, such as the Arctic Circle.
> That's enough about garbage collection. Tomorrow we will discuss cultural anthropologists and the issue of grave robbing.

10. What are the people listening to the speaker probably interested in?
11. Why does the speaker mention orange peels?
12. What would most likely be found in a Stone Age garbage dump?
13. Why does the speaker regret that most garbage is organic?

Exercise L42   Listening Section Practice Test

Part A

Now we will begin Part A with the first conversation.

1. M: How did you get Peter to help out at the Student Activities Center?
   W: It wasn't easy – I had to twist his arm.
   What does the woman mean?

2. W: Classes will be over the week after next.
   M: And that's not a minute too soon for me.
   What does the man imply?

3. W: Was Robert elected student body president?
   M: Of course he was. He promised to help students with housing problems.
   What did Robert do?

4. M: Jane had no problem passing calculus.
   W: She sure has a head for it, doesn't she?
   What does the woman say about Jane?

5. W: Do you have the camera? I'd like a shot of the façade of that building for my photography class.
   M: That would be a nice photo, but we're out of film.
   What does the man mean?

6. M: I wouldn't have failed that test if I'd gone to the course review.
   W: And if you had read the books and done the homework.
   What does the woman imply?

7. W: I don't have enough money to buy gas for the geology trip.
   M: We could go halves.
   What does the man mean?

8. M: Is it snowing out?
   W: Is it snowing! You can't even see the Student Union across the street.
   What does the woman mean?

9. M: I'm so burned out I don't think I can finish this term.
   W: You can do it. Our final exams are over the week after next.
   What does the woman mean?

10. W: How will Sue ever get around Germany?
    M: Don't worry. She's signed up for a crash course in German.
    What does the man say about Sue?

11. M: Margaret had better apologize to Dr. Morris for having mislaid that nutrition research paper he asked her to send off.
    W: I should say so.
    What does the woman mean?

12. W: Have you forgotten about the book I lent you?
    M: No, I haven't. But can you wait another week for it?
    What does the man imply?

13. M: Is Jason ready to audition for the Drama
    Department's new production?
    W: Ready? He's memorized his lines backwards
    and forwards.
    What does the woman mean?

14. M: There's an exhibition on costume design
    at the Fashion Institute.
    W: Shall we go?
    What does the woman mean?

15. M: Why don't you sign up for a course in botany?
    W: I'd do better in zoology.
    What does the woman mean?

16. M: Are you going to the library today?
    W: Not until after lunch.
    What does the woman mean?

17. W: I thought you tried to arrange your schedule
    so that you only had morning classes.
    M: I did. But my ten-o'clock history class was
    canceled, and the only other class open that
    would fulfill my course requirements was
    at two o'clock.
    W: Well, I suppose it's better than taking
    an evening class.
    What does the woman mean?

18. M: I've come about the photocopier.
    W: Oh, good. It hasn't been working properly
    for almost a week, and the students are getting
    annoyed. Photocopiers in university libraries
    get a lot of use.
    M: That's true. So, what's the problem?
    W: The copies are coming out with dark streaks
    on them, and it's making a peculiar noise.
    Why has the man come to the library?

Part B

Now we will begin Part B with the first conversation.

W: Are you going to meet me at the Student Union?
M: Yes, I think that would be the easiest place
to meet. Then we can share a taxi to the theater.
W: What time should I be there?
M: My evening archaeology class finishes at about
seven o'clock, so I can be at the main entrance
of the Student Union by 7:15 at the latest.
W: Unless your professor gets carried away with
his lecture. That's happened before.
M: That's true. If he does, I shouldn't be more than
fifteen minutes late though, and that will still
give us time to get to the theater.
W: You've already reserved the tickets, haven't you?
M: Yes, but I haven't gone to get them.
W: I'll be downtown this afternoon, anyway. I could
go to the ticket office and pick them up. Then
if you're late it won't matter. We'll be able
to go right in.
M: That's a great idea. Thanks. See you this evening.

19. What are the two people discussing?
20. Why does the woman think the man might be late?
21. What does the woman intend to do in the afternoon?

M: I was supposed to buy a lot more books, but I
didn't have enough money.
W: Did you try that used-books store on University
Avenue or ask whether you could check out
copies from the library?
M: Both. The library had a couple of them, and I
bought all the used ones I could find.
W: You're always short of money. Why don't you
look for a part-time job?
M: I'm afraid a job would interfere with my studies.
W: I don't think so. They're always looking for
people to work at the concession stands during
the university sports events and concerts.
M: Hey, I could see the games and concerts for free
while I earned money!
W: That's right. And it wouldn't take that much
time away from your studying.

22. What is the man's problem?
23. What does the woman suggest he do?
24. What will the man probably do?

Listen to part of a talk in an art history class. The professor
is talking about silhouettes.

The silhouette portrait, in which the shadow of a
sitter's profile is captured on paper, is still a popular art
form at fairs and school carnivals. Originally, this kind
of portrait was called a "shade." Once the artist captured
the shade on paper, it could be transferred onto ivory,
plaster, porcelain, or glass. It could also be reduced to fit
into brooches, lockets, or rings.

The word "silhouette" was taken from the surname
of Étienne de Silhouette, an eighteenth-century French
finance minister who was infamous for his cost-cutting
policies. In ridiculing these policies, opponents coined the
term "à la silhouette" to mean "done cheaply." This phrase
was passed on to the art of profile drawings because it
was so inexpensive. However cheap they may have been
in the eighteenth century, today these curiosities, which
might be mistaken for junk, could be worth large
amounts of money depending on the date they were
made and the artist who made them. Eighteenth-century
silhouettes continue to be auctioned at high prices.

25. What were silhouettes originally called?
26. What is NOT mentioned as one of the materials
    artists transferred portraits onto?
27. Who was Étienne de Silhouette?
28. Why are the discussed art forms known as silhouettes?
29. Which picture is an example of a silhouette?

Listen to a conversation between a professor and a student.
The professor is giving the student information about a job.

M: Professor Cline?
W: Yes?

M: I'm Robert Daley. The work-study office sent me.

W: Oh, I've been waiting for them to send someone. Did you say your name was Robert?

M: Yes.

W: What's your major, Robert?

M: Zoology.

W: Good. You have some science background, then. Let me show you what we're doing in our lab.

M: Will I be working in the biology lab?

W: Yes. We're studying the speed of reproduction of paramecia, which are the most complex single-celled organisms.

M: Oh, that sounds interesting.

W: Well, what we need you to do is probably not so interesting.

M: And what is that?

W: We'll need you to come in every day at the same time and count the paramecia.

M: Count paramecia?

W: Yes. It's very important to keep an accurate count and fill the numbers in on a form. I'll show you where the forms are and explain how to complete one later. After you have completed the form, you'll need to give it to Nancy. She is the woman that you met in the lab office. She'll enter your numbers into the computer for our statistical analysis. Right now though, I want to introduce you to the other members of our team so that we can arrange a convenient time for you to come in.

30. What are the people mainly discussing?
31. In what department is the professor probably working?
32. What will the man's job be?
33. Why might it be important that the man come in at the same time daily?
34. The professor briefly explains a process. Summarize the process by putting the events in order.

Listen to part of a talk in a media studies class. The professor is talking about a well-known event.

Shortly after eight o'clock on Sunday evening, October 30, 1938, many Americans became anxious or even panic-stricken while listening to a live, one-hour radio play realistically depicting a fictional Martian landing at a farm in the tiny hamlet of Grovers Mill, New Jersey. The broadcast could be heard in all regions of the continental United States, but those living in the immediate vicinity of the bogus invasion appeared to have been the most frightened. The play included references to real places, buildings, highways, and streets. The broadcast also contained prestigious speakers, convincing sound effects, and realistic special bulletins. The drama was produced by a twenty-three-year-old theatrical prodigy named George Orson Welles, who was accompanied by a small group of actors and musicians in a New York City studio. The actual broadcast script was loosely based on the 1898 book *The War of the Worlds* by the acclaimed science-fiction writer H. G. Wells. (In the original Wells novel, the Martians had landed in nineteenth-century England.) Even today, the 1938 broadcast remains arguably the most widely known deception in the history of the United States, if not the world, and many radio stations continue to broadcast the original play each Halloween.

The panic produced by the fictional Martian landing demonstrates the enormous credibility that the media enjoys in contemporary society. Moreover, in an ironic twist, there is a growing consensus among sociologists that the extent of the panic was greatly exaggerated. The irony is that for many years the public may have been misled by the media to believe that the panic it caused was far more extensive and intense than it actually was. However, there is little doubt that many Americans were genuinely frightened and some did try to flee the Martian gas raids and heat rays depicted in the drama.

35. What is the talk mainly about?
36. According to the professor, what is true about the broadcast?
37. What can be said about the event?
38. Why were people convinced of the invasion?
39. The professor explains a sequence of events. Summarize the sequence of events by putting the events in order.
40. What is the ironic twist the professor mentions?

Listen to part of a discussion in an environmental-science class. The people are talking about an environmental problem.

W1: As it is now well established, our planet's protective ozone layer has been thinning in recent decades. The ozone layer lies between 15 and 30 kilometers above the Earth's surface and absorbs ultraviolet rays emitted by the sun. The thinning of the ozone layer occurs when artificial chemicals called chlorofluorocarbons (CFCs) and other chlorine compounds combine with the oxygen atoms of the ozone and this depletes the amount of ozone. Ozone depletion has serious consequences because more ultraviolet light can reach the Earth's surface and damage DNA in humans and animals. The most well-known effect of this is the recent dramatic increase in skin cancers.

M: So, who is actually responsible for creating these CFCs?

W1: Well, in a sense, we all are. CFCs are a main component of dry-cleaning and refrigerating chemicals. They are also produced in various manufacturing processes, in nitrogen fertilizers, and by aerosols used in products such as hair sprays and polishes. Fortunately, their use in aerosols has been phased out in most countries. These chemicals disperse in the lower atmosphere, where they linger for years before migrating to the stratosphere, where the damage to the ozone takes place.

W2:   Dr. Alameda, this sounds very pessimistic. Haven't there been international agreements to phase out CFCs?

W1:   Yes, in fact, since 1985 several international conventions have produced agreements.

M: Would you say you are optimistic about the future of the ozone layer?

W1:   I would say I'm guardedly optimistic for the long-term future. The various agreements are beginning to take effect. The problem is that it takes many years for the CFCs to disperse, and not all countries are enthusiastic about phasing out their production for economic reasons. However, it is generally expected that the ozone layer will recover completely by the year 2060 as long as we all abide by the international agreements.

41. What is the discussion mainly about?
42. According to the professor, how do CFCs get into the atmosphere?
43. Why does the professor mention hair sprays and polishes?
44. The professor briefly explains a process. Summarize the process by putting the events in order.
45. Why is the professor cautious in her prediction of the future?

Listen to a talk given in a criminology class. The professor is discussing the juvenile justice system.

The basic principle of the American juvenile justice system is that children are different from adults. It follows that the justice system that deals with children should reflect these differences. When the principle was established a hundred or so years ago, it provided for the individualizing of treatment and services to vulnerable children. Today this system is under threat as critics say it is not tough enough on juvenile offenders and it fails to rehabilitate them.

Some of you may think that these criticisms are justified. After all, criminal statistics seem to point to a steadily increasing problem with young people. It's true that there has been an increase in the rates of criminal offenses by juveniles. But my concern is that the critics of the juvenile justice system are trying to dismantle it and will start to treat young offenders as adults, rather than rationally examining how to reform the system for the benefit of all citizens.

Before reforms are made, an examination of the whole system needs to be undertaken. As I see it, there are three key areas of research: The first is the area of accountability. In other words, how are juveniles different from adults in their understanding of criminal behavior? How do we assess their responsibility? Secondly, we need to evaluate risk. How can we determine the chances of a given youth committing an offense, and is it possible to use this information to prevent juvenile criminal activity? Finally, we need to discover how susceptible young people are to change. Can we assess an individual's likelihood of changing his or her behavior or of responding to treatment?

All these inquiries should be fully and accurately based on a thorough understanding of child and adolescent development. Experts from all relevant fields, as well as the general public, should contribute to the debate on future directions and goals. More needs to be learned about the origins, development, prevention, and treatment of juvenile crime, and that knowledge has to be spread among professionals and the community. In this way, eventual reforms of the system may truly be able to tackle the growing problem.

46. What is the talk mainly about?
47. What resulted from the basic legal principle that children are different from adults?
48. Why is the professor concerned about reforms to the juvenile justice system?
49. What do the three key areas of research examine?
50. What does the professor recommend?

PRACTICE TEST 1

Section 1 Listening

Part A

Now we will begin Part A with the first conversation.

1. M: Where was Bob going in such a hurry?
   W: He was going to pick up an application for a student loan.
   What was Bob going to do?

2. W: Did the Drama Club members make all the scenery for the play?
   M: Yes, but a carpenter advised them on the design.
   What does the man say about the scenery?

3. M: We've been driving around for an hour, and I can't find Elm Street.
   W: There's not a single soul to ask, is there?
   What does the woman mean?

4. W: Did you see the results of the poll?
   M: Yes, they were posted on the bulletin board in the union.
   What did the man say about the poll?

5. M: It's a little early for lunch, isn't it?
   W: I had to leave home before breakfast was ready.
   What does the woman imply?

6. W: Gloria's giving her presentation this afternoon.
   M: Oh, I don't want to miss that.
   What does the man mean?

7. W: Professor Wilson said we'd have a quiz on Monday.
   M: That's nothing new.
   What does the man imply about Professor Wilson?

8. M: We should meet once a week to discuss our term project.
   W: Wednesday afternoons would be a good time for me.
   What are the people discussing?

9. W: You sure have spent a long time on that calculus problem.
    M: And that's just one on a long list.
    What does the man mean?

10. M: Would you like to join me for a stroll along the river?
    W: What a pleasant way to spend a warm evening!
    What does the woman imply?

11. M: Is Mary around? We have our karate class tonight.
    W: She's practicing the piano.
    What does the woman say about Mary?

12. M: You were studying part-time for a master's degree, weren't you?
    W: Yeah, I used to take evening classes after work, but it got to be too much.
    What does the woman mean?

13. M: You could go to the infirmary and have that callus removed.
    W: I guess I should. I've been putting it off for weeks.
    What does the woman mean?

14. M: Have you finished that assignment for your telecommunications class?
    W: The script is too long, so I'll have to edit it.
    What does the woman mean?

15. W: Would you mind your own business?
    M: I'm sorry, I didn't mean to upset you.
    What does the man mean?

16. W: There was a large crowd buying your Engineering Department T-shirts. You must have collected a lot of money for your fund-raiser.
    M: Not as much as we would have liked.
    What does the man mean?

17. W: Even with student discounts, this conference sure has been expensive.
    M: I know. Look at this bill.
    W: What's it for?
    M: The charge for the hotel room, and it doesn't even include our breakfast.
    What does the man mean?

18. M: The physics midterm exam is next week, isn't it?
    W: No, it's the following week.
    M: Are you sure? I have next week marked in my calendar.
    W: That was the original date it was set for, but Professor Peters announced the change in our last class meeting.
    M: Oh, I missed that day because I had to make an emergency trip to the dentist.
    Why was the man confused about the date for the midterm exam?

Part B

Now we will begin Part B with the first conversation.

Listen to a conversation between two people.

W: Aren't you too old to be reading comic books?
M: This isn't just any comic book. It's a Walt Disney classic.
W: Walt Disney classic or not, this is a university.
M: Don't be such a snob. I'll have you know that this is required reading for my American popular culture course.
W: I can't believe it. Here I am reading stacks of major works by important authors like Flaubert, Dickens, and Tolstoy for my survey of nineteenth-century literature course, and you're reading comic books.
M: Hey, this isn't the only required reading material in the course. We have to read a lot about the historical events that affected the comic-book writers, and study contemporary art movements, and how women and minorities are depicted in the comics. And this is only one aspect of the course.

19. Why is the woman critical of the man's reading material?
20. What does the man imply about his American popular culture course?
21. What is one of the assignments the man has to do in the course?

Listen to a conversation between a student and a university office staff member. They are discussing financial aid.

W: I'm afraid your student-loan money won't be available for another two weeks because your application arrived a few days after the deadline.
M: Two weeks! Oh, no! Does that mean I might not get a loan?
W: No, but we had to wait until those applications that met the deadline were processed before we knew if there was going to be enough money for late applicants.
M: How will I complete my registration without my loan money? The registrar drops students if they don't pay their tuition fees by September 20.
W: Students in your situation usually apply for an emergency loan. An emergency loan must be paid back within a month or a very high interest rate will be charged. As soon as you receive your student loan, you use it to pay back your emergency loan.
M: So I need to take out an emergency loan to pay my tuition, and then when the student loan comes through, I pay back the emergency loan.
W: That's right. Emergency loans are usually granted on the same day you apply for them,

so you could get one and complete your registration today. Here's the form. Be sure to sign it here and . . . here. When you have finished filling it out, take it to Mr. Schultz in the office next door. He'll tell you what to do after that.

M: Thank you very much.

22. What is the student's problem?
23. Why wasn't the student's loan ready?
24. What can the student do in order to complete his registration?
25. The woman briefly explains a process. Summarize the process by putting the events in order.
26. When will the student be able to complete his registration?
27. What will the student probably do immediately?

Listen to part of a lecture in an architecture class. The professor is talking about an architectural style in North America.

Today I'd like to focus on the Prairie School of Architecture, which developed the foremost architectural style in North America in the first decades of the twentieth century. The impetus for the movement can be found in the philosophy and practice of Louis Sullivan, who was also instrumental in the building of the first skyscrapers. Other important influences were the English Arts and Crafts Movement and traditional Oriental themes. The students and followers of Sullivan, the most famous of whom was Frank Lloyd Wright, developed Sullivan's ideas into a quintessentially American style, expressing an underlying belief in the unity of man and nature.

When many people think of architecture, they think of large public buildings, but most of the effort of the Prairie School was devoted to domestic buildings. The most visible external feature of this architecture was the predominance of horizontal lines and heavy projecting roofs. The shapes were designed to both harmonize with and reflect the broad, flat prairies of the midwestern United States. The guiding principle behind the interior of these houses was an emphasis on reducing the number of separate rooms to a minimum, opening up living space, and designing internal divisions so that the light and vista created a sense of unity. The interior corners typical of traditional European houses were abolished to create a feeling of movement and freedom. This aesthetic ideal was an attempt to make the living space more compatible with human proportions and living requirements. In line with their belief in the importance of nature, these architects related the interiors to the surrounding landscape by their use of windows that were continuous ribbons of glass, of projecting terraces with parapets that were used as planting boxes, and of deeply cantilevered roof overhangs that led the eye towards the horizon. Often natural rocks formed a broad fireplace anchored at the center of the design.

Ornamentation was only permitted to complement the overall expression of the building. To this end, the Prairie School architects tended to use simple, unmixed, natural materials, sometimes with geometric or Oriental motifs. For example, many of the Prairie houses had a "turned-up" roof edge reminiscent of traditional Japanese houses.

28. What is the talk mainly about?
29. What can be said about the nature of Prairie School architecture?
30. Select the building that could be classified as an example of the Prairie School style.
31. According to the professor, how did the Prairie School architect make living space more compatible with human needs?
32. Why does the professor mention traditional Japanese houses?

Listen to a talk given in a library science class. The professor is discussing how libraries acquire resources.

It is simply not feasible for every university library in the nation to contain all the books and journals that university students and faculty need for their research. To meet the needs of their users, libraries have made many innovations. While some money is used for the yearly purchasing of hardcover books and current journals that are recommended by professors, other funds are used to obtain materials that have been put on microfilm and microfiche. These techniques have proved extremely useful for adding informative materials to a library's collection at a low cost and without taking up much space. Most libraries now have computers that connect with other libraries. Professors and students can ask their librarian to use a computer search to find a library that has the material they need. The material is then ordered and checked out through this interlibrary loan system, which costs the user only a nominal shipping fee.

33. What is the main idea of the talk?
34. What can be inferred from the talk?
35. How do librarians decide what to purchase?
36. According to the talk, what can students do if they can't find a book in the library?
37. The professor briefly explains the steps that a library user would follow to obtain materials. Put the steps in order.

Listen to part of a lecture given in an economics course. The professor is talking about microenterprises.

An enduring problem facing small-scale entrepreneurs in developing countries has been the difficulty in obtaining capital to start and run a business. A traditional route has been to borrow money from informal moneylenders who often attach exorbitant interest rates and thus reduce the net income of the borrower. This arrangement can trap a small-scale entrepreneur in a cycle of debt from which it is impossible to escape. An initiative pioneered in Bangladesh in 1983 by the Grameen Bank is an attempt to remedy this situation. The goal of this initiative was to help poor people escape from poverty by allowing them to borrow small amounts of money at reasonable interest rates without the necessity of providing collateral. The idea has now spread throughout much of the world and has been responsible for making significant inroads into both rural and urban poverty in developing countries.

The founder of the Grameen Bank, an economics professor named Mohammed Yunus, understood that because of the risk and expense involved, traditional banks would not lend money to poor people who have no property to use as collateral. But he discovered that poor borrowers would maintain a good loan repayment rate if interest rates were realistically set and if certain other conditions were applied. These conditions included the use of peer-group pressure to monitor the loans and guarantee repayment.

The peer group typically consists of five borrowers linked together through the life of a loan. The group undergoes a training session and attends weekly meetings with a bank official. The members monitor how the money is used and scrutinize the business plan of their peers because any one individual's chances of being awarded a loan are dependent on the repayment proficiency of every other member. This arrangement reduces costs for the bank and makes the borrowers manage their businesses well.

Another important factor in the success of the scheme is that the loans tend to be short-term and small, averaging about seventy U.S. dollars. This minimizes the bank's risk and does not overwhelm the borrower. If the money is fully repaid after a year, then a further and larger loan may be awarded.

The success of such schemes can be judged by the exceptionally high loan-repayment rate, and by the fact that a high percentage of borrowers have been able to work themselves out of poverty through the borrowers' diligence and the support of the microloans.

38. What is the main topic of this lecture?
39. The professor briefly explains a traditional cycle of borrowing. Put the steps of the cycle in order.
40. According to the professor, why did Mohammed Yunus found the Grameen Bank?
41. What problem facing small-scale entrepreneurs does the professor discuss?
42. How can the success of the microenterprise scheme be judged?
43. According to the professor, how is the Grameen Bank different from traditional banks?
44. Who would be most likely to receive a loan from the Grameen Bank?

Listen to a discussion in a physical-education class. The participants are talking about jumping in sports.

W1: The largest and strongest muscles in the body are in the hips, legs, and torso. These are the ones that give the most power to your total body movements. We have discussed the development of training methods for these muscles, especially those used for jumping. Many sports require a large repertoire of jumping skills. In such sports, players must respond in a variety of ways to different situations that occur in the course of the game or activity. For example, think about a volleyball player who may have to jump immediately after landing from a previous jump.

Now, certain other sports require highly specialized types of jumping. Can you think of any particular sport in which a specialized type of jumping is required? Yes, Susan?

W2: High jumping would require the same kind of jump to be repeated over and over.

M: So would a long jump. And what about a high dive? Would that be considered a kind of specific jump? I mean, a diver has to practice the same kind of movement in jumping off the board, right?

W1: Yes, Bill, that's right. To perfect these sport-specific moves, an athlete has to repeat the motion literally thousands of times to ingrain its pattern into the subconscious memory of movement. This repetition strengthens the muscles so that the movement can be performed with less effort, more power, and often greater speed. Most athletes work their leg muscles hard in their fitness program. But they tend to neglect their arm muscles. Arms are at least as important as legs when it comes to carrying through a jumping motion. So, why is it a mistake for athletes to neglect these muscles when training?

M: Well, one reason an athlete trains is to reduce the risk of injury by strengthening muscles, bones, joints, and connective tissue. I suppose this is just as important a consideration for the arms as it is for the legs.

W2: Also, the motions of the arms can increase the effectiveness of a jump. So, even though the arms aren't the actual muscles used in the jump, having strong arms could improve one's ability to perform the required sports skills.

45. What is the class discussion mainly about?
46. Why does the professor bring up the topic of arm muscles in a discussion about jumping?
47. The professor mentions volleyball as an example of which of the following?
48. According to the professor, what can an athlete do to improve efficiency of movement?
49. What is probably true about training methods to improve jumping in different sports?
50. Based on the discussion, classify the training requirements for the sports that are illustrated.

PRACTICE TEST 2

Section 1 Listening

Part A

Now we will begin Part A with the first conversation.

1. W: Did the drama students make all the props for the show?
   M: No, they posted an announcement asking for donations.
   What does the man mean?

2. W: Did you get a ticket for the concert tomorrow?
   M: They were sold out weeks ago.
   What does the man mean?

3. M: I don't imagine Nancy will want to borrow my notes, will she?
   W: Not the way you write.
   What does the woman mean?

4. W: Jennifer is very close to finishing, but she won't graduate this spring.
   M: She has to face facts.
   What does the man mean?

5. M: Did you find the flowered stationery you wanted?
   W: No, I had to settle for the pale blue.
   What does the woman mean?

6. W: You don't care for your chemistry class, do you?
   M: I'll say I don't.
   What does the man mean?

7. M: When did Susie pay you back?
   W: The week before last, when she got her Christmas bonus.
   What does the woman mean?

8. W: Would you have remembered the box if I hadn't called?
   M: Yes, because I tied a string around my finger.
   What did the man do?

9. M: You're within walking distance of the new stadium, aren't you?
   W: That's right. From our house, you can hear the crowds cheering in the stands.
   What does the woman mean?

10. M: There's just no stopping Jane.
    W: That's true. Nothing is more certain than her determination to succeed.
    What does the woman say about Jane?

11. M: I heard the physics test was difficult.
    W: No kidding. Only Mary scored high enough to pass it.
    What does the woman say about Mary?

12. M: I'm going down to the lobby.
    W: Would you check if my newspaper has come yet?
    What does the woman ask the man to do?

13. W: I can't possibly meet Dr. Joyce's deadline.
    M: Why don't you ask for an extension?
    What does the man suggest the woman do?

14. M: We're supposed to pass out the flyers this afternoon.
    W: Oh, so they have been printed, huh?
    What had the woman assumed about the flyers?

15. M: Since Diane wants to type your essay, why don't you let her?
    W: Have you ever seen the work she does?
    What does the woman imply?

16. M: Since Rhoda's exams kept her from coming with us to this conference, I think I'll bring her back a souvenir. I saw a very nice turquoise bracelet in the gift shop.
    W: Are you sure she wouldn't prefer a necklace?
    What does the woman imply about Rhoda?

17. W: Do you know who Dr. Carson picked for the lead part in this year's musical?
    M: Angela, I think.
    W: Angela? I thought that Terry did a much better job of acting.
    M: Perhaps, but she doesn't sing as well and when it comes to dancing, a bear could do better.
    According to the woman, who does the best acting?

18. W: The way David went on about that terrible virus, I thought that Mary was deathly ill.
    M: What was the matter with her?
    W: It wasn't her at all. He was talking about her computer.
    M: Oh, no. She let me use her computer to write my history research paper. That means I turned it in on a diskette that might be infected.
    W: Let's hope your professor has an anti-virus program.
    What is the man's concern?

Part B

Now we will begin Part B with the first conversation.

Listen to a conversation between two friends.

   W: I just can't get excited about this coming semester.
   M: Once classes start, you'll feel differently.
   W: I hope so. But what if I don't?
   M: Maybe you should drop one of your required courses and add one to take just for fun.
   W: That's a good idea. I'm feeling better about classes already.

19. What is the woman's problem?
20. What will the woman probably do?

Listen to a conversation between two friends.

   M: Hey, Jane, how was your first day of classes?
   W: Great. I signed up for an American history course that concentrates on the period surrounding the Revolutionary War.
   M: Sounds boring to me. I never did like history.
   W: That's because you've never had a teacher as exciting as Professor Lewis. He describes the events so vividly that it seems as though you

are actually involved. It's like getting caught up in a movie.

M: That sounds interesting.

W: Why don't you take it? It's not too late to add courses.

M: Well, I don't need it for my major, and there are other courses I'd rather take as electives.

21. What are the people discussing?
22. What does the man say about history classes?
23. What does the woman encourage the man to do?

Listen to a lecture given in a food science course. The professor is talking about saffron.

Treasured since ancient times, the spice saffron is obtained from the autumn-flowering *Crocus sativus*. The dried flower stamens – the three slender threads in the center of each flower – are the source of saffron. In New York, this "king of spices" can fetch up to sixty dollars a gram, making it one of the world's most prized and expensive foodstuffs. The finest variety is grown in La Mancha in the central plateau of Spain. The cultivation of saffron in Spain goes back to the Moorish invasion of the eighth century, when the crocuses were first introduced from the Middle East. Spain is by far the biggest producer of saffron. It contributes 70 percent of the world's output, with India and Iran the only other producers of note. Not only is Spain the largest producer of saffron, but it is also the largest consumer. Up to one-third of the Spanish saffron is bought domestically, while the remainder is exported. The biggest importer is Saudi Arabia. Other countries that import a large amount of saffron are Bahrain, the United States, Italy, and France.

24. What is the lecture about?
25. Which part of this plant is used to produce saffron?
26. What reason is given for saffron being known as the "king of spices"?
27. Besides Spain, which countries produce a significant amount of saffron?
28. Which country is the biggest consumer of saffron?

Listen to a conversation between two people. The man is giving the woman information.

W: By the way, Bill, could you tell me where the University Shuttle Bus stop is?

M: Well, it depends on the bus. Both the Family Housing Bus and the Recreation Center Bus stop in front of the bookstore, but the bus to the Music Complex stops around the corner.

W: Oh. How can I tell which one is the Recreation Center Bus?

M: It has the letters "RC" above the windshield. All the buses have the initials of their final destination posted there.

W: Do you know the schedules?

M: For the "RC" bus, about every twenty minutes during the day, but after five o'clock, it runs every hour until midnight.

W: Is it usually on time?

M: Yes, except during rush hour.

W: So I should go now if I'm going to catch it?

M: Not quite so soon. Look, I have to catch the Family Housing Bus. The Recreation Center Bus should come before mine. We can go together and I'll let you know which one to get on.

W: Oh, thank you.

M: Not at all.

29. What is the relationship between the man and the woman?
30. What does the woman want to know?
31. What can be inferred from the conversation?
32. How can the woman recognize the bus she wants?
33. What can be said about the woman?

Listen to a lecture given in a geology class. The professor is talking about the fossil record.

For a fossil to be found, a complicated series of steps must occur in sequence. The first is that the animal (or plant) must be buried quickly. Animals that die on the plains or in the mountains are soon found by scavengers, such as hyenas, and rapidly reduced to bone chips. Most animals that are fossilized are caught in a flash flood, die in or near a river and are buried in a sand bar, or are caught in a sandstorm. If the current in the river is fairly strong, even those few animals that die in the water are soon torn apart and their bones scattered over acres of river bottom.

The second condition necessary for an animal to be fossilized is that it must be buried in a depositional area; that is, layers and layers of mud or gravel must be laid down over it. If the area is subject to erosion – and nearly all land surfaces are – the fossil will soon be washed out and destroyed.

The third step is that this depositional area must at some time become an erosional area so that wind and water wear it down and uncover the buried remains.

The fourth step necessary for the recovery of a fossil is that when the fossil is uncovered, someone knowledgeable has to locate the fossil and recover it. The time frame for this recovery varies, but it is necessarily short. The fossil is protected, but also invisible, until it is exposed. As soon as it is exposed, wind and water attack it and destroy it quickly. The best fossils are found when someone spots an exposed bone that turns out to be part of a buried skeleton and is, therefore, still well preserved. But many fine fossils have been washed away because no one happened to see them when they were first exposed, or the people who saw them didn't realize what they were seeing.

34. What is the lecture mainly about?
35. What circumstances causing death will most likely ensure fossilization of an animal?
36. Why does the professor mention hyenas?
37. What is the professor's attitude toward finding animal fossils?
38. The professor briefly explains a process. Summarize

the process by putting the events in order.

Listen to part of a discussion in a criminology class. The people are talking about the trade in stolen art objects.

W1: Today I want to discuss with you the problem of theft of cultural antiquities and art. Illicit trafficking in cultural property has become a massive criminal activity, which today ranks in economic terms alongside illegal trading in weapons and drugs. No part of the world is immune from this problem. Works of art are stolen from museums and looted from historic and religious buildings everywhere, eventually finding their way to wealthy buyers. Frequently, smaller stone or wooden carvings are simply cut or chopped away from a wall or base, thus destroying the integrity of the work that had contained them. In some regions of the world, such activities have seriously depleted the stock of national treasures. What kinds of measures do you think are most appropriate for dealing with this situation? Yes, Tom?

M: Well, electronic surveillance of exhibitions and historical monuments might help.

W1: Well, yes, no doubt that would act as a deterrent. But that's not always an affordable or practical option, especially since many cultural objects are located in remote places.

W2: Isn't there a movement afoot to get owners to make thorough catalogs of their cultural possessions?

W1: Yes, indeed, Mary. Remember that one of the chief problems in policing this kind of crime is that very often the original owners – whether governments, museums, or private collectors – cannot furnish an accurate description of their stolen property and, therefore, cannot prove their ownership. Several organizations concerned with combating this illegal trade are now stressing the importance of owners making accurate inventories. These inventories should include relevant data about the object such as date of fabrication, kind of material, shape, size, the presence of identifying markings, etc. Of course, they should also include detailed photographic illustrations.

M: Would inventories in themselves prevent this trade? Information like this can only be really useful if it's made widely available.

W1: You're absolutely right, Tom. In fact, the development of electronic networks allows the International Police Organization to use inventories to identify objects and disseminate information about them to all of its offices worldwide. This information can also be used by customs agencies, the insurance industry, and cultural-heritage organizations. Can you think of any other measures that might help

stem this illegal trade?

W2: Well, it seems that many people unwittingly purchase artifacts without being aware of their historical or cultural value or of the possibility that the object may have been looted. Perhaps travelers should be alerted to this danger. This might go some way to reduce the trade.

39. What are the people discussing?
40. Why does the professor mention the trade in weapons and drugs?
41. What does the professor say about electronic surveillance?
42. For which of the following pieces would the use of electronic surveillance be impractical?
43. Which problem in policing the trade in national treasures was discussed?
44. What does the professor say about inventories of cultural properties?

Listen to a lecture in a music appreciation class. The professor is talking about a specific genre of music.

The importance of background music in a film cannot be overstated. Background music is instrumental in creating the mood the moviemaker wants to evoke. During the infancy of cinema, the importance of music was understood, but the relationship between music and the action on the screen was not fully appreciated. Thus, early musical material consisted of whatever was available and often bore little relationship to the movie. Since the technology for movies to include sound had not yet been developed, music was provided by live musicians who played whatever they wanted. A pianist good at improvisation was highly regarded.

As the commercial potential of the cinema became apparent, producers realized the advantage of each film having its own music. In 1908, Camille Saint-Saëns was commissioned to compose music specifically for a French film. However, this idea was ahead of its time and was not embraced by the movie industry. Perhaps cinema musicians weren't ready to learn new pieces for each movie that came along, or perhaps the costs were too high.

By 1913, special catalogs of music for specific dramatic purposes were available. Thus, musicians had at their disposal music that could be used for any scene from any movie. Much of this music consisted of works by famous composers and predated the advent of motion pictures. For example, Mendelssohn's "Wedding March" was a typical catalog piece for wedding scenes and had been written before the appearance of motion pictures.

In 1922, a system that made possible the synchronization of recorded sound and image was developed. The era of talking pictures began, thus making music an integral part of filmmaking. At first, background music was used only if there was an orchestra or performer on screen because it was believed that people would be bewildered about the origin of the sound.

A 1930s' Western called *Cimarron* was the first film to experiment with background music without a visible means of production. The composer for this sound track was Max Steiner, a pioneer of film scoring. Steiner also composed the film score for *Symphony of Six Million* in 1932, the first film to have music underscoring dialogue. The simple, somewhat naive music of early film scores quickly developed into the sophisticated musical experience that moviegoers encounter today.

45. What is the lecture mainly about?
46. The professor mentions three different composers. How does the music discussed in the lecture relate to the composers mentioned?
47. The professor briefly explains a process. Summarize the process by putting the events in order.
48. Why does the professor mention Mendelssohn's "Wedding March"?
49. According to the professor, in what ways was Max Steiner a pioneer of film scoring?
50. What event probably had the most influence on film music?

INDEX

TERMS AND CONDITIONS OF USE OF CD-ROM

1. License

(a) Cambridge University Press grants the customer the license to use one copy of this CD-ROM (i) on a single computer for use by one or more people at different times, or (ii) by a single person on one or more computers (provided the CD-ROM is only used on one computer at one time and is only used by the customer), but not both.

(b) The customer shall not: (i) copy or authorize copying of the CD-ROM, (ii) translate the CD-ROM, (iii) reverse-engineer, disassemble, or decompile the CD-ROM, (iv) transfer, sell, assign, or otherwise convey any portion of the CD-ROM, or (v) operate the CD-ROM from a network or mainframe system.

2. Copyright

All material contained within the CD-ROM is protected by copyright and other intellectual property laws. The customer acquires only the right to use the CD-ROM and does not acquire any rights, express or implied, other than those expressed in the license.

3. Liability

To the extent permitted by applicable law, Cambridge University Press is not liable for direct damages or loss of any kind resulting from the use of this product or from errors or faults contained in it, and in every case Cambridge University Press's liability shall be limited to the amount actually paid by the customer for the product.

INSTALLATION INSTRUCTIONS

Windows: Insert the disc in the CD-ROM drive. The installer will auto-start. If the installer does not auto-start, click on Run from the Windows Start menu and type "D:\Install.EXE" (where "D" is the drive letter of your CD-ROM drive). Follow installer instructions.

Mac: Insert the disc in the CD-ROM drive. Click on the disc icon and then on the Cambridge Practice Installer icon. Follow installer instructions.

For product information and technical support, visit http://esl.cup.org/toeflprep/